CRITICAL
PERSPECTIVES
ON
DEREK WALCOTT

CRITICAL PERSPECTIVES ON DEREK WALCOTT

Compiled and Edited
By Robert D. Hamner

An Original by Three Continents Press

Copyright © by Three Continents Press 1993

Three Continents Press, Inc.
1901 Pennsylvania Avenue, N.W.
Washington, D.C. 20005

Library of Congress Cataloging-in-Publication Data
Critical perspectives on Derek Walcott / compiled and edited by Robert D. Hamner.
        p.   cm. — (Critical perspectives series : 26)
    Includes bibliographical references and index.
    ISBN 0-89410-141-2 : $36.00. — ISBN 0-89410-142-0 (pbk.) : $18.00
    1. Walcott, Derek—Criticism and interpretation. 2. West Indies in literature. I.
    Hamner, Robert D. II. Series: Critical perspectives : 26
PR9272.9.W3Z57   1992
823—dc20
                                                                92-3588
                                                                CIP

Cover photo © by Robert D. Hamner

For the muse of my other life

Roseau
Allamanda   Oleander
Casuarina   Laburnum
Eddoes   Jasmine
Lotus   Tamarind
Ixora   Avocado
Immortelle   Nightshade
Aglaia

ACKNOWLEDGMENTS

I gratefully accord recognition to the following firms and individuals who have granted permission to reprint original and copyrighted primary material.

Derek Walcott, for permission to publish "The Figure of Crusoe." Although this essay was originally presented in oral form at the University of the West Indies, St. Augustine, Trinidad in 1965, Mr. Walcott has agreed to allow its publication, as I have edited it here, for the first time.

Laurence Goldstraw for permission to publish his original essay, "Reminiscences of Derek Walcott and the Trinidad Theatre Workshop," which he wrote at my request.

Derek Walcott and the *Journal of Interamerican Studies and World Affairs* 16.1 (Feb. 1974) for permission to reprint "The Caribbean: Culture or Mimicry?"

Derek Walcott and the Trinidad Publishing Company, Ltd. for permission to reprint "History and Picong . . . in the Middle Passage," "Necessity of Negritude" and "Tribal Flutes."

Derek Walcott and *London Magazine* for permission to reprint "Leaving School."

Derek Walcott for permission to reprint "Meanings" from *Savacou*.

Derek Walcott and the National Library of Jamaica on behalf of *Public Opinion* for permission to reprint "Society and the Artist."

I am grateful to the following firms which have kindly granted permission to reprint copyrighted excerpts from the works of Derek Walcott that have been quoted throughout the secondary essays in this collection.

Faber and Faber, Ltd. for the British Commonwealth, excluding Canada. Reprinted

Calvin Bedient and *Parnassus: Poetry in Review* for "Derek Walcott: Contemporary."

Robert Bensen and the editor of *The Literary Review* for "The Painter as Poet: Derek Walcott's *Midsummer*."

Sven Birkerts' "Heir Apparent." Reprinted by permission of *The New Republic* © 1984, The New Republic, Inc.

Stephen Breslow and *World Literature Today* for "Trinidadian Heteroglossia: A Bakhtinian View of Derek Walcott's Play *A Branch of the Blue Nile*."

Lloyd Brown and the *Caribbean Quarterly* for "Dreamers and Slaves — The Ethos of Revolution in Walcott and Leroi Jones."

D J. R. Bruckner's "A Poem in Homage to an Unwanted Man," in *The New York Times*, copyright © 1990 by The New York Times Company. Reprinted by permission.

Frank Collymore's "An Introduction to the Poetry of Derek Walcott." Reprinted by permission of *Bim*.

Theodore Colson and *World Literature Written in English* for "Derek Walcott's Plays: Outrage and Compassion."

Benjamin DeMott's "Poems of Caribbean Wounds." Reprinted with permission from *The New York Review of Books*. Copyright © 1979 Nyrev, Inc.

Aubrey Douglas-Smith's review of *Henri Christophe*. Reprinted by permission of *Bim*.

Richard Dwyer and the *Caribbean Review* for permission to reprint "One Walcott, and He Would Be Master."

John Figueroa's "Some Subtleties of the Isle: A Commentary on Certain Aspects of Derek Walcott's Sonnet Sequence, 'Tales of the Islands.'" Permission granted by *World Literature Written in English*.

Robert E. Fox and *The Journal of Commonwealth Literature* for permission to reprint "Big Night Music: Derek Walcott's *Dream on Monkey Mountain*."

John Grimes' "Company of Players Win Praise for 'Ione.'" Permission granted by *Trinidad Guardian*. Copyright © 1957 by the Trinidad Publishing Co., Ltd.

Christopher Gunness' "White Man, Black Man." Permission granted for *People* by Imprint Caribbean, Ltd.

Seamus Heaney and *Parnassus* for "The Language of Exile." Subsequently retitled "The Murmur of Malvern" from *The Government of the Tongue* by Seamus Heaney. Originally appeared in *Parnassus*. Copyright © 1989 by Seamus Heaney. Reprinted by permission of Farrar, Straus & Giroux, Inc. (United States, in English only). For the British Commonwealth, reprinted by permission of Faber and Faber, Ltd. from *The Government of the Tongue* by Seamus Heaney.

Edward Hirsch's interview with Derek Walcott, "The Art of Poetry." Copyright © 1986 *The Paris Review*, Inc.

G. A. Holder's "B. B. C. Broadcast of 'Henri Christophe.'" Reprinted by permission of *Bim*.

Patricia Ismond and *Caribbean Quarterly* for "Walcott Versus Brathwaite."

Patricia Ismond and *The Trinidad and Tobago Review* for "Breaking Myths and Maidenheads" which appeared originally in *Tapia*.

Biodun Jeyifo for "On Eurocentric Critical Theory: Some Paradigms from the Texts and Sub-texts of Post-colonial Writing," in *Kunapipi*.

Bruce King and the *Southern Review* for permission to reprint "*The Collected Poems and Three Plays* of Derek Walcott."

Mary Lefkowitz's "Bringing Him Back Alive," Copyright © 1990 by The New York Times Company. Reprinted by permission.

Earl Lovelace's "The Last Carnival." Permission granted by Trinidad Express Newspapers. Ltd.

J. D. McClatchy and *The New Republic* for "Divided Child."

Mark McWatt's review of *Remembrance* from *Caribbean Contact*. Permission granted by *Caribbean Contact*.

Anthony Milne's interview, "Derek Walcott." Permission granted by Trinidad Express Newspapers, Ltd.

Sule Mombara's "'O Babylon!'— Where It Went Wrong" from *Caribbean Contact*. Permission granted by *Caribbean Contact*.

Mervyn Morris and *Caribbean Quarterly* for "Walcott and the Audience for Poetry."

Edith Oliver and *The New Yorker* for "Displaced Person." Reprinted by permission; © 1979. The New Yorker Magazine, Inc.

Victor Questel's "Interlude for Rest or Prelude to Disaster" from *Tapia*, Vol 6, No 13 of March 28, 1976. Permission granted by the Trinidad and Tobago Institute of the West Indies.

Norman Rae's "*Ione*: Colourful but Academic" from *The Gleaner*. Permission granted by The Gleaner Company, Ltd.

Kenneth Ramchand for "Readings of 'Laventille'" from *Tapia*.

Gordon Rohlehr's "Withering into Truth" which appeared in three segments in the *Trinidad Guardian*. Although the *Trinidad Guardian* had no objections to my reprinting this review article, I have been unable to elicit a response from Dr. Rohlehr, despite numerous letters over a period of several years. Since Dr. Rohlehr has aided my work in the past, I trust that his approval will be forthcoming.

Vernon Shetley and *Poetry* for Shetley's review of Walcott's *The Arkansas Testament*. This review of *The Arkansas Testament* first appeared in *Poetry* © 1988 by The Modern Poetry Association. Reprinted by permission of the Editor of *Poetry*.

Harold Simmons' "A West Indian Poet Fulfills His Promise" from *The Gleaner*. Permission granted by The Gleaner Company, Ltd.

Judy Stone's "Warner's *Beef, No Chicken* an Inspired Production." Permission
    granted by *Caribbean Contact.*

Patrick Taylor and *World Literature Written in English* for "Myth and Reality in
    Caribbean Narrative: Derek Walcott's *Pantomime.*"

    The facsimile reproduction of the photograph of Derek Walcott is provided by
Robert Hamner. The photograph was taken in Trinidad in September, 1975.

CONTENTS

PREFACE

Although Derek Walcott's work may be unfamiliar to some who examine this collection, by now most readers know of his rise from West Indian colonialism to become one of the finest writers in the English language. The purpose of this anthology is to provide beginners and scholars a concise overview of the criticism that has attended Walcott's development from the 1940s to the present.

Had he confined himself to one genre, verse or drama for example, or even chosen one of the usual forms of prose fiction, the number of contributors and the length of this book could have been considerably reduced. Walcott is, however, not only an accomplished poet and playwright; he is prolific in both fields, sometimes combining them in verse drama, enhanced with music and dancing. In order to deal with his complex style, critics have resorted to a variety of approaches. That diversity is reflected in the different kinds of material comprising this anthology.

Since Walcott wrote an arts column for the *Trinidad Guardian* for many years and he has eloquently articulated his ideas elsewhere in essays and introductions to his own works, I have brought together ten of his articles to complement the material offered by secondary critics. The latter comprises the bulk of my collection. Herein may be found reviews of books and reports on live performances of many of his plays. Longer studies of individual works—of specific themes and techniques—analyze the depth and breadth of Walcott's creativity.

Given the number of exceptional essays available, the process of selection has not been easy. Relevance is necessary, of course—aesthetic as well as historical. Walcott is the product of a society involved in establishing its independence; therefore, passions sometimes run high among commentators, especially those attached to the Caribbean. Although not all of the opinions offered here are disinterested, scholarly criticism, they reflect the controversy surrounding a writer who bridges two worlds. Since there are too many excellent essays that might well have served my purposes, I have attempted to limit inclusion to the most clearly focused materials that gave timely coverage to poems and plays and the context in which they appeared. In addition, while I wish to avoid unnecessary repetition of accepted conclusions, I also want to provide examples of principal interests and diverse approaches to the primary works. Readers desiring further information may consult the annotated bibliography appended to this volume.

I should be remiss were I to overlook the assistance of several people who made this collection possible. Foremost, of course, is Derek Walcott. His willingness to allow the use of representative material is greatly appreciated. His advice has been invaluable. Donald Herdeck of Three Continents Press has been understanding and very helpful at each stage of the work. My wife, Carol has proofread and encouraged me from the beginning. Librarians at the St Augustine campus of the University of the West Indies, the University of Texas at Austin and Hardin-Simmons University have provided aid on numerous occasions—Irma Goldstraw, Alice Specht and Corrine Shields in particular. I owe a great debt to the Hugh Roy Cullen Fund for Faculty Enrichment at Hardin-Simmons University for research grants and other monetary support enabling me to complete this project. Last, I wish to pay tribute to Victor D. Questel, a contributor to this collection who might have been its editor were it not for his untimely death in 1982.

TRINIDAD THEATRE WORKSHOP
WORLD PREMIERE

O BABYLON!

The New Musical By

DEREK WALCOTT
and
GALT MAC DERMOT

Choreography : Carol La Chapelle
Lighting : John Andrews
Designed and Directed By : DEREK WALCOTT

LITTLE CARIB THEATRE

Opens FRIDAY MARCH 19th to SATURDAY APRIL 2nd 8.30 p.m. $8.00; $6.00
BOOKINGS : Singer Mall, Frederick Street, RESERVATIONS : 637-4028

INTRODUCTION

In early youth, Derek Walcott fell in love with language and dreamed of becoming a poet. What makes his dream all the more incredible is the fact that he was born in Castries, capitol of the small Caribbean island of St. Lucia. The obstacles he had to overcome were formidable. Not only was he fatherless in a backwater of fading colonial empire but, as he put it in his autobiographical poem *Another Life*

> The dream
> of reason had produced its monster:
> a prodigy of the wrong age and colour. (3)

Nevertheless, on the dust jacket of *In a Green Night* (1964), his first major collection of verse, Robert Graves proclaimed, "Derek Walcott handles English with a closer understanding of its inner magic than most (if not any) of his contemporaries." And by the time he was in his forties, Walcott counted among his circle of mentors and personal friends Robert Penn Warren, Robert Lowell, Joseph Brodsky and Seamus Heaney.

In the wake of colonialism, Walcott has acquired an international reputation that enhances the growing stature of West Indian literature. The fact that Walcott's life coincides with the Caribbean's independence movements makes his career significant for historic as well as aesthetic reasons.

His father Warwick Walcott died while Derek and twin brother Roderick were hardly a year old. Their mother, Alix Walcott, headmistress of a Methodist grammar school in Castries, assumed the burden of educating the twins and their older sister, Pamela. At St. Mary's College, young Walcott thrived on the traditional curriculum of Western classics. At home he was surrounded by the delicate watercolors and witty, satirical poems left by his father. Then there was the influence of his father's old friend Harold Simmons, an artist who encouraged Walcott to express himself both with brush and pen.

The city of Castries had no book publisher, but by the time he was eighteen, Walcott wanted to see some of his poems in print. Borrowing $200 from his mother, he sent his manuscript off to Trinidad and then sold copies of *25 Poems* (1948) to friends and people in the street until he repaid his mother's investment.

1

Poetry was only one of his primary vocations. He turned some of his verse into drama for the stage. Along with brother Roderick, and a few others, he founded the St. Lucia Arts Guild in 1950 and produced his earliest plays, such as " Henri Christophe."

After completing his undergraduate education at the University of the West Indies in Jamaica in 1953, and following a brief stint at teaching, he accepted a Rockefeller fellowship to study theater in New York in 1958.

Finding that there were few opportunities for serious black playwrights and actors in the United States, he moved to Trinidad where he wrote a column for the *Trinidad Guardian* and founded his second theatrical troupe, the Trinidad Theatre Workshop in 1959. Since that time, his volumes of poetry and play collections have appeared at regular intervals. Walcott now teaches at Boston University, living parts of each year in Boston and the West Indies.

Walcott has risen from colonial obscurity to international prominence as a direct result of his ability to assimilate and express the disparate elements of a rich social milieu. European exploitation of the West Indies, entails the history of slavery and indentured servitude; yet, along with that history, it also means the ingestion of Renaissance, African, Asian and Oriental cultures. Despite V. S. Naipaul's bleak assertion that nothing has been created in the West Indies (27), Derek Walcott seizes upon the fragments at hand to demonstrate that something new can arise, like the phoenix, out of imperial ashes.

Throughout the social disturbances of the independence-minded fifties and the Negritude and Black Power sixties and seventies, Walcott kept his finger on the pulse of the times without relinquishing his own aesthetic principles. While his models have changed over the years, he began by assimilating European values. As he has matured, his own voice has emerged: a voice informed by the masters of western literature, yet personal and resonant in the lyrical register of the islands.

I   Walcott: Artist and Critic

The following collection of essays records Walcott's unique career in two ways. The first ten selections, taken from Walcott's own articles and interviews from 1957 to the last of the 1980s, allow him to speak for himself. The second, larger, group of essays and reviews, introduces a representative sampling of varied critics and their approaches to Walcott from the time he was a teenager until his poetry and plays became accepted as among the best the English language has to offer.

Although Walcott's writings are too extensive to be summarized briefly, the ten pieces comprising part one of this collection exemplify recurrent personal views, major themes and the tenor of his discursive voice. Four newspaper articles between 1957 and 1967 — "Society and the Artist," "History and Picong," "Necessity of Negritude" and "Tribal Flutes" — establish positions that remain virtually unchanged up to the present. He outlines the obstacles confronting artists in the West Indies, admits reservations regarding Negritude and reviews books by fellow Caribbean writers V. S. Naipaul and Edward Brathwaite.

Three more extensive essays provide valuable insights into Walcott's development as a writer and critic. In "Leaving School," he reminisces about childhood, schooling, and sources of inspiration during his early formative years until he left St. Lucia for Jamaica on a Commonwealth Development scholarship. "The Figure of Crusoe" (which is published here in this collection for the first time) details Walcott's utilization of Robinson Crusoe as a literary symbol. Because of Crusoe's mixed accomplishments, his ambivalent existence as a castaway, Walcott sees him as more appropriate than Caliban as a paradigm of West Indian identity.

What "The Figure of Crusoe" suggests for Walcott's poetry, "Meanings" supplies for his early plays. Herein, he conceptualizes the elements of West Indian theater: an authentic creation with origins in Asian, African and oriental art forms but molded by western order and discipline. Ironically, Bertolt Brecht influenced him to reclaim disparate cultural fragments already available in his native West Indian environment and made him aware of the potential in classical Kabuki and Noh theater. By his own admission, *Malcochon* is based on Akira Kurosawa's *Rashomon*. This play as well as his famous *Dream on Monkey Mountain* seek the physical assertion, the inarticulate directness of Japanese film ("Meanings" 48).[1]

"The Caribbean: Culture or Mimicry?" addresses the vital questions inherent in his unapologetic assimilation of foreign influences. While well-meaning nationalists prefer racially pure art, Walcott insists on the authenticity of his complete New World identity. He accepts the central dilemma of his birth. Since inhabitants of the West Indies are descendants of transplanted African, Asian and European forebears, their ancestral roots are detached from modern Africa, China, Europe and India yet they may view their native island as alien soil. The choice of allegiances is highly charged — determining racial identity, political alignments, cultural values, even the language of expression. It is no wonder that many artists have preferred exile to this maelstrom.

Concluding this section of articles are two interviews. The first, conducted in Trinidad by Anthony Milne in 1982, inquires into Walcott's strained relationship with the Trinidad Theatre Workshop after he has taken up residence in the United States for several years. The second interview, by Edward Hirsch in 1986, touches on Walcott's personal and professional career including his friendship with such luminaries as Robert Lowell, Joseph Brodsky and Seamus Heaney.

These selected reviews, essays and interviews render insights into Walcott's perspective on himself, his work and the world in which he writes; however, as informative and refreshing as his candor may be, it yields but one man's vision.[2] The modern distrust of an author's personal interests abetted by the revelations of psychological analysts, deconstructive critics and new historicists demand additional (if not equally biased) interpretations.

II The Critical Reception

The second division of this volume contains representative criticism of both Walcott's plays and his poetry. There is an overall chronological arrangement according to a specific work's date of publication. Within this framework, Walcott's career is subdivided into four periods of development. Despite aesthetic and thematic links among all the plays and poems, there are distinguishable periods corresponding roughly with the four phases of his professional life from the late 1940s through 1990.

A. "The Divided Child" (1948-1959)

Walcott's juvenilia may well be said to extend into his first commercially published book, *In a Green Night* (1962), since it contains versions of some of his first poems. However, not only did those poems undergo extensive revision and editing, but a major portion of *In a Green Night* is reproduced in *Selected Poems* and belongs more properly among the work of the 1960s.

As should be expected, Walcott's earliest critics are close to home. Seven of the nine articles in the first subdivision come from regional periodicals: *Bim*, Barbados; *The Daily Gleaner*, Jamaica; *The Trinidad Guardian*. Frank Collymore, influential editor of *Bim* — and therefore a pioneering force in West Indian literature — recognized an "accomplished poet" in the nineteen-year-old author of *25 Poems*. He is also among the first to perceive the unmistakable lineage of Gerard Manley Hopkins, W. H. Auden, Dylan Thomas and Christian theology. Even closer to Walcott's origins, Harold Simmons points up his protege's sensual imagery, the elusiveness of his erudition, before citing vestiges of Rilke and Dylan Thomas in *25 Poems*. The only other poem covered from the 1940's is "Epitaph for the Young." In it, Keith Alleyne sees T. S. Eliot not as just an influence but rather a "complete formula."

Performances of the play "Henri Christophe" are assessed by Aubrey Douglas-Smith and G. A. Holder. For Douglas-Smith, it is important to find a West Indian writer making use of West Indian subject matter with valuable implications for indigenous people. Holder is attuned to audience response in his account of a group of peasants stopping to listen to a radio broadcast of the play.

In contrast with these basically favorable assessments of "Henri Christophe," two reviewers are highly critical of *Ione*. For Norman Rae, *Ione*, is an academic exercise, awkward in its Aristotelian conventions. Because of the way the playwright combines music, dance, atmosphere and style, Rae makes one observation that is prophetic for Walcott's evolving technique. Rae concludes, ". . . it seems a West Indian theatrical production of a straight play is no longer just a collection of persons making conversation on a platform" (115). John Grimes offers encouragement to a cast he sees struggling valiantly to overcome what is essentially melodrama.

Despite mixed and negative reviews, Walcott continues to experiment with material and styles, seeking a blend of theatrical conventions closer to West Indian experience. This leads to three folk plays — *The Sea at Dauphin* (1954), inspired by J. M. Synge's *Riders to the Sea; Ti-Jean and His Brothers* (1957); and *Malcochon* (1959), suggested by Akira Kurosawa's film *Rashomon* (Walcott, "Meanings" 48). Walcott's growing assurance and success are reflected by the inclusion of these plays in *Dream on Monkey Mountain and Other Plays* (1970), and by the fact that they continue to appear on stages internationally.

More extended articles by Albert Ashaolu and Theodore Colson indicate emerging critical awareness of Walcott's complexity. In "Allegory in *Ti-Jean and His Brothers*," Ashaolu examines six layers of meaning and stresses linkages with Aristophanes' *Frogs* and Aeschylus' *Prometheus Bound*. In "Derek Walcott's Plays: Outrage and Compassion," Colson argues that the juxtaposition of polar elements in *The Sea at Dauphin, Ti-Jean and His Brothers*, and *Malcochon* embodies the racial and cultural reality of post-imperial existence. Blackness, whiteness and their mixture are archetypal. By the time of this analysis in 1973, Colson enjoys the advantage of having seen the culmination of Walcott's assimilation process — the Obie award-winning *Dream on Monkey Mountain*.

B. "The Estranging Sea" (1960-1969)

During the sixties the figure of outcast Crusoes is ubiquitous, whether in Walcott's first collection of plays with protagonists like Chantal (in *Malcochon*) or Makak (in *Dream on Monkey Mountain*) or in each of his four books of poetry: *In a Green Night, Selected Poems, The Castaway* and *The Gulf*. By 1960 Walcott is settled in Trinidad, having lived briefly in Kingston and New York. His travels serve only to confirm the validity and relevance of his West Indian experience.

Concomitant with Walcott's affirmation of native materials is the growing self-awareness of indigenous critics and their struggle toward authentic West Indian values. As a matter of fact, six of the seven critics representing coverage of Walcott's work during the sixties, are themselves West Indian (Robert E. Fox the exception). The first three authors, John Figueroa, Kenneth Ramchand and Mervyn Morris focus not only on Walcott's poetic text but also the difficult milieu within which he writes.

Figueroa and Ramchand elect close examination of individual poems. Drawing upon the linguistic mixture of "Tales of the Islands," Figueroa interprets the Creole/ Standard tension Walcott exploits within the traditional sonnet form. Ramchand uses his explication of "Laventille" from *The Castaway* to complement other critics' easy generalizations regarding themes and trends. He explicates the poem to illustrate how interwoven themes, imagery, syntax and metrics compound meaning. As they illuminate Walcott's intricate verse, Figueroa and Ramchand also exercise their own ingenuity. While Walcott's verbal dexterity rewards careful study, it poses difficulties for unsophisticated readers. In "Walcott and the Audience for Poetry," Jamaican poet Mervyn Morris condemns the system of colonial education and moribund reviewers for inadequate grounding in younger, more "difficult" poets. He rejects Barbadian poet Edward Brathwaite's classification of Walcott as a "humanist," as opposed to a "folk," poet (because he allegedly directs himself away from the people). Morris argues that critics who accuse Walcott of addressing a foreign, elite audience are so obsessed with his style that they overlook the highly relevant content of his work:

> Poems which happen to be about death, love, evil, art, the loss of faith,
> are not relevant enough for those who find compassion or complex

ambiguity decadent luxuries in our emerging society, and call instead for
poems which speak stridently of politics, class and race. (Morris 178)

Analyzing poems in *The Castaway*, Morris emphasizes the greater particularity, tighter rhythm and increasing significance that result from Walcott's meticulous revisions. He detects richer complexity beneath a more natural-sounding simplicity in his newer verse. Walcott's experiments with non-standard usages even lead Morris to anticipate within dialect poetry greater potential than he had previously expected.

Both Morris and Walcott are realistic enough to know that not everyone will understand, much less respond to, serious poetry. The fact remains that Walcott's text yields meaning according to the reader's tenacity and powers of perception. His most famous play, *Dream on Monkey Mountain* is a good example. Two essays, by Lloyd Brown and Robert Fox, take different approaches, yet they center on the play's dream element. Brown compares *Dream on Monkey Mountain* with Leroi Jones' *The Slave* (1964) to illustrate crucial parallels. Both plays are revolutionary, utilizing symbolism within fantasy sequences that are simply more explicit in Walcott's hands. Makak can then be used as an antidote for literalists who misinterpret Jones' implications.

Given the correspondences between the plays — the need for dreams and for revolutionary violence to rid the black man's psyche of self-hatred — Brown insists on the oneness of Caribbean and black-American experience. Interestingly, Brown uses Walcott, whose racial credentials are questioned by purists because of his Eurocentric style, to clarify the deeper meaning of *The Slave* which some critics dismiss as a "naïve and suicidal" race-war play authored by "an hysterical monomaniac" (Brown 194).

Robert Fox goes beyond racial implications in his study of *Dream on Monkey Mountain*, asserting the mythological proportions of Walcott's drama. There is more to the play than the theme of imagination's power to redeem the downtrodden of the earth. Walcott uses the stage to dramatize "the disparities between a consciousness that is creative and metaphoric, and one that is straightforward and imprisoning" (Fox 204). Alter egos embodied in an apparition, in Moustique, and in Corporal Lestrade tempt the protagonist successively toward whiteness, blackness, materialism, then power and revenge. What is liberating about Makak's dream — collective and universalized according to Fox — is that he outgrows and throws off external values to return to himself. Rather than provide easy escape into a prescribed framework, the dream awakens Makak to personal roots.

Having begun coverage of this phase of Walcott's career with explications of two particular poems, I close with two surveys of his work culminating in *The Gulf* (1969). *The Gulf* brings out the ironic fact that isolation is the common denominator for all Walcott's castaways. The distance separating alien shores links individuals in a brotherhood of loneliness. Gordon Rohlehr reasons that after *In a Green Night* and *The Castaway*, imagery in the *The Gulf* indicates that Walcott's "vitality and inner affirmative music" are withering into a dryness of spirit. His themes of loneliness, exile, and the chasms separating people may be overly internalized, leaving the poet too skeptical and too detached to remain a part of the West Indies.

Another consideration of Walcott's place in the Caribbean is Patricia Ismond's "Walcott Versus Brathwaite." Like Rohlehr, Ismond refers to Walcott's three main poetry collections from the sixties. The device of comparing Edward Brathwaite, a Barbadian "people's poet" with Walcott's Eurocentric humanism, provides more than a definition of the issues dividing two types of poetry. Ismond capitalizes on the opportunity to outline the strengths and weaknesses of conflicting aesthetics within the context of her emerging society. She concludes that although Walcott's is a personal quest, his insistence on self reliance is a broader, positive assertion, "not to be derivative and beholden, or to deem ourselves secondary in status" (235).

C. "Homage to Gregorias" (1970-1979)

The decade of the seventies confirms Walcott's West Indian roots and his conviction that these roots tap the deepest human resources. An autobiographical thread weaves through *Another Life*,(1972), the dialect poem "Sainte Lucie" in *Sea Grapes* (1976), the politically oriented *Remembrance* (1977) and *The Star-Apple Kingdom*,(1979). At the same time, Walcott dramatizes cultural affinities between modern Trinidad and 16th-century Spain in *The Joker of Seville* (1975), between Jamaica's Rastafarians and Ethiopia in *O Babylon!* (1976), then works a reversal of Daniel Defoe's Crusoe-Friday tandem in *Pantomime* (1978). All three of these plays are to some extent creolized musicals, incorporating more or less successfully such native forms as calypso and reggae.

Walcott draws details from his early years in St. Lucia for *Another Life* a veritable poetic "Portrait of the Artist as a Young Man"; yet he insists that he is recording the "biography of an 'intelligence,' a West Indian intelligence, using it in the Latin sense of spirit" (Hamner 411). Edward Baugh, who has written extensively on Walcott, demonstrates in "Painters and Painting in *Another Life*" the extent to which the structure and content of the poem depend on the visual arts. In painting, as in poetry, Walcott exhibits early inclinations toward the Renaissance. Counterbalancing these foreign leanings are the immediate influences of Harold Simmons and his childhood friend, the painter Dunstan St. Omer. As Baugh indicates, Walcott's perception of correspondences between 16th-century European creative vigor and St. Lucia's artistic awakening inspires much of the rich allusiveness of the poem.

On the stage, the Spanish Golden Age informs Walcott's *The Joker of Seville:* his adaptation of Tirso de Molina's classic *El Burlador de Sevilla* (1630). In "Breaking Myths and Maidenheads," Patricia Ismond delineates not only the striking parallels between Port-of-Spain, Trinidad and Tirso's Spain, but she analyzes the existentialism of Walcott's Don Juan character. Since she has viewed different runs of the play, she is in a position to report the effects of various technical changes for subsequent productions.

While Ismond approves the performances she has viewed, two separate reviewers react negatively to Walcott's treatment of Jamaica's Rastafarians in his next play, *O*

Babylon! Sharing part of the blame is Galt MacDermot who scored the lyrics for the two musicals. Both Victor Questel and Sule Mombara agree that the play fails to overcome the incompatible differences between metropolitan musical traditions and Rastafarian culture. The perceived weaknesses in idiom, music and acting lead Questel to hope that the play is merely an interlude in Walcott's progress and Mombara to argue that the dramatist needs to sink his roots among the people, to deliver messages that will alter his decaying society.

This kind of oversimplification is not likely to be taken seriously by Walcott since his aim is art rather than propaganda. Of course he delves into the society he knows, with all its complicated ambiguities. His next volume of poetry, *Sea Grapes* (1976), is a case in point. Edward Baugh's review "Ripening with Walcott" considers the book in light of Walcott's evolving style: the manner by which personal experience serves as an image of the human struggle against bitterness, corruption, and the ravages of age to achieve reconciliation. As Baugh points out, the central poem "Sainte Lucie" with its blend of languages, fuses the artist with the common people of Roseau Valley.

Although Walcott's next two plays, *Remembrance* (1977) and *Pantomime* (1978), are equally embedded in the West Indian scene, neither is as ambitious or extravagant as his previous musicals. Their reception in the West Indies has been favorable and a New York production of *Remembrance* starring Roscoe Lee Brown has received high marks from veteran *New Yorker*, critic Edith Oliver. Oliver's review is followed by Mark McWatt's report on a Barbados run of the play. His commentary on the director's innovative use of sets underscores the drama's rightful venue: live performance. The play is contemplative; yet it comes alive with humor, music and vivid representation of Trinidad's rancorous independence movement.

Since *Pantomime* is a tour de force on the classic *Robinson Crusoe* it possesses a unique literary element that goes beyond the basic stage script. Therefore, complementing Christopher Gunness' short review of a Port-of-Spain production, Patrick Taylor's close analysis of the play's narrative structure probes deeper relevance. Taylor argues that Walcott's reversal of the master-slave relationship constitutes a "liberating narrative." The creativity extends beyond "the authentic Creole appropriation of the classical traditions," avoids ethnic critics' demands that he forge a new "African mythology" and addresses the innermost needs of any degraded outcast. In this particular role transferal, the black man assists the white man to confront the reality beneath his delusions.

In a sense, the theme of this play and of major poems in *The Star-Apple Kingdom* (1979) culminates Walcott's treatment of castaway figures in the seventies. Shabine, the "red nigger" poet-sailor of the opening poem "The Schooner *Flight*," celebrates his "nation of the imagination" in sure-handed dialect. The unnamed politician of the book's title poem comes to terms with his heritage while preparing his breakfast within the estate-house his ancestors could enter only as slaves. Two poets in their own right, Benjamin DeMott and Seamus Heaney are struck by the linguistic accomplishment of *The Star-Apple Kingdom*. DeMott believes that Walcott's years of casual experimentation with dialect account for the range and grandeur of his language, although he still lapses occasionally into portentousness. Heaney, an Irish expatriate, compares Walcott's accomplishment with that of John Millington Synge — the creation of a singular idiom capable of the most subtle expressiveness. DeMott and Heaney testify to the distance Walcott has traveled since his defense of cultural assimilation in introducing *Dream on Monkey Mountain and Other Plays* in 1970.

D. "A Simple Flame" (1980-1990)

Despite laudatory reviews in major professional journals for over twenty years, critical opinion regarding each new collection always seems to divide over the individual critic's perception of Walcott's literary debt to predecessors. What is one reviewer's derivative reliance on the Jacobeans, T. S. Eliot, Dylan Thomas, or Robert Lowell is another reviewer's brilliant acquisition fused into a unique, personal voice. The pattern continues into the nineties where Walcott reaffirms his position on familiar issues, leading to the release of his *Collected Poems 1948-1984* and the epical *Omeros* (1990). A new development that becomes increasingly evident in recent works is his use of intertextuality itself as content. Two collections of verse in the eighties precede *Collected Poems*. Calvin Bedient condemns *The Fortunate Traveller* (1981) for being imitative and disproportionately verbose. Richard Dwyer, on the other hand, is primarily concerned with subject matter. He suggests that Walcott has played up the bifurcation in his nature so long that commentators often mistake his polarized subject matter for the poet's own self-conception. He defends the multiplicity of Walcott's voices as the poet merges them into his own idiom.

Reviewing *Midsummer* (1984), Sven Birkerts echoes Dwyer's reference to Walcott's "Ovidian gift": meaning that his "compressions, associations, and transformations appear effortless" (331). For Birkerts, Walcott's subject matter is not landscapes but words, "language becoming poetry." When he notices subtle linkages within *Midsummer*,he touches on the theme of Robert Bensen's detailed study "The Painter as Poet." Bensen is impressed with the particularity of Walcott's reliance on the visual arts for subject, imagery, light and color throughout *Midsummer*. Beyond that, he also traces significant changes in Walcott's relationship with painting since *Another Life*.

As may be expected, publication of *Collected Poems*, elicits overviews of Walcott's cumulative oeuvre. Concerning the early poems up to *Another Life*, Peter Balakian remarks on their modest intention. J. D. McClatchy brands them rhetorical, consciously derivative and literary. When he comes to *Another Life*, McClatchy finds the book to be one of the finest autobiographical poems in English. By the time of *The Star-Apple Kingdom*, Balakian sees in Walcott the same capacity to revitalize and renew himself that characterizes Yeats, Neruda, and Rilke. Bruce King takes exception to a policy of selection that appears to emphasize universal themes and the mythology of Walcott's life, at the expense of "more topical, argumentative poems" (King 361).

In addition to his succinct coverage of *Collected Poems*, Bruce King's dual review also affords a transition into Walcott's second major publication of 1986: *Three Plays*, which includes *The Last Carnival, Beef, No Chicken* and *A Branch of the Blue Nile*.

Although *A Branch of the Blue Nile* dates back to 1983, *Beef, No Chicken*, dates back to 1981 and *The Last Carnival* dates back to the unpublished "In a Fine Castle" from 1970, King very properly argues that their collected versions conform to a "new phase of withdrawn, introspective, more traditional drama, directly rooted in Walcott's life and focused on the social realities of the post colonial West Indies" (King 367).

Single reviews hardly do justice to serious plays which, by their very nature, must vary with each production; nevertheless, there are informative reviews available which capture not only something of the immediacy of live performance but also the reviewer's frame of reference. Judy Stone, for example, managed to see a flawed premier of *Beef, No Chicken* in 1981, and later a markedly improved staging in 1985. She is witness, then, to specific authorial revisions and to the impact of a new director's interpretation. Bruce King indicates major revisions leading from "In a Fine Castle" to *The Last Carnival* and Trinidadian novelist/playwright Earl Lovelace analyzes a Port-of-Spain production of the play. Aside from the evaluation of acting and thematic content, Lovelace charges that the importation of American actors prevents native audiences from seeing their story dramatized by their own people. Walcott's response to just such concerns appears in his 1982 interview with Anthony Milne (59-60).

A Branch of the Blue Nile has been received favorably by audiences, but it demands special treatment because of the way in which it departs from Walcott's previous drama. In several of his later poems ("The Forest of Europe," "The Star-Apple Kingdom," "The Hotel Normandie Pool," "Marina Tsvetaeva"), and to some extent in *The Last Carnival*, Walcott seems to have begun experimenting with the interrelationship between the writing process and subject matter. His flirtation with this kind of intertextuality bursts into full bloom in *A Branch of the Blue Nile*. In Steven Breslow's words, the play literally "reverberates with reflexive consciousness of itself" (389).

The Arkansas Testament closes out the eighties in keeping with the internalized particularity of Walcott's recent work. Vernon Shetley refers once again to the paradox of a writer from the margins of English literature having acquired such an abundance of insight and expressiveness. Although he notes that Walcott has restrained much of his earlier rhetorical excess, Shetley contends he is still prone to elevate style over matter. Recognizing Walcott's maturation as an artist, Shetley echoes sentiments of critics throughout his career. It is ironic that having absorbed Western culture in a colonial outpost, Walcott persistently challenges the establishment to accommodate this West Indian phenomenon. Walcott's first entry in the nineties is no exception.

With the appearance of *Omeros* in 1990, Walcott undertakes nothing less than a modern adaptation of the time-honored genre of the epic. Although he confesses that as a youth he longed to continue the "line of Marlowe and Milton" ("What" 31), the sheer magnitude of such a project may account for his insistence that the poem is not actually an epic. Then again, perhaps his denial signifies a more radical agenda: redefining classical assumptions in a modern third world mode.

As J.D.R. Bruckner reviews *Omeros*, he quotes Walcott's contention that he wants to avoid the "heroic" elevation of battles and warriors in order to emphasize inherently humble people. In keeping with that sentiment, Mary Lefkowitz focuses on the down-to-earth quality of the Narrative. The story advances in a spiral of memory and action which emulates thought processes. In the end, universal and personal, past and present are juxtaposed not in superhuman demigods but in natural, unassuming men and women. The definitive study of this monumental work remains to be written; however, its fundamental dimensions are readily apparent. Greeks, Romans, French, Italians, Germans, Spaniards, and Britons all have their national epics. Those of Dante and Milton may even be said to project Western culture as universal. Walcott's venue, while not that comprehensive, is international in scope.

In the tradition of his classical predecessors, Walcott adheres to the basic formula. Influences are frequently explicit and occasionally as unobtrusive as a familiar turn of phrase or parallel plot device. Characters may not be superhuman, yet they resonate extended cultural significance. Battles may not rise to Olympic heights, yet they determine the survival of an emerging race. The language of Walcott's sustained *terza rima* stanzas ranges from highly rhetorical periods to colloquial earthiness, not unlike the rising and falling cadences of Dante's *Divine Comedy*.

Other epic devices add their flavor: invocation of the muse, statement of theme, beginning *in medias res*, catalogs, formal speeches, communication with the dead. The supernatural intervenes through dreams, visions and the incantations of the old shamanMa Kilman. The past and the present are brought together episodically as the progeny of Europe and Africa carve out their New World identity. The list of comparisons could go on; however, despite the formal similarities, Walcott offers new perspectives, a re-writing of tradition.

What is unique about Walcott's epic is not so much the particular geographic montage or the lowly station of his characters. The outstanding feature of his creation is its reflexive consciousness. Like Dante, Walcott participates in his own Narrative, occasionally addressing the audience more or less directly. But beyond that, he plays with the intertextuality of autobiography and fiction, the postmodern recognition of words and margins as poetic content.

On the literal plane, the story concerns a Caribbean Helen who inspires two interconnected Narrative lines. One recounts the contest between West Indian fishermen, Achille and Hector, for her hand. The second involves British expatriate Major Dennis Plunkett's ambition to give Helen a history of her own. On the figurative level, the story uses Helen as the embodiment of Walcott's native island, St. Lucia. Whether they are descendants of African slaves or representatives of declining empire, the author and the protagonists ultimately discover that through their efforts to possess metaphorical Helen, the real island asserts its possession of them.

It is St. Lucia's place in the larger struggle among European powers for control of the New World that gives Walcott all the reason he needs to synthesize Greek and African mythology as they wash up on West Indian shores. The pervasive motif of the poem is closure. Whether it be the letter "O," mouths of poets, vases, caves, conch shells, statues or lovers, the shoreline of an island surrounded by ocean, the circuit of sea swifts or peasant fishermen out to sea and back each day, the journeys of various characters, past and present—all the dominant imagery of the poem suggests circular completion. Achille loses, then regains Helen. Plunkett learns to appreciate Helen as the living woman rather than as a symbol.

Walcott has not essayed the epic of African diaspora any more than he has assumed the guise of a black Homer. In "The Muse of History," Walcott rejects the epic of the tribe which needs forgotten gods and a dead speech based on shame or revenge. He argues, "The epic poem is not a literary project. It is already written; it was written in the mouths of the tribe, a tribe which courageously yielded its history: (8-9). *Omeros* is his epic of the dispossessed, regardless of nationality or race.

When I speak of Walcott's uniqueness, I am not suggesting that he stands alone. He has his peers and several masters. What is original in Walcott is the use he makes of his manifold voice, his particular combination of imagination and experience. For a poet often given to confessional verse, he is remarkably other-oriented. Even in passages where he is most topical, he translates personal immediacy into human insight. Walcott has maintained his right to diverse cultures so consistently that he might well embody the ideal expounded in T.S. Eliot's "Tradition and the Individual Talent." Eliot describes a depersonalized artist with an historical sense that enlightens his contemporaneity well beyond any reference to self or cause (49). In poetry, as on stage, Derek Walcott rewrites tradition, expanding and renewing in the most profound sense of the word. Perhaps the crowning recognition of this achievement is his Nobel Prize for Literature, awarded in December 1992.

Endnotes

[1] Hereinafter, page references to articles that are reprinted in this *Critical Perspectives* volume apply to pagination within this present book. References to all outside sources observe pagination of their original publication.

[2] In reproducing the ten items for section one, occasional errors may be indicated by [sic]. Typographical matters, such as diacritical markings and the presence or absence of italics, are left as in the original publication.

References

Eliot, T.S. "Tradition and the Individual Talent." *The Sacred Wood: Essays on Poetry and Criticism*. 1928. London: Methuen, 1950. 47-59.

Hamner, Robert. "Conversation with Derek Walcott." *World Literature Written in English* 16.2 (Nov. 1977): 409-20.

Naipaul, V.S. *The Middle Passage*. London: Andre Deutsch, 1962.

Walcott, Derek. *Another Life*. New York: Farrar, Straus & Giroux, 1972.

_____. "Meanings." *Savacou* 2 (1970): 45-51.

_____. "The Muse of History: An Essay." *Is Massa Day Dead?* Ed. Orde Coombs. Garden City, N.Y.: Doubleday, 1974: 1-28.

_____. "What the Twilight Says." *Dream on Monkey Mountain and Other Plays*. New York: Farrar, Straus & Giroux, 1970: 3-40.

I

WALCOTT, ARTIST AND CRITIC

SOCIETY AND THE ARTIST (1957)

Derek Walcott

Where history is being made now, in these islands, is not in the quick political achievements, not in the large agricultural schemes, but in the deepening stream of the way we are now learning to think. To see ourselves, not as others see us, but with all the possibilities of the new country we are making.

Naturally, when we think of our independence we think in political terms. We will point to the riots we won and the other actions which are so natural now that it seems difficult to imagine that we did not always have them.

Whether we are socially different, and whether our racial hatreds still smoulder inside, the people of all these islands know that they must share their countries. They may think of minorities, or of the large, backward mass of people, Indians and Negroes, but they do not think principally of race. They are now a people who possess the land in thought and share it.

All except the inevitable minority, their artists. I do not think that there is any minority in the entire archipelago with more pride in the islands, with a deeper love for their roots, with a more anguished sense of a people's suffering and progress, than the old men and their younger inheritors, who think that they write for themselves, who long for the metropolitan centres of civilization, temporarily conquer them, and then yearn for more than the sunlight and the sea. They know where they are planted, and know where they should like to die.

Some of them, like Mais, Dunkey and Daley died when the praise came late or not at all.

When they are dead, they are blessed with the usual ironic praise of the safer ones, who are glad to have them silent. Their violently public statements of love of country, whether in pamphlet, rum-shop, or drawing room, whether aesthetic or in politics has always been embarrassing. But nothing has been more valuable than the honest cursing of abuses which they could not stand or prevent. Their names must be kept alive until their work has settled as part or our tradition.

But after we have turned from the safe dead, we face some of those who are stupid enough to follow in the paths of self-destruction and isolation. They are those whom we say we cannot help. Perhaps we cannot. They are the voices which the Government cannot hear, since nothing can make a government uncomfortable in a democracy. When the democratic government is disturbed, it is hearing the total voices of its own conscience. It is not disturbed when a painter or a writer succumbs to despair, suffers continual frustration and abuses its lack of patronage.

It is not like begging, for the state must look after beggars, it does not have to feed every ranting idiot who claims his indispensable genius. The only difficulty is that until they are dead we feel that we cannot know. Their lives must follow the romantic pattern of neglect, mockery and inbreeding argument.

Year after year, these men remain. They remain because they are not in search of environment. The land-scape is their home. They are not in search of better jobs, like the emigrants, because Europe is tougher, and they can work more comfortably here.

They are urged to remain, and these islands kill them. They are killed by acclaim without cash, praise without purchase, killed by too much drinking which like the praise of friends bloats and distends their ego. They are killed by the humiliation of borrowing from people who always knew they would never mean anything. They are tortured by the insistence with which amateur expatriates and returned dilettantes tell them of the work that is done or has been done in Europe. What is worse they are swamped by the amateurs who prefer posture to the serious discipline that must be acquired.

In a sense, every artist is on his own. But it is the most difficult profession in the world to be on your own when you are, if you are any good, the property of this world and not of the next.

The poets know the hopelessness of the situation. A man writes probably two good poems a year, and that by the finest standards is plenty. For a poem of reasonable length, he will be paid a half guinea locally. This does not pay for the poem, but it is called a gesture. He then loses his property to the publisher, or the newspaper. If he is an honest poet, he will print only the poems which succeed. As an honest working man, he will have earned perhaps four pounds a year, and it is pretty certain that he will do any other work reluctantly.

It seems better sometimes to agree with Plato, who chased artists out of his ideal community, or to have a petition in verse presented to the Almighty to please stop making poets, as people do not know what to do with them.

There is no serious West Indian artist, painter or poet, who would not prefer to say something of his country than of a view of Venice. Europe does not belong to them. But they still live in a green culture where, unless they are camouflaged in grey flannel suits, or sell insurance, or pretend that they are happy Civil Servants who are simply dying to own a new Chevrolet, they are not pleasant to have around.

There is not a good publisher in the islands. There is one art dealer in Jamaica. There is no true theatre building in the entire archepelago, and you will hear popular talk about Elizabethans and new Greeks. There is no such thing as a real collector or patron of the plastic arts, but hotels change hands every day.

Scholarships which our artists receive are given by foreign governments, if you can call the British government foreign, and these, only when their work has won merit or been printed in the scholarship's country of origin.

There are no schools for actors, no theatres, no backers of plays, and they will talk about a national theatre.

Nobody buys paintings because they know the artists drink too much, or talk too much about themselves, or detest criticism, but they talk about the inevitable gaiety of West Indian art. No one will print verse and who can blame them.

Consequently they pack their manuscripts and head for Europe. In two years they are acclaimed and their work has all the vigour of a fresh memory, all the style of years of isolation, all the beauty of nostalgia, and then the deterioration begins, and the fog closes around the memory.

They are rootless, and then they teach themselves to deny the loves which they had earliest and the faith which perhaps their own communities made them betray.

Our artists and writers should not be forced, like soldiers to die on foreign soil, or to return wounded and crawl famously into a hole. They are part of what can be one of the finest and most beautiful of countries. I mean these islands. Without them Greece would have been a Tourist resort, and these island will be beautiful but dumb.

HISTORY AND PICONG ... IN THE MIDDLE PASSAGE (1962)

Derek Walcott

If there ever were, there are no earthly paradise [sic] left. Those picturesque archipelagoes, the West Indies and the South Sea Islands, have for their moral and financial improvement been captured by UNESCO guerillas, international hoteliers, tourists, anthropologists, religious sects and travel writers.

Marshes, mosquitoes and seedy expatriates of Greene and Maugham are passing away with the nineteenth century, which in those far-flung outposts is a long time dying. Yet the best travel books have been by these nineteenth century writers who could look at the filthy backyards of the Empire with a proprietary and corrective eye.

None of them knew that their eye was that of the auctioneer; that, less than a century later, another nineteenth century relic would refuse to preside over the dissolution of their Empire. They saw history and the destiny of the white man steadily and whole, as logical in direction as a Roman road.

Those tours of Empire, taken as if by carriage by parsonical zealots like Trollope, Froude and Kingsley concern themselves with the climate more than with the people and with people more than the individual. This is natural, since they wrote for their own time.

It is curious to find however, that possibly our best West Indian novelist, Mr. V.S. Naipaul, has chosen to do our Grand Tour, Trinidad, Guiana, Martinique, Surinam, Jamaica, with his Victorian spectacles on, and that in his "Impressions of Five Societies, British, French and Dutch, in the West Indies, and South America," he has given us a number of idyosyncratic, neo-classical engravings of these societies.

Every experience is bent to his style, historical judgments made in mannered aphorisms, and the writing once again is brilliant. It is the result that is doubtful. Everything is made to seem touching and ridiculous. The people he encounters have an antic, desperate pathos. More often they are vulgar and we can imagine Mr. Naipaul recoiling in terror from their exuberance.

18

The benefit of style is that it can conceal emotion, and in the hand of an excellent ironist like Mr. Naipaul little will be revealed of the vulgar emotions like homesickness, love or disgust. It is a case of history versus the aphorist, landscape versus art, compassion versus wit. It produces strange contradictions:

"How can the history of this West Indian futility be written?" Mr. Naipaul writes: "What tone shall the historian adopt? The history of the islands can never be satisfactorily told. Brutality is not the only difficulty. History is built around achievement and creation: and nothing was created in the West Indies. . ." Nothing? Come, come, Naipul. V. S., know your literature, how about "A House for Mr. Biswas?"

"Sir, that book was not created in the West Indies."

"Where was it created?"

"In England, sir."

"My apologies, again. You may sit down, Naipaul. And don't smile before ah make George Lamming hold you!"

The difference in viewpoint between Lamming's "The Pleasures of Exile" and "The Middle Passage" is striking. For all his occasional incoherence Lamming is a visionary, which means that his despair is profound, closer to anger and translatable into action. Naipaul, a neater writer, is reflective, more weighed down by the sense of the past, not by the chains of slavery but by a chronic dispiritedness. It makes his book depressing. The flashing wit shines like a mirror in a rubbish heap.

I become uncomfortable when a people or a race are a source of infinite amusement or benign tolerance to a writer, even such a gentle humorist as Mr. Naipaul, and his mixture of history and picong, however exotic is a forgettable recipe.

He has chosen some striking ingredients of our society and pointed out how tasteless they are: the society columns of our newspapers are cunningly ridiculed, the worst aspects of our 'Americanisation,' the belligerence of our humour, Negro churlishness. East Indian apathy, canned coffee, tourists, stray dogs and noise, including folk-art and steelbands. On the other hand he must prefer things as they are, since they are rich resources for the satirist.

The section on Trinidad, with which he deals with affectionate loathing, is the best part of his book. Despite its flavour of "An Englishman's Guide To The Colonies," it stings with the home truths of a family quarrel. Like any such catharsis, it draws him nearer to us.

But it is not near enough to hatred, to that holy rage which a great exile like Joyce poured on Dublin, or to the savage indignation of Swift. It is more like a supercilious pat on the head, or a friendly volley of insults. But, as Mr. Naipaul must know, it is hard to insult a West Indian subtly. We like we noise.

NECESSITY OF NEGRITUDE (1964)

Derek Walcott

The fact that neither Aime Cesaire nor Leopold Senghor, two major poets of our time, are included in a volume I own called "The Concise Encyclopaedia of Modern World Literature", (although Amos Tutuola is registered), may illustrate the necessity of "Negritude".

There is a concept of language and literature as being white that on one hand divides writers racially — anthologies of Negro poetry for example, are becoming popular — and which on the other claims that art is universal.

The division has spread to popular art forms like jazz, which is now exclusively claimed by the American Negro as his "soul music", and it is an assertion that has impelled a great deal of "separatist" poetry.

Many Negro poets are conducting an experiment in racial self-analysis which involves finding those qualities in their personality which they consider distinctive from those of the white writer. This sort of poetry has led to an emphasis on certain modes which the Negro formerly resented when they were applauded by the white spectator or reader; rhythms, simplicity, "barbarism," splendour.

It is the opposite of the integration movement. A great deal of modern Negro poetry and prose belligerently asserts its isolation, its difference, and sometimes its psychic superiority.

Yet it is extremely difficult to create a natural poetry that is technically identifiable as Negro without distorting language or feeling, and most Negro poets writing in English arrive at a point where to progress technically, to develop complexity of structure appears like treachery, a betrayal of the cause.

It is more artificial when the Negro in the Western World, so long cut off from Africa, with his language, religion, customs and politics an entirely different experience, attempts to force a fusion.

As Eliot once wrote, "you gotta use words," and the words he uses, to stretch the point to absurdity, are the white man's words.

So, in the Western World, are his God, his dress, his machinery, his food. And, of course, his literature.

In the West Indies the most powerful expression of Negritude has come from Cesaire, whose poem "Cahier d'un Retour au Pays Natal" has only now begun to have an influence on the writers and intellectuals of the Caribbean.

But Cesaire's great poem is not so much a work of protest of exaltation: it is a work of magnificent optimism, one that goes higher in feeling than the paternalistic, cataloguing of Whitman.

His riposte to the usual claim that Negroes have contributed little or nothing to the progress of the world is:

> "Hurrah for those who never invented anything
> "Hurrah for those who never explored anything
> "Hurrah for those who never conquered anything
> "But who, in awe, gave themselves up to the essence of things. . ."

And further on, he proclaims:

> "But preserve me, heart, from all hatred
> do not turn me into a man of hate whom I shall hate
> for in order to emerge into this unique race
> you know my worldwide love,
> know it is not hatred against other races —
> that turns me into the cultivator of this one race
> for what I want
> arises from infinite hunger
> from infinite thirst
> finally to demand them to be free,
> freely in their secluded soul
> to create the ripening fruit."

This is a West Indian poem, and its subject is race as openly, though with much more complexity of expression, as the Guadeloupean poet, Saint John Perse's "Eloges" or "Pour Feter Un Enfance" is about being a white child in the tropics.

The two poems make an interesting contrast, but their resemblances, their primal sources are very alike. They are separated from the poetry of Senghor by an entire experience, by geography and by traditions.

Senghor is an African poet and the mythology from which he writes is one that is part of him. For Cesaire it is a nostalgia, a legend, a number of intuitions which he gives shape.

Ulli Beier, that arduosu, [sic] white German publicist of Negritude has written on "The Theme of The Ancestors in Senghor's Poetry," that:

"Those African poets who most strongly assert their Negritude, are often the most sophisticated and — on the surface at least — the most assimilated Africans.

One might ask oneself therefore, whether this new proclamation of 'Negritude' is a genuine rediscovery of African attitudes and values in the poet's soul, or whether it is merely a deliberate, self-conscious intention, a kind of cultural manifesto. Since 'Negritude' has become a kind of literary and cultural movement, some people will no doubt suspect that if Senghor makes use of Balafongs and Khalams in this poetry when he speaks of the princess of Elissa and the night of Mahgreb when he envisages the Lamantines drinking at the source and the procession of the dead on the beach — that all these are merely picturesque trappings intended to provide atmosphere and an African flavour to his poetry. . . ."

Herr Beier, in this penetrating article (*Black Orpheus* No. 5. May, 1959), proves that the poetry of Senghor is a natural exhalation of tribal mythology, that, for example, the African veneration of ancestors, its ritual pieties, in fact, its "joy" in the presence of the dead, is not European, in fact, the dead opposite of the Hebraic-Christian attitude.

German excavators like Herr Beier and Mr. Janheinz Jahn, author of "Muntu" have done some valuable definition of the African personality.

Sometimes their enthusiasm carries them to the frontiers of the absurd, as when Herr Jahn praises Selvon for the African quality of his story telling.

Two English-educated poets, the Nigerians John Pepper Clark and Wole Soyinka have ridiculed the idea of Negritude as a poetic principle, Mr. Soyinka's remark about the tiger not going around proclaiming its tigritude already becoming famous.

It is significant that the assertion has come from those islands, and countries formerly ruled by the French, since the French process of assimilation in its colonies has been very different from the non-interference of the British. Negritude, like Presence Africaine, are French concepts, just as the surrealism of Perse—and Cesaire come from the genus of that language.

It is a language that is flexible to ideas, to abstraction, to a philosophy-poetry, and its qualities in prosody are different from English. There has never been a good surrealist poet in English, whereas in the Romance languages, in Spanish, French, Italian, Portuguese, surrealism has flourished.

Neruda, Lorca, and Cesaire, are to a fair degree, untranslatable.

In Senghor's poetry it has been pointed out that the symbols, the materialised concepts that he uses have votive, totemic, magical use. Because of this, because of its incantatory use, its function of poetry as ritual, its quality hardly comes over in English.

The mnemonic use of words, of naming things and blessing them by naming, is something which has gone out of English, since it is possible that the more complicated in syntax a language becomes the more its original impulses, worship and communication weaken.

Although Senghor writes in French, he writes as an African who is putting that language to a particular, restricted use, the ancient, tribal one of the poet as an oracle. He himself has requested a poetry whose tone is monodic, recitation accompanied by traditional African instruments.

In this way he has tried to restore, even if it is through an intellectualisation of the process, poetry to its right place, to the language of the tribe.

For us, whose tribal memories have died, and who have begun again in a New

World, Negritude offers an assertion of pride, but not of our complete identity, since that is mixed and shared by other races, whose writers are East Indian, white, mixed, whose best painters are Chinese, and in whom the process of racial assimilation goes on with every other marriage.

But both the concepts of Negritude and the assertion of the African personality have restored a purpose and dignity to the descendants of slaves.

In the art of poetry, it has shown, through the translations of Senghor, Cesaire, and Perse, a freer, more natural expression, one that need not confine itself in the dated rigidities of certain forms, but which will demand its own discipline and power.

In this way, the poetry of Senghor may be assimilated into the experiment of not only a West Indian language, but of a West Indian personality, one in which all our races are powerfully fused.

LEAVING SCHOOL (1965)

Derek Walcott

> 'Sometimes an ancient and infinitesimal detail will come away like a
> whole headland; and sometimes a complete layer of my past will
> vanish without a trace.'   Tristes Tropiques

Our climate has two seasons, heat and rain. Sometimes, in childhood, this rain was like a sadness entering the earth, penetrating me with longing for our father. Even now, approaching the island, there are steaming grey piles of cumuli, the colour of boiled laundry, heaped on its mountains. It looks impenetrable or abandoned. Brown, broken precipices with the tattered grey lace of ocean, the single, tilted flag of a canoe, while the noise of the engines carries the memory of rain, of cold, clean cataracts pitching through gulches of giant fern, and the smoky, sulphurous sound of 'Sainte Lucie'.

Yet, when I think of my own headland, Vigie, it is never in rain, but the colour of that epigraph, copied in Brown ink; the colour of burnt seagrape leaves, and of roofs rusting in drought.

In elementary school we had been taught that Saint Lucia was 'The Helen of The West' because she was fought for so often by the French and British. She had changed hands thirteen times. She had been regularly violated. In fact, her final capture by the British had the quality of a cuckold's surrender, since she remained faithful to her French colonial past. Her name was clouded with darkness and misfortune; Columbus had named her after the blind saint; her saint's day was December thirteenth. Even her natural history was tragic. I had seen enough in childhood to believe it: a landslide that swallowed a mountain village after heavy rains, the memory of Saint Pierre, and, the year after I left school, a fire that destroyed half of the town.

Now, when I stood on the long wooden verandah of St Mary's College, I could see clear across the charred pasture of Castries to the Vigie promontory. 'The balcony' was a position I had earned as a prefect, but now, as an assistant master, I could loiter or strut there if I chose. It ran past the headmaster's study, and had been proscribed as sacred ground by our last head, a choleric, absent-minded English Catholic, whose name was T.E. Fox-Hawes. Mr. Fox-Hawes had also defined the 'alley' back of the College as out-of-bounds until five minutes before school, a decree which sent a

24

schoolboy population in blue serge blazers and blancoed cork 'bughouses' wandering through the town before the 'bell'. Bells obsessed the Head. He selected his bell-ringer carefully. It was a post more responsible than a prefect's. If a wind tilted the bell and the clapper rang lightly, the school shuddered, since Foxy would be out roaring, 'Who rang the bell?' It had been the same with the school balcony. But now, Foxy's era was over. The Irish Brothers of the Presentation had taken over the College.

Despite his short-fused temper, we had worshipped Foxy, and hated to see him go. So did he. He hated displays of sentiment. So we hung back under the roof of the galvanized iron customs shed, by a rusty gate and waved when we were sure his ship was headed for England, turning between La Toc point and Vigie. Our last English headmaster, he had been a lonely man, devoted to parades, fond of sailing and Conrad's prose, proud of the benignity of his Empire. He left the names of battles drumming in us, Blenheim, Waterloo, Malplaquet, of heroes who had actually quartered here, Sir John Moore, victim of Corunna, Admirals Abercomby and Rodney and the graves of an Inskilling Regiment on the Morne, where there were barracks built by the Royal Engineers, with the same rational, Romanesque brickwork as those at Vigie. Apart from the Cathedral, they were our only 'architecture'.

The only important buildings left after the fire were in the two blocks on either side of the verandah: one was the Convent and the Ave Maria Girls School, the other was the Presbytery with its French priests, and the Roman Catholic Boys' Primary School divided from the College by 'the Alley'. Leaving school had meant half-circling the block. I had been editor of its weekly Wall magazine, of its first Annual and a prefect. Little else.

I had given up sports early. In first or second form. Because I had been christened a prodigy, I couldn't endure failure, except it was so ridiculous that it looked like self-sacrifice. I had been considered a promising, conventional off-break bowler, but 'conventional' had no promise in it. All those promises were a long way behind me, all those angry, urgent cries to leave the life of a young silverfish and get out in the sun, and in the swim.

'Walcott, man!' Man was the cry, whatever your age. 'Get out there and give Abercomby a point, boy!' Once Walcott had tried. Pale, sallow, big-headed, the blue heart of his house blazoned on his singlet, the blue stripe of his house running down the seams of his shorts, flailing away towards the tape. Then how come fathead Simmons, who he was sure was bound to come last, put up a desperate burst for Abercomby (his own house) to save himself? Also, what was the point of being a wicketkeeper when some full toss, meant by an ambitious stylist to be swept to leg, just missed my Adam's apple by a gulp? I was so furious that I stretched out flat behind the stumps, playing dead until the team collected around me, then rose, threw off the gloves and left. Abercomby had to look elsewhere for points: in essays, and in conduct. In addition to the Black Book, where canings were noted, and the Detention Book for minor crimes, the Brothers had introduced the Alpha book for academics. I concentrated on getting points for Abercomby there.

Behind me on the balcony, the classrooms were humming with a generation being introduced by the Brothers to the wonders of natural science. Above the remaining town, were the thick green hills boiling all day with their broadleaved, volcanic vegetation. That was the nature I had learned to love in childhood. The one road inland coiled out of Castries up Morne Fortune, where the graves of the Inskillings were, the harbour below wide and hazing rapidly between trees. It crested that view that took in the Martinique channel, and sinuated through a cane-green valley towards snake country. It climbed again across the spinal ridge of the island, then it fell into the wide, heart-breaking Atlantic coast with its dirty breakers, its grey, unpainted villages with their squat Norman-style cathedrals, to split on to the clean, windy Southern plain of Vieuxfort, with its runways and arrowing highway, where the Americans had built an air base. I had known that road by heart from boyhood, travelling on its brightly painted trucks loaded with passengers, creaking with freight the names of its villages plaiting into each other like straw, Forestière, D'Ennery, Ravine Poisson (where the village was buried), Praslin, Micoud, D'Aubaignan, and the odours of its fruits, moubain, corrosol, gouyave, and the very strong odour of the sea.

In those days I would leave our house on Chaussée Road, equipped for such pilgrimages with a small, brown cardboard suitcase of clothes and painting and writing materials. I would bid my mother goodbye, and the cook would see me down to the country bus terminus on the wharf. I was going off alone into the country, 'en betassion', to write.

I spent those vacations at the large, wooden roadside hotel of a farmer-spinster who had been my father's friend, writing poems which I showed her, one or two a day, preparing myself for the life I had chosen. She treated me with amused respect, introduced me to the writings of Whitman, and at other times she would indulge in reminiscences of my father whom she had loved.

I had come from a genteel, self-denying Methodist poverty. My mother, who was headmistress of the Methodist Infant School, worked hard to keep us at college, even if my brother and I had both won scholarships, by taking in sewing. My mother's friends, those who had survived my father, had been members of an amateur dramatic group, some cultural club which had performed Shakespeare and given musical concerts, when my father was their 'moving spirit'. These friends included a violinist, an ex-merchant seaman, an inveterate reciter who had seen Barrymore's Hamlet, and a professional painter named Harold Simmons.

Their existence, since most of them were from a religious minority, Anglican, Methodist or lapsed Catholic, had a defensive, doomed frailty in that steamy, narrow-minded climate. Perhaps because of this they believed in 'the better things of life' with a defiant intensity, which drew them closely together. Their efforts, since the pattern would be repeated for my brother and me, must have been secretly victimized. Their presentations were known as 'The Anglican consette' (concert) or 'The Methodist School' or 'Teacher Alix Concert', with all the vague implications of damnation. My brother Roderick and I would go through the same purgation later.

All through adolescence I had experienced some of this mockery and persecution, even public damnation. The hell of others, of limbo and purgatory was something that, being an outsider, I learned to envy. I learnt early to accept that Methodists went to purgatory or hell, a Catholic hell, only after some strenuous dispensation. I was thus, in boyhood, estranged not only from another God, but from the common life of the island.

Perhaps it was this that made me find in the actual hell of the great fire, a certain exultation, since it had destroyed that other life.

From then on Saint Lucians would refer to it as an historical phrase, as they had once of 'en temps cholera'; all that year I lived in the traumatic wake of a heat wave. The air above the ruins, for months after, seemed to ripple like a washboard. There was a powerful sense of the unreal, the absurd. It was long after the shock of that destruction that the shapes of houses vibrated in memory and could be, in our imagination, placed rigidly into their foundations. This was a plain of blackened walls, ridiculous arches of doorways, of steps that marched in air.

The older life was unimaginable. The fire had humiliated the smug, repetitive lives of those Civil Servants, merchants and Creole professional men who had lived in rambling wooden houses with verandahs and mansards, attics for mongoloids, alcoholic uncles and half-racked, ageing aunts, that rigidly constructed, French-colonial life of the petit-ponche and the evening stroll. Down to the wharf to look at the island schooners and back, always along the same streets. All that had disappeared in smoke.

Down by the wharf, past the coal dunes near my grandfather's house, I had watched during childhood the crossing freizes of erect, singing women carrying huge panniers of anthracite coal, each weighing a hundredweight, but the port was no longer a coaling station. That had gone too. What still remained was the rhythm of the Church's calendar year, its bannered, chanting processions, Les Enfants De Marie, Retreats, and Friendly Society parades. During such processions I would feel that the town was empty and belonged to me. Every dusk the Cathedral of the Immaculate Conception flamed palely for vespers, drawing your friends from games in Columbus Square. Now, all those people, and they were a large part of the town's population, who had their properties destroyed by this Act of God, had been moved to the Romanesque barracks on the Vigie headland, a cantonment of refugees and destitutes. In fact Vigie was temporarily the new town, and when evening came those of us whose houses had survived preferred to go out there than to stay on that depressing, scorched plain where most of the City had been.

Still, all of those refugees on Fire Relief, poor man and merchant, seemed happier during those chaotic months, sharing in a common elation of having suffered. On moonlight nights, all around the barracks of the cantonment, from Married Women's Quarters to Officer's Mess, you could hear laughter, screams and singing across the broken water. The promontory had once been the green preserve of the Vigie Golf and Country Club, a haunt of retired white or near white Civil Servants and Army Officers. The buildings on the crest of the hill still were occupied by them, but they too would be gradually invaded, besieged.

In fact, the topographical changes of that headland chart the social evolutions of the island. It is now an airfield, but in our house on Chaussée Road, we still had a pale water-colour of my father's of 'The Coconut Walk', an avenue that I could only vaguely remember now that I was eighteen, that showed what it had been like. Now, everyone that I loved lived out there. From the balcony I could make out the Army morgue which Harry Simmons, who was now Fire-Relief officer, had converted into a studio, and Barnard's Hill, where Dunstan St. Omer, Hedwig Henry, Claude Theobalds (the son of the amateur violinist) and I, had studied painting.

This was a low hill shelved with white walled, red-roofed villas that formed the thick end of the Vigie headland. We had been invited to study painting with Harry Simmons on Saturday mornings when he heard that we were interested in art, that St. Omer was a prodigious draughtsman for his age, that Henry and I wrote verse and painted, and that Theobalds, apart from being an athlete, was also his father's son.

Wherever you grow up as a writer, even with the limitations of a colonial boyhood, you depend with filial piety on older intelligences that help to shape your mind. I had been very lucky. In addition to the intelligent indulgence of the farmer-spinster, my adolescence fed on the approval and faith of teachers, professional and instinctual who had loved my father, and those who were amazed at my industry. These included one of the brothers of the Presentation, a college master who gave me extra lessons in French poetry and who read my verse, a Dominican lawyer and that astigmatic, garrulous, and benevolent man who had been botanist, editor, anthropologist and painter.

Harold Simmons had been my father's friend. It was my father who had interested him in painting. My father had died in his thirties, when my twin-brother and I were a year old, my sister three, but on the drawing room walls of our house there were relics of his avocation: a copy of Millet's *The Gleaners*, a romantic original of sea-birds and pluming breakers he had called *Riders of the Storm*, a miniature oil portrait of my mother, a self-portrait in water colour, and an avenue of pale coconut palms. These objects had established my vocation, and made it as inevitable as that of any craftsman's son, for I felt that my father's work, however minor, was unfinished. Rummaging through stuffed, dark cupboards, I sometimes came across finely copied verses, evidence of a polite gracile talent, and once on a sketchbook of excellent pencil studies. I treasured the books he had used: two small, blue-covered volumes on *The English Topographical Draughtsmen* and on *Albrecht Dürer*, and the thick-ridged, classical albums of John McCormack and I think, Galli Curci. It was this veneration that drew his friends to me.

They may have realized that I had no other ambition. Below where I stood on the balcony was a plaque on the Fourth Form wall with a gilded list of Island Scholars who had become doctors and lawyers, or, infrequently, engineers. There was no writer or painter among them, and I had failed to win the Island Scholarship because of my poor mathematics. In Foxy's era it had been awarded biennially on achievement in the London Matriculation. I had failed the exam once, and I might have won the Scholarship if, as happened under the Brothers, it had been awarded for special subjects, but by the time the Higher School Certificate was introduced I was seventeen and too old.

Those boys who knew the hopelessness of their one chance, for whom a 'classical' education meant a rut for life in the Civil Service grabbed at the opportunity to make money working in the oil refineries of Curaçao. By the time I had reached the Sixth, they had left in batches, their school life broken, their education incomplete. They left as frightened boys and returned hardened men. The life there was rough. It was tireless, materialistic, but you could not afford to break, because there was nothing to return to, you were indentured anyway, and sending part of what you made back home, or else, on that sterile, cactus ridden boom-camp, where everyone spoke papiamento, you whored on Campo Allegre, or gambled, or tried at nights to educate yourself.

Until Curacao, for every doctor, or lawyer the Board numbered it destroyed the ambitions of his classmates. It even took its toll among the winners, some of whom collapsed from tension and the exhaustion of new studies in Edinburgh, Oxford, London or McGill. It was a grinding, merciless system. Those who surrendered hope and became Civil Servants went through accepted, brief periods of protest with idleness or drink, then settled desperately into what they had feared, early marriage, a large family, debt and heavy drinking. Some who had slid to the gutter preferred to stay there, or go mad. They had 'missed it by one mark', or by being born a month too soon. But the 'The Schol' was what made or broke you. It was the only way out, and once every two years, it let just one boy through.

These things are not written without pain, for their heroes still suffer the abrasions of that life; but since our apprentice days on Barnard's Hill, Dunstan and I knew what our professions were. We would be what we could do, what we loved best. Mr Simmons had set up that example. But now Dunstan had gone to Curaçao. I was not lonely, though. I was in love.

Here I imagine myself on that balcony, in an inherited heavy brown sports jacket, grey flannel trousers, a tin of Country Life cigarettes in my pocket, waiting for late afternoon, when I would go across the harbour to her house.

A., who was still a schoolgirl at the Convent, lived with her parents and innumerable sisters in a stone bungalow with a concrete landing stage below Harry's house. Every dusk now I would walk through the burnt-out town to the yacht basin and hire a rowboat and oarsman to take me across the still, dark-green harbour towards Vigie. Sitting there on the stern, with the town's cries fading, and the only noise the feathered oars creaking in the oarlocks, I felt suspended, as if the world around me were unreal, the white-pillared, gutted Government Offices and the Morne, and the brickwork, yellow cubes of the Barracks growing larger.

The trip cost only a shilling. The boatman, who would begin to cast off from the wharf as soon as he saw me coming, hardly spoke. To arrive after that still, twilit voyage and find A. playing with her sisters on the small pier, or waiting at the doorway, was even deeper peace. Years afterwards, when I had to study Dryden, I would think of his poem on the Great Fire of London and his Annus Mirabilis as one poem, since both blent in that year.

Love of that kind never returns. It contains, because of its innocence, its own extinction. It is so self-content, so assured of immortality that it irradiates not only the first-loved but her landscape with a profound benediction. I was content to spend hours in A.'s vicinity, not always in her physical presence. In fact, we must have had few moments alone. There were always others about: shrieking children, other schoolboys, or the guests of her father's club. Yet we were so happy that we could ignore each other. It is easy to dismiss all this as adolescent, to prove that at that age we love ourselves, that underneath such calm, there are the first intuitions of loss and the ennoblings of sexual desire. Maybe. But A.'s presence was consummation enough. She gave off a nimbus whose quality was golden, the colour of the light itself, and it made her the generator of those canoes that returned at dusk, and of the stillness of the water. There was nothing frail about her. She had a firmness of sinew and purpose that sometimes made her petulant, quarrelsome, stubborn, and coarse. She was graceful, gentle, resolute. I surrendered my heart to her as wholly as I had surrendered my imagination to her landscape.

Luna Park, where A. lived, had been converted from an unprepossessing concrete shed into cramped family quarters to one side, and a spacious restaurant-nightclub on the other. Her father, a little man given to the most fiercely ornate monologues, had great faith in me as 'an artist, my boy', but none as a prospective son-in-law, whose only prospects seemed to be a lifetime's teaching at the College. He wanted better for his daughters, and it was to impress and placate him, as well as to be near A. that I offered to decorate the restaurant walls with 'panels'.

These were simply slabs of concrete bedded against the walls by a prison corporal who was a part-time mason. Their design was neo-Nicholson. Circular cement plaques horizontally cut by a narrow slab, and for real daring, a collage of torn newspaper, the outline of a fish etched in with the edge of the trowel, and other Cubist left-overs of bottles and guitars. For A.'s father, who had once prophesied that the name 'Walcott would blaze like a meteor across the black midnight sky of Saint Lucia', the panels confirmed my talent but not my prospects. But he treated me courteously, cunningly, his bushy eyebrows and corrugated forehead fixed in perpetual amazement that a mind like mine, bent on higher things, should be another banal worshipper of his beautiful daughter. He would win in the end.

For me, though, everything was beginning, the culmination of a secretive childhood spent in reading, writing, and playing with my brother for hours with stick-puppets in our backyard, elaborating our own cowboy and detective plots, into public poems, plays, and paintings like those at Luna Park. Some months before, when I felt that I was ready to be 'published', I had sat on the landing of the stairs and asked my mother, who was sewing at the window, for two hundred dollars to put out a booklet of poems. She did not have that kind of money, and that fact made her weep, but she found it, the book was printed, and I had hawked it myself on street corners, a dollar a copy, and made the money back. It went into a 'second edition'. I was writing plays or sketches for the school and for a group we had formed, and I had already painted two huge backdrops for a Convent Concert that had taken me six months.

What made me feel more 'professional' was that Harry would let me have the use of his studio on Saturdays and during vacations. This meant permission to play his classical records on the grey-metal, red-buttoned radiogram as loudly as I wanted, the use of his neat, battered Royal typewriter, his library and his liquor cabinet. I was drinking a lot, for I was now moving in a circle that included hard, talkative, and intelligent drinkers: Simmons himself, and the Dominican lawyer, another lawyer who had won an Island scholarship and had recently returned, an English architect and his painter wife.

What names, what objects do I remember from that time? The brown covered *Penguin Series of Modern Painters*: Stanley Spencer, Frances Hodgkins, Paul Nash, Ben Nicholson: the pocket-sized Dent edition of Thomas's *Deaths and Entrances*, the Eliot recordings of *The Four Quartets*, dropped names like Graham Sutherland, and Carola and Ben Fleming's and Harry's reminiscences of ICA student days, and Harry's self-belittling anecdote of how he had once heard that Augustus John was aboard a cruise-ship and he had rushed up to see him with a pile of canvases and how John, agreeing to look at them, had glared back and said 'you can't paint a damn, but I admire your brass!', *BIM* magazine, Henry Swanzy's Caribbean Voices programme, *Caribbean Quarterly*, and the first West Indian novels, *New Day* and *A Morning at the Office*. Once Mittelholzer had sat in our drawing room and warned me to give up writing verse-tragedies, because 'they' would never take them.

That year I was hardly ever at home. My life lay between A.'s house at Luna Park and along the path that wriggled up the hill to Harry's Morgue. At school, I now felt more sympathy with the Brothers. They were at least young and outspoken. Besides, I found in their accents and in their recollections of Irish events and places, in their admiration for Synge and Yeats, for Pearse, and even for Joyce, an atmosphere, fortified by those martial Irish tunes that the school choir was taught, by the morning and evening litany droned out by the assembled school under the galvanized iron roof of the college yard, an atmosphere that summoned that of my current hero, the blasphemous, arrogant Stephen Daedalus.

> 'Help Of the Sick,
> We are Sick of Help,
> Towers of Ivory,
> Pay for Us,
> Comforter of the Afflicted
> We are afflicted with Comfort. . .'

I was now consumed by poetry, whatever expression it took. I shared with one of the Brothers, a flushed, tubercular-looking mathematician, who also wrote verse and had composed the new school song (did we have one before?), a new cynicism for the Empire and a passion for James Clarence Mangan's poem:

> O, my dark Rosaleen,
>   Do not sigh, do not weep!
> The priests are on the ocean green,
>   They march along the deep . . .

for Fergus and Cuchulain, and in the struggle and wrestling with my mind to find out who I was, I was discovering the art of bitterness. I had been tormented enough by the priests, and had even been savaged in a review in the *Port-of-Spain Gazette* by the

Catholic Archbishop. Like Stephen, I had my nights of two shilling whores, of 'tackling in the Alley', and silently howling remorse. Like him, I was a knot of paradoxes: hating the Church and loving her rituals, learning to hate England as I worshipped her language, sanctifying A. the more I betrayed her, a Methodist-lecher, a near Catholic-ascetic, loving the island, and wishing [I] could get the hell out of it.

My adolescence was over.

But nearly two more years of this life would go by before I left the school, A., and the island. In those years Dunstan would return, fed up with the materialism of Curaçao, dedicated to God and to a career, right here in his own island, as a painter, while I was beginning to acquire a little fame from abroad: kind reviews from Roy Fuller, a recommendation to Longman's from Christopher Fry . . .

In those years my love for A. strengthened. When I was at last given a Colonial Development and Welfare Scholarship, for which I had mechanically applied, I felt that it was breaking up a settled, purposeful life.

Yet, on that last morning at the Vigie airport, how cruel, selfish and unsurprising was this exhilaration of departure! Of farewell to A., who arrived late and hung back shyly in the crowd, to Harry, to Dunstan smiling wisely, and how merciless to hope that the island and A. would preserve herself (since they were one), under some sacred, inverted bell of glass, and that I was incapable of betrayal! All those island mothers, brothers, and first-beloveds who had seen us go, they knew an older pain than ours. We felt a gentle pity for their familiar clouds, roads and customs. We imagined that their lives revolved around our future. We accepted as natural their selfless surrender.

Under the engines, as it did when you climbed the Morne, the promontory hazed and widened, until there were no more figures, only houses, roads, and a landscape narrowly receding into cloud.

THE FIGURE OF CRUSOE (1965)

Derek Walcott

[This paper was presented orally at the University of the West Indies, St. Augustine, Trinidad, 27 October 1965. Derek Walcott has graciously allowed its publication for the first time as edited by Robert Hamner.]

As I get older I find that there is little I can say in public about a private calling that can be of interest. As a poet in the West Indies I find my position more and more idiosyncratic. I have no real wish to be a public person, but since there are so few of us who continue to practice poetry, and even fewer who have elected to remain behind, these unhappy few are always called on to make pronouncements. We stand behind lecterns and send the same audiences away if not emptier than they came, then cramped with a kind of indigestion. This is because all such exchanges of this kind are really lies. We should be incoherent. There should be offered, not sanity and reason, but something more frightening but more truthful, an impossibility of communication. The last thing I want you to do tonight, then, is to understand me.

This is partially due to the fact that I am addressing you in prose, which is the most immoral form of feeling. But, on either side of this lectern, some kind of public duty is being performed. A kind of patronage is being offered. What has driven us both to this position is a sense of duty. In my case there is also a fee attached.

All forms of preamble, aside and digression are part of the poet's evasion of his public. He has nothing to offer but his work. But people do not want poetry. They want its concomitants: explanation, justification, order. They want not the poetry, but the poet. Not revelations, but instruction, and a formal lecture gives the poet an approved chance of avoiding all of those agonizing truths. Already, as you can see by this preamble, I am going through all the motions of ritual.

The American poet and parodist e. e. cummings once titled a series of public talks "Six non lectures." Cummings could have meant that the poet, whose breath is very short, will do anything to avoid being confessional in prose. Lectures can be the first signs of waste, of moral deterioration, and the Muse is merciless to those of her brood who relish the limelight.

33

More than all this is the fact that poets are in one way, nature's idiots. They are inarticulate. They are capable only of speaking in poetry, for the poetic process, in every morning of the poet's life is an agonizing humiliation of trying to pronounce every word as if he had just learnt it, and was repeating it for the first time. Behind him, of course, is a morphology that comes to life when the word is set down, and when it is pronounced, but all that dead bush of tradition, of naming things anew can only come to life through some spark. It is now unfashionable to call the spark divine. It has been called, through different phases of our evolution, frenzy, imagination, inspiration, or the subconscious or unconscious. Whatever it is, and wherever it comes from, it exists.

An image may do better. It is that of a lonely man on a beach who has heaped a pile of dead bush, twigs, etc., to make a bonfire. The bonfire may be purposeless. Or it may be a signal of his loneliness, his desperation, his isolation, his symbol of need for another. Or the bonfire may be lit from some atavistic need, for contemplation. Fire mesmerizes us. We dissolve in burning. The man sits before the fire, its glow warming his face, watching it leap, gesticulate, and lessen, and he keeps throwing twigs, dead thoughts, fragments of memory, all the used parts of his life to keep his contemplation pure and bright. When he is tired and returns into himself, then he has performed some kind of sacrifice, some ritual.

The hermit is thrown back on magic. By magic I do not mean forms of incantation, the summoning of spirits. I mean only that for him, such simple chores as lighting fires for food, for warmth, for contemplation, for light, repossess their primitive, original use. Each object around him, every texture becomes a household god. Hermits, however, are monotheists, not pantheists. The terror of loneliness is so intense, so wide, that it cannot fragment itself into other small presences.

I have used that image of the hermit and the bonfire because I have found that it has a parallel for the poet. The metaphor of the bonfire, in the case of the West Indian poet, may be the metaphor of tradition and the colonial talent. More profound than this, however, is that it is the daily ritual action of the poet creating a new poem. He burns what he has made the day before by adding new wood to the flame. All becomes pure flame, all is combustible, and by that light, which is separate from him, he contemplates himself.

Dante has said it better: *Paradiso:* The final Canto, XXXIII, the ultimate vision:

> Oh grace abounding, wherein I presumed to fix my look on the
> eternal light so long that I wearied my sight thereon!
>   Within its depths I saw ingathered, bound by love in one volume, the
> scattered leaves of all the universe;
>   Substance and accidents and their relations, as though together fused,
> after such fashion that what I tell of is one simple flame.

That is the shape of the poem, the spirit of the bonfire, *un semplice lume!* Madmen are fond of boasting like eagles of how long they can stare at the sun. The contemplation of fire induces trances, not to mention hallucinations. In Plato's cave, I hear from second hand, our lives are shadows cast on the walls, transitory things. I am not describing, in that image of the bonfire and the hermit, the visitation of the saint, the catatonic visions of the madman. Not all if any, poetry, is delirium. The supreme vision of Dante is not frenzied, but one of calm, order, and of a serene, steady, unearthly light. I am also not talking about an abandonment of the world, the confining of its rubbish to flame, in the sense that Donne wrote after his mistress's death:

> She, she is gone. She's gone. When thou know'st this,
> What fragmentary rubbish this world is
> Thou knowest. . .

Nor am I describing, in that image, a figure of self-pity that of some felon abandoned by the world, a castaway.

What am I saying then? I am trying to make a heretical reconciliation between the outer world, and the world of the hermit, between, if you wish, the poet and the objects surrounding him that are called society. By objects I mean everything that can be loved, person, animal or thing, because a poet has no more respect for one noun, the thing by which an object is called, than he has for another, whether this is fish, stone, wife, cloud or insect, all are holy as he names them, although in his other life he cannot love them all equally, since he is not a saint. Now that I have said this, I realize what I meant by a poem of mine entitled "Crusoe's Journal," (*The Castaway* 51-53). The epigraph is from *Robinson Crusoe*:

> I looked now upon the world as a thing remote, which I had nothing
> to do with, no expectation from, and, indeed no desires about. In a word,
> I had nothing indeed to do with it, nor was ever like to have, so I thought
> it looked as we may perhaps look upon it hereafter, viz., as a place I had
> lived in but was come out of it, and well might I say, as Father Abraham to
> Dives, "Between me and thee is a great gulf fixed."

I have, as you heard, summoned the figure of Crusoe. It is not the Crusoe you recognize. I have compared him to Proteus, that mythological figure who changes shapes according to what we need him to be. Perhaps my mythology is wrong. I am, however, also summoning, in the combination of Crusoe and Proteus, the Old Man of the Sea with whom a mythological hero wrestled. The commercial Crusoe gives his name to our brochures and hotels. He has become the property of the Trinidad and Tobago Tourist board, and although it is the same symbol that I use, you must allow me to make him various, contradictory and as changeable as the Old Man Of the Sea. In the poem I have evidently seen him in several shapes, and I bore you with a catalogue of these shapes because, to me, they represent various problems organic to West Indian life. My Crusoe, then, is Adam. Christopher Columbus, God, a missionary, a beachcomber, and his interpreter, Daniel Defoe. He is Adam because he is the first inhabitant of a second paradise. He is Columbus because he has discovered this new world, by accident, by fatality. He is God because he teaches himself to control his creation, he rules the world he has made, and also, because he is to Friday, a white concept of Godhead. He is a missionary because he instructs Friday in the uses of religion; he has a passion for conversion. He is a beachcomber because I have imagined him as one of those figures of adolescent literature, some derelict out of Conrad or Stevenson, or Marryat. In the poem he also becomes, in one line, Ben Gunn, the half-crazy pirate who guards Treasure Island, and finally, he is also Daniel Defoe, because the journal of Crusoe, which is Defoe's journal, is written in prose, not in poetry, and our literature, the pioneers of our public literature have expressed themselves in prose in this new world. A footnote on Defoe, and on our writers, I have tried to say in these lines:

> out of such timbers
> came our first book, our profane Genesis
>   whose Adam speaks that prose
> which, blessing some sea-rock, startles itself
>   with poetry's surprise,
> in a green world, one without metaphors.
> (*The Castaway 51*)

I have tried to say this. That given a virgin world, a paradise, any sound, any act of naming something, like Adam baptizing the creatures, because that action is anthropomorphic, that is, like the pathetic fallacy, it projects itself by a sound onto something else, such a sound is not really prose, but poetry, is not simile, but metaphor. It is like that well known joke about Adam calling that shape a rhinoceros and when asked by God why he had called it that, Adam answered, 'Well, sir, because it looks like one." We surprise ourselves by watching, say, our children grow to resemble the names we give them, and for Adam, as for Crusoe, and as it should for prose writer and poet, the named thing should have an exact surprise.

I am claiming, then, that poets and prose writers who are West Indians, despite the contaminations around us, are in the position of Crusoe, the namer. Like him, they have behind them, borne from England, from India, or from Africa, that dead bush, that morphology I mentioned earlier, but what is more important is that these utterances, these words, when written, are as fresh, as truly textured, as when Crusoe sets them down in the first West Indian novel. The exhilaration that still carries across, like a gust of salt air, from the most putrid West Indian writing owes its health to this. Besides, it is the figure of Crusoe, as certain critics have found in the figure of Prospero, that supplies the anguish of authority, of the conscience of empire, rule, benign power. The metaphor can be stretched too far. There is now a fashionable, Marxist-evolved method of analysing figures from literature as if they were guilty. These analyses, we have seen them happen in brilliant re-creations, to Prospero as the white imperialist, and to Caliban as the ugly savage. If, as I shall, I draw a similar parallel to Crusoe and Friday, it is because all such dialectic is there in the text. It exists in Defoe the pamphleteer as it does in Defoe as a novelist, not a poet, and a novelist deals with the human condition under pressure. In *Robinson Crusoe* the pressure is that of isolation and survival.

I once read somewhere that a survey conducted on the most successful films proved that they were ones which dealt with endurance and survival, much more so than those whose themes were sex, or romance. We must allow this plain purpose to Defoe, who decided to write the story of Alexander Selkirk for a public. I am simply saying that Defoe's plot, which couldn't be plainer, needed all that other commercial excitation of savages and cannibal feasts, that compared, for instance, to that poem by Cowper which we all learnt at school,

> I am monarch of all I survey,
> My right there is none to dispute,
> From the centre all around to the sea,
> I am lord of the fowl and the brute,

compared to that poem, the novel, any novel needs to radiate from different centres. A novel, least of all the written forms, is not a definition of the ego. Crusoe, in Defoe's novel, is a "subject," and he is observed by his inventor with dispassion. In Cowper's poem the centre of creation is the "I," the "lord of the fowl and the brute," and we need no "interpretations" of the hermit's statement. In Defoe's Crusoe, Crusoe is a symbol, an example.

I am claiming nothing exaggerated when I state that Crusoe, through Defoe's multiple combination of adventure story, religious Protestant tract of trust and self-reliance, and Christian zeal for converting brutish tribes, not with the belligerence of Kipling, but with honest, tender belief in the superiority of his kind, has given us a more real symbol than critics claim for Prospero and Caliban. Crusoe is no lord of magic, duke, prince. He does not possess the island he inhabits. He is alone, he is a craftsman, his beginnings are humble. He acts, not by authority, but by conscience.

It is his and Friday's children who have generated this disturbing society. Disturbing to others, because on one hand there is resolution in landscape and in faith in God, and on the other a desperate longing to leave these island prisons forever and to survive on nostalgia.

Besides, Crusoe is a figure from our schoolboy reading. He is a part of the mythology of every West Indian child. I have recorded this in an essay on which I am now engaged. If there are repetitions, forgive me, and consider them as variations and emphasis. I am afraid that what emerges from this portrait is as different as one poem is to another, although they be on the same subject. I have here almost an existentialist Crusoe, but he changes shape, as I warned, with Protean cunning.

In our primary school reader there were two reproductions that terrified me. The terror was a child's incomprehension of despair. One figure was G.F. Watt's mournful symbol of "Hope." She sat, blindly playing her lyre, side-saddle on the turning globe. To me, she was the embodiment of "despair." The other figure was in a painting of Robinson Crusoe. If what I remember of "Hope" is its damp grayness, like wet gravecloths, I associate a dull, smouldering red, more brown than really red, with Crusoe.

In the painting the figure seems to have resigned itself not only to abandonment,

but to discomfort. The rusty, chafing goat's hide, touched by a tropical sunset, and
looking, like the sea and sky, dully on fire, doesn't seem to itch him. Nor does the
peaked, ruddy, goatskin hat. The patron saint of shipwreck, he sits in his hair-shirt
looking out to the horizon out of habit. He seems bored with the idea of salvation,
because he has resolved his own. He has reached, as he sits there on his sand dune with
parasol and dog, an anonymity so complete, that it is past despair. To me, he seemed
neither animal nor human, but a combination of both.

Of course Crusoe has now gone mad. He has already shouted to God, which is
the echo of his own voice, all sorts of terrified obscenities. He is saved, for a time, by
the consolation of that other voice, which is his own. So he looks out on his six
thousandth sunset as an old man will look out from a balcony. But his verandah is
sand, and the sea has that great emptiness of motion that he no longer studies just as
he learned to stop counting sunsets. He has learned the indifference of his dog, but
their separate lonelinesses are terrible. Empty his mind as assiduously as he tries, he
cannot become a dog because he has more than a dog's desires. Their dependence
exists without language, and their companionship is a kind of affliction. He has no
wish to return to his fortress. Yet, in that picture, you feel that if a sail should pass,
the blasphemy of his enervation would let it go about the business of the world.

He publishes every day the newspaper of himself in the journal he now keeps. The
craftsman, the artisan, has become the writer. Crusoe can now look at Crusoe as at
another object. It is this act that saves his sanity. The essay proceeds to describe the
arrival of Friday, the cannibal whom Crusoe converts.

It is only when Friday arrives that Crusoe again withdraws into himself. He learns
the fear of another. Now he stops becoming a writer, hermit, saint, and becomes by
necessity, a master. He reverts to what he was taught and becomes self-righteous on
such subjects as God, civilization, art and human nakedness. And, of course, race. He
returns to a commonplace sanity, to the puritanism that he had abandoned, when,
unlike most men, he once really understood nothing.

Crusoe now arms himself with the divine folly of the missionary and adapts
Friday to himself. He cannot understand that for the savage, this could mean an
abandonment as deep or deeper than his own, for it means not a denial but an
exchange of gods. The savage thus surrenders his name, language, religion and
nakedness for another man's, and his reward is servitude. The imperialist concept
sees all this as inevitable, and it binds its servants to it by creating a sin new to them,
ingratitude. Then, of course, it may have struck Friday as strange that the God of
Crusoe was killed and eaten. Confrontation with Friday, with Friday's barbarism
and limited knowledge of language and its graces creates homesickness in Crusoe.
He has made the island his own home, but now he sees its "shortcomings." All that
he has learned he now relegates to the level of experience and adventure. His sanity
is preserved, his language and his equilibrium restored. And so, too, is the old order
of things.

The Crusoe I describe there is, of course, not the Crusoe of Defoe; it is the
distorted, surrealist Crusoe of Bunuel. For everyone else, this must be exaggeration
and distortion, but it was not until my imagination settled on that symbol that I

understood what Yeats meant when he wrote: "Give a man a mask, and he will talk the truth."

In another one of my poems, "The Almond Trees" (*The Castaway* 36-37), trying to describe the absence of history, tradition, ruins, I saw the figures of ancient almond trees in a grove past Rampanalgas on the north coast, as a grove of dead, transplanted, uprooted ancestors.

We must not commit that heresy of thinking that because we "have no past," we have no future. If we read the commentary of exiles, we will think that my position which is that of Crusoe or Friday, or more truly, a mixture of their imagined progeny, has been made defensive when it is in fact logical. Here is Mr. Keith Botsford, an American, writing on Brazil:

> Often it's been a matter of pure panic. I fled the Caribbean with a sense that I was talking to myself and that if I stayed longer, I'd be like a breadfruit swaying on a tree in idyllic sunshine, ready to rot on the ground.

Brazil! What would have happened to Mr. Botsford if he had found himself washed up on one of our rocks. We know. The answer is in our own writers. First, Mr. Naipaul :

> The years I had spent abroad fell away and I could not be sure which was the reality in my life: the first eighteen years in Trinidad or the later years in England. I had never wanted to stay in Trinidad. When I was in the fourth form I wrote a vow on the endpaper of my Kennedy's *Revised Latin Primer* to leave within five years. I left after six; and for many years afterwards in England, falling asleep in bedsitters with the electric fire on, I had been awakened by the nightmare that I was back in tropical Trinidad .
>
> I had never examined this fear of Trinidad. I had never wished to. In my novels I had only expressed this fear; and it is only now, at the moment of writing, that I am able to attempt to examine it. I knew Trinidad to be unimportant, uncreative, cynical. . . . Power was recognized, but dignity was allowed to no one . Every person of eminence was held to be crooked and contemptible. We lived in a society that denied itself heroes. (*The Middle Passage* 41)

Both Mr . Naipaul, and Mr . Lamming , as you will hear shortly, are speaking the truth, not only their truths, but general truths. It is only that I am attempting to accommodate a third truth. Mr. Lamming on "The Pleasures of Exile":

> So we come back to the original question of the West Indian novelists living in a state of chosen exile. Their names make temporary noise in the right West Indian circles. Their books have become handy broomsticks

which the new nationalist will wave at a foreigner who asks the rude
question; "What can your people do except doze?"

Why don't these writers return? There are more reasons than I can
state now, but one is fear. They are afraid of returning . . . because they
feel that sooner or later they will be ignored in and by a society about
which they have been at once articulate and authentic. You may say that a
similar thing happens to the young English writer in England. There is
the important difference that you cannot enjoy anonymity in a small
island. . . In spite of all that has happened in the last ten years, I doubt that
any one of the West Indian writers could truly say that he would be happy
to go back. Some have tried; some would like to try. But no one would
feel secure in his decision to return. It would be worse than arriving in
England for the first time. *(The Pleasures of Exile* 46-47)

To each his own terror, to each his own isolation. We evidently become more
frightening, more vulgar every day to these writers, and I myself tend to agree with
that judgment. But I have tried to show that Crusoe's survival is not purely physical,
not a question of the desolation of his environment, but a triumph of will. He is for
us, today, the twentieth century symbol of artistic isolation and breakdown, of
withdrawal, of the hermetic exercise that poetry has become, even in the New World,
he is the embodiment of the schizophrenic Muse whose children are of all races.
Crusoe's triumph lies in that despairing cry which he utters when a current takes his
dugout canoe further and further away from the island that, like all of us uprooted
figures, he had made his home, and it is the cynical answer that we must make to
those critics who complain that there is nothing here, no art, no history, no architecture, by which they mean ruins, in short, no civilization, it is "O happy desert!" We
live not only on happy, but on fertile deserts, and we draw our strength, like Adam,
like all hermits, all dedicated craftsmen, from that rich irony of our history .

It is what feeds the bonfire. We contemplate our spirit by the detritus of the past.

TRIBAL FLUTES (1967)

Derek Walcott

Rights of Passage
by Edward Brathwaite

The image which Edward Brathwaite's long lyric meditation conjures is of a bundle of antique tribal instruments; a bark and skin drum, ceremonial fifes, rattle and bones. Each suite of the poem is "accompanied" by a particular instrument, and the melody threading them all is plaintive and tenuous.

Even when the poet lays aside the ancient tribal modes and takes up a modern instrument the melody is still melancholic, the introspective, meandering of a blues saxophone in the wee hours.

Mr. Brathwaite's melodic exterior is cool. The spurts of rage, once his cool is lost, sound raw and tinny. He is also a poor exhorter.

There is nothing in "Rights of Passage" that equals the fan-poem "Cahier d'un Retour Au Pays Natal", or the sustained ram's horn splendours of Perse's "Eloges" and "Pour Feter Un Enfance". Wry, self mocking, melancholic. Brathwaite is at his best.

The structure of his poem recalls the symphonic suites of Archibald MacLeish, the poetic documentary overlaid by the soothing voice of the poet-narrator, in a language whose linkings depend on biblical conjunctions and on liturgical response.

This manner, popular in the late twenties, invented by Eliot and Pound, later thinned out to epical proportions in writers like Pare Lorenz and Hart Crane.

Mr. Brathwaite has a chosen subject: the rootless migrations of the African tribes, the loss of tribal memory, degradation and humiliation. His title is a pun. The drifting tribes have the right to choose a final anchorage, but their forced excursions, the unfinished rhythm of their exodus contains elements of ritual. The "rites" are those of evocation. They try to remember what they were. They try to see what they will become. The exorcism is the realisation of self. Mr. Brathwaite, in fact, has been ambitious and patient enough to orchestrate that old West Indian cliché of the 'quest for identity' very skillfully.

His title deliberately invokes Naipaul's "The Middle Passage". It may even challenge it, and the area on which it throws the challenge is that of compassion and understanding.

Where Naipaul fumes with exasperation at the deracinated wreckage that makes every island a compost heap, Mr. Brathwaite picks his way through the wreckage, selecting broken artifacts, unshaped memories.

Poets, like anthropologists, have a fascination for middens, but their way of looking at history is glazed.

The held object dilates before their vision. Mr. Brathwaite is a professional historian, but he offers us no cyclical evolution. His poem is without economics. It is not history. One of his favourite similes is of glitter, silica flashing signals, quartz, shining rubble. His perceptions reflected from these microcosmic messages, he makes long observations and proceeds to the next signal.

Naturally his poem requires order. It is a single work eighty-three pages long, and even then, to quote the publisher's blurb, it is the first part of a trilogy. Mr. Brathwaite's ambition is astounding, but as the reader settles into the poem his ear becomes accustomed to its modesty of expression.

The poet does not wish us to approach the poem as a compression of epic experience. His vision is oblique, his tone modulated, "Rights of Passage" is a succession of lyrics, almost casually arranged in terms of epochs and historical changes, and like every lyric it is self-centred.

The journeys and sojourns which the poet has made have entered his experience without his addressing them in prophetic terms. Everything has been honed down to a silver-thin essential, to bare bone, to the sound of a single instrument.

Mr. Brathwaite, from his earliest pages, keeps to a light finger-melody. The initial rhythm is faint, light, and studied. The poem, read aloud, subdues and arrests the onrush of its subject by closely packed rhymes, by the tautness of its short stresses,

> Here clay
> cool coal clings
> to glass, creates
> clinks, silica glitters,
> children of stars.

As the single melody begins the evocations rise. Smoky flutes, the faint drumming of dancers. The maternal landscape recedes like smoke and mist, and the children, looking back to a shore that is beginning to acquire the anonymity of a map, begin to forget, to force themselves to remember. The beginning of their rites,

> It will be a long time before we see
> this land again, these trees
> again, drifting inland with the sound
> of surf, smoke rising
> It will be a long long time before we see
> these farms again, soft wet slow green
> again: Aburi, Akwamu,
> mist rising.

The delicate melancholy behind these lines tends to liquefy into a vague feeling. The structure is fragile, and the tone, as the poem proceeds, is often more pleading than plaintive. It makes Mr. Brathwaite's later rages petulant and sometimes nasty without irony. In the savage sequences the reader's voice is required to rise without being buoyed up by the surging fury of rhetoric.

We are pulled and nearly drowned by Cesaire's tidal wave of exasperation at the stupidity of all men, including the 'good nigger', whereas Mr. Brathwaite often sounds like someone at a dance who is being ignored.

> To rass
> o' this work-song singin' you singin'
> the chant o' this work chain
> gang, an' the blue bell
> o' this horn that is blowin' the Lou-
> eee Armstrong blues; keep them
> for Alan Lomax, man, for them
> swell
> folkways records, man

. . . as bitterness, this is hardly raw enough.

It is this division of several sensibilities all coiling around the spine of the poem simultaneously that gives it its nervous look. Self-pity, in itself a kind of folkways blues very seductive to colonial poets alternates with another kind of attraction, four-letter fury. When Mr. Brathwaite proclaims with a Leroi Jones viciousness that he is an effing Negro, one is equally tempted to shrug acceptance as at:

> Ever seen
> a man
> travel, more
> seen more
> lands
> than this poor
> land—
> less, harbour—
> less spade?

Yes. The Jews, for one. And it is Jewish mythology that supplies Mr. Brathwaite with his epigraph: 'And they took their journey from Elim, and all the congregation of the children of Israel came unto the wilderness of Sin, which is between Elim and Sinai, on the fifteenth day of the second month after their departing out of the land of Egypt.' The sorrowing grandchildren of Noah, cursed with darkness. The poet must either believe or mock it, but Mr. Brathwaite tries to balance these opposites.

His position is vaguely between Malcolm X's celebrated remark that he was sick of hearing Negroes compared to Jews, and John Hearne's "the pathetic nostalgia for

Africa that corrupts so many Negroes", and neither can be wholly explained away by calling Malcolm X a prophet or Hearne a racial hybrid. Yet both extremes are contained in what Mr. Brathwaite is trying to excise as the West Indian Negro sensibility. There are divisions among the tribes themselves and Mr. Brathwaite's thin, generic blanket does not cover all their quarrels.

If we remain disappointed at the general tone of "Rights of Passage", its near mission-school melancholy, we can at least be grateful that they are sketched in for us, that the anguish is real even if it is not excruciatingly anatomised.

It is very difficult for foreign readers to understand the vacuum at the core of West Indian sensibility, a kind of deadness that no exhortations about community and achievement can stir, one that is suspicious and uncertain.

The wavering, querulous note that "Rights of Passage" sounds is right for us. We recognise it in the vacillations and aggressions of the nonheroes of our novelists. It is in Ian Macdonald's phrase about East Indian music, 'the soft peculiar wail searching for sadness'. The search for our own sadness is the progression of that sensibility towards being named.

Mr. Brathwaite, an excellent critic of West Indian fiction, has in several passages, adapted its prose and in some other cases its 'characters' to his poem. This is not imitation but a serious attempt at cohesion.

In several sequences, but particularly in "The Dust", "The Emigrants" and "Wings of a Dove," we are in the worlds of Lamming and Mais. Beyond the mere presence, however, there is stylistic achievement that one hopes will urge other or younger poets to study.

It is Pound's well-known dictum that verse should be at least as well written as prose, and in our case that West Indian verse should be as well written as West Indian prose.

The excellence of Mr. Brathwaite's style lies in the steely fragility of his lines. His overall design looks as tenuous but is as resilient as a spider's web. It is not overblown, our ideas, and the ideas of 'history,' and 'epic poetry' blow through its spaces, yet it is all the more lissome. The tone is of a refined, anguished sensibility bent on achieving not power, but grace, not grandeur but sharp, piercing truths. It is a tone, filtered through Eliot, through Cesaire, through Carlos Williams, but its sound is strangely indigenous. In that it is West Indian. It is several things at once, and yet triumphantly itself. One only has to read and reread the penultimate sequence "The Dust" to know how masterful a technician Mr. Brathwaite has become.

MEANINGS (1970)

Derek Walcott

My mother, who was a school-teacher, took part in amateur theatre. My father was a civil servant, but also wrote verse and was an excellent draughtsman. He was also a good portrait painter in water-colour. Our house was haunted by his absence because all around the drawing room there were his water-colours and water-colour portraits. He had a meticulous style with an innate humility, as if he were a perpetual student. He must have plotted his own development carefully, proceeding from drawing to full-bodied painting when death interrupted it. He died quite young. In another situation I think he would have been an artist. He evidently had a great influence on his friends. One of them, under whom I later studied painting, went on to become a professional painter. I have an immense respect, in fact, an awe, for that kind of spiritual strength; I mean here was this circle of self-civilizing, courteous people in a poverty-ridden, cruelly ignored colony living by their own certainties. So to begin as a poet was, for me, a direct inheritance. It was natural. I feel that I have simply continued where my father left off.

I go back as far as this because it is almost death to the spirit to try to survive as an artist under colonial conditions, which haven't really changed with our independent governments. The fall-out rate among artists and actors, in fact, all creative people, is considerable. They either abandon their talents or emigrate, which is the same thing.

I really became involved in theatre when my brother suggested I write a play about the Haitian revolution. He had read a book about it and gotten excited. So I said, all right, I'll try one, and I wrote a play, *Henri Christophe*. This was in Saint Lucia, where I was still living. We formed a group there called The Arts Guild — mainly school-boys, and we performed this play. Then I began to write more plays for them. We performed them in Castries, my home town; the whole island's population must be about eighty thousand. The plays may have been seen by a few hundred people in all. But The Arts Guild still exists. My twin brother, who also writes plays, continued it. At the university in Jamaica, we formed another group. Then I got a Rockefeller Fellowship to go to America in '58.

While I was in America I was supposed to study scene design as well as directing, but because I was so isolated I felt very alone in the United States. I knew I did not

45

want what was going on. Not on Broadway, but in a way, not off-Broadway as well. I think the pressure of that loneliness made me realize I had to do something which was true to the kind of company I wanted to have. I used to go to José Quinterós classes and to the Phoenix Theatre.

The first real experience I had of writing a stylized West Indian play was in New York. It was a West Indian fable called *Ti-Jean and His Brothers*. For the first time I used songs and dances and a narrator in a text. That was the fastest play I'd ever written. I wrote it on my first trip to New York — before I got the Rockefeller — in four or five days. It astonished me. I probably wrote the damned thing because I was afraid to go out. Out of that play, I knew what I wanted.

Then I came back [to] New York to take up the Fellowship and I began to study Japanese films. I had seen the dancers of the Little Carib Company in Trinidad and I felt that what would spring from our theatre need not be a literary thing — not the word, not the psychology — not the *detailed* psychology of character so much as a mimetic power, in the dance particularly. I had a company in mind who would be both dancers and actors . . . a dance company mixed with an acting company. Then the Little Carib and the workshop separated, so what happened was that an actor had to try to be a dancer.

Sooner or later, I had to decide whether to go back to the West Indies at all. Luckily, my brother was still with The Arts Guild. They went to Trinidad, and he asked me if I would come and help him, so I went down there. I used it as an excuse. I didn't finish my Fellowship. I was very tired and was feeling very depressed about New York theatre and about any chance I might have of ever doing anything there. Plus, of course, at that time in '58, plays about the West Indies, or black actors — well, there wasn't much of a chance of getting anything going. There was no such thing in New York as a company of black actors. So I went back to Trinidad and began the Trinidad Theatre Workshop. Most of the people who came to this Company had some experience in amateur theatre or with other companies in Trinidad. But we began very modestly. I didn't do any work on production at first. Having gone through the American experience of seeing improvisations and direct- ing, watching American actors and 'the method', I knew that initially I had to get discipline. I had to work for three or four years doing improvisations, letting the actors lead themselves with all of us exploring together before we finally could put on a play. It was seven years before we really decided we were fit to produce something. We chose two very modest plays — modest in scale: *The Zoo Story* and *The Sea at Dauphin*, a play I had written earlier about a fisherman.

When the improvisations began, I saw that there was something extra about the West Indian because of the way he is so visibly, physically self-expressive. If that were combined with the whole self-annihilating process of who you are and what you're doing, which you get from method acting — if those two were fused together, you could get a terrific style. So that's what we aimed at. And once improvisations began to go well, then I would know in what direction the company could move. So I was after . . . and am still after . . . a theatre where someone can do Shakespeare or sing Calypso with equal conviction.

In 1966, we did our first production in a very small abandoned bar called The Basement Theatre. We only had seats for sixty people. We thought we would just be on for two nights, but we went on for a week. We were amazed. The response was so good that we decided that we were now a producing company, and we put on other West Indian plays which got equally good report. The theatre itself was very crude: a platform very loosely made and some lights. Then we put on our first repertory season, which ran successfully for 26 nights. We did *The Blacks*, and a West Indian play called *Belle Fanto*, and *The Road* by Soyinka. By that time the actors were working very hard — working by day at eight-to-five jobs and coming back at night to perform. So there is a terrific energy that exists in the Company.

From then on we began to do a lot of plays. I can't remember them all now. I try to keep a balance in the repertory between classic or great contemporary plays and West Indian material. There are things I want to do, but not yet. Eventually, we are going to do some kind of Shakespeare, but it must have its own style — not just exotic. I am talking about a real, true style — true to our own experience. It would be very cheap to do certain things — a black *Hamlet* — just for that kind of effect. I know I have a good Hamlet in the Company, but I don't want that kind of thing.

At this time, I began to revive my own plays because I now had the company to express them. *The Dream on Monkey Mountain*, for example, I had begun in the States in '59. We were going on tour; we had just completed our first repertory season and needed a new play. I remember I wrote the second act very rapidly because we had to have a play, and I always fiddle around a long time with my plays. Now, a strange thing happened: I had a prepared text, but there was one figure at the back of my mind, a death figure from Haitian mythology, that wasn't written in. There was an actor, Albert Le Veau, who had just finished doing *The Zoo Story* and *Dauphin*. We were going on tour, but there was no part in it for him. So I worked in the figure from the center of the play's design,and the part radiated through the whole text — the part of Basil. I think that this figure tightened, webbed its structure. It's one of the beautiful accidents that can happen when you have a good company.

Our sin in West Indian art is the sin of exuberance, of self-indulgence, and I wanted to impose a theatre that observed certain rules. The use of choruses required precise measure; the use of narration required precise mime. There was one dance step that, when it was arrested, seemed to be exactly what I wanted — powerful, difficult, precise. It came out of the bongo-dance. It is a male challenge dance played at wakes, obviously derived from warrior games, and I saw in that moment the discipline of arrest, of revelation from which a mimetic Narrative power could spring like some of the *mies* in Japanese theatre.

Furthermore, I do a lot of drawing for my plays. In fact, I visualize them completely in terms of costume and staging, even certain group formations, before I go into production and while I am writing the play. In New York, I came to the Chinese and Japanese classic theatre through Brecht. I began to go to the texts themselves and, because I draw, I used to look very carefully at the woodcuts of Hokusai and Hiroshige. There was then a very strong popular interest in Japanese cinema — in Kurosawa, and films such as *Ugetsu*, *Gate of Hell*, *Rashomon*, etc. I had written one play which was derivative of *Rashomon,* called *Malcauchon.* It was the story of a woodcutter and people gathered together under a hut. This was a deliberate imitation, but it was one of those informing imitations that gave me a direction because I could see in the linear shapes, in the geography, in the sort of myth and superstition of the Japanese, correspondences to our own forests and mythology. I also wanted to use the same type of figure found in this material, a type essential to our own mythology. A woodcutter or charcoal burner.

To me, this figure represented the most isolated, most reduced, race-containing symbol. In addition, I have my own associations of our forests, of rain, of mists, plus of course, the inherent violence or despair in a person of that type — the mad woodcutter. In the kind of play I wanted to do, it was natural to have someone who was narrating the text since, in a sense, that is Oriental as well as African. What I wanted to do was reduce the play almost to an inarticulateness of language. I would like to have had a play made up of grunts and sounds which you don't understand, like you hear at a Japanese film. The words would be reduced to very primal sounds.

But in writing the play another more literary tradition took over, so that I made the figures voluble. In a sense, I feel that is still what I am going after. I am a kind of split writer: I have one tradition inside me going in one way, and another tradition going another. The mimetic, the Narrative, and dance element is strong on one side, and the literary, the classical tradition is strong on the other.

In *The Dream on Monkey Mountain,* I tried to fuse them, but I am still after a kind of play that is essential and spare the same way woodcuts are clean, that dances are clean, and that Japanese cinema is so compressed that gesture does the same thing as speech. That is where our kind of conflict is rich. I think the pressure of those two conflicts is going to create a verbally rich literature, as well as a mimetic style. This happens in Wole Soyinka. It happens as well in the kind of plays that we are writing at home.

When we first did *Monkey Mountain,* I told the actors exactly what I was after. It was easy to communicate with them because I knew what was being generated in the actors' minds. All of these actors move well. They don't dance in the ballet or modern idiom; they are not abstract dancers. They can do dances which are spontaneous yet precise and have more to do with acting than with dance. Any one of them in the Company, for instance, can do a bongo step, and the bongo step was the step which, as I said, crystallized the kind of movement I was after; it is a kind of Russian thing, low-stepping, leg-crossed, and it's just one of those associations that generated a style for me.

The bongo is a wake dance, a spiritual celebration at death of the triumph over death. I suppose two warriors would challenge each other to divert the attendant grieving people from the death. It is a very foot-asserting, earth-asserting, life-asserting dance in contradiction of the grief that has happened through the death. In that dance, when the legs are crossed, and the dancer is arrested for a second, there is all the male strength that I think has been absent for a long time in Western theatre. The emphasis is on virility. This ancient idea of the actor in a theatre where women are not allowed to take part or are uninterested was true of colonial society in the West Indies and in Africa, whether in Soyinka's Company or in mine. Very few women took part in our theatre when we began, so initially all of our plays had more male characters than women. Still, it's good. I think that in a theatre where you have a strong male principle, or where women aren't involved at the beginning, a kind of style will happen; there will be violence, there will be direct conflict, there will be more physical theatre and there will be less interest in sexual psychology. From this step, the bongo step — came a private mythology associated with the warrior-figure — the African warrior, or the Japanese samurai. In that sense, it is more like early medieval plays or early Shakespeare plays where the conflict is always a male conflict.

This is in some part affected by our being an island culture. I think that an archipelago, whether Greek or West Indian, is bound to to be a fertile area, particularly if it is a bridge between continents, and a variety of people settle there. In the West Indies, there are all these conditions — the Indian heritage, the Mediterranean, the Lebanese and Chinese, etc. I don't want to look too far ahead, but I think there will be a playwright coming out of the Indian experience and one out of the Chinese experience; each will isolate what is true to his own tradition. When these things happen in an island culture a fantastic physical theatre will emerge because the forces that affect that communal search will use physical expression through dance, through the Indian dance and through Chinese dance, through African dance. When these things happen, plus all the cross-fertilization — the normal sociology of the place — then a true and very terrifying West Indian theatre will come. It's going to be so physically strong as to be something that has never happened before.

On any island, when the night comes in — and it's true for the Japanese peasantry too — we gather around the story-teller, and the tradition is revived. A style is emerging, because you've got the story-teller at the fire, and you've got the hero whose quest is never done. This quest figure, who is a warrior, a knight, endures experiences that resolve what he is. There is a geography which surrounds the story-teller, and this is made physical by things like mist or trees or whatever — mountains, snakes, devils. Depending on how primal the geography is and how fresh in the memory, the island is going to be invested in the mind of the child with a mythology which will come out in whatever the child grows up to re-tell.

In the West Indies, from a slave tradition adapted to the environment, the slaves kept the strength of the stories about devils and gods and the cunning of certain figures, but what was missing in the folklore was a single heroic warrior figure. We had the cunning of certain types, representative of the slave outwitting his master, like Br'er Rabbit or Tar Baby, done in West Indian dialect.

My Makak comes from my own childhood. But there was no king, no tribal chief, no warrior for a model in those stories. So the person I saw was this degraded, humble, lonely, isolated figure of the woodcutter. I can see him for what he is now, a brawling, ruddy drunk who would come down the street on a Saturday when he got paid and let out an immense roar that would terrify all the children in the street. When we heard him coming we all bolted, because he was like a baboon. He is still alive, and there is no terror anymore — except in the back of my mind. This was a degraded man, but he had some elemental force in him that is still terrifying; in another society he would have been a warrior.

There is another strange thing for me about the island of Saint Lucia; its whole topography is weird — very conical, with volcanic mountains and such — giving rise to all sorts of superstitions. Rather like what Ireland was for Yeats and the early Irish poets — another insular culture.

Whether you wanted to accept them or not, the earth emanated influences which you could either put down as folk superstition or, as a poet, accept as a possible truth. I think that is why a lot of my plays remain set in Saint Lucia, because there is a mystery there that is with me from childhood, that surrounds the whole feeling of the island. There was, for example, a mountain covered with mist and low clouds to which we gave the name of La Socière, the witch.

Does an island tradition impose limitations on a company such as ours? This goes back to the whole question of provincial, or beyond that, colonial experience, and of how we can broaden the base of the arts in the West Indies, and through that reach the larger audiences we should like. To me the only hope is in communal effort, just as I think some form of socialism, evolved from our own political history, is the only hope for the archipelago. When people like me ask the state for subsidy, we aren't asking the state to support the arts; we are informing the state, which is as poor and as spiritually degraded as we have been, of its true condition. The state is being asked to share the condition of its artists, to recognize its experience. The indifference is the same as it was under colonialism, but without that charming, avuncular cynicism of the British.

Yet I feel absolutely no shame in having endured the colonial experience. There was no obvious humiliation in it. In fact, I think that many of what are sneered at as colonial values are part of the strength of the West Indian psyche, a fusion of formalism with exuberance, a delight in both the precision and the power of language. We love rhetoric, and this has created a style, a panache about life that is particularly ours. Our most tragic folk songs and our most self-critical calypsos have a driving, life-asserting force. Combine that in our literature with a long experience of classical forms and you're bound to have something exhilarating. I've never consciously gone after this in my plays, nor do we go after this kind of folk-exuberance deliberately in my theatre company. But in the best actors in the company you can see this astounding fusion ignite their style, this combination of classic discipline inherited through the language, with a strength of physical expression that comes from the folk music.

It's probably the same in Nigeria with Wole Soyinka's Company. It's the greatest bequest the Empire made. Those who sneer at what they call an awe of tradition forget how old the West Indian experience is. I think that precisely because of their limitations our early education must have ranked with the finest in the world. The grounding was rigid — Latin, Greek, and the essential masterpieces, but there was this elation of discovery. Shakespeare, Marlowe, Horace, Vergil — these writers weren't jaded but immediate experiences. The atmosphere was competitive, creative.

It was cruel, but it created our literature.

THE CARIBBEAN: CULTURE OR MIMICRY? (1974)

Derek Walcott

We live in the shadow of an America that is economically benign yet politically malevolent. That malevolence, because of its size, threatens an eclipse of identity, but the shadow is as inescapable as that of any previous empire. But we were American even while we were British, if only in the geographical sense, and now that the shadow of the British Empire has passed through and over us in the Caribbean, we ask ourselves if, in the spiritual or cultural sense, we must become American. We have broken up the archipelago into nations, and in each nation we attempt to assert characteristics of the national identity. Everyone knows that these are pretexts of power if such power is seen as political. This is what the politician would describe as reality, but the reality is absurd. In the case of my own identity, or my realness if you like, it is an absurdity that I can live with; being both American and West Indian is an ambiguity without a crisis, for I find that the more West Indian I become, the more I can accept my dependence on America as a professional writer, not because America owes me a living from historical guilt, nor that it needs my presence, but because we share this part of the world, and have shared it for centuries now, even as conqueror and victim, as exploiter and exploited. What has happened here has happened to us. In other words that shadow is less malevolent than it appears, and we can absorb it because we know that America is black, that so much of its labor, its speech, its music, its very style of living is generated by what is now cunningly and carefully isolated as "black" culture, that what is most original in it has come out of its ghettos, its river-cultures, its plantations. Power itself is ephemeral, unstable. It is the least important aspect of any culture, who rules.

So, in the Caribbean, we do not pretend to exercise power in the historical sense. I think that what our politicians define as power, the need for it, or the lack of it should have another name; that, like America, what energizes our society is the spiritual force of a culture shaping itself, and it can do this without the formula of politics.

To talk about the contribution of the black man to American culture or civilization is absurd, because it is the black who energized that culture, who styles it, just as
it is the black who preserved and energized its faith. The most significant experience
in America's recent past is this revolution, and it is a revolution that was designed by
the poets and intellectuals of our powerless archipelago, by West Indians like Garvey,
Cesaire, Fanon, Padmore, and Stokely if you wish, and so our definitions of power
must go beyond the immediately political. We can see this and still keep distinctions.
In fact it is only because these leaders could make distinctions that they could see the
necessity for certain actions. And that is what I mean by being both West Indian and
American. This is not schizophrenia. Remember our experience of different empires.
Those experiences have been absorbed. To us, in many ways, America is a young
country, and that is why the metaphor exists in the minds of every revolutionary.
Many of us in the Caribbean still hold the ideal of the archipelago, just as you here
hold to the metaphor named America. If I speak in the tone of metaphor among men
who are more practical in their approach to problems, it is because I do not think that
as men of the Americas, we are different. Our society may be less complex. It is
obviously powerless. What I hope to explore is that society's validity, its reality.

To begin with, we are poor. That gives us a privilege. The poor always claim
intimacy with God over the rich. Emergent countries simplify man's political visions
in like manner because they are reduced to essentials. Like faith, it remains the
American problem, how to be rich and still good, how to be great and exercise
compassion.

Perhaps powerlessness leaves the Third World, the ex-colonial world, no alternative but to imitate those systems offered to or forced on it by the major powers, their
political systems which must alter their common life, their art, their language, their
philosophy. On the other hand, the bitterness of the colonial experience, its degradations of dependency and its cynicism of older "values" tempts the Third World with
spiritual alternatives. These alternatives will be violent, the total rejection through
revolution, for example, or cunning, or conservative, by which I mean the open
assimilation of what is considered from the metropolitan center to be most useful.
But whichever method is applied, it is obvious that the metamorphosis is beginning.
Large sections of the population of this earth have nothing to lose after their history of
slavery, colonialism, famine, economic exploitation, patronage, contempt. But the
tragedy is that most of its politicians are trapped in the concept of a world proposed
by those who rule it, and these politicians see progress as inevitability. They have
forgotten the desperate authority of the man who has nothing. In that sense Naipaul
is right, that their mimicry of power defrauds their own people. Such politicians insist
on describing potential in the same terms as those whom they must serve; they talk to
us in the bewildering code of world markets, and so forth. They use, in short, the
calculus of contemporary history, and that gives them and us the illusion that we
really contribute to the destiny of mankind, to foreign policy. We align ourselves to
this bloc or that, to that way of life or the other, and it is this tiredness, which falls so
quickly on the powerless, that horrifies Naipaul; but the truth is that there is
something else going on, that this is not the force of the current, and that its surface

may be littered with the despairs of broken systems and of failed experiments, that the river, stilled, may reflect, mirror, mimic other images, but that is not its depth.

It could not be. You see, the degradations have already been endured; they have been endured to the point of irrelevancy. In the Caribbean history is irrelevant, not because it is not being created, or because it was sordid; but because it has never mattered. What has mattered is the loss of history, the amnesia of the races, what has become necessary is imagination, imagination as necessity, as invention.

The phrase "The Mimic Men," which so many English-speaking West Indian intellectuals have so eagerly, almost masochistically taken to themselves, originates in the East Indian novelist Vidia Naipaul, who uses it as the title for one of his novels. Mr. Naipaul's epitaph on all West Indian endeavor has not aborted the passion with which West Indian culture continues to procreate this mimicry, because life, if we can call it that in the archipelago, defiantly continues.

To mimic, one needs a mirror, and, if I understand Mr. Naipaul correctly, our pantomime is conducted before a projection of ourselves which in its smallest gestures is based on metropolitan references. No gesture, according to this philosophy, is authentic, every sentence is a quotation, every movement either ambitious or pathetic, and because it is mimicry, uncreative. The indictment is crippling, but, like all insults, it contains an astonishing truth. The only thing is that it is not, to my mind, only the West Indies which is being insulted by Naipaul, but all endeavor in this half of the world, in broader definition: the American endeavor.

I use the word American regardless of genetic variety and origin. Once the meridian of European civilization has been crossed, according to the theory, we have entered a matter where there can only be simulations of self-discovery. The civilized virtues on the other side of this mirror are the virtues of social order, a lineally clear hierarchy, direction, purpose, balance. With these things, so we were taught, some social justice and the exercise of racial memory which is tradition. Somehow, the cord is cut by that meridian. Yet a return is also impossible, for we cannot return to what we have never been. The truth in all this is, of course, the amnesia of the American, particularly of the African. Most of our definitions of American culture are fragmentary, based on the gleam of racial memory which pierces this amnesia. The Old World, whether it is represented by the light of Europe or of Asia or of Africa, is the rhythm by which we remember. What we have carried over, apart from a few desultorily performed customs, is language. When language itself is condemned as mimicry, then the condition is hopeless and men are no more than jackdaws, parrots, myna birds, apes.

The idea of the American as ape is heartening, however, for in the imitation of apes there is something more ancient than the first human effort. The absurdity of pursuing the anthropological ideal of mimicry then, if we are to believe science, would lead us to the image of the first ape applauding the gestures of what we must call the first man. Here the contention crumbles because there is no scientific distinction possible between the last ape and the first man, there is no memory or history of the moment when man stopped imitating the ape, his ancestor, and became human. Therefore, everything is mere repetition. Did the first ape look at his reflection in the mirror of a pond in astonishment or in terror? Could it, or he, identify its or himself, and what name was given to that image? And was it at that moment of the self-naming grunt, a grunt delivered either in terror or in amusement, that the ape became man? And was that the beginning of the human ego and our history?

Advance some thousand years, protract the concept of evolution to the crossing of the mirror and the meridian of Alexander VI, and, like that instant of self-recognition or self-disgust, which are the same, what was the moment when the old ape of the Old World saw himself anew and became another, or, was paralyzed with the knowledge that henceforth, everything he did in the New World, on the other side of the mirror, could only be a parody of the past? Of course there is no such moment, just as there is no such moment for science of the transition from ape to man.

Columbus kneels on the sand of San Salvador. That is a moment. Bilbao, or Keat's Cortez looks on the Pacific. That is another moment. Lewis and Clark behold whatever they beheld, and that is yet another moment. What do they behold? They behold the images of themselves beholding. They are looking into the mirror of the sea, (the phrase is mimicked from Joseph Conrad), or the mirror of the plain, the desert, or the sky. We in the Americas are taught this as a succession of illuminations, lightning moments that must crystallize and irradiate memory if we are to believe in a chain of such illuminations known as history. To make a swift leap, probably without the mimicry of Aristotelian logic; because these illuminations are literary and not in the experience of American man, they are worthless. We cannot focus on a single ancestor, that moment of ape to man if you wish, or its reverse, depending on what side of the mirror you are favoring, when the black felt that he had crossed the meridian, when the East Indian had, or the Portugese, or the Chinese, or the Old World Jew. There was no line in the sea which said, this is new, this is the frontier, the boundary of endeavor, and henceforth everything can only be mimicry. But there was such a moment for every individual American, and that moment was both surrender and claim, both possession and dispossession. The issue is the claim.

The moment then, that a writer in the Caribbean, an American man, puts down a word—not only the first writer whoever he was, in Naipaul's view, but every writer since—at that moment he is a mimic, a mirror man, he is the ape beholding himself. This is supposed to be true as well of the dancer, the sculptor, the citizen, anyone in the Caribbean who is fated to unoriginality. So, of course, is Mr. Naipaul, whose curse extends to saying of this place that "nothing has ever been created in the West Indies, and nothing will ever be created." Precisely, precisely. We create nothing, but that is to move from anthropological absurdity to pseudo-philosophical rubbish, to discuss the reality of nothing, the mathematical conundrum of zero and infinity. Nothing will always be created in the West Indies, for quite a long time, because what will come out of there is like nothing one has ever seen before.

The ceremony which best exemplifies this attitude to history is the ritual of Carnival. This is a mass art form which came out of nothing, which emerged from the sanctions imposed on it. The banning of African drumming led to the discovery of the garbage can cover as a potential musical instrument whose subtlety of range, transferred to the empty oil drum, increases yearly, and the calypso itself emerged from a sense of mimicry, of patterning its form both on satire and self-satire. The impromptu elements of the calypso, like the improvisation and invention of steelband music, supersedes its traditional origins, that is, the steeldrum supersedes the attempt to copy melody from the xylophone and the drum, the calypso supersedes its ancient ritual forms in group chanting. From the viewpoint of history, these forms originated in imitation if you want, and ended in invention; and the same is true of the Carnival costume, its intricate, massive and delicate sculpture improvised without a self-conscious awe of reality, for the simple duplication of ancient sculptures is not enough to make a true Carnival costume. Here are three forms, originating from the mass, which are original and temporarily as inimitable as what they first attempted to copy. They were made from nothing, in their resulting forms it is hard to point to mere imitation.

But more significant than this is the attitude to such a prolixity of creative will that is jeered at as the "Carnival mentality." The carnival mentality seriously, solemnly dedicates itself to the concept of waste, of ephemera, of built-in obsolescence, but this is not the built-in obsolescence of manufacture but of art, because in Carnival the creative energy is strictly regulated to its own season. Last year's intricate sculptures are discarded as immediately valueless when it is midnight on Shrove Tuesday, last year's songs cannot be sung this year, nor last year's tunes, and so an entire population of craftsmen and spectators compel themselves to this regeneration of perpetually making it new, and by that rhythm create a backlog of music, design, song, popular poetry which is as strictly observed as the rhythm of cane harvest and cane-burning, of both industry and religion. The energy alone is overwhelming, and best of all, on one stage, at any moment, the simultaneity of historical legends, epochs, characters, without historical sequence or propriety is accepted as a concept.

Mimicry is an act of imagination, and, in some animals and insects, endemic cunning. Lizards, chameleons, most butterflies, and certain insects adapt the immediate subtleties of color and even of texture both as defense and as lure. Camouflage, whether it is in the grass-blade stripes of the tiger or the eyed hide of the leopard, is mimicry, or more than that, it is design. What if the man in the New World needs mimicry as design, both as defense and as lure. We take as long as other fellow creatures in the natural world to adapt and then blend into our habitats, whether we possess these environments by forced migration or by instinct. That is genetics. Culture must move faster, defensively. Everyone knows that there are differences between say plains cultures and sea cultures, or mountain cultures and jungle cultures, and if we see that in the Caribbean particularly, creatures from these different regions, forced into a common environment, still carry over their genetic coloring, their racial or tribal camouflage, the result, for a long time, can only be a bewildering variety that must race its differences rapidly into stasis, into recognition. The rapidity with which this is happening in the Caribbean looks like confusion.

But those who see only disorder, futility, and chaos must look for the patterns which they produce, and they will find in those patterns contradicting strains which often were not meant to adapt, far more survive. There were those who did not survive, not by weakness but by a process of imperialistic defoliation which blasted defiance; and this process, genocide, is what destroyed the original, destroyed the Aztec, and American Indian, and the Caribbean Indian. All right, let us say what these had was not a culture, not a civilization, but a way of life, then, a way with their own gods and language and domestic or marital customs. The point is that they broke, that they were resilient for awhile but were broken. These have gone. They left few ruins, since the ego was tribal, not individualistic, pagan if you want, not Christian. We can praise them for not imitating, but even imitation decimated them, or has humiliated them like the aborigine and the American Indian. What have we been offered here as an alternative but suicide. I do not know if apes commit suicide—their mimicry is not that far advanced—but men do, and it appears too, certain cultures.

That is the process by which we were Christianized. The imitation of Christ, the mimicry of God as a man. In that sense the first Christian is also not only the first man but the first ape, since before that everything was hearsay. The imitation of Christ must be carried into human life and social exchange, we are responsible for our brother, we are not responsible to ourselves but to God, and while this is admirable and true, how true is it that the imitation of God leads to human perfectibility, how necessary is it for us to mimic the supreme good, the perfect annihilation of present, past, and future since God is without them, so that a man who has achieved that spiritual mimicry immediately annihilates all sense of time. "Take no thought of the the morrow" is the same as "history is bunk"; the first is from Christ, the second from Henry Ford. But Ford is the divine example of American materialist man. Ford is an inventor, Ford created cars, Edison created light, and so it goes. What surrounds all of us as mimic men is that gratitude which acknowledges those achievements as creation. We are thus taught specific distances between the word invention and the word creation, between the inventor and the creator. We invent nothing, that is, no object. We do not have the resources, we can argue. Well, neither did Ford, neither did Edison. But electricity and light and even the idea of the car existed before they were discovered. They were not creations, they are also mimicry, originating from the existence and the accidents of natural elements. We continue far enough and we arrive at Voltaire confronting Nietzsche: "It is necessary to invent God," and "God is dead." Join both, and that is our twentieth-century credo. "It is necessary to invent a God who is dead."

Where have cultures originated? By the force of natural surroundings. You build according to the topography of where you live. You are what you eat, and so on; you mystify what you see, you create what you need spiritually, a god for each need.

If religion is not a life, if it is not itself mere mimicry of some unappeasable fear, then is not the good man a man who needs nothing? And I do not mean a man who does not need a car, nor electricity, nor television or whatever else we have failed to invent in the Caribbean, but a man who does not need them in the religious sense, a man who is dependent on the elements, who inhabits them, and takes his life from them. Even further, the ideal man does not need literature, religion, art, or even another, for there is ideally only himself and God. What he needs he makes, and what he makes will become more subtle in its uses, dependent on the subtlety of his needs or the proliferation of his creature comforts. That pursuit takes him further away from his mystical relation to the universe, thins its mystery, distances the idea of prayer, awe, spiritual necessity, until he can ask, surrounded by his own creations, "who needs God?"

No, cultures can only be created out of this knowledge of nothing, and in deeper than the superficial, existential sense, we in the Caribbean know all about nothing. We know that we owe Europe either revenge or nothing, and it is better to have nothing than revenge. We owe the past revenge or nothing, and revenge is uncreative. We may not even need literature, not that we are beyond it, but in the archipelago particularly, nature, the elements if you want, are so new, so overpowering in their presence that awe is deeper than articulation of awe. To name is to contradict. The awe of God or of the universe is the unnameable, and this has nothing to do with literacy. It is better for us to be a race of illiterates who retain this awe than to be godless, without mystery. A pygmy is better than an atheist. Sophistication is human wisdom and we who are the dregs of that old history, its victims, its transients, its dispossessed know what the old wisdom brought. What is called mimicry is the painful, new, laborious uttering that comes out of belief, not out of doubt. The votive man is silent, the cynical is articulate. Ask any poet which he would prefer, poetry or silence, poetry or wisdom, and he would answer wisdom. It is his journey to self-annihilation, to beginning again.

History, taught as morality, is religion. History, taught as action, is art. Those are the only uses to which we, mocked as a people without history, can put it. Because we have no choice but to view history as fiction or as religion, then our use of it will be idiosyncratic, personal, and therefore, creative. All of this is beyond the sociological, even beyond the "civilized" assessment of our endeavor, beyond mimicry. The stripped and naked man, however abused, however disabused of old beliefs, instinctually, even desperately begins again as a craftsman. In the indication of the slightest necessary gesture of ordering the world around him, of losing his old name and rechristening himself, in the arduous enunciation of a dimmed alphabet, in the shaping of tools, pen or spade, is the whole, profound sigh of human optimism, of what we in the archipelago still believe in: work and hope. It is out of this that the New World, or the Third World, should begin.

Theoretical and idealistic though this sounds, it is our duty as poets to reiterate it. The embittered despair of a New World writer like Naipaul is also part of that impatience and irascibility at the mere repetition of human error which passes for history, and that irascibility is also a belief in possibility. The New World originated in hypocrisy and genocide, so it is not a question for us, of returning to an Eden or of creating Utopia; out of the sordid and degrading beginning of the West Indies, we could only go further in decency and regret. Poets and satirists are afflicted with the superior stupidity which believes that societies can be renewed, and one of the most nourishing sites for such a renewal, however visionary it may seem, is the American archipelago.

DEREK WALCOTT (1982)

Anthony Milne

Derek Walcott was in Trinidad last week. While here he gave a reading at the Royal Victoria Institute, and met with members of the Trinidad Theatre Workshop who are to produce his play, "The Joker of Seville", later this year.

Walcott was staying, as is his wont, at the Hotel Normandie, and when EXPRESS feature writer Anthony Milne went to see him he was lounging by the pool. The interview was conducted beneath a poolside umbrella until the wind and the rain made this impossible. The rest of the interview took place in Walcott's hotel room, in between interviews with members of the Theatre Workshop.

EXPRESS: What is it like living in the United States, and what are you doing there?
WALCOTT: I used to teach in a university there one term, or semester, at a time. I was making my living that way. Of course, the money was rapidly consumed; whatever I saved went very quickly while I was in Trinidad. I was living in hotels while I was here. I decided last year, having got an offer from Boston University, that I would take a permanent job there because it would involve the reality that my children would get a free university education.

Just to try to create a kind of continuity I thought I would take the job for a period of time and test it and see how long I wanted to remain there. Then I got the MacArthur award, which is a good amount of money, and one has to live in a place that is one's own, so I got a place in Boston quite near to the university.

But I genuinely consider that I have a kind of even balance, geographically and even mentally now between the United States and Trinidad, or the Caribbean, because another place I like to go to in summer, I do a workshop up there, is St. Thomas in the Virgin Islands. I run a playwrights' workshop there, and I'm going to go back there this summer with my daughters, to do a combined work-vacation type of thing.

Then, of course, I'm here in Trinidad during the vacations, and the summer vacation is quite long, beginning at the end of May and continuing till the first week in September. I am very active. There are a lot of things I plan to do here, with the theatre particularly.

Since I have got this grant from the MacArthur Foundation, and since the grant included $36,000 annually to be used by any institution I associate myself with, that sum will go, on alternate years, to Boston University and to the Trinidad Theatre Workshop.

So I think I have achieved a kind of balance which I have sought for a long time. I'm not doing enough, and one needs a hell of a lot more money, but this whole question of exchanging talent, which I am continuing with, is not just for my sake; it's something that needs to be done. The actors here need to have fresh professional actors come down to work with them. And the actors who come down from New York, or wherever, will also benefit from the experience of coming to the Caribbean.

EXPRESS: Who now constitute the Theatre Workshop?

WALCOTT: Just recently Albert La Veau was appointed to be a new director of the workshop, and there is evidently going to be a new board. I created the workshop, but I'm not in it, I'm outside of it, so that's where the interest lies. There is also an executive board, and also a board of trustees which has to be there before the grant can be administered.

But what I want to do in a broader sense, if it's possible (and this is where one can test whether there is any guided philanthropy in Trinidad), if that $36,000 goes to the workshop, which is quite likely, then what will be necessary, to ensure there is enough money for a solid programme, are matching grants either from the government or from business people. Because generally the situation has always been that you go and beg and so on, and there have been instances of people endorsing things, and signs that they will do so again. But if you have that initial sum, from the grant, you can go to people and ask whether they will match the amount, and that way you can find out if people are really interested in developing the theatre here; the arts on the whole.

I'm not saying that there has been no funding in the past, but at times the funding is minimal (it certainly has been sporadic), and sometimes it has been overblown. In other words there has been immense investment in things that are basically ephemeral. Over the next five years during which that grant is administered, I want to get people to come down here.

I have spoken to some very important actors and directors in America who say they will come down. Lloyd Richards, who is the artistic director and Dean of the Yale Drama School, will be coming down in the summer to do a ten-day master-class in acting. I've spoken to another American director who did a play of mine; and I've also spoken to a world-renown[ed] actress, a terrific actress, I won't tell you her name now, because the thing is still being negotiated, and there are a couple other people who will come down to help create this widening, mutual area of experience.

It is about time the experience of the theatre here be expanded, and certainly it shouldn't contract itself racially. That is a danger here as well. You can see that there is almost beginning to be a division in terms of colour in the theatre. People may say I'm talking nonsense, but I'm watching it and I think that the more nationalistic you get, because of the nature of the bulk of the population here, the more the thinking may tend to be only in black or in Indian, and that is not what the West Indies is supposed to mean, or Trinidad certainly.

So I'm talking about white actors too. I'm not interested in making a black theatre in the Caribbean, absolutely not, because that would exclude everybody, apart from the black.

EXPRESS: Do you know about the controversy over the role of theLittle Carib Theatre?

WALCOTT: Yes, that is a complicated question. I suppose I'm skirting the question, but let me say that I think that one of the problems is that this country is a very small place, and the biggest danger here is for people to self-inflate their reputations, and to become disproportionately blind about what is really valuable. I find that increasingly frightening, and distressing. It's all around. Very inexperienced people who may have zeal (which in itself is allright) but whose zeal gets transformed into very large egos, can do a lot of damage in terms of restraining or misdirecting certain things.

This is a place where if you just get something published a couple of times you are automatically a poet; if you write a play you are a playwright; if you go on the stage you are an actor. Because of nationalism, because of this greed to have an identity that is purely Trinidadian, with the loss of the sense of patience and building that is necessary in any craft, people have overblown reputations, and tend after a while to believe in their own reflections.

I think it's all around now. I have come back here and seen people's names billed as stars, and I'm talking about totally inexperienced young actors. I've seen directors' names put above the names of authors; so that playwrights established worldwide get second billing. It's insanity, and it looks foolish, because I have had friends down here, professional theatre people, and it makes us look damn silly, that's all I'm saying. There's some sanity required to get back into a modesty of discipline and direction that has been derailed by this inflation of egos here.

I go through a hell of a lot in terms of this kind of thing. I've just had two plays done in America that have got very bad reviews and these are sobering experiences. Down here my reputation is big, but when I'm in America I'm among other people who can be sliced in a review the next day, so I always have that chastening experience of knowing I'm not finished working. A lot of people here have the feeling that in six months' time they can become actors or directors or producers. I think that's the worst aspect of things here now.

EXPRESS: There was an article about Vidia Naipaul in last Sunday's EXPRESS which was perhaps evidence of the kind of thing you are talking about. The writer joined in the criticism of both Naipaul and yourself, apparently because you don't always say the things a certain kind of person likes to hear. It seems as though that type of person feels he must revile those who, by international standards, are the finest literary products of the region.

WALCOTT: I don't think that is of any importance whatsoever, because no matter what is said in terms of being criticised locally, it is expected. You have a village mentality, and if you walk down a village street dressed differently you get people heckling you at a street corner. So when you encounter a village mentality you ignore it, otherwise you would never work. And a village mentality can exist on an official level, on very responsible levels. It still remains a village mentality.

Certainly anyone can say what they want about Naipaul, in terms of his philosophy or his attitude to Trinidad, but it is impossible to degrade him as an artist, because the work is there. So that is only village jeering and is of absolutely no consequence; that is just standpipe criticism.

EXPRESS: Would you say that this kind of thing, this attitude, and the danger of assuming an inflated ego makes it difficult for a person who is trying to become a serious writer or artist in Trinidad?

WALCOTT: In days gone by, and this may seem like nostalgia because I am 52, a different kind of thing happened. There were values in the colonial system of education, and the colonial system of hierarchy that were over-turned with independence, but people revert to them. One of the obvious symptoms of hierarchy is the hierarchy of language.

If you live in a society in which bad language (and by bad I don't mean immoral, but ill-expressed language) is acceptable not only as a norm but as an expression of Patriotism (so that if you don't speak badly you become an enemy of the people, because the people don't talk that way) you get a deterioration of syntax. A deterioration of syntax is related to the threat of deterioration in a society. Because the next thing that happens is that anyone with any talent or with any ambition is called a showoff, because there is an attempt to force that person to become democratic.

But art is not democratic, art is hierarchical, and all artists know that. They know that it takes all your life to achieve some level where you can be among your peers. But if immediately your peers are made to be illiterate, or the people who feel education is restricted entirely to self-expression without craft, then the society is in danger. It is in more danger than it is from terrorists or revolutionaries.

But I think the standard of education here, just from speaking to my daughters, is high, it remains high. That is one good aspect of the colonial heritage. We mustn't look on colonialism simply as oppression, there are certain things in it that, however irascible they make some people, form the basis of the kind of democratic society that exists here. It is not a matter of race. It is a matter of racelessness, really.

For us to teach art as race, which is typical independence type of thinking, that will go away. Because I don't think anyone is going to prevent the artist from having a universal type of mind. But I will say again that I think the standard of education here remains high, because it depends on the severe discipline of studying, which I think is good.

EXPRESS: It seems that what you are saying is that there is sometimes a confusion between colonial standards and standards which are universal; that people reject a certain standard saying that it is colonial, when it is important to maintain that standard.

WALCOTT: Yes, or they make the silly mistake of confusing race with culture. Now I'm not saying that colonial culture is the only culture. I am saying that the exclusion of good speech, the exclusion of books, of art, or whatever, as a sort of historical revenge, as a revenge on history, is very short-sighted, and is fatal.

The question of emphasing [sic] an African or Indian identity is irrelevant, because you are African or you are Indian and no one can take that away in terms of identity. To exclude yourself, like some other Third World countries would do, to think that everything there is tainted and poisoned, is immature.

EXPRESS: So that the same way that the primitive Britons benefited from Roman Colonialism?

WALCOTT: Exactly. The whole process of civilization is cyclical. The good civilization absorbs a certain amount, like the Greeks. Empires are smart enough to steal from the people they conquer. They steal the best things. And the people who have been conquered should have enough sense to steal back.

EXPRESS: But is there a difference between Roman-British colonialism and British-West African colonialism because of greater racial differences in the latter?

WALCOTT: Colonialism is often based on race. You are going out there to subdue heathen races, and so on. But it isn't always based on race, it isn't always that you are subduing the heathen, although you have to think of people as heathen. It depends on how much power exists at the moment, in the empire. For example, when Britain invaded India it was invading a civilisation older than its own.

All of what is called the Third World is now confronted by this crisis of restoration. The Moslem thing that Naipaul talks about in his recent book, though it is not a very profound book, but one of the things it talks about is the extreme and frenzied rejection of everything Christian in Islamic countries; that's not what you want.

To be told by politicians, or by critics, or by anyone at all, or by Naipaul himself (this is where he contradicts himself), that you are imitating is odd. On the one hand you say embrace, and on the other you say don't imitate. But you cannot embrace without imitation. The trouble with it is that when the empire does it, it is known as acquisition and when it is done by colonials it is known as imitation. The amorality of that is absurd.

My main concern is not with any political refutation of the past, but with the reality of the day to day experience of language and literature, and so on. I think that the situation here is almost obscene in the fact that there isn't a good library still, and other things. All those things that should be there.

These things are not false. It isn't that you are putting up the structure and hoping to fill it. The point is that you have the personnel, you have the people, you have the enthusiasm, the drive, you have the reality of people's becoming; but what you don't have is those moulds to contain and shape that expression. What you do have, unfortunately, is a government, which has been re-elected, that is not going to suddenly get a new vision of the situation.

It may be that their vision will broaden and they will see the obvious need for certain things which one has been crying out for a quarter of a century. I am not cynical any more. I am just resigned to the fact that I don't expect anything to be done. But that does not mean that I don't have the faith that another generation of people will insist on their right to have civic buildings where they can express themselves: museums, theatres, and so on. Another generation is going to make damn sure they get these things.

EXPRESS: With regard to what you were saying about language and its deterioration, does that have to do with the way in which language and thought are connected, in that subtlety of thought needs subtlety of language?

WALCOTT: It is hard to measure that, but I don't think you can say that a thought is more subtle in an imperial language than it is in a colonial dialect. I know a feeling cannot be. I think that artists have acute, more accentuated, more mercurial feelings, because they train their minds towards this daily. They become over-sensitive and more receptive.

But the average person in one culture is not more sensitive than the average person in another culture, because the same experiences go through each culture, whether it is death or fear, just to take the large ones. In terms of subtleties of feeling no man is different from another man.

The acuteness of the artist in terms of representing or experiencing those feelings is a difference, definitely. But you cannot be an artist without the discipline of thought, and that discipline of thought must be within a structure of language. That structure of language may begin in dialect, originate in dialect.

I don't think we have as yet managed to express fully the subtleties that are possible in dialect. They have been expressed, but as a generic thing, as a large thing. You have the kind of dialect writing that is h[u]morous or satirical, which pretends to be nationalistic, but which [is] really poking fun at itself. You also have, as with Naipaul or Selvon, artists working in the language and making some masterful little variations in the language. So that it is there.

But to say that when someone is writing a dialect story that person is thinking in the imperial language, I don't know if that's true. I think that the confidence you have in the language is that you are saying that one is no better than the other. It's like Dante writing "The Divine Comedy" in the vulgar tongue, or Chaucer, or Joyce, or Synge.

EXPRESS: But what about the other functions of language, in philosophy, for example?

WALCOTT: Well, the language in art is the language that is used in schools. And unless we look very carefully and realise, for instance, that the diction of teachers in schools cannot be tolerated purely as being nationalistic diction. In other words, to mispronounce words, to say "de" instead of "the" is not a nationalistic thing.

It is crippling and limiting the width of a child's mind if at an early age what is correct speech (and there is no question about what is correct speech, correct speech is agreed upon by what grammar is) we are talking about schools principally. And if the subtlety of a philosophical thought contradicts itself in dialect then you have no confidence in the dialect and you have more confidence in the imperial language, the source of the language.

So that whole problem is centred in education, because every artist either is self-educated to the same degree that he was his own teacher, very rigidly, or he had a formal education in which he was trained by teachers who had enough confidence to be what they were.

EXPRESS: Do you think that syntactical breakdown is part of a process by which something new may be formed?

WALCOTT: Certainly, because that happens with the artist; but what I'm saying is that the artist has the duality of confidence in either language. If Naipaul wants to write a dialect story, like "Tell Me Who To kill," which is a little masterpiece, he does that, then he does another kind of story, in English. He can choose either tool he likes. But when you have someone else who is not a writer, or an artist, patriotically affirming that this is our language then just purely as an academic exercise, for the sake of an examination, or for the sake of getting a job, beginning to treat English as some kind of device by which one can advance oneself, purely for that reason, then you are limiting what I still think is the range of the West Indian experience. Which is world-wide range. It's like teaching bad Hindu, or Hebrew, or Swahili.

EXPRESS: In spite of all the attendant problems, how do you feel about living and working in Trinidad again.

WALCOTT: My whole thing about Trinidad is that it is more enriching, however embittering or degrading or frustrating sometimes. It is a richer experience for me to be in Trinidad than it is to be in America. The challenge of the experience of what it means to be at the beginning of a society is more exciting than to be in one that is too large to influence, to help direct. As I explained, I think I have achieved a balance between being in the United States and Trinidad.

THE ART OF POETRY (1986)

Edward Hirsch

I went to visit Derek Walcott on his home island of St. Lucia in mid-June, 1985. St. Lucia is one of the four Windward Islands in the eastern Caribbean, a small mountainous island which faces the Atlantic Ocean on one side and the Caribbean Sea on the other. For a week Walcott and I stayed in adjacent bungalows, called "Hunt's Beach Cottages," just a few miles from the harbor city of Castries where he was born and raised. Outside of our large, mildly ramshackle cottages, a few stone tables and chairs were cemented into a strip of grass; beyond was a row of coconut trees and then, just a few yards away, what Walcott has called "the theater of the sea," the Caribbean. One is always aware of the sea in St. Lucia—an inescapable natural presence which has deeply affected Walcott's sense of being an islander, a new world poet.

*Derek Walcott was born in 1930. He was educated at St. Mary's College in St. Lucia and at the University of the West Indies in Jamaica. For many years he lived in Trinidad—he still spends most of his summers there—where from 1959 to 1976 he directed the Trinidad Theater Workshop. Since then he has spent much of his time in the United States, living first in New York City and more recently in Boston. Currently, he holds a MacArthur Fellowship and teaches at Boston University. Walcott's first three booklets—*25 Poems *(1948),* Epitaph for the Young *(1949), and* Poems *(1951)—were privately printed in the West Indies. His mature work begins with* In a Green Night: Poems 1948-1960 *(1962) and* Selected Poems *(1964). Since then he has published seven individual poetry books:* The Castaway *(1965),* The Gulf *(1969), the book-length autobiographical poem* Another Life *(1973),* Sea Grapes *(1976),* The Star-Apple Kingdom *(1979),* The Fortunate Traveller *(1981) and* Midsummer *(1984). At the time of this interview Walcott was looking forward to the publication of his* Collected Poems*—which appeared in the winter of 1986. Considering himself equally a poet and a playwright, Walcott has also published three books of plays in America:* Dream on Monkey Mountain and Other Plays *(1970),* The Joker of Seville and O Babylon! *(1978), and* Remembrance and Pantomime: Two Plays *(1980).*

To live next door to Walcott, even for a week, is to understand how he has managed to be so productive over the years. A prodigious worker, he often starts at about 4:30 in the morning and continues until he has done a four or five hour stint—by the time most people are getting up for the day. On a small easel next to a small blue portable typewriter, he had

65

recently done a pencil drawing of his wife, Norline, and a couple of new watercolors to serve as storyboards for a film version of Pantomime *(he is doing the film script); he had also just finished the draft of an original screenplay about a steel band, as well as an extended essay about the Grenada invasion (to be called "Good Old Heart of Darkness"), and a new manuscript of poems, "The Arkansas Testament" (Spring, 1987). At the time of this interview the cuttings for two more films were all but complete: a film version of his play,* Haitian Earth *(which he had produced in St. Lucia the previous year), and a documentary film about Hart Crane for public television. At times one gets the impression that the poetry for which he is primarily known has had to be squeezed between all his other projects.*

And yet while I was in St. Lucia, most of Walcott's other activities were suspended as he worked on a new poem, "The Light of the World." It is a homecoming poem, a Narrative lyric about returning to Castries. The poem is set on a transport—what we would call a mini-bus—and characterizes the poet's sense of feeling both separated from, and connected to, the life of the people around him. Once more he is struck by the grace as well as the difficult poverty of his people; he reexperiences the beauty of St. Lucian women and feels the weight of their daily lives. "The Light of the World" is a large poem of guilt and expiation, and it gives a good sense of Walcott's inner feelings during the time of our interview.

Our conversation took place over three days—beginning in the late afternoon or early evening and continuing until dark. We talked at the table and chairs outside our cottages where we could hear the wind in the coconut trees and the waves breaking on the shore. A compact man in his mid-fifties, Walcott was still dressed from his afternoon on the beach—barefoot, a pair of brown beach trunks and a thin cotton shirt. Often he kept a striped beach towel draped around his shoulders, a white flour-sack beach hat pushed forward jauntily on his head. He seemed always to be either smoking or about to start.

INTERVIEWER: I'd like to begin by asking you to talk about your family background. In many ways it was atypical for St. Lucia. For example, you were raised as a Methodist on a primarily Catholic island. Your family also seems to have been unusually oriented toward the arts.

DEREK WALCOTT: My family background really only consists of my mother. She was a widow. My father died quite young; he must have been thirty-one. Then there was my twin brother and my sister. We had two aunts as well, my father's sisters. But the immediate family consisted of my mother, my brother, my sister, and me. I remember from very early childhood my mother, who was a teacher, reciting a lot around the house. I remember coming across drawings that my father had done, poems that he had written, watercolors that were hanging in our living room—his original watercolors—and a terrific series of books: a lot of Dickens, Scott, quite a lot of poetry. There was also an old victrola with a lot of classical records. And so my family always had this interest in the arts. Coming from a Methodist minority in a French Catholic island, we also felt a little beleaguered. The Catholicism propounded by the French provincial priests in St. Lucia was a very hide-bound, prejudiced, medieval, almost hounding kind of Catholicism. The doctrine that was taught assigned all Protestants to limbo. So we felt defensive about our position. This never came to a head, but we did feel we had to stay close together. It was good for me too, to be able to ask questions as a Protestant, to question large authority. Nobody in my generation at my age would dare question the complete and absolute authority of the church. Even into sixth form, my school friends and I used to have some terrific arguments about religious doctrine. It was a good thing. I think young writers ought to be heretical.

INTERVIEWER: In an essay called "Leaving School" you suggest that the artifacts of your father's twin avocations, poetry and painting, made your own sense of vocation seem inevitable. Would you describe his creative work and how it affected you?

WALCOTT: My mother, who is nearly ninety now, still talks continually about my father. All my life I've been aware of her grief about his absence and her strong pride in his conduct. He was very young when he died of mastoiditis which is an ear infection. Medicine in St. Lucia in those days was crude or very minimal; I know he had to go to Barbados for operations. I don't remember the death or anything like that, but I always felt his presence because of the paintings that he did. He had a self-portrait in watercolor in an oval frame next to a portrait of my mother, an oil that was very good for an amateur painter. I remember once coming across a backcloth of a very ordinary kind of moonlight scene that he had painted for some number that was going to be done by a group of people who did concerts and recitations and stuff like that. So that was always there. Now that didn't make me a morose, morbid child. Rather, in a sense, it gave me a kind of impetus and a strong sense of continuity. I felt that what had been cut off in him somehow was an extension that I was continuing.

INTERVIEWER: When did you first discover his poems?

WALCOTT: The poems I'm talking about are not a collection. I remember a couple of funny lyrics that were done in a southern American dialect for some show he was probably presenting. They were witty little satirical things. I can't remember any poems of a serious nature. I remember more of his art work. I remember a fine watercolor copy of Millet's "The Gleaners" which he had in the living room. The original is an oil painting and even now I am aware of the delicacy of that copy. He had a delicate sense of watercolor. Later on I discovered that my friend Harold Simmons, who was a professional painter, evidently was encouraged by my father to be a painter. So there's always this continuity in my association with people who knew him and people who were very proud to be his friend. My mother would tell us that, and that's what I felt.

INTERVIEWER: Your book-length autobiographical poem, *Another Life*, makes it clear that two painters were crucial to your development: your mentor Harold Simmons, called Harry in the poem, and your friend Dunstan St. Omer, renamed Gregorias. Would you talk about their importance to you?

WALCOTT: Harry taught us. He had paints, he had music in his studio, and he was evidently a good friend of my father's. When he found out that we liked painting, he invited about four or five of us to come up to his studio and sit out on his veranda. He gave us equipment and told us to draw. Now that may seem very ordinary in a city, in another place, but in a very small, poor country like St. Lucia it was extraordinary. He encouraged us to spend our Saturday afternoons painting; he surrounded us with examples of his own painting. Just to let us be there and to have the ambience of his books, his music, his own supervision and the stillness and dedication that his life meant in that studio was a terrific example. The influence was not so much technical. Of course, I picked up a few things from him in terms of technique: how to do a good sky, how to water the paper, how to circle it, how to draw properly and concentrate on it, and all of that. But there were other things apart from the drawing. Mostly, it was the model of the man as a professional artist that was the example. After a while, the younger guys dropped out of the drawing thing and Dunstan St. Omer and I were left. We used to go out and paint together. We discovered it at the same time.

INTERVIEWER: Did you have a favorite painter then?

WALCOTT: The painter I really thought I could learn from was Cézanne—some sort of resemblance to oranges and greens and browns of the dry season in St. Lucia. I used to look across from the roof towards Vigie—the barracks were there and I'd see the pale orange roofs and the brickwork and the screen of trees and the cliff and the very flat blue and think a lot of Cézanne. Maybe because of the rigidity of the cubes and the verticals and so on. It's as if he knew the St. Lucian landscape—you could see his painting happening there. There were other painters of course, like Giorgione, but I think it gave me a lot of strength to think of Cézanne when I was painting.

INTERVIEWER: What would you say about the epiphanic experience described in *Another Life*, which seems to have confirmed your destiny as a poet and sealed a bond to your native island?

WALCOTT: There are some things people avoid saying in interviews because they sound pompous or sentimental or too mystical. I have never separated the writing of poetry from prayer. I have grown up believing it is a vocation, a religious vocation. What I described in *Another Life*—about being on the hill and feeling the sort of dissolution that happened—is a frequent experience in a younger writer. I felt this sweetness of melancholy, of a sense of mortality, or rather of immortality, a sense of gratitude both for what you feel is a gift and for the beauty of the earth, the beauty of life around us. When that's forceful in a young writer, it can make you cry. It's just clear tears; it's not grimacing or being contorted, it's just a flow that happens. The body feels it is melting into what it has seen. This continues in the poet. It may be repressed in some way, but I think we continue in all our lives to have that sense of melting, of the "I" not being important. That is the ecstasy. It doesn't happen as much when you get older. There's that wonderful passage in Traherne where he talks about seeing the children as moving jewels until they learn the dirty devices of the world. It's not *that* mystic. Ultimately, it's what Yeats says: "Such a sweetness flows into the breast that we laugh at everything and everything we look upon is blessed." That's always there. It's a benediction, a transference. It's gratitude, really. The more of that a poet keeps, the more genuine his nature. I've always felt that sense of gratitude. I've never felt equal to it in terms of my writing, but I've never felt that I was ever less than that. And so in that particular passage in *Another Life* I was recording a particular moment.

INTERVIEWER: How do you write? In regard to your equation of poetry and prayer, is the writing ritualized in any way?

WALCOTT: I don't know how many writers are willing to confess to their private preparatory rituals before they get down to putting something on paper. But I imagine that all artists and all writers in that moment before they begin their working day or working night have that area between beginning and preparation, and however brief it is, there is something about it votive and humble and in a sense ritualistic. Individual writers have different postures, different stances, even different physical attitudes as they stand or sit over their blank paper, and in a sense, without doing it, they are crossing themselves; I mean, it's like the habit of Catholics going into water: you cross yourself before you go in. Any serious attempt to try to do something worthwhile is ritualistic. I haven't noticed what my own devices are. But I do know that if one thinks a poem is coming on—in spite of the noise of the typewriter, or the traffic outside the window, or whatever—you do make a retreat, a withdrawal into some kind of silence that cuts out everything around you. What you're taking on is really not a renewal of your identity but actually a renewal of your *anonymity* so that what's in front of you becomes more important than what you are. Equally—and it may be a little pretentious-sounding to say it—sometimes if I feel that I have done good work I do pray, I do say thanks. It isn't often, of course. I don't do it every day. I'm not a monk, but if something does happen I say thanks because I feel that it is really a piece of luck, a kind of fleeting grace that has happened to one. Between the beginning and the ending and the actual composition that goes on, there is a kind of trance that you hope to enter where every aspect of your intellect is functioning simultaneously for the progress of the composition. But there is no way you can induce that trance.

Lately, I find myself getting up earlier, which may be a sign of late middle-age. It worries me a bit. I guess this is part of the ritual: I go and make a cup of coffee, put on the kettle, and have a cigarette. By now I'm not too sure if out of habit I'm getting up for the coffee rather than to write. I may be getting up that early to smoke, not really to write.

INTERVIEWER: What time is this?

WALCOTT: It can vary. Sometimes it's as early as half-past three, which is, you know, not too nice. The average time would be about five. It depends on how well I'm sleeping. But that hour, that whole time of day, is wonderful in the Caribbean. I love the cool darkness and the joy and splendor of the sunrise coming up. I guess I would say, especially in the location of where I am, the early dark and the sunrise, and being up with the coffee and with whatever you're working on, is a very ritualistic thing. I'd even go further and say it's a religious thing. It has its instruments and its surroundings. And you can feel your own spirit waking.

INTERVIEWER: Recently, I heard you say that you were deeply formed by Methodism. How?

WALCOTT: In a private way, I think I still have a very simple, straightforward foursquare Methodism in me. I admire the quiet, pragmatic reason that is there in a faith like Methodism, which is a very practical thing of conduct. I'm not talking about a fanatical fundamentalism. I suppose the best word for it is "decency." Decency and understanding are what I've learned from being a Methodist. Always, one was responsible to God for one's inner conduct and not to any immense hierarchy of angels and saints. In a way I think I tried to say that in some earlier poems. There's also a very strong sense of carpentry in Protestantism, in making things simply and in a utilitarian way. At this period of my life and work, I think of myself in a way as a carpenter, as one making frames, simply and well. I'm working a lot in quatrains, or I have been, and I feel that there is something in that that is very ordinary, you know, without any mystique. I'm trying to get rid of the mystique as much as possible. And so I find myself wanting to write very simply cut, very contracted, very speakable and very challenging quatrains in rhymes. Any other shape seems ornate, an elaboration on that essential cube that really is the poem. So we can then say the craft is as ritualistic as that of a carpenter putting down his plane and measuring his stanzas and setting them squarely. And the frame becomes more important than the carpenter.

INTERVIEWER: *Another Life* suggests that eventually you gave up painting as a vocation and decided to concentrate on poetry. Recently, though, you seem to be at work on your watercolors again. What happened?

WALCOTT: What I tried to say in *Another Life* is that the act of painting is not an intellectual act dictated by reason. It is an act that is swept very physically by the sensuality of the brushstroke. I've always felt that some kind of intellect, some kind of preordering, some kind of criticism of the thing before it is done, has always interfered with my ability to do a painting. I am in fairly continual practice. I think I'm getting adept at watercolor. I'm less mucky. I think I could do a reasonable oil painting. I could probably, if I really set out, be a fairly good painter. I can approach the sensuality. I know how it feels, but for me there is just no completion. I'm content to be a moderately good watercolorist. But I'm not content to be a moderately good poet. That's a very different thing.

INTERVIEWER: Am I correct that you published your first poem, "The Voice of St. Lucia," at the precocious age of fourteen? I've read that the poem stirred up a considerable local controversy.

WALCOTT: I wrote a poem talking about learning about God through nature and not through the church. The poem was Miltonic and posed nature as a way to learn. I sent it to the local papers and it was printed. Of course, to see your work in print for any younger writer is a great kick. And then the paper printed a letter in which a priest replied (in verse!) stating that what I was saying was blasphemous and that the proper place to find God was in church. For a young boy to get that sort of response from a mature older man, a priest who was an Englishman, and to be accused of blasphemy was a shock. What was a more chastising thing was that the response was in verse. The point of course was to show me that he was also capable of writing verse. He did his in couplets and mine was in blank verse. I would imagine if I looked at both now that mine was better.

INTERVIEWER: Most American and English readers think of *In a Green Night* as your first book. Before you published abroad, however, you had already printed three booklets at your own expense in the West Indies. How did you come to publish the first one, *25 Poems?*

WALCOTT: I used to write every day in an exercise book, and when I first wrote I wrote with great originality. I just wrote as hard and as well as I felt. I remember the great elation and release I felt, a sort of hooking on to a thing, when I read Auden, Eliot, and everyone. One day I would write like Spender, another day I would write like Dylan Thomas. When I felt I had enough poems that I liked, I wanted to see them in print. We had no publishing house in St. Lucia or in the Caribbean. There was a Faber collection of books that had come out with poets like Eliot and Auden, and I liked the type-face and how the books looked. I thought, "I want to have a book like that." So I selected a collection of twenty-five of them and thought, "Well, these will look good because they'll look like they came from abroad; they'll look like a published book." I went to my mother and said, "I'd like to publish a book of poems, and I think it's going to cost me two hundred dollars." She was just a seamstress and schoolteacher, and I remember her being very upset because she wanted to do it. Somehow she got it; —a lot of money for a woman to have found on her salary. She gave it to me, and I sent off to Trinidad and had the book printed. When the books came back I would sell them to friends. I made the money back. In terms of seeing a book in print, the only way I could have done it was to publish it myself.

INTERVIEWER: Frank Collymore wrote a very appreciative essay about your early poetry. That must have been a heady experience for a nineteen year-old. After all, he was the editor of the ground-breaking Caribbean literary magazine, *Bim*, a man that Edward Braithwaite once called "the greatest of West Indian literary godfathers."

WALCOTT: Frank Collymore was an absolute saint. I got to know him through Harry Simmons. I have never met a more benign, gentle, considerate, selfless person. I'll never forget the whole experience of going over to Barbados and meeting him. To be treated at that age by a much older man with such care and love and so on was wonderful. He treated George Lamming the same way. There are people like that, people who love other people, love them for their work and what it is. He was not by any means a patronizing man. He never treated you as if he were a schoolmaster doing you good. I had great fortune when I was young in being treated like that by people, by people much older than I was who treated me, who treated my mind, as if I were equal to them. He was the best example of that.

INTERVIEWER: You once described yourself at nineteen as "an elated, exuberant poet madly in love with English" and said that as a young writer you viewed yourself as legitimately prolonging "the mighty line" of Marlowe and Milton. Will you talk about that sense of yourself?

WALCOTT: I come from a place that likes grandeur; it likes large gestures; it is not inhibited by flourish; it is a rhetorical society; it is a society of physical performance; it is a society of style. The highest achievement of style is rhetoric, as it is in speech and performance. It isn't a modest society. A performer in the Caribbean has to perform with the right flourish. A Calypsonian performer is equivalent to a bullfighter in the ring. He has to come over. He can write the wittiest Calypso, but if he's going to deliver it, he has to deliver it well, and he has to hit the audience with whatever technique he has. Modesty is not possible in performance in the Caribbean, and that's wonderful. It's better to be large and to make huge gestures than to be modest and do tiptoeing types of presentations of oneself. Even if it's a private platform, it's a platform. The voice does go up in a poem. It is an address, even if it is to oneself. And the greatest address is in the rhetoric. I grew up in a place in which if you learned poetry, you shouted it out. Boys would scream it out and perform it and do it and flourish it. If you wanted to approximate that thunder or that power of speech, it couldn't be done by a little modest voice in which you muttered something to someone else. I came out of that society of the huge gesture. And literature is like that, I mean *theatrical* literature is like that, whether it's Greek or whatever. The recitation element in poetry is one I hope I never lose because it's an essential part of the voice being asked to perform. If we have poets we're really asking them, "Okay, tell me a poem." Generally the implication is, "Mutter me a poem." I'm not in that group.

INTERVIEWER: There is a confident, fiery sense of privilege in your early work. In a recent poem, *Midsummer*, you write "Forty years gone, in my island childhood, I felt that/the gift of poetry had made me one of the chosen,/that all experience was kindling to the fire of the Muse."

WALCOTT: I never thought of my gift—I have to say "my gift" because I believe it is a gift—as anything that I did completely on my own. I have felt from my boyhood that I had one function and that was somehow to articulate, not my own experience, but what I saw around me. From the time I was a child I knew it was beautiful. If you go to a peak anywhere in St. Lucia, you feel a simultaneous newness and sense of timelessness at the same time—the presence of where you are. It's a primal thing and it has always been that way. At the same time I knew that the poor people around me were not beautiful in the romantic sense of being colorful people to paint or to write about. I lived, I have seen them and I have seen things that I don't need to go far to see. I felt that that was what I would write about. That's what I felt my job was. It's something that other writers have said in their own way, even if it sounds arrogant. Yeats has said it; Joyce has said it. It's amazing Joyce could say that he wants to write for his race, meaning the Irish. You'd think that Joyce would have a larger, more continental kind of mind, but Joyce continued insisting on his provinciality at the same time he had the most universal mind since Shakespeare. What we can do as poets in terms of our honesty is simply to write within the immediate perimeter of not more than twenty miles really.

INTERVIEWER: How does your sense of discovery of new subject matter integrate with the formal elements in your work?

WALCOTT: One of the things that people have to look at in West Indian literature is this: that what we were deprived of was also our privilege. There was a great joy in making a world which so far, up to then, had been undefined. And yet the imagination wants its limits and delights in its limits. It finds its freedom in the definition of those limits. In a sense, you want to give more symmetry to lives that have been undefined. My generation of West Indian writers has felt such a powerful elation at having the privilege of writing about places and people for the first time and, simultaneously, having behind them the tradition of knowing how well it can be done—by a Defoe, a Dickens, a Richardson. Our world made us yearn for structure as opposed to wishing to break away from it because there was no burden, no excess of literature in our heads. It was all new.

INTERVIEWER: Well, then how do you see yourself in terms of the great tradition of poetry in the English language?

WALCOTT: I don't. I am primarily, absolutely a Caribbean writer. The English language is nobody's special property. It is the property of the imagination: it is the property of the language itself. I have never felt inhibited in trying to write as well as the greatest English poets. Now that has led to a lot of provincial criticism: the Caribbean critic may say, "You are trying to be English," and the English critic may say, "Welcome to the club." These are two provincial statements at either end of the spectrum. It's not a matter of trying to be English. I am obviously a Caribbean poet. I yearn for the company of better Caribbean poets, quite frankly. I feel a little lonely. I don't see what I thought might have happened—a stronger energy, a stronger discipline, and a stronger drive in Caribbean poetry. That may be because the Caribbean is more musical: every culture has its particular emphasis and obviously the Caribbean's poetry, talent, and genius is in its music. But then again the modern Caribbean is a very young thing. I consider myself at the beginning, rather than at the end, of a tradition.

INTERVIEWER: Would you say that your relationship to English poetry has changed over the years? As your work has progressed you seem to have increasingly affiliated yourself with a line of New World poets from Whitman through St. John Perse to Aimé Césaire and Pablo Neruda.

WALCOTT: Carlos Fuentes talked in a *Paris Review* interview about the essential Central American experience, which includes the whole basin of the Caribbean—that it is already a place of tremendous fertility. The whole new world experience here is shared by Márquez as it is by Borges, as it is still by American writers. In fact, too many American poets don't take on the scale of America. Not because we should write epics but because it seems to be our place to try to understand. In places that are yet undefined the energy comes with the knowledge that this has not yet been described, this has not yet been painted. This means that I'm standing here like a pioneer. I'm the first person to look at this mountain and try to write about it. I'm the first person to see this lagoon, this piece of land. Here I am with this enormous privilege of just being someone who can take up a brush. My generation of West Indian writers, following after C. L. R. James, all felt the thrill of the absolute sense of discovery. That energy is concomitant with being where we are; it's part of the whole idea of America. And by America, I mean from Alaska right down to Curaçao.

INTERVIEWER: How do you respond to V. S. Naipaul's repeated assertion— borrowed from Trollope—that "Nothing was created in the British West Indies"?

WALCOTT: Perhaps it should read that "Nothing was created *by the British* in the West Indies." Maybe that's the answer. The departure of the British required and still requires a great deal of endeavor, of repairing the psychological damage done by their laziness and by their indifference. The desolation of poverty that exists in the

Caribbean can be very depressing. The only way that one can look at it and draw anything of value from it is to have a fantastic depth of strength and belief, not in the past but in the immediate future. And I think that whenever I come back here, however desolate and however despairing I see the conditions around me to be, I know that I have to draw on terrible reserves of conviction. To abandon that conviction is to betray your origins; it's to feel superior to your family, to your past. And I'm not capable of that.

INTERVIEWER: Why is the figure of Robinson Crusoe so important to you?

WALCOTT: I wrote a poem called "The Castaway." I told my wife I was going to stay by myself for a weekend somewhere down in Trinidad. My wife agreed. I stayed in a beachhouse by myself and I wrote the poem there. I had an image of the West Indian artist as someone who was in a shipwrecked position. I'm not saying that's the origin of my Crusoe idea. But it's possible. The beaches around here are generally very empty—just you, the sea, and the vegetation around you, and you're very much by yourself. The poems I have written around the Crusoe theme vary. One of the more positive aspects of the Crusoe idea is that in a sense every race that has come to the Caribbean has been brought here under situations of servitude or rejection, and that is the metaphor of the shipwreck, I think. Then you look around you and you have to make your own tools. Whether that tool is a pen or a hammer, you are building in a situation that's Adamic; you are rebuilding not only from necessity but also with some idea that you will be here for a long time and with a sense of proprietorship as well. Very broadly that is what has interested me in it. There are other ironies, like the position of Friday as the one who is being civilized. Actually, the reverse happens. People who come out to the Caribbean from the cities and the continents go through a process of being recultured. What they encounter here, if they surrender to their seeing, has a lot to teach them, first of all the proven adaptability of races living next to each other, particularly in places like Trinidad and Jamaica. And then also in the erasure of the idea of history. To me there are always images of erasure in the Caribbean—in the surf which continually wipes the sand clean, in the fact that those huge clouds change so quickly. There is a continual sense of motion in the Caribbean—caused by the sea and the feeling that one is almost traveling through water and not stationary. The size of time is larger—a very different thing in the islands than in the cities. We don't live so much by the clock. If you have to be in a place where you create your own time, what you learn, I think, is a patience, a tolerance, how to make an artisan of yourself rather than being an artist.

INTERVIEWER: Your recent play *Pantomime* explores the racial and economic side of the relationship between Crusoe and Friday. In the play, a white English hotel owner in Tobago proposes that he and his black handyman work up a satire on the Crusoe story for the entertainment of the guests. Is the play a parable about colonialism?

WALCOTT: The point of the play is very simple. There are two types. The prototypical Englishman is not supposed to show his grief publicly. He keeps a stiff upper lip. Emotion and passion are supposed to be things that a trueblood Englishman avoids. What the West Indian character does is to try to wear him down into confessing that he is capable of such emotion and there's nothing wrong in showing it. Some sort of catharsis is possible. That is the main point of the play. It's to take two types and put them together, put them in one arena and have that happen. I have never thought of it really as a play about racial conflict. When it's done in America, it becomes a very tense play because of the racial situation there. When it's done here, it doesn't have those deep historical overtones of real bitterness. I meant it to be basically a farce that might instruct. And the instruction is that we can't just contain our grief, that there's purgation in tears, that tears can renew. Of course, inside the play there's a point in which both characters have to confront the fact that one is white and one is black. They have to confront their history. But once that peak is passed, once the ritual of confrontation is over, then that's the beginning of the play. I've had people say they think the ending is corny, but generally that criticism has come when I'm in America. The idea of some reconciliation or some adaptability of being able to live together, that is sometimes rejected by people as being a facile solution. But I believe it's possible.

INTERVIEWER: How would you differentiate your work of the middle and late sixties, *The Castaway* and *The Gulf*, from your previous writing?

WALCOTT: There's a vague period in any poet's life between thirty and forty that is crucial because you can either keep working in one direction, or you can look back on your earlier work as juvenilia, a nice thing to look at from a distance. You have to head toward being forty with a certain kind of mindset to try to recreate chaos so you can learn from it. Yet you also have the fear that your work really has been basically mediocre, a failure, predictable. You find yourself at a point at which you say, ah, so you have become exactly what you were afraid of becoming: this person, this writer, with a certain name and a certain thing expected of you, and you are fulfilling that mold. The later books attempt to work against the given identity. At this point I don't think they're deep enough in terms of their sense of sin. Their sense of guilt could be more profound. In a way a lot of these poems smooth over while seething underneath the surface. One can always put a sort of poster over the rough, you know. A smoothness of attitude over something that's basically quite null and chaotic and unsettling. A lot of the roughness is missing in these books, but then that dissatisfaction continues all one's life.

INTERVIEWER: Would you talk about your experience in the Trinidad Theater Workshop which you founded in 1959 and finally left in 1976? You once stated that you wanted to create a theater where someone could produce Shakespeare and sing Calypso with equal conviction. Did the idea succeed?

WALCOTT: Yes, I think I made that happen. The best West Indian actors are phenomenal. Most West Indian actors have gone to West Indian secondary schools. The classical training and reading they get there is pretty wide and impressive—a lot of Shakespeare, and all the great English writers. Once that happens people read much more widely than if they hadn't done the great poets. So most West Indian actors have a familiarity with the classic theater of the English language. They also have an accent, not an affected accent, but a speech that is good diction. Some of the finest Shakespeare I have ever heard was spoken by West Indian actors. The sound of

Shakespeare is certainly not the sound we now hear in Shakespeare, that androgynous BBC-type, high-tone thing. It's a coarse thing—a great range between a wonderful vulgarity and a great refinement, and we have that here. We have that vulgarity and we also have that refinement in terms of the diction. The West Indian actor has a great rhetorical interest in language. In addition to that, the actor is like the West Indian writer in that he is a new person: what he is articulating has just begun to be defined. There's a sense of pioneering. For me writing plays was even more exciting than working on poems because it was a communal effort, people getting together and trying to find things. When I won a fellowship to go to America in 1958, I wanted to have, much as the Actors Studio did, a place where West Indian actors, without belonging to any company, could just come together and try and find out simple things such as how to talk like ourselves without being affected or without being incoherent, how to treat dialect as respectfully as if we were doing Shakespeare or Chekhov, and what was our own inner psychology as individuals, in a people, as part of a people. The first couple of years we had a very tough time. Very few people would come. We didn't know what we were doing; we just improvised and explored and tried things. I was determined not to do a production until I though we had some kind of ensemble. I had no intention of forming a company. At that time, all I wanted to do was to have the actors come and begin to work together. It took a very long time. But eventually we did put on a play and for about seventeen years I had a terrific company. It also began to involve dancers and some great actors. I remember Terry Hands came once (he is now one of the associate directors of the Royal Shakespeare Company) for a performance of *The Joker of Seville* that Margaret, my then wife, suggested we do. We had this little arena, like a bullfight ring, or a cockfight ring, and we served sandwiches and coffee and oranges and so on, and the crowd by that time had begun to know the songs and they were singing along with the actors. Terry said to me, "Derek, you're doing what Brecht tried to do." Well, I felt terrific because I knew what he meant. Brecht's idea of the participation of the audience, the whole idea of the boxing ring as a stage or the stage as an arena, had happened. But after several years of falling out and fighting and coming back together, eventually, for all sorts of reasons, the thing wore down. Although I still use actors from the company singly, I no longer run the company. But seventeen years is a long time to run a theater company.

INTERVIEWER: You've written that you first began writing drama "in the faith that one was creating not merely a play, but a theater, and not merely a theater, but its environment." But by the time you came to write the prologue to *Dream on Monkey Mountain* in 1970, the feeling of pride was replaced mainly by exhaustion and the sense of innocence seems to have given way to despair. What happened?

WALCOTT: Well, right now I'm writing a play called *A Branch of the Blue Nile*— about actors, a small company of actors and how they fall apart. I don't know up to now—and I'll have to decide pretty quickly—if it's going to end badly. The epiphany of the whole thing, the end of it, is a question that remains.

INTERVIEWER: Is the problem at all related to questions of whether the state should support the arts?

WALCOTT: I'm fifty-five now and all my life I've tried to fight and write and jeer and encourage the idea that the state owes its artists a lot. When I was young it looked like a romance: now that I'm older and I pay taxes, it is a fact. But not only do I want roads, I want pleasure, I want art. This is the terrible thing in the Caribbean. The middle class in the Caribbean is a venal, self-centered, indifferent, self-satisfied, smug society. It enjoys its philistinism. It pays very short lip-service to its own writers and artists. This is a reality every artist knows. The point is whether you say that and then turn your back on it and say to hell with it for life. I haven't done that and I don't think I'm capable of doing it. What's wrong is this: a legacy has been left by the British empire of amateurism. What we still have as an inheritance is that art is an amateur occupation. That attitude is combined with some of the worst aspects of bourgeois mercantilism, whether it is French, Danish, British, or Spanish bourgeois. The whole of the Caribbean that I can think of has this stubborn, clog-headed indifference to things around them. The philanthropy that exists in the Caribbean is negligible. Money is here—you just have to see the houses and the cars, and to look at the scale of living in any one of these islands—but nobody gives anything. If they do, I don't know what they give to, but that penny-pinching thing is typical of the petty-bourgeois merchant, the hoarder of money. Without any bitterness I can say that anything that I have gotten, whether earned or not, has been from America and not from the Caribbean.

INTERVIEWER: What constitutes an artistic generation in the Caribbean?

WALCOTT: An artistic generation in this part of the world is about five years. Five years of endurance. After that, I think people give up. I see five years of humanity and boredom and futility. I keep looking at younger writers, and I begin to see the same kind of despair forming and the same wish to say the hell with it, I'm getting out of here. There's also a problem with government support. We have come to a kind of mechanistic thinking that says, a government concerns itself with housing, food, and whatever. There will always be priorities in terms of sewage and electricity. If only a government could form the idea that any sensible human being wants not only to have running water, but a book in hand and a picture on the wall. That is the kind of government I had envisaged in the Caribbean when I was eighteen or nineteen. At fifty-five, I have only seen an increase in venality, an increase in selfishness, and worse than that, a shallow kind of service paid to the arts. I'm very bitter about the philistinism of the Caribbean. It is tough to see a people who have only one strength and that is their culture. Trinidad is perhaps the most concentrated example of a culture that has produced so many thousands and thousands of artisans at Carnival. Now Carnival is supported by the government, but that's seasonal kind of thinking. I'm talking about something more endemic, more rooted, more organic to the idea of the Caribbean. Because we have been colonies, we have inherited everything and the very thing we used to think was imperial has been repeated by our own stubbornness, stupidity, and blindness.

INTERVIEWER: Your prologue to *Dream on Monkey Mountain* also blasts the crass, state-sponsored commercialization of folk culture. One of your subjects in both poetry and essays has been how negatively tourism has affected the West Indies. Would you discuss that?

WALCOTT: Once I saw tourism as a terrible danger to a culture. Now I don't, maybe because I come down here so often that perhaps literally I'm a Tourist *myself* coming from America. But a culture is only in danger if it allows itself to be. Everybody has a right to come down in the winter and enjoy the sun. Nobody has a right to abuse anybody, and so I don't think that if I'm an American anybody should tell me, please don't come here because this beach is ours, or whatever. During the period I'm talking about, certainly, servility was a part of the whole deal—the waiters had to smile, and we had to do this and so forth. In tourism, it was just an extension of master/servant. I don't think it's so anymore. Here we have a generation that has strengthened itself beyond that. As a matter of fact, it can go beyond a balance and there's sullenness and a hostility toward people who are your guests. It can swing too far as well. But again, it's not enough to put on steel bands and to have people in the hotels entertaining and maybe to have a little show somewhere to keep them what they think is light-minded and happy and indifferent and so on. If that's the opinion that the government or culture has of itself, then it deserves to be insulted. But if it were doing something more rooted in terms of the arts, in terms of its writers, its painters, and its performers, and if there were more pride in that and not the kind of thing you see of guys walking around town totally bored and hoping something can happen. . . . I'm not one to say that you can't do things for yourself because certainly having spent all my life in the Caribbean theater and certainly seventeen very exacting years in the workshop, I do say, yes—get up and do it yourself and stop depending on the government. But there is a point where you have to turn to the state and say, "Look man, this is ridiculous. I pay my taxes. I'm a citizen. I don't have a museum. I don't have a good library. I don't have a place where I can perform. I don't have a place where I can dance." That's criminal. It's a carry-over of the same thing I said about the West Indies being seized and atrophied by a petty-bourgeois mentality from the metropolis that has been adopted by the Creole idea of life which is simply to have a damn good time and that's it, basically. I mean that's the worst aspect of West Indian life: have a good time, period.

INTERVIEWER: What do you have against folklorists and anthropologists? Some people think of them as an intellectually respectable lot.

WALCOTT: I don't trust them. They either embarrass or elevate too much. They can do a good service if they are reticent and keep out of the way. But when they begin to tell people who they are and what they are, they are terrifying. I've gone to seminars in which people in the audience who are the people the folklorists are talking about, are totally baffled by their theories.

INTERVIEWER: One of your most well-known early poems, "A Far Cry from Africa," ends with the question, "How can I turn from Africa and live?" However, by 1970 you could write that "The African revival is escape to another dignity," and that "Once we have lost our wish to be white, we develop a longing to become black, and those two may be different, but are still careers." You also assert that the claim to be African is not an inheritance but a bequest, "a bill for the condition of our arrival as slaves." These are controversial statements. What is your current sense of the West Indian writer's relationship to Africa?

WALCOTT: There is a duty in every son to become his own man. The son severs himself from the father. The Caribbean very often refuses to cut that umbilical cord to confront its own stature. So a lot of people exploit an idea of Africa out of both the wrong kind of pride and the wrong kind of heroic idealism. At great cost and a lot of criticism, what I used to try to point out was that there is a great danger in historical sentimentality. We are most prone to this because of suffering, of slavery. There's a sense of skipping the part about slavery, and going straight back to a kind of Eden-like grandeur, hunting lions, that sort of thing. Whereas what I'm saying is to take in the fact of slavery, if you're capable of it, without bitterness, because bitterness is going to lead to the fatality of thinking in terms of revenge. A lot of the apathy in the Caribbean is based on this historical sullenness. It is based on the feeling of "Look what you did it me." Well, "Look what you did to me," is juvenile, right? And also, "Look what I'm going to do to you," is wrong. Think about illegitimacy in the Caribbean! Few people can claim to find their ancestry in the linear way. The whole situation in the Caribbean is an illegitimate situation. If we admit that from the beginning that there is no shame in that historical bastardy, then we can be men. But if we continue to sulk and say, "Look at what the slave-owner did," and so forth, we will never mature. While we sit moping or writing morose poems and novels that glorify a nonexistent past, then time passes us by. We continue in one mood, which is in too much of Caribbean writing: that sort of chafing and rubbing of an old sore. It is not because one wishes to forget; on the contrary, you accept it as much as anybody accepts a wound as being a part of his body. But this doesn't mean that you nurse it all your life.

INTERVIEWER: *The Fortunate Traveller* is filled with poems set in a wide variety of places. The title poem itself elaborates the crisis of a fortunate traveller who goes from one underdeveloped country to another. And in "North and South" you write that "I accept my function/as a colonial upstart at the end of an empire,/a single, circling, homeless satellite." Has The Castaway given way to the Traveller? Do you still feel the old tugs between home and abroad?

WALCOTT: I've never felt that I belong anywhere else but in St. Lucia. The geographical and spiritual fixity is there. However, there's a reality here as well. This afternoon I asked myself if I would stay here for the rest of my life if I had the chance of leaving. The answer really is, I suppose, no. I don't know if I'm distressed by that. One is bound to feel the difference between these poor, dark, very small houses, the people in the streets, and yourself because you always have the chance of taking a plane out. Basically you are a fortunate traveller, a visitor; your luck is that you can always leave. And it's hard to imagine that there are people around you unable, incapable of leaving either because of money or because of any number of ties. And yet the more I come back here the less I feel that I'm a prodigal or a castaway returning. And it may be that as it deepens with age, you get more locked into what your life is and where you've come from and what you misunderstand and what you should have understood and what you're trying to reunderstand and so on. I'll continue to come back to see if what I write is not beyond the true experience of the person next to me on the bus—not in terms of talking down to that person, but of sharing that person's pain and strength necessary in those pathetically cruel circumstances in which people have found themselves following the devastations of colonialism.

INTERVIEWER: What led you to assert, as you do in *Midsummer*, that "to curse your birthplace is the final evil"?

WALCOTT: I think it is. I think the earth that you come from is your mother and if you turn around and curse it, you've cursed your mother.

INTERVIEWER: You've written a number of poems about New York City, Boston, old New England, and the southern United States. I'm thinking in particular of the first section of *The Fortunate Traveller* where one of the poems is entitled "American Muse" and another asserts "I'm falling in love with America." What are your feelings about living in the United States? Do you think you've been Americanized in any way?

WALCOTT: If so, voluntarily. I don't think I've been brainwashed. I don't think I have been seduced by all the prizes and rewards. America has been extremely generous to me—not in a strictly philanthropical sense; I've earned that generosity. But it has given me a lot of help. The real thing that counts is whether that line is true about falling in love with America. That came about because I was travelling on a bus from one place to another, on a long ride looking at the American landscape. If you fall in love with the landscape of a place the next thing that comes is the people, right? The average American is not like the average Roman or British citizen. The average American doesn't think that the world belongs to him or her; Americans don't have imperialist designs in their heads. I find a gentleness and a courtesy in them. And they have ideals. I've travelled widely across America and I see things in America that I still believe in, that I like a lot.

INTERVIEWER: What are your feelings about Boston, which you have called the "city of my exile"?

WALCOTT: I've always told myself that I've got to stop using the word "exile." Real exile means a complete loss of the home. Joseph Brodsky is an exile; I'm not really an exile. I have access to my home. Given enough stress and longing I can always get enough money to get back home and refresh myself with the sea, the sky, whatever. I was very hostile about Boston in the beginning, perhaps because I love New York. In jokes, I've always said that Boston should be the capital of Canada. But it's a city that grows on you gradually. And where I live is very comfortable. It's close to the university. I work well there, and I very much enjoy teaching. I don't think of myself as having two homes; I have one home, but two places.

INTERVIEWER: Robert Lowell had a powerful influence on you. I'm thinking of your memorial poem "RTSL" as well as the poem in *Midsummer* where you assert that "Cal's bulk haunts my classes." Would you discuss your relationship to Lowell?

WALCOTT: Lowell and Elizabeth Hardwick were on a tour going to Brazil and they stopped off in Trinidad. I remember meeting them at Queen's Park Hotel and being so flustered that I called Elizabeth Hardwick, Edna St. Vincent Millay. She said, "I'm not that old yet." I was just flabbergasted. And then we became very friendly. My wife Margaret and I took them up to the beach. Their daughter, Harriet, was there. I remember being up at this beach house with Lowell. His daughter and his wife, I think, must have gone to bed. We had gas lanterns. *Imitations* had just come out and I remember that he showed me his imitations of Hugo and Rilke and asked me what I thought about them. I asked him if two of the stanzas were from Rilke, and he said, "No, these are mine." It was a very flattering and warm feeling to have this fine man with this great reputation really asking me what I thought. He did that with a lot of people, very honestly, humbly, and directly. I cherish that memory a lot. When we went back to New York, Cal and Lizzy had a big party for us with a lot of people there, and we became very close. Cal was a big man in bulk but an extremely gentle, poignant person, and very funny. I don't think any of the biographies have caught the sort of gentle, amused, benign beauty of him when he was calm. He kept a picture of Peter, my son, and Harriet for a long time in his wallet, and he'd take it out and show it to me. He was sweetly impulsive. Once I went to visit him and he said, "Let's call up Allen Ginsberg and ask him to come over." That's so cherishable that it's a very hard thing for me to think of him as not being around. In a way, I can't separate my affection for Lowell from his influence on me. I think of his character and gentleness, the immediacy that was part of knowing him. I loved his openness to receive influences. He was not a poet who said, "I'm an American poet, I'm going to be peculiar, and I'm going to have my own voice which is going to be different from anybody's voice." He was a poet who said, "I'm going to take in everything." He had a kind of multifaceted imagination; he was not embarrassed to admit that he was influenced even in his middle-age by William Carlos Williams, or by François Villon, or by Boris Pasternak, all at the same time. That was wonderful.

INTERVIEWER: What about specific poetic influence?

WALCOTT: One of the things he said to me was, "You must put more of yourself in your poems." Also he suggested that I drop the capital letters at the top of the line, use the lower-case. I did it and felt very refreshed; it made me relax.It was a simple suggestion, but it's one of those things that a great poet can tell you that can be phenomenal—a little opening. The influence of Lowell on everyone, I think, is in his brutal honesty, his trying to get into the poetry a fictional power that wasn't there before, as if your life was a section of a novel—not because you are the hero, but because some of the things that were not in poems, some of the very ordinary banal details, can be illuminated. Lowell emphasized the banality. In a sense to keep the banality banal and still make it poetic is a great achievement. I think that's one of the greatest things that he did in terms of his directness, his confrontation of ordinariness.

INTERVIEWER: Would you tell the story of your first poetry reading in the States? It must have been rewarding to hear Lowell's extravagant introduction.

WALCOTT: Well, I didn't know what he said because I was in back of the curtain, I think it was at the Guggenheim. I was staying at the Chelsea Hotel, and that day I felt I needed a haircut, so, foolishly, I went around the corner and sat down. The barber took the electric razor and gave me one of the wildest haircuts I think I've ever had. It infuriated me, but you can't put your hair back on. I even thought of wearing a hat. But I went on anyway, my head looked like hell. I had gotten some distance into the reading—I was reading "A Far Cry From Africa"—when suddenly there was

the sound of applause from the auditorium. Now I had never heard applause at a
poetry reading before. I don't think I'd ever given a formal poetry reading, and I
thought for some reason that the applause was saying it was time to stop, that they
thought it was over. So I walked off the stage. I felt in a state of shock. I actually
walked off feeling the clapping was their way of saying, "Well, thank you, it's been
nice." Someone in charge asked me to go back and finish the reading, but I said no. I
must have sounded extremely arrogant, but I felt that if I went back out there it would
have been conceited. I went back to Trinidad. Since I hadn't heard Lowell's introduction, I asked someone for it at the Federal Building, which had archives of radio tapes
from the Voice of America. I said I would like to hear the Lowell tape, and the guy
said, "I think we erased that." It was only years later that I really heard what Cal said,
and it was very flattering.

INTERVIEWER: How did you become friends with Joseph Brodsky?

WALCOTT: Well, ironically enough, I met Brodsky at Lowell's funeral. Roger
Straus, Susan Sontag, and I went up to Boston for the funeral. We waited somewhere
for Joseph, probably at the airport, but for some reason he was delayed. At the service
I was in this pew when a man sat down next to me. I didn't know him. When I stood
up as the service was being said, I looked at him and I thought, if this man is not going
to cry then *I'm* not going to cry, either. I kept stealing glances at him to see if anything
was happening, but he was very stern looking. That helped me to contain my own
tears. Of course it was Brodsky. Later, we met. We went to Elizabeth Bishop's house,
and I got to know him a little better. The affection that developed after that was very
quick and, I think, permanent—to be specific about it is hard. I admire Joseph for his
industry, his valor, and his intelligence. He's a terrific example of someone who is a
complete poet, who doesn't treat poetry as anything else but a very hard job that he
does as well as he can. Lowell worked very hard too, but you feel in Joseph that that is
all he lives for. In a sense that's all any of us lives for or can hope to live for. Joseph's
industry is an example that I cherish a great deal.

INTERVIEWER: When did you first become friends with Seamus Heaney?

WALCOTT: There was a review by A. Alvarez of Seamus's book a very upsetting
review—to put it mildly—in which he was describing Heany as a sort of blue-eyed
boy. English literature always has a sort of blue-eyed boy. I got very angry over the
review and sent Seamus a note via my editor with a little obscenity in it. Just for some
encouragement. Later, in New York we had a drink at someone's house. From then
on, the friendship has developed. I see him a lot when he is in Boston at Harvard. I
just feel very lucky to have friends like Joseph and Seamus. The three of us are outside
of the American experience. Seamus is Irish, Joseph is Russian, I'm West Indian. We
don't get embroiled in the controversies about who's a soft poet, who's a hard poet,
who's a free verse poet, who's not a poet, and all of that. It's good to be on the rim of
that quarreling. We're on the perimeter of the American literary scene. We can float
out here happily not really committed to any kind of particular school or body of
enthusiasm or criticism.

INTERVIEWER: Over the years your style seems to have gotten increasingly
plainer and more direct, less gnarled, more casual, somehow both quieter and fiercer

at the same time. Is that an accurate assessment of the poetic style of your middle age? I can't imagine a book like *Midsummer* from the young Derek Walcott.

WALCOTT: It varies, of course. When I finished *Another Life*, I felt like writing short poems, more essential, to the point, things that were contracted. They didn't have the scale of the large book and so on. It goes in that kind of swing, in that kind of pendulum. In the case of *Midsummer*, I felt that for the time being I didn't want to write any more poems, although that sounds arrogant. I just felt perhaps I was overworking myself. I was going to concentrate purely on trying to develop my painting. While painting, I would find lines coming into my head. I would almost self-destruct them; I'd say, all right, I'll put them down . . . but with antipoetic vehemence. If they don't work, then I'll just forget it. What kept happening is that the lines would come anyway, perhaps out of that very irritation, and then I would make a very arbitrary collage of them and find they would take some sort of loose shape. Inevitably, of course, you try to join the seams. I was trying to do something, I think that was against the imagination, that was not dictated in a sort of linear, lyrical, smooth, melodic—but rather something that was antimelodic. For a poem, if you give a poem personality, that's the most exciting thing—to feel that it is becoming antimelodic. The vocabulary becomes even more challenging, the meter more interesting, and so on. So what happened was that by the very wish not to write, or to write a poem that was against the idea of writing poems, it all became more fertile and more contradictory and more complex. Gradually a book began to emerge. Inevitably you can't leave things lying around with unjoined shapes, little fragments and so on. I began to weld everything together—to keep everything that I felt worthwhile. I thought, well, whether this is just an ordinary thing or not, it has as much a right to be considered as something a little more grandiose. That's what I think happened to *Midsummer*.

INTERVIEWER: How do you feel about publishing your *Collected Poems?*

WALCOTT: You're aware of the fact that you have reached a certain stage in your life. You're also aware that you have failed your imagination to some degree, your ambitions. This is an amazingly difficult time for me. I'm absolutely terrified. It's not because I have a kind of J. D. Salinger thing about running away from publicity. It's really not wanting to see myself reflected in that way. I don't think that that's what the boy I knew—the boy who started to write poetry—wanted at all, not praise, not publicity. But it's troubling. I remember Dylan Thomas saying somewhere that he liked it better when he was not famous. All I can say is this: I do have another book about ready, and I hope it will be a compensation for all the deficiencies in the *Collected Poems*, something that will redeem the *Collected Poems*.

II
THE CRITICAL RECEPTION

A. "The Divided Child"
1948-1959

AN INTRODUCTION TO
THE POETRY OF
DEREK WALCOTT

Frank Collymore

A talk given to the Literary Society. Mr. Alan Steward of the British Council read the selections from "25 Poems".

I should like to introduce to you this evening the work of Derek Walcott of St. Lucia: a small volume recently published entitled *25 Poems*. His name may be familiar to some of you, for I remember being shown a few years ago some manuscript poems of a schoolboy of that name, and being greatly impressed by their promise. That promise has now been fulfilled, and *25 Poems*, although the product of one who has not yet attained his majority—he is just nineteen years of age, must be regarded as the work of an accomplished poet.

I use the word "poet" advisedly. There are some of us who write poetry: to us the spirit comes and goes and we are deeply grateful if at some time in our lives it is our good fortune to be blessed with the divine gift. But there are others, a select band, who are poets from birth: to them poetry is all in all, the very breath of life; and I do not think I am mistaken when I make this high claim for Derek Walcott.

I am indebted to Mr. Harold Simmons of St. Lucia for the following biographical data:—

"Derek was nineteen years old on the 23rd of January this year. He won an exhibition scholarship to St. Mary's College where he is now an assistant master teaching English to the Higher Certificate Class, and French. He is a prolific writer, and this volume represents his own selection. He is also a painter in water colour and oils. His father, Warwick Walcott, was a Barbadian. His mother is a prominent social worker, one of our most successful head teachers, and a producer of amateur dramatics."

With this brief introduction I now pass on to the important matter of the evening: the reading of some selections from *25 Poems*. First, a sonnet occasioned by the recent disaster in Castries:

"A CITY'S DEATH BY FIRE"

After that hot gospeller had levelled all but the churched sky,
I wrote the tale by tallow of a city's death by fire.
Under a candle's eye that smoked in tears, I
Wanted to tell in more than wax of faiths that were snapped like wire.
All day I walked abroad among the rubbled tales,
Shocked at each wall that stood on the street like a liar,
Loud was the bird-rocked sky, and all the clouds were bales
Torn open by looting and white in spite of the fire;

By the smoking sea, where Christ walked, I asked why
Should a man wax tears when his wooden world fails.

In town leaves were paper, but the hills were a flock of faiths
To a boy who walked all day, each leaf was a green breath

Rebuilding a love I thought was dead as nails,
Blessing the death and the baptism by fire.

You will have noticed many component elements in this poem, the swarming imagery, the deft turn of phrase, the religious motif—above all, the high poetic fervour. Here, one feels, is the spirit of poetry shaping its own ends through the mastery and sincerity of the writer. Perhaps some of you may think he has taken too great liberty with the traditional sonnet form; but this is a matter which lies outside the scope of this talk.

Let us now listen to another poem:

"ELEGIES"

On a couch of arsenic, smelled with staling fame, no sun
Will dupe the boy flung dead on the soiled linen of his tale.
Was dying foul or music to that one?
The hand of the sorrowful sun has smothered the pale
Young and stillborn dreams on the verge of his lips.
His fierce and serene death, tolled in an absent time,
Was dumb under the business of coin, cloth and ships,
And makes of him, how fate, a limb of naked and dead Greece
In a London flat. Hunger for bread, gnawinger than shame,
Stormed him to drink his blood in an anguish of peace.
That power of the soul over the asylum of hunger,
Threatens me with the ghost of the boy who died younger.
Innocence is wrecked early, but on their mountaindeath flames
Their flag of bloody words, by death how deep, so stronger.

Stretch him out on the world's rack no longer;
Time has her false trumpets, and fake is the word
The hibiscus blows, whisper of windy resurrections.
The beautiful and young are always dead, a brood
From time's harsh wing springs, a bevy of recollections.
When will Lazarus publish their torn words, for most flung the
Tattered bloods in a killing wind, and some died in war, or warring.
The power of the turnkey who can wreck the suffering
Body; some were made beautiful only by the crude
Hands of a world that later made monument their deaths.
And in London, Rome, Skyros, Castries or Kingston, gave to their weak
    breaths
A column of praise, professor's tear, offal of a famemonger.

I am as young as they died, and am proud in a trade of fames,
I fear death, inmate of my hand, leaps wall to join their names.

I would ask you to note how the unusual flood of imagery shocks, startles or convinces us into acquiescence; and the last couplet with its echoes of Keats' "half in love with easeful death":

I am as young as they died, and am proud in their trade of fames,
I fear death, inmate of my hand, leaps wall to join their names.

Only a poet, conscious of his calling, could have written that.

Echoes.... there must always be echoes. Every artist must draw upon the accumulated heritage of his particular art; and so one is aware of many echoes in these poems; of Gerard Manley Hopkins, whose genius so profoundly influenced the trend of modern poetry; of Auden, especially in the skillful use of half-rhyme and assonance, and of the arresting generalisation; and, above all, of Dylan Thomas, with whom our poet seems to share a close affinity. But there is no suggestion of pastiche: it is obvious that Walcott's style is derived from many sources as a result of his wide and sympathetic study of the moderns, but it is his own compound.

There are other formative influences also. It is difficult to read any of his poems without observing the great part played by the ever-vital myths of the Christian Tradition. This religious imagery is apparent everywhere, and is one of the focal points of the young poet's experience. The others are the social and geographical background of his environment. Let us listen to Derek Walcott, the West Indian, in some stanzas from

"TRAVELOGUE"

Come to my island here, whose fallen numbered blood
Of battalions drummed to death, our name is proud of,

See, even here the world lulls with its ambitions.

Its people are small and build their architecture
Of futures, in small rooms late at night, in corners
On accountancy, the violin and shorthand.

Observe how later here your same boredoms will grow
Concealed like cancer, in magistrate, tennis champ—
Ion, in doctor, doctor's wife and pensioner.

How here are two pence loves, loss, whispered vanities.
Plans of sour conquest, illegal love-affairs,
And a kind of democracy and politics.

Outside your window the upward sighs of the earth
Transform to leafless trees, and the dry walks outside
Are aloof in their tame riots of green, continue

Their natural indifference as when redcoats would roll
Down rocks, and blue gunsmoke paler than sky, wrote what
Men thought of as signals of history in air.

For these lands belong to no one but the luckless;
(Not to the conquering teeth of foreign engines)
To lost red and black tribes, and keep looks of their gods.

Seldom occasion brings white and black together,
Yet often proves as in singing of schoolboys
In a bus, possible temporal democracy.

But History asks "Do not exhort men to build worlds
Shallower than their slow ebbing loves and fortune,
Or taller than sky or the bird-frightening chimney.

Let all on the islands of the heart construct the day
Of the federated archipelago, black
And white live apart, if so, but dream the same dreams.

Then might God and his wise machines elect to cross
With a shower of blossoms, and make if no Eden
Then such peace as traveller expects of islands."

You will note that this poem is altogether different in feeling and in treatment from those you have already heard; the style is astringent, harsh even; the author labours under no false delusions; and you will find this Caribbean pride exemplified in many other of his poems.

Derek Walcott is still a youth, and so you will find in his work the concomitants of the youthful vision: all its idealism with its capacity for love and friendship, and, too, the reverse side of the picture—all its swift capacity for being hurt, its uninhibited despair. For, to the youth, the progress of time is not to be measured by the same clock as it is to those who have attained maturity. In our youth we are able to keep pace with time—its progress is ours; later, we lag behind, and, as we watch its waters outpace us we are only too conscious of its rapid flight. But, in the first flush of early manhood, when we are able to keep abreast of the river, days and months are disconcertingly long, and there seems to be little, if any, prospect of accomplishment.

Here in these stanzas is this tragedy of youth unfolded:

"IN A YEAR"

A whole year turned to stale as salt afternoons.
That sea from my window, pale
As dreams I struck once, on a hill leaved with tunes.
I sink in a sea of discord, with gone hopes;
Wise that dreams founder; now in a June's
Weather of chains and ropes,
I look at greengay seas, leaves, through an eye's jail
And how the heart gropes
For the windstrewn words said on a hill.
Will I be searching long, or the searching fail?
There was a place I know, windy with spinning voices,
And that year hope called to me like a happy sail,
But I was duped no worse than any boy is.

·   ·   ·

How have I changed?
Do I not write still
Of love of nature? Yet if I ranged
The windy wood, golden in the memory of that hill
Homing a prodigal in sound of the still young seas,
Would there be yellow wisdoms strewn under the leaves?
Ah if I go again, what will
I tell to the sea that I have learned?
The place is near this window and the grave of my age still
Cries in yellow, when the seas are churned
By a hand of memories; changed
With the year and slowly is the boy time and I kill.

•   •   •

> O harped seas, hills, waves
> Walking like a minstrel that lied to me of joy,
> O leaves that were school to a learning boy,
> What is it that any man saves,
> A broken blossom, a ruined rhyme.
> Are you the same wind that revels, the sea that raves,
> As I am both the boy's ghost, and one of Time's slaves?
> O time that murders time,
> I move from fasts of mercy to new crime,
> And these are brown and dead words that I now talk,
> O sea you shall never be plucked like leaves again, o waves
> You shall never walk.

But there is no real cause for despair. You will recall the strong religious element in these poems. Poetry springs from tension. Such tension may spring from a variety of causes. In his case I would suggest that this tension is the result of the consciousness of the conflict of life caught between love and hatred, between the spiritual and the material, between the terrible beauty and the callous indifference of nature. From such cosmic opposites he strives to find release. The pattern of this striving is his poetry. And here he realises the futility of purely human effort—hence the omnipresent relgious imagery.

In what is perhaps his most ambitious attempt, the strange and deeply-moving "ST. JUDAS," he has attempted to reconcile these opposites. Of this unorthodox conception of ultimate values Mr. Harold Simmons writes in his review of *25 Poems*.

"This poem is divided into five sonnets, each of which is a link in the chain of fate that leads to the crucifixion of Christ. . . Sonnet by sonnet traces the conflict in the mind of Judas Iscariot—Iscariot, the sentimentalist attracted to Christ by his loquacious poverty; the development that destiny had ordered that the most sentimental of the apostles will betray Christ; Judas doubting that Christ is God's son; then darkness over the earth, the guilt of Christ; the light out of the darkness, Judas' guilt and suicide—all in all. History and Fate are one."

"ST. JUDAS" is not an easy poem to read. The technique, essentially modern in concept is, very briefly, an attempt to reveal the form of an experience by the substitution of image for the more formal statement of the theme in abstract and nonpictorial terms. We must bear this in mind when reading many of Walcott's poems else we will only too aptly incline to label them obscure, and miss both their beauty and their significance.

I have chosen the second sonnet of the poem as being perhaps the one to be the most readily comprehended by the listener.

> Death is the guest of the bone, and the running ribs
> Pace for a while, but doom is patient, a glory

To God's legend was timely the red crime I did:
Stays on the hill of the three trees as foul side of the story,
But I graced no less God's will by my cradleborn crime.
For deep in the night of bread in the speaking hush of the wine
I hated the thorns he foretold; in the doubter time
I wept with the all is-it-I faithful for the love gone hoary
After the summers of the powerful corn we roved;
I loved him as any, and I am still beloved
By the stranger God who killed His unwombed son.
Among the cunning priests caught in the web of history
I heard the silver blood of Christ flowing in wounds of coin
And thorns sprang from my roseless and sadder than his story.

There are so many other poems I should like you to hear this evening; but as this would entail a reading of practically the whole volume, a few extracts must suffice.

Here are two stanzas in which is conveyed the dazzling sunlight of the Caribbean from "AS JOHN TO PATMOS:"

As John to Patmos, among the rocks and the blue live air, hounded
His heart to peace as here surrounded
By the strewn silver on waves, the wood's crude hair the rounded
Breasts of the milky bays, palms, flocks, and the green and dead

Leaves, the sun's brass coin on my cheek, where
Canoes brace the sun's strength, as John in that bleak air.
So am I welcomed richer by these blue scapes Greek there.
So I will voyage no more from home, may I speak here.

and here a complementary picture of spring in a fogbound land from "LETTER TO A PAINTER IN ENGLAND:"

It is April and already no doubt for you
As the journals report, the prologues of spring
Appear behind the rails of city-parks,
Or the late springtime must be publishing
Pink apologies along the black wet branch
To men in overcoats, who will conceal
The lines of songs leaping behind their pipes.

Here is the second part of an elegy for two young airmen, fellow St. Lucians, who were killed in their bombers over Germany, taken from " BOTH SIDES OF THE QUESTION:"

You cannot break their deaths with any dividing dawn,

They fell like the flares dreams are, and war makes her fools;
And when sky no more held them, a traitor to each one,

Peace stood always in her old use. Needing no price she rules
High in their massive misled midnight like a star.
She knows no martyrs, that tigersome is all war.

Remains perpetual in spite of boys and schemers that make wars,
And our science only builds death nearer cheerless stars.
Now may the slipping airman, popular by death,

Find dying private, watching the downward needle of his breath
In mortal comedy curse city-castrating angers,
And sleep secure in spite of fog and dangers.

Behaving in grace, for history who is God, demands
That men shall die not for their sakes but man's.

Here is another poem by Walcott, the West Indian, looking forward beyond the confines of a smug materialism to the limitless realms of the creative imagination set free to work in his own community. "Love is here and under your feet" he writes in "CALL FOR BREAKERS AND BUILDERS:"

Whether you are brown, lonely, golden or black, young
Man, construct the day of companions, and found
The industrious solitude: o raise
From these half-cities the prejudices
At last, o raise the world your fathers did not make.

There are no worlds to conquer, but worlds to recreate.
No houses to build except from the falling timbers.
And though the pastures are not new we can plant new grass.
Leave your girl, forget your parent's reluctance
Be bold to make faults History pardons and understands.

We do not ask a landscape of tall chimneys, there
Would be a greater need of blasting again the air
If we know anything, we know we can have a better
Island, bright as advertisements let it lose its litter
Of hovels, hunger, and let there be no loss of anger
Infectious in the peasant, which is the worst danger.

Almost impossible and absurd the distant love for
England. Love is here, and luck under your

Feet; the world is green outside, you rot in rooms;
Be proud of the anarchy of will, make dooms
Your dreams; it is never (though men die) too late for
The painting, the bridge and the exploding door.

The creative imagination working through love, perhaps the answer to all poets'
seeking: the theme is again apparent in the last lines of the long poem which I have
chosen to round off this evening's reading, "THE YELLOW CEMETERY:"

A swallow falls, and perhaps the sole spoken prayer
Is the hand of a leaf crossing the cold curled claws.
Where is the God of the swallows, is He where
Lives the One whom you flew young from, who all life was yours?

And yet for all these gifts, the gift that I can pray,
The mountain music, the pylon words, the painting they are
Enough, and may be all, for they add grace by day
And night give tears as harshly as a telling star.
Were there nothing, and this the only
Life, a man has still to save the cliché of his soul, to live
With, I will say it, grace, to atone for the
Sins that all the worlds awoke before he ailed alive,
Climb there, go to the hill while another sun is warning
That the wicks weaken, and in the halls of the heartsun, love,
For love is the stone speech that outlasts our ash and mourning.

Before concluding this talk I should like to emphasise what I consider to be Derek
Walcott's two greatest qualities. I have said but little of his technical accomplishments. I have not attempted to criticise his work; I have preferred to approach this
collection from a purely personal standpoint: these poems have given me very great
pleasure, and I wanted, if possible, to communicate this pleasure to others. But I
consider that you have heard enough to be aware of the remarkable power and range
of his imagery, that sine qua non of all poetry; and enough too to convince you of his
sincerity. These two qualities then, imagery, the vital product of the poetic imagination, and sincerity, the ballast by which the former is kept in touch with the here and
now of the human heart, combine in a poetic fervour sufficient to assure me that
Derek Walcott is a poet of whom any community might well be proud.

Let us hope then that this significant voice in West Indian literature may continue
to be heard often in the many years to come.

A WEST INDIAN POET FULFILLS HIS PROMISE

Harold Simmons

25 Poems: Derek Walcott

Derek Walcott has commenced to emerge from the chrysalis of his promise of great creative force. His first publication, 25 POEMS, clamours for recognition, not because the poet is a young man of 19 years, but because the poetry is already distinctive with merit.

Twenty-five Poems has all the qualities of good poetry, and apart from the imagery and beauty, emotional fixation, there is the power of great thought refusing to be crushed. This is a collection with nothing false or superfluous in the search for truth and beauty. Derek is a prolific writer, and selected the poems presented without assistance from anyone, otherwise meddling opinions may have resulted in the declension of the merit of the present collection.

> Go by the heart, the head is heartless, tears are
> Children: exile seed-sucking reason.
> The bitter and bright children make from a prison,
> A church of the brain . . .
>
> In the island of himself, in that garden
> Of his tearwatered love, man is light and lovely as a star,
> Legend pours love in the clay's genesis and no more.
> The logic of genitals is the rule by reason.
> Learn that love only, that builds on either shore
> Of our twin islands in an indifferent season,
> A bridge of white stone where the souls berth like swallows.

This extract from the poem "Go by the Heart" is so emphatic that it leaves no room for sentiment, or even comment.

In this appreciation I will not attempt to dissect 25 POEMS, a poem dissected, decomposes. I would like to state briefly the concept of modern poetry which Derek meets satisfactorily. These are the writings of a seer, who expresses intuitions and experiences in language that tends to arouse the imagination by sensual images, with qualities of rhythm and melody, or sometimes dissonance. These writings may be difficult owing to elusiveness, obscurity of subject or the profundity of thought. In creating "The Yellow Cemetery," he records:

> All grains are the ash to ashes drowsing in the morning,
> Wearing white stone. I passed them, not thankfuller to be
> Their living witness, not noisy in salt like the near sea,
> Because they are spaded to the dirt, our drowning.

When these lines [are] being written, images, words, ideas, dance in the mind, jostling, coming and going: the poet chooses, rejects, concentrates, accepting a rejected phrase or image. The reader too also experiences the dance of thoughts that originally jostled the poet's mind, flickering on the fringe of understanding, or fading into thoughts newly found by the reader. "It is a mistake to ask the poet what he means by an obscure phrase in a poem, as he may mean one thing or several things. The answer is that it means just what it says in the poem."

There is a strong skein of fatalism threaded throughout the work, showing the influence of Rilke through the medium of Sidney Keyes and latterly Dylan Thomas (for whom Derek has a great love). He pays tribute to those poets in a "bevy of recollections," and laments, "I am as young as they died, and am proud in a trade of fames./ I fear death, inmate of my hand, leaps wall to join their names."

"Saint Judas" is the most profound work (and to the anti-intellectual the most 'obscure'). This work is divided into five sonnets each of which is a link in the chain of fate that leads to the crucifixion of Christ. This work shows the influence of Ezra Pound and Dylan Thomas' sonnets and deserves a review all by itself. Sonnet by sonnet traces the conflicts in the mind of Judas Iscariot—Iscariot the sentimentalist attracted to Christ by His loquacious poverty, the development that destiny had ordered that the most sentimental of Apostles will betray Christ, Judas doubting that Christ is God's son, then darkness over the earth, the death of Christ, the light out of the darkness, Judas' guilt and suicide—all in all. History and Fate are one.

Perhaps the most personal poem in the collection is "Letter to a Painter in England," which Walcott addressed to me, and its nostalgic, almost reproachful force, expresses perfectly the understanding that is grown within us. The contrast of the "strict grey industry of cities of fog and winter fevers", with the languishing reminder "of personal islands for which Gauguins sicken," is but an example of the poet's capability of creating atmosphere and vivid telling. In fact throughout the volume, the reader will find many memorable lines—lines that shock sometimes, but do not repel.

Derek Walcott's maturity in spite of his age will be a pleasant surprise for many— and he needs not fear adverse criticism from the real lovers of poetry—those persons who recognise that the poet of today must symbolise the disorders of the present day. This poet has lit a beacon that will shine far beyond the horizon of the Caribbean.

EPITAPH FOR THE YOUNG

Keith Alleyne

The world's whole sap is sunke:
The generall balme th'hydroptique earth hath drunk,
Whither, as to the bed's-feet, life is shrunke,
Dead and enterr'd; yet all these seem to laugh,
Compared with mee, who am their Epitaph . . .
                    "A Nocturnall Upon St. Lucy's Day"—Donne.

It seems natural that Derek Walcott, on joining the ranks of poets of crisis, should don the garb. With Walcott, Eliot is not merely an influence, but a complete formula, through the whole succession of Joyce and Stephen Daedalus, Buck Mulligan and Hamlet, Telemachus and Dante and Virgil. In his second book of poems, *Epitaph for the Young*, Walcott has assumed a whole tradition. This at first is a shock to Walcott, a shock to the Negro West Indian.

Rebellion is the death I suffer from . . .
And the revolt is insistent.
A classical Atlas,
For naked pickanninies, pygmies, pigs and poverty,
Veiling your inheritance, you kneel before
The sessile invocation of the thrush, the sibilant yew-trees,
By broken and flaked languages, near a drying river,
You practice the pieties of your conquerors,
Bowing before a bitter god.

The language of crisis can resolve its own dilemma. It, too, condenses and reaches deep into a universal past for valid symbols of the present. The traditions of the human race merge in the past and a formula with its source in a common heritage becomes universally acceptable.

In Canto IV there is the raving Walcott:

> Where is your culture? Prejudice is white
> As the spittle from an estaminet.
> A tradition is not made, it evolves
> Through those who are not concerned with history.

It is necessary, for those West Indians at least who read Walcott, to recognize the dilemma in which he finds himself, and which, from the uneasiness one may detect in so many of his lines, betrays an embarrassed self-consciousness that they may experience themselves—the embarrassment of borrowed clothes, no matter how legitimately acquired—the top hat in the tropics.

> A tradition is not made, it evolves
> Through those who are not concerned with history.

Doubtless Walcott means the future, for he too, like the moderns who have come under the spell of Eliot, has tried to abstract the essences of the past, and to give us a classicism distilled through ages of history. Donne's:

> I am begot
> Of absence, darknesse, death; things which are not.

In Cantos IX and X of the *Epitaph*, the re-incarnated personality of the son of Ulysses, Stephen son of Daedalus: hence Icarus, and the recurrence of the son seeking the spirit of his father, hence Hamlet, the telescoped literary images so directly inspired by Joyce. Suddenly coming upon the lines

> Greatest of all mysteries, no hand made,
> I know from here, that I and distant others,
> Alien only by twang and dialect, have unity . . . (Canto VII)

it seemed that Walcott was about to acknowledge his debt of literary allusion. But no, he immediately restricts the reference to his friends in the islands—

> Whispers under the thunder of neurotic continents.

How bitter the struggle merely for a form! The same problem of style which confronted him in his *25 Poems*, has now sharpened against the background of the reaction to that effort. Let him speak for himself:

> Suffering is applauded, encouraged, and dissolves
> In a kind Englishwoman's smile among the olives,
> My soul, neatly transfixed in toothpick proportions

Is spread among the lenient, lovely patrons.
By 25 gestures of a lame mind,
The privately prejudiced pretended to be tamed, . . .
Dissected at each tea-party the surprising abortion
Of my contradicting colour. They prevailed
In being nice, as in the Restoration
The dowagers to the pickanninies were almost kind.
At every sandwich on a polite plate,
Each delicacy should melt in my mouth like hate,
Performing puppet on the string of history. (Canto X)

The sources of West Indian language sometimes are at conflict with the sources of West Indian emotion. Lyric poets may find no hardship in this. At the first literary awakening their material must appear fresh and original and it is the content which sounds the note. Because it is the content which matters most, their voices are often original and authentic Caribbean—the genuine folk-song. With this Walcott is not satisfied. His preoccupations are intellectual, but he has not discovered a native intellectual diet which is palatable. He is therefore transplanted and lonely. His escape is to regurgitate not one tradition, but a mixture of several cultures, African, English, French, with a West Indian drop-scene for a sociological background.

Can the West Indian historically project and edit Dante, Baudelaire, Eliot, *et al.* and claim them as being the right landing stage for our literary adventure? Walcott makes the most liberal use of literary allusion and experience which sketch and strengthen his personal quandary, and yet he makes this use reluctantly: ". . . armful of traditions in your fumble for a voice. . . ." That is the traditional-fixation of *Epitaph for the Young.* Just as Stephen Daedalus tried to "forge the uncreated conscience of my race in the smithy of my soul", so must the poet for his ultimate individuality, forge a language and background native to him, before his tongue can leap nimbly into its groove. Till then—always the mocking voices of former masters:

. . . Inviolable and veiled
Across the unshrinking sea . . .

Is not the answer a denial of that intellectual nationalism which the attitude suggests? Walcott has arranged some sort of fealty with classicism and is uneasy under stress of the need for something more national—ultimately, more personal. I believe the later Walcott will be less obscure than the earlier imitative, cautious Walcott; that a thorough digestion of his chosen spiritual diet will lead him to present through poetic vision the simple, familiar universal things, at one with his classicism and at one with his personal and national aspirations. The promise is implicit:

The flutes from antique woodlands usurp the ear,
We are too drunk to look for them on walks,
With cigarettes and beer

> We'll drink to any West Indian who
> Strips speech of tie and socks. . . . (Canto X)

Here perhaps one may leave Walcott's unsolved riddle of form which indeed runs through the whole of *Epitaph* and is one of its central problems, and go to the message of the poem. *Epitaph for the Young* is an allegory in twelve Cantos depicting the voyage of life from birth to manhood, the boat—the human spirit—moving through an archipelago of experience. Each Canto may contain an actual experience, that experience translated into a literary similarity, a philosophical passage, and the allegory of the voyage.

The allegory: "... from egg to flight ...", the human spirit passing through successive circles of trial as portrayed in the Cantos:—

     I.   Birth
    II.   Solitude
   III.   Awakening and disillusion of love.
   IV.   Ambition.
    V.   Wreck of Faith.
   VI.   Drought and sterility.
  VII.   Escape to sordid reality.
 VIII.   Contemplativeness of life and death.
   IX.   Lust and sensuality.
    X.   Thirst for knowledge.
   XI.   Love, cleansing and purifying.
  XII.   Assertion of faith.

The poem includes a satirical portrait of the West Indies within the frame of autobiography. Canto I opens with echoes of *Four Quartets*, the world compressed "aux yeux du souvenir ..." against the background of the charred city.

> Remembering
> My youth, in the crater of the year.
> Here I was born.

The ode is reminiscent of Anatole France's contemplation of the opening words of Dante's *Divine Comedy* ... "In the middle of the road to Chicago, or to think that road the same for all and leading to age. Is it the point at which life loses hope and cannot say tomorrow without sadness or anxiety?" And Eliot's: "Teach us to care and not to care."

Louis Macneice in a note on *Eliot and the Adolescent* remarks that "anyhow *lacrimae rerum* are not a monopoly of the mature adult." Indeed the *lacrimae rerum* of the adolescent are likely to be far more bitter and consuming than those of the mature adult learning to care and not to care. "C'est un bien fait que le souvenir," says Anatole France, "Nel messo del cammin di nostra vita ..." To Derek Walcott, remembering youth in the crater of the year

> Memory is a mad woman
> Draining a dry glass emptier . . .

So the journey begins, and the evaluation of the self in relation to the rest depends on the facts of memory—the moment in the garden.

Canto I: When one has forgiven the faithful imitativeness of the opening passage, it holds its own freshness of imagery

> Daylight unlatching the door of the bird's throat, brings
> Old water in new vases, these time-stale tears,
> The Studebaker and sterility.

The hyphen in "time-stale" removes, I think, a possible obscurity.

Canto II takes up the allegory

> Voyaging
> In the first strong wind, gathering purpose,
> We observed the wreckage drifting by at morning.
> Signifying
> Land, and the flotsam of other purposes.

The lands of desire, ambition and temptation now pass before us amid sudden flashes of introspection

> The doomed lushness of a green mind
> Beginning to nurse its death with images. . . .

and

> The gifted, seeking out gnarled holes of solitude,
> Separate in crowds, lonely and laughing,
> Transfer their hate of self to love of objects.

We voyage through the pain of unrequited adolescent love in Canto II to the theme which against the background of this chapter of autobiography is a central one in *Epitaph.* Canto IV is the climax of the satire on West Indian social life. It opens with drums beating a basic savagery and winds up with crushing sarcasm at the expense of the civil servant:

> Died most as Suppressor of His Majesty's Conscience in the Colonies,
> Inspector of Civil Service lavatories.
> Vulgar, respectable, horrid at home, in the Forum. blest
> As fathers of their countries.
> Voucher and Report undid them, *dulce indecorum est*—

> Attaché to the Assistant Attaché.
> Requiescat in papier.

It sketches the assimilation of races, complexes and cultures which compose the polyglot society of the West Indies and the sum a blank:

> History, a dull pupil, poises a pen in air,
> Believing pawns, her silence speaks epitaphs
> On all our wooden actions. . . .

Does not Prof. Toynbee fail to attribute any contribution by the race to any of the civilisations he studied? The young poet comes out and cries against the city.

The message of Canto V is therefore not surprising—faith shaken into a wavering agnosticism and the echo of Eliot's "Ash Wednesday" "Will the veiled sister . . . pray for those who offend her?" Canto V is given over to the philosophical aspect of the work and with the problem of style and language and the satire on West Indian life completes the trinity of challenges which is *Epitaph for the Young*. From here to the end of the poem the philosophical struggle is in the foreground. Does one generalise as to how and when the religious, moral, ultimately philosophical struggles of the adolescent arise? It is undoubtedly true that for many these struggles arrive as a sudden shadow across the joy and exhilaration of youth's awareness of intellectual power, not to say sufficiency. Then the seeking to reconcile the evidences of intellect and the cherished acceptances of faith. Then despair and bewilderment. We are discussing *Epitaph* but I cannot resist borrowing the words of the Archbishop in *Henri Christophe* (an as yet un-published dramatic poem of Derek Walcott)—

> Our faiths, Henri, are no more than crooked divers crouched
> To leap into negation.

Canto V is not blasphemy, but the symbolical balancing on the brink of negation; the Virgin, the ultimate symbol of surrender and belief as in Dante, Eliot and Joyce. In this season of life nothing is certain, only bewilderment is complete. No longer does the poet voyage "towards . . ." anything. Canto VI closes:

> Condemned to wander.
> Without purpose.

The cry is Baudelaire's

> "Nous nous embarquerons sur la mer des Tenèbres
> Avec le coeur joyeux d'un jeune passager."

Because there is no guide, but only the belligerence of youth we are given the symbol of shipwreck:

> After the shipwreck, shaken but not spirit
> Retaining belligerence on the secure sand. . . .

and as in David Gascoyne's poetry a reckless negation—

> And may we know Thy perfect darkness
> And may we in Hell descend with thee.

so in Canto V using the symbol "Our Lady of Fishermen"

> Prevent us the necessity of coming to Thee
> Or coming to Thee from necessity.

There is the brief unrepentant phase of lustful fulfilment in Canto VI with Baudelaire re-echoing out of a depth of agony: (here are the lines completed)

> "Criant à Dieu dans es furibonde agonie
> O mon seblable, O mon maitre, je te maudis."

   Were this the last Testament of negation the poem would end here in death and dissolution, but youth finds diversions to

> Motor to Vigie on Sundays, sleep in the afternoon
> And nightly, the urge of democracy, and the urge to dress
> The cinema on Sunday. . . .

Cantos VII, VIII, IX are divertisements—after the exhausting voyage: Canto VII

> Descend, Don Juan, stone bird, Icarus. . . .

and VIII

> I moved my three master to the goal of grief. . . .

as Baudelaire said of the soul—

> "Notre ame est un trois-mats cherchant son Icarie."

Here the poet has been ruminating over death—

> If aught I should hear of my father returning alive. . . .

and part of the diversion is a parody of Dante with Eliot as guide followed by a parody of the *Four Quartets*.

In Canto IX the fading hope is seen reviving: "I must live"—still in the echo of despair as the Canto ends under the inspiration of a painting by Breughel, *The Fall Of Icarus*—two pink legs disappear under lucid water while a ploughman "turning his green trades" is oblivious of the disaster.

So the hope develops into a longing to proceed again on the voyage—thus Canto X:

> O Appius and Ulysses for the first ship!

The new philosophy revives the "Matelot;"

> ... I pray to be a normal man,
> Proudly insecure, ignoring pardon. ...

and again—"to care and not to care" and the new philosophy completely abandoning Baudelaire for Eliot's

> We must be still and still moving
> Into a further intensity.
> A deeper communion.

As the poem closes in Canto XI and XII images of peace compete with each other. The poet meets his symbolic lady of flowers;

> I walked in a sweet path away from sharp fires,
> And there I saw, her solitary, culling flowers,
> By love beyond myself I came to Thee. ...

and in Canto XII the images of Neptune, pagan God of the sea, and Mary, symbol of surrender, merge in the colours of the sea—blue, green and white—

> Mary, in blue and green
> Holding a stalk of foam,
> Two fingers stuck in blue and green mercy
> Speaking an invitation to forgiveness.

Epitaph for the Young is a poem and not a philosophical work. Its intuitions, the preoccupations of its author with his surroundings, leave much unargued and unresolved; its triumph is that serious poetry in a short space is able to present so sharply; the closing note from Joachim du Bellay's sonnet neatly sums the purpose, and for the artist the supreme triumph is a personal one

> "Heureux qui comme Ulysse a fait un beau voyage."

REVIEW OF
"HENRI CHRISTOPHE"

Aubrey Douglas-Smith

We are not flattering Derek Walcott by saying that the appearance of a play by him is important. Here in the West Indies it is the more important for having a West Indian subject. The result confirms our belief in his talents and his future.

Like many other modern writers, Walcott perhaps assumes knowledge in his readers. West Indians ought to know more of the epic story of Haitian independence than the average Englishman such as myself; but there may be West Indians too who, after reading a page or two of *Henri Christophe*, will reach for a history book before proceeding further. We probably know something of the towering figure of Toussaint L'Ouverture; we may not be as pat as we might be with the events which followed his death in 1803.

What I found in the book on my shelves was this. Haiti under the French was very rich, and Port-au-Prince had Parisian elegance and three theatres. It was also a country where black slaves were treated with more appalling cruelty, on occasions, than in most; at least, I hope my further Caribbean reading will discover nothing worse. Mackandal attempted a rising, was burned alive, but left behind him a remembered war-hymn of prayer against the whites. There was a great rebellion in 1791; the negroes killed two thousand whites and the whites hanged ten thousand negroes. Then there arose Toussaint L'Ouverture a slave employed as a coachman, born in Africa and son of a reigning chief. General and diplomat of genius, he formed an army and allied himself with Spain, then at war with France. Then the French of the Revolution, in 1793, declared slavery abolished. Toussaint became their general, drove the invading English and the planter-French out of the island, and conquered Santo Domingo from the Spanish. He had able lieutenants, especially Dessalines, and Henri Christophe, both ex-slaves. Dessalines often behaved with monstrous cruelty, of which Toussaint, who showed many examples of magnanimity and clemency, greatly disapproved. When Napoleon emerged, Toussaint did not show the deference the First Consul desired. Napoleon sent one of his largest expeditions to Haiti under his brother-in-law Le Clerc, with treacherous instructions to show Toussaint every honour until the time was ripe to seize and execute him if he would not submit. But Toussaint was too clever, and bought thirty thousand rifles. Christophe declined to receive Le Clerc at Cap François, and burned the city when the French entered with Napoleon's sister Pauline. But Le Clerc in time prevailed, for Toussaint's generals betrayed him. Toussaint made peace and retired to his home in the hills. Then the French, when there were ready, invited him to a friendly conversation, kidnapped him and took him to France, where Napoleon (of whom Tolstoy suggested that we should define the word greatness before we call him the Great) shut him up to die in prison, as Caesar did the valiant Vercingetorix. But his spirit lived, and Napoleon had not won. Dessalines had himself crowned King (or was it Emperor?) as Jacques I. Pétion, a Republican, one of the best of the generals, disapproved, for Toussaint had been a democrat; and there was civil war. Toussaint had made roads and built schools; Dessalines built twelve palaces, a church for his coronation, and fortresses in the hills. The fortresses at least were necessary, for the vengeful Napoleon was preparing to crush the insolent Negroes who resisted the conqueror of Europe. Dessalines was assassinated. Christophe became King as Henri I. Like Dessalines, he was obsessed by blood, cruelty, and massacre, but he made the island ready to meet Napoleon's coming expedition, and created the huge citadel of La Ferrière in the mountains, equipped to resist a siege of years. Napoleon watched with snarling teeth, and, busy enough elsewhere, did not send the expedition after all. Even for him it would have been a difficult invasion, and he would have met what finally ruined him in Europe,—the resistance, not only of generals and an army, but of a people determined to be free. Had he tried it, would the Haitian mountains have anticipated the Moscow snows? King Henri I reigned till 1820, when Pétion's Republic followed.

Walcott's play opens as the news reaches Haiti of Toussaint's death in France. The people's grief is swept aside by the impatient egoism of Dessalines, scheming immediately for a crown, and planning to prevent the opposition of Christophe. In Christophe's camp, waiting also for the dreaded news from Europe, the great leader's loss finds better expression. The First Soldier speaks:

> I cannot wait to hear what I fear and expect,
> That if Toussaint is dead, we have lost our respect
> We stand like gargoyles in the angelus
> That spells a cruelty we cannot endure, and the ship's bell
> Clappers a lost creed to a ruined army. . .

And Christophe here is noble in his reactions:

> Fold up your hopes to show them to your children,
> Because the sun has settled now
> Behind the horizon of our bold history.
> Now no man can measure the horizon
> Of his agony; this grief is wide, wide,

> A ragged futility that beats against these rocks, like
> Sea-bell's angelus.
> The man is dead, history has betrayed us . . .

Christophe in fact might seem at first the proper leader of the young democracy against Dessalines, who wants to use it as a tool for his own power. But Walcott's lines bring out the subtle difference of protest between the generals and Christophe himself:

Vastey.   No, general, you misunderstand. I do not consider
                     Dessalines democratic as, say, Toussaint taught:
                     He nurses whispers, imperial ambitions,
                     He will work without council, and oppress the poor.

1st. G.   He will want to be king. Toussaint
                     Never assumed this.

Christophe.   History has duped me; I who was a leader
                     Shall now play school to a pawn . . .

And later the First General sums him up:

> Christophe is a two-sided mirror; under
> His easy surface, ripples of dark
> Strive with the light, or like a coin's two sides,
> Or like the world half-blind when moons are absent.
> And brilliant in the glare of sun.
> Under that certain majesty he hides
> The teaching of Toussaint, the danger of Dessalines.

Scene III gives us Dessalines as King Jacques I. He is drunk with blood and the massacre of whites, a lunatic, as he knows himself. Pétion and Christophe plan his removal. Scene IV is a bizarre and powerful scene of assassination, which will be very successful on the stage. (The best hints of success in the career of a professional murderer are "First, be a vegetarian, second, be kind to animals, third, keep in practice'"). The fifth Scene shows Christophe acclaimed king by a doubtful and half-hearted crowd, whose hesitating cheers are led by a soldier who has been bribed. Pétion the Republican has turned against Christophe.

Will the new king, Henri I, be an improvement on Dessalines? Sylla, an old general,

> . . . had hoped for, first, faith,
> People singing, eating leisurely

Under the green ease of councils, a federation
Of complexions; but Hayti will never be normal . . . .

Christophe's dreams of royalty are marred by the selfish glorying in power, as he himself realises: "This nigger search for fame Dragged like a meteor across my black rule"—and also by his murderous, uncontrollable hatred of his white foes, a hate conditioned by his days of slavery and branded on his soul. He has genius; he makes ready for Napoleon with the skill of a soldier, the imagination of a poet, the megalomania of a despot.

I shall build chateaux
That shall obstruct the strongest season,
So high the hawk shall giddy in its gyre
Before it settles on the carved turrets
My floors shall reflect the faces that pass over them,
And foreign trees spread out the shade of government;
On emerald lawns I will hold councils.
I'll pave a room with golden coins, so rich,
The old archbishop will smile indulgently at heaven from
The authenticity of my chateaux . . .
I who was slave am now a king; after my strength
Not England, Jamaica, or Napoleon
Shall send ships to disgorge invasions, but search for
Trade and quite. Hayti will flourish.
When I am king.

The great citadel is built, and Napoleon will not come; but Christophe, taught by the greatness of Toussaint, is still tainted with the mad cruelty of Dessalines. Brelle, the white archbishop who endeavoured to serve the new monarchy, is murdered. Christophe, torn between his instinct to justify himself and his own understanding of the truth, discusses it with Vastey:

Christophe.   He was white.

Vastey.   In death, Henri, the bone is anonymous;
Complexions only grin above the skeleton.
Under the grass is an anthology of creeds and skins.
Who can tell what the skull was?
Was it for that we quarrelled?

Alone, Christophe sees reality as by lightning flashes:

Time is the god that breaks us on his knees, learning
Our ruin and repeating epitaphs

Like a dull pupil; it is one that flings
That moon, a wild white spinning coin in grooves of time;
But death returns as the bright thrown dust falls, and walks
Into the memory, the death, the dark.

So the play moves to a close, as Christophe, still questioning himself in alternate pride, laughter, and despair, hears the drums of Pétion's approaching army, and slowly raises the pistol to his own head.

This is a play of genuine power. At first I asked myself why Walcott had not rather told the story of Toussaint; but as I read on I realized the greater value of the tragedy he has made. It is a tragedy of a people breaking through to freedom and the light, their feet still enmeshed, their souls cumbered by the ineradicable memories of the cruelties they had undergone. I found myself thinking of the play's profound significance even for our own day, and of that magnificent utterance by a South African Negro: "My one fear is that we shall have learned how to hate before you have learned to love." We, at least, black and white alike, should have grown a century and a half further out of savagery towards true civilisation (how far away even now!) than Napoleon and Dessalines.

Probably there will be argument about the curious short rhymed couplets in which Walcott has written much of his dialogue. I began by being disconcerted, and ended by finding them effective. I do not see much point in the quotations from Shakespeare which preface the two Parts of the play. I would rather have had a précis of the history of Haiti between 1791 and 1820 instead. It is to be hoped that this splendid drama of West Indian history will be widely performed by amateurs and professionals throughout the islands. It is to be hoped that the young poet and dramatist will give us more. Perhaps one day he will continue the story of Pétion who asked no reward for his services to Bolivar except that the slaves of Venezuela should be free.

B.B.C.'S BROADCAST OF "HENRI CHRISTOPHE"

G.A. Holder

In February Derek Walcott's play "Henri Christophe" was broadcast, in two instalments, in the B.B.C's "Caribbean Voices". I think it a pity that more time could not have been given to the broadcast for, in fitting it to an hour's reading, its most powerful scene had to be omitted completely. I refer to the scene in which Dessalines, king of Hayti, is assassinated. Nevertheless, what was done should have given listeners unfamiliar with the play a desire to read it and enjoy its inconsiderable [sic] merits.

Let me say frankly that I thought the production uneven. One got the impression that the producer was not quite decided whether the play was to be acted or merely read, with the result that the first instalment was very mediocre indeed. I suspected an insufficiency of rehearsals. Again, there was the present-day tendency to be embarrassed by poetry and to evade its demands by trying to make it sound like prose. *Brelle* was especially guilty, with his 'ums' and 'er-s', and only *Dessalines* and *Christophe* seemed unafraid to let their listeners realise that they were hearing a verse play. Naturally, the poetry and the drama suffered from this indecisiveness and I hope that listeners were not dissuaded from returning to the second instalment which was delightfully thrilling.

The second instalment suffered from none of the defects criticised above. The grandeur, passion and beauty of the lines were given their full value and Walcott himself, who, had he been listening, must have been pleased. I had a splendid opportunity to test this effect. On this occasion, I was listening at a wayside loud-speaker when the rain began to drizzle and three or four people took shelter. Two men, barefooted, were talking when *Christophe* momentarily flared up; then his voice grew quieter.

> Anyway he died, broken, grey and quiet
> White-haired as the moon and stumbling just as lost
> Through peace-fleeced colonies of clouds, a foolish, mad old man.

The two men stopped talking and even when the rain had ceased, they remained listening to the end of the play. At that late stage they could not have followed the events; they were held by the poetry, striking in its vividness and beauty and spoken with sympathy and sincerity. I through of the Elizabethans. It was a pleasing rendition. The defaulters of the first instalment had corrected their errors and come to life and beauty, and Edrich Connor as *Christophe* gave a performance memorable for its power and passion.

The faithful who listened to the second instalment will be very grateful to the producer Errol Hill and will, I am sure, want to form groups to read and act this ambitious and satisfying play.

IONE: COLOURFUL BUT ACADEMIC

Norman Rae

In 'Ione', which opened to a crowded house on Saturday evening at the Ward Theatre, Derek Walcott has fallen fatally in love with the outward conventions of the classical theatre as expounded primarily by Aristotle. Not only does he adhere to the theory of the three unities of time, place and action — the story shall take place within the compass of a day, shall unfold in one place, and shall concern itself with a single line of plot — but he also re-presents something of the formal structure. All violence occurs off-stage and is reported, there is experimental work with the chorus, characters pronounce their sentiments most often in 'tirades'.

The flow of action sweeps before the ever-present figure of an ancient clairvoyant, something like a Delphic Sybil, who, from time to time, becomes inspired and utters prophetic words of doom. All events are pre-ordained and what must come, must inevitably come. It is a matter of time.

Walcott has woven a story to match the Greeks, as full of blood and thunder as *Agamemnon,* of women's matters as *Electra.* But, the exercise remains an academic one. He presents the people and he presents the plot and hardly ever do the twain meet. The manipulation of the people for plot purposes is even more overt than in the Greek plays and because of the brevity of character exposition they do not make themselves very well known.

The idea is impeccable according to Aristotle, but Mr. Walcott forgets the tremendous religious and philosophical background to the ancient theatre. Sophocles and Eurpides and Aeschylus unfolded their plays against the relationship of gods and men. Walcott seems to suggest two things only, that men and women differ and that a beautiful woman will cause destruction.

However, the old conventions retain their life and 'Ione' sustains an exalted tone for the greater part of the way. Walcott achieves this through the language heightened — though sometimes pseudo-heightened as in the 'Ione, daughter of Victorin, wife of Pamphile etc., etc'. method — to a great degree.

Many of the poetic images are felicitous, the needle of God stitching, the bereaved father's request that the pennies of the cold moon be placed on his eyes for he cannot

113

face the sun. Nevertheless, when the language runs away with itself as it frequently does in the apostrophes of the father, the beggar, the husband and occasionally Ione, the play becomes full of sound and fury signifying little.

To return to the matter of tone. Walcott gives himself away sadly in the last act when he breaks it. The old conventions are hard and jealous masters. 'Ione' builds up a certain power in spite of drawbacks. Then, inexplicably, Walcott introduces a low comedy character in the person of Mercure to read the letter which Ione has been awaiting. At one fell swoop, playwright destroys himself. He reveals even more plainly that the play possesses no internal cohesion, no binding economic force. He ruins the tremendous final moments of the Ione-figure, the 'cold rock', as she goes off to commit suicide.

Indeed, as far as motives and manipulation go, Ione is among the least successful of Walcott's figures. She broods while sister Helene, lover slain in bed by her angry husband, child also slaughtered by him, is banished from the land. She waits for a letter from an American University professor who, while doing research in the island, got her with child, a letter which will summon her to the States and out of the island's feudal setting. When the American sends her fifty dollars just in case the child is really his, Ione jumps from a cliff or the equivalent.

'Ione' demonstrates something which often happens with a poorish play in the commercial theatre. One of the best all-round casts assembled recently works hard at it and under imaginative direction supplied by Ronald Llanos and Errol Hill brings as much of the bacon home as is possible.

The directors succeed in making 'Ione' colourful and atmospheric by all the theatrical means at their disposal, costumes, set, vivid lighting, sound effects (although there are inevitable difficulties in interspersing recorded with natural sound) and many of its most moving moments, though possibly indicated by the playwright, seem attributable to them.

The derisive handclapping of the men as Victorin, Ione's father, is forced to relinquish power; the rejection and stoning of Helene; the angry figure of Ione confronting the men of the tribe; the dignity of movement and attitude generally; the big style of the production.

Among the actors, who must be complimented incidentally on being audible, most realised that to deal with 'Ione', the best method of defence was attack. They played with sustained vigour. The figure of Lois Kelly-Barrow in the title role stands out in the memory. Statuesque, firmly planted as though on the cold rock which is her symbol in the play, dressed in black, she commanded attention and never relaxed her hold.

Annie Perkins handling the difficult role of the clairvoyant Theresine turned in a remarkably sustained performance, making use of all the tricks of breaking up lines with odd inflections to great advantage and yet blending them in without effort. Carmen Manley as Helene, not given much chance by the script, carried off her rejection scene wordlessly and movingly. The Washerwomen Chorus struck a bright little spark in their humorous chatterings.

The production was not quite so well-served by its men. Errol Hill playing the

father Victorin could not summon enough heart to cover some of the self-consciousness of the verse. Archie Hudson-Phillips, as the betrayed husband of Helene, carried
over some of the comic propensities of his previous role in the University Players'
'Man Betta Man'. Keith Sasso in the Greek-y role of the Beggar spoke well, unlike
Hugh Morrison, playing the brother of Victorin and leader of the rival tribe, who
produced accents worthy of 'The Green Pastures'.

Delroy Mendes extracted all the comedy from the wrongly-conceived role of
Mercure and, in lesser roles, Douglas Fairweather and Richard DaCosta were adequate.

The most interesting thing of all about 'Ione', however, is that with the directors
weaving in dance, song, atmosphere, style, so forth and so on, and in conjunction
with the recent presentation of 'Uncle Robert' it seems a West Indian theatrical
production of a straight play is no longer just a collection of persons making
conversation on a platform.

COMPANY OF PLAYERS
WIN PRAISE FOR *IONE*

John Grimes

Any group of players who could make presentable Derek Walcott's unbalanced cocktail of love, hate, greed, lust, incest, murder, voodoo, and degeneracy that flourished in a small West Indian fishing village, deserve the highest credit.

For if they had deliberately set out to do the almost impossible, the Company Of Players could hardly have attempted anything but Walcott's "Ione," now being staged at the Community Education Extension Workshop, St. Ann's.

Indeed, it is one of the few occasions when the author, and not the players, draws the fire of an audience.

Walcott evidently wanted to get away from normal people, whose lives contain more hidden drama than he gives credit for. In their place, he painted the emotions and gave them names.

Fortunately, The Company Of Players, reversed matters, and achieved some measure of glory. The fact that they managed to link together the melodrama and fatuous comedy of the play is indicative of the hard work, imagination and skilful casting of the producer and director.

Briefly, the story, as told in a day of the lives of a split family, tells of the old grudges, greed, loose living, jealousies and hates that rule the lives of two clans of farmers and fishermen.

That it is unconvincing, does not even take into consideration the established beliefs that such types are hardly ever associated with such goings-on.

Fortunately, Jean Herbert, as the main character "Ione," Eunice Bruno, as the old hag "Theresine," who all but steals the play, George Kangalee, as Victorin, whose daughters betray his family pride, and Roslyn Borel, the scarlet lady of the village, headed an intelligent cast, who brought some measure of human appeal into the discordant melodrama.

With the exception of Miss Bruno the others have already made their bows to the public. Yet, as the voodoo priestess she paced them all the way, most of the time dominating the stage. She can count "Ione" as a personal triumph.

Seldom, too, have there been such creditable performances by supporters, whose main unspeaking roles were confined to glowering at each other, looking menacing or merely helping to fill the stage.

Indeed, all the praise belongs to the actors, unassisted as they were by the play itself, the bare "props," a feeble-voiced Narrator and the thousand and one ills that beset each and every local production.

And again, they were forced to work the harder as the story progressed through its three acts, with the second and third growing weaker and weaker to fade away into the weakest part of all, the climax.

In the final analysis, the play demonstrated that local theatre has progressed a great deal over the past few years. The actors have apparently grasped the idea, at long last, that it takes hard work, talent and imagination to produce a play worthy of a paying audience.

"Ione" deserves to be seen for these considerations alone.

ALLEGORY IN
TI-JEAN AND HIS BROTHERS

Albert Ashaolu

The significance of Walcott's *Ti-Jean and His Brothers*[1] lies in its pluralistic allegory. Theodore Colson observes that the play "is a parable of mankind's various confrontations with the devil, and more particularly of black man's confrontation with the white devil."[2] No doubt, the deceptive simplicity of *Ti-Jean* reveals on the surface only the levels of interpretation pointed out by Colson. However, the allegory in the play may be likened, in a way, to an iceberg drifting down a river, with only one-ninth of the mass visible above water. And like a myth which Northrop Frye terms as "a centripetal structure of meaning,"[3] the play contains at least six built-in allegories: the allegory of the artist, and historical, political, moral, Christian, and class allegories.

The first allegory identifiable in *Ti-Jean* is that of the artist. The Frog hops out to tell the tale of a mother and her three sons. Sneezing, the Frog, rather than say "God bless me," as one might do after sneezing, calls out, "Aeschylus me!" This is as curious as it is significant.

The numerous classical allusions in Walcott's works are proof of the poet-playwright's familiarity with classical works. One such work is Aristophanes' *The Frogs*,[4] a satirical drama in which Euripides is made the butt of the joke. In "The Argument" provided by J. Hookham Frere and prefixed to the play, it is stated that "Dionysus, the patron of the stage, in despair at the decline of the dramatic art . . . determines to descend [to] the infernal regions with the intention of procuring the release of Euripides." In Hades, Aeschylus already occupies the "tragic chair," an honour which Euripides now vies for with vigour. Dionysus is faced with the problem of judging who deserves the coveted "tragic chair." A contest, or *agon* is set in which the two rivals contend for recognition. In the end Dionysus who is obviously a mouthpiece for Aristophanes gives the victor's prize to Aeschylus. Pluto's speech, following this decision, is worth quoting for its relevance:

> Farewell then, Aeschylus, great and wise,
> Go, save our state by maxims rare

Of thy noble thought; and the fools chastise,
For many a fool dwells there.

And so, Aeschylus, "the poet triumphant," is led out by the Chorus who wish him success in his mission.

The significance of all this to our study is that the choice of Aeschylus by Dionysus, with the approval of Pluto, reflects Aristophanes' preference for Aeschylus over Euripides; and Walcott's invocation of Aeschylus' name, as put in the mouth of the Frog, is an implicit recognition of Aeschylus as the great and wise poet-playwright endowed with "maxims rare" and "noble thoughts" which a Narrator like the Frog needs as its muse and source of inspiration. And by invoking the name of Aeschylus, the Frog has elevated itself from the low status of a mere folktale animal to that of an inspired poet-Narrator with a vision.

Commenting on the opening of the play, Lloyd Coke observes that "Critics reared on Metropolitan theatre immediately see Greek chorus translated into folk-tale animals. Africanists recognize the village storyteller and keeper of legends, in which the frog is usually a model of sagacity."[5] The allegorist would go a step further and recognize in the Frog a clever representation of the role of Aeschylus the dramatist. The Frog is as much Aeschylus as it is Walcott the artist himself presenting us with the well-crafted drama of *Ti-Jean*. To miss this allegory of the artist is to lose sight of the significance of Walcott's stylized dramaturgy.

Ti-Jean is a modern presentational drama in which the Frog combines the function of a traditional storyteller with something of the Stage Manager as exemplified in Thornton Wilder's *Our Town*. The "Greek-croak" opening is a modified adaptation of the riddle formula with which the storyteller in patois opens his tale:

Storyteller:	*Tim-tim* (The draining of sap out of wood).
Audience:	*Bois sech* (The wood is dry.).
Storyteller:	*Tout ça Bon Dieu mettais a sou la terre?* (What did God put on the earth ?) .
Audience:	*Tout chose* (Everything).

The story which follows this introduction is often enlivened with music and dancing. By adopting this pattern of introduction, the storyteller arouses the interest of his audience and commands their attention. This is precisely what Walcott attempts at the beginning of *Ti-Jean*, and we, his audience, are invited to listen to his tale which operates at five levels .

More obvious than the allegory of the artist are the historical and political allegories, which constitute the pivot on which the action in the play revolves. The West Indies has a long tradition of slave rebellion, characterized by bloodshed and mass murder of the slaves, whose invincible courage is recorded in General Lemmonier-Delafosse's memoirs: "But what men these blacks are! How they fight and how they die! One has to make war against them to know their reckless courage in braving danger when they can no longer have recourse to strategem [sic]. I have

seen a solid column, torn by grapeshot from four pieces of canon, advance without
making a retrograde step. The more they fell, the greater seemed to be the courage of
the rest. They advanced singing, for the Negro sings everywhere, makes songs on
everything."[6]

In *Ti-Jean,* the West Indies is symbolized by the helpless Mother of the three
brothers who, in turn, represent the black slaves in their relentless fight for emancipa-
tion. The tyrannous colonial slavemaster is aptly allegorized in the Devil who masks
up as an Old Man, or as Planter, as occasion demands. Gros Jean and Mi-Jean[7] would
then become a metaphor for the suicide squads of Negro fighters who, in
Lemmonier-Delafosse's memoirs, defied cannons and sacrificed their lives in the
cause of freedom from oppression. Ti-Jean may therefore be regarded as a dramatic
re-creation of any or all of those who successfully led slave rebellions in the West
Indies, among them Toussaint L'Ouverture of San Domingo.

We do not pretend for a moment that these parallels can be worked out in their
fine details. Nevertheless, we may further examine the allegorical nature of some
individual characters in Ti-Jean. In a sense, the play reminds us of Aeschylus'
Prometheus Bound which Romantic poets like Goethe and Shelley hail as a parable of
human revolt against autocracy and established religion. *Ti-Jean* is an allegory of any
revolt against any authoritarian or tyrannical government, like the successful revolt
led by Old Lem against Brutus Jones in Eugene O'Neill's *The Emperor Jones.*

Given this political allegory, Gros Jean may loosely be likened to Prometheus, a
Titan who foolhardily pitches himself against the tyrannical, almost villainous god
Zeus. Although the parallel between the two cannot be a neat one, Gros Jean's
prideful reliance on his physical strength in his encounter with the Devil is reminiscent of the titanic strength upon which Prometheus relies in confronting Zeus
without much success. Prometheus by befriending the experimental race of men,
much against the plans of Zeus, becomes himself a victim of divine oppression; but
his liberation does not lie in his own titanic force. In like manner, the decline of the
Devil in *Ti-Jean,* which invariably means the liberation of the race of Gros Jean and
his brothers, does not lie in the brute force of Gros Jean whose defeat by the Devil is
well-deserved.

Mi-Jean, a shade better than Gros Jean, also fails in his revolt because he is an
unimaginative man of rhetoric, a shallow philosopher without the spirit of persever-
ance when persecuted. The triumph of the Devil over him may therefore symbolize
the victory of a political tyrant over a force of resistance that lacks persistent courage
and endurance.

Unlike his two brothers, Ti-Jean is an embodiment of intuition, courage, humility, vision, and endurance. He is very much like the small animal in folk tales,
outwitting the bigger and stronger animal. But the ruthless method adopted by Ti-
Jean in overcoming the Devil is not unlike those which the slaves employed in getting
rid of their overbearing masters or overseers. Negro slaves are known to have resorted
to vile tricks, like poisoning with corrosive sublimate. In his Journal of January 28,
1816, Lewis records: "A neighbouring gentleman . . .has now three negroes in prison,
all domestics, and one of them grown grey in his service, for poisoning him with

corrosive sublimate; his brother was actually killed by similar means."[8] Mischievous conspiracies against white overseers were also common among the slaves. One such conspiracy recorded by Lewis on March 16, 1816, reveals that "besides their occasional amusements of poisoning, stabbing, thieving, etc., a plan has just been discovered in the adjoining parish of St. Elizabeth's, for giving themselves a grand fete by murdering all the whites in the island. The focus of this meditated insurrection was on Martin's Penn, the property of Lord Balcarres. . . . Luckily, the plot was discovered time enough to prevent any mischief."[9]

It is doubtful if Ti-Jean could have succeeded against the Planter had he not resorted to vile tricks and outright mischief in getting the cane plantation burnt down. His success against the Devil symbolizes the success of a revolt led by a man who is capable of combining the meekness of a lamb, the instinctive wildness of a tiger, and the cunning of the fox, qualities which when in proper balance can stun even the Devil.

Closely related to the fate of each of the three brothers in both the historical and political allegories is their fate in the moral allegory. The Frog concludes its tale, saying, "And so it was that Ti-Jean, a fool like all heroes, passed through the tangled opinions of this life, loosening the rotting faggots of knowledge from old men to bear them safely on his shoulder, brother met brother on his way, that God made him the clarity of the moon to lighten the doubt of all travellers through the shadowy wood of life." However, there is more to learn from the tale than these closing remarks reveal.

Gros Jean's fate demonstrates the truth of the saying that pride goes before a fall. His mother warns him against reliance on his physical strength, and advises him to be humble, tactful, and careful:

> When you go down the tall forest, Gros Jean,
> Praise God who make all things; ask direction
> Of the bird, and the insects, imitate them;
> But be careful of the hidden nets of the devil,
> Beware of a wise man called Father of the Forest,
> The Devil can hide in several features,
> A woman, a white gentleman, even a bishop.
> Strength, ça *pas tout*, there is patience besides;
> There always is something stronger than you.
> If is not man, animal, is God or demon.

This advice is reminiscent of Teiresias' warning to Pentheus:

> Mark my words, Pentheus.
> Do not be so certain that power is what matters in the life of man; do
> not mistake for wisdom the fantasies of your sick mind.
>   (Euripides, *The Bacchae*, 11. 309-12)

But Pentheus, blinded with pride, neglects these words of advice and his end is as disastrous as his cousin Actaeon's. Similarly, Gros Jean utterly disregards the advice of his mother out of sheer pride in his muscular strength. And like Pentheus and Actaeon he comes to a dreadful end.

Very much like Gros Jean, Mi-Jean is too proud to listen to the warnings against danger offered by the Frog, the Cricket, and the Bird. However, his is an intellectual pride which, ironically enough, does not stand him in good stead in his philosophical argument with the Planter (Devil) about the divinity of man ("All I say is that man is divine!"). The Planter claims that "A man is no better than an animal," that "he is a kneeling hypocrite who on four legs, like a penitent capriped, prays to his maker, but is calculating the next vice," that a "goat . . .may be a genius in its own right," and that, eloquent as Mi-Jean is, he is but a "descendant of the ape." Moved by his intellectual pride, Mi-Jean grows full of precocious rage and consequently forfeits his life.

Unlike Gros Jean and Mi-Jean, Ti-Jean attentively listens to his mother's words of advice, and before leaving home, asks for and receives his mother's blessings. He compares himself with David, hoping to be as victorious over the Devil as David was over Goliath. His humility in recognizing the smaller creatures as part of the ordered universe enables him to be well informed about the impending danger in his way. Fully equipped with his mother's advice and blessings, the knowledge acquired from the smaller animals, his humility and natural instincts, and an invincible determination, he successfully beats the Devil in his own game, outwitting him at every point. The victory of Ti-Jean over the Devil reminds us of the achievement of Orestes which compels Zeus in Jean-Paul Sartre's *The Flies* to admit: "Well, Orestes, all this was foreknown. In the fullness of time a man was to come, to announce my decline. And you're that man, it seems."[10] Ti-Jean has defeated the Devil, but the fight is anything but over, because the Devil threatens: "We shall meet again, Ti-Jean. You, and your new brother! / The features will change, but the fight is still on." The point being made here is that the struggle against evil is an unending affair. The best we can do, like Orestes come to announce the decline of Zeus, is to mitigate the destructive power of the Devil as Ti-Jean has done.

This moral allegory can be extended further to include a Christian allegory. The victory dance with which Ti-Jean makes his exit recalls to mind the dance of victory usually performed by the Acrobat in the crude mime show put on by Masqueraders at Christmas time in St. Lucia. Papa Diable (The Devil), with a following of Ti Diables (little devils), is challenged to a duel by the Acrobat who is knocked down by the Devil. However, with the help of two friends, or so, the Acrobat, sword in hand, revives and attacks Papa Diable whose weapon is a pitch-fork. This time, the Acrobat emerges as the winner. Then he performs an acrobatic dance of victory. This crude mime reenacts the death of Christ (in the initial fall of the Acrobat) and his resurrection and ascension, his symbolic victory over Death. The song of the Devil in *Ti-Jean*,

Bai Diable-là manger un 'ti mamaille,
Un, deux, trois 'ti mamaille!

(Give the Devil a child for dinner,
One, two, three little children!),

is the same as that sung by the groups of Masqueraders performing in the streets at Christmas at St. Lucia. The entire play, *Ti-Jean*, may therefore be seen in terms of a Christian allegory in which man (Gros Jean, Mi-Jean) is defeated by Satan, but is later redeemed through the salvific mission of Christ, which is ingeniously allegorized in the person of Ti-Jean.

A discussion of the allegory in *Ti-Jean* cannot be complete without a mention of the class allegory. The pronunciation of "Jean" strongly suggests a deliberate pun on *gens* which means folk, people, men. Gros Jean whose name suggests the gross (burly) individual therefore symbolizes the big power class in society. Mi-Jean would then represent the people of the middle class, with their new-found learning and intellectualism. Ti-Jean, "the little man," is a name associated with the little man in the moon in West Indian folk tale. Lloyd Coke has also suggested that Ti-Jean's name "sounds like 'ti-zanges,' (spirits of Haitian children who die too young to have been sinful)."[11] Ti-Jean would then be a metaphor for the "little" people in society, the low class, usually noted for their inevitable humility and practical common sense. It is to this class that Bolom belongs. Once he is "reborn," he becomes, as Lloyd Coke aptly puts it, the "foetus of Caribbean aspirations, who chooses the pain of selfhood rather than continue to be the Devil's emmissary."[12]

The various levels of interpretation of *Ti-Jean* attempted in this study have been made possible by the pluralistic nature of the allegory with which the play is laden. Derek Walcott may not have consciously designed the play the way it is now being perceived. But, as Eldred Jones once commented, "good works of art are notorious for yielding more than their authors consciously put into them."[13] This comment made with reference to J. P. Clark's *The Raft* is quite true of *Ti-Jean*, which is a monumental play in its own right, next in grandeur and artistic design only to *Dream on Monkey Mountain* in the hierarchy of Walcott's plays.

NOTES

[1] All citations from this play, which will henceforth be referred to as *Ti-Jean*, are taken from Derek Walcott, *Dream on Monkey Mountain and Other Plays* (New York: 1970), pp. 81-166, *passim*.

[2] T. Colson, "Derek Walcott's Plays: Outrage and Compassion," *WLWE*, 12, 1 (April 1973), 83.

[3] N. Frye, *Anatomy of Criticism* (Princeton: 1957), p. 341.

[4] See Aristophanes, *The Frogs*, trans. by Benjamin B. Rogers, in John Gassner, ed., *A Treasury of the Theatre* (New York: 1935; rev. 1967), v. I, pp. 73-95. All references to the play in this study are from this edition.

[5] Lloyd Coke, "Walcott's Mad Innocents," *Savacou*, 5 (June 1971), 121.

[6] Cited in C. L. R. James, *The Making of the Caribbean Peoples*, p. 14. (A guest lecture delivered at the second conference on West Indian Affairs held in Montreal, Summer 1966.)

[7] Walcott's reference in "What the Twilight Says: An Overture" to the sin of pride, and the

ultimate defeat of Dessalines and Christophe, two generals involved in the War of Independence, suggests that he may have had at the back of his mind these two historical figures in creating the two characters Gros Jean and Mi-Jean in his play.

[8] M. G. Lewis, *Journal of a West Indian Proprietor 1815-17* (London: 1929), p. 126.

[9] Ibid., p. 184.

[10] In John Gassner, ed., *A Treasury of the Theatre* (New York: 1935; rev. 1967), v. II, p. 494,

[11] Lloyd Coke, 122.

[12] Ibid.

[13] E D. Jones, "African Literature 1966-1967," *African Forum,* 3, 1 (Summer 1967), 5.

DEREK WALCOTT'S PLAYS: OUTRAGE AND COMPASSION

Theodore Colson

Dream on Monkey Mountain and Other Plays (Farrar, Straus and Giroux, Noonday Press, 1970) is Derek Walcott's first collection of plays; and just because they are so intensely of and about the West Indian people and places, they are intensely for the world. The four plays are prefaced by a remarkable essay, "What the Twilight Says." The twilight here is an immensely rich metaphor, starting with the actual twilight of Trinidad, with "the destitute in their orange-tinted backyards, under their dusty trees, or climbing to their favelas," but immediately spreading, resonant with meaning. The West Indies are a zone of twilight of the setting sun of the British Empire, and of a people light and dark and mixed; and Walcott becomes the voice of the light and the dark and the mixed. He had written in "A Far Cry from Africa":

> The gorilla wrestles with the superman.
> I who am poisoned with the blood of both,
> Where shall I turn, divided to the vein?

Where he turns is to speak, through the same themes, from the twilight area of poetry and drama.

That twilight speaks to those of us who are in the still nearly full blaze of empire—be it American, British, or whatever. And there is no mistake that we hear the note of a rage for revenge, the sons of slaves rebelling—but Walcott embodies, "divided to the vein," the dilemma of that rebellion, since he is the descendant of master as well as slave.

One of the things that the twilight says is that those who are literally the children of slaves, and whose blackness pronounces it, become metaphors for the slavery of us all—and simultaneously whiteness becomes the metaphor for the slavedealer in us all. Painful as this is, we cannot escape it; nor should we want to. And it provides one of the tensions that contribute to the greatness of current West Indian writing.

125

The first play, of one act, is *The Sea at Dauphin.* While it is a poetic drama, in which men speak verse when emotion peaks—and it always feels right—this is the most naturalistic of the plays in theme. The malcontent Afa's outrage is like Job's:

> Where is compassion? Is I does make poor people poor, or this sea vex?
> Is I that put rocks where should dirt by Dauphin side, man cannot make
> garden grow? Is I that swell little children belly with bad worm, and
> woman to wear clothes white people use to wipe their foot? (p. 53)

Hounakin, an old man desolate with poverty and age, but mostly with the loss of his wife, wants to take up fishing with Afa and his partner—not for a new livelihood, he finally reveals before the fishermen leave without him, but, "I did feel to die in Dauphin sea, so I could born." When they return Hounakin has fallen to his death from the cliff by the sea. Afa does not apparently, like Job, finally accept God's power with good grace:

> God is a white man. The sky is his blue eye.
> His spit on Dauphin people is the sea.
> Don't ask me why a man must work so hard
> To eat for worm to get more fat. Maybe I bewitch.
> You never curse God, I curse him, and cannot die,
> Until His time. (p. 61)

When asked, "Why you must curse the priest?" he answers, "I was vex. . . . It mean nothing." The play ends on the note of Ecclesiastes, that the sun also rises and goes down; a generation goes, and comes; but Afa's concern is with the going:

Afa:	Last year Annelles, and Bolo, and this year Hounakin . . . .
	And one day, tomorrow, you Gacia, and me . . . . And
	Augustin . . .
Gacia:	Sun going down . . .
Afa:	The sea too . . .
Gacia:	Tomorrow again. *Un autre demain* . . .
Afa:	Your woman crying for you. . . . Help me with this sail. . .
	(p. 80)

Despite the pessimism Afa looks to the morrow.

Outrage and compassion are the emotional and thematic poles of the whole book—summed up in the concluding lines of *Malcochon, or The Six in the Rain:*

> The rage of the beast is taken for granted,
> Man's beauty is sharing his brother's pain. (p. 206)

While Afa's rage, like Lear's, is wild, it is not that of a beast; for it is intense with consciousness and compassion. Afa raging against the dying of the light for the people of Dauphin is one more voice of what the twilight says.

In contrast to *The Sea at Dauphin's* naturalism, *Ti-Jean and His Brothers* is pure fairy tale. The two plays have a common note in vexation, though the first is tragic, the second, comic. There are the archetypal three sons, Gros-Jean, Mi-Jean, and Ti-Jean. The oldest is disastrously proud of his physical might, the second is a self-educated fool; they each in turn try to get ahead by dealing with the devil (in the form of a white planter). The deal with the devil is that the first to become vexed will be eaten. The first two brothers, one relying on his brute force, the other on his learning, both become vexed, and that's the end of them. But Ti-Jean is sent out by his mother with this blessing:

> Instinct be your shield,
> It is wiser than reason,
> Conscience be your cause
> And plain sense your sword. (pp. 133-134)

The devil's tasks are to keep his goat tied up, to count his canes and to clean his house. Ti-Jean "fixes" the goat (and later eats it), burns the cane field, and burns the house. The devil does get vexed, but as he says, "I never keep bargains." But Ti-Jean's course is supported by the Bolom, who is the ghost of a hideous abortion. So the devil pays Ti-Jean money, but in revenge shows Ti-Jean his mother dying, and taunts, "Now, can you still sing?" But Ti-Jean, though faltering, does sing:

> To the door of breath you gave the key,
> Thank you, Lord,
> The door is open, and I step free,
> Amen, Lord . . . . (p. 162)

The devil (whom the Bolom had earlier revealed "is dying to be human") is moved to tears. For this experience (that "Man's beauty is sharing his brother's pain") he grants Ti-Jean a wish, and Ti-Jean responds to the Bolom's pleading for life. So Ti-Jean goes off with a new brother.

Bolom is the play's most strikingly symbolic figure; the devil says to him, "For cruelty's sake I could wish you were born"; and Ti-Jean says, "Is life you want child? You don't see what it bring?" He is "child of the devil," and it is strongly implied that he *is* Ti-Jean's brother; for as Ti-Jean represents all fool-heroes, the Mother is all mothers, and Bolom is—whatever else he is—all aborted human potential, in a world of black mothers and white planters. Bolom is such a monster that the mother said of him:

> The sight of such horror, though you are brave,
> Would turn you to stone, my strong son, Gros-Jean. (p. 98)

But with Bolom's "birth" the play, like *Dream on Monkey Mountain*, ends with morning light, the twilight of hope.

The play is a parable of mankind's various confrontations with the devil, and more particularly of black man's confrontation with the white devil. Vexed force, vexed learning play into his hands; instinct, wisdom, conscience, sense—and good humour—defeat him, as far as the devil is ever defeated. But that Ti-Jean resists vexation hardly means that he is passive. He avoids vexation by "fixing" the devil's goat and fields and house.

But what makes the play so great is the sheer fun of it. This devil is one of the great comic devils, and driven by Ti-Jean, he goes on a great comic drunk. For example, he sings:

> When I was the Son of the Morning,
> When I was the Prince of Light.

Then breaks off, "Oh, to hell with that! You lose a job, you lose a job." And what a moment when the drunken devil sings:

> Leaning, leaning,
> Leaning on the everlasting arms . . . ! (p. 152)

How I envy those who have seen this play.

In the one-act play *Malcochon, or The Six in the Rain*, a jealous husband and his wife (who has a bottle of *Malcochon*, cheap rum, as a present from an overseer), along with an old man and his nephew and the Moumou, a simple-minded deaf mute, take refuge from the rain in a shed. They are joined by Chantal, an old man who is a perpetual fugitive, with a life-long reputation of violence and crime, a man whose name has been used to frighten children. The husband and wife continually quarrel, and the old man advises them (with imagery which is a continuing motif through all the plays):

> We not tigers and serpents and dogs, we are men.
> We don't murder and curse, we leave the old savagery,
> When you ask for justice make sure is not revenge,
> And when you ask for truth make sure you don't mean justice.
> (pp. 191-192)

And he appeals to Chantal, revealing that he knows who he is, "Chantal the madman. Tiger of the forest." The husband roars with laughter:

> This old man there with the broken teeth and the crack voice,
> with one crooked eye and marks on his face, this is Chantal the
> wood demon, that we was frighten of as children? (p. 193)

But at this moment comes the fine dramatic climax; the wife sees the body of the planter, Regis, tumbling in the stream nearby. Chantal, who is armed with axe and cutlass, had come in with Moumou, who had silver spoons marked with an *R* to sell. It is immediately assumed that Chantal is the murderer, and that he is desperate and dangerous. Chantal is drunk on the woman's rum, and disgusted with the quarreling he decides to confess the distraught wife and threatens to behead her. The result is an intense, over-wrought "theatrical" little orgy of repentance. And even the old man gets into the act: "Kill me, kill me. Let the others go. I am tired of this life." Chantal's judgment is really that wild man's grasping toward the responsibility of the knowl-edge of good and evil, the tiger man's rejection of "the rage of the beast" for man's unique beauty:

> I drunk, friends. Drunk and hungry. I don't know what to do.
> I always on the other side of the law. But life funny,
> Today I must play judge. I will let you all go.
> But if I let you all go, who will speak for Chantal ?
> All my life I just do what I want and leave the rest,
> The responsibility, you follow, to the men who run the world,
> The priest and magistrate, the rich man, the . . .
> (p. 200)

And at this ironic moment the deaf mute, Moumou, plunges a knife into Chantal's back, and grins at the others to show that he has saved them. Chantal, dying, reveals it was the Moumou who killed Regis, but that is not important. Chantal wants no priest, and only asks that his head be lifted up to see the mountain:

> Three years I working there, and sometime in the morning when
> the sun coming up, I did only feel to roar like a mad tiger.
> "Praise be God in His Excellence!" And look at the sun making
> diamond on the wet leaves. That's all the money I ever had in
> this life. A man should not leave that forest, eh? (p. 205)

The raging and exultation of Chantal is a nice contrast to the rage of Afa in *The Sea at Dauphin*. Chantal is magnificent where Afa is surly. But Afa lives his whole life with a knowledge Chantal approaches in his end. The old man's answer to Chantal is, "Man have to live with man, Chantal." And the play closes with his death:

> The rage of the beast is taken for granted,
> Man's beauty is sharing his brother's pain;
> God sends the wound where a wound is wanted,
> This is the story of six in the rain. (p. 206)

The old man looking toward his home on the mountain is an image common to *Malcochon* and *Dream on Monkey Mountain*, and these last lines are a fitting transition to the major play of the collection. "The rage of the beast"—however we pity it there is nothing we can do about it finally, philosophically, except take it for granted, whereas the outrage of man can have tragic beauty. In *Dream on Monkey Mountain* Makak, the monkey, flanked by Tigre and Souris, the rat, struggles for freedom and manhood. The Corporal in that play, however, is associated with no beastliness but man's—or white man's culture, and his job seems to be repressing animality (black, of course). His theme is "animals, beasts, savages, cannibals, niggers." The Corporal who does "white man work" and "black man work" is beastly in just the sense that he is alienated from what makes humanity of some value—that " man's beauty is sharing his brother's pain."

The heart of the whole book, which is unified by various themes, is embodied symbolically in the climax of *Dream on Monkey Mountain*, when Makak beheads the apparition of a white woman. Makak, a poor, ugly, old charcoal burner who lives on Monkey Mountain, *Morne Macaque*, is visited in a vision by a white woman,

> The loveliest thing I see on this earth,
> Like the moon walking along her own road. (p. 227)

She tells him he is the son of kings and as a king should return to Africa. In Part I with his poor squire, Moustique, Sancho Panza to his Don Quixote, indeed Judas-treasurer to Makak as black Messiah, Makak sets forth, in a role rather like a prophet. Moustique, all practicality and scepticism, humours him, but after Makak cures a man of a fever, Moustique becomes disciple, agent; and finally, when Makak is not showman enough, he impersonates Makak. But he is revealed by Basil—the carpenter, coffin-maker, figure of death—and is beaten to death by a mob.

In Part II Makak breaks out of jail after wounding Corporal Le Strade (the Corporal is a mulatto who does "white man work" as jailer, judge, overseer, white hunter, and converted does black man work as lieutenant to King Makak as black judge). Makak sets off for Africa again, this time as king and general, with Souris and Tigre (two thieves in a supporting role like those by Christ's crucifixion). The Corporal pursues, but "goes native," and when Makak is king on the Golden Stool, the Corporal becomes the mouthpiece of black law, condemning all that is or has been white: "Some are dead and cannot speak for themselves, but a drop of milk is enough to condemn them." At the climax of the play the apparition, the white moon queen is condemned, and Makak, alone, beheads her.

But it has all been a dream, and in the epilogue, Makak wakes up in jail (put there for mashing up Alcindor café) and returns home to Monkey Mountain with Moustique.

In "What the Twilight Says" Walcott writes, particularly of his actors, but it is true of all actors:

> If I see these as heroes it is because they have kept the sacred urge
> of actors everywhere: to record the anguish of the race. To do
> this, they must return through a darkness whose terminus is

amnesia. The darkness which yawns before them is terrifying. It
is the journey back from man to ape. . . . The children of slaves
must sear their memory with a torch. The actor must break up
his body and feed it as ruminatively as ancestral story-tellers fed
twigs to the fire.Those who look from their darkness into the
tribal fire must be bold enough to cross it. (pp. 5-6)

I am immediately reminded of Marlow in Conrad's *Heart of Darkness:* "You
wonder I didn't go ashore for a howl and a dance? Well, no—I didn't. Fine
sentiments, you say? Fine sentiments be hanged! I had no time. . . . I had to watch the
steering and circumvent those snags, and get the tin pot on by hook or by crook.
There was surface truth enough in these things to save a wiser man." But Walcott
observes for us that the surface truth, by keeping us from the dance, the tribal fire, has
indeed *not* saved western culture:

The cult of nakedness in underground theatre, of tribal rock, of
poverty, of rite, is not only nostalgia for innocence but the
enactment of remorse for the genocides of civilization, a search
for the wellspring of tragic joy in ritual, a confession of aboriginal
calamity, for their wars, their concentration camps, their millions
of displaced souls have degraded and shucked the body as food
for the machines. These self-soiling, penitential cults, the Theatre
of the Absurd, the Theatre of Cruelty, the Poor Theatre, the
Holy Theatre, the pseudo-barbarous revivals of primitive tragedy
are not threats to civilization but acts of absolution, gropings for
the outline of pure tragedy, rituals of washing in the first darkness.
Their howls and flagellations are cries to that lost God which they
have pronounced dead, for the God who is offered to slaves must
be served dead, or He may change His chosen people. (p. 6)

Marlow drags Kurtz back from the howl and dance, but he does look over into the
depths where Kurtz fell. And he goes from Africa and Kurtz's black queen to London
and that white lady the "Intended," who is "all in black, with a pale head, floating towards
me in the dusk." Marlow, who hates lies above all else, lies to her for her happiness:

The heavens do not fall for such a trifle. Would they have fallen,
I wonder, if I had rendered Kurtz that justice which was his due?
Hadn't he said he wanted only justice? But I couldn't. I could
not tell her. It would have been too dark—too dark, too dark
altogether. . . .

Surely Marlow is only humane: she could not have understood as Marlow does,
and to crush her would not render justice to Kurtz. But the case of Kurtz (who cried
out "exterminate all the brutes" and who was himself exterminated) *is* symbolically

the case of black and white, slave and master, and it cries out for justice. And so the pale head floating in the dusk must sooner or later be chopped off. That is precisely the climax of *Dream on Monkey Mountain*. As the woman is beheaded, Makak can say, "Now, O God, now I am free."

Marlow, in character, exercises restraint. Makak's beheading of the woman for Makak personally, through his dream, has the effect of ritual sacrifice and absolution, and should also have that effect on the audience, through the dramatic enactment. This beheading is also precisely the climax of Joe Christmas's relationship with Joanna Burden in Faulkner's *Light in August,* but that beheading is represented not ritually but naturalistically; Joe Christmas's life and action carry out the crude raw material of myth and ritual; there is no vicarious sacrifice for Joe Christmas; he is the sacrifice for the community.

All three situations represent justice, for that pale head is in and of us all (black, white, or whatever); the Corporal defines and judges her:

> She is the wife of the devil, the white witch. She is the mirror of
> the moon that this ape look into and find himself unbearable.
> She is all that is pure, all that he cannot reach. You see her statues
> in white stone, and you turn your face away, mixed with
> abhorrence and lust, with destruction and desire. She is lime,
> snow, marble, moonlight, lilies, cloud, foam and bleaching
> cream, the mother of civilization, and the confounder of
> blackness. I too have longed for her. She is the colour of the law,
> religion, paper, art, and if you want peace, if you want to
> discover the beautiful depth of your blackness, nigger, chop off
> her head! When you do this, you will kill Venus, the Virgin, the
> Sleeping Beauty. She is the white light that paralysed your mind,
> that led you into this confusion. It is you who created her, so kill
> her! kill her! The law has spoken. (p. 319)

This seems self-contradictory, but she is the colour of white law, while the law which pronounces, "Kill her!" is black law. The Corporal distinguishes between Roman law and "tribal law," "jungle law." We are reminded of black magic and white, but we live in the realm not of absolute black or white, but of the "tinged with black," tinged with white. To absolute white intellect all magic is black, all flesh is black, all feeling is black. And to absolute black, all unmagical reasoning is "the colour of law, religion, paper, art." When white law is isolated from feeling, flesh, from its blinding light it says, "Restrain, Imprison," and that is why the play begins with Makak brought into a prison cage. And when black law is shackled it must finally break out, "kill her."

The present Black movement is a necessary corrective to the sickly dominance of that white lady. And this is precisely what *Dream on Monkey Mountain* is about. It is true that "white" language has preconceptions, stereotypes, embedded in it, but they may not be so deep, so incapable of correction as black outrage feels—at least, not as far as literature is concerned. The horror of sepulchral white is as old as humanity and it is represented convincingly in works like Melville's. *Dream on Monkey Mountain* is, I think, a classic statement on this subject.

That pale head both must and must not be chopped off. Please—not actually my head or my wife's, or my neighbor's Intended. As Marlow sees, no real justice lies in that—though there are places where it seems that the only approach to justice might have to come through actual violence. That is the point. If it is not done in ritual, in dream, in art, in religion, spiritually, it *will* be done in actuality, or if it is not done it will hold us, as it has and does, in the most awful slavery.

Of course the drama is playing with the idea that the black man, Makak, is closer than the white to our evolutionary primate ancestors (an idea probably invented by white racists). How black man is different from white has infinitely more to do with myths than physiology, but the myths are fascinating—do they come from the built-in psychological archetypes as described by Jung, or from archetypes on the pattern of literary conventions, like those described by Northrop Frye? I am really convinced that Negritude is an invented myth rather than a physiologically based one, but *practically* that couldn't matter less. Practically we have the one extreme of Marlow restrained with the help of nuts and bolts, and the other of the "savages" exulting in the dance, and a multitude caught between—blacks and browns on the weary road to whiteness, the tormented Joe Christmas who doesn't know *what* he is, and Makak and all of us looking toward Africa. One tiny note of real "progress" in the twentieth century has been the beginning questioning in revulsion of the idea of "progress." Inextricably part of this must be the questioning of the preferability of white, as represented by those apparition-ladies, over black as represented by Makak. To become more human—in what is good in the concept of humanity—we must all go back through the tribal fire. But how can we? We can't all go literally back to Africa, as Edward Brathwaite did. We are like poor old Makak; he must go vicariously, back to Monkey Mountain.

To achieve freedom Makak must reject mimicry, his—what shall I call it? "monkeyness." In the Prologue of the play the chorus of judges at Makak's "trial" sings, "Everything I say this monkey does do / I don't know what to say this monkey won't do." But Makak does not altogether deny "monkeyness," for his freedom is precisely achieved through his dream on Monkey Mountain. What of Monkey Mountain he affirms rather than rejects is represented in the "conversion" of Corporal Le Strade:

Corporal:	Grandfather. Grandfather. Where am I? Where is this? Why am I naked?
Makak:	Because like all men you were born here. Here, put this around you. [He covers him with the sack] What is this?
Corporal:	A gun.
Makak:	We don't need this, do we?
[Tigre *and* Souris *approach cautiously*]	
	They reject half of you. We accept All. Rise. Take off your

> boots. Doesn't the floor of the forest feel cool under your
> foot? Don't you hear your own voice in the gibberish of the
> leaves? Look how the trees have opened their arms. And in
> the hoarseness of the rivers, don't you hear the advice of all
> our ancestors. When the moon is hidden, look how you sink,
> forgotten, into the night. The forest claims us all, my son. No
> one needs gloves in his grave. (pp. 300-301)

But Tigre and Souris will not accept the Corporal, and beat him, and so Makak must turn to "jungle law":

> I have brought a dream to my people, and they rejected me. Now
> they must be taught, even tortured, killed. Their skulls will hang
> from my palaces. I will break up their tribes. (p. 301)

But although Makak had earlier broken out momentarily in a regal manner, while he is on the stage as king, the Corporal steals the show, and Makak has little to say: "I am only a shadow." Just before the white apparition is brought in the Corporal condemns Moustique along with all the others, and Moustique says to Makak:

> That is not your voice, you are more of an ape now, a puppet.
> Which lion? [Sings: I don't know *what to say this monkey won't
> do.* . .] (p. 315)

To destroy the moon because it is white is, ironically, still to act as ape—but necessary to his manhood. Makak's dream is full of ironies and conflicts, and Makak is a confused old man—but not just a confused old man; for the conflicting elements of his dream are the conflicting elements of humanity.

In the conclusion of "What the Twilight Says" Walcott writes:

> The last image is of a rain-flushed dawn, after a back-breaking
> night of filming, in a slowly greying field where the sea wind is
> like metal on the cheek. In the litter of the field, among black
> boxes of equipment and yellow, sleekly wet tarpaulins, stands a
> shawled girl caught in that gesture which abstractedly gathers
> cloth to shoulder, her black hair lightly lifting, the tired, pale skin
> flushed, lost in herself and the breaking camp. She was white,
> and that no longer mattered. Her stillness annihilated years of
> anger. His heart thanked her silently from the depth of exhaus-
> tion, for she was one of a small army of his dream. She was a
> vessel caught at the moment of departure of their Muse, her clear
> vacancy the question of a poem which is its own answer. She was
> among the sentries who had watched till dawn. (p. 39)

The essay, like the play, moves from the twilight of nightfall to that of dawn. Hatred and frustration purged and *played* out, that damnable white-goddess ritually killed, Walcott the man can say, "She was white, and that no longer mattered." What does matter is that she is a person, in a relationship: "I am bound within them, neither knowing which is liana or trunk." The solution to racism is not our merging into one neutral likeness. How I admired recently the complexions of two girls together, one white, one black, both beautiful. When white is purged of the meaning of purity so utter it means nothing but death, when black is purged of the stereotype of meaning only outer spiritual darkness, then they no longer matter.

Makak kills the apparition and says, "Oh, God, now I am free," and his next words are in the epilogue: "Felix Hobain, Felix Hobain." He has recovered his real name as a *man*. "My name is Felix Hobain . . . Hobain," he says. "I believe in God. I have never killed a fly." He has killed in his dream, so he has and has not killed (he eats his cake and has it too), and apparently not to have actually killed is just as important to his sense of manhood as is the dream beheading.

The final tone of Makak's experience is acceptance. We've all got to accept the universe, finally; and it can be a despairing acceptance. Makak is threatened with that:

> I was a king among shadows. Either the shadows were real, and I
> was no king, or it is my own kingliness that created the shadows.
> Either way, I am lonely, lost, an old man again. No more. I
> wanted to leave this world. But if the moon is earth's friend, eh,
> Tigre, how can we leave the earth. And the earth, self. Look
> down and there is nothing at our feet. We are wrapped in black
> air, we are black, ourselves shadows in the firelight of the white
> man's mind. Soon, soon it will be morning, praise God, and the
> dream will rise like vapour, the shadows will be real, you will be
> corporal again, you will be thieves, and I an old man, drunk and
> disorderly, beaten down by a Bible, and tired of looking up to
> heaven. You believe I am lost now? Shoot, go ahead and shoot
> me. Death is the last shadow I have made. The Carpenter is
> waiting. (p. 304)

That is what the Corporal will always believe. At the end he has been in Makak's dream, but has had no dream conversion of his own; his tune is still the same:

> Niggers, cannibals, savages! Stop turning this place into a
> stinking zoo. Believe me, old man . . . it have no salvation for
> them, and no hope for us. (pp. 323-4)

The Corporal's role must be an accomplished actor's delight; the Corporal is not an Everyman figure but a whole set of roles; the actor plays an actor who is nothing but an actor and can see no possibility of his being a person. But Makak can reject the mask (of the white apparition) which the Corporal holds out to him:

Makak:	And what day is this?
Corporal:	It is market Saturday, it was, when you came. It is Sunday morning now. [*Singing can be heard.*] That noise is from the Church of Revelation. You want this? [*Makak shakes his head*] (p. 324)

The Corporal's very last words are, "Here is a prison. Our life is a prison. Look is the sun." But Makak's last words, for his kind of acceptance is very different from the Corporal's, are:

> Lord, I have been washed from shore to shore, as a tree in the
> ocean. The branches of my fingers, the roots of my feet, could
> grip nothing, but now, God, they have found ground. Let me be
> swallowed up in mist again, and let me be forgotten, so that
> when the mist open, men can look up, at some small clearing
> with a hut, with a small signal of smoke, and say, "Makak lives
> there. Makak lives where he has always lived, in the dream of his
> people." Other men will come, other prophets will come, and
> they will be stoned, and mocked, and betrayed, but now this old
> hermit is going back home, back to the beginning, to the green
> beginning of this world. Come, Moustique, we going home.
> (p. 326)

Forgive me for quoting so much, but it is all so necessary and inevitable .

Makak has parallels to Christ throughout the play, but not because this is a silly little attempt of Walcott's to plug into some of the power of the Christ myth. Rather, Makak is a true scapegoat figure for us, for our time; if we can imaginatively with him be washed from shore to shore, and with him go home to the green beginning—well we won't be saved; drama and religion are not reunited yet—but we will have had an imaginative contact with damnation and salvation.

The colonies and slaves had to study white culture. Walcott and other West Indian writers of stature are having their revenge; the white culture is now going to have to study theirs. This revenge is a great comic irony, and really, divine comedy, full of grace. For this revenge will be just, not with the justice of retribution, but of rehabilitation. In an ultimate sense we must all be rehabilitated to Monkey Mountain.

These are important plays.

B.
"THE ESTRANGING SEA"
1960-1969

SOME SUBTLETIES OF THE ISLE:
A Commentary on Certain Aspects of Derek Walcott's Sonnet Sequence 'Tales of the Islands'[1]

John Figueroa

> You do yet taste
> Some subtleties o' the isle, that will not let you
> Believe things certain.
> Prospero, *(Tempest* V, I)

I. Introduction

This treatment of Walcott's *Tales of the Islands* forms part of a long study in five parts and was in its substance originally presented at the ACLALS meeting at York University, Toronto, in April 1974.

This particular version deals in detail with the Sonnet Sequence under two perspectives only: one as illustrative of some concerns which seem to appear often in Walcott's work, and two, as a study of the language he uses—bearing in mind the creole/standard continuum and tension that is indigenous to the West Indies.

We first look briefly at a summary of the five perspectives in the original long study and then deal fully with the two mentioned above which in fact appear in the following summary as sections 4 & 5.

(Section 1) Summary of Large Study

The intra-comparative perspective, i.e. *Tales* as a stage in Walcott's development as a poet. This aspect can be looked at first, and less importantly, by comparing some of the earlier versions of this Sonnet Sequence, as published for instance in *Bim,* with the present finished product. Similarly, and more importantly, the jellied texture of the Sequence could be compared with the ragout-like quality of some of the early poems, or with the rather more direct and sparse locutions of later poems.

Tales emphasizes a tendency away from chunky marmalade to a more clarified, though not less nourishing, jelly, from mechanical mixtures (always interesting) to chemical compounds (not as "visible" but more full of controlled usable energy). This tendency goes even further in Walcott's remarkable *Another Life* [2] as the following passage will show, especially when compared with his very early work:

> For I have married one whose darkness is a tree,
> bayed in whose arms I bring my stifled howl,
> love and forgive me!
> Who holds my fears at dusk like birds which take
> the lost or moonlit colour of her leaves,
> in whom our children
> and the children of friends settle
> simply, like rhymes,
> in whose side, in the grim times
> when I cannot see light for the deep leaves,
> sharing her depth, the whole lee ocean grieves.
> (*Another Life,* p. 140)

(Section 2) The Sonnet

The Sonnet Sequence can also be examined from the perspective of the sonnet, and its development. For instance, a careful study of the rhyme schemes in *Tales* seems to indicate a move towards, or at least an experiment with, the substitution of assonance and half-rhymes for the more traditional full and end-stopped rhymes. Further, the formal aspects of sonnets within the sequence are related to the fact that we are dealing with a sequence. The first and last sonnet, for instance, form a firm frame within which the others work. The first introduces the persona, I, the Narrator; and this Narrator returns to prominence in the tenth and final sonnet, having apparently wandered, in the meanwhile, through a path of contemplation where he meets a series of events some of which he simply contemplates, others of which he actually takes part in— as well as contemplates. More relevant to our present concerns is the fact that from the point of view of the sonnet form, the first and last sonnets are, although not regular in rhyme, less experimental than most of the other sonnets, and "feel" more like traditional sonnets. Walcott's use of the "Volta" in *Tales of the Islands* is worth close examination.

(Section 3) The "I" Who Narrates

Tales could also be studied from the point of view of the pattern of appearance, and involvement or non-involvement, of the "I," the persona who narrates. In Chapter I—each sonnet is called a chapter—we start with an "I" who is not merely a Narrator but really an involved persona. In Chapter II no ego persona emerges; in Chapter III, there is a weak appearance; until in Chapter X he reappears fully to contemplate his state of mind on leaving one island for another. There is a meaningful pattern here.

(Section 4) Creole/Standard Tension

Another perspective on the sonnets would be that of the language of the poems in relation to the standard dialect tension which exists throughout the Anglophone Caribbean, and which has been such an embarrassment to some people as to inhibit their language production, and to repress in them all adventure in language usage. Walcott has few inhibitions about using the whole range of his dialects so as to express and embody values and attitudes not otherwise easily expressible. He is also adept at using different registers within each dialect.

V.S. Naipaul, in *The Middle Passage* places the apparent predicament of many in this way:

> The insecure wish to be heroically portrayed. Irony and satire, which might help more, are not acceptable; and no writer wishes to let down his group. For this reason the lively and inventive Trinidad dialect, which has won West Indian writing many friends and as many enemies abroad, is disliked by some West Indians. They do not object to its use locally; the most popular column in Trinidad is a dialect column in the *Evening News* by the talented and witty person known as Macaw. But they object to its use in books which are read abroad. "They must be does talk so by you," one woman said to me. "They don't talk so by me." (pp. 68-9)

Walcott's use of the full range of his language repertory is worthy of the most careful study.

(Section 5) Special Concerns

Finally, the Sonnet Sequence can be examined as illustrative of some of the concerns which seem to appear over and over again in Walcott's work as a poet.

> I thought of nothing; nothing, I prayed, would change

is the second to last line of the sequence, and it is related to the earlier lines

> . . . each mile
> Dividing us and all fidelity strained
> Till space would snap it.

Compare these with

> Nothing her mouth, my east and crimson west,
> Nothing our restless, separated sleep;
> Nothing is bitter and is very deep.
> ("Nearing La Guaira,"
> *In a Green Night,* p. 22)

Again compare

> Teach our philosophy the strength to reach
> Above the navel

and

> The sunwashed body, past the age of sweat
> Sprawls like a hero, curiously inert.

and his eventual departure, at the end of the sonnet with

> The place seemed born for being buried there.
> ("Return to D'Ennery, Rain,"
> *In a Green Night,* p. 33)

and with

> . . . we ask
> O God, where is our home?
> ("Return to D'Ennery, Rain,"
> *In a Green Night,* p. 34)

In fact a subtitle for the Sonnet Sequence could well be *"O God, where is our home?"* provided it be taken to apply not only to the returning persona but to wide sets of situations and personae in *Tales:* to "one of them Oxbridge guys"; to Franklin assaulted by "memories of his own country where he could not die" (Chapter VIII); to Miss Rossignol; to Cosimo de Chrétien; and to many others in *Tales.*

This concern has not been infrequent in Walcott's work and reappears in various ways in his recent *Another Life.*

Despite the ending of *Tales* or because of the cumulative effect of the sequence, we know that his prayer is necessary, but in a sense, vain:

> Then, after a while
> I thought of nothing; nothing, I prayed, would change;

And in *Another Life*, at least in one aspect, one feels that the quest for home is nearer resolution and deepening, and the concern with Nothing gets closer to the Todo y Nada of John of the Cross:

> I leapt for the pride of that race
> at Sauteurs! An urge more than mine,
> so, see them as heroes or as the Gadarene swine,
> let it be written, I shared, I shared,
> I was struck like rock, and I opened to His gift! . . .
>
> O simultaneous stroke of chord and light,
> O tightened nerves to which the soul vibrates,
> some flash of lime-green water, edged with white—
> "I have swallowed all my hates."
> (Chapter 21, *Another Life*,
> pp. 139-40)

A little later in the poem he refers to

> those who remain fascinated,
> in attitudes of prayer

with the past, with the fathers' manacles, those who cry

> . . . at least here
> something happened

and then he says

> they will absolve us, perhaps, . . .
> and then nothing.
> (Chapter 22, section ii,
> *Another Life*, pp. 144-45)

II. Concerns and Language

Detailed Study of sections 4 & 5:

On this occasion we omit 1, 2, and 3 above, and will deal with some of Walcott's main concerns as they show themselves in this Sequence, (5) above, and with his use of the varieties of dialects and registers he so well controls, (4 above).

1. Special Concerns, (section 5 above): "*O God, where is our home?*"

The Sonnet Sequence seems concerned throughout with a kind of heteronomy; the personae seem not really to be in charge of themselves; they are either somewhat displaced, or wandering or looking back to other days—or in a way, each can be seen as

> Peering from balconies for his tragic twist
> (Chapter II, line 14)

Chapter I introduces a sharp division within the Ego-persona, the Narrator:

> Touring its Via Dolorosa I tried to keep
> That chill flesh from my memory

Before these, the 7th and 8th lines, we have had at the very beginning:

> . . . the Dorée rushing cool
> Through gorges of green cedars, like the sound
> Of infant voices from the Mission School, . . .
> The stone cathedral echoes like a well,
> Or as a sunken sea-cave. . . .

The "chill flesh" juxtaposed with "Via Dolorosa" introduces a sharp division, a sharp contrast with the green and gold and the sound of infant voices (from the Mission School—and another green is yet to come, in Chapter IV: the green light in the local bawdy house).

The eleventh line (Chapter I) is

> Teach our philosophy the strength to reach
> Above the navel;

This introduces very early the feel of and for the layered universe, in which the layered persona lives and moves, as we also do; and it is with the delight of self-recognition that we read the first two lines of Chapter II,

> Cosimo de Chrétien controlled a boarding house.
> His maman managed him. No. 13.

And—to run forward a bit—we will move (in Chapter III) from Miss Rossignol's present state

> . . . in the lazaretto
> For Roman Catholic crones; . . .
> . . . tipsy as a bottle when she stalked

to her previous state—her division from herself, her tragic twist, because once

> . . . that flesh knew silk
> Coursing a green estate in gilded coaches.

Indeed, "*O God, where is our home?*" expresses one of the main concerns of this Sonnet Sequence: what are we? Are we what we have been? Where shall we set up our everlasting rest?

But this age-old concern is not reduced in *Tales* to anything as boring, trivial and misleading as racial or national "identity." The sonnets manage to embody universal human concerns in the very context of St. Lucia. From the very streams, earth, "loupgarou" ritual slaughterings, fake tourist posters of the Caribbean, Walcott calls forth the *angst*, the "all fidelity strained," the "nothing" ("Nothing, I prayed, would change") of the human "fête," of the "bare room," which we all enter. For it is our humanity that we taste and shudder at in such lines as those that end in Chapter II.

> Devouring Time, which blunts the Lion's claws,
> Kept Cosimo, count of curios fairly chaste,
> For Mama's sake, for hair oil, and for whist;
> Peering from balconies for his tragic twist.

All of the personae are searching for something; all of them are not quite at home; they are, in a way, in a state of going beyond themselves. They seem to hasten to meet their tragic twist. For instance, the exile

> . . . who fought
> The Falangists en la guerra civil. . .
> now
> . . . past the age of sweat
> Sprawls like a hero, curiously inert.
> (Chapter VIII)

His "sunwashed body" has come to rest—but what a rest!

> In the Hotel Miranda, 10 Grass St., . . .

He, like the Ego-persona, is in exile, but not an exile in his own land as, in a sense, the "Black writer chap" is. Rather this "hero" is more like Franklin in Chapter VII whom

> . . . Each spring, memories
> Of his own country where he could not die
> Assaulted him.

Notice incidentally that most exiles can't *live* in their own country; Franklin can't die there. But his kind of *life* in the new country is limited in the extreme, and his attempt to come awake is pathetic:

> He shook himself. Must breed, drink, rot with motion.
> (Chapter VII)

Whereas

> . . . In the tea-coloured pool, tadpoles
> Seemed happy in their element.

These tadpoles are almost the only "at home" things in the whole Sequence, and yet there is great irony here for their "element" is mud.

There is a twist even in their happiness, for the tea-coloured pool was "blocked by/ Increasing filth." And it is in a kind of mud, "their element," an inactive mud, that they seem *happy*. But for Franklin, of course, the act of coming alive is an active one, but none the less it is an activity taking place in another kind of mud:

> He shook himself. Must breed, drink, rot with motion.

In Chapter IX we have the most powerful example of being displaced, of real wandering beyond one's home, of being an "exile"—"le loupgarou." For here we are told through the "greying woman sewing under the eaves" of

> . . . how his greed had brought old Le Brun down,

of how, in fact,

> He changed himself to an Alsatian hound,
> A slavering lycanthrope hot on a scent,

and with what lasting damage to himself. Le Brun's "tragic twist" is the most startling of all. Yet note where it ends,

> . . . back to its *doorstep*, almost dead.
> (Emphasis added)

His tragic twist is not really of a different order from the kind of displacement embodied in the images which are "Remembered from the dark past whence we come" into the twist by which

> . . . one of the fathers was himself a student
> Of black customs;
> (Chapter V)

and by which the "Black writer chap" thinks that

> . . . 'Each
> Generation has its *angst*, but we has none'

Nor is it too fanciful to see connections between Le Brun "hot on a scent," seeking "knowledge," "satisfaction"—

> Ruined by fiends with whom he'd made a bargain.

—and the main persona, the Narrator, who sought his home-coming where it could no longer be; in a sense, almost sought *his* tragic twist where, in the end, it had to be "folded in cloud,"

> . . . each mile
> Dividing us and all fidelity strained
> Till space would snap it. Then, after a while
> I thought of nothing; nothing, I prayed, would change;
> When we set down at Seawell it had rained.
> (Chapter X)

One is left wondering whether that almost lustral shower, at the end of the Sequence, will be

> . . . a green breath
> Rebuilding a love I thought was dead as nails,
> Blessing the death and the baptism by fire.
> ("A City's Death by Fire,"
> *In a Green Night*, p. 14)

"Where is home?" is not necessarily an easy question for everyone. Only the Jingo nationalist, or racist, is likely to think that the answer to that question is bound to be automatic and very clear. But once one allows the possibility of choice in these matters, and of rising above "right or wrong my country," then the question can be difficult. Even the very meaning of "home" is likely to change, particularly for one who is from that part of the "New World" known as the Caribbean, and has noticed certain tendencies in the *weltanschauung* of the twentieth century.

This concern with home, or with the meaning and, as it were, location of "home," is not uncommon in Walcott's poetry; it shows itself in *Tales of the Islands* partly under the guise of where do we find our being. Is it an attempt to find our "being-there" that tempts us to go beyond ourselves, to peer from balconies for our tragic twist? What is the end of travelling the Via Dolorosa; is it in travelling; in the quest; in the leaving home? This concern together with "Nothing" looms quite large in the poetry of Walcott not only up to the *Gulf*[4] (1969) but also through *Another Life*

(1973). Further, it comes up in a special way in the splendid Introduction to *Dream on Monkey Mountain* (1970):

> Pastoralists of the African revival should know that what is needed is not new names for old things, or old names for old things, but the faith of using the old names anew, so that mongrel as I am, something prickles in me when I see the word Ashanti as with the word Warwickshire, both separately intimating my grandfathers' roots, both baptising this neither proud nor ashamed bastard, this hybrid, this West Indian. (p. 10)

Walcott has earlier touched upon this concern in "The Train"; as he travels on a train in England he asks

> Where was my randy white grandsire from?
> He left here a century ago
> to found his 'farm,' . . .

> Black with despair
> he set his flesh on fire,
> blackening, a tree of flame.
> That's hell enough for here.
> His blood burns through me as this engine races,
> my skin sears like a hairshirt with his name.
> On the bleak Sunday platform
> the guiltless, staring faces
> divide like tracks before me as I come.
> Like you, grandfather, I cannot change places,
> I am half-home.
> ("The Train," from *The Gulf*, p. 54)

Another Life was written April 1965-April 1972, and published in 1973. Since it deals partly with his growing up, many of the old concerns reappear, but, as would be expected, they also have grown. This is particularly true of his concern with "Nothing," which as has been pointed out, is strongly heard in "Nearing La Guaira," and comes out in the last sonnet of *Tales*; as we will shortly see, it has taken on a new form in *Another Life*.

One of the sonnets originally published in *Bim*, along with early versions of Chapters VI and VIII, and at that time apparently meant for *Tales*, was replaced in the Sequence. It now turns up on p. 113 of *Another Life* in a slightly altered form. It was originally to be number X, and significantly bore the epigraph "You can't go home again." Moreover the present Chapter X appears very slightly altered, on p. 115 of *Another Life* incorporated into the end of Part Three, which is subtitled "A Simple Flame," linking it, at one level with the disastrous fire in the Castries of

Walcott's youth—that fire which he celebrated in his youthful poem "A City's Death by Fire" which started

After that hot gospeller had levelled all but the churched sky,

and *fourteen lines* after ended

Blessing the death and the baptism by fire.

We have incidentally touched upon but cannot now further examine, one of Walcott's ways of working. He obviously reconsiders, rewrites, reincorporates; one of the sonnets in *Tales*, Chapter VII, subtitled 'Lotus eater,' brings forward

Franklin . . .
. . . Each spring, memories
Of his own country where he could not die
Assaulted him.

Walcott was later to write a play called *Franklin, a Tale of the Island.* Much of it is about a man who just could not leave the island, which was and was not his home. And *Another Life* picks on the concern shown in "The Train" in this way

But I tired of your whining, grandfather, . . .
I tired of your groans, . . .
I cursed what the elm remembers,
I hoped . . .
for the sea to erase
those names a thin,
tortured child, kneeling, wrote
on his slate of wet sand.
(Part Two, Chapter 10,
section iv, *Another Life*, p. 67)

The concern with "Home" appears at a somewhat different level in Walcott's "A Letter from Brooklyn" which is really a most moving poem, and appears in his earliest collection, *In a Green Night: Poems 1948-1960.*

In that collection we have another aspect of this same theme in his well-known lines

(a) Where shall I turn, divided to the vein?
("A Far Cry from Africa,"
from *In a Green Night*, p. 18)

(b) All in compassion ends

So differently from what the heart arranged:
'as well as if a manor of thy friend's . . .'
("Ruins of a Great House,"
from *In a Green Night*, p. 20)

We shall not pause long over these as they are well known and have even been, in
a sense, the cause of controversy, because some have found them not to be side-
taking, to be too understanding. "All in compassion ends" has, in one's experience,
caused quite a furor among certain blacks in New York.

In these quotations we have once again the concern with "home" and with the
travelling, the journeying—to what end, to whose home? Always towards some sort
of twist, though not necessarily, as appears to be the case in *Tales of the Islands*, a tragic
twist.

The answer to the question posed in "where shall I turn. . ." is an awareness and
acceptance of both the Kikuyu slaughter and the drunken officer of British rule, of
the question necessary, but inherently not answerable on a *simplistic* basis:

. . . how choose
Between this Africa and the English tongue I love? (p. 18)

And in "(b)" we have the journey of experience, awakened, and symbolized, by the
Great House, ending, not in hatred, although hatred has been aroused, but in
understanding,

So differently from what the heart arranged:

Despite the ending of *Tales*, or because of the cumulative effect of the sequence,
we know that his prayer is necessary, but in a sense vain:

. . . Then, after a while
I thought of nothing; nothing, I prayed, would change;
(Chapter X)

It is not possible for nothing not to change once the plane turns to the final north;
fidelity must be strained even when we return

. . . trailing wet
With blood back to its doorstep, almost dead.
(Chapter IX)

Nothing is bitter and is very deep.
("Nearing La Guaira,"
In a Green Night, p. 22)

In a way, *Tales of the Islands* is a sort of transition between the concerns evident in "Nearing La Guaira" (written about 1955) and those coming to life in "A Letter from Brooklyn." But in the "letter" the coming home is in the realm—as it might always have to be—of faith, dedication, and a transmogrification of the everyday world of experience.

> 'I am Mable Rawlins,' she writes, 'and know both your parents;'
> He is dead, Miss Rawlins, but God bless your tense:
> . . . .
> 'He is twenty-eight years buried,' she writes, 'he was called home. . . .'

Here we have, persuasively put in the mouth of an old lady, ("Of her I remember small, buttoned boots") another answer to "where is our home":

> 'He is twenty-eight years buried,' she writes, 'he was called home. . . .'
>
> Heaven is to her the place where painters go,
> (from "A Letter from Brooklyn,"
> *In a Green Night*, p. 53)

In *Another Life*, at least in one aspect, one feels that the idea of the quest for home is being deepened, that the concern with Nothing is also changing, coming closer to the Todo y Nada of St. John of the Cross.[6] The meaning of place and history is not solved simplistically but enriched and accepted in all its complications; nothing is no longer only the experience of the negative, the depriving, the bitter. It is at the very least, the emptying that is the necessary condition of creativity, of the fresh start.

So we read:

> I leapt for the pride of that race
> at Sauteurs! An urge more than mine,
> so, see them as heroes or as the Gadarene swine,
> let it be written, I shared, I shared,
> I was struck like rock, and I opened
> to His gift!
> . . . .
>
> O simultaneous stroke of chord and light,
> O tightened nerves to which the soul vibrates,
> some flash of lime-green water, edged with white—
> 'I have swallowed all my hates.'

A little later in the poem he refers to:

> those who remain fascinated,
>   in attitudes of prayer

fascinated with the past, with their father's manacles, those who cry

> . . .at least here
> something happened—
> they will absolve us, perhaps, if we begin again,
> from what we have always known, nothing,
> from that carnal slime of the garden,
> from the incarnate subtlety of the snake,
> from the Egyptian moment of the heron's foot
> on the mud's entablature,
> by this augury of ibises
> flying at evening from the melting trees,
> while the silver-hammered charger of the marsh light
> brings towards us, again and again, in beaten scrolls,
> nothing, then nothing,
> and then nothing.
> (Chapter 21, section iii, and Chapter 22,
> section ii, from *Another Life*, pp. 139-45)

But, as I hope to show at the very end, as well as cumulatively, the dislocation, and "tragic twist," and "nothing," of *Tales of the Islands* is not a merely negative concern. It is a deep self-knowledge, and a society knowledge. It is absolutely necessary, though none the less *harrowing* for that reason!

For we also read in *Another Life*:

> Anna, I wanted to grow white-haired
> as the wave, with a wrinkled
>
> brown rock's face, salted
> seamed, an old poet,
> facing the wind
>
> and nothing, which is,
> the loud world in his mind.
> (Chapter 22, section vi, *Another Life*, p. 148)

2. Language, (section 4, above)

Let us turn our attention now to the language of *Tales* inasmuch as that language exhibits a variety of registers and relates to the "standard" dialect tension which exists throughout the Anglophone Caribbean. Walcott shows, in this Sonnet Sequence, and elsewhere, a remarkable control of a remarkable variety not only of registers and styles, but also of dialects.

Clearly, "being at home" or being uneasily *not* "at home" or being consciously "half-home" are all connected with language. (The concern with "good language" and with "broken English," and with "the dialect"—a concern noted by Naipaul, Rex Nettleford, Mervyn Morris et al.—is connected with the question of *Home.*) For we do not feel comfortable, to be in command, or at least not to be at a loss, whenever our language antennae cannot pick up with ease and accuracy the subtle movements in the ether of the spiritual environment.

I have dealt previously[7] with the use which Walcott makes in Chapter VI of a wide language continuum comparing it with Evan Jones's work. He goes through the exclamatory creole of "Poopa, da' was a fête!" to the idiomatic creole of "it had / Free rum free whisky . . ." to the colloquial standard (but not unaffected by creole and creole intonation) "everywhere you turn," which stands cheek and jowl with the creole syntax "was people eating/ And drinking." He then introduces the creole lexicon by way of "tests" ("with two tests up the beach") and makes a telling point by having the "Black writer chap" unintentionally break into creole just when he is being most pretentious and pontifical:

> . . . quoting Shelley with 'Each
> Generation has its angst, but we has none'
> (Chapter VI)

(has we not? one is tempted to ask). Walcott then for the next five lines uses standard syntax, lexicon, intonation and sonority, but ends on a slightly slangy (but standard) note.

He sharpens the irony of the situation by his use of the slangy "jump and jive" especially as this phrase appears in juxtaposition to the more weighty "But that was long before." He does not hesitate to place "chap" and "guys" within a single line. Furthermore, the language uses referred to here and above are not mere variations of alternatives; they are meaningful, substantive uses which gain and mean more by being structured together. This structuring arises not only out of being used as part of the formal construct of a sonnet, but also because of the immediate shape of what is about to be expressed and is being expressed. The sonnet (Chapter VI) is framed, both in ironic significance and in expressive intention, by two phrases:

> Poopa, da' was a fête . . .

at the very beginning and

> . . . before this jump and jive

at the very end.

These variations are part and parcel of the meaning and the message. For here "the medium is very much the message." The remarkable thing to be noted and studied linguistically is that Walcott (in Chapter VI) has exploited a wide area of the language medium, which he controls so well.

What Walcott's control of the dialects and languages (and his use of them) should signify to the Caribbean person is that *here* in this kind of language situation is he really *at home!* And when he has to, or chooses (as is his right) to use only one section of the language(s) he controls, he is necessarily limiting both his expressive and communicative resources. Of course, questions of *context* and *audience* loom very large here, underlining the excruciating problem of any Anglophone Caribbean writer who has so constantly to write mainly for those who really know only one small section of the creole/standard continuum.

It is interesting that the other sonnet in which this kind of language usage is seen is in Chapter IV which is subtitled "Dance of Death." In it, in a sense, the heart of a young child is being torn from it alive: "Y'all too obscene" on the one hand, and, on the other, the smart aleck: "Don't worry, kid, the wages of sin is birth."

With respect to Walcott's use of a variety of levels of language, let us further note that those subtitles of the Chapters which appear in French are not in French for an exotic, learned or courtly effect. In the St. Lucia scene the exotic would be to subtitle them all in English. And the feeling of return to home and at the same time of displacement must call for, lean upon, and evoke the mixed language situation. But we are not to be left with a generalized mixed language situation, but rather with those specifics which give meaning to a deeply complex situation, which again is ever individualized, made specific and so used to be, and to embody, what is often an excruciatingly exact but subtle, direct but ambivalent, disturbance of our human sensitivity.

> . . . He watched the malarial light
> Shiver the canes . . .
> He shook himself. Must breed, drink, rot with motion.
> (Chapter VII)

In fact, the specificity of each of the poetic acts and processes, which go to make up this Sequence, is what makes a constant rereading of the text itself so urgent. It also makes copious quotations necessary; just as it makes useful critical comment more difficult. It also focuses on the difficulty of the kind of comment or interpretation which rests heavily on general psychological insights, such as archetypes, or on general ideological or mythic concerns.

For instance, to digress from our present concern with language for a moment, the rain falls on two occasions at the end of a chapter. But this natural phenomenon, not incapable of bearing deep symbolic meaning, has quite different feeling-tone on each occasion. At the end of Chapter IV "Dance of Death" the young men are leaving the brothel. The Narrator, who just has returned home is recalling an event in his early life before he had gone out beyond his island:

> . . . 'Our mother earth,'
> I said. 'The great republic in whose womb
> The dead outvote the quick.' 'Y'all too obscene,'
> The Indian laughed. . . .
> . . . We entered the bare room.
> In the rain, walking home, was worried, . . .

The same "event" of rain falling at the end of a significant incident has quite a different feeling when it comes at the end of Chapter X, ('Adieu foulard'), which is also the end of the Sequence:

> . . . Then, after a while
> I thought of nothing; nothing, I prayed, would change;
> When we set down at Seawell it had rained.

Seawell is the airport in Barbados; a new world, so different from St. Lucia, is there touched and set upon—". . . it had rained." There is here almost a ritual washing, "after the fashion of the Jews," now at the end of the long journey; an ablution, an absolution—a bath after adultery. But also the tautness of "all fidelity strained" has been left behind: now there is, not the glare of bright, cloudless harsh light, but the feeling of muted colors just after the rain; consummation; a coming. . . .

> . . . each mile
> Dividing us and all fidelity strained
> . . . Then, after a while
> I thought of nothing . . .
> . . .it had rained.

We must now return to the other *specificities* and particularly to language. Chapter VII—"Must breed, drink, rot with motion."—has for its subtitle 'Lotus eater.' And the name of the man lost in that lotus land is Franklin, an English-sounding name, despite its semantic content, a stranger who is assaulted each spring with memories. . .

> Franklin gripped the bridge-stanchions with a hand
> Trembling from fever.

Notice that "Chapter," subtitle, or epigraph, wherever it appears has a significant, and often highly ironic, relationship with its sonnet. Only two are in English: "Lotus eater" (note the singular) in Chapter VII for Franklin; and "Dance of Death" in Chapter IV with its line "the wages of sin is birth."

The others are

| La rivère dorée. . . | Chapter I |
| 'Qu'un sange impur. . . | Chapter II |

La belle qui fut . . .	Chapter III
moeurs anciennes'	Chapter V
'Le loupgarou'	Chapter IX
'Adieu foulard . . .'	Chapter X

Although Chapter I (La rivière dorée. . .) is written in quite straightforward "Standard English," it does convey the feeling of a place not quite "English," of, in fact, that mixed language—culture background of St. Lucia to which reference has been made before. This is done mainly by the introduction not only of the French subtitle, but also within the first four lines of "Dorée" ("the Dorée rushing cool") with "ici, Choiseul."

"Dorée" is of course but a name, albeit a French name, but the use of "ici" in the second phrase quoted, suggests a consciousness which, in identifying to itself just where it finds itself, has to fall back upon not only a French name, not only on "Choiseul," as the place it recognized, but also on the full phrase as the recognition is accepted, ("ici, Choiseul").

Like leaves like dim seas in the mind; ici, Choseul.

The non-Anglo-Saxon feeling is further aided by the introduction of "Via Dolorosa," "a Sancta Teresa" (in her nest of light)

The cherub, shaft upraised, parting her breast.

The specific ambience, feel of a place like St. Lucia is suggested, subtly, not only in the instances just quoted, but also in:

. . . like the sound
Of infant voices from the Mission School

and

. . .black bodies, wet with light, . . .

The directness of the sentence structure, the lack of inversions, together with the comparative simplicity of the flow of sentences, plus the use of "I" help the impression remarked upon earlier, that the opening sonnet, together with the last, form a firm framework for the rest. Within this sonnet itself, Chapter I, the first two lines and the last two lines likewise work together to enclose the rest.

"The marl white road" (the first half of the first line) is contrasted with "black bodies, wet with light" (the second half of the penultimate line); but "the Dorée rushing cool" (the second half of the first line which introduces the water theme, the wetness contrasted with the dry marl) is continued and reinforced by the last line of the sonnet:

> Rolled in the spray as I strolled up the beach.

In this, the first of the Sequence, the feeling that an opening melody is being introduced, that a first plateau is being reached on which further developments will take place, is communicated not only by the semantic contrast but also by the tone and intonation of the language.

> Teach our philosophy the strength to reach
> Above the navel . . .

We have not only internal rhymes, but also the magisterial invocation with its inversion of the verb position to the powerful beginning of the sentence, and to the beginning of the line, where the previous line has been end-stopped.

Chapter II ('Qu'un sang impur. . .') is also in fairly straightforward "Standard English"; the language level is even, but once again the non-Englishness of the locale is conveyed semantically rather than structurally or supra-segmentally.

We have, for instance, *perroquet*, which certainly is more often known in English as *parakeet*. As the O.U.D. has it: "Parakeet, also paroquet etc. 1581 1/2." The historical forms are of three types:

> (a) O. F. *paraquet*, F. *perroquet* parrot; (b) from its possible source It. *parrochett*, dim. of *parroco* parson (cf. F. *moineau* sparrow, fr. *moine* monk) (c) Anglicized forms of these typified by *parakeet.*

Notice, we do not have one of the "anglicized forms" here, but the French historical form *perroquet*, which if used in the Jamaican or Barbadian situation, could, I think, be quite rightly considered affected or purposely *quaint*. Not so in this sonnet where we also find Cosimo de Chrétien; maman; Rue St. Louis; French barquentine; count and lineage. The first listed, who is a "count," is a good reminder that it is not only in St. Lucia that the French language and the "English" had to interact, co-exist, and bring forth good fruit. It is a moot point, of course, which one dominated, so that "naught nowhere never was to be found!"

Of "count," incidentally, let it be noted that O.U.D. says

> Count 1553 a AF, counte=O.F. cunte, conte. . .

Unlike Countess the word never passed into English till used in the sixteenth century to represent "Fr. conte . . .A foreign title . . ."

"It had" in line 3, especially coming after "Rue St. Louis," has a slightly unstandard sound; in fact it has a strong creole overtone, well suited to this displaced count's dwelling, this count of curios who somewhat like his parsonic parroquet is

> Peering from balconies for his tragic twist.

In Chapter III ("La belle qui fut . . .") we do have the name Miss Rossignol. Otherwise the language appears straightforward and "standard" but there are a few cases of tense which seem worth looking at.

> (1) My mother warned us how that flesh knew silk
> Coursing a green estate in gilded coaches.

and

> (2) Whose pride had paupered beauty to this witch
> Who was so fine once, whose hands were so soft.

In (1) "that flesh knew silk" reads somewhat awkwardly; the sequence of tenses, even allowing for "poetic license," seems unstandard, but unfortunately not deliberately so. What we need is "that flesh had known silk." To say

> My mother warned us how that flesh knew silk

is to suggest, in standard usage, it seems to me, that the lady in question, Miss Rossignol, is knowing silk at the time that the mother is warning; this is clearly not the sense intended, as is clear from the whole poem but particularly in (2) where "once" is called upon to reinforce the anteriority of her having been "so fine." (2) also is awkwardly phrased; the last line is rhythmically weak—ten monosyllables all in a row. Further, coming after "Sang to her one dead child," "whose hands were so soft" suggests that the hands are now soft, that is, are so soft while she was singing in the cathedral loft. But this is hardly what is to be conveyed.

Creole languages in the West Indies are notoriously problematic with respect to indicating shades of tense through the morphology of the words. In the above it could just be that "my mother," suggesting psychologically the creole influence—she would have spoken, one supposes, various forms of creole—that "my mother" influences the tense marker to be "knew" rather than "known." However, this kind of explanation would not hold for (2).

It is that a poet, working within the limiting and releasing confines of the sonnet structure, might well be expected not to be completely circumspect about his tenses, or is it that the creole tense systems have affected, perhaps at an unconscious level, even such an *aficionado* of English English as Derek Walcott?

Of the one hundred and six words used all seem quite standard, and some eighty-two of them are used once only.

Chapter IV is clearly made up of a variety of dialects and of formality within even one dialect. Of its one hundred and sixteen words eighty are used only once, and a number can be immediately identified as being either West Indian or "informal standard": "'He's a damned epileptic'; 'Let's join . . .'; '*The beer and all looked green*';[8] 'The next talked . . .'; 'Y'all too obscene'; 'Y'all . . . ain't worth the trouble'; 'Don't worry kid.'"

There are in this sonnet some thirty-one words which can be grouped in the informal "non-standard" category; which is fairly high out of a total of one hundred and sixteen words, since there is anyway a certain common ground between the Creole-English occurrences and those of "Standard English." Specifically West Indian in tone are

> We all looked green. The *beer and all* looked green . . . .[9]
> The next talked politics . . . .
> . . . 'Y'all too obscene,'
> . . . 'Y'all college boys ain't worth the trouble.'

And sort of quasi, "take off" West Indian is also

> 'Don't worry, kid, the wages of sin is birth.'

The question that arises about the dialect-mix here is to what extent it is used to gain verisimilitude, and to what extent really to deepen insight and embody significant meaning. There is an element of verisimilitude. Two very young men are speaking, first outside a brothel, then with "les girls" inside, and then outside "In the rain, walking home." So they, coming from a mixed language background, in which Standard English is not standard for intimate chatter and banter, would not be expected, even within the formal confines of a sonnet, to be uniformly standard. The situation would look forced and would lack verisimilitude if they "stuck to standard."

But there is more to it than that. The persona who has returned to his native island is recalling an incident in his youth, when in fact, not unlike the lamb in Chapter V, he had been led to the slaughter (one feels, partly for the satisfaction of the onlooker and initiator, Doc) almost "for the approval of some anthropologist" (Chapter V, 2nd line). So that it adds a further aspect of meaning when Doc says:

> 'Don't worry, kid, the wages of sin is birth.'

Similarly, the voice in recalling his youthful inexperience, gives itself that kind of bravado, of "he-man" talk which would not easily have come to him in the "standard."

> . . . 'He's a damned epileptic
> Your boy, El Greco! Goya, he don't lie.'

Notice here that there is a significant tension set up between the quasi learnedness of the art talk—El Greco and Goya—and "he don't lie." Nor is it only the use of the names which contrasts meaningfully with the "he don't lie"; it is also the quasi "being on the inside," of being really able to *explain*, which strikes off "He's a damned epileptic." Further note how his inexperience and displacement come out in:

> . . . In the queer light
> We all looked green. The beer and all looked green.

The last sentence of the quotation really phrases it in a way appropriate to the intimacy and strangeness of the surroundings: this kind of verbalization suits perfectly the situation and the awakening consciousness of the young man, whose very being grows in, and out of, the mixed "creole" standard background.

So the mixture of language levels which appears in Chapter IV is not then only for "added interest," or to entertain those who like the "exotic" ("What is your native dress?"), nor is it there only to make the scene more acceptable, more probable, more "true to life" in a limited sense. Rather the language is used to embody and show forth, in a structured meaningful way, a certain consciousness and experience which can only be fully embodied by the use of a variety of dialects and registers.

In Chapter V ('moeurs anciennes') we return to a fairly straightforward, unmixed, "standard" language use. But even here at the very beginning of the sonnet, we have the West Indian word "fête." Of course it is an acceptable word elsewhere, but in the Eastern Caribbean it does not signify what we used to call "garden fêtes" during my Jamaican boyhood. The word fête which is usually applied, in the Eastern Caribbean, to a rather lively get-together, at which drink, dance, loud talk, and an amorous situation or two, are *de rigeur*, has wide application, not unlike the word "party" in England. "Where's the fête?" and "Who's giving the party?" are almost congruent. Of course, no one has yet invented a "reading fête" in the West Indies!

But there is an irony in referring to the reenacting of the "moeurs anciennes" as "the fête."

> The fête took place one morning in the heights
> For the approval of some anthropologist.

And this ironic twist, indicated early by the use of that West Indian word, is intensified by the use of a fairly slangy standard English word:

> The whole thing was more like a *bloody* picnic.[10]

One should also notice that, of course, "white rum" as used here is a particularly West Indian locution, not unconnected with "brawling." And once again it is wholly appropriate . . . , so appropriate that one might miss the appropriateness of its use, but hardly the non-Englishness of its intonation.

Finally, the last line calls upon another part of the oral tradition of the West Indies, a very English, and slightly comic part, but a very genuine part: "Great stuff, old boy"; and then turns, through semantic suggestion, rather than language mixture, to a very un-English image: "sacrifice, moments of truth," where the reality giving that part of the image vigour and resonance is the bullfight, a ritual, "a bloody picnic," "Dancing with absolutely natural grace," "savage rites / In a Catholic country." A bullfight is very nearly a certain kind of fête!

Of the one hundred and eleven words used in Chapter V, some seventy-eight appear only once, and only two are particularly West Indian, but, as shown above, they are important to the overall effect, as is the occasional shift of register, within the Standard English used. Comparatively "unimportant" words, such as particles, occur more frequently than in the other sonnets: (the) seven times; (a) four times; (of) four times. Chapter VI has been dealt with at length in Volume II of my *Caribbean Voices*.[11]

Chapter VII (Lotus eater . . .) is very nearly as English as its subtitle. Maingot, the name given by the fisherman to "that pool blocked by / Increasing filth" is the only French-sounding word in the sonnet, and there seems to be nothing particularly creole about the language. "Composition of place" is given semantically rather than structurally or suprasegmentally: "filth that piled between ocean / And jungle," "dry bamboo," "Through urine-stunted trees / A mud path wriggled," "Poor, black souls."

Of the one hundred and sixteen words used in this sonnet, some eighty-three are used once only; there appear to be no particular creole words or structures. Chapter VIII has no subtitle, and from the point of view of the creole "standard," tension and mixture is unremarkable. However, it does suggest the extraordinary variety of the cultural situation through which the consciousness of the Narrator has passed. We now find added to the previously met "black bodies wet with light," Cosimo de Chrétien, count of curios, Miss Rossignol, the Indian girl, the ritualists, the anthropologist, the Oxbridge guy, "some fellars beating / Pan from one of them band in Trinidad" and Franklin—added to all these we now find the Spanish and Jewish element: Hotel Miranda (this exile) "who fought / The falangists en la guerra civil"; "with the wry face of a Jew"; and "an ant, caballo, rides"; "a dish of olives." But not only is the strong cultural heterogeneity stressed, the figure and theme of the exile is reinforced:

> The sunwashed body, past the age of sweat
> Sprawls like a hero, curiously inert.

And in the distance

> . . . a girl plays
> A marching song not often sung these days.

Of the one hundred and eleven words in this sonnet, some eighty-six are used only once; no creole words appear. But the first six lines, while in no way non-standard, are curious in their syntax.

This Chapter VIII is very much the creation of a painter[12] and the first long clause stretching five lines, from "in the Hotel Miranda" to "his pamphlets," gives a feeling of the static. The inverted and rather involuted syntax helps this static impression, for we wait for six lines for the closure and full point of the first sentence. The exile has, unlike other exiles, at last come to rest, "curiously inert."

Near him a dish of olives has turned sour.

Chapter IX ('Le loupgarou'), while not simple, is syntactically direct and standard. There is a slightly awkward use of the colloquial "was how."

A curious tale . . .
Was how his greed had brought old Le Brun down, . . .

Note the one "French" touch of the name Le Brun, and that here we have "had brought" rather than simply "brought" which would have been more in keeping with the form used, and commented upon in Chapter III, line 9 ("how that flesh knew silk").

Of the one hundred and six words used in this sonnet as many as eighty-nine are not repeated—a higher density of "new words" than in the other sonnets. This is even more so inasmuch as "a" is repeated six times. One of the repetitions, that of "its," is very effective as it helps with giving the impression of the total displacement of Le Brun, of, in fact, his exile to the realm of the non-human.

He changed himself to an Alsatian hound,
....
But his own watchman dealt the thing a wound
Which howled and lugged its entrails, trailing wet
With blood back to its doorstep, almost dead.

Note. ". . . his own watchman dealt the thing a wound" and then we move to "its entrails." Partly because of the word "entrails," the "its" does not hit as hard as it does in "its doorstep," "doorstep" being in every way much more civilized, human and humane in its overtones than "entrails." The antithesis of "its" with "doorstep" is particularly effective.

Certainly Walcott's use here of "the thing" must be one of the best examples in literature of the extent to which the sharpness, and propriety, of an image need not depend on visual sharpness, or visual suggestivity, but can be pointedly effective through a process of "concept reduction" or, as Shakespeare has it, by being "Diminished."[13]

Chapter X ("Adieu foulard . . .')[14] is straightforward in its syntax and seems to have no trace of creole, nor any shift in register. It is the final sonnet in the Sequence and has the touching dignity and sadness of the last post. The shape of the first sentence underlines this valedictory quality; the poem starts: "I watched the island . . ."; in the middle of the fourth line the same form is repeated. "I watched . . ."; again in the middle of the eighth line we have "I watched . . . the shallow green." All these phrases begin sentences. We later, at the end of the sonnet, have "I" plus the past tense repeated, but the shape of the sentence is slightly different.

. . . Then, after a while
I though of nothing; nothing, I prayed, would change. . . .

Of the one hundred and ten words in this sonnet, some seventy-seven occur only once. What is interesting is the words which are repeated. In this strongly valedictory sonnet, in which the persona-Narrator states clearly a position and his involvement in it, "I" is repeated six times in all, twice in the penultimate line. "Nothing" is also repeated twice in that penultimate line. "Watched" is used three times (each time, of course, with "I"—"I watched"); and "till" three times. "Turned," like "nothing," is used twice in the same line.

The last line achieves a certain kind of objectivity, in contrast to the strong personal-subjective tone of the first thirteen lines. This is done partly by the image "it had rained" in conjunction with "Seawell" as has been discussed above.

But the calm and finality and switch to the solid outside world is also achieved by the move from "I" to "we"; and then to the impersonal:

> When we set down at Seawell it had rained.

III. Conclusion

> ... the isle is full of noises
> Sounds, and sweet airs, that give delight and hurt not ...
>
>   When I waked,
> I cried to dream again. ...
> (*The Tempest*)

Before concluding this long study we should call to mind (gratefully?) that it is but two fifths of a longer study! Except by implication and suggestion we have not touched upon the central points mentioned in summary fashion in Part I, sections 1, 2, & 3. So that we have in no way dwelt upon the many aspects of *Tales* as a stage in oeuvre of the poet; nor have we examined his "technical" and meaningful development and stretching of the sonnet form. Further, we have not examined the interesting pattern of appearance and nonappearance of the "I" Narrator throughout the Sequence. These have all been worked upon carefully elsewhere, but could not, in all conscience, have been included in this already long essay. But the Sequence seems to me central enough to Walcott's work and development as a poet, and outstanding enough as poetry, to warrant a few concluding comments.

"Exultent insulae; let the islands rejoice." In olden days, in St. John of the Cross, and in the Old Testament before him, there was a fascination with "strange islands." In modern days it is no different; tourist boards recommend the Greek or the Caribbean Islands; and for a long time the "South Sea" islands, and then the Hawaiian, were put forward as the new Paradise. And now, on the left, Cuba! It would be fascinating to trace the attraction which islands have held for so many—not least of all the West Indian islands. It might be that a certain security, in the days

before planes, rockets, or even steamships, attached to the isolation of an island; this
isolation by being whole (not peninsular) was not only secure, but also integral.[15] It
might be also that islands tend to be small and perhaps more easily "identified with,"
and certainly not too difficult to "sail all around; to get a feeling of, to come to know."
And in the far reaches of the vast oceans a shipwrecked man could only hope for an
island. But, perhaps, tired of the ways of man, he hoped for an empty island, even as
tourists, flocking in their millions, still speak of finding some "unspoilt" place.

This is the strength and flavour as well as drawback and potential weakness of
islands: they must sooner or later bring their people into close daily contact with each
other. The quality of this contact and of this living together, especially in the only
world we know, where competition of ideologies, of commerce, of political units
tends to keep people in tightly competing groups—the quality of being pressed
together can be oppressive, frustrating, confusing, even when it is at the same time
intimate, warm and public. At least as much as other islands, those of the West Indies
have often appeared to their children to be dry nurses or constantly intruding
mothers. Again, the mixtures of the cultures, of languages; the history of bloodshed,
exploitation, self-doubt and heteronomy, and of growth and endurance have all made
of the Caribbean islands *potentially* a really new world, but actually, only too often, a
very un-brave world from which escape seems the only answer.

The islander, shipwrecked on his own shores, longs for the ocean—where is home?
Within this context we find *Tales of the Islands*. Within this context we must read it.
The Sequence is really one of illumination and recognition of the "tragic twist" so
often only seen as a series of "moments of truth"—great stuff! Illumination with
respect to the scenes, the activities, the "realities" of the living and the dead—"The
great republic in whose womb / The dead outvote the quick"; but also the recognition
by the narrator-persona of certain things about himself:

> . . . I tried to keep
> That chill flesh from my memory . . .

> Teach our philosophy the strength to reach
> Above the navel;

> . . . until all that I love
> Folded in cloud;

> . . . each mile
> Dividing us and all fidelity strained
> Till space would snap it. Then, after a while
> I thought of nothing; nothing, I prayed, would change. . . .

Recognition of the true situation of the inner self is the first necessary step. Le Brun,
we have every reason to believe, hardly recognizes the role which his "bargain" had played
in his life; it reduced him to a thing, "trailing wet / With blood"; "A dying man licensed

to sell sick fruit." The "exile" in Chapter VIII is "past the age of sweat," beyond the toil, beyond the exertion, beyond the response to the sun; beyond, in fact, knowing what the situation is: he cannot know that there is some grace, some life out there—

> . . . the children's street cries, a girl plays
> A marching song not often sung these days.

But Miss Rossignol and Franklin have a life of some kind; the former suffered for one she loved; the latter stirs himself even if only to "breed, drink, rot with motion."

Some sort of grace visits Miss Rossignol, crone though she is; and she has movement. And an element of grace moves also through Chapter V, 'moeurs anciennes'

> Dancing with absolutely natural grace
> Remembered from the dark past whence we come.

All of the personae seem to be attempting to transcend themselves, to be other than themselves; they all have, or are looking for, their tragic twist. The Oxbridge guy has bought, with one half of himself, the notion of the tourist island *without angst*; but his slip in speech shows how thin the facade is, the facade that separates all kinds of fêtes from each other—"jump and jive"; rolling with tests on the beach while one's husband drinks himself drunk because he is so happy, happy! And that particular fête not unlike a bloody picnic in which

> . . . the heart
> Of a young child was torn from it alive
> By two practitioners of native art. . . .

The facades (and the fêtes) separate people from people, groups from groups, often in the very act of bringing them together!

Transcendence is a kind of alienation, and vice versa. It is more easy, it appears, to try to be something else rather than to remake one's self. And in any case fate exiles us often: Franklin, the hero of la guerra civil, Miss Rossignol. Sometimes we make a bargain as old Le Brun did, because we are "hot on a scent"; we all seem anxious to join the count of curios

> Peering from balconies for his tragic twist.

But what of the Narrator-persona? Has he made a bargain? He too is leaving his usual estate; he has walked the path and has seen and acted, and now as he leaves he watches

> . . . till the plane
> Turned to the final north

> . . . until all that I love
> Folded in cloud. . . .

He has left all that he loves; for he must; and once again he prays; but there is ambiguity in his prayer:

> . . . After a while
> I thought of nothing; nothing, I prayed, would change.

Will his departure be an attempt at transcendence which will meet *its* tragic twist; or will it be a remaking through the recognition and insight which he has gained by contemplation and action?

> 'Each
> Generation has its angst . . .'

> 'Don't worry, kid, the wages of sin is birth.'

The light shines here and the light shines there. But there is not a great deal of it. Whence comes the grace—from Miss Rossignol? "From the dark past whence we come?" What of the narrator's alienation, exile, exodus—straining all fidelity? The whole of this Sequence answers that question: insight and illumination have come. No longer "Blessing the death and baptism by fire" but rather

> When we set down at Seawell it had rained.

When we wake from his dream will we cry to dream again?

That question might well have been answered in the negative, if only *Tales of the Islands* were in question. Even then it would have been wiser to notice that self-recognition-realization of that desire to "go beyond," to look for the tragic twist, is part of human growth and maturity. Now with the publication of Walcott's *Another Life* we can see that *Tales* was not only an important accomplishment in itself, but also an important step on the way to understanding Todo y Nada, a step from Exorcism to Benediction—a real entering into *Some subtleties o' the isle.*

Footnotes

[1] *Tales of the Islands* available in Derek Walcott's *Selected Poems* (New York: Farrar and Straus, 1964); and in *In a Green Night* (London: Cape, 1968); and in *Caribbean Voices*, Vol. II, John Figueroa, ed. (London: Evans Brothers, 1970).
[2] Derek Walcott, *Another Life* (New York: Farrar and Straus, 1973).
[3] V.S. Naipaul, *The Middle Passage*, (New York: Macmillan, 1963).
[4] Derek Walcott, *The Gulf* (London: Jonathan Cape, 1969).
[5] Derek Walcott, *Dream on Monkey Mountain* (New York: Farrar, Straus, and Giroux, 1970).

[6] John Figueroa in *Revista Americana* (Puerto Rico: Inter-American University, Fall 1974).

[7] In *Caribbean Voices*, Vol. II, Appendix.

[8] Emphasis added.

[9] Emphasis added.

[10] Emphasis added

[11] London: Evans Brothers, 1970.

[12] One is reminded not only of Auden's "About suffering they were never wrong the old Masters," but also of the fact that Derek was, and is, a painter of some accomplishment, and that his St. Lucian friend and mentor Harry Simmons, R.I.P., was also a painter of merit, as is that other St. Lucian friend Dunstan St. Omer, both "heroes" in Walcott's latest book, *Another Life*, the former appearing as Harry, the latter, as Gregorias.

[13] cf. Lear, especially Act IV, Scene vi, lines 11-25.

[14] From a "farewell song" in the French islands.

[15] Recall the famous speech in Henry V.

READINGS OF
"LAVENTILLE" [sic]

Kenneth Ramchand

For obvious reason of convenience, the criticism of modern poetry tends to be made up of studies of themes, touching upon a large number of poems in piece-meal fashion. This useful method sometimes allows a critic to be evasive (especially when dealing with difficult poets or poems), but even when there is no bad faith, the method seldom shows us the critic making a response to a whole poem and organising that response into an orderly account.

Too often, the emphasis falls upon what the poet is held to be saying (erroneously called the 'meaning' of the poem), with little respect for the ways in which the 'how' contributes to the total effect of the poem.

A further disadvantage of this method is that it can be made to yield patterns, generalisations that cannot be sustained by a reading of any complete poem; on the strength of such generalisations, indeed, the critic may pass over particular poems as 'uncharacteristic' or 'untypical'.

The approach used in the following reading of "Laventille" is brought into play as a necessary complement, at this stage in our critical history, to some of the general approaches to Derek Walcott's poetry that have been in evidence in recent articles.

"Laventille" appears in the volume *The Castaway and Other Poems* (1965), whose main device is the Robinson Crusoe figure, and whose unifying experience, expressed and explored in various situations is the sense of being cast away and having to begin again:

> . . . We left
> somewhere a life we never found,
> customs and gods that are not born again,
> some crib, some grill of light
> clanged shut on us in bondage, and withheld
> us from that world below us and beyond,
> and in its swaddling cerements we're still bound (p. 35)

The naturalness with which this notion fits the West Indian scene is obvious enough; and it is interesting to note that Naipaul's *The Mimic Men* uses the notion of shipwreck with associated imagery similarly in the presentation of Ralph Singh.

But Walcott's exploration in *The Castaway* is richer than Naipaul's to a large extent, because the poet interprets the attempts of The Castaway figure to possess his green world as a type of the literary artist's attempts to invent an appropriate language:

> . . . So from this house
> that faces nothing but the sea, his journals
>   assume a household use,
> We learn to shape from them, where nothing was
> the language of a race
> "Crusoe's Journal"(p. 52)

The identification between the Crusoe figure and the poet is one of the ways in which Walcott wears the mask in the *Castaway* poems. But in "Laventille" there is no intervening mask between the person of the poet, and the living material he journeys to confront.

For convenience, the poem may be divided into four broad movements. In the first, lines 1-30, there is a description of a slum settlement in the hills overlooking a city; and we meet the poet and his companion making a foot journey to a church at the top of the hill.

The next section, lines 31-43, is more reflective; in it the poet realises with a growing compassion that living conditions in the settlement of Laventille are no better than the cramped conditions in which his and their ancestors on the slave ships covered the middle passage from Africa to the West Indies.

In the third section (lines 44-77), which takes place before and during the Christening ceremony that he has come to be a godfather at, the poet overcomes an initial contempt for the apish habits of those with whom he has a common ancestry; he recognises that they are still under the influence of that religion which had suffocated him as a child, but he is not prevented by his progress from seeing that he and they are derelicts in the new world.

This feeling dominates the last section of the poem (lines 78-89), where the poet watches the sunlight falling on Laventille and spreading over the city towards which Laventille crawls, and he feels again the communal anguish of being in the limbo passage between two worlds.

Any attempt to produce something akin to a Narrative account of a poem like "Laventille", or of any poem for that matter, inevitably leads one into oversimplifications. Yet it is something we do unconsciously all the time. We do it not because our summary or 'story' can ever become a substitute for a sensuous grasp of the whole poem, but because it helps us to a rudimentary sense of the structuring of the poem and to a quick hold of its more immediately apparent themes.

From the summary given above, for example, we can see that "Laventille" is concerned about the socio-economic plight of these 'lives fixed in the unalterable groove of grinding poverty' throughout the West Indian islands; and that the poem moves beyond the expression of a socio-economic plight to an awareness of something unhealthy in the mentality even of the earth's wretched, symbolised in the postures of the Blacks at the Christening.

The poem recognises, too, the wide gap between rich and poor ('the impossible drop'), the defensiveness of the class structure separating the two main groups, and the insecurities of the stratified and devitalised inhabitants ('merchant, middleman, magistrate, knight') of 'the flat coloured city'.

Still dealing broadly, the poem comments ironically on the empty ritualistic nature of a Christian religion imposed upon descendants of Africans since the middle passage; it suggests how this religion cloys the sense of its adherents into gratitude for arrival ('across the troubled waters of this life . . . .') at a promised land that is a nightmare:

> Which of us cares to walk
> even if God wished
> those retching waters where our souls were fished
> for this new world? . . . (p. 34)

If the language of literary works is more complex than the language of sociology or history, our grasping of themes should only be the beginning of a literary criticism that will not be satisfied with itself until it responds to a complex verbal ordering, and begins to see how that ordering deepens the themes of the work.

An examination of lines 1-30 shows how what seemed like pure description contains or anticipates meanings that only begin to clarify themselves after we have gone through the whole poem.

The description of crows as '*episcopal* turkey-buzzards' is not only visually appropriate; their dropping down from the church images the sense we gather later of religion's pickings among these left-overs of The Middle Passage.

If this is going too far, we can still see how the vocabulary 'episcopal', 'miraculous', 'shrine' prepares us for the explicit concern with the Church that comes in lines 44-67, and which, in any case, is inherent in a poem built around a Christening.

The simile in line 11, which likens the rooftops of Belmont, Woodbrook, Maraval, St. Clair to 'peddlers' tin trinkets in the sun' contains some contempt for the materialism of an uncreative commercial class who can only peddle, and peddle only 'tin trinkets'.

Again, this may be reading in too much, but the simile at least refers to that class; and a sense that the homes and values of the rich are merely show, that something is missing in their lives, too, seems to come out in the 'flat' of the 'flat coloured city' in line 24, catching on to the accumulating impressions of 'fell', 'fall', 'drop', (lines 4, 5, and 8) and leading into the literally true but spiritually ironic 'To go downhill from here was to ascend' in lines 26 and 27.

What is even more remarkable, in this opening movement, is the way in which the description of the Settlement's physical properties also contains suggestions about the lives of the inhabitants—what they are, what they can become under continued oppression, and the music that is part of their technique of survival.

The sound of the steel pans heard on the approach to the settlement is made to merge sharply into the colour of the hot sky ('steel tinkling its blue painted metal air' line 2), those who play the pans being like the pans themselves 'tempered in violence'.

Long before we actually meet 'the inheritors of the middle passage' (lines 19-22) our sense impressions have been built up by Walcott's apparently objective description of things seen on the journey up. The alliterating gutturals in 'gutters growled and gargled wash' (line 13) suggest both the harshness of the lives in those 'raw brick hovels', and the morning sounds of a crowded tenement without privacies; the '*lank electric* lines and tension cables' (lines 16-17) gives a physical picture of the slum dwellers and of the their explosive state as well as suggesting the criss-crossing of their lives.

The gutters growling past the Youth Centre fittingly enacts the rapidity with which childhood is bypassed here; the rigidity of 'a rigid children's carousel of cement' applies to the rigidities hardening the children, and contains an apparent contradiction if even their roundabouts or merry-go-rounds are rigid.

Even more tellingly upon our senses, the whirling motion of the water, the circular movement implied by carousel (= whirligig, merry-go-round, roundabout), the turning over of the round pot contained in stewed, the quick cycle of life and death in 'breeding' meet in the word 'revolve' in line 22 'whose lives revolve round prison, graveyard, church', and spin outward to the deepening striations of lives fixed in the unalterable *groove of grinding* poverty' (of lines 76-77.)

We can now return to the opening line of the poem and see how the suggestiveness of the descriptions in this first movement of the poem is also contained in the peculiarly apt verb 'huddles'. The primary reference is to the shacks heaped confusedly together, but by the time we come to the end of the first movement, the word draws into itself the sense of something, coiled up, ('It huddled') waiting to strike.

The rich verbal effects looked at above suggest an imaginative understanding which must penetrate deeper than surface truths and surface animosities between classes; and an involvement by the poet more inward than that of a detached observer.

As "Laventille" develops we are drawn into recoginising a common fate, different forms of being cast away awaiting poor and rich, uneducated and educated, those who live perilously on the hill or those who reside flatly in the city. And we follow as the concomitant of this reveals itself to the poet that he is part of the wreckage that he had begun by registering from the point of view of an observer in the opening movement. The process can be traced in the alternating use of the pronouns 'we' and 'I' over the course of the poem.

In the second section of "Laventille" (lines 31-43), the detached observing 'we' of the preceding movement comes closer to the other descendants of slaves who are less fortunate, it seems, than the poet and his companion.

The journey to the church through the slum becomes a type of journey through the horrors of the middle passage to the new world; and the sight of waves of heat rising from the roof-tops down below shimmers into a vision of that historical trauma '. . . the hot corrugated iron sea / whose horrors we all / shared . . .'

But the poet, who has come from the city below to be godfather to the child being christened, has made more progress socially than the slum dwellers. So the 'climbing' with which this section begins is charged with two sets of meanings, giving tension to his life: 'Climbing, we could look back / with widening memory'. The 'climbing' refers both to his social evolution (educated, middle-class, writer) and to the physical journey which is becoming a psychic journey into his own past.

Similarly, the 'widening memory' is both the forgetting of links with 'the inheritors of the middle passage' which occurs during the social ascent, and the memory now spreading out to reclaim kinship with 'those who suffered, who were killed and who survive'.

We can see in the second section of the poem, therefore, a personalising of the theme of the relationship between the middle class and the masses in the developing drama of the observing poet's relationship with the observed of Laventille. But in the third section, lines 44-77, there is a move back again from the rapprochement of the common 'we'.

An alienated 'I' bursts into the poem, irritated by the sight of

> . . . The black, fawning verger
> his bow tie akimbo, grinning, the clown-gloved
> fashionable wear of those I deeply loved
> once, (pp. 33-34)

The phrase 'those I deeply loved / once' hints at the poet's earlier involvement in the process the verger and others are now undergoing; and the same phrase suggests the effect his involvement in that climbing has had upon him in his relationship with the people.

But if in section two, we see the dividing effect of social and economic striving, in section three the poem deals with the stifling effect of an imposed religion that teaches gratitude to the shipwrecked inhabitants of such desolations as Laventille, and allows them under heavy influence to be close to death on alien earth and not know it.

The odour of 'bay rum and talc' and the intoning of 'the supercilious brown curate' waft the poet back to his 'childhood fear of Sabbath, graveyards, christenings, marriages', reminding him how far he has travelled compared with those churchgoers. The droning of the curate does not in fact heal the rickets of the undernourished slum children already suffering, the poet ironically observes, from original sin, which the Christian religion has taught them about since the middle passage.

The poet's awareness of the fact of death (they are in the churchyard), of spiritual death, and of the living death he has just seen in the journey through the slums makes him feel this Christening to be a baptism into death.

Nevertheless, the poet does not separate himself from the congregation. The 'We' returns with a confirmed sense of identification with a betrayed Laventille:

> Which of us cares to walk
> even if God wished
> those retching waters where our souls were fished . . .
> for this new world? (p. 34)

The penetration of 'Laventille' comes from the way in which the journey into a hill-top slum becomes for the poet a journey into his own darkness which has a direct bearing upon his relationship with words.

The 'I' who now (line 77) 'stands out' on a balcony watching the sun 'pave its flat golden path' is the poet (his Laventille kinship established) yearning for a language that can march, like the sun spreading over Laventille and the city, with elemental directness and healing.

For the 'swaddling cerements' which images either the still-birth and mummification of the society or its need to subsist on its own deprivations (bandaged even in grave-clothes for healing) can also be seen as having to do with the poet working with an inherited language and in a heavily influenced culture. ('Cerements' according to the *Concise Oxford Dictionary* refers figuratively to the 'influences that restrain freedom of action or thought.')

To justify this reading we must return to lines 74, 75, and 76:

> . . . desperate words,
> born like these children from habitual wombs
>
> From lives fixed in the unalterable groove
> of grinding poverty. (p. 34)

The restraining influences lie in a language worn down in certain ways by its previous usage, fixed in an apparently 'unalterable groove' which he must mimic because of his history of spiritual and cultural impoverishment ('some deep, amnesiac blow').

It is nevertheless out of these 'swaddling cerements' that the poet must temper his 'desperate words' and find his own voice in the same way that the music of the steel pans, 'tempered in violence', tinkling in the blue metal air over Laventille represents a triumph of creativity and endurance.

WALCOTT AND THE AUDIENCE FOR POETRY

Mervyn Morris

The burden of immediate communication lies heavier on the man of the theatre than on the poet, but if he submits his work for publication, the poet too — even when he is at base the lonely artist grappling with private experience — manifests a desire to communicate. This evening we consider both the poet and his possible audience.[1] First, we consider why in the West Indies an audience for serious contemporary poetry scarcely exists, and some practical suggestions are offered of ways in which the situation could be improved. Then we introduce and discuss some of Derek Walcott's work, particularly as it relates to a putative West Indian audience.

"If," writes George Lamming in *The Pleasures of Exile*, "we accept that the act of writing a book is linked with an expectation, however modest, of having it read; then the situation of a West Indian writer, living and working in his own community, assumes intolerable difficulties. The West Indian of average opportunity and intelligence has not yet been converted to reading as a civilized activity, an activity which justifies itself in the exercise of his mind. Reading seriously, at any age, is still largely associated with reading for examinations."[2] My own experience on this campus frequently supports Lamming's assertion. Time after time students who complain that they do not get enough West Indian literature on their English course turn out to have read practically none of the West Indian writing not actually prescribed. Walcott was not always prescribed; but he is now. Not only on University courses but in at least one Jamaican teacher-training college; and shrewd secondary school teachers can persuade Sixth Formers that it is actually *useful* to have read some Walcott if they are facing University Scholarship examinations. I daresay Walcott knows this is a mixed blessing, being prescribed for examinations. The poet's work receives, in some instances, attention which is, from the poet's point of view, far worse than no attention at all, his work seen as necessary academic information not as shared experience. (Question: What main literary influences in Walcott can you detect in *In a Green Night*, and how successfully have they been assimilated?) The readers the poet no doubt craves are people who will take up — maybe even buy — his book because they enjoy reading poetry and are interested in his. Not only in the

West Indies is the audience for poetry small in comparison to the audience for prose fiction, but here we have, it seems to me, an educational problem more acute than in many other countries. Many West Indian persons who profess an interest in poetry cannot actually read it; not, that is, unless it is in imitation of the English Romantics: Wordsworth, Keats, Shelley or their Victorian successors. School after school in Jamaica selects the Romantics for the special paper in "A" level English, rejecting (no doubt for sound practical reasons of examination convenience) the twentieth century paper available and the paper 1550-1660 which relates fairly intimately to much contemporary verse. The Great Romantics are, of course, worthy of study, but the observable effect on some pupils has been the hardening of the idea that poetry is "beautiful", "sublime" thoughts and images drawn from nature, and the undervaluing of the intellectual tightness, the unillusioned verbal intelligence, of so much contemporary verse. The great emphasis on the Romantics may also, because the poetry is so often involved with the seasons of a temperate climate, help to foster the idea that poetry does not much relate to the life of its readers. Let me not seem to say that we need a diet of the obviously local. The suggestion rather is, that in some schools the diet might be better balanced — poems from various periods of literature, poems from various countries including the West Indies. Anthologies of West Indian poetry are beginning to appear.

Yet — nervously, tentatively — one fears that the trouble is not so much the concentration on the Romantics as the lifeless way in which they have so often been taught; poetry as information, not poetry as experience.

Teachers who believe in literature as experience are likely to believe in having children write poems or imaginative prose of their own. Intensive writing, such as recommended by Margaret Landon in *Let the Children Write*[3] is not only invaluable in developing writing skills, it fosters an interest in the creative imagination, which should produce more receptive readers of poetry. And class discussion of good work can be the beginning of training in how to articulate an aesthetic or moral response.

Higher in our schools, careful training in Practical Criticism would be a major contribution to the development of a discriminating West Indian public. By "training in Practical Criticism" I mean: guided practice in looking closely at words on the page, and in relating the particular area of scrutiny to some larger aesthetic and moral response, not the dreary business of pedestrian technical comment divorced from values, meaning or arguable intention. There are a number of school texts, among them James Reeves' *The Critical Sense* [4], which I like because it makes Practical Criticism seem not a police inspection, but something more like a natural outgrowth of reading: a flexible, courteous, essentially humble, talking about a response.

The inadequacy or the absence of Practical Criticism in West Indian schools is part of the reason why few West Indians read contemporary poetry; they have not learnt to give it the concentrated attention it sometimes demands. W. I. Carr (who has left us for Guyana) and J. E. Ingledew (a member of our English Department still) published in *Caribbean Quarterly* Volume 8 No. 4, an analysis of English Literature scholarship examination papers of February 1962. Of 134 candidates, 98 failed to reach the pass mark of 34 out of 100. There were, the authors point out, "errors suggesting a total incapacity to see what words can do and to use words in the making of elementary points." Answers on the poem for comment included: "irrelevant moralizing at the expense of the poet, counting of feet and purely metrical analysis, attempts to explain the poem in terms of something read elsewhere, and false notions of the poetic . . ." From the numerous examples quoted from scripts, here are a very few. (There are) "no devices such as onomatopoeia or alliteration to suffuse the atmosphere of the poem with the sounds and pleasures of life." Similarly, answering the question, "How would you define a major poet?", this — "We should see whether he ends his poem with rhyming couplets. If he uses verse, we must see whether he uses the decasyllabic or octosyllabic verse or whether he uses four line verses of abab, aabb, or abbba." (And the candidate actually counted the last one wrong.) "If his diction and metre is such that it does not present any difficulty to the reader then he can be defined as a major poet." From another candidate, the dangerous view, so popular with students in the Social Sciences: "An artist who appeals to a limited circle is not an artist of real value." My own personal contact with the 1966 final examination training college scripts in English Literature confirms the impressions drawn in Carr's and Ingledew's article. My experience was perhaps even more frightening: the scholarship candidates did, after all, hope to study at the university, where no doubt they would improve; the training college graduates were shortly to go out into our schools: as teachers — trained! — hundreds of persons who simply cannot read with close attention.

Among the reasons why we do not have much of a West Indian audience for poetry such as Walcott's, the teaching in our schools must rank quite high. But, of course, formal education is only one of the educative agents in any society. Some of our book reviewing, for example, tends to reflect and reinforce the unfortunate training in many schools. When *In a Green Night* [5] was reviewed in *The Sunday Gleaner*, we were offered two-thirds background information, a small amount of general description, and then: "On many occasions in this collection Walcott will impress the reader with delightful lines"— whereupon, without further comment (then or later), the delightful lines follow, and the review, winningly entitled "The Magic of Words", concludes: "This is highly recommended for layman and scholar alike."[6] Usually, the more detailed reviews which focus on texts or make the kind of evaluative-descriptive comment that can only be earned from grappling with the text appear in the small-circulation journals, such as *Bim, Caribbean Quarterly, New World;* though in Trinidad, *In a Green Night* was carefully reviewed in *The Trinidad Guardian,* by C.L.R. James.

More careful formal education and more helpful newspaper reviewing may tend to develop and train an audience. But they may not, of course, get very far very quickly: the nature and values of the society are the major controlling factors. A grossly materialistic society will not read serious poetry unless it is prescribed for examinations. You may remember that, addressing the graduates in the 1963 graduation ceremony, Dr. Eric Williams actually found it worth his while to recommend that they read!

"The second obligation," he said, "is . . . your duty to read, to cultivate the habit of reading. I have here tonight one of the most damning indictments of West Indian society ever written. It was written by one of the most distinguished abolitionists as far back as 1831. This is what he said of the West Indies and the West Indian people: 'Their lives are passed in a contracted circle amidst petty feuds and pecuniary embarrassments. There is no civilized society on earth so entirely destitute of learned leisure, of literary and scientific intercourse and even of liberal recreations.' One hundred and thirty years ago," said Dr. Williams, "but perhaps some of it still applies to the West Indies today."[7]

In "Castiliane," Walcott makes a similar point, with bitter irony:

> A merchant claims the daughter,
> A man who hawks and profits in this heat,
> Jeering at poets with a goldtoothed curse.
> Girl, you were wise, whoever lived by verse?
> The future is in cheap enamel wares.

And so we turn to Walcott more specifically.

Given the kind of society we have described, the kind of conditions which have produced and been the product of this particular society, for whom then do our poets write? The poet may well be a man speaking to men, but — which men?

In a seminar here on campus in 1965, someone wondered whether our West Indian poets might not aim at reaching a wider audience. This provoked from Walcott a merry passage in which he pictured the earnest bard, his newest poem completed, rushing up to the hills and saying to a labourer: "Have you heard this one?" Poetry, Walcott at that time argued, is high art which the ordinary man will not understand. In his book on obscurity in poetry,[8] the English poet-critic, John Press, fully represents what was the Walcott position then. "Although," wrote Press, "few people have the audacity to blame mathematicians or physicists for being difficult to understand, there is a general belief that poetry should be immediately comprehensible even to the meanest intelligence. The truth is that much poetry of the highest quality demands of its readers a degree of mental alertness and of general culture which most people do not possess." Asked at that seminar to read one of his poems, Walcott chose "Origins", which he introduced as "reminiscent or deliberately modeled on Césaire and Perse. But what I was trying to do in this poem was to try to get the same quality that exists in French West Indian Poetry in English." That difficult poem "Origins", appeared in the American *Selected Poems*[9] but was dropped before *The Castaway*.[10] Walcott was taken to task by Edward Brathwaite: "It is very difficult," said Brathwaite, "for these poems to immediately communicate to society in general." Brathwaite suggested that there were three main approaches to West Indian writing: What he called the humanist approach, the personal approach and the folk approach. The distinctions do not seem to me very helpful, especially as there are very few instances indeed in which a poet can be found attempting only one of these approaches at a time. But Brathwaite's most important point is really about Walcott. "The humanist poet," said Brathwaite, "naturally takes his inspiration from his society, and his voice is often speaking away from that society rather than speaking in towards it. I think this is one reason why many people claim that poetry is irrelevant. It does not mean anything to them, simply because it is not speaking directly to them on a matter of great concern."[11] Now, speaking directly to them or communicating directly to society in general would be self-denying ordinances indeed, for a poet of any subtlety. Brathwaite's suggestion that Walcott speaks away from the society relates in fact, not to the direction of Walcott's address, but to level and mode of communication. In this specific instance of "Origins," the point would partly be: that near as we are to the French West Indies, Walcott is more likely to find in some foreign metropolis a reader who can understand his attempt to do as Césaire and Perse had done. I believe that is true. I do not, myself, have the necessary experience of Césaire and Perse. But if we restrict our poets to speaking directly to this society in general we will never get any deeper than Louise Bennett or The Mighty Sparrow, both superb performers and sharp-eyed, ironic critics but both, by the immediate clarity to which they are committed, limited to external satiric comment. Miss Lou and Sparrow speak to the society in general all right, but the modes in which they work preclude any deeply personal human expression.

Walcott, some say, is not West Indian enough. He is too much concerned with world literature and international sophistication. Of course, the fact that Walcott has actually chosen to live in the West Indies is given little weight by West Indian pundits who assert their commitment from some address in London. The central content of Walcott's verse is not much examined. The accusers get stuck with allusions to world literature or with stylistic influences. Poems which happen to be about death, love, evil, art, the loss of faith, are not relevant enough for those who find compassion or complex ambiguity decadent luxuries in our emerging society, and call instead for poems which speak stridently of politics, class and race. Poems are fine if they are black enough. In actual fact Walcott has written many poems about race, but usually they are exploratory enough to displease the propagandists. The propagandists want, they prefer, McKay: When a nigger is lynched:

> Little lads, lynchers that were to be,
> Danced round the dreadful thing in fiendish glee.[12]

Or they want stirring cries to racial battle, arising out of the extreme situation:

> If we must die, let it not be like hogs
> Hunted and penned in an inglorious spot.[13]

Confronted in America with extreme racial conflict, Walcott still chooses not to abandon his discriminating sense of the individual experience:

> Outside,
> more snow had fallen. My heart charred.
> I longed for darkness, evil that was warm.

> Walking I'd stop and turn. What had I heard,
> Wheezing behind my heel with whitening breath?
> Nothing. Sixth Avenue yawned wet and wide.
> The night was white. There was nowhere to hide.

Artists are always having to contend with people who want not art as understanding or recreated experience, but art as a spur to action. They even find persons who tell them whom to address. The analytical, compassionate James Baldwin, for example, has been attacked for a preoccupation with white liberal conscience.

Walcott has been attacked by *New World* for what it calls pre-occupation with being published abroad.[14] This seems to me unusually unfair. Walcott first published in the West Indies at his own expense. He writes, in *The London Magazine:* "I had sat on the landing of the stairs, and asked my mother, who was sewing at the window, for two hundred dollars to put out a booklet of poems. She did not have that kind of money, and the fact made her weep, but she found it, the book was printed, and I had hawked it myself on street corners, a dollar a copy, and made the money back."[15] City Printery did a book for him before Jonathan Cape. Further, not only is publication in reputable foreign magazines such as *The London Magazine* or *Encounter* some encouraging indication that a certain level of achievement has been reached, it is also a virtual guarantee of readers who may understand a serious poet's art. Also, it is a melancholy fact (examined in Lamming's *The Pleasures of Exile*) that our society is still timid to acknowledge excellence before it has had the stamp of foreign approbation. It still too often has to be by success abroad that one establishes one's right to this society's serious attention.

Like any worthwhile poet, Walcott speaks to people anywhere, but very often his primary significance is for his own West Indian people or for Negroes.

"Ruins of a Great House" has been much explicated. But you will forgive me if I use it here again. It is an excellent example of a poem which in range of reference may seem to "speak away from the society" but which is saying something important not just to any people, but to West Indian people in particular. The poem depends on a passage from a meditation by Donne — a passage which includes the very famous, ask not "for whom the bell tolls; it tolls for thee." But Walcott alludes to parts of that passage which are less well-known. The poem, you will remember, ends:

> All in compassion ends
> So differently from what the heart arranged:
> 'as well as if a manor of thy friend's . . . '

which is an unfinished quotation from Donne.

The Donne passage runs:

> No man is an *iland*, intire of it selfe; every man is a peece of the
> *Continent*, a part of the *maine*; if a Clod be washed away by the Sea,
> *Europe* is the lesse, as well as if a *promontorie* were, as well as if a *Mannor* of

thy *friends* or of *thine owne* were; any mans *death* diminishes *me*, because I
am involved in *Mankinde*. And therefore never send to know for whom
the bell *tolls*; It tolls for *thee*.[16]

Now, in the poem the allusions are an integral part of the experience explored, not
just a means of conducting the enquiry. Donne's "peece of the *Continent*, part of the
maine" has been appropriately introduced earlier, and the reference to a Manor nicely
relates to the poem's starting point — "Ruins of a Great House" or manor. The
"friends" of the last line is superbly ambivalent. Is it ironic? And if so, how far? Some
of the colonialists mentioned earlier, where the West Indian was angry, were

> Men like Hawkins, Walter Raleigh, Drake
> Ancestral murderers and poets

but the "and poets" has meant a kinship between the "I" of this poem and some of the
colonialists he seems to wish to abhor. Now, bearing all this in mind, listen again to
the last lines:

> Ablaze with rage, I thought,
> Some slave is rotting in this manorial lake,
> But still the coal of my compassion fought
> That Albion too was once
> A colony like ours, 'part of the continent, piece of the main'
> Nook-shotten, rook o'er blown, deranged
> By foaming channels and the vain expense
> Of bitter faction.
> All in compassion ends
> So differently from what the heart arranged:
> 'as well as if a manor of thy friend's . . .'

Are they friends or are they not? It is a question important in the West Indies at this
time. That it is unanswered is the meaningful subtlety of exploratory poetry.
    While we are on this poem, let us look at something else. In *In a Green Night*, the
text runs:

> Ablaze with rage, I thought
> Some slave is rotting in this manorial lake.

In *Selected Poems*, the American book, the first section of which selects from *In a
Green Night*, these lines run:

> Ablaze with rage I thought,
> Some slave is rotting in this manorial lake.

Now looking closely at Walcott emendations, one is not always sure the punctuation is his. In places it is very likely to be a printer's error, a publisher's convention, or an omission. But here, one can discern intention. Grammatically the poet wishes to introduce the thought so he requires a pause; but also, by omitting the comma after "rage", he has introduced a nice syntactical ambiguity. The line means:

> Ablaze with rage, I thought (so and so),

as in the first version. But it now also means: "I thought I was ablaze with rage, but perhaps I wasn't really, perhaps I had already begun to recognize my kinship to all men (especially poets — ancestral murderers and poets — remember?) so that I was probably just faking anger in an automatic and unexamined anti-colonial gesture." So much a comma can do. This, I believe, is part of what poetry is about: controlling, refining language so intricately that it traps for the poet much more meaning than its ordinary day-to-day usage.

"Ruins of a Great House" may have seemed difficult, but insofar as it was, it did advertise much of its difficulty. But there are many other lines, many other poems, that are no more likely to be widely understood, in spite of their apparent simplicity. Here, for example, are the opening lines from "A Village Life", which is from *The Castaway*.

> Through the wide, grey loft window,
> I watched that winter morning, my first snow
> crusting the sill, puzzle the black,
> nuzzling tom. Behind my back
> a rime of crud glazed my cracked coffee cup,
> a snowfall of torn poems piling up
> heaped by a rhyming spade.
> Starved, on the prowl,
> I was a frightened cat in that grey city.

The difficulty (and the excellence) here resides in the poet's verbal concentration. Introduced by "black" that "tom" should recall to us "Uncle Tom", the poems torn up are snow inside like the snow outside, the rime (that is, hoar frost) of crud in the coffee cup is again suggesting snow inside like snow outside. And "rime" shades into "rhyming". "Spade" means not just the literal spade shoveling snow, but "spade" as English slang for a black man. "I was a frightened cat" is a precise use of American slang (like cool cat, man). But the cat is also tom-cat, the Uncle Tom, the frightened black man. Here is the passage again:

> Through the wide, grey loft window,
> I watched that winter morning, my first snow
> crusting the sill, puzzle the black,
> nuzzling tom. Behind my back

a rime of crud glazed my cracked coffee-cup,
a snowfall of torn poems piling up
heaped by a rhyming spade.
Starved, on the prowl,
I was a frightened cat in that grey city.

—which for its subject matter, vaguely brings to mind Edward Brathwaite's *Rights of Passage*, a poem worth reading but one which lacks, I think, that verbal concentration which we find so often in Walcott.

Walcott's care for precision, his patient craft, are easily demonstrated. He is, and has been, a very keen reviser. Poems which appear in *Bim* or *Caribbean Quarterly* in one form appear in one of the books in a different form and in a later book in yet another form. Almost always the emendation is towards a greater particularity (a "this" for a "the" would be a typical change), or the changes are for tighter packing of significance or a tighter rhythm. No doubt, however Walcott may shudder, some future scholar will one day publish parallel versions line by line. One of the most notable for examination is "The Wedding of an Actress" which jumps from *Bim 37* to a version in the American *Selected Poems* and another version in *Castaway* which brings back several of the readings in *Bim*. More obvious (and therefore better suited to a lecture which you must hear, but cannot see) is "Margaret Verlieu Dies" a poem in *Poems* (a book published by City Printery). The poem "Margaret Verlieu Dies" becomes "A Country Club Romance" in *In a Green Night*. Some of the more pathetic bits are now; for example, the stanzas:

She took an occasional whisky,
Mr. Harris could not understand.
He said, "Since you so damn frisky,
Answer this backhand!"
Next she took pills for sleeping,
and murmured lost names in the night;
She could not hear him weeping:
"Be Jeez, it serve us right."

The language and rhythm of the poem are tightened even while extra beats are added. Let us look at the punctuation again. The early version runs:

Love has its little revenges
Love whom man has devised;
They wed and lay down like Slazengers
Together and were ostracized.

The poem is, as you know, about the tragic marriage of a black Bajan to a white socialite.

"Love has its revenges"

becomes less tripping in the new version, becomes slower in movement and therefore more ominous. Instead of "Love has its little revenges",

> O love has its revenges,
> Love whom man has devised;
> They married and lay down like Slazengers
> Together.

— where "married" replaces "wed". But instead of "and were ostracized", we get a full-stop after "together". Instead of "they were" we get "she was". As the main focus of the poem is on the white social group, to involve black Mr. Harris in problems from his own group would blur the point, so:

> O love has its revenges,
> Love whom man has devised;
> They married and lay down like Slazengers
> Together. She was ostracized.

Two of the emendations in "Crusoe's Island" may be noted. In stanza three "the simple plaid" of Scarborough (Tobago's capital) becomes "the picnic plaid", relating more deeply to the "hedonist philosophy" the poet talks about. Thus:

> Below, the picnic plaid
> Of Scarborough is spread
> To a blue, perfect sky,
> Dome of our hedonist philosophy.

And the "transfixing" chapel bell of the last stanza becomes the "transfiguring" bell, suggesting the re-enactment of a religious operation rather than a startling memory of belief.

In "The Swamp" we have some very interesting alterations. The American book has the first two stanzas running:

> Gnawing the highway's edges, a black mouth
> Cries quietly: 'Home, come home . . .'
>
> Below its viscous breath, the very word 'growth'
> Grows fungi, rot;
> White speckling its root.

Revising for *The Castaway*, the poet evidently wishes to intensify the brooding menace of "The Swamp" so he darkens some of his lighter vowels. He replaces "cries" with "hums":

> . . . a black mouth
> hums quietly: 'Home, come home . . .'

where that "hums" is also picking up the later "Home, come home . . ." It is a tight
unit of sound. And he substitutes "mottling" for "speckling".

> White mottling its root.

As a gloss to "Tales of the Islands" — that is, to the version which appeared in *Bim
26* — Walcott wrote:

> What I have been trying to do with them over the last five years is to
> get a certain factual, biographical plainness about them. I suppose the idea
> is to do away with the prerogative of modern prose in narration. Also to
> dislocate the traditional idea of the sonnet as a fourteen-line piece of
> music. The idea is the same as in prose; dispassionate observation. Say
> nothing, but cut the bronze medallion and present it to the normal poetry
> reader saying, "Here you are; verse was here first, and it's time we got back
> what they took from it." As a result the pieces may read flat. But as much
> selection goes into making them work as into the traditional lyric . . .

Now, five years' work on them was evidently not enough for Walcott. Between
their *Bim* appearance in 1958 and *In a Green Night* in 1962, the poems are largely
rewritten. They are certainly no longer flat. In some instances they have been made
more surely conversational. Sometimes the ironies have been sharpened. In Chapter
III, for example, Miss Rossignol in the later version who "flew like bats to vespers
every twilight"; Chapter III repays close examination. The rhythms are tightened, the
images altered so they inter-relate more closely. Chapter V is that one about the
anthropologist. In it the emphatic "it was most ironic" becomes the throw away "it
was quite ironic". That delicate ironic line "Dancing with absolutely natural grace"
was once rather regular, "And dancing with that customary grace." "The whole thing
was just like a bloody picnic" becomes more casually conversational and more West
Indian: "The whole thing was more like a bloody picnic". The earlier, rather
workaday: "They tie the sheep and then cut off its head" becomes the sharply,
unassertively but so exactly, West Indian cadence:

> They tie the lamb up, then chop off the head.

The standard English "took" becomes the West Indian conversational "take" (in the
past tense):

> And ritualists take turns drinking the blood.

The final line is made more ironic: "Great stuff all right", becoming, "Great stuff,

old boy;" and the pause after it is strengthened by a semi-colon instead of a comma.
This is the final version:

> The fête took place one morning in the heights
> For the approval of some anthropologist.
> The priests objected to such savage rites
> In a Catholic country; but there was a twist
> As one of the fathers was himself a student
> Of black customs; it was quite ironic.
> They lead sheep to the rivulet with a drum,
> Dancing with absolutely natural grace
> Remembered from the dark past whence we come.
> The whole thing was more like a bloody picnic.
> Bottles of white rum and a brawling booth.
> They tie the lamb up, then chop off the head,
> And ritualists take turns drinking the blood.
> Great stuff, old boy; sacrifice, moments of truth.

It is more useful to compare closely the Chapter V's, I think, than the famous
Chapter VI, for the reason that the alterations in Chapter V, though smaller, are no
less significant. But Chapter VI, I think you will want to hear; it's been completely
transformed. It ran:

> Garcon — that was a fête — I mean they had
> Free whisky and they had some fellows beating
> Steel from one of the bands in Trinidad,
> And everywhere you turn people was eating
> Or drinking and so on and I think
> They catch two guys with his wife on the beach,
> But, there will be nothing like Keats, [sic] "each
> Generation has its angst, and we have none,"
> And he wouldn't let a comma in. edgewise
> (Black writer, you know, one of them Oxford guys),
> And it was next day in the papers that the heart
> Of a young child was torn from it alive
> By two practitioners of the native art.
> But that was far away from all the jump and jive.

The famous present version runs:

> Poopa, da' was a fête! I mean it had
> Free rum free whisky and some fellers beating
> Pan from one of them band in Trinidad
> And everywhere you turn was people eating

> And drinking and don't name me but I think
> They catch his wife with two tests up the beach
> While he drunk quoting Shelley with 'Each
> Generation has its *angst*, but we has none'
> And wouldn't let a comma in edgewise.
> (Black writer chap, one of them Oxbridge guys.)
> And it was round this part once that the heart
> Of a young child was torn from it alive
> By two practitioners of native art,
> But that was long before this jump and jive.

For its language this is an exciting and an important poem. Critics have not always made so much, however, of what it means. This is a rapid dramatic glimpse of a hedonistic society which explodes easily into a party (especially when there is free-ness); the lively party on the tropical beach has had plenty of food, women and a choice of liquor. Set against the whole scene, but yet a part of it all is the alienated writer — a black man quoting the foreign white idealist Shelley; a black man out of the foreign university of Oxford or Cambridge. He senses vacuity in this hedonistic society of which he is a part. Or is he? Is he drunk to kill the pain or is he drunk because he likes the booze?

"Each generation has its *angst*" — that is, its anxiety about the human condition — "but we has none". The error in grammar may signify either that the drunk, alienated writer wishes (in spite of quoting Shelley, in spite of using a fashionable German word) to identify with the West Indian dialect class; the cultured West Indian wishes to feel peasant. Or it may signify that the foreign culture is only an overgrowth. Or, least interestingly, the grammar may be the narrator's, not the writer's actual usage. And, obliquely, by placing that final anecdote next to the hedonistic scene and the writer's comment, Walcott suggests that there is indeed a West Indian *angst*, and that may be why we fête so very much.

Here I take a chance to clarify a position: or, if you like, discreetly to recant. In an essay on Louise Bennett in 1963, I referred to Dennis Scott's "Uncle Time":

> Uncle Time is a ole, ole man . . .
> All year long 'im wash 'im foot in de sea
> long, lazy years on de wet san'
> and shake de coconut tree
> dem quiet-like wid 'im sea-win' laughter.
> scraping away de lan' . . .
>
> Uncle Time is a spider-man, cunning an' cool,
> him tell yu': watch de hill an' yu' si me.
> Huhn! Fe yu' yi no quick enough fe si
> how 'im move like mongoose; man, yu' t'ink 'im fool?

> Me Uncle Time smile black as sorrow,
> 'im voice is sof' as bamboo leaf
> but Lawd, me Uncle cruel.
> When 'im play in de street
> wid yu' woman, — watch 'im! By tomorrow
> she dry as cane-fire, bitter as cassava:
> an' when 'im teach yu' son, long after
> yu' walk wid stranger, an' yu' bread is grief.
> Watch how 'im spin web roun' yu' house, an' creep
> inside an when 'im touch yu' weep. . .

My comment in 1963 was,

> Here we have a poet using dialect, as Walcott does in "Poopa, da' was
> a fête:", for artistic purposes that don't seem natural to dialect at all. The
> poem has been thought, so to speak, in standard English. Louise Bennett
> uses dialect more or less as we can believe the normal speakers of dialect
> might use it, if they were skilled enough; Walcott and Scott borrow
> dialect for the literary middle-class. The image, "smile black as sorrow" is
> too abstract for the eminently concrete medium of dialect. It must be said,
> however, that this poem has a careful, exquisite beauty that I cannot claim
> for anything in Louise Bennett.[17]

Now, I still hold more or less those opinions, though (in that last sentence) "It must
be said, however" is a rather reluctant tribute to a subtle poem. It is possible to get
deeper effects than Louise Bennett without being false to the dialect: some folk song
instances have been cited in that Bennett essay, and Edward Brathwaite, in *Rights of
Passage*, achieves this in "The Dust".

Where my comment was most inadequate was in its failure to indicate ways in
which meaning and apparent intention may make the "borrowing of dialect" triumphantly artistic. Walcott and Scott are not trying to be faithful to dialect, they are
trying to convey their complex perceptions. At the request of the Caribbean Artists
Movement, Scott has recently written a note on this poem, "Uncle Time". The
presentation of Anancy as a threatening and dangerous figure is a comment in fact on
Jamaican mythology and therefore the Jamaican national character. The web is a
Jamaican symbol of peace, so that there is critical menace in:

> Watch how 'im spin web roun' yu' house, an' creep
> inside, an' when 'im touch yu', weep.

About the mixture of standard English and dialect, Scott makes the penetrating
comment:

> Creole speech permits — indeed often, I think, *encourages* and *sustains*

the tones of irony wonderfully well. But when the poet requires a complexity of levels of meaning in an image or a line, somehow the dialect
form shatters under the tensions he tries to set up, and he has to have
recourse to traditional "English" language patterns and stresses. Gordon
Rohlehr seems to make this point in some CAM Comments on the end of
Walcott's dialect poem: "Poopa, da' was a fête":

And it was round this part once that the heart
Of a young child was torn from it alive
By two practitioners of native art . . .

   "A change of tone, a change of metre," [says Rohlehr] "a swing back to
the traditional. Is it ironic that the voice of serious recollection should
be so traditional and so English?"

   Walcott himself, in introducing "Some West Indian Poets" in *The London Magazine*, makes a similar point. "What makes the West Indies a complex challenge to the
West Indian poet is the same thing that eventually wearies him: how to find his
specific tone without being distant, how to invent natural forms. He suspects the raw
spontaneity of dialect as being richer in expression, but is not willing to sacrifice the
syntactical power of English. Naturally enough," says Walcott, "where the conflict is
realized, the poetry is strongest. That dramatic ambivalence is part of what it means to
be a West Indian now."[18]
   Yet what Walcott calls a conflict is not always seen to be that. There are many
West Indians who with natural voice interweave dialect and Standard English in their
speech. Chapter V of "The Islands" seems to me to do it fairly effectively. ("The fête
took place one morning in the heights"). There are, elsewhere in Walcott's poetry
interesting small examples of West Indian vocabulary placed unemphatically in a
Standard English setting. The word "galvanize" (southern Caribbean for "zinc roof-
ing") for example, appears in solemn context:

He wept again, though why, he was unsure,
At dazzling visions of reflected tin.
So heaven is revealed to fevered eyes,
So is sin born, and innocence made wise,
By intimations of hot galvanize.
("Orient and Immortal Wheat", p. 48)

"Feteing" appears in "The Glory Trumpeter":

Now it was that, as Eddie turned his back
On our young crowd out feteing, swilling liquor,

In "Cadaver" the dead dog lying in the road is "the mashed beast".

Personally, I find unobtrusive natural West Indianism more congenial than the art-speech wrought from dialect as in "Parang". I have a preference for the recognizable speaking-voice in poetry. The kind of dialect poems Walcott has written, do not, I may add, speak any more directly to his society than the other poems in his books.

Walcott's development has been towards a cunning, more natural sounding simplicity. The early rhetoric is being deliberately pruned away. In the early "Choc Bay" he could exclaim:

> All that I have and want are words
> To fling my griefs about.

*But that large a*nd noisy gesture was already under criticism in In a Green Night. For in "Islands" he wrote:

> I seek
> As climate seeks its style, to write
> Verse crisp as sand, clear as sunlight,
> Cold as the curled wave, ordinary
> As a tumbler of island water . . .

The development of greater complexity at the same time as there is a simpler surface may be judged if we compare that bit from "Islands" with the following two short quotations which are from much later poems. From "Sea-Crab":

> The sea crab's cunning, halting, awkward grace
> is the syntactical envy of my hand;
> obliquity burrowing to surface
> from hot, plain sand.

When in "Tarpon" the poet asks:

> Can such complexity of shape,
> such bulk, terror and fury fit
> in a design so innocent,

he is, in part, reflecting on his search for a style more "innocent", more simple on the surface.

In "The Castaway" Walcott preaches withdrawal at the same time that he examines involvement. In "Lizard" asserting: "The impotence of rescue or compassion" in the face of death, he concludes:

> Withdraw and leave the scheme of things in charge . . .

And yet, Walcott's commitment to the West Indies and to the Negro Struggle is also very much present in the books, present *enough* to pacify the most militant activist. His examination of Othello, for example, rejects the stereotype of the Negro. The poem is worth setting against that compelling but grotesque caricature, Lawrence Olivier's performance. Othello, to Walcott, is a man driven by horror at "the corruption of an absolute". Walcott sees Othello as a

> . . . mythical, horned beast who's no more
> monstrous for being black.

The poem "Laventville" is a somber analysis of class and colour gradations, a relic of the middle passage. Up the hill at Laventville:

> the middle passage never guessed its end.
> This is the height of poverty
> for the desperate and black.

Very firmly Walcott places real, and yet symbolic, people:

> . . . The black, fawning verger
> his bow tie akimbo, grinning, the clown-gloved
> fashionable wear of those I deeply loved
>
> once, made me look on with hopelessness and rage
> at their new, apish habits, their excess
> and fear, the possessed, the self-possessed.

His cry of anguish, at the end, is informed by an analysis of history:

> Something inside is laid wide like a wound,
>
> some open passage that has cleft the brain,
> some deep, amnesiac blow. We left
> somewhere a life we never found,
>
> customs and gods that are not born again,
> some crib, some grill of light
> clanged shut on us in bondage, and withheld
>
> us from that world below us and beyond,
> and in its swaddling cerements we're still bound.

The slave left a culture behind in Africa — "customs and gods that are not born again" — but nothing has taken its place. The image of birth, recalled in "crib" and in "swaddling", shades into an image of death, "its swaddling cerements" (that is, graveclothes). Culturally speaking, the black West Indian baby is born dead.

In "grinding poverty" up the Laventville hillside the people find withheld from them "the world below them and beyond" — a separate world of culture, economics, social class.

Walcott is concerned too, about the dominance of mediocrity in this society. In "Codicil" he wearily laments:

> Once I thought love of country was enough,
> now, even I chose, there's no room at the trough.
>
> I watch the best minds root like dogs
> for scraps of favour.

Everybody is a nationalist these days. "Trough" nicely suggests the poet's dislike of the crude concourse. "Troughs" have water for animals, especially sheep.

A recurring concern is religion and the absence of religion. In "The Wedding of an Actress" we see the poet

> Wrestle with prayer and fail ·
> It is no use.
> In any church my brain is a charred vault
> Where demons roost,
> A blackened, shifting dust.

In "Crusoe's Island", the children return for vespers; and the poet reflects that art will not give the happiness that truly felt religion can.

> At dusk when they return
> For vespers, every dress
> Touched by the sun will burn
> A seraph's, an angel's,
> And nothing I can learn
> From art or loneliness
> Can bless them as the bell's
> Transfiguring tongue can bless.

Walcott is deeply concerned with West Indian problems, black problems, problems of faith, problems of art. This is the work of a patient artist, but also (even in the crudest sense) of a man who cares. In "A Village Life" he wrote:

> And since that winter I have learnt to gaze
> On life indifferently as through a pane of glass.

But this is modified by other statements in the very same book. The trumpeter,

Eddie, plays with a "fury of indifference"; and, finally, at the end of "Codicil" (the last poem of Walcott's latest book) a reminder: that we must not demand of the poet a crudely released commitment: if the work of art seems indifferent to our lives, we should remember:

All its indifference is a different rage.

There should be no doubt of Walcott's relevance to our society. The development of a reacting public for subtle West Indian poetry is one of our many educational needs.

Footnotes

[1] A lecture delivered at the Creative Arts Centre, U.W.I., on Monday 18th March, 1968.
[2] *The Pleasures of Exile* (Michael Joseph, 1960), p. 42.
[3] Longman's 1967.
[4] Heinemann Educational Books.
[5] Jonathan Cape, 1962.
[6] *Sunday Gleaner*, 13 May, 1962.
[7] Reported in *The Daily Gleaner*, 23 February, 1963.
[8] *The Chequer'd Shade* (Oxford University Press, 1958; Oxford Paperback 1963).
[9] Farrar, Straus & Company, 1964.
[10] Jonathan Cape, 1965.
[11] "West Indian Poetry, a Search for Voices", seminar sponsored by the Extra-Mural Department, U.W.I., 14 March 1965, fifth in a series on "The State of the Arts in Jamaica".
[12] From "The Lynching".
[13] From "If We Must Die".
[14] "The Intellectual Tradition and Social Change in the Caribbean", *New World Fortnightly*, Nos. 27 & 28, 12 November 1965.
[15] *The London Magazine*, September 1965, Vol. 5, No. 6.
[16] Devotions XVII (Nonesuch Library, Donne p. 538).
[17] "On Reading Louise Bennett, Seriously", *Jamaica Journal*, Vol. 1, No. 1, December 1967.
[18] *The London Magazine*, September 1965, Vol. 5, No. 6.

DREAMERS AND SLAVES —
The Ethos of Revolution in Walcott and Leroi Jones

Lloyd Brown

In January 1962 a Lower East Side theatre in New York presented *Moon on a Rainbow Shawl* with a cast headed by James Earl Jones who was later to receive national acclaim as Jack Johnson in Sackler's *Great White Hope*. Eight years later, in 1970, the National Broadcasting Company televised a play, *Dream on Monkey Mountain*, a few months before the stage version made its debut across the United States. Errol John, the author of *Moon on a Rainbow Shawl*, is a Trinidadian playwright. *Dream on Monkey Mountain* is the work of Derek Walcott, a St. Lucian now residing in Trinidad. The West Indian dramatist had finally arrived in the United States. Not in a flood, admittedly, neither with the reverberating impact of political activists like Marcus Garvey (Jamaica) and Stokeley Carmichael (Trinidad); nor with the loud acclaim of other literary predecessors like Claude McKay, the Jamaican poet-novelist of the twenties. But, however limited in number and general impact, the arrival of the West Indian dramatist in the United States of the sixties and seventies is of special significance for the contemporary history of Black America as a whole, and for the evolution of Black American theatre in particular. West Indian playwrights like Errol John and Derek Walcott are engaged in the kind of ethnic themes which imply significant parallels between the Black Caribbean and Black America, and which, in the process, appeal to the Pan-American sympathies of Black nationalism in the United States. John's *Moon on a Rainbow Shawl* explores the slum backyards of Port-of-Spain with the frank realism that we find in current images of the Black ghetto in Black American theatre. In Walcott's *Dream on Monkey Mountain* the quest for an African identity becomes an exploration of that revolutionary consciousness which is the subject of Black (revolutionary) theatre in America. And among Black American plays, Leroi Jones' *The Slave* offers the closest and most revealing parallels with Derek Walcott's work.

These parallels are revealing on two counts. First they demonstrate the cultural and psychological similarities — the Pan-African affinities — which link all Blacks who are in contact with a White world. The impoverished visionary/dreamer who inspires an imaginary crusade for a Black African heritage in Walcott's play is substantially similar, in kind, to the rebel-slave archetype who leads a Black insurrection in Jones' work. Secondly, these parallels shed some much needed light on *The Slave* itself. Ever since its first appearance in 1964 Jones' play has been the target of a fearful literalism that has been incapable of grasping the dramatist's symbolism or the metaphoric forms and rhetorical structures in which that symbolism is rooted. Instead of searching analysis and contributive insights we have been treated to a succession of short-sighted invectives — ranging from the charge that Jones' race-war theme is naive and suicidal to the allegation that the playwright is an hysterical monomaniac.[1] Of course Walcott's play is painstakingly explicit about *his* symbolic structure. The overt emphasis of both the "dream" title and the Narrative phantasmagoria is unmistakable. So are the explicit statements of the author's "Note on Production"; "The play is a dream, one that exists as much in the given minds of its principal characters as in that of its writer, and as such, it is illogical, derivative, contradictory. Its source is metaphor and it is best treated as a physical poem with all the subconscious and deliberate borrowings of poetry. Its style should be spare, essential as the details of a dream."[2]

From here it is not difficult to accept the play's "revolution" as a dream, a vision which symbolically projects the revolutionary potential of Makak, Walcott's peasant hero. In other words, the play is an analysis of whatever exists in the minds of the hero and his contemporaries — his messianic dream about a Back-to-Africa pilgrimage from the oppressive poverty of the Caribbean, or his obsessive ambivalence towards the White world. And contrary to hackneyed allegations about Jones' "suicidal monomania", I would suggest that the insurrection in *The Slave*, lends itself to a symbolical approach which does far more justice to the play's complexity than the familiar literalism. In short, Jones' Vessels Walker is conceived and presented in the play, not only as the literal leader of an actual insurrection, but also as the dreamer-revolutionary. The insurrection does have some significance as a futuristic or prophetic reality. After all, racial violence in the United States is both an historical fact and a continuing probability. But quite apart from *that* reality, the play is also a dream; its action exists in the mind of Jones' rebel-slave archetype; and on this basis it is a symbolical analysis of the paradoxes and self-conflicts which are inherent in Black revolutionary consciousness, or, indeed, in the very notion of Black revolution.

Conversely, the revolutionary "dream" or the visionary quest of Walcott's Makak symbolically projects the psychological realities of the Black man's relationship with both the White West and with the African past. Makak (Felix Hobain), a charcoal vender on a West Indian island, is jailed overnight for disorderly conduct. Strictly speaking, the play's action represents the fantasies which constitute Makak's dream-world and which are re-enacted in his mind during his overnight imprisonment; he is a Black Messiah whose quest for an African identity (he plans to return to Africa) is inspired by an "Apparition" (an image of the White woman). But Walcott does not allow us the luxury of viewing Makak's dream as an isolated, individual fantasy. For we are a part of his dream. And *our* implication is dramatized by the manner in which the "spectators" *within* the play/dream are incorporated into Makak's visionary world; his cell-mates, Tigre and Souris, the jailor Corporal Lestrade, and Makak's partner, Moustique — they are all principal actors in Makak's "fantasies" because, although they see him as a weak-headed old man, the dream also exists in *their* minds, and, implicitly, in the minds of the play's Black (theatre) audience.

In one sense, of course, our African dream and our revolutionary transcendental-ism are a kind of escape. On its most elemental, sexual level, Makak's dream of a White goddess/apparition compensates for the fact that he is ugly ("macaque," the monkey), sexually repulsive, and lonely. And beyond this, his dream lifts him above the harshness of his everyday poverty; the vision of an African splendour compensates for the self-hate that is ingrained in the Black psyche in a White world. As Makak himself summarizes, "I have left death, failure, disappointment, despair in the wake of my dreams" (*Dream on Monkey Mountain,* p. 305). But the nature of Makak's dream also touches upon the ambiguities and ironic self-conflicts of a Black revolutionary consciousness. For our revolutionary dreams are not merely a form of escape. They are also, paradoxically, a psycho-existential affirmation of self, of Black selfhood. However overly idealistic his revolutionary cause may be, and despite the romantici-zation of his "royal" African heritage, Makak affirms his human identity precisely because the capacity to dream has survived within him. Before his vision Makak is despised and self-hating, an impoverished hermit whose ugliness (that is, *Black* ugliness) makes Monkey Mountain an appropriate habitat (Monkeys are ugly, Black is ugly, and, of course, Blacks are monkeys/"makaks"). But at the end of his dream Makak expresses a triumphant sense of his own humanity which has been confirmed for us by his proven capacity for dreams. So that when he is released from prison the regaining of physical freedom is analogous to a birth, to revolutionary beginnings for Makak and his people.

> . . . . I have been washed from shore to shore, as a tree in the ocean.
> The branches of my fingers, the roots of my feet, could grip nothing,
> but now, God, they have found ground. Let me be swallowed up in
> mist again, and let me be forgotten, so that when the mist open, men
> can look up, at some small clearing with a hut, with a small signal of
> smoke, and say, "Makak lives there. Makak lives where he has always
> lived, in the dream of his people." Other men will come, other prophets
> will come, and they will be stoned, and mocked, and betrayed, but now
> this old hermit is going back home, back to the beginning, to the green
> beginning of this world. (p. 326)

In other words, the romantic fantasies about an African "home" of royal lions act as a catalyst, enabling Makak and his people to come home to their human selves. The dream-fantasy about revolution involves and confirms a very real revolutionizing of self-perception.

But this fantasy-reality paradox does not account for all the ambiguities which Walcott attributes to Makak's dream and its revolutionary ethos. For the very nature

of Makak's vision emphasizes a certain tension or self-conflict in the development of
a revolutionary consciousness. Makak first hears the "call" to a Black awareness from
the "Apparition" in his dream; "She say I should not live so any more, here in the
forest, frighten of people because I think I ugly. She say I come from the family of
lions and kings" (p. 236). But the apparition is a White woman, the "loveliest thing I
see on this earth,/Like the moon walking along her own road" (p. 227). Makak's
fascination with her White beauty is really the instinctive result of his self-hate as an
old man who is "ugly as sin." He is a man

> Without child, without wife.
> People forget me like the mist on Monkey Mountain.
> Is thirty years now I have look in no mirror,
> Not a pool of cold water, when I must drink,
> I stir my hands first, to break up my image. (p. 226)

And her whiteness compensates for his self-hate as a Black man. In his own crude way
Moustique who is really Makak's alter ego embodies this self-hate. Moustique's, and
Makak's ugliness and Blackness make the White woman (and, by extension, the
White world) inaccessible — and therefore more desirable. According to Moustique's
bitter reminder, "You is nothing. You black, ugly, poor, so you worse than nothing.
You like me. Small, ugly, with a foot like a 'S.' Man together two of us is minus one"
(p. 237).

   In effect, Makak's revolutionary consciousness is closely linked with the self-hate
and whiteness of his pre-revolutionary phase. The revolutionizing of his self-perception depends upon an intense awareness of the whiteness and self-hate; the Black man
must recognize the latter for what they are — as integral parts of his own psyche —
before he can deal with them. So that, initially, Makak's "Black" pride, his reaching
for some glorious African past of "lions and kings," is an affirmation, rather than a
negation, of his whiteness. For it is all aimed at proving some notion of humanity to
the White world rather than to himself. And his revolutionary Black awareness can
only be fully developed once he recognizes that the Apparition represents his continuing and subconscious allegiance to the White world which his rhetoric rejects. Hence
Corporal Lestrade, Makak's bourgeois alter ego, reminds him that he can only realize
his total Black humanity by destroying an allegiance that saps his revolutionary
potential.

> What you beheld, my prince, was but an image of your longing. As
> inaccessible as snow, as fatal as leprosy. Nun, virgin, Venus, you must
> violate, humiliate, destroy her; otherwise, humility will infect you . . .
> She is lime, snow, marble, moonlight, lilies, cloud, foam and bleaching
> cream, the mother of civilization, and the confounder of blackness. I too
> have longed for her. She is the colour of the law, religion, paper, art, and
> if you want peace, if you want to discover the beautiful depth of your
> blackness, nigger, chop off her head! When you do this, you will kill

> Venus, the Virgin, the Sleeping Beauty. She is the white light that
> paralysed your mind. (p. 319)

When Makak obeys, when he beheads the Apparition, the self-conflict ends, because in his words, he is now "free" — free of White value systems and images which have stunted his Black self-awareness.

Altogether then, Makak's dream is a mirror which reflects the paradoxes in his emergent self-awareness. The full development of a Black revolutionary conscious-ness depends upon a frank recognition of the Whiteness within, and of the Black-White tensions which account for the Black man's notorious double-consciousness, but which, ironically, also spark his perceptual revolution by forcing him to confront his self-contradictions. And having recognized his self-hate and Whiteness for what it is, then he must destroy it before he can progress from his initial ambiguities (Black rhetoric, White Apparition) to the unequivocal freedom of Black self-acceptance. This is the kind of progression that the Black American critic Larry Neal describes; the Black revolution is an internal violence, "the destruction of a weak spiritual self for a more perfect self. But it will be a necessary violence. It is the only thing that will destroy the double-consciousness — the tension that is in the souls of the black folk."[3]

This, too, is the progression that is dramatized by the relationship between Makak and those who both inhabit and share his dream. Moustique, his coal-vending partner in real life, and Corporal Lestrade, the mulatto policeman who takes him in custody for the night, enter the dream as Makak's alter egos. And as such they join the Apparition herself to complete the contradictions of Makak's undeveloped Black consciousness. Moustique's ugliness is a physical reflection of Makak's self-loathing. Moreover, when Moustique turns Makak's popularity into a quick, monetary profit, he represents the exploitive motives that are inherent in the initial stages of Makak's revolutionary development. In the absence of a fully developed Black awareness, Moustique remains faithful to his racial self-loathing by using Makak's idealism as a means of exploiting a gullible and impoverished community. So that taken together, Makak and Moustique represent the ambiguity of the undeveloped revolutionary psyche. It combines the new revolutionary idealism with the exploitive instincts of the old self-loathing; and this destructive ambiguity can also be resolved when Moustique, like the Apparition, is purged from Makak's consciousness through a ritualistic execution.

By the same token, the extreme, anti-Black neuroses of the mulatto Lestrade re-enact Makak's self-hate. When Lestrade is "converted" to Makak's Black cause his rampaging militancy is a guilty reflex which seeks to compensate for the old bourgeois self-hatred. Hence, like Makak, Lestrade can only be truly free when he recognizes the central paradox of the Black revolutionary consciousness — the psycho-existential link between the old self-hate and the new self-discovery. And he acknowledges this connection when he lectures Makak on the latter's need to destroy the Apparition ("I too have longed for her. She is the colour of the law, religion. . ."). In effect, Lestrade's earnest injunction to Makak is also a crucial confession of his own double conscious-ness. But, in symbolical terms, this is really Makak's confession, since Lestrade is his alter ego. Consequently, the Lestrade/Makak confession joins the execution of Moustique/Makak and the beheading of the Apparition; they are the initial purging which releases Makak into an untrammelled Black selfhood. The revolutionary psyche which Makak's dream projects is now complete. He now returns to that other reality represented by the jail cell. But, as we have already seen, the very capacity to dream has confirmed his revolutionary possibilities.

These are the "possibilities" which Jones' *The Slave* is also exploring. And, like his West Indian counterpart, Jones' analysis illuminates the paradoxical links between the new revolutionary psyche and the Black man's old double consciousness. Of course, on the more obvious political level, Vessels Walker's Black revolution does emphasize, and predict, the counter-productive effects of White repression. And in this sense *The Slave* is a rhetorical justification of Black violence against White society. But, once again, the literal and more obvious statements of Black revolutionary theatre do not account for all the crucial conflicts of the play. And in *The Slave* these tensions involve the Black man's perceptual values, the kinds of self-awareness which retard or promote his cultural revolution. In this regard we must view Vessels Walker and his two White antagonists, Grace and Bradford Easley in the same light in which we perceive Makak and his alter egos. They are three interrelated parts of a single whole — that whole being Walker's dual personality as a Black man in a White world. For quite apart from their obvious roles as symbols of that White world around Walker, Easley and Grace are projections of Walker's White values, of those criteria and desires which have inhibited his ethnic self-awareness. Moreover, this dramatization of Black self-perception is integrated with the aesthetic issue. For Walker is also a poet. And the symbolic emphasis on revolution as individual perception touches upon his role as an artist. His poetry is "White". As he reminds Easley, "It's changed to Yeats. Yeah, Yeats . . . Hey Professor, anthropologist, lecturer, loyal opposition, et cetera, didn't recognize those words as being Yeats'? Goddamn, I mean if you didn't recognize them . . . who the hell would?"[4] Easley is expected to recognize Walker's poetry because Walker's literary tastes and the professor's irrelevant intellectuality ("et cetera") are one. Walker hates Easley as the White enemy outside, but he loathes and fears him even more as the whiteness within.

In this respect, Grace is comparable with Easley, as well as with Makak's Apparition in Walcott's *Dream*. She represents that White femininity, that myth of the white goddess, which has historically held a fatal fascination for the Black man. Thus Walker's earlier love for Grace, and their former marriage, represent a psycho-sexual obsession which has always been destructive of the Black man's self-awareness. It is an obsession which has formed the racial triangle of the Black man, White woman and White man — even in Shakespeare; "remember when I used to play a second-rate Othello? Oh, wow . . . you remember that, don't you, Professor No-Dick? You remember when I used to walk around wondering what that fair sister was thinking? Oh, come on now, you remember that . . . I was Othello. . . Grace there was Desdemona . . . and you were Iago" (*Dutchman and the Slave*, p. 57).

In short, the racial treachery inherent in the Black man's white sex images is represented by Iago Easley — just as his exploitive self-loathing is symbolized by

Derek Walcott's Moustique/Makak. And this self-destructive whiteness is embodied in Jones' play by the half-man (Professor No-Dick) whose impotence symbolizes Walker's castrated Blackness. In reviling Grace and manhandling Easley, Walker tries to exorcize his own crippling Whiteness. Hence the contrast between Walker, the strong masterful male, and Easley, the weakling, represents an internal conflict between racial integrity and self-acceptance, on the one hand, and on the other, the half-manhood that results from the sexual and intellectual denial of one's own identity.

Easley, then, is the living personification of the aesthetic and racial values which threaten Walker's role as revolutionary. This is the point of the title, for having progressed from the slave status of the prologue, Walker is experiencing a transitional stage in which he recognizes his spiritual serfdom incarnated in Easley, his cultural alter ego. But this is precisely the point which escapes a fearfully literal reading of the play. The useful hysteria about the play's (successful) Black insurrection is gratuitous. The "race war" is less important as a literal happening, than as a symbolic, emotional catalyst for Walker's self-revelation and self-security. Indeed, the manner in which Jones presents Vessels Walker at the beginning of the play strongly suggests that the race war is not an objective event to all, but a projection of Walker's own highly subjective self-analysis.

All of which brings us to another significant parallel with Walcott's play — the dream structure. For, in a very real sense, the physical violence and the emotional confrontations in the main body of Jones' play are all a kind of dream, the self-vision of the old man (Vessels Walker) who appears in the prologue. In his own words,

> "we know, even before these shapes are realized, that these worlds,
> these depths or heights we fly to smoothly, as in a dream, or slighter,
> when we stare dumbly into space, leaning our eyes just behind a last
> quick moving bird, then sometimes the place and twist of what we are
> will push and sting, and what the crust of our stance will ring in our ears
> and shatter that piece of our eyes that is never closed. An ignorance. A
> stupidity. A stupid longing not to know . . . which is automatically
> fulfilled. Automatically triumphs. Automatically makes us killers or
> foot-dragging celebrities at the core of any filth." (*Dutchman and the
> Slave*, pp. 43-44)

Walker is preparing his audience for a "dream," a self-revealing vision that will disturb and awaken — it will "push and sting," and "ring in our ears." And since this is to be a form of self-recognition, it will shatter the apathy or the "stupid longing not to know" which characterizes the slave mentality. The shattering of this apathy will create either "killers" (real revolutionaries) or "foot-dragging celebrities" (jive revolutionaries who turn their militant image into personal profit). Applied to the events which follow the prologue, Walker's remarks imply that the race war incidents, and the meeting with Grace and Easley, are a visionary self-scrutiny. Or, to return to Walcott's preface to *Dream on Monkey Mountain*, Walker's experiences are all "a dream, one that exists as much in the given minds of the principal (character) as in that of its writer." And as a dream, these experiences project Walker's physical relationship with the main action suggesting a dream sequence — not unlike the psycho-Narrative structure of Walcott's *Dream*. He is an old man in the prologue, and at the end of his introductory speech, he assumes "the position he will have when the play starts." If this physical transformation suggests, as it should, that there is a "fading-in" to the main-action dream-sequence, then the physical metamorphosis at the end of the play is equally symbolic; as Walker the rebel-leader stumbles out, he becomes "the old man at the beginning of the play" — signifying the "fade-out" of the dream.

All of which brings up the question of Walker's identity. He himself points to its ambiguity in the prologue; "I am much older than I look . . . or maybe much younger. Whatever I am or seem . . . to you, then let that rest. But figure still you might not be right." He is warning us against a literal approach to his character, for he is an archetypal symbol of the Black psyche and of Black history. He is *both* younger and older than he looks because he incorporates the past and the present — and his dream opens up future possibilities. The "old" field-slave personality is the key to this archetypal role. That role is ambiguous. In one sense his servile status symbolizes the subjection to white images like those embodied by Grace and Easley. But in another sense, his identity as a *field* slave points up his revolutionary potential, for in this regard, he fulfils Malcolm X's remarks about the field slave in Black American history! Unlike the house Negro who loved the white slave-master, the field Negroes "were in the majority, and they hated the master. . . If someone came to the field Negro and said, 'Let's separate, let's run,' he didn't say 'Where we going?' He'd say, 'Any place is better than here.' You've got field Negroes in America today. I'm a field Negro. The masses are the field Negroes."[5]

Walcott's Makak, Malcolm X's field Negro, and now Jones' field slave are all linked by their potential for revolution; and in Jones' play the "race war" vision is an introspective exploration of this potential within Walker, the archetype of past and present ("older" and "younger") militancy. Hence Walker's visionary conflicts are comparable with the psycho-ethnic tensions in Makak's dream; they represent the contrast between the White images and the self-hating implications of his servile status, on the one hand, and on the other hand, the rebellious predisposition of the field-slave figure. To return to Walker's cryptic prologue, his "ideas," or "theories" (dreams) are expressed through borrowed (White) concepts and language. "As: Love is an instrument of knowledge." But they also involve the discovery of an image that belongs to a long tradition of Black revolution/resistance; "old, old blues people moaning in their sleep, singing, man, oh nigger, nigger, you still here, as hard as nails, and takin' no shit from nobody" (p. 45). Indeed, the ability to dream and to explore his psyche through the dream symbols, confirms this rebellious pre-disposition — even after the dream inevitably comes to an end, as it does in Walcott's *Dream*. And it is this self-exploration that links Jones' slave with Walcott's dreamer. They are *both* dreamers whose visions are, in one sense, symbolical of that fantasy/escape which colours the prophetic ideal. But in a more pressing sense these visions also imply the capacity to revolutionize self-perception. Hence although the dreams themselves must end, in both plays this ending is actually a beginning — the existential beginnings of a new Black self-definition.

Footnotes

[1] Donald P. Costello, "Black Man as Victim," *Commonweal* LXXXVIII (June 28, 1966), 436-440; Edward Margolies, *Native Sons; A Critical Study of Twentieth-Century Negro American Authors* (Philadelphia, 1968), pp. 192-198.
[2] *Dream on Monkey Mountain and Other Plays* (New York, 1970), p. 208.
[3] "And Shine Swam On," in *Black Fire: An Anthology of Afro-American Writing*, eds. Leroi Jones and Larry Neal, Apollo ed. (New York, 1969), p. 656.
[4] *Dutchman and the Slave*, Apollo ed. (New York, 1964), p. 51.
[5] *Malcolm X Speaks*, Evergreen ed. (New York, 1966), p. 11.

BIG NIGHT MUSIC:
Derek Walcott's
Dream on Monkey Mountain
and the
"Splendours of Imagination"

Robert E. Fox

— Dream. Ona nonday I sleep. I dreamt of a somday. Of a wonday I shall wake.[1]

In Derek Walcott's own words, "The play is a dream, one that exists as much in the given minds of its principal characters as in that of its writer, and as such, it is illogical, derivative, and contradictory. Its source is metaphor. . ."[2] This statement is crucial to any profound understanding of the work, and my purpose in this essay shall be to examine the nature and function of dreams in the play in an effort to elucidate one essential level of meaning in Walcott's *magnum opus*.

I

In the world of the work — that is, within the context of the play itself — we are presented with a dream and a dream-within-a-dream. But in the context of the work within the world — that is, beyond the text or enactment of the drama — we are also confronted with a dream: Walcott's creative vision which informs the play, and which is itself a part of a larger dream in the mind of mankind, an edenic dream of elemental freedom.[3] Beginning on a "realistic" level in the play we move rapidly into the realm of *poetic* reality, spiraling evermore inward toward an essential core of meaning before ascending once more to the "logic" of the waking world,[4] But this essential core of meaning, discoverable by the individual through an internal voyage, exists beyond the individual — or any individual work of art — in a collective consciousness which Art as a spiritual endeavor has always striven to articulate. So, at the play's conclusion, when we are told that "Makak lives where he has always lived, in the dream of his people" (p. 326), the world within the work and the work within the world merge at the crossroads of the imagination. Makak comes from, and he returns to, the world of myth.[5]

One of the perennial motifs of myth is that of the seeker, the defier of odds and gods, and his redemptive quest; and one of myth's lessons to mankind lies in the articulation of the rhythms of recurrence, the repetitive nature of experience. Walcott grasped these concepts early. He "recalls the familiar scene in his childhood when the story teller would sit by the fire to narrate stories involving a 'hero whose quest is never done', and explains how it became necessary for him to appropriate the image of that hero in his plays."[6] And his brother, Roderick Walcott, has noted that "The legends of Papa Diablo, Mama Glos, lajables, and the sukuya can remain if only we tell them over and over again."[7]

Imagination solidified itself in the ambiguous person of an actual individual whom Walcott vividly remembers. "My Makak comes from my own childhood. I can see him for what he is now, a brawling, ruddy drunk who would come down the street on a Saturday when he got paid and let out an immense roar that would terrify all the children . . . When we heard him coming we all bolted, because he was like a baboon . . . This was a degraded man, but he had some elemental force in him that is still terrifying; in another society he would have been a warrior."[8]

These images from Walcott's past, folkloric and literal, are fused in the character of Felix Hobain, whose metaphoric identity is Makak, the monkey-man, the lion and king. Makak, one of the lowliest of the low, is the one in whom the dream is invested. The dream that transforms Makak is, in a very real sense, Walcott's own dream, his artist's vision which espies the potential for greatness in "a degraded man", which recognizes the raw power behind seeming impotence.

> These dead, these derelicts,
> that alphabet of the emaciated,
> they were the stars of my mythology.[9]

Makak then becomes representative of the downtrodden and impoverished blacks who long to be redeemed, and of the transformation that brings about, or at least prefaces, such redemption.

II

Speaking specifically of the anguish of the West Indian, Walcott says, "we have not wholly sunk into our own landscapes" (p. 20), thus defining an inherent rootlessness. It is a concern that numerous writers share, but Walcott, like Wilson Harris, attempts the absorption into the indigenous landscape along with a corresponding exploration of a mind — or dreamscape: "a country for the journey of the soul" (p. 24), as Walcott calls it. Both of these geographies — the literal and the imaginative — are recreated and fused through *language*.

It is through language, in fact, that Walcott envisions the salvation of "the New-World Negro." "What would deliver him from servitude was the forging of a language that went beyond mimicry, a dialect which had the force of revelation as it invented names for things, one which finally settled on its own mode of inflection, and which began to create an oral culture of chants, jokes, folk-songs and fables . . . " (p. 17). The poet in his primal role as maker is the one who can forge this recreative language that will provide a vehicle for the liberation of consciousness from its colonized state. But it is obvious here that the way forward is the way back: to roots. "For imagination and body to move with original instinct, we must begin again from the bush. That return journey, with all its horror of rediscovery, means the annihilation of what is known . . . On such journeys the mind will discover what it chooses . . ." (pp. 25- 26). But a choice made via the annihilation of the known can only be instinctual, unconscious, intuitive, it will not be *rational.*

The true arena of the drama, then, is that of the mind, of imagination. Its vehicle is dream, which enables Walcott to dispense with normal logic, linearity, literalness, and emphasize instead myth, recurrence, ambiguity.[10] When the cages rise out of sight during Makak's deposition — his first recital of his dream — we have a graphic representation of the liberating power of the imagination. This is Walcott's strategy throughout: to demonstrate the disparities between a consciousness that is creative and metaphoric, and one that is straightforward and imprisoning. Makak, for instance, is said to be in a state of "incomprehensible intoxication" (p. 224). He may literally be drunk, or this could be merely a pejorative characterization of his dream and madness by someone who remains untouched by them. Especially the dream is described as "vile," "obscene" and "ambitious". The charges of being "uppity" and sexually depraved are those traditionally leveled at blacks by racists, and Corporal Lestrade has absorbed this mentality, or rather, he has been possessed by it.

"Incomprehensible intoxication" might be one label a modern, scientific mind would apply to the trance states of mystics, seers and shamans. When Makak declares, "Spirits does talk to me" (p. 225), a "rational" person would perhaps dismiss this as hallucination, but a "primitive" individual would know that Makak is in touch with the traditional world, which encompasses a nonmaterial reality.[11] Makak is a visionary, and the visionary stance is fraught with peril. He is able to exorcise a dying man's sickness when "priest," "white doctor," and "bush medicine" fail, and he tries to do the same with his people, only to be rejected by them because they are incapable of belief. Makak is struggling with a pejorative limitation on his psyche and being which his dream helps him transcend. Failure to "dissolve in his dream" means that one remains imprisoned. Moustique, for example, masters the rhetoric of salvation but he lacks vision; he has not experienced the power of the dream but merely wishes to exploit it. Hence Basil says of him, when unmasking him in the marketplace, "The tongue is on fire, but the eyes are dead"(p. 269).

In his recital of his dream, Makak describes himself as walking through white mist to the charcoal pit on the mountain. He is ascending the slope of consciousness, journeying through whiteness to blackness, through vagueness toward a solid identity. "Make the web of the spider heavy with diamonds/And when my hand brush it, let the chain break" (pp. 226-27) — that is, the chain of slavery, both psychological and actual. The spider's web represents the entanglements of history, racism, colonialism; the diamonds are the oppressed. In his role as saviour, Makak is able to shatter this evil beauty with an almost casual gesture. The dream transcends time, telescopes spiritual and physical evolution, so that Makak moves, in the infinite space of a poetic moment, from ape to God[12]:

> I have live all my life
> Like a wild beast in hiding . . . .
> And this old man walking, ugly as sin,
> In a confusion of vapour,
> Till I feel I was God self, walking through cloud. (pp. 226-27)

Again, in the healing scene, Makak stands with a burning coal in his palm, chanting a formula for salvation, striving to save the sick man from an actual death and his people from the living death of degradation and despair. "Faith! Faith! / Believe in yourselves" (p. 249). The energy released by the burning charcoal symbolizes the spiritual energy released by Makak's positive confirmation of his blackness. "You are living coals," he tells them, "/ you are trees under pressure, / you are brilliant diamonds . . . " The decomposed matter from primeval vegetation was transformed into coal, and diamonds are the result of coal under enormous pressure, over great periods of geological time. Burning coal brings light; diamonds reflect and refract light. Hence Moustique's echo, in the marketplace, of Makak's metaphor: "One billion, trillion years of pressure bringing light, and is for that I say, Africa shall make light" (p. 268). Here, of course, Moustique is speaking better than he knows. The "revelation of my experience" that he talks of is that of his people, the broader dimensions of which Makak's dream calls back from a darkness of oppression, forgetfulness and ignorance.

The dream which redeems, the imaginative reversal that transforms a poor charcoal burner into royalty, has its roots in historical fact. In his book *The Loss of El Dorado*, V.S. Naipaul relates how the black slaves in Trinidad at the beginning of the nineteenth century created kingdoms of the night, with their own kings, queens and courtiers, elaborate uniforms, and other regal paraphernalia. During the day the blacks laboured and endured the cruelty and contempt of their masters; but beneath the moon these same slaves were for a time themselves metamorphosed into masters, issuing commands and miming splendours, while their white owners became the objects of mockery and fantasies of revenge.[13] One of these nocturnal regiments, led by a King Sampson, was known as the Macacque regiment.[14] In light of the condemnations meted out during the apotheosis scene in *Dream*, it is significant to note as well from Naipaul's account that "the role of the Grand Judge, who punished at night as the overseer punished by day was important."[15]

This nighttime pageantry was redemptive drama, an elaborate masquerade which enabled the oppressed to vivify their ancestral memories while at the same time reversing, if only momentarily, the bitter realities of the present. Naipaul remarks,

"Negro insurrection, which seemed so sudden in its beginnings and endings and so casual in its betrayals, was usually only an aspect of Negro fantasy; but an adequate leader could make it real."[16] It never came to this. In 1805, the imaginary kingdoms were revealed — practically voluntarily, as if the secret were too good to keep — and the slave aristocracy was executed or whipped. Still, until such time as the powers of rebellion proved to be sufficiently substantive, the dream remained as a possible vehicle of escape from despair; and, while they lasted, the kingdoms of the night must have been a positive force, a means of sustaining the slave in what were otherwise intolerable circumstances. There are those who would argue — and indeed the same criticism has been directed against *Dream* — that the blacks would have been better off had they refrained from fantasy and resorted instead to violence. But this is itself a form of romanticism. When you have been reduced to a dehumanized state, you must first regain your dignity; when you have been relegated to physical toil, the mind must sometimes soar above the body. If you are an animal, why not be a lion? If you are a slave, why not dream of being a king (especially when you may be the descendent of kings?)[17] Dreams may be attacked as nothing more than dreams, but in the beautiful words of Delmore Schwartz, "In dreams begin responsibilities."

III

Monkey Mountain is depicted in the Prologue as "volcanic" (p. 212), which suggests unpredictability, slumbering violence, submerged and smouldering energies that will one day demand release. Makak's dream taps these hidden energies and gives them form and substance in a way that the criminality of Tigre or Souris or the oppressive mentality of the corporal (themselves crude manifestations of the need for self-assertion, of a refusal to accept identitylessness) cannot. Makak repeatedly insists that his dream is not a dream, whereas others characterize it, not only as a dream, but a *bad* one. They are literalists, fatalistic and unimaginative, like the politicians whom Walcott describes as "generation after generation / heaped in a famine of imagination."[18] Even though the charges that the corporal addresses against Makak clearly include incitement to rebellion (pp. 224-25), even though Makak himself declares that it is "better to die, fighting like men, than to hide in this forest" (p. 242), *Dream on Monkey Mountain* cannot be said to advocate revolution in the circumscribed political sense. What Walcott thinks about colonialism, racism, oppression — the "dream of milk" as he calls it (p. 290) — ought to be evident from the play; but Walcott is equally clear about an opposite but attendant danger, characterized by him as "Witchdoctors of the new left with imported totems" (p. 35). The solution is not politics. "The future of West Indian militancy lies in art" (p. 18).[19]

One reason why this should be so can be adduced from the tension in the play between a fulfilling, integrative sensibility — represented by Makak and his dream — on the one hand, and divisive, reductionist tendencies — manifested in the likes of the corporal and Moustique — on the other. Plurality of experience is suggested by the number of doublings and pairings we find in the play. Makak and Moustique provide one dual, complementary partnership; Tigre and Souris present another pair who offer a similar contrast. Basil seems sometimes to be paired with the dancer, sometimes with the white apparition. The corporal is really a double in himself: he is both black and white, and shifts from one pole of being to the other partway through the play.[20] The sun and the moon form another pair, the former representing "reality" and the latter "dream." The prevailing tendency — which the play implicitly condemns — is to emphasize one aspect of identity or experience at the expense of all others. The corporal tries to be white, then reverses the process and strives to be as black as possible. The pragmatic aspect of Makak, symbolized by Moustique, dies twice. The moon is slain in order to free the sun. White supremacy is established on the myth of black inferiority, then black supremacy asserts itself.

According to Walcott's stage directions, the moon reversed becomes the sun; the two are opposed but joined, Janus-like. Makak "kills" the moon so that the sun can rise and free them all from the dream in which they are locked "and treading their own darkness" (p. 305). Sun and moon each have their particular clarity; it is only that all things appear equal under the sun (Makak, Moustique, the corporal, the thieves are all "imprisoned"). It is the moon and its attendant world of dreams beneath which we experience vital contrasts, revealing differentiations.[21]

In the contradictory dreamworld, these differentiations become ambiguous; distinctions between things keep shifting, altering. But characters with restrictive, "logical" mentalities keep struggling to reduce things to simple black and white, and Corporal Lestrade is perhaps the preeminent example of this behavior. In his role as the upholder of the rules of Her Majesty's government, the corporal functions as Makak's prosecutor. Later, in the important apotheosis scene, where the power of shaping history now lies with Makak and his retinue, the corporal is still functioning as a prosecutor, but this time upholding the law of the tribes against the threat of whiteness. He has changed his allegiance but retains his legalistic devotion, with its logic and rationalism. (When the corporal says of Makak, "I can both accuse and defend this man" [p. 220], he is articulating his ability to switch sides easily, a testimony to his innate opportunism and uncertain sense of identity.[22]) For him, the white goddess, who represents the negative aspect of his own previous possession (by "English" and all that it implies), is much more of a threat than she is to Makak, for whom she functions as muse. The corporal has reduced her to one (especially for him) damaging context: the mother of (Western) civilization — in other words, Europe. (Eur-opë = "she of the broad face" — that is, the full moon.[23])

IV

Walcott himself characterizes the apparition as having four roles (or phases): the moon, the muse, the white goddess, a dancer. All of these manifestations coalesce into a simultaneous complex of meaning, splendidly articulated by Robert Graves in *The White Goddess*. He writes, "Her name and titles are innumerable. In ghost stories she often figures as 'The White Lady,' and in ancient religions, from the British Isles to the Caucasus, as the 'White Goddess'." She is the Muse, "the Mother of All Living, the ancient power of fright and lust — the female spider or the queen-bee whose embrace is death."[24] The Night Mare is one of her cruelest aspects.[25] But it is she who inspires the magical language of poetic myth which "remains the language of true poetry."[26] Hence the goddess has complementary moods of creation and destruction.[27]

One of the further aspects of the muse is Mnemosyne, "Memory": and this is important for the play in that it is through the dream inspired by the white goddess that Makak journeys back to the roots of his heritage, to the time when he was both "lion and king."[28] Before his inspiration, Makak could declare, like the speaker in Walcott's poem "Names": "I began with no memory. I began with no future."[29] And when he does make a beginning, it is "where Africa began: / in the body's memory."[30]

Since Makak is clearly posited in the play as a kind of Christ-figure, one is likely to question the simultaneous emphasis on the rather pagan white goddess, since, as Graves reminds us, the concept of such a creative anima was banned by Christian theologians nearly two thousand years ago and by Jewish theologians even earlier.[31] But if we move outside the mainstream of orthodoxy, as artists are wont to do, there is no real contradiction or incompatibility, for the ancient Irish and British poets "saw Jesus as the latest theophany of the same suffering sacred king whom they had worshipped under various names from time immemorial."[32] Furthermore, the Gnostics held that Jesus "was conceived in the mind of God's Holy Spirit, who was female in Hebrew"[33] — which is enlightening in view of the fact that Makak refers to himself as "responsible only to God who once speak to me *in the form of a woman* on Monkey Mountain" (p. 226; my emphasis). Graves goes on to remark that the "male Holy Ghost is a product of Latin grammar — *spiritus* is masculine — and of early Christian distrust of female deities or quasi-deities."[34] The corporal's indictment of the apparition — "She is the wife of the devil, the white witch" (p. 319) contains strong echoes of this intolerance.

Makak in his role as the King of Africa and the saviour of his people is an image of the Sacred King who is the moon goddess's divine victim, who dies and is reborn in the cycle of perpetual renewal; and, as the madman, the dreamer, the visionary poet, he is also the muse's victim, for the two roles interpenetrate.[35] But Makak refuses to die this death, slaying the white goddess instead, under the pressure of the corporal's vehement prosecution and the collective animosity of the tribes. In doing so he frees himself from the dream, but only on one level — a level on which, as Moustique correctly diagnoses, a betrayal of the true cause is taking place, blindness replacing vision, maleficent madness driving out beneficent madness. It is Moustique who dies, and, in so doing, attains wisdom; he who had himself betrayed the dream by attempting to market it is later able to see that the dream is now being prostituted by others for political ends.[36] And the corporal has to go to the verge of death before he experiences a necessary (but not thoroughgoing) transformation.

Makak has to kill the white goddess for several reasons: one, because he cannot forever go on depending upon his source of inspiration but has to begin to rely upon himself[37] (just as he had earlier insisted that the people have faith in themselves as well as in an outside force); two, he has to come back from the world of visionary truth to the everyday world, in order to translate and transmit the fruits of his experience; and, three, he has to escape from the somewhat perverted role of tyrant which the corporal and others have thrust upon him, as well as from the complementary role of saviour that is so fraught with agony and peril.

When Makak divests himself of his royal robe before he beheads the apparition, he is symbolically freeing himself from the bondage of kingship as well as that of the dream and all externally-imposed definitions of selfhood. Indeed, Makak's real name, Felix ("happy") is only revealed in the Epilogue, after he has finally discovered who he is. It is not quite as simple as waking up, because, paradoxically, on one level the dream continues right to the play's end. What happens is that Makak moves from his personal dream back to the realm of collective dream, where his experience becomes universalized and undifferentiated.

In an early poem by W.B. Yeats, Fergus of the Red Branch tells a druid of his desire to "Be no more a king / But learn the dreaming wisdom that is yours."[38] Taken as an admonition, these words could apply appropriately enough to Makak, who in the apotheosis scene witnesses the clarity of his vision being distorted by the blindness of revenge, the salvational role of leadership reduced to a rallying-point for fanaticism. Just as he must escape from the thrall of the muse, Makak must free himself from the perversions of power. The recogniton of kingliness, the possibility of triumph, are sufficient for the satisfaction of the psychic hunger for reinforcement. It is similar to the realization that it is enough to travel to Africa in one's mind; indeed, that such an imaginative journey may be ultimately preferable to an actual one. Ironically, the dream seems to reassert reality once more, though on a higher plane of recognition. Makak, after all, is no king; he is merely himself — but that self is now endowed with dignity and a certain prophetic wisdom. As long as the dream remains a dream, we can awaken from it or dream it again. The danger is when people like Corporal Lestrade try to make the dream literal. Then there is no more imagining and no more awakening; no true freedom, only another confining structure.

Footnotes

[1] James Joyce, *Finnegans Wake*, New York: The Viking Press, 1959, p. 481.
[2] "A Note on Production," in *Dream on Monkey Mountain and Other Plays*, New York: Farrar, Straus and Giroux, 1970, p. 208. All citations are from this edition. Subsequent references appear in parentheses in the text.
[3] Schiller declared that "Freedom belongs only to the realm of dreams." (Quoted by Victor Ehrenberg in *Man, State and Deity* [London: Methuen, 1974], p. 24.)I take this to mean, not that there is no such thing as freedom, but that freedom rather persists in the mind, in the visionary aspect of man, even when the world conspires to stamp it out.
[4] It is worth noting here that the structure of the play recapitulates that of the rites of passage — separation: trial/initiation: return — which may be seen as a paradigm for the black experience.
[5] I have said that we move in the play from a "realistic" level to a poetic one before re-emerging on a "normal" plane. Yet this seems an oversimplification, which is why I have enclosed the word realistic in quotation marks; for the very first mention of dream comes in the Prologue, in the song "Mooma, momma," and it alludes to prophecy and

clairvoyance (one of many crucial thematic undercurrents): "Forty days before the Carnival, Lord, / I dream I see me funeral" (p. 213). Indeed,as the mimed action at the very outset of the play reveals quite clearly, we are in the world of dreams, of myth and folklore, to begin with. Suddenly and profoundly in Walcott's work we delve into what Joyce called "the Deepsleep Sea" (*Finnegans Wake*, p. 37), the communal source of metaphor.

6 Quoted in Samuel Omo Asein; "The Growth and Reputation of Derek Walcott as a Playwright" (unpublished Ph.D. dissertation, University of Ibadan, Nigeria, 1974), p. 232.

7 *Ibid.*, p. 235.

8 Ibid., p. 304.

9 Derek Walcott, *Another Life*, New York: Farrar, Straus and Giroux, 1973, p. 22.

10 In so doing, he is confirming an important feature of African art. See Jean Laude, *The Arts of Black Africa*, Berkeley: University of California Press, 1971, pp. 244-45.

11 It is significant that Makak also has a traditional knowledge of herbs; he is a healer. At one point, Tigre refers to Makak as a "crazy ganga-eating bastard" (p. 289*)* — the literalist view again — whereas Makak himself is emphasizing the shamanistic and ritual qualities of herbs when he tells Souris, "When your eyes open, you will be transformed, as if you have eaten a magic root" (p. 291*)*.

12 Cf. these lines from *Malcochon*: "Between beasthood and Godhead groping in a dream" *(Dream on Monkey Mountain and Other Plays*, p. 205).

13 Harmondsworth: Penguin Books, 1973, pp. 291-99.

14 *Ibid.*, p. 295.

15 *Ibid.*, pp. 296 and 386.

16 *Ibid.*, p. 292.

17 Lloyd W. Brown makes a similar point: " [O]ur revolutionary dreams are not merely a form of escape. They are also, paradoxically, a psycho-existential affirmation of self, of Black Selfhood. However overly idealistic his revolutionary cause may be, and despite the romanticism of his 'royal' African heritage, Makak affirms his human identity precisely because the capacity to dream has survived within him." — "The Revolutionary Dream of Walcott's Makak," in Edward Baugh, ed., *Critics on Caribbean Literature*, London: George Allen & Unwin, 1978, pp. 58-59.

18 "Party Night at the Hilton," in *Sea Grapes*, London: Jonathan Cape, 1976, p. 26.

19 In his essay, "The Muse of History," Walcott refers to the "great poets of the New World, from Whitman to Neruda," whose vision is Adamic and for whom man "is still capable of enormous wonder." "This", he declares, "is the revolutionary spirit at its deepest," where fact "evaporates into myth," recalling "the spirit to arms." — Edward Baugh, ed., *op. cit.*, p. 39.

20 The following description of Raymond Kassoumi, from Yambo Ouologuem's novel *Bound to Violence*, London: Heinemann, 1971, p. 137, seems perfectly applicable to the corporal: "The white man had crept into him and this white presence determined even the moves that he, a child of violence, would make against it."

21 It is worth noting here that "the psychic characteristic of all Black African civilizations is lunar and not solar . . .," according to Boris de Rachewiltz, *Introduction to African Art*, London: John Murray, 1966, p. 48.

22 Cf. the politicians who "explain to the peasant why he is African" but do not really appear to understand what it means themselves, in *Another Life*, p. 127.

23 Robert Graves, *The White Goddess*, London: Faber and Faber, 1961, p. 173.

[24] *Op. cit.*, p. 24.

[25] *Ibid.*, p. 25.

[26] *Ibid.*, p. 10. Graves also notes, "Poetry began in the matriarchal age, and derives its magic from the moon, not from the sun" (p. 448)

    In the "Ion," Plato also makes an interesting reference to the Muse, whom he says inspires the poet, not to art, but to enthusiasm, to a kind of delirium. This clearly seems to be her effect on Makak.

[27] *The White Goddess*, p. 178.

[28] *Lion* can be seen as a homophone for *king.* Cf. Jan Vansina, *Oral Tradition,* Harmondsworth: Penguin Books, 1973, p. 69.

[29] *Sea Grapes*, p. 40.

[30] *Another Life*, p. 25 .

[31] *The White Goddess*, p. 490.

[32] *Ibid.*, p. 143.

[33] *Ibid.*, p. 157.

[34] *Ibid.*, p. 157.

[35] *Ibid.*, p. 489.

[36] Moustique in the apotheosis scene is the voice of reason in its timeless conflict with blind authority. Moustique has always been down-to-earth, practical. He will sell Makak's dream to fill his belly (he is compelled, in other words, by necessity, not avarice), but he is incapable of fanaticism, which is one dangerous pitfall for visionaries.

[37] Makak at one point declares that if the moon goes out, he will still find his way (p. 286). In a sense he has already learned to do without her before he is forced to kill her. Thus for him the killing is an anticlimax, while for the tribes it is a ritual act, an iconoclasm which destroys a negative or potentially disparaging symbol, while at the same time providing vivid dramatic impact.

[38] "Fergus and the Druid," in *Collected Poems,* New York: Macmillan, 1956, p. 32.

WITHERING INTO TRUTH:
A Review of Derek Walcott's
The Gulf and Other Poems

Gordon Rohlehr

The publication of Derek Walcott's *In a Green Night* (1962) was a landmark in the history of West Indian poetry, liberating it at once from a simple, mindless romanticism, a weak historicism, over-rhetorical protest and sterile abstraction. That volume of poems was a remarkable attempt by a West Indian to come to terms with a tangled cultural heritage which offered both the vision of unbearable brutality, and the promise of rich variety. There Walcott echoes a number of very different English poets from Shakespeare and Marvell to T.S. Eliot, Yeats and Dylan Thomas, but, what is more important, transposed those echoes into his own peculiar music, so that for the first time West Indian landscape was being genuinely seen, and interpreted by a British West Indian poet.

What clearly distinguished Walcott's verse then from that of his English contemporaries was not only its rich variety, but its controlled vitality and inner affirmative music, which could be heard even in exceedingly melancholy poems like "Nearing La Guaira." But even then, there were disquieting hints of the void beneath the amazing vitality, and a kind of dryness qualifying the lyricism.

Homecoming showed its ironies, and the joy of "As John to Patmos" with its assertion that "This island is heaven — away from the dustblown blood of cities," became the disillusion of "Return to D'Ennery, Rain."

> Despairing in action we ask
> O God, where is our home? . . .
> The passionate exiles believe it, but the heart
> Is circled by its sorrows, by its horror
> And bitter devotion to home. (p. 34)

Underlying all this too, was a fear that poetic energy would waste away as experience began to seem increasingly more banal.

212

No Florida loud with citron leaves
With crystal falls to heal this age
Shall calm the darkening fear that grieves
The loss of visionary rage
Or if Time's fires seem to blight
The nature ripening into art,
Not the fierce noon or lampless night
Can quail the comprehending heart.
("In a Green Night" p. 73)

The Castaway (1965) and *The Gulf* (1969) read like fulfilments of this prophetic fear. In *The Castaway*, significantly, a recurring image is that of fire. The sun suggests an inferno, a kiln, whose blazing harshness withers rather than purifies. Time's fires not only ripen experience into art, but wither the mind into dry despair. The consequences of Walcott's imperfect homecoming are beginning to be felt. Ocean becomes a placid void, image of the life emptiness of the Crusoe-like castaway figure who haunts the book.

The theme of alienation demands a difference in style, a hardening of the verse which also becomes much less regular, more fragmented, and more studied. There is also a growing sense that the poet is inhabiting a region inside his head, from which he turns a dry bleached stare on external phenomena. Exile at home has an immediacy and an inner frenzy quite distinct from the grey tedium of exile in the metropolis.

If the sense of ice and fog pervades books like Lamming's *The Emigrants* and Selvon's *The Lonely Londoners*, the sense of fire and calm vacuity pervades *The Castaway* . . . The bitter anger of a poem like "Laventville", for example, is occasioned by much more than the economic poverty, empty mimicry and psychic castration which Walcott identifies as the main elements of Creole culture in Trinidad. The fire runs through that poem, which is really a measure of his own sense of alienation from the people in this, the country of his adoption. On the one hand, there is a dry loneliness, on the other hand a frenzied, helpless rage. Both are the distinct moods of exile, the consistent elements of tropic death. Between these extremes, there is detachment, a kind of indifference.

Walcott ends *The Castaway* with a quest for such indifference. But in the last line of the ominously named final poem "Codicil" (a codicil is an appendage to one's last will and testament), he insists that such indifference, the cold eye which he would like to cast on death and life, is a "different rage", another kind of frenzy which, presumably, indicates a severer commitment.

The Gulf (1969) is the logical successor of the other two volumes, beginning where *The Castaway* left off. The scene of the title poem is an aeroplane travelling over The Gulf of Mexico. In this plane, the poet, like the lovers' souls in Donne's "The Extasie," separated from terrestrial attachments, is free to contemplate the meaning of things like human struggle, revolution, democracy, the Civil Rights' Movement, the seasonal assassination of Presidents, the whole macabre farce that is the American Dream, the total failure of men to learn from experience even of death; and more personal things like his own angst, the meaning and tenuity of human love, the finality of death.

In other words, "The Gulf" deals with the general chasm separating peoples, cultures and even individuals within the closed unit of a family, who seek to erect their frail barrier of love against change, time and death. In a sense, the title poem contains all the major themes of the entire volume. But The Gulf-image signifies more than this. It is the image of the general sense of life — emptiness which afflicts Walcott; for the poet has retreated even farther into the region of the void within his head.

Indeed, the image of The Gulf appeared before in *The Castaway*. It is explicitly mentioned in the epigraph to the poem "Crusoe's Journal."

> I looked now upon the world as a thing remote, which I had nothing
> to do with, no expectation from, and, indeed, no desires about . . . and
> well might I say, as Father Abraham to Dives, "Between me and thee is a
> great gulf Fixed." *(Robinson Crusoe)*

This might well be the epigraph to *The Gulf* also, a volume where the image of the poet looking at the world through darkened glass, or from a moving vehicle recurs time and again. An odd sense of abstraction hangs about the world he describes, as if each image were surrounded by its individual void. The poet has in Yeats' phrase, "withered into the truth." He continually hunts out images to express this withering." In the opening poem, symbolically named "Ebb", he describes this withering in terms of the gradual bulldozing of the landscape to build the new industrial city. "Scurf-streaked bungalows and pioneer factory" replace.

> . . . a dark aisle
> of fountaining, gold coconuts, an oasis
> marked for the yellow Caterpillar tractor. (p. 37)

The image is one of desecration — "aisle" suggests church — and blight. The "caterpillar" is also the pest which will attack the palm and eat the green from its fronds. But the poet is not talking about urbanisation alone. He is also describing the growth of the wilderness inside him, the spread of the caterpillar.

[Walcott certainly has not lost the art of extracting maximum ambiguity from the word or situation. "The Gulf" for instance begins with a long chain of serious — and at times laboured — puns. The method is also used in "Corn Goddess"].

But to return to "Ebb". Boyhood, like a schooner out at sea, is too far away to be recalled; the moon, symbol of romance, is unattainable now. But, the poet declares, the time for romanticism is past.

> there's terror enough in the habitual,
> miracle enough in the familiar. Sure. . . (p. 38)

The sense of withering is also powerfully present in the Guyana poems. The empty Guyanese savannah is the perfect image of the void. It simply extends, and the slightly absurd figure of the government's surveyor mapping out the limitless landscape for the five-year plan and making his pathetic little marks on paper, is in fact at one with the poet, who also must survey his own inner void, and make his marks too on paper. But the Great Falls offer no revelation, no window into meaning, as it did the dead crew in Wilson Harris's *Palace of the Peacock*, at their reburial. The smoke and thunder of the falls, wither to the chaos of bicycles and the banal noise of Georgetown at midday.

Georgetown itself appears to be a white-washed wasteland. Images of sluggishness, festering and stagnation abound. At times, too, the "Georgetown Journal" is not at all coherent. But there are flashes of brilliant insight like "white washed houses outstaring guilt." How correct is this description of Georgetown in the sun. "Outstaring guilt." Looking at the white modern innocence and feeling the static grace of "the Garden City," as Guyanese proudly describe their capital, one finds it hard to associate it with racial hatred, civil war, bloody holocausts, the C.I.A., and the myopic political imbecility of the last decade. Nor would the calm graciousness of the Guyanese people suggest that guilt were at all possible, in that hospitable, white-run world.

It is in "A Georgetown Journal," too, that the clearest and most moving declaration of Walcott's poetic ends occurs.

> If the poem begins to shrivel
> I no longer distend my heart,
> for I know how profound is the folding of a napkin
> by a woman whose hair will go white,
> age, that says more than an ocean,
> I know how final is the straightening of a sheet
> between lovers who have never lain . . . (p. 79)

Domestic truths, he claims, are as absolute and more important than more public ones. At the same time, he declares his quest for a plain, honest style (he also did so in the poem "Islands" in *In a Green Night*) and a dry hardness which has really become a psychic necessity now, and which resembles the reticence of much contemporary English and American poetry.

> Lines which you once dismissed as tenuous
> because they would not howl or overwhelm, . . .
> harden in their indifference, like this elm.
> ("Homage to Edward Thomas", p. 55)

Later in the volume in "Nearing Forty" he claims to seek

> the household truth, the style past metaphor

that finds its parallel, however wretched
in simple, shining lines, in pages stretched
plain as a bleaching bedsheet . . . (p. 106)

Power in desolation certainly exists in this volume. The dry bleached style is
especially successful in "Blues," "Elegy," "Washington" and "Negatives." "Blues" gets
down to the origin of all genuine folk blues, which are essentially an attempt to come
to terms with an irreconcilable harshness of irony either in men's actions, or at the
root of existence itself. The best blues, those sung by Bessie Smith or Billie Holiday,
express not merely desolation, but almost absence of emotion, a melancholy gone
beyond itself.

In Walcott's poem, a "yellow nigger" is beaten "black and blue" by a street gang of
black youths with whose cause he sympathises. The bitter pun on "black and blue"
contains the profound irony of the entire situation. For in the stereotyping eyes of
white America, the yellow nigger is "black." The fact that he becomes a victim too
binds him in "blackness" to his assailants. He too is suffering. And he is also blue, not
only from the blows, but with the heartbreaking irony of the whole situation. The
prosaic conclusion seems quite logical . . . If love is so tough, "forget it." Alienation
makes more sense: again a genuine blues conclusion.

I love my man I'm a liar if I say I don't
But I'll leave my man, I'm a liar if I say I won't

That is how Billie Holiday put the same thing in "Billie's Blues."

The same involved detachment occurs in "Washington" and "Negatives." "Washington," lines written for a postcard, sees in the American autumn an image of the
self-immolating fires which Buddhist priests have chosen in Viet Nam.

while bombs of sumac burst below my window
and the live oaks catch fire,
and saffron beeches, gay
as a Buddhist's robes,
charred,
drop their rags, naked.
("Washington," p. 65)

"Negatives" is like "A Far Cry from Africa" without either its implied self-
contempt or its self-righteousness. There are no more lines like" . . . Kikuyu, quick as
flies/Batten upon the bloodstream of the veldt" or "I who am poisoned with the blood
of both." What replaces them is a dry restraint and a bewildered incomprehension at
the idea of such disaster. "Negatives" seems to me to be a much more honest record of
how one does feel when one tries to comprehend remote disaster.

Walcott, at the launching of "The Gulf," said that constant contemplation of
disaster teaches one a greater faith in the small community of family and friends.

Ultimately, love is a way out of absurdity. These sentiments are certainly not borne
out in the poetry itself, where love appears to be constantly fighting a losing battle
against death. In "The Gulf" he learns that

> ... the gifts, multiplying
> clutter and choke the heart, and that I shall
> watch love reclaim its things as I lie dying.
> My very flesh and blood! Each seems a petal
> shrivelling from its core. I watch them burn ...
> ("The Gulf," p. 59)

The void is within the poet's mind and heart, and therefore imposes itself on all he
sees, making love itself look more like despair. Yet, poems like "Star," "Landfall:
Grenada" and "Love in the Valley," show something of a marriage between lyricism
and dryness, which may be the basis of a new departure.

Our final exploration concerns the vexed question of Walcott's stature as a
sensitive commentator on the West Indian scene. It has recently been argued by
Lynne Griffith, in an article on Walcott in "Art and Man," that there is little use for
introspection or pessimism in the West Indies, because "the West Indians have newly
found their national identities" and are "a people whose attention is focussed outside
themselves and toward the future." [If by "outside themselves" she means outside the
West Indies, she's probably quite right.] She is simply the spokesman for a large
number of people, who believe that art should foster what they vaguely term a
national spirit, and that an introspective art cannot satisfy this end.

It is doubtful, however, how far an artist can go on nationalism alone, or whether,
in Walcott's case, exploration of a personal predicament does not cast a powerful, if
oblique light, on the society of which he is a product. The tensions,which we have
been noting in Walcott's poetry are rooted in West Indian society — which is a much
more gloomy and anxiety-ridden place than is normally imagined by anthem-and-
flag enthusiasts.

It is palpably untrue that "the West Indians have found their national identities."
Much more real is the betrayal of people by politician and intellectual alike (some-
times the two are one and the same person) as noted by Walcott in poems like
"Codicil," or "Gib Hall Revisited."

> A generation late, I sadden
> that the brightest ones were sold
> to a system ...
> that our first Christmas riots hid the sick
> envy of Caliban for our master's gown
> of ersatz ermine. (p. 105)

Thus the old radicals, huddled into their shabbily respectable black-gowned groups,
like so many colonial Privy Councillors and Companions of Honour, welcome each

fresh generation of academic frauds to the establishment fold. And, Walcott suggests, the betrayals will continue.

> Now, in the black, processioned and approved,
> old hands acknowledge us by our first names,
> the red gowns mark the same betrayals down.
> ("Gib Hall Revisited," p. 105)

Where Walcott does fall short, if one can call it falling short, is in the failure to look for positives in those poems where he does directly observe the society. In "Hic Jacet," he claims to have returned not for the cheap adulation which our society metes out to the supposedly brilliant, but because he is "convinced of the power of provincialism," and feels that by consciously losing his identity within the group, he might be able simultaneously to awaken group consciousness and achieve his own rebirth.

One wonders at this though. He seems rather to regard himself as one crushed by the power of provincialism, whose only hope lies in a detached preservation of identity from the crippling narrowness of the group.

A poem like "Mass Man" is a case in point. Here Walcott is observing the Carnival crowd, "the people" and finds it quite impossible to do what in "Hic Jacet" he says he does in provincial society — "pretend subtly to lose (himself) in crowds." Here he can't even pretend, much less lose himself. In fact he stresses his distance from the masqueraders in a dry humour which only partially redeems the poem from its essential desolation.

> Hector Mannix, water-works clerk, San Juan, has entered a lion,
> Boysie, two golden mangoes bobbing for breastplates, barges
> like Cleopatra down her river, making style
> "Join us," they shout, "O God, child, you can't dance?"

Is Mannix meant to be scanned as Man-Nix"? That is, a man who is not a man, a mas' man without a true face of his own? This interpretation, if true, would make Walcott's irony even sharper. But isn't the deeper irony against the poet himself who is not part of the dance? He seems to feel this, because he explains why he is detached from the crowd's frenzy. "My mania is a terrible calm," the calm of detachment which is necessary if he is to write at all, while Trinidad chips along like one long 'ole mas.'

> Upon your penetential morning
> some skull must rub its memory with ashes,
> some mind must squat down howling in your dust,
> some hand must crawl and recollect your rubbish
> someone must write your poems. (p. 48)

A sharp rebuff indeed; but whose poems will be written on Ash-Wednesday? Hardly Hector Mannix's. And this will not merely be because Mannix, Walcott's archetypal Trinidadian, does not possess the serious vision of self or the empathy to understand the bleak poetry of self-knowledge, but because for him the dance itself was the final poetic statement. The Dionysiac masquerader knows, perhaps better than the Apollonian poet, that Carnival is a dance of death. Some of the greatest calypsonians, those most accomplished wearers of the comic mask, were lonely men whose lives were tragedies.

In "Nearing Forty," Walcott quotes Dr. Johnson to reinforce his arguments for a verse of dry disillusion. It may be that he also knows the passage where Dr. Johnson says that life must either be enjoyed or endured. Since Walcott seems to be growing less and less capable of enjoying life, and is clearly too sceptical to wear a mask of any sort and is obviously too old, nearing forty, to learn to tango much less shango, he needs to learn to endure an existence, which must be quite burdensome.

Indifference might be a way out, an ultimate stoicism; but indifference requires some talent, since it normally leads to silence.

WALCOTT VERSUS BRATHWAITE

Patricia Ismond

Since Edward Lucie-Smith's pronouncement that the West Indies must choose between Walcott and Brathwaite, there has arisen something of a controversy about these two figures. There is a sense in which this kind of quarrel was inevitable in the present atmosphere of liberation, and one of the first things that needs to be established is that it is not an irrelevant question within this context. Some attempt has been made to resolve the issue by pointing out that it is futile to attempt a comparison when the two are obviously doing such widely different things. Those who take this position have not, as far as I can gather, tried to examine the differences if only to prove their point. Others think that the whole thing falls into place when we see them as complementary rather than opposed. This is the view that Rohlehr expresses in his essay on *Islands*, entitled "The Poet as Historian."[1] Here again no one has really ventured to show in what ways they are complementary. There remains, as a result, a great deal of indeterminacy surrounding this matter, and it has tended to give rise to a Brathwaite faction versus a Walcott. It is obvious that behind this state of affairs is an issue that needs to be faced. Either, on the one hand, there are deficiencies in the poets concerned that makes this an authentic cleavage. Or, on the other hand, there are limitations in the attitudes of the audience that get in the way of a proper appreciation. There are accordingly, ghosts that need to be laid, and the effort to come to terms with these issues becomes necessary.

The cliché attitudes towards these two poets must be taken as starting points, because behind every cliché attitude is a hard core of significance which must be the true target of any such argument. Brathwaite is hailed as the poet of the people, dealing with the historical and social themes that define the West Indian dilemma. Walcott is a little more difficult to place — appears at times to pay passing attention to these matters, but more consistently he seems to be a type of poet's poet, the kind of luxury we can ill afford, and which remains Eurocentric. The European literary postures he continues to assume are evidence enough of this. These are the stock attitudes, and it is quite clear that Walcott does get the worse of the deal. Those who, recognising some undeniable strength and relevance in his work, have risen to his defense, have not really dealt adequately with the essential Walcott. Mervyn Morris, for example, in trying to show that Walcott is indeed concerned with the problems of his environment, cites only those poems which deal overtly with the themes of the colonial and middle-passage experience.[2] In bringing these two poets together, therefore, it would be dishonest not to recognize at once that it is Walcott above all that needs to be vindicated. At the same time, the true nature of Brathwaite's achievement has been somehow blurred by the very excesses of the enthusiasm with which he has been hailed. Walcott, as a craftsman, towers far above Brathwaite — but I think this is a matter that can be temporarily put aside in a consideration of the content of their works and the type of sensibility that emerges in each case. It seems to me, moreover, that our best appreciation of each does gain from looking at them vis-a-vis each other in this way. It seems, also that this kind of investigation, properly conducted, will shed some light on the multiple aspects of the West Indian malaise.

Brathwaite sets out, in his trilogy, to recreate the historical experience of the Black race in the New World, and to express the various aspects of their condition as a dispossessed people. Walcott is primarily the artist — a man for whom, as an individual, art is a means of exploring and seeking a hold on reality. This general outline of their purposes of course merely skims the surface, but it is noticeable that Walcott's purpose is the more vague and insubstantial at this point. To state these basic purposes in this way, however, is a necessary introduction into the argument. It immediately raises the question of Brathwaite as a public poet versus Walcott as a private poet. In the essay already alluded to, Rohlehr dismisses this approach as false and misleading. "Each of these poets is in his different way at once 'public' and 'private,'" he says.[3] The distinction remains valid however. When one regards Brathwaite as a "public" poet, it is not at all to underestimate his capacity for a deep personal involvement in the psychic and spiritual disturbances he presents. The point is that Brathwaite has undertaken to present certain aspects of the experience of a group, suffers in his own person for them as a representative, and always in relation to his vision of their collective destiny. The epic endeavour behind the trilogy demands the heightened awareness and sensitivity without which the poem could not begin to be written. There is not the sense of Brathwaite as an isolated figure — which is pervasive in Walcott's poetry — for this very reason: that his is a representative posture.

The essential nature of Walcott's "personal" endeavour, on the other hand, is not so readily discernible. It is something which emerges only when we watch the patterns unfold from the whole corpus. We are aware, first of all, of the variety of scenes and situations he moves through, and the unflagging tone of seriousness which he brings to bear upon all of them in turn. He dwells upon the domestic and provincial scenes of the islands and the peculiar nature of the "tragic twist" within the confines of their own experience ("Tales of the Islands" — *In a Green Night*). He withdraws into the world of the private symbol to examine the psychic disturbances of an almost existential condition ("The Swamp" — *The Castaway*); he enters into the agonized fantasies of the old fiddlers at Parang to show how doomed these are to disillusionment ("Metamorphoses" — *The Gulf*). Directing all these, however, are spiritual and moral energies that seem ever to be seeking to fulfill themselves — in *Green Night* he aspires towards "the mind that enspheres all circumstance"; in *The Castaway* towards conditioning himself to the fact of "domesticity, drained of desire"; in *The Gulf*, towards an apprehension of the awe which life's "plainness" evokes. In working through to these there is a certain expansiveness and elasticity in Walcott's world that results in the variety already indicated. It is a feature that conveys the impression of a man responding to the chance encounter, almost extempore, and there is a quality of the unusual and unexpected in most of the events and situations that feature in his world. If Walcott is conscious of one abiding motivation in his search for a hold on reality — which is by definition essentially vague — it is the important part his art must play in affording him this realisation. The keynote is struck in the "Prelude" when he suddenly rises out of the curious dearth in which both he and his island lie prostrate:

> I go, of course, through all the isolated acts,
> . . .
> Until from all I turn to think how
> In the middle of the journey through my life
> O how I came upon you, my
> Reluctant leopard of the slow eyes.
> (*In a Green Night*, p. 11)

It is this sense of a personal salvation that directs Walcott, and makes his a private enterprise sharply distinct from Brathwaite's. It is one of the sources of all the major differences between them and provides a significant point of departure for a comparison of the two.

The central value of Brathwaite's collective enterprise is succinctly stated in Jean D'Costa's review article, "The Poetry of Edward Brathwaite":

> . . .while others like Cesaire and Baldwin have treated this world (the
> New World Negro's) fragment by fragment, Edward Brathwaite attempts
> a synthesis of a splintered, shattered area of experience, and manages to
> bind it together in a single poetic vision. . .[4]

Behind this effort his main objective remains, as he puts it in the concluding lines of *Islands*, to make out of the rhythms of these fragments "something torn, and new". The rhythms are accordingly chosen to convey the qualities of suffering and the type of sensibility that unites the Black race. To mention a few at random: the plaintive blues of the Southern Negro; the frenzied jazz of his urban brother; the powerful pulsations of limbo therapy; the resonances of the dark mystery of African religious ritual. For Brathwaite the enaction of these rhythms is finally aimed at one thing; to set in vibration an awareness that is predominantly black; to liberate a way of thinking and feeling that is essentially new in so far as it is devoid of all the strains and elements of the Western myth. His tone, if one may put it this way, is the theme of the dispossession of the black man and the spiritual torpor resultant on it. But his aesthetic motivation, the creation of a Black Word separate and distinct from the Western Word, is what predominates. The concluding lines of the trilogy already cited point to this, and his preoccupation with resisting Western tradition is made explicit time and again in his poems. Now he considers our total alienation from the Western Word, the sentiments and visions of the "masters."

> So the stars
> remain my master's
> property. . .
> . . .
> . . .
> . . . we have no name
> to call us home, no turbulence
> to bring us soft —
> ly past these bars to miracle, to god,
> to unexpected lover.
> ("Homecoming" — *Islands*, p. 19)

and again:

> it is not enough to be free
> of the whips, principalities and powers
> where is your kingdom of the Word?
> ("Negus" -*Islands*, p. 65)

At other times he examines its pernicious effects, as he watches Christianity, as mythical expression of the Western tradition, reclaim Tizzic from the outlet the carnival ritual seemed to offer:

> . . . Behind the masks, grave
> Lenten sorrows waited: Ash —
> Wednesday, ashes, darkness, death.
> After the *bambalula bambulai*
> he was a slave again.
> ("Tizzic"— *Islands*, p. 105)

This sort of attitude obviously belongs somewhere in the same ethos of liberation as Cesaire's vision, but an important distinction emerges from a comparison of the two. The latter sustains an impassioned dynamic of protest that derives from an original moral outrage at the unparalleled insult to the Negro race, and it is this one purpose that informs and discovers its own rhetoric. Brathwaite takes the suffering of the negro as a given subject, and is mainly concerned with sounding the varying strains that will create a language, a way of thinking and feeling peculiar to the experience.

This makes Brathwaite's a predominantly aesthetic undertaking, by contrast with
Cesaire's direct gesture of assertion and protest. Finally, Brathwaite's most serious
opposition is aimed at the Western Word, and his craft works carefully at expunging
it from black modes of feeling and expression.

Which is precisely the point which the division between himself and Walcott
begins. Walcott, aware of the growing resistance towards what is called his fascination
with the Western tradition, has been stung recently into what seems a rather
reactionary remark. In an article entitled "Meanings", he states rather squarely:

> Yet I feel absolutely no shame in having endured the colonial experi-
> ence. There was no obvious humiliation in it. . . It was cruel, but it
> created our literature.[5]

It would be terribly simplistic to conclude from this that Walcott is rejecting the
past, our turbulent history, as having no bearing upon our present predicament. The
statement has to be taken in context. Walcott has been examining the dual elements
of the African and Western traditions in the West Indian experience, and how the
two might unite to produce a peculiarly West Indian drama. For him the one has
bequeathed an exuberance which must be subjected to the discipline of the classical
tradition introduced by the other. The particular emphasis that needs to be noted
here, however, is his readiness to acknowledge the relevance of both these traditions
in the West Indian experience. It is no helpless submission to a fascination with
Western myth that makes him continue to work within its medium. He is quite
conscious of his relationship to it, as he fashions it to cater to his indigenous needs
and experience. He refers to this relationship in "Exile" (*The Gulf*) as his "indenture
to her Word." His essential approach is expressed in "Crusoe's Journal":

> into good Fridays who recite His praise,
> > parroting our master's
> style and voice, we make his language ours,
> > converted cannibals
> we learn with him to eat the flesh of Christ. (p. 28)

This awareness of his indenture to the word of the Western tradition — its
concept of man in relation to creation, its peculiar apprehension of man's
spiritual destiny — amounts to almost an obsession with Walcott. Yet one
needs to be careful in trying to grasp the true nature of his position here.
There is in Walcott an active scepticism that reflects a generic condition of
spiritual dispossession, the spirit of which is captured in "The Castaway"
(*The Castaway*). It turns, of necessity, on a criticism of the Western myth, its
betrayals and failures for believer and convert alike. To recognize this however, is to grasp as well that his resistance of it involves an immersion in its
qualities of awareness. This two-fold aspect of his involvement is brought out

in a passage like the following, permeated with fragmentary allusions to the
gospels and the crucified Christ:

> Godlike, annihilating godhead, art
> And self, I abandon
> Dead metaphors. . .
>
> . . .
>
> . . .
>
> That green wine bottle's gospel choked with sand,
> Labelled, a wrecked ship,
> Clenched seawood nailed and white as a man's hand.
> ("The Castaway" — *The Castaway*, p. 10)

Thus, the "green wine bottle" has associations with the symbol of "new wine
bottles" of the gospel, except that here, contrary to the promise of its greenness, it is
choked with sand — symbolizing spiritual putrefaction. Similarly, behind the references to "clenched seawood nailed" and "man's hand" hovers the image of the
crucifixion that has become perverted and menacing. Walcott is very much immersed
in the Western spiritual atmosphere. While Brathwaite rejects it as an imposture and
imposition on the grounds of its being alien to the sensibility of the Black people,
Walcott consciously faces it to resist the perplexities and confusions with which it is
fraught. For him, to maintain this sceptical awareness is to work out, through modes
of apprehension bequeathed by Western influence, his own sense of humanity and
"God's loneliness." This question of acceptance of the Word is perhaps the fundamental issue between the two poets. To appreciate its full significance one needs to
look closely at this aspect of their work.

The peculiar anguish of dispossession from which Brathwaite starts sends him in
quest of some sort of spiritual baptism. The basic scheme of the trilogy follows the
three stages given in M. Arnold Van Gennep's book entitled *Les Rites de Passage*. In
this latter, which may well have provided Brathwaite with his title for the first part of
the trilogy, the French anthropologist sees all primitive ceremonies as a passage
through three states: first, the effort to withdraw from a profane world that revolves
round one's awareness of it; second, a withdrawal during which experiences move on
a sacred plane; and third, a reinstatement into the ordinary world.[6] *Masks* represents
that second stage of withdrawal into a sacred world, and it is symbolic of Brathwaite's
quest for some kind of initiation into the mysteries of the heart of darkness. Jean
D'Costa rightly draws attention to the tentative nature of this movement in the
poetry,[7] where he seems, at his best, to be hovering on the brink of two worlds, one
dead, the other powerless to be born. The former seems to prevail, so that despite the
birth-pangs aroused by the powerful pulsations of the drum ritual, he returns to this
sense of negation:

> But my spade's hope,
> shattering stone,
> receives dumbness back

for its echo.
Beginnings end here
in this ghetto.
("Sunsum" — *Masks*, p. 66)

At other times he reaches very close to a discovery of the possibilities of suffering and renewal in the intensities of African religious ritual. This is enacted in the section "Eating the Dead" (*Islands*), a mode of communion with the supernatural that belongs in the African metaphysic and its concept of evil:

It seems
a long way now from fat, the shaking bone, the laughter. But I
can show
you what it means to eat
your god, drink his explosions of power

and from the slow sinking mud of your plunder, grow. (p. 64)

Behind the multiple aspects of his presentation of Black reality, Brathwaite is indeed burrowing his way into the depths of a spiritual consciousness and a language of belief. This search for gods runs parallel with his desire for discovering a new Word. It is a search that revolves round an African twilight of the gods, and hovers between the condition of limbo and inferno in the ways already suggested. It is also in passages like these that he acquires the greatest strength, as he moves beyond the "surfaces of things."

Walcott's experience of spiritual conflict also moves between similar levels of limbo and inferno, arising from a generic strife between the will to believe and the glaring conditions of a reality that mock this desire. His efforts to gain access to these levels of consciousness involve energies just as violent self-immolating. In a poem like "Dogstar" (*The Castaway*) this is very much the principle at work. The intense heat of his own tropical setting seems to join forces with the elemental energies of the raging Dogstar, as Walcott becomes aware of the destructive dynamic at the heart of things. It opens for him the prospect of hell, and the eternal menace of death. Out of the intensities of this inferno glow images of a corresponding heaven, and he is tossed between this double vision in such a way as to be left utterly confused:

Shovelled in like sticks to feed earth's raging oven,
consumed like heretics in this poem's pride,
these clouds, their white smoke, make and unmake heaven. (p. 13)

Walcott starts from a contemplation different from the initiation rites in which Brathwaite is engaged, but what seems most important to both is the near-overwhelming strain of the spiritual effort. In each it draws upon the same dynamic of holy rage and awe. The main point here, however, is that Walcott enacts this drama within the mythical symbols of Christianity, not as an orthodox system, but for the traditional power of its images of heaven and hell, of paradiso versus inferno. To stress this point is to draw attention to an aspect of poetry in general that is much overlooked in the present clamor for "literature engagee". Every poet reverts now and then into the most private recesses of "pure" poetry. To begin to deal with mysterious rites or a confrontation with death readily lends itself to the visionary frontiers of such "pure poetry". Thus, when Walcott in his retreats into the visionary draws upon the Christian symbols of heaven and hell, he is following much the same artistic course as Brathwaite is in seeking inspiration in the symbols of African traditional religion. Conversely, given the nature of visionary exploration, Brathwaite is no more engaged in creating a Word that communicates more powerfully to us by virtue of its being African. The ceremony of "Eating the Dead", as Brathwaite presents it, explores a mystique that arouses a response in us because the emotive drives point to the quality of the spiritual crises — despite our unfamiliarity with its modes and ritual. The Christian symbols feature in the same way in Walcott's spiritual overtures. Any rejection of his poetry on this score comes finally from a failure to understand the ultimate processes of poetry, and on a blind concept of what protest truly involves. It is not the mere gesture of supplanting in poetry one set of symbols *qua* symbols, by another that makes for an act of self-assertion. That aspect of Brathwaite's poetry which proposes this sort of thing — and it is very much present — is claiming much more for itself than it is really doing. Yet, one needs to proceed cautiously and draw the distinction between this attempt at installment of an African concept of reality and his effort to distill the sense of a people broken in spirit, that movement in his work which has more to do with protest. It strikes a characteristic note in a passage like this, describing the pathos of Tom's failure:

> poised
> in that fatal attitude
>
> that would have smashed
> the world, or made it, he
> let the hammer
>
> down; made
> nothing, un-
> made nothing;
>
> his bright
> hopes down,
> his own
>
> bright future
> dumb,
> his one

heroic flare
and failure
done.
("Anvil" — *Islands*, p. 94-5)

There remains, I think, at the heart of his aesthetic a basic irresolution between these two movements, or rather, a confounding of the one with the other. On the one hand his desire to rehabilitate an African pantheon and mythology as the medium for suffering. On the other, his aim to capture the peculiar anguish of Black oppression. They are not the same thing, though the fragmentary technique of the trilogy helps to create the illusion of an orchestration of these two intentions. It is on this second level rather than on the first that Brathwaite shows a meaningful involvement. Against this can be measured the peculiar quality of involvement that emerges from Walcott's orientation towards reality. The most authentic differences between them arise from here — and the wider implication of Walcott's immersion in the Western tradition emerges as something far more positive and less of an anachronism than it is made out to be. It takes its place, within the specific terms of poetry, in the complex directions of the struggle for liberation.

In a seminar on West Indian poetry, Brathwaite considers Walcott a humanist and points out the limitations of this approach. The humanist poet, Brathwaite thinks "is often speaking away from that society rather than speaking in towards it."[8] Brathwaite concedes that the humanist poet draws his inspiration from the society, but what is implied in the quotation given above is that all such inspiration is sophisticated away from any relevance. A humanist Walcott certainly continues to be, and the tradition of humanism in which he tries to find his bearings derive again from the Western orientation. That is to say, Walcott's awareness of man in search of fulfillment and man the victim of adversity follows the patterns evolved in the Western imagination. Western philosophy, going as far back as Plato, conceives of man as a creature endowed with the capacity for Truth and Beauty through which he can attain transcendence over the dark forces that threaten to undermine his humanity. African wisdom follows another angle of approach. Arising out of the exigencies of the African experience, it sends the African imagination in search of a more precipitate contact with Evil. The spiritual energies are engaged in a direct placating of Evil that involves an absorption in its darker mysteries — something of what Conrad perceives in his *Heart of Darkness*. Brathwaite captures the essence of this philosophy in the following lines, hinting at the significance of the fetish for the African:

symbol sickness fetish for our sickness.
For man eats god, eats life, eats world, eats wickedness.
This we now know, this we digest and hold;
this gives us bone and sinews, saliva grease and sweat;
("Adowa" — *Masks*, p. 29)

In the Western imagination the thrust is upwards; in the African downwards.

The above explications aim at drawing the distinction between the two, in order to recognise more clearly *how* Walcott is involved in the Western tradition of humanity. It is important to understand how, working within this broad perspective Walcott evolves a humanism that relates to the West Indian condition. Anyone who fails to come to grips with this aspect of his sensibility, will in attempting to find him "relevant", be glossing over a significant part of his achievement. To illustrate this point one need only take a look at the group of poems entitled "A Tropical Bestiary" (*The Castaway*). These represent the essential Walcott just as strongly as "Tales of the Islands" (*Green Night*). In the former, however, he is directly engaged in orienting himself to reality on a philosophical level. He starts from a recognition that his attempts to achieve transcendent vision remain ineffectual, and strives towards the resilience that will accept this as a *fait accompli* of human limitations. With the poetic concentration that such an external image affords him, he sees the reality enacted in the fate of the Ibis that "fades from her fire.";

> Pointing no moral but the fact
> Of flesh that has lost pleasure in the act,
> Of domesticity, drained of desire.
> ("Ibis," p. 19)

The painful pulsations of desire still linger, though, in the human psyche:

> Pulse of the sea in the locked, heaving side.
> ("Octopus," p. 19)

When Walcott passes from this reflective level into the human scene, the perspective is still the same. This is true of a poem like "Hawk" (*The Gulf*). He enters into the spirit of the folk festivity as the old fiddlers play at Parang. The agonised strains of their "tension lines" expresses their yearning for some keen spur to drive them to their dreams, and they look back nostalgically to the powerful purpose that spurred on the violent Caribs, for example. The presiding genius of the hawk is involved, symbol of strife and torture, but, abruptly, the sharp dissonance of the hawk of their actual surroundings brings them back to earth and the futility that mocks such sentiments:

> Slaves yearn for their master's talons,
> the spur and the cold, gold eyes,
> for the whips, whistling like wires,
> time for our turn, gavilán!
> But this hawk above Rampanalgas
> rasps the sea with raw cries.
> Hawks have no music. (p. 45)

These are the reaches of Walcott's humanism and they are inspired by the kind of

destitution he sees about him. In following these movements between desire and
negation, he does not point directly to its sources in social or historical deprivation —
but the sense of defeat concentrated in his treatment does recreate the world of these
old rum-guzzlers in their rustic setting, caught within the confines of their vegetable
life, cheerless and hopeless but for their drunken visions and the occasional rhythms
of the old parang. That Walcott approaches them through these modes of apprehension does not refine away the concreteness of their world and its specific conditions. It
does not thin into "irrelevance."

This consideration of Walcott's humanism is a necessary preliminary if we are to
weigh it against Brathwaite's mission of protest. The questions then become: How
does Walcott's humanistic approach serve the West Indian dilemma as compared to
Brathwaite's kind of protest? How do these peculiar positions reveal their respective
types of involvement in their environment — always bearing in mind a comment of
Dennis Scott's, that neither of them is offering us a programme for social reform.[9]
And since every diagnosis of a malaise hints at possibilities of renewal and relief,
however indirectly, how do their visions of West Indian hope and renewal compare?
These are among the questions that must arise in a comparison of the two.

The essential tone of Brathwaite's protest is captured in one of his most-quoted
passages. It is one in which he rises to a rare flash of original imagery:

> and we float, high up over the sighs of the city,
> like fish in a gold water world
>
> we float round and round
> in the bright bubbled bowl
> without hope of the hook,
> of the fisherman's tugging-in root.
> ("Jah" — *Islands*, p. 3)

Brathwaite's vision of the destitution of the Black people rests on this final diagnosis
of their plight; they are a people doubly benighted in a lost world, and the hopelessness of this condition is perhaps his most insistent theme. The circumstances behind
this plight have their origin in our history of displacement and subjugation. It is the
historical consciousness, quite obviously, that provides him with his viewpoint, and
leads him to penetrate the sinister aspects of our unnatural encounter with Europe.
He traces the interrelations between the material, psychological and spiritual effects
in such portraits as that of the Rasta man. The lingering presence of Babylon, a legacy
of the colonial system that fixed the relations between colour and prosperity, has
relegated the Rasta man to the absurd dimensions of his world. The sources of the
oppression that prompt his ironic hallucinations are shown to be indeed sinister:

> Brother Man the Rasta
> man, hair full of lichens
> head hot as ice

watched the mice
walk into his poor
hole, reached for his peace
and the pipe of his ganja
and smiled how the mice
eyes. . . .
. . . .like rhinestone
and suddenly startled like
diamond.
("Wings of a Dove" — *Rights of Passage*, p. 41)

These are matters of fundamental concern in West Indian reality, and Brathwaite implies that our very alertness to these injustices will engender a positive condition of restlessness. In this lie the greatest possibilities of assertion and realisation. Gerald Moore grasps this condition of restlessness as Brathwaite's main positive:

> Only by embracing this restlessness can the Negro conceive it as a forward movement. . . The search is what defines the race giving it purpose and momentum. [10]

In the article already cited, Rohlehr witnesses a prophetic fulfillment of this vision. As he watches the protest marches in Trinidad, Brathwaite's insight into the continued tribal wanderings of the Black race strikes home:

> Right now it is drought in Trinidad, and those young men with fixed faces looking blankly into an unimaginable future and marching are fulfilling a deep tribal dream.[11]

In this kind of criticism there is a hint of "mythologizing — there is a point at which, on its own terms, this becomes archetypal and is no longer peculiar to the African tribal experience. Be that as it may, Brathwaite's restlessness aims at feeling its way out of the trappings of such oppression. The conflicts and confrontations that set it in motion are directly associated with the historical aftermath.

Walcott's approach does not bring him to quite this kind of diagnosis. That he brings a certain type of diagnosis to bear upon various aspects of his society cannot be denied. But the humanistic angle from which he starts eschews the sense of direct protest and the vision of our release from the repercussions of history as our only means of escape. His approach works on the level of a morality and internal psychology that turns on a confrontation with self. This is not to say that Walcott does not allow for the effects of the historical experience in aggravating the problems of the environment — but, rather, that he does not see this as the main feature standing in the way of self-realisation. A typical example of his approach is his analysis of the kind of megalomania that finally defeats the hero of "Junta" (*The Gulf*). He begins with the observation of the kind of illusions that the carnival psychology is

fraught with. As the hero marches through in the guise of Vercingetorix, there is
already a premonition that for him this fantasy is in dead earnest, and the illusions of
power are being engendered in the very spirit of carnival:

> He fakes an epileptic, clenched salute,
> taking their tone, is no use getting vex,
> some day those brains will squelch below his boot
> as sheaves of swords hoist Vercingetorix! (p. 46)

The ironic approach here retains its sympathetic poise, but almost unobtrusively
Walcott shows how this fantasy finds its way through the political outlet of the junta,
and the curious twist it takes in leaving the coup, which is to prove his undoing, just
as much a matter of fantasy for Vercingetorix. What had been for him a symbol of
fulfillment retains the emptiness of an over-desperate and rash gesture, without the
authentic purpose of the coup to give it direction:

> . . . He clears his gorge and feels the bile
> of rhetoric rising. Enraged, that every clause
> "por la patria, la muerte" resounds
> the same, he fakes a frothing fit and shows his wounds,
> while, as the cold sheathes heighten, his eyes fix
> on one black, bush-haired convict's widening smile.
> ("Junta" — *The Gulf*, p. 46-7)

These insights finally turn upon an intense type of confrontation with self. Walcott's
humanistic concern leads him to explore this kind of delusion as a condition
ultimately arising from shortcomings within the individual consciousness — although they arouse sympathy, as in the case of Vercingetorix in showing how
vulnerable man really is. In other words, his approach shifts the emphasis away from
the external targets that Brathwaite keeps in view. One notices how the turbulent
political atmosphere is brought in almost as a matter of course; and in fact, Walcott's
approach does carry its environment with it as inevitably. But in bringing the irony to
bear directly on the processes of his mania, Vercingetorix' disoriented state becomes a
matter of private tragedy for which he alone is, ultimately, responsible. This is the
peculiar achievement of Walcott's approach, and it is closely related to his dogged
pursuit of a personal hold on reality.

Brathwaite, however, does opt now and again for the stability of traditional
morality as a tentative avenue of "liberation". This is proposed every so often as he
returns to the theme of Mammon as another major source of the disruption of
possible order and the good life:

> when only lust rules
> the night. . .
> when men make noises

louder than the sea's
voices; then the rope
will never unravel
its knots, the branding
iron's travelling flame that teaches
us pain, will never be
extinguished. . .
("Islands"— *Islands*, p. 48)

He seems to concede intermittently, therefore, that some sort of poise between the
protesting consciousness and a moral vigilance will show the way out of the morass.
This moral responsibility, summarily included in his mission of protest, is the very
dimension on which Walcott concentrates. One last comparison between the two
will serve to underscore this point — their treatment of carnival, an indigenous
cultural feature. Brathwaite sees carnival as an expression of a positive and vital
impulse, instinctual in the race. So that, in his presentation of Tizzic's case, he
denounces the tyranny of a foreign imposition such as Christianity that robs Tizzic of
its powers of enrichment: Through carnival's "stilts of song" Tizzic comes near to
attaining the seventh heaven, but he is doomed to failure:

. . . In such bright swinging company
he could no longer feel the cramp
of poverty's confinement, spirit's damp;
. . .
. . . But the good stilts splinter-
ed, wood legs broke, calypso steel pan
rhythm faltered. The midnight church

bell fell across the glow, the lurch-
ing cardboard crosses. Behind the masks, grave

Lenten sorrows waited. Ash-
Wednesday, ashes, darkness, death.

After the *bambalula bambulai*
he was a slave again.
("Tizzic" — *Islands*, p. 105)

Brathwaite's mission of protest leads him to this kind of exposé of the hopelessness
of Tizzic's thraldom, held as he is within the fastnesses of an alien religion. He seems
to be offering carnival as a possible outlet. In a poem like "Mass Man" (*The Gulf*)
Walcott harbours no such illusions about it. As he watches the frenetic gaiety behind
the carnival extravaganza, he is conscious of the emptiness behind it all; and the
sensuality, devoid of any significance beyond the most Philistine type of self-indul-

gence, assumes sinister resonances. So that the child "rigged like a bat", far from
experiencing any genuine merriment, is aware of the absurd scene of its isolation:

> But I am dancing, look, from an old gibbet
> my bull-whipped body swings, a metronome!
> Like a fruit-bat dropped in the silk-cotton's shade
> my mania, my mania is a terrible calm. (p. 48)

All this must end in a dispirited sense of negation and futility, Walcott thinks with
misgiving. His manner of expressing this latter has tended to mislead a number of his
readers into thinking that he is merely judging from a sickeningly orthodox and self-
righteous viewpoint, based on an acceptance of the Christian religion. His reference
to Ash Wednesday is primarily figurative, hinting at the violation of sensibility, the
kind of self-desecration that this attitude involves. He continues to stress this sense of
aberration with metaphorical intensity:

> some mind must squat down howling in your dust,
> some hand must crawl and recollect your rubbish,
> someone must write your poems. (p. 48)

Put beside Brathwaite's view as champion of such cultural features, Walcott's
seems to be hopelessly negative. Yet his diagnosis of the carnival psychology in the
decadent urban atmosphere of Port-of-Spain where the gesture serves mainly as a
means of license, does uncover an authentic aspect of present day carnival. The
morality that informs his sardonic appraisal does arise from a genuine humanistic
concern, as his tableau of the child "rigged like a bat" does show. It is the same
approach which sees these shortcomings and deficiencies in terms of our own failures,
places the onus of guilt upon us, and shows us to be victims of ourselves primarily.
This is instinctively Walcott's purpose, and by comparison Brathwaite's notion of the
liberating influences of carnival seems curiously half the truth, if not altogether off the
mark. It presupposes a kind of "innocence" which we have quite lost; and this is what
Walcott is fundamentally realistic about. This is the peculiar strength of his approach.
Yet Brathwaite's attempt to draw attention to such indigenous cultural features and
his move to preserve them through his artistic medium remains an important
undertaking. If, in his enthusiasm to retain what is our own — and this relates closely
to his larger purpose of creating Black aesthetic — he gets carried away into half-
truths, much shall be overlooked, because he hath meant well. . . At the same time, it
is exactly here that the two become complementary. In dwelling on his peculiar
emphases, Walcott takes such cultural features for granted; while Brathwaite's mode
of protest brings them to the fore and points to the importance of preserving them.
Walcott is not proposing a rejection of carnival, but denouncing the vulgarization
resulting from our unwholesome attitudes towards it. Yet without Brathwaite's
attempt, its presence as an indigenous feature worth salvaging from this
unwholesomeness might well be glossed over. . .

The different positions of these two poets does, however, assume peculiar relevance when viewed within the larger context of liberation. Walcott's humanistic approach, in its insistence on searching within for the attitudes of mind that will set us free, signifies this: he accepts himself, in his time and place as a man who, with the ravages of history behind him, is willing to rise above any surviving fetters by a courageous expression of his intrinsic stature as a man. There is this spirit of independence in his approach, completely unselfconscious that shows him to be altogether free of that historical legacy, a sense of inferiority — a point from which the movement of protest does start. The significance of his "acceptance" of the Western Word is closely related to this attitude: it has availed him of a strategy for consciousness that, having been absorbed and modified in his environment over the centuries, become as much his property as that of the former masters. So that he feels free to mould it, bend it to his own purposes, now to expose its shortcomings, now draw upon its strengths — as competently as the original possessors. This is the sense of freedom that makes him recognise the positive aspects of the double-heritage of the West Indies, fraught as it is with all the contradictions that precipitate the crisis of liberation. Nor is it merely a matter of an abdication of the historical sense on Walcott's part. It suggests instead of a man, who, realising that there is no turning back, believes that the destiny of the West Indian peoples must depend on the resources they find within themselves for acting with confidence towards what has been left, negative as well as positive. Only with this attitude, can we begin to make them ours. Moreover, this is not to be derivative and beholden, or to deem ourselves secondary in status. The very confidence and tenacity of his approach challenges and defies any such notions of inferiority. His reaction to the Southern States in "The Gulf" (*The Gulf*) is revealing in this respect. He recoils instinctively from the Negro's condition there, his "secondary status as a soul". Its strangeness communicates an uncanny sense of fear to him. Somehow Walcott has managed to achieve a sense of self-mastery, and it begins with the attitude of a mind that makes the most strenuous demands upon itself, and takes for granted its right to do so. This is the peculiar strength of his personal quest, and it is, in its own way, *a most powerful gesture of assertion.* Yet perhaps not all can rise to the level of courage that he represents. He stands out curiously among his contemporaries in this respect, in his refusal to leave the West Indian setting. It is finally a refusal to see the area as confining, or as a secondary order of existence. The attitude he stands for is a valid and acceptable one, though difficult for it opens up a definite possibility, even through the elusive reflections of such a medium as poetry.

This is one mode of assertion, and the next most effective is through protest such as Cesaire's: an outright insistence on the intrinsic stature of the Black man that aims at exploding that myth of his inferiority, and makes an absurdity of all the lingering effects of that myth. There is just so much poetry can do and no more, however committed it is to such a cause. Cesaire's gesture represents the rousing call to manhood and defiance that epitomises this kind of commitment. This spirit is finally lacking in Brathwaite, and it is a direct result of his peculiar conception of his artistic purpose. Concerned to create Black poetry first and last, he depends on the painful lyricism of Black suffering for the anguish of protest. Protest itself remains a subordinated theme, accordingly, and the elegiac mood that pervades it tends to weigh too heavily upon us to leave us any positive attitude. There is not, in its brooding lament, the defiant will to strive. It is for this reason that his protest, even taken on its own terms remains weaker, in the final analysis, than Walcott's kind of assertion. Yet what he has achieved in missing the mark is indeed valuable, even though it seems to offer more of an escape into its rhythmical movements. If we can resist the lotus-eating atmosphere of the appeal they tend to exert — Brathwaite's attempt to draw attention to the latent possibilities of these rhythms as modes of awareness, is indeed a positive and timely contribution.

Footnotes

[1] "The Historian as Poet," *The Literary Half-Yearly* Vol. XI No.2, July 1970, p. 178.

[2] "Walcott and the Audience for Poetry," *Caribbean Quarterly* Vol. 14 Nos. 1 and 2, March-June 1968, pp. 22-24.

[3] "The Historian as Poet," *The Literary Half-Yearly* Vol. XI No.2, July 1970, p. 178.

[4] The Poetry of Edward Brathwaite," *Jamaica Journal* Vol. 2 No. 3, September 1968, p. 24.

[5] "Meanings," *Savacou* No. 2, September 1970, p. 51.

[6] *The Rites of Passage* (Translated from the French by M.B. Vizedom and G.L. Caffee), London, Routledge and Kegan Paul, 1960.

[7] "The Poetry of Edward Brathwaite," *Jamaica Journal* Vol. 2 No. 3, September 1968, p. 25.

[8] "West Indian Poetry, a Search for Voices," seminar sponsored by the Extra-Mural Department, U.W.I., 14 March 1965; fifth in a series on "The State of the Arts — in Jamaica."

[9] The present writer has heard him make this comment at several seminars on West Indian poetry at the U.W.I.

[10] *The Chosen Tongue* (London, Longmans, 1969), p. 36.

[11] "The Historian as Poet," *The Literary Half-Yearly* Vol. XI No. 2, July 1970, p. 174.

C.
"HOMAGE TO GREGORIAS"
(1970-1979)

PAINTERS AND PAINTING IN *ANOTHER LIFE*

Edward Baugh

In recreating the St Lucia of his memory in *Another Life*, Walcott draws heavily on images from painting and related arts, especially photography. Sculpture, etching, pottery, dance also contribute, and music provides a major "cluster" of images and allusions. This deliberate and extensive use of imagery from the arts is appropriate to the recall of the youthful dream of a society dedicated not to power but to art. As he says at the end of the essay "What the Twilight Says": "When twenty years ago we imagined cities devoted neither to power nor to money but to art, one had the true vision."[1] So the art imagery in *Another Life* helps to convey the poem's meaning partly by being counterpoised against the martial imagery (soldiers, bugles, cannon smoke and battle-charges), connotative of power, of history as a saga of great battles, of victors and vanquished.

It is particularly appropriate that imagery of painting, including allusions to actual painters and paintings, should figure as prominently as it does in *Another Life*, since the lost life which the poem celebrates was a life of very active involvement in painting, one dominated by two painters, Harold Simmons and Dunstan St Omer, the Harry and Gregorias of the poem.[2] By using painting so much as part of the poem's technique, Walcott pays homage, over and above anything he *says* in the poem, to that life and those painters. The poem not only recounts that period of his life when he saw his future to be that of a painter; it not only fits that period into the shape of meaning which he sees his life as having taken; it also *uses* that life (painting) as a major factor or vehicle in the poem's way of expressing meaning. To put it another way, painting is not only a subject of the poem, but also an important aspect of its style and texture. Walcott's poetry has always shown a marked interest in and influence from painting. *Another Life* is likely to remain the most profound and elaborate expression of this feature.

Throughout the poem Walcott describes with a painter's and draughtman's eye:

> the frieze of coal-black carriers, *charbonniers*,
> erect, repetitive as hieroglyphs (p. 29)[3]

> A peel of lemon sand
> curled like a rind across the bay's blue dish. (pp. 65-66)

> ... the hills stippled with violet
> as if they had seen Pissarro. (p. 74)

> . . . the framed yellow jungle of
> the groyned mangroves meeting
> the groyned mangroves repeating
> their unbroken water-line. (p. 149)

Every view is composed and coloured and framed as for a painting. We read of "every view/assembling itself to say farewell" (p. 111), and "A landscape of burnt stones and broken arches/arranged itself with a baroque panache" (p. 84). At the beginning of the poem we are taken into the mind of the young Walcott straining to record his beloved Vigie landscape in line and colour; in chapter 9 he achieves a remarkable evocation of the act of painting; and one of the controlling images of the poem is that of the island seen as a painting, particularly a Renaissance painting, "a cinquecento fragment in gilt frame" (p. 4).

Many of the painterly images and the references to famous paintings derive from one book which greatly influenced Walcott in his youth, Thomas Craven's *A Treasury of Art Masterpieces: From the Renaissance to the Present Day* (New York, 1939) He mentions it twice in the poem: once at the beginning of chapter 4 ("Thin water glazed/the pebbled knuckles of the Baptist's feet. In Craven's book" (p. 23); and again in chapter 12, when he asks his remembered young self, "Starved, burning child,/ remember 'The Hay Wain'/in your museum, Thomas Craven's book?" (p. 78). In the unpublished first version of *Another Life*, Walcott refers to it as

> a book that I used as my imaginary museum and where I had learnt all
> I now knew about the old masters and the great painters . . . a large black
> book from which I copied, in watercolour, a number of great paintings:
> Turner's "The Fighting Téméraire Towed To Her Last Berth", Goya's
> "Night Execution" as my father had once copied Millet's "The Gleaners."[4]

The many references to Renaissance painting and painters whose acquaintance he made or maintained through this book, not only attest to the hold which Renaissance art had on Walcott's imagination, but are also very apt for delineating the vision of *Another Life*. In the Renaissance he found a supreme example of a great age defined by its art, so to speak, the idea that it is the art that brings the age to fullest self awareness, that "signs" the epoch. So, "as conquerors who had discovered home" (p. 53), he and St Omer, Walcott tells us,

> . . . swore,
> disciples of that astigmatic saint,

> that [they] would never leave the island
> until [they] had put down, in paint, in words,
> as palmists learn the network of a hand,
> all of its sunken, leaf-choked ravines,
> every neglected, self-pitying inlet . . . (p. 52)

In the early poem "Roots", Walcott, wishing himself to be the Homer of his own people, had prayed that his poetry would

> . . . *make* without pomp, without stone acanthus,
> In our time, in the time of this phrase, a "flowering of islands,"
>
> . . .
>
> *Make* the rice fields and guinea-corn waving,
> The creak of the bullock-cart, *make*
> The fields with bent Indians in the rice marsh.[5]

Walcott keeps the idea of the Renaissance alive in the reader's mind through imagery, as when he thinks of Pinkie, the dead child, as having "(g)one to her harvest of flax-headed angels, /of seraphs blowing pink-palated conchs" (p. 9). These angels and seraphs are details from Renaissance painting, as, for example, is the "chiton-fluted sea" (p. 5).[6] And his account of his "conversion", the epiphanic moment of dedication to Art, which was at the same time a dedication of himself to his country, is expressed through allusions to Renaissance art:

> Our father,
>   who floated in the vaults of Michelangelo,
> Saint Raphael,
>   of sienna and gold leaf . . . (p. 44)

A passage such as this also illustrates the fact that Renaissance art, by virtue of its religious connections, was most helpful to Walcott in conveying the notion of the identification between art and religion in his remembered life, as well as his transference of much of his religious feeling to art. So, for instance, chapter 4, which recalls some aspects of the religious life of St Lucia, begins by way of reference to one of the Renaissance paintings reproduced by Craven:

> Thin water glazed
>   the pebbled knuckles of the Baptist's feet.
> In Craven's book.
> Their haloes shone like the tin guards of lamps.
> Verrocchio. Leonardo painted the kneeling angel's hair.
> Kneeling in our plain chapel,
> I envied them their frescoes.

> Italy flung round my shoulders like a robe,
> I ran among dry rocks, howling, "Repent!" (p. 23)

The painting is "The Baptism of Christ" by Andrea del Verrocchio and Leonardo da Vinci. Walcott no doubt got his information about the painting of it from a comment by Craven:

> The picture is memorable for the vaporous landscape in the distance, and for the kneeling angel at the left, whose carefully drawn hair and delicate features touched with radiance were not of Verrocchio's fibre. These additions were painted by an apprentice, a boy of seventeen named Leonardo da Vinci.[7]

In the comparison of the haloes to "tin guards of lamps", the reflectors on the kerosene lamps which were common in his childhood,[8] we see Walcott relating art, and foreign art, to his day-to-day experience of life. So too with the "seraphs blowing pink-palated conchs", the conchs, replacing the more usual trumpets in the religious paintings, being commonplace in the West Indies and used in St Lucia to border graves. These details, like his general "envy" of Renaissance art, underscore how much Walcott's view of life and religion was coloured by his experience of art. Furthermore, they contribute to the exploration of one of the main themes of the poem, the relationship between art, life and reality—the idea, for example, that we are driven by a desire to make life over into art. The centrality of this area of interest is indicated by the quotation from Malraux's *Psychology of Art* which forms the epigraph to Book One of *Another Life*. Also of special significance in this connection are those instances in the poem in which a scene or a person fixes itself/himself in the poet's mind in terms of some scene or character from a painting or a book. An outstanding example is the case of the child Pinkie mentioned above — the girl whom Walcott knew being confused with/made more real by Sir Thomas Lawrence's famous portrait.

The connotative identification of art and religion extends into many specific details of the poem and enhances the impression of a richly integrated whole. For example, our first glimpse of Simmons is of the scholar-artist-priest, with intimations of sainthood about him, yet another image out of Renaissance painting and one to which Simmons' baldness lent itself:

> Within the door, a bulb
> haloed the tonsure of a reader crouched
> in its pale tissue . . . (p. 5)

This imaging of Simmons deepens the significance of the master-apprentice aspect of the Simmons-Walcott relationship, evoking all such situations in Renaissance art, as, for example, the Verrocchio-Leonardo relationship alluded to above. This initial image of Simmons develops easily into that of Simmons as martyr and saint, a kind of soldier-Christ:

> I see him bent under the weight of the morning,
> against its shafts,
> devout, angelical . . . (p. 138)

Eventually, the idea of Simmons as having been "crucified" by his society, by a world which knew him not, assumes inevitable rightness within the structure of the poem, and is itself instinct with all the meaning of the art-religion nexus. So when Walcott pronounces his curse (chapter 19) on that society for what it did to Simmons, what it does to its artists, he ends with a reassurance against whatever destruction the "enemy" can perform; he ends with the vision of a "risen" Simmons/St Omer/ Walcott:

> their vision blurs, their future is clouded with cataract
> but out of its mist, one man,
> whom they will not recognise, emerges
> and staggers towards his lineaments. (p. 128).

And Gregorias/Simmons is transfigured, translated, lifted up to be one with the painter-"saints":

> Every muscle
> ached like a rusting hawser
> to hoist him heavenward towards
> his name, pierced with stars
> of Raphael, Saint Greco . . . (p. 125)

Walcott's portrait of Anna is also influenced by Renaissance art:

> profile of hammered gold,
> head by Angelico,
> stars choiring in gold leaf. (p. 89)

> her golden plaits a simple coronet
> out of Angelico, a fine sweat on her forehead,
> hair where the twilight singed and signed its epoch. (p. 45)

Even his description of her as Judith with the head of Holofernes (p. 89) obviously derives from one or other of the Renaissance paintings on that favourite theme, as much as from Dante's description of the headless trunk of Bertrans, "that bears for light/Its own head swinging, gripped by the dead hair,/And like a swinging lamp. . ."[9]

The art-inspired descriptions of Anna, as indeed all the allusions to Renaissance art in *Another Life*, help to convey the sense of epoch[10] which attaches to Walcott's memory of that life, the feeling that he was participant in an epoch-making moment

of artistic awakening in St Lucia and the West Indies, the feeling that St Omer and
he, under Simmons' tutelage, were seeing and re-creating their world with new eyes,
in the same way that the Renaissance artist had rediscovered the world. Simmons
"had beheld/a community of graceful spirits/irradiating from his own control and
centre . . " (p. 120), and Walcott sees St Omer as a St Lucian (Giotto or Masaccio,
"his primitive, companionable saints" (p. 61), since Renaissance art just about began
with Giotto and Masaccio, especially the former, who arose almost self-created as it
were to create a new world.

   Giotto and Masaccio, then, like some other painters mentioned in the poem, are
used by Walcott to define Gregorias, just as Gauguin is used in chapter 19 to define
Simmons.[11] Giotto and Masaccio connote the "primitive", original force of
Gregorias, as Van Gogh, "saint of all sunstroke" (p. 56), connotes his vibrancy and
compulsive energy, his "madness."

> . . . Every muscle
> ached like a rusting hawser
> to hoist him heavenward towards
> his name, pierced with the stars
> of Raphael, Saint Greco, and later,
> not stars, but the people's medals,
> with Siqueiros, Gauguin, Orozco,
> Saint Vincent and Saint Paul. (p. 125)

In the original version of this passage, Walcott spells out the symbolism in his
references to these painters:

> You [Gregorias] wanted to be not only Raphael, your "sweet painter"
> (that was your Catholic side) but Orozco, Siquerios [sic] and Rivera as
> well (your violent Trinity, the new world rebel in you) but Gauguin and
> Van Gogh (madness and isolation) . . .[12]

The Mexican muralists — Orozco, Siqueiros and Rivera — represent not only the
idea of a revolutionary New World art, to which Walcott and Gregorias dreamed of
contributing, but also the idea of art for "the people." This idea of community is held
in tension against that of isolation/madness as a major theme of the poem — the artist
as man of the people against the artist as outcast and alienated.

   Even more essential to the web of the poem than the painterly descriptions and the
allusions to particular paintings and painters, is the poet's use of certain images
relating to colours and techniques of painting.

   At the very beginning of the poem, when he is describing Vigie and Castries at
sunset, he uses "amber" three times in two pages to convey the quality of the light.
The glare, he says,

> . . . mesmerised like fire without wind,

> and as its amber climbed
> the beer-stein ovals of the British fort
> above the promontory, the sky
> grew drunk with light. (p. 3)

As the painting completes itself in the boy's mind, the "silence waited"

> . . . for the tidal amber glare to glaze
> the last shacks of the Morne till they became
> transfigured sheerly by the student's will.
> a cinquecento fragment in gilt frame. (p. 4)

This amber glow glorifies his memory of the island and his young life:

> There
> was your heaven! The clear
> glaze of another life,
> a landscape locked in amber, the rare
> gleam. . . (p. 3)

Like the amber glaze used by the Old Masters, the poet's imaginative memory modifies and enriches the "colours" of the world which it recreates. In this connection, the amber image also comes from the theatre — the amber gel which provides basic stage lighting — and is used by Walcott in the opening sentence of "What the Twilight Says", a sentence which in mood, meaning and imagery parallels the opening of *Another Life*. "When dusk heightens, like amber on a stage set, those ramshackle hoardings of wood and rusting iron which circle our cities, a theatrical sorrow rises with it, for the glare, like the aura from an old-fashioned brass lamp is like a childhood signal to come home."[13]

The notion of the amber glaze "locking", sealing, fixing, preserving the painting is also crucial, and Walcott's language in the lines just quoted from the poem is reminiscent of a comment by Craven on Vermeer's technique: "His textures are such perfect replicas that his table covers and stuffs strike the eye, not as painted illusions, but as actual materials preserved in amber glazes."[14] The amber glaze of the poet's memory/imagination, therefore, not only transfigures the remembered world but also transfixes the memory and the vision. Paradoxically, it actualises and idealises at the same time. It catches and holds the remembered object in its quiddity. This is a feature of Vermeer's work which Walcott has cherished. Vermeer is explicitly mentioned once in *Another Life* ("the Vermeer white napery of the altar", p. 23). In "A Map of Europe", pursuing "the gift/To see things as they are", Walcott had praised Vermeer's skill in reproducing the very essence of objects in his paintings:

> . . . A cracked coffee cup,
> A broken loaf, a dented urn become

Themselves, as in Chardin,
Or in beer-bright Vermeer,
Not objects of our pity.[15]

The desire to catch or fix once and for all the essential quality of the remembered
life is the central point of the epigraph to *Another Life*, the quotation from Glissant's
novel *La Lezarde*. The sealing effect of the glaze also connotes the poet's attempt to
preserve his memories, which are his life, himself, against time and oblivion, against
the "amnesia" (temptation, horror, inevitability) which is mentioned more than once
in the poem. The amber signifies the dream of art to be indestructible, to preserve
man's finest moments against the flux. (And here we note that amber is also the
yellowish, translucent fossil resin which encloses and preserves the bodies of insects of
past ages). Hence the motif of the numerous images of preserving, locking, enclosing,
holding. These are almost invariably drawn from the arts, mainly the pictorial arts.
Indeed, the impulse of the poem to recreate the remembered life as a painting is most
apposite to the idea of arresting the moment; for of all the arts, painting, by the very
nature of its artifacts, is the one which most suggests in itself the idea of arresting
actuality through art. We experience a painting, even a painting which depicts swift
movements, as a moment arrested, enclosed within the frame and perceived whole in
an instant.

Small wonder, then that the image of the picture frame, in various permutations,
contributes much to the poem's unity, from the first reference to the Vigie landscape
as "a cinquecento fragment in gilt frame", through the memory of the "white face/ of
a dead child [which] stared from its window-frame" (p. 7), to the picture of the poet
and Anna walking "near the lagoon", where

dark water's lens made the trees one wood
arranged to frame this pair whose pace
unknowingly measured loss. (p. 93-4)

and the account of his return to St Lucia, when he

. . . would wake every morning surprised
by the framed yellow jungle of
the groyned mangroves . . . (p. 149)

The lens image, in the last quotation but one, is one of many images from
photography which extend the fixing/preserving connotations of "glaze" and
"frame." Through the images from photography, Walcott is able to complicate the
attractive connotations of "holding" life with the tragic implications. Remembering
Anna twenty years after their golden year of love, he catches through imagery the
essential tragedy of life and the tragic paradox of art:

your gaze haunts innumerable photographs,

> now clear, now indistinct,
> all that pursuing generality,
> that vengeful conspiracy with nature,
>
> all that sly informing of objects,
> and behind every line, your laugh
> frozen into a lifeless photograph. (p. 95-6)

The snapshot holds the moment, preserves the laugh from decay, but the laugh, the girl so preserved is "frozen", "dead." Similarly, the insect preserved in amber is splendidly undecayed, and dead. Amber heightens, makes luminous the life preserved in memory; looked at in another light, what it does is merely embalm that which is dead. Amber is also the colour of the spirits in which pathological specimens are preserved. In "Origins", Walcott recalling his childhood, had written:

> Memory in cerecloth uncoils its odour of rivers,
> Of Egypt embalmed in an amber childhood.[16]

These connotations of amber carry over into *Another Life*. Ultimately, any one of the many occurrences of the image evokes all its various and often contradictory associations, and the image itself is an embodiment of that ambiguity, that dwelling in contradictions which is of the essence of life. So even the most idyllic or idealized moments of *Another Life* are deepened into that complete vision of life which Walcott sees as a "tragic joy",[17] the vision which sees art as a "noble treachery" (p. 94). The poet has indeed preserved his paradisal moments, but their sweetness is rendered all the more poignant because the artistic realization of such moments is deepened by the knowledge that in actuality they cannot last; the artistic preservation is only a "second best."

So when he remembers "green lagoons/whose fading eye held Eden like a transfer" (p. 63), the "fading" and the "held" balance each other in an all-inclusive tension. So do "Eden", with its connotations of timelessness, and "transfer", with its connotations of the fragile and ephemeral. The same principle operates in the image which climaxes the re-creation of Walcott's St Lucian life and constitutes a major turning-point in the narrative. It is the image, significantly enough from the arts again, of the model ship assembled in a bottle, which figures the vow that he makes when he decides to leave the island. Incidentally, the passage in question (p. 108), which itself images the poem as a whole, is an example of how Walcott sometimes takes up again, and uses with a new depth and urgency, some detail from his earlier poetry, as if that detail, fascinating from the first, has to wait, gestating in his mind for a long time, before it can yield up its full potential. The glaze-glass-frame combination had been the basis of a little-remembered early poem, "Simply Passing Through",[18] while the ship in the bottle recalls the "old French barqentine anchored in glass", which had itself imaged so well "Cosimo de Chretien, count of curios", in chapter II of "Tales of the Islands."[19] The ship in the bottle is a curio, something to be marveled at; the art by

which the poet preserves his memories is a kind of miracle, all the more marvelous for
being instinct with the awareness of inevitable loss and separation.

The alchemy of Walcott's imagination, amber is transmuted easily into gold,
another key image in *Another Life*. (The alloy amber, it may be worth noting, consists
of four parts of gold to one part of silver; and "amber" was in Latin *elektrum*, from
Greek *elektron*, akin to *elektor*, "bright" or "gleaming as the sun.") The two colours,
sufficiently similar to begin with, merge into each other. In his use of gold in the
poem, Walcott takes a hackneyed image and infuses new vigour into it by means of
the concreteness of autobiographical fact which informs his use of it. It is not just a
random metaphor taken from a ready tray of stock metaphors; rather its appropriateness springs naturally from its specific, literal place in the poet's memory. So when he
speaks of the year just before he left St. Lucia as his "golden year", (p. 50) the trite
image is burnished by the memory of all the "gold leaf," "golden haloes and gilt
frame(s)" which figure in the poem, by the memory of Anna's golden hair and the
"bossed brass" (p. 23) on the altar of the Methodist chapel, no less than by the golden
vibrancy of Van Gogh and the golden glory of a Vigie sunset. Eventually all this gold
is metamorphosed back to its original source so to speak, into the holy, life-giving sun
which the poet invokes, and against which he sits in calm fulfillment, the sun itself his
golden halo:

> I sit in the roar of that sun
> like a lotus yogi folded on his bed of coals,
> my head is circled with a ring of fire. (p. 146)

Gold, too, is the allamanda, and the burnished bugles which it evokes. But in the
life-giving radiance of the gold image is also *its* opposite, the darkness and finality of
death. The allamandas fall and "rust", and rust — the "donkey's rusty winch" (p. 85),
the "rusting hawser" (p. 125) — is decay and death, the ship's bleeding wash (p. 32)
and Simmons' bleeding wrists. The variations on the imagery of rust and blood
recurring throughout the poem inter-connect to form a crucial motif, one that is
instinct with the painter's, the watercolourist's vision. So when the poet begins the
account of his departure from St Lucia with the line "One dawn the sky was warm
pink thinning to no colour" (p. 114), this seemingly "straight" piece of painterly
description is loaded with intimations of death (specifically Simmons' bleeding
wrists), separation, the encroaching blankness of disillusion, the diminishing vitality
of faith and purpose which the poem negotiates.

Such examples illustrate how imagery works as an essential, unifying force in
Another Life, a force particularly valuable in a poem as long and, in its way, as loose as
this. The refractions of images throughout the poem may be appreciated not only in
terms of the poem's forward movement in time, but also in terms of its spatial
existence. We can see the poem spread out before us in its totality, like a painting or
tapestry, presenting a subtle design of intermeshing webs of images and a rich texture
of many-layered meaning at any point. But this aspect of the poem, its richness and
complexity of metaphor, is at the same time an important part of whatever keeps the

poem true to its own medium, as distinct from the medium of paint. Yet another use
to which Walcott puts painting in *Another Life* is that of helping him to define, by
contrast with painting, what appeals to him in the medium of poetry. He does this in
chapter 9, when, after his recreation of what it feels like to toil at a canvas and to fail,
he rationalises his "failure" as a painter and explains what made him concentrate on
poetry:

> . . . I rendered
> the visible world that I saw
> exactly, yet it hindered me, for
> in every surface I sought
> the paradoxical flash of an instant
> in which every facet was caught
> in a crystal of ambiguities,
> I hoped that both disciplines might
> by painful accretion cohere
> and finally ignite,
> but I lived in a different gift,
> its element metaphor . . . (p. 58-9)

To acknowledge the otherness of the painter's medium is itself a gesture that
enhances the poet's tribute to painters. At the same time, *Another Life* represents a
remarkable attempt, within the one discipline, to make "both disciplines . . . cohere."

Footnotes and References

1 Walcott, *Dream on Monkey Mountain*, New York, 1970, p. 40.
2 See Baugh, *Derek Walcott: Memory as Vision*, London, 1978.
3 All quotations from *Another Life* are taken from the London and New York editions of 1973,
  the pagination being the same in both.
4 Walcott, *Another Life, MS*, in library, University of the West Indies, Jamaica, p. 59. Millet's
  painting is not reproduced by Craven.
5 Walcott, *In a Green Night*, London, 1962, p. 60; my emphasis.
6 See, for example, Boticelli's "The Birth of Venus", also reproduced by Craven.
7 Craven, *op. cit.*, p. 56.
8 Cf. "the old-fashioned brass lamp", *Dream on Monkey Mountain*, p. 3.
9 From Canto 28 of *Inferno*. This translation is taken from Ezra Pound's "Near Perigord."
10 Cf. *Another Life*, p. 4:
   but if the light was dying through the stone
   of that converted boathouse on the pier,
   a girl, blowing its embers in her kitchen,
   could feel its epoch entering her hair.
11 See Baugh, *Derek Walcott*, pp. 63-64.
12 *Another Life*, MS, p. 18.
13 *Dream on Monkey Mountain*, p. 3.
14 Craven, p. 166.

[15] Walcott, *The Castaway*, London, 1965, p. 42. In an earlier version of these lines, Walcott had made the point even more explicitly, though somewhat more heavy-handedly: " . . . become/ More than themselves, their SELVES, as in Chardin . . " *Selected Poems* New York, 1964, p. 79.

[16] *Selected Poems*, p. 52.

[17] *Dream on Monkey Mountain*, p. 25.

[18] *In a Green Night*, p. 75.

[19] *Ibid.*, p. 26.

BREAKING MYTHS AND MAIDENHEADS

Patricia Ismond

The Joker of Seville completed its second run at the Little Carib Theatre on Sunday 30th March, a run which was very successful despite the setbacks posed by the country's industrial crisis. As Walcott observed in a short commentary (*Trinidad Guardian*, March 22), this second production of the play, barely three months after the first, represented a new attempt to introduce continuous theatre in the region. *The Joker* was well able to carry off this experiment.

We are accustomed to a high standard of theatre from Walcott, however controversial in content. But he has certainly found fresh levels of accomplishment in this musical, responsible for the tremendous reception it got from its large audiences. The play reached out, in fact, to expand the country's theatre audience. Already its musical score has passed into our everyday experience, much as the music of Carnival does. It is a sure sign of the way in which good theatre becomes part of a people's cultural experience. This is a measure of the strong regional appeal of *The Joker*.

When we consider that Walcott is adapting an original distant both in time and setting — seventeenth century Spain — this regional appeal becomes all the more impressive, even curious. It is necessary to take a close look at Walcott's effort in recasting the original, to appreciate the factors which were responsible for this remarkable achievement.

Walcott is working to two main principles in adapting De Molina's *El Burlador de Sevilla*. Firstly, he frees the timeless significance of an ancient legend, and, releasing a theme close to the spirit of modern times, angles it to draw out an intrinsic relevance to our own situation. Secondly, he exploits the dramatic style of the musical to serve this basic purpose. Its open, non-naturalistic form allows him to ply between foreign and local strains to bring out this relevance in "seamless transitions". It is a technique which serves to bring out the parallels by showing sameness in difference.

The "difference" is always the more immediate feature in this kind of fusion, and it accounts for the single most original element in the play: the use of native Creole rhythms drawn from West Indian folk forms, song and dance. They are imaginatively exploited to distill the relevance of the Don Juan legend to the native experience, in our own terms and modes of expression. The play is working all the time to find rhythmic counterparts between the foreign and the local.

Thus, at the centre of the play, is the figure of the stickfighter, the local counterpart to the Spanish courtier. The spirit of Juan's triumph is caught in the rhythms of the local stickfight, corresponding to the sword-fight of the Spanish original. This is not to overlook the combination of foreign and local elements present especially in the musical content of the play. Many remained unhappy with this combination, resulting from the joint effort of Walcott and Galt McDermot.

But the point is that this blend is well subordinated to the underlying effort to realise the correspondences in native rhythms. The play is controlled in such a way that all the major climaxes where foreign and local coalesce are rendered in West Indian terms. The shipwreck sequence which brings Juan to the New World is dramatised in terms of the middle passage experience. The celebration of Tisbea's rape, where the New World takes up the burden of Juan's quest for freedom, is patterned on local forms of possession cults. Juan's climactic duel with Don Gonzalo, the embodiment of repressive traditions, is symbolic of his will to triumph over adversity: it is performed to the ritual strains of the stickfight. This is an important aspect of the play to which we will return later.

Walcott retains the framework of De Molina's plot to free the universal significance of the legend. It serves as the base from which he appropriates the wider meanings. Juan, the rebel courtier of Seville, makes a career of seducing women. He offends, thereby, against the Spanish codes of honour and chastity. But Juan's sexual exploits serve a positive purpose. In engaging his women in these violations he brings out into the open the libido, the inordinate appetite which is the root element of all human desire. Its excesses and desperation are provoked by the very fact of human limitations and denials, and are thus existential. It begins from the lust for an impossible completion, fraught with the fears and anxieties posed by these limitations.

The violation which Juan practices mirrors this existential truth. The Spanish tradition of honour shortcircuits and conceals this disturbing truth. Its codes of propriety and chastity are held out as absolutes which fix men's rightful place above the reaches of appetite. Libido is thus proscribed as unnatural: which means that the code is erected on a principle of repression and self-deception. There is a basic human failing responsible for this deception. It is the desire to find a definitive system which will rule out the contradictions, and thus provide a sinecure. The Spanish code is such a sinecure: a substitute for God. In the king's words to Isabella, honour "isn't owned by you or me, it is the word of God". It must be upheld by the God-given rule of Justice, whose necessary instrument is merciless vengeance.

In rebelling against its rigid formulas, Juan exposes the lie on which the Spanish code is founded. He explodes its repressive sinecures to come into stark confrontation with the chaos of our natural subjection to these appetites. He gains freedom to indulge them fully. It is through this very course that he comes to recognise the moral challenge they pose as the sole medium of human struggle for fulfillment. This is the kind of awareness Juan arouses in the women he violates. Their loves, broken free from the prescribed codes of chastity, assume their true incontinent and troubled features.

Significantly, most of the women had been planing for secret meetings with their lovers to take what was theirs "a little before" the rules allowed. Juan takes the place of these lovers to show up the true image of these desires in its most naked guise. The freedom Juan brings them is thus two-sided and complex. It begins with the freedom to enter fully into the violations; and from there to face two final possibilities: either to succumb to the threats and destructive forces of these violations, or to take up the challenge of finding a measure of love within those tragic necessities, without hope of any outside justification. It is the choice of losing or finding themselves.

This is the fundamental moral dialectic at the heart of the play, and it represents Walcott's abiding perspective on the meaning of freedom. Freedom carries this dual burden: it is the choice either to *lose* or *find* oneself.

The relevance of the Don Juan legend to our own situation begins from here. The dialectic is presented in terms of Women's Liberation, but the whole issue of paternalism versus independent, self-deterministic effort is one which includes but goes further than Women's Lib. If, in the hierarchies of society's establishments women are subjugated to men, men higher up the scale are no less subjugated to the paternalistic principle which runs through the system. In the terms of the play the need for liberation applies as much to men as to women. The women, representing the creative principle, serve a mainly symbolic role in *The Joker*.

Juan's role in arousing this awareness is at once demonic and beneficent, since he must violate in order to free. His penetration of the contradictions involve bitterness and outrage, at the absurd gap between human aspirations and limitations. Juan takes up the challenge defiantly. He assumes the character of the joke played by existence itself, his irrelevant attitudes reflecting its mockery.

The strategy of the joker is to laugh in the face of this grave mockery. The defiance of his laughter carries the will to exult over it — "to change to elation each grave situation" — though the strains are perhaps more mocking than exultant. The blend finds expression in the devilish charm of Juan's personality. Nigel Scott captured its impish spirit very effectively, though, at times the effort to sustain that dynamic left him somewhat breathless, and blurred his words.

Yet, while the affirmative purpose of Juan's role as the joker prevails in the play, he is himself doomed as an individual to a tragic end. It is an ironic twist in the drama. The irony of the situation is that Juan has become immured in the very resistance which is supposed to free him: he cannot move beyond it. It has hardened into the unyielding force of the superman, from the very intensity with which he penetrates the mockery. The struggle becomes a matter of matching his own force against the odds, to overwhelm or be overwhelmed by them — an effort in which he is destined to be the loser. He cannot find the strength of humility, which is the strength of "surrendering" to creative choice within the pattern of tragic necessity.

Thus, when he tries to repent towards the end, the voice of a woman comes to counsel this humility and love in surrender. But, "irresolute and proud/(he) can never go back" (Walcott, "Crusoe's Island" — *The Castaway*). In the course of this proud struggle he has become "not a man, but a force" as he puts it, drained of humanity. Incapable of destroying the odds, he falls victim to the rigours of a hell which he himself has allowed to become relentless.

It is important to understand the meaning of Juan's failure in the dialectic of the play. Walcott is not adhering to the anachronistic code of vengeance. Juan's error is at the opposite extreme of the imprisonment in codes. The true principle of moral freedom, the principle which comes to fruition in the women, lies in the middle ground between these two negative poles — the imprisonment in codes, and Juan's unyielding resistance.

It is this positive principle which the joker pursues in spirit, and it prevails to affirm the values of the play. Juan the joker thus survives as the genius of this message: to find elation in facing the challenge unflinchingly, without self-pity, *sans humanite*. The burden is expressed in the theme song *Sans Humanite*, with which the first production concluded (it is replaced by *Little Red Bird* in the second production to stress the theme of freedom). It is Walcott's own emphasis, and represents the meaning he distills out of the timeless theme of freedom preserved in the original legend.

What authentic bearings does this theme have on the West Indian situation? This is the motivating concern behind Walcott's adaptation. In passing on to this final question, it is impossible to miss the close link between Juan's rebellious role and the spirit of modern times. Juan's effort as arch-rebel is the paradigm of modern man's effort to resist orthodoxies and establishments in order to confront existential contradictions and the imperatives of choice.

The twentieth century motto "God is dead" heralded this awareness — which does not necessarily extend into existentialist doctrine. To the existentialist, the contradictions spell an absurdity which undermines man's very being and leaves him a non-entity; to the existential joker the chaos means a mockery he must elude. The one begins from the sense of life as a void; the other from a sense of active crisis which never questions the reality of life. But whether or not it ends in existentialism, modern belief finds its point of departure in the recognition of an existential challenge.

The legend of Don Juan thus speaks immediately to the modern consciousness on the most essential levels. The Juan who sets out to wage love, not war in defence of creeds, is truly close to the spirit of modern times. This "timeli-ness" is a measure of his timelessness, and the latter, the basis of his shifting persona in the play. He is "nobody" and everybody (a recurrent motif in the play), belongs nowhere and everywhere. He moves with ease from Spanish to West Indian setting, glances in passing at the contemporary metropolitan scene.

To Walcott, this intrinsic relevance of the Don Juan legend applies uniquely to our own situation as a people emerging out of a certain history. The challenge which the joker uncovers is the very challenge that the denials of history have left us to face; the promise of freedom which this challenge holds is uniquely our own promise as a New World people.

The middle passage experience dispossessed the peoples of the region of their parent traditions, especially the black man of his roots in Africa. Its corruption and violence were, moreover, a product of the collapse of the Old World civilization, the failure of the traditions of the master. We were shipwrecked onto these shores with this breakage. As victims of these dual privations — dispossessed of parent traditions and left only with a heritage of broken values — we are truly in a position of "traditionlessness", a new race existing outside cultural establishments.

A people, therefore, who are in a unique position to see through the falsehoods and constraints of such systems, and who must, to use the popular phrase, "do their own thing". To put it another way, we start off with an advantage over the Old World Juan. While he has to go through the process of stripping the customs bare to expose the truth — we are already placed in the original condition through history. The condition is a predicament; but, as with Juan, this very predicament becomes our advantage.

Without any props to rely on, we are open to a more intense experience of the chaos, and a greater lucidity into its imperatives. In this lies the potential advantage of being roused to the authentic challenge, as in Juan's case. Catalinion, Juan's servant, is referring to this advantage when he rebukes Anfriso for betraying the promise of his freedom. Anfriso is the freed slave who aspires to remake himself only in the image of Spanish honour. Catalinion says "You have a chance to remake things, instead you accept them. That's disgraceful".

Old and New World Juan thus meet at this point in *The Joker*. The Spanish Juan passes from the Old World scene to the New in the middle-passage sequence. The image of shipwreck combines both the Old World's crisis of disillusionment and the ravage and destitution of the New World. Juan looks to a fresh undertaking of the challenge in a setting bare of all the old illusions and props. His encounter with Tisbea is the symbol of this new effort. Their sexual relationship signifies the rape of the New World, and its awakening to experience. In Tisbea Juan looks forward to ideal resources which have been missing from his earlier conquests. He looks forward to a "simple, unremorseful Eve" — that is, an innocence free from the repressive guilt and recriminations built into man's orthodox compromises, and capable of a fearless, native vitality in meeting the strife.

But what Juan actually finds falls far short of this expectation. The new region has betrayed its promise, and failed to exploit its potential. *The Joker* is thus engaged in a close critical focus on the region, as it examines the parallels between the mistakes of the older societies and our own. The New World too yearns for sinecures, for the earnests of success deceptively meted out in codes and customs. At root the yearning harbours the same failing identified in the Spanish code. It withholds independent confrontation with the existential challenge, and involves the same kind of deception perpetrated in the Old World creeds.

Walcott's general critical outlook on the society is based on a view which begins from this insight — that "society has taken the old direction". This is what continues to impel the colonial towards the values and customs of the former master. They still exert fascination as measures of a tangible prosperity. Tisbea seeks her self-esteem in the proprietorship of marriage to Juan, equating this esteem with its codes of respectability and stability. Juan, encountering the same disillusionment, has "wasted a trip": "Old World, New World, they're all one". "The Ballad of The Middle Passage" sums up the common failing which makes Old and New World one:

> But I'm not sure, now I'm alive,
> which is the worse disaster.
>
> For this new world, its promised feasts,
> is nothing but the old one,
> as long as men are beasts, and beasts
> still bear their master's burden.

The issue is further examined in the case of Anfriso, who eventually attacks Juan in the form of a mad bull-fighter. Anfriso is the prototype of the free native who pursues realisation and dignity in the traditions of the master. In the play he makes a symbolic journey to the Spanish motherland to secure its faith. He finds instead only the mockery and travesties of this ideal in the Old World. He has been duped and deceived — which is what his image as the mad bull-fighter signifies. Juan stands generally for the shattering of these illusions. To the distracted Anfriso, Juan is the despoiler responsible for his betrayal and deception. He seeks revenge on Juan, still harbouring the illusion that he is defending the principle of honour. But Juan expresses the truth as Anfriso falls: "It is not honour but madness kills for the revenge of cuckoldry". Anfriso falls victim to his own self-destructive rage and distraction when he is duped by his own misconceived ambitions.

Walcott is dwelling here on the self-betrayal and moral suicide involved in this adoption of the master's burden on the part of colonised peoples. The basic moral complex being examined in this context reflects on failings that may still be embedded in the attitudes of the society. This is of fundamental significance. In revolutionary times, when we no longer pay deference to foreign values and customs — at least ostensibly — we like to think that we have passed that stage of servitude and dependence. We may not have gone so far beyond that stage as we imagine, which is part of what *The Joker* is saying.

But over and above this, there is an implicit point which extends outside this immediate context. Walcott believes that the same fundamental failing may still be at work in our righteous devotions to Black Power and the cult of Africa. He has one insistent reservation about these revolutionary directions. They may still serve as substitute ideals replacing those of the master, and answering to the misguided needs for absolute props. This has earned him the reputation of being insensitive to the needs of the region, but it deserves serious reflection.

He puts the case in an important essay, "What the Twilight Says", which sums up his position: "The African revival is escape to another dignity. . . . The West Indian mind . . . prefers . . . to narrow its eyelids in a schizophrenic daydream of an Eden that existed before its exile. Its fixation is for the breasts of a nourishing mother".

Walcott has made the most penetrating study of this complex in the figure of

Corporal Lestrade, a central character in his climactic play, *Dream on Monkey Mountain*. Lestrade is representative of the endemic, schizophrenic split between black and white in the colonial psyche. Lestrade is ungrounded: he switches from total dependence on a white order to a black one as times change in the region. In the colonial era he finds his ballast in white culture. He is committed to its law as the sole means of eradicating the conflicts and contradictions which make for disorder. The black man must be drilled to the white code to escape his native savagery, which threatens the given order.

When he switches over to Black Power in revolutionary times, it holds the same basic value for him. The externals change but the ethic remains the same: he looks to the black code to regulate an order obliterating all native contradictions. It entails the same evasion of choice in struggle and short-circuiting of self-deterministic effort. It is a valuable criticism, one which urges a moral stock-taking necessary to reinforce revolutionary purpose, and set it along the right tracks. What it says, finally, is that it is just as easy for the black man to wear a *black* mask as it is to wear a white one — which is an even more weird state of affairs. Blackness then remains artifice rather than true consciousness.

The Joker's concern with servitude to white values is thus far from irrelevant to the current movements in the society. It also raises the question, as earlier observed, whether the region has gone so far past that servitude at this stage. The play moves to take a direct look — by contrast with the symbolically ordered Tisbea and Anfriso incidents — at local attitudes and features where the failing survives in various guises and disguises. We get such a close-up of the society in the wedding festival Juan storms during his exile to Lebrija. The peasant wedding is celebrated in courtly pageantry: all the country folk don the finery of dukes and duchesses for the occasion. The spectacle is a very West Indian one in tone, spirit and character, and mirrors the native flair for pageantry and play-acting on the grand scale. The scene is in fact modelled on certain French Creole flower festivals surviving in St. Lucia.

La Rose and *Marguerite* represent rival loyalties, which are dramatised in terms of a feud between royal factions. West Indians have always had this tendency to adopt the modes and styles of "high" culture to satisfy their natural love of fantasy. This genius for mimicry carries its creative aspects. There is imaginative vitality in the invariable effects of comedy and parody present in such play-acting.

But these more happy effects stem from a susceptibility which is quite deeply entrenched in our serious intentions and objectives. Mimicry is not only a matter of play-acting but becomes woven into the very life-style of the region. The styles and fashions of more "sophisticated" societies are cultivated as standards of advancement and social mobility. They are exploited as means to those ends. It is a bourgeois mentality to which the common man, no less than the middle class is prone.

To the canaille at Batricio's wedding, the pageantry has marketable value. Batricio's profit-minded attitudes reveal this quite clearly. He measures his worth in terms of the borrowed dignities his money can buy; and these illusions, vulgar though they remain, are just as frenetic as the more "noble" aspirations of Anfriso. They represent "another kind of lust". We get a freeze of the pageant as Juan makes a critical appraisal of these buried motives. (The second production was considerably improved by the freeze technique, which served to highlight these critical perspectives). Juan is the detached spectator commenting on the scene:

> . . . . just like the bourgeois
> because their forced prosperity
> is based on what goes on at court,
> all that shrewd eccentricity
> is profit. They still sell you short.
>
> . . .

> . . . . they despise the age
> they live in like their own natures,
> so, they dress up in the image
> of dons, princes and duchesses.
> Isn't that another kind of lust:
> to curse the court, then say "Let us
> dress like those who grind us in the dust"?

Juan has earlier exposed another travesty nestling in the bourgeois pretensions to propriety and respectability. The society still depends on borrowed formalities and sophistications to maintain the illusion of being self-possessed:

> . . . The New World that I saw
> wasn't Eden. Eden was dead
> or worse, it had been converted
> to modesty. No Indian goes
> naked there. They're all dressed
> to kill. . .

All these concerns derive from Walcott's fundamental insight into a new society "taking the old direction", and leave the relevance of *The Joker* intrinsic. They all radiate from one central perspective, contrary to Denis Solomon's criticism that Walcott "has never been able to resist an incidental theme" (*Tapia*, 8 December 1974).

The first part of this appreciation examined the moral significance of the Don Juan legend, and considered its authentic bearings on the society, present in the plot with varying degrees of obliqueness. It is, however, where action is deployed in song and dance elements that the original spiritual values of the theme are being most fully crystallised and communicated. These basic values relate quite closely to our own circumstances, forming the basis of the critical parallels Walcott draws between the old societies and the new.

Creole rhythms of song and physical expressiveness are orchestrated to enact the correspondences. They become identified and immediate in West Indian strains. The general principle behind this technique — the use of song and dance to present action — is characteristic of the musical. Walcott exploits it resourcefully for the "seamless transitions" from Spanish classical setting to local folk setting.

The Joker thus advances through a number of major sequences consisting of the total orchestration of sung, mimed and danced performance. These sequences all represent climaxes of action and meaning in the play. They dramatise its central themes. In The Middle Passage sequence, the experience of shipwreck and chaos is performed to "The Ballad of The Middle Passage". In the celebration of Tisbea's initiation into sexual experience, the complex burden of freedom is performed to the strains of "Tisbea Went and Bathe". While the joker's will to find a life-asserting power in struggle is recaptured in the local stickfight — "Let the resurrection come from the stickfight".

Foreign passes into local at these climaxes; and, most importantly, they are all unmistakably West Indian in tempo and sensibility. The burden of The Middle Passage, for example, combines the predicament of master and slave. The journey is mimed in patterned movements which blend elements of the limbo dance with gestures indicating lack of direction and disaster. The movements thus capture the effects of oppression and shipwreck typical of that historical experience, while Catalinion's "Ballad of The Middle Passage" recites this very burden in choric accompaniment:

> El captain was a drunken wreck
> el first mate muy borracho,
> los crew, who staggered round the deck
> didn't know arse from elbow.
> . . .
>
> El cargo was a raving lot,
> of Negroes, coon and bimbo,
> who screamed the blues when they were not
> up practising el limbo

The "Ballad of The Middle Passage" allows scope for different theatrical interpretations, and the non-West Indian producer can draw upon dance-styles peculiar to his own culture to mime the action. But in moral substance it remains closest to the experience of the region. In Walcott's theatre, the physical style and its peculiar vigour are vitally West Indian, and the black experience predominates.

It is in the sequence celebrating Tisbea's sexual awakening that the deepest moral strains are being sounded, and this form of orchestration is at its most powerful. Tisbea, seduced by Juan, has been awakened to the conflicts and violating forces of libido. This brings her, like Juan's other women, to the threshold of final moral discovery.

The Sisters who dance Tisbea's fall to the strains of "Tisbea Went and Bathe" are giving theatrical expression to this process of discovery. She now faces the dual choice: either to find creative control in desire, or to submit to its mocking tyrannies and be confounded. She is therefore being urged by the Sisters to hold fast to the struggle, and maintain control with a hardihood equal to its rigours — to "hold on to the rod".

Deliverance lies in this very effort — that "rod is the rod of correction:" but like "the miraculous serpent/it point to the promised land" (The sexual image, together with the implicit allusion to the myth of Eden make these points quite eloquently). The real crux of the struggle is to resist becoming a slave to appetite and being overwhelmed by its excessive forces — Tisbea must mind lest the rod "jump out (her) hand". In short it is an aspiration to maintain the true tension of freedom and avoid the negative aspect of its twofold burden: the danger of losing oneself.

The chorus of "Tisbea Went and Bathe" sums up these realisations:

> Hold on to the rod, Sister Tisbea
> Hold on the rod,
> though it turn like the staff of Aaron
> to a miraculous serpent
> mind it jump out of your hand!

The Sisters capture the vibrations of these moral sentiments in physical rhythms, so that strains of dance and song fuse for a live imitation of this process of awareness. Through these living rhythms, the Sisters are apprehending the meanings organically. Here Walcott is superbly assisted by the imaginative choreography of Astor Johnson. The tension of "holding on to the rod" is caught in a "steady rocking" beat, drawn from basic Jamaican dance-rhythms, which themselves originated in possession cults such as pocomania. The emotive rhetoric of the Baptist preacher rises in counterpoint to the singing, whipping up religious fervour as the whole performance builds up to a pitch. Song rises into choral chant, dance into ritual observance, and the Tisbea sequence builds up into a veritable communal celebration.

In Walcott's production (especially the December run) the sequence reached an elation which caught in all audiences. As in the true folk festival, ritual purposes found elation in sheer sensuous and aesthetic expression — a feature which was also powerful in the stickfight sequence.

This elation, excelled only by the verbal richness of the play, was one of the most immediate sources of the enjoyment *The Joker* brought to its audiences. The spirit of communal participation caught in most of its audiences during these musical sequences. Walcott's arena stage helped to encourage a response itself integral to that style of theatre. It seems to me that the communal power of the Tisbea sequence was stronger in the first production.

In the second run the performance was pared down. The number of dancers and singers was reduced, by contrast with the first production, where Chorus and dance-movement expanded to include the whole cast. In the second production Walcott seemed to be making the stylisation more spare and clean-cut, with the net result of losing the original communal impact.

But Walcott is not merely satisfying our natural love of dance and song in this musical treatment of the play. He exploits much more than the aesthetic appeal in reaching towards these communal effects. He is recovering the deeper psychic principle that lies behind this natural love of dance, song and mime. It reaches back to an instinct rooted in the psyche of the folk, and true to our own sensibility as a people still close to the folk. It is the instinct to enter into religious experience organically, through the pulsations of the body. Meaning is realised through the language of the body, rather than through the mental, reflective disciplines and abstract processes typical of more intellectual, "civilized" cultures.

This is the source of the ritualistic modes of observance which prevail in folk culture. What survives as the love of dance and song in the West Indian temperament goes back to this root instinct. Walcott thus seeks to revive the power of dance and song in his theatre, in his effort to create a style based on our own dramatic resources. This has been developing as a central aspect of his style, very successfully in plays like *Ti-Jean* and *Dream on Monkey Mountain*.

The most vital purposes of the musical-conception of the play culminate in these creolised sequences. At base, they function on a mimetic principle — that is, dramatic states and attitudes are not being directly presented, but rhythms and gestures are stylised to mime the experience. The wider, total style of *The Joker* is an extension of this mimetic pattern. Vocal expression — both speech and song, symbolic gesture and movement, are generally working together to present action.

An outstanding example of this is the incident where Juan, like the shipwrecked Ulysses, is discovered on the beach by Tisbea, the local Nausicaa. Juan proceeds to seduce Tisbea. The highly allusive and rhetorical dialogue between the two; the bawdy sexual mime presented in the basket-and-eel image; Tisbea's exaggerated, mannered declamations which break into song at one point — all these interact to dramatise the seduction in a nonrealistic mode. Walcott has in fact developed an inbuilt property of the musical form to fashion a total style where symbolic gesture, elements of mime, verbal expression — song and speech alike — support and interpret each other. Dialogue therefore, is just as important as song and dance in this wider style.

What this means is that *The Joker* as a musical does not follow the classic operatic form, but draws close to total theatre. Musical expression is not the main vehicle of communication in the play. Song, speech and gesture are being co-ordinated to serve this purpose. At the same time, within the expansive pattern of total theatre, Walcott can isolate any of these modes to function independently at certain points. The composite nature of total theatre allows scope for this.

This bears, though indirectly, upon the incidence and distribution of songs based on Western traditional airs in the play, for example the "Divina Pastora" and "The Sower". Many felt that the mixture of foreign and local airs made for discordance and unevenness in *The Joker* (though both types have proved equally popular since the release of the record). But the points at which these Western songs enter are so controlled that they take nothing away from the central role played by creolised music in the play.

A song like "La Divina Pastora" serves as a further, heightened expression of the character's sentiments, occurring at a point where these sentiments have already been registered in the character's reaction on the direct realistic plane. The song serves to intensify the strains of these sentiments, but it is external to the action. It functions on a choric dimension to *extend* feeling rather than to *enact* it, by contrast with the local music in the creolised sequences.

Songs like "La Divina Pastora" and "The Sower" mainly provide a choric background to the action, following the more classic principle. The significant point is that in serving this role they are confined to their immediate contexts, "localised". They do not permeate through the whole moral content of the play as do those in the creolised sequences.

"Placed" in this way, a song like "La Divina Pastora" exists independently in its pure form, requiring the pure singing talent which was so outstanding in Syd Skipper's rendition of the hymn in question. (By contrast with the pure song we have in a piece like "The Ballad of The Middle Passage" the sung recitative which, combining with mime, remains close to speech). Most of the Western songs functioned in this way, and though a few of the singers were competent, none approached the professional excellence of Syd Skipper, and Andrew Beddoe doing "The Sower." Treated in this way, the foreign songs fitted in as local details in the composite tapestry of *The Joker*, serving to enrich rather than impair its total texture.

Some critics were also uneasy about the use of pop elements in the style of the play. It was felt that the inclusion of these elements was indulgent and arbitrary and contributed nothing to the effort to make the content of *El Burlador de Sevilla* meaningful in our time and place.

The first point to be noticed here is that the theme of *The Joker* is on an important dimension timeless and placeless. By virtue of this the play remains "open" and can accommodate styles and elements from a variety of sources, both formal and popular in character. So that the few music-hall and slapstick features which enter, skilfully engaged, do fit into its design. They are, in fact, minimal.

A few such elements are blended in, for example, in things like the horse-riding mime to which Juan and Catalinion make their entrances and exits. The mime is in the vein of slapstick comedy. Juan and de Mota flash back to a vaudeville scene as they recall their days with "the hags (they) found so pretty/in every Port of Spain". Such elements contribute important dramatic effects. Walcott exploits them to vary the pitch from high to low comedy — effects which are very active in a play made rich by a range of vibrations from high seriousness to sheer vulgarity.

An incident like de Mota's last fling with the prostitutes — which is a popular version of Juan's promiscuity — comes down to this lower pitch to provide comic relief. These pop elements are one of the many sources Walcott mines for the vitality and energy of the process of "vulgarisation" at work in the play.

In the second run, these effects were enhanced with the introduction of the prostitutes in the short brothel sequence. Noble Douglas gave an outstanding performance as one of the prostitutes. She is a very fine dancer whose every movement has a special West Indian freedom and eloquence. Controlled so skilfully for these variations in dramatic pitch, the diversity of *The Joker* was, far from being discordant, an enrichment.

There is one common source of energy and vitality running through these diverse theatrical effects, to sustain a unity of tone in *The Joker*. It is the language of the play, its sheer verbal richness. It is characterised by a peculiar brand of wit and an accent which remains consistent throughout these changing pitches and settings. These qualities are, moreover, distinctly West Indian in character. Walcott states in a programme that one of his main objectives was to make the adaptation "vulgar enough for audiences here to enjoy it". The real strengths of this vulgarisation, and its West Indianess, are present especially in the language. Basically the "high", dignified style of the original classic is being brought closer to and modulated by the earthy style of popular West Indian expression. The popular interacts with the grand style to remint the latter in its own coinage.

This works in various ways. The dignified and proper are being reduced and undercut by bawdy puns. In the courtly milieu Juan's misdeeds are defined in the elevated terms of chastity and defilement. This is constantly being decoded in bawdy sexual puns — which captures the true spirit of Juan's irreverence.

This reductive technique works through a highly imaginative process. It manages to retain and add to the poetic, metaphorical content of the language. The grand style takes its elaborate metaphors seriously. What is serious on the grand level becomes sheer verbal extravagance on the vulgar plane: the elaborate metaphors are retained to serve reductive purposes. The result is a kind of mock-rhetoric which blends both the serious implications and ribald humour. There is imaginative vigour and ebullience in this kind of rhetoric, and they are vitally West Indian in spirit. The West Indian has this genius for extravagant pun and parody. It is present in the spirit of robber talk, *mamaguy*, and enters into the calypso.

Juan's first meeting with Tisbea is rich in these effects. The seduction of Tisbea is an incident of high seriousness. As Juan persuades her to go into the garden with him, the metaphors allude to the Serpent's seduction of Eve. But the images are being wittily redirected to the raw physical facts of the situation. The mythic allusions are still present, but the metaphors now function as an elaborate rhetorical pun. Juan persuades Tisbea:

> Well, but never release him, and we'll go over to . . . to that Eden
> there, my salty Eve, and cast him out, angel with the flaming sword, keep
> the eel in the basket where it belongs, and lead us on. . .

There are also more immediately recognisable strands of this West Indian style in things like "Tisbea Went and Bathe". Its idiom recalls that of the old calypso "Miss Elsie River" — "I went to bathe in a river". The witty West Indian idiom which enters in these various ways, carries the inflections and accent of the region intact.

Except for the formal exchanges within the Spanish court, it was remarkable how West Indian the language remained in inflection and accent. It was especially remarkable in the performance of Hamilton Parris, who played the role of Rafael. As leader of the troupe of actors he served as general Chorus, and had to carry a good deal of the play's philosophical overtures. He managed to preserve an open style and his delivery retained the native inflection throughout. Hamilton Parris is always the most relaxed and unstrenuous of the actors in the Company. His style shows best of all how intrinsic the basic rhythms of West Indian dialect remain in Walcott's diction. Walcott can move naturally from a more literary medium to plain West Indian vernacular, as when Parris expresses the fate of the artist in this speech: "In this business, every man so catching his arse we soon come to resemble one another." And in that most felicitous touch where Norline Metivier as Aminta deflates Juan's grandiose ardours with this Trinidadian rejoinder: "You joking yes."

In moral and stylistic conception *The Joker of Seville* is a well integrated play, and Walcott's adaptation is altogether successful. It succeeds in finding meaningful bearings on the society, and captures in the process the rhythms of our own forms of expression. (I think a good deal of the peculiar richness of the play will be lost in the Royal Shakespeare Company production — and this is as it should be). There were flaws in the production, but these were flaws in execution, arising from local weaknesses on the part of the actors.

This relates to the character and needs of the Theatre Workshop. Walcott's style is the style of total theatre, as *The Joker* shows most clearly. This means that his actors must combine the arts of acting, singing, dance, and mime with some degree of competence, whatever their individual professional skills — as every properly trained performing artist does. Walcott has tried to develop the Theatre Workshop along these lines. But quite a few of the company lack this versatility, and this was responsible for the flaws in the performance.

Norline Metivier, for example, is a competent singer and dancer, but quite weak in acting. She gave a hesitant performance in the bedroom scene with Juan, which was well below the standard of acting in *The Joker*. Carol La Chapelle as Ana showed similar limitations. She is a dancer, and her movements are supple and eloquent; but in the scene where the three women discuss Juan's bequest to them, her performance as the outraged, vengeful daughter was quite strained. By contrast we had Anthony Hall, in the role of Don Pedro, who combines considerable acting ability with great miming skills. Physical and verbal flourishes interacted richly in his portrayal of the comic personality of Don Pedro. His is representative of the kind of training Walcott's actors need.

Most of the veterans in the troupe have acquired this versatility. Stanley Marshall, for example, can switch from the sustained immobility of the statue, which requires a serious piece of classic acting, to a remarkable display of body language as stickfighter. On the whole, the uneven patches were counterbalanced by the performances of such experienced actors in the Company. Among these were veterans like Errol Jones, and Nigel Scott himself, a relative newcomer whom the role of Juan has turned into a serious actor overnight.

INTERLUDE FOR REST OR PRELUDE TO DISASTER?

Victor Questel

O Babylon! the musical by Derek Walcott and Galt MacDermot now playing at the Little Carib is, in every sense of the word, average. It challenges nothing, achieves nothing. It lacks authority and vision. The music is tame and the acting is without the fierce integrity that the Rastafarian cult deserves and demands. The play is staged by the Trinidad Theatre Workshop for six and eight dollars per ticket. The music is tame because the man who has composed it hears reggae as "rock' n' roll turned around a bit". The acting is without authority and integrity because the playwright/director is constantly looking for excuses, or if you like, occasions for songs rather than dramatic situations growing out of the play that could be aided by song. Thus songs set to music remain on the one side, while the drama develops on the other.

No one will doubt Walcott's devotion to honesty and his fidelity to words and actions; but the play seems to have been too easily, too glibly put together. Walcott, it would seem, is using this production as a rest period before going on to greater things. The play looks and sounds like an interlude piece. The unsuspecting audience, and the dull witted camp follower quick to see an "attack" in every critique, might well find my words too harsh and the play a "masterpiece". The fact is, it is not — it is an interlude work reflecting an effort supported by a memory of Jamaica that goes back to the 1950's. A memory supported by a musician who after listening to reggae for 10 years still hears it as rock' n' roll turned around a bit. The play's foundation is therefore not simply weak but completely decayed.

O Babylon!, has the thinness of spirit and will reflected in the acting of Norline Metivier. Miss Metivier as the common-law wife of Brother Aaron, the wood-carver, has just somehow failed to internalise the role. It is not enough, though, to say that she was miscast, because the play as a musical needs voices and Miss Metivier can sing. The problem that arose is related to the fact that after *The Joker* and *The Seagull* Miss Metivier's acting has not improved.

The problem goes beyond all that of course. The fact is, the Company looked too happy, too happy, too much the product of Rude Bwoy's Big Apple stage illusion. Wilbert Holder as Rude Bwoy has the right panache and flair without the much needed conviction. The play should have moved easily but frighteningly between the poles of cool and dread. Even the importation of one of Trinidad's imitation Rastas gave the play a further element of absurdity rather than reality and clarity. Like the Rastafarian's rocket fueled by ganja, the play never gets off the ground. So many possibilities seem to have gone up in smoke.

O Babylon! demonstrates that one needs more than respect for another's belief to make a success of a staging of that belief. A vision matching that belief, along with an integrity equal to that belief is required.

At a lower level, the Mafia represented by the efforts of Christopher Pinheiro and Laurence Goldstraw are too pleasant without the required menace that should lie beneath the surface smile. The song "The Mafia Care" contains no latent threat either in tone or gesture. Errol Jones as Deacon Doxy, politician and hotel manager, therefore finds himself falling between two stools — the non-dread comic Rastas on the one hand and the non-violent paper thugs from the North. The humour although needed, never has the undercurrent of a threat or a presence that is calculated to tighten the tension. In other words, the humour is never accompanied by the required unease.

The choreography never for one step really tries to come to terms with the current movement in Jamaica. Carol La Chappelle might say that is not necessary; but at least we should be given dances that reflect the underlying sense of explosion the situation demands. The situation is that Brother Aaron is squatting on a piece of land that the Mafia want, so that they can build another large hotel in Jamaica and further expand their control over Caribbean politicians and people. The local politician is in the pay of the Mafia and he is arranging things so that Brother Aaron and his common-law wife Priscilla will be forced to move.

Meanwhile the Rastas are all keyed up since His Imperial Majesty Emperor Haile Selassie is coming to Jamaica and this means repatriation for the true followers of Jah. Finally only a limited number are chosen and the most ardent believers, General Sufferer and Brother Aaron, are left out for very dubious reasons.

The actors failed to transcend the Trinidadian ethos of confronting Babylon with humour, whereas the Jamaican and especially the Rastafarians confront Babylon with dread and a flair for ritual. Moreover pronunciation of the Jamaican dialect by the actors is woefully inconsistent. The two actors who put any kind of feeling and purpose into the opening night's exercise are Anthony Hall as General Sufferer and Syd Skipper as Brother Aaron. Anthony Hall does so by his acting which was true and consistent for about three-quarters of the play. Syd Skipper does so by his intense energy and rich vocal control. Too often in the play the element of humour comes too close to caricature, but Brenda Hughes as Miss Dolly, the good time girl, works well within her area outlined.

The set is as unimaginative as most of the music. The song "Se-las-sie Ah Come" is well sung and is the most moving piece. *The Four Horsemen*, the carving by Brother Aaron, invites his own demise and thus the play ends with the four horsemen arriving to take Brother Aaron along "a journey without an ending that starts with an ending".

> Spears shoot on the edge
> of the wave every moonlit night.
> The horsemen will keep their pledge,
> the knights of Burundi
> (Derek Walcott)

If *O Babylon!* is a rest piece, a quiet rest by Walcott before he goes on to greater things, then one may be a little more sympathetic. If, on the other hand it reflects the apocalypse of the Workshop or even a suicidal tendency, then things are very grave for us all.

O BABYLON! — WHERE IT WENT WRONG

Sule Mombara

O BABYLON!, Derek Walcott's musical presentation in cooperation with Galt McDermot, completed a successful run at the Little Carib Theatre in Trinidad last month. *Contact's* first review was made last month while the production was still being staged.

Since then, we received a very critical review from Sule Mombara (Horace Campbell) of the Department of Government, UWI, St. Augustine. He does not conceal his deep disappointment with the production, and is even making a very personal criticism, in what follows, of Derek Walcott.

His views, contrast sharply with those expressed in last month's review, and came while Walcott was concentrating on revising his work for a second presentation next month.

> "SING not the songs . . . of make believe. Draw
> not the pictures . . . of fanciful delusions, but
> create to relate to the struggle of our people."
> (Ainsley Vaughan)

The attempt of the petty bourgeoisie to come to grips with the popular culture is always fraught with contradictions. The impact of the culture of oppressed peoples has always piqued the interest of political and cultural leaders who seek to exploit the cultural values of the people for diverse reasons. The attempt by Michael Manley in Jamaica to exploit the symbols of Rastafarian culture in calling himself "Joshua" and walking with a "rod of correction" is but one of the most recent examples of the petty bourgeoisie bastardising and exploiting the cultural advances of the people.

The recent musical by Derek Walcott and Galt McDermot is but another attempt to trail behind the leadership of Caribbean people. The musical *O Babylon!* was an attempt to fuse the European musical drama into the tense political day to day life of the oppressed peoples of Western Kingston called Rastafarians.

The plot of the play centres around the life of an exploited community in Kingston. The central characters of the play, Brother Aaron (Syd Skipper) and Rude Bwoy (Wilbert Holder), are the focal point for a community challenged by a number of forces, poverty, lack of proper recreational facilities, by the police, by politicians, the international bourgeoisie in the mafia, and by desperation. The musical score attempts to bring out the people's view about the impending visit of Emperor Haile Selassie to Jamaica, about the combined efforts of politicians and the mafia to expropriate their land and the reaction of Brother Aaron in burning down parts of Kingston. *O Babylon!* attempted to bring a number of crucial themes of Rastafarian life into a three hour performance in such a way that the performance seemed incomplete.

However, this seeming incompleteness is in fact the limitation of the playwright trying to present a volatile and political theme in a light European musical for predominantly white and black petty bourgeoise who could afford to go to the Little Carib Theatre. The one positive aspect of the play is the recapture of the high level of tolerance between people of different world outlooks. The divergence of political beliefs between neo-colonial prostitutes — "Rude Bwoy" and "Dolly" — on the one hand and Brother Aaron and Brother Samuel on the other shows that the lack of tolerance at the level of political bureaucracy is not duplicated in the day to day lives of Caribbean people.

O Babylon! broke down as a dramatic performance, given the sharp contradiction between the tradition of European musicals, the African orientation and culture depicted by the Rastafarian movement. The fact that the play was a musical demanded that the leading actor and actress be singers. However, the sudden break into song by Brother Aaron and Sister Priscilla did not remind us of a sufferer and his queen "sitting under a logwood tree drinking cornmeal porridge." Instead the roles reminded one of the boring musicals of Mario Lanza and his serenading scenes. The picture of Sister Priscilla kneeling at the knee of Brother Aaron is most uncharacteristic of the Rastafarian Brethren.

This contradiction of the musical detracted from the content of the play even for the serious spectator who did not come to laugh at the Rastafarian belief. The music not only made light the day to day struggle for survival but also obscured a very real content or message of the play. The clearest example was the lawyer of Brother Aaron — Mr. Goldstein — breaking into a crisp song losing the otherwise promising court scene where the Rastafarian Brethren were pitched against the legal machinery of the state.

The inconclusive ending of dramatic scenes was a dominant feature of the production. The scenes dropped flat without the kind of message which could have lifted the whole performance out of mediocrity. The impact of the mafia and the supposedly raped white developer were so badly located in the whole sequence of events as to make light the ever-present fact of European domination of the neo-colonial Caribbean societies. However, one is reminded that the part of the white developer was hastily included so that the producers would not incur the wrath of the European members of Trinidad Theatre Workshop.

The inconsistency in the attempt to use the Jamaican vernacular was a clear demonstration of the actors removal from the Rastafarian culture. In fact, the language of the Rastafarian Brethren represents not only their creativity but the long quest to mutilate the English language such that only other sufferers can understand their discourses. It would have been better if the actors sought to speak with a clear Trinidadian accent instead of mimicking "Rasta words". One has to understand the experimentation with language by suffering Jamaicans. For example, when Bob Marley in "Talking Blues" sings about a "permanent screw" he is in fact referring to a particular facial expression which characterises the anguish of the oppressed Jamaicans.

The music and choreography depicted the same misunderstanding of the dominant cultural force in the English speaking Caribbean — the Rastafarian movement. While the scenes of the play were located in 1965, the year when Rock Steady was beginning to give way to the political expression called reggae, the music of the band lacked the strong emotional chord which characterises reggae music. The music was very appropriate for a musical with dancers jumping hither and thither but was out of place with the mood of suffering Caribbean peoples, especially the Rastas. The physical gyrations of the Rudettes was out of place. Any participant in a social function in the urban and poor section of Jamaica would be struck by the absence of rapid moves like those necessary for funky music. For dancing to reggae is a reflective and political experience: an experience called "skank". This is why Carol la Chapelle's dancers were misplaced in the same fashion as their European name "Rudettes".

The foremost problem of the play was its metaphysical and idealistic content. The theme of the play was supposed to represent a confrontation between poor suffering Jamaicans and the neo-colonial state machinery. But the constant political struggle ends with Brother Aaron idealistically going into the clouds — possibly leaving the house to be bulldosed [sic] by the mafia for a new hotel. The idealistic and "cloud nine" ending of the play is unrepresentative of the thrust of the Rastafarian culture. Even though in its origins the Rasta Brethren believe in the divinity of his Imperial Majesty Haile Selassie, the Rastas have been at the forefront of challenging the shameless imitation of everything European by Afro-Saxon political leaders. This is why the Prime Minister who loves Bach and Beethoven cannot understand Bob Marley when he says "it takes a revolution to make a solution." This is the essence of the Rastafarian culture fighting against the old order.

The political nature of the Rastafarian movement has placed the Brethren in clear confrontation with the neo-colonial and colonial cultural and political leaders. This is why the slavery laws banning the "Dreads" were passed in Dominica and the police in St. Kitts and Jamaica try to cut the locks of the Brethren. While the Rastafarian movement becomes more political, the Jamaican ruling class seeks to promote the religious aspect of the culture by institutionalising the Ethiopian Coptic Church in an effort to control the development of the movement. However the young Rasta of Tobago, Dominica and Antigua are forging communal forms of production, neglecting crass materialism and a political belief in the redemption of Africa. The potential for the political mobilisation of these people has so far only been discovered by Walter

Rodney. There is therefore no wonder that the political ideas of Marcus Garvey and Walter Rodney buttress the movement's everyday ideas in the reggae music. At present in Jamaica it is the Rastafarian Movement Association which is calling for the removal of the ban on Rodney from Jamaica.

O Babylon! does not seek to influence the audience. *O Babylon!* is a cynical castigation of oppressed Jamaicans which sought to merge European musical forms on African movements and song. The possible enlightening scenes in the drama were eroded by musical interludes which bored many. Throughout the Caribbean the popular culture remains one of protest against injustice, poverty and unemployment. It was not coincidental that the dominant themes in the present crop of calypsoes are songs of protest ramified by Chalkdust's reminder that there are too many struggles in the world for us to sing about smut. It is time the playwright — like the calypsonian — sink his roots among the people, drawing inspiration from them to provide dramatic messages of how we can change the decaying order. The cynicism of *O Babylon!* in 1976 is a backward step.

REMINISCENCES OF DEREK WALCOTT AND THE TRINIDAD THEATRE WORKSHOP

Laurence Goldstraw

[At my request, Laurence Goldstraw kindly agreed to write out a few of his memories of the years 1972-82 when he was a member of the Trinidad Theatre Workshop. Given the diverse backgrounds of Walcott's troupe over the years from 1959 to 1982, it is understandable that impressions of working within the company should vary with each individual. For this very reason, Goldstraw's perceptions lend a unique insight into the day to day experiences of amateur actors joining in Walcott's theatrical experimentation. During his tenure with the Workshop, Goldstraw acted in Walcott's *Franklin, The Charlatan* (unpublished), *The Joker of Seville, O Babylon!, Remembrance* and his film *The Rig.*] RDH

My main impression of the Trinidad Theatre Workshop, at least during the time I was involved (roughly 1972-1982), was that contrary to some lip-service to the opposite it was a one-man-band. Derek made virtually all the decisions himself, perhaps discussing them with a select committee post facto; and generally, we in the company were quite prepared to go along with this. This arrangement was usual in such areas as selection of plays, casting, and production arrangements. There would on occasion be the odd grumble, but it appeared that Derek had always done things this way, and the group were generally quite happy to go along with it. As previously noted, there was a committee which ostensibly met with Derek to decide policies and other matters, but when I was a member of the Workshop I was never fully aware of the activities of this committee, nor was I sufficiently interested to inquire.

At the onset of a production there would be a first reading and then parts would be assigned. Very often the major parts would have been decided beforehand—by

272

Derek, and sometimes several of the cast would have been informed. This may not sound very democratic, and I suppose it wasn't, but the company went along with it and the committee did likewise. (Most if not all of these were senior members of the Workshop, and so reasonably sure of a part, but I am not implying that this is why they went along with the system; they just accepted it *faut de mieux*.)

Unless a play was some way into rehearsal, the early sessions had to be held wherever was available to us, and wherever Derek could find a venue—preferably one that did not require paying rent, as funds were always somewhat scarce. Schools, church halls and even the local museum were all utilised. Quite a few of the early rehearsals for *O Babylon!* were held in a small restaurant in the Holiday Inn — thanks in this case probably to Galt MacDermot, who was staying in the hotel. Galt, of course was a great favourite with the members of the Workshop. In spite of his international standing and success he never put on airs, and was very much one of the company. Quite often, when we were rehearsing for either *The Joker of Seville* or *O Babylon!* the cast, crew and others would congregate outside the Little Carib Theatre, waiting for Derek to arrive with the only key, and let us in; and I recall on more than one occasion I would arrive to find Galt, dressed in his shirt and slacks, sitting on the steps of the Little Carib, eating chicken and chips from a cardboard box and looking quite relaxed. This business of "waiting for Walcott" could be a bit irritating, as most of us there waiting had all been at our normal jobs during the day. Some, including myself, had been unable to go home after work, but had to go straight to the theatre. We thought that Derek might have paid a bit more attention to this little problem, as he had no daily timetable to adhere to and need not have kept us waiting with such regularity. But of course, Derek never paid much attention to this. We all either had regular jobs, or were busy housewives with children and households to run.

Once rehearsals started in earnest, our domestic lives were put on "hold". For instance, prior to the first performances of *The Joker,* for weeks we would rehearse almost every night, from 6:30 p.m. sometimes up to midnight, plus all day Saturday or Sunday (occasionally, Saturday *and* Sunday!) At this time, there were no chairs or seating of any kind in the Little Carib Theatre. Chairs were hired and bleachers constructed for performances. There were no dressing rooms either—nor were there any for the early actual performances, since the backstage area was partly open to the sky, and so could not be used when it rained. There were two temperamental toilets and a cold-water tap. All the forgoing sounds like a big complaint, which it possibly is, but there were no mutinies, and in fact we were all prepared to (and did) accept these conditions because we knew that we were part of something artistically exciting and rewarding—eventually!

Being somewhat older than most of the other members, and therefore not so spry, my particular dislike was to do the dancing. The singing I didn't mind. In fact, I often enjoyed it since the songs were lively and fun to sing. The singing coaches were enthusiastic and talented, and could usually motivate us well—even me! "Voice exercises" were a bit boring, but we realised they were necessary and did our best. Dancing, however, was something else. There were in the company several young, trained dancers, male and female, who did their numbers very well, enjoyed doing it.

However, when it came to pressing all the company into dance routines for various effects—like mass entrances, exits or wedding processions—the non-dancers found it tedious and often difficult. Sometimes, it turned out to be fun and enjoyable, but not often. Of course the dance teachers, who were also actors, were well aware of who were sheep and who were goats in this respect, and dealt with us sympathetically. Round about this time, Derek had become obsessed with the idea of the all-singing, all-dancing, all-acting performer found everywhere in the American entertainment world; and yearned to have us conform. It was useless to point out to him that the Sammy Davises of this world did not also have to run an office or a home, or bring up children, or work as a builder's labourer to earn his or her daily bread. For instance, there is the case of Winston [Goddard], normally a construction worker down south in San Fernando. He was a faithful member of the Workshop, and during rehearsals, having no car, he would take a taxi to Port of Spain each evening (thirty-five/forty miles), make his way to the Little Carib, and join in the rehearsals till half past eleven. He would then have to beg a lift to Port of Spain and take a taxi back to San Fernando, reaching home about 1:30 a.m. He had to be at work by 7:00 a.m. and he would often do this every weekday when rehearsals were in full swing, and come up on Saturday or Sunday as well. Even when he had quite a small part, he seldom if ever missed a rehearsal.

Having the author of a play as its director can be a mixed blessing. Once rehearsals get underway, the director comes across snags and shortcomings in the script, which the playwright then attends to overnight. Perhaps there are no actual snags, but as rehearsals proceed the director/playwright perceives room for improvement; so it's back to the typewriter for a more polished script. This is fine as far as the script goes, but pity the poor player who, having carefully learned the part, arrives at rehearsal next day to receive yet another dreaded rewrite; and now has to unlearn the old version to get a grip on the new. Because *The Joker*— for one reason or another — was in rehearsal for a long time, the re-write phenomenon became very prevalent. As a consequence, the actor or actress would get to rehearsal, be handed the latest "insert" and retire to the back of the hall with one or more fellow-sufferers to try to learn the new lines. This was not made any easier by the nagging thought that lurking somewhere in Walcott's brain was the rewrite of the rewrite we were trying to learn.

As I say, the rewrite problem was chronic with regard to *The Joker*, but considerably less in other plays. However, one character I played in the first versions of *O Babylon!* subsequently disappeared from the play completely. I have in my house a large travelling bag containing a number of discarded acting scripts of *The Joker* alone. Of course, there was a plus side to all this rewriting for those willing to see. It was often fascinating to observe how the playwright's mind was working as each rewrite came up; and one could nearly always see where the improvement lay.

On the whole, I quite liked being directed by Derek, and I learned a lot from it. His approach to the directing process was really unpredictable. Sometimes it would be fairly passive, and then sometimes vividly active. He was very thorough and painstaking, and most of the time extremely patient. Now and again however, his safety-valve would blow and there would be a minor, mercifully short-lived explosion. Generally he would go over and over a few lines to get the effect he was after. He had an irritating little habit which developed into a sort of humorous catch-phrase in the whole company. After having worked for a long time on a short scene, or even a few lines, he would express his satisfaction by saying "That's great! . . . Let's do it again!"

Sometimes in order to get the effect he wanted, Derek would give a demonstration. These were often very helpful to the actor concerned—at least I know they were for me. Walcott is, of course, a great punster, and equivocal lines appear in all of his plays. Derek never forgets any of them, and roars with laughter each time they make an appearance, no matter how venerable these puns and jokes may be. I played the lead in *Charlatan* for two productions, and this play has some of Walcott's oldest jokes. Each time one of these ancient puns occurred—whether in rehearsal or performance, I knew without looking that Derek was convulsed with laughter. This I found somehow very comforting and reassuring, and it eased the tension a lot. I often wondered how Walcott the director could stand listening to some of his marvelous words and phrases being subjected to verbal butchery as sometimes occurred when a player did not understand what he was speaking or reading. I have seen a look of pure anguish on his face when such a catastrophe occurred; but usually the resultant outburst was surprisingly mild.

Perhaps his worst time in this respect was during rehearsals for *The Joker*. Poor Derek had slaved away, putting this play into quite beautiful octosyllabic verse. This meant, of course, that unlike an ordinary play, any mistake with the words, or any substitution of one word for another was a minor disaster. It also meant that one had to be word-perfect with one's lines; as ordinary ad-libs (which actors can usually get away with) just would not work in this case. Derek would try manfully to impress this on the cast; but not always with success, alas. Very occasionally, there would be the situation when a player really did not follow what was going on, and, in the early stages of rehearsal, would be reading from the script quite automatically. The classic case occurred during early rehearsals for *The Joker,* but it could have happened in any play. The character had but one word on a line, which was the command "Eat." Now there was a typing error in the script, and the initial capital "E" had been mistakenly replaced by an "F." For several rehearsals the company were astonished to hear the actor concerned say "Fat", in a commanding tone. Well, eventually someone said something about it and all was well; we had a little laugh and then got on with the business in hand.

Derek's visual artistic talent of course, stood him in good stead with regard to set design and costume. Of course, he never reached the splendid heights achieved by Richard Montgomery in Jamaica, with his stunning sets for *Franklin* and *The Joker;* but Derek could conjure up some smashing visual effects of his own, often with little actual material alteration. One innovation he conceived in the Jamaican production of *The Joker* I will always remember. Montgomery had established a country grave-yard for the setting, and upstage was a clutter of bamboo crosses, candles and tattered wreaths. Derek conceived the idea of having the dead "Boy" of the travelling players' group, to pass (as a ghost) through this background, singing quietly in a little thin voice as it made its way through the graveyard. I found this intensely moving, besides being very effective, and it brought tears to my eyes every time.

In spite of the various privations—or perhaps because of them—due to the constant shortage of funds, we were generally a happy group. We mixed well, and on tour would move freely between rooms, talking and having an occasional drink. Many of the group had been with the Workshop for many more years than I, and had a long series of plays to their credit. There was always singing whenever the opportunity arose, so that songs from *Ti Jean, Dream on Monkey Mountain* and others would mingle with the current songs from *The Joker* or *O Babylon!*. I recall that on our way back home from Jamaica once, the aeroplane had to shut down an engine and make a stop in Puerto Rico, where we had to wait for another plane to pick us up and take us on home. Of course, as very few of us had U.S. visas, we were not allowed out of the transit lounge. We were plied with sandwiches and soft drinks, and as we had our musicians with us we were soon singing all our songs. Of course, we were all well versed in these selections, so we didn't sound too bad. In fact we soon had an admiring audience of other passengers who stopped to listen.

There was generally a good camaraderie amongst the Workshop members, both actors and crew. We also managed to put up with the various vicissitudes which we encountered. When we toured St. Lucia to put on *The Joker* (in a banana warehouse on the docks) we had to save money by each of us carrying—as hand luggage—one of the theatre lights. It was all part of the experience, but I can vouch for the fact that such lights are not the most comfortable of travelling companions. Of course, the stage crew were in the same boat as the actors in having normal nine-to-five jobs during the day. Our versatile, accomplished lighting man, John Andrews, is now the Permanent Secretary in the Ministry of Finance.

I found my time with the Workshop—which included performances of *Franklin, The Charlatan* (twice), *The Joker of Seville* and *O Babylon!*, with three tours to Jamaica and one to St. Lucia—very rewarding. Very demanding, very wearing at times, but very rewarding. Working with Walcott could be irritating, sometimes tedious, sometimes frustrating and often exhausting. He can be a hard taskmaster who will not settle for anything less than the best you can do. He is also prepared to go on and on until he has got that best out of you. When Derek was directing a play, or even conducting Workshop sessions, he would treat everyone equally and impartially.

My wife and I had been good friends with Derek and his wife Margaret for a number of years. We lived quite close, and spent lots of time in each others' houses. We often spent time together at seaside holiday houses, and Billy and I are Anna Walcott's godparents. This made not the slightest difference to the way Derek treated me as a member (and a fairly new member at that) of the Theatre Workshop; and I would come in for my share of the rough edge of his tongue whenever he reckoned I deserved it.

Until *The Joker* came along, Walcott productions in Trinidad were not often box-office successes. The Friday and Saturday performances were popular and always well attended; but the size of weekday audiences was predictably small. Everyone in the group accepted this, realising it was due to Walcott's fidelity to himself and to the artistic standards he had set for himself and, by association, for us. When *The Joker* came along, and we played to full houses night after night for weeks it was a bit bewildering. I remember as we came off the stage for an intermission on the first night to the roar of applause, the player next to me said in an amazed tone, "They like it!" Of course, it is moments like this which make up for all the previous trials, tribulations and occasional bursts of temperament. It certainly wasn't the money. For although Derek was insistent that we should all be paid, the amounts we got were quite small, and it should be remembered that we all paid a monthly subscription to be members of the Workshop.

So what was it that kept us coming back for more? I think it was pride in eventual achievement, pleasure in the camaraderie amongst us in the group, plus affection for Derek and deep respect for his genius.

RIPENING WITH WALCOTT

Edward Baugh

To follow Derek Walcott's progress over more than a quarter of a century, through several books of poetry, from feverish, precocious youth to mellow middle age, is to follow a process of self-discovery and self-creation. Walcott's binding theme is Walcott, the pursuit and delineation of a fictive character based on an actual person named Derek Walcott. The self-portrait emerges as an interplay between the man's recognition of weaknesses and deficiencies in himself and a definition of ideal strengths, values and virtues, by which he seeks to determine himself.

This activity is no narrow or selfish introspection. To confront experience is, with him, to confront his own reactions to experience, but so as to purify and understand those reactions, to make himself worthy of experience. He contemplates himself in order to burn through to a condition where he will lose himself in the greatness of everything that is greater than himself, where he will be reconciled with all experience, where he will

> . . . have learnt to love black days like bright ones,
> the black rain, the white hills, when once
> I loved only my happiness and you. (p.80)[1]

This is, of course, the model, the ideal; the actuality is the day-to-day, poem-by-poem, uneven, unending struggle to realise it, in life and on the page. The actuality is an oscillation between polarities of mood, a manoeuvering between seeming opposites. So, for example, in one poem he extols "the desert dignities of silence" (p.22), while in another he

> . . . look[s] forward to age
> a gnarled poet
> bearded with the whirlwind,
> his metres like thunder. . . (p.93)

In a third we can see how the opposites, silence and thunder, are reconciled in paradox:

even love's lightning flash
has no thunderous end,

it dies with the sound
of flowers fading . . .

till we are left
with *the silence that surrounds Beethoven's head.* (p. 71; my
italics)

Such a silence, surely, is a kind of thunder. The same paradox was expressed before, in
Another Life (1973), in a similar image of an old poet, weathered by experience and
calm in the midst of whirlwind:

. . .I wanted to grow white-haired
as the wave, with a wrinkled

brown rock's face, salted,
seamed, an old poet,
facing the wind

and nothing, which is,
the loud world in his mind. (p.148)

The mind of this old poet had been prefigured long before, in the title-poem of
Walcott's first volume to achieve metropolitan publication — *In a Green Night*
(1962). In that poem, the orange tree and the orange, the cycle of flowering and
fruiting as well as the sphere of the "full" fruit, symbolised the ideal of "the mind
[which] enspheres all circumstance" (p. 73). This ideal has governed all of Walcott's
work. It has taken various aspects, e.g. his cultivation of what he has called his "sense
of season" (*The Castaway*, 1965, p. 15), the condition of attuning oneself so perfectly
to the rhythm of life that one is reconciled to the inexorability of change, of pain and
cruelty and loss, while being keenly sensitive to them; So now he says (to himself?),

. . . The zone
that is your sadness rings you,
but sadness is your season
like the apples, as you ripen
to a fullness that can endure
that blazing lie of summer; for,
at the core of passion, you've
always sensed the cold. (p.16)

What is strongest now is not the sadness which comes with the sense of cold, the "icy

intuitions/that seasons bring" (*Castaway*, p.45), but the ripeness and the fullness that
can endure them. Now, to be reconciled is to accept with a kind of joy the fact of
change, to be happy "that fine sprigs of white are springing from my beard" (p. 92). It
is to be able to set against the "blazing lie of summer", which dazzles us in youth, the
subtler sensitivity to the variegations of "grey":

> grey has grown strong to me,
>
> it's no longer neutral,
> no longer the dirty flag
> of courage going under,
>
> it is speckled with hues
> like quartz, it's as
> various as boredom,
>
> grey now is a crystal
> haze, a dull diamond,
> stone-dusted and stoic . . . (p.93-94)

The short poem "The Morning Moon", which ends with the line about "fine
sprigs of white", begins by confessing the poet's long-lived obsession with change and
mortality , and proceeds to encapsulate his latest mood of grave and joyful acceptance. Such acceptance includes accepting that no matter how ready one composes
oneself to be, one is never quite ready for the downward turning of time; grief always
takes us by surprise:

> You prepare for one sorrow,
> but another comes.
> It is not like the weather,
> you cannot brace yourself,
> the unreadiness is all. (p.85)

Nor does the mood of ripeness, of a calm and mellow acceptance, mean that we won't
hear any more the bleaker Walcott, the moods of ennui, frustration and despair, the
cynicism and the horror. The ripeness enspheres and transcends the phases of
bitterness, but still *includes* them. The vision of the ripeness and the transcendent
calm have now been caught, held, but this state of being is attainable only momentarily, as in

> . . . the great pause
> when the pillars of the temple
> rest on Samson's palms

and are held, held,
that moment
when the heavy rock of the world

like a child sleeps
on the trembling shoulders of Atlas
and his own eyes close,

the toil that is balance. (p.94)

Broadly speaking, the arrangement of *Sea Grapes* parallels the progression of
moods in Walcott's poetry as a whole, from sadness to celebration, though in the
former the latter was always present, while the latter is fuelled by a deep awareness of
the former. In the opening poem, "Sea Grapes", the protagonist/poet is a world-
weary Odysseus, condemned forever to fight (in himself) the "ancient war between
obsession and responsibility" (passion and duty, poetry and action?), and not really
cheered by the knowledge that others have suffered the same agony throughout
history and literature. Still, the question of shirking the fight never arises, and the
poem sustains, beneath the weariness, a fortifying sense of the continuity of human
struggle and endurance.

"Sea Grapes" is followed by three poems about Frederiksted, a town in the U.S.
Virgin Islands, which describe a more or less typical, meretricious Caribbean tourist
"paradise" gone tawdry — the New World "lost to vipers" (p.20) and to money, as is
made explicit in the very cynical "New World", one of a handful of Eden-myth
poems which also occur early in the volume and extend Walcott's interest in his idea
of New World man as "Adamic".

[So] when Adam was exiled
to our New Eden, in the ark's gut,
the coined snake coiled there for good
fellowship also; that was willed.

Adam had an idea.
He and the snake would share
the loss of Eden for a profit.
So both made the New World. And it looked good.
(pp.18-19)

A poem like "New World" leads naturally to Walcott's most directly political
poems to date. Some of these, if we include chapters 18 and 19 of *Another Life*, which
belong to the same period, are also his most vitriolic. "The Brother", "Party Night at
the Hilton", "The Lost Federation" and "Parades, Parades" (and the uncollected
"Commune" *Tapia*, 17 Dec. 1972) are curse-poems. They are political not in the
sense that they advance any ideology or party-line — in fact they are anti-party — but

because they attack in straightforward invective, political con-manship and corruption, the betrayal of "the people" in the West Indies, whether the betrayers are the entrenched, reactionary bosses and dictators, or bigoted and hypocritical radicals. He "tongue-lashes" "the evangelical hyenas" (p. 22) and the "smiler next to you who whispers /brother" (p.23) as well as the "pimp Nkrumahs", "venal, vengeful party-hacks" (p.26) and "ministers administering/the last rights to a people" (p.28). In "Parades, Parades" he satirises the paternalistic, petty dictators feasting on the adulation of their worshippers:

> Here he comes now, here he comes!
> Papa! Papa! With his crowd,
> the sleek, waddling seals of his Cabinet . . .(p.30)

"Dread Song" identifies these "bastard papas" (p. 28) even more pointedly:

> Brothers in Babylon, Doc! Uncle! Papa!
> Behind the dark glasses (p.33)

In "Preparing for Exile" he has a nightmare vision of a steadily encroaching police-state tyranny, and in "The Silent Woman" he commemorates a Trinidadian middle-class girl, Jean Miles, who had the courage to expose some of the corruption of "the executives in business suits." All of these poems belong to the early seventies and directly or indirectly express something of Walcott's reaction to a central political event of that period in the West Indies, the abortive revolution in his adopted homeland, Trinidad.

But eventually, above whatever notes of cynicism or anger or terror or despair this volume utters, there begins to rise dominant the note of joy, a solemn joy of life, which resounds longest and sinks deepest. It rises in the face of pain and bitterness and negation; it is mellowed and tempered by them. The progression is the same as in *Another Life*, where eventually all the experiences lived through are reconciled and "blessed" in the prayer-benediction-hymn to life which climaxes the poem in chapter 22. Walcott has earned his vision of ripeness and calm which reconciles all clashes and confusions. He has earned, precociously no doubt, this latest mask, of the seamed, gnarled, grizzled face of the old poet, which is a variation on the mask of the "old sea-almond [tree] / unwincing in spray" (p. 93), the

> . . . obdurate almond
> going under the sand
> with this language, slowly,
> by sand grains, by centuries. (p.95)

Poems like "To Return to the Trees", "At Last", "Oddjob, a Bull Terrier", and "The Bright Field" are "large" poems. In their comparatively short lyrical flights, they attain the heights of human feeling. Firmly rooted in the personal and concrete reality of the visible world of the poet's experience, they move upwards and outwards to a visionary, world-encompassing dimension. Although, in typical Walcott fashion, they depend essentially on a process of metaphorical associations, the matrix of metaphor is not so dense or complex as before. Imagery tends to be stripped down to elementals — earth, wind, sea, rock, tree, moon, light, dark, and so on. There is also a marked use of repetition to produce an incantatory effect which heightens the feeling of epiphany and celebration. These features are well exemplified in "Oddjob", which was occasioned by the death of a pet dog that belonged to a couple, the poet's close friends, in whose sea-side cottage the poet was staying at the time. The poem celebrates the deep silences of grief-stricken love:

> the silence is all
> it is deeper than the readiness,
> it is sea-deep,
> earth-deep,
> love-deep.
>
> The silence
> is stronger than thunder,
> we are stricken dumb and deep
> as the animals who never utter love
> as we do, except
> it becomes unutterable
> and must be said,
> in a whimper,
> in tears,
> in the drizzle that comes to our eyes
> not uttering the loved thing's name,
> the silence of the dead,
> the silence of the deepest buried love is
> the one silence,
> and whether we bear it for beast,
> for child, for woman, or friend,
> it is the one love, it is the same,
> and it is blest
> deepest by loss
> it is blest, it is blest. (pp. 85-86)

"The Bright Field" brings back to mind the famous "Ruins of a Great House", written some twenty years before, and a comparison of the two shows how Walcott is continuously working over his basic themes and yet not just repeating himself. Nor does the new poem, even though it goes beyond the earlier one, supersede it. In both we see compassion getting the better of anger and bitterness. There are similar key words and images in both: rage, compassion, great house, the tolling bell (of Donne),

grave reminder of the ultimate one-ness of mankind. But whereas "Ruins" is primarily about a West Indian's experience of trying to come to terms with the anguish of
West Indian history, "The Bright Field" is primarily one man's vision of his involvement in mankind, in the commingled grief and glory of the human condition. But
the vision is authenticated in terms of the specific historical point of view of the poet,
that is to say, by his West Indian experience. In "Ruins" the imaginative energy of the
poem is concerned most with recreating the painful act of confrontation with history,
while in "The Bright Field" it is most concerned with recreating the glow of the one
dying light which illuminates and unifies all (seeming) opposites—past and present,
the crowd and the individual, colonising conqueror and colonial victim, London and
insignificant, remote Balandra (on the east coast of Trinidad), the powerful techno-
logically advanced world of conveyor-belts and underground railways with the agricultural, pastoral and underdeveloped world of cane-field and bullock cart.

The vision of this reconciling light is achieved, in the overall arrangement of *Sea
Grapes* as in the overall structure of *Another Life*, after, and no doubt partly as a result
of an imaginative return to his beginnings, to his St. Lucia. *Another Life* was a
confrontation of and homage to the St. Lucia which produced him. In the middle of
Sea Grapes he returns again, to resume the homage in a sequence of five poems
entitled simply "Sainte Lucie". Part II, untitled, is largely a plangently nostalgic litany
of the flora and the girls of the island, ending with as direct and final an act of self-
identification as we could wish:

> O Martinas, Lucillas,
> I'm a wild golden apple
> that will burst with love,
> of you and your men,
> those I never told enough
> with my young poet's eyes
> crazy with the country,
> generations going,
> generations gone,
> moi c'est gens St. Lucie.
> C'est la moi sorti;
> is there that I born. (p.47)

The swift modulations of language, from standard English through St. Lucian patois
to a West Indian English equivalent, not only bring to an authoritative summation
the whole problem/richness of identity for Walcott, but also triumphantly answer his
cry, earlier in the poem, "Come back to me/my language" (p. 44).

The concluding poem in the sequence, "For the Altar-piece of the Roseau Valley
Church, Saint Lucia", is one of the finest in the book, and it treats again another
major topic from *Another Life*, the "homage to Gregorias." Gregorias was the name
with which Walcott has "christened" Dunstan St. Omer, the painter, his school-mate
and friend, whose early life and work he had sung in *Another Life*. But that account

had had to end with a "beaten", disillusioned Gregorias, one whose youthful dreams
for his art and his country had come to seem doomed to non-realisation. Now
Walcott provides the sequel of fulfillment to that story. For St. Omer has recently
begun to enjoy a resurgence of creative power and stability, and the altar-piece which
Walcott praises is one of a few such murals in various St. Lucian churches which mark
this latest period of St. Omer's career and constitute his most ambitious work.

The poem fuses the painter, the painting and the common folk of the Roseau
Valley who are represented in the painting. That fusion is a central point of the poem,
the inter-rootedness of the place, its people and its art. Walcott's vision of this ideal,
his mythologising of the valley as his Garden of Eden, is tempered by his awareness of
the harsh and unenviable aspects of the lives of the painter and the people. The valley
is a "rich valley", but it is also a "cursed valley":

> ask the broken mules, the swollen children,
> ask the dried women, their gap-toothed men . . .(p.53)

But the curse, the harsh reality, no less than the "simple" faith by which the people
have endured, are all part of their nobility, and if we can see them with the eyes of
imagination, through the eyes of the artist who "signs" them with his own faith and
love, we shall be able to see "the real faces of angels", which is to say the faces of real
angels. In their humanity is their divinity. Here is the religious faith of the people
which Walcott had in earlier poems simultaneously envied and pitied (if not despised); but now he does not set against it any cynical detachment of his own, neither
pity nor self-conscious envy, "it is there", the faith, as the painting "is there" (p.53)
even when "[n] obody can see it"; and when Walcott values the painting as something

> which comes from the depth of the world,
> from whatever one man believes he knows of God
> and the suffering of his kind . . . (p.54)

we feel that he has come to accept and to offer his own work as "whatever [he] believes
he knows of God/and the suffering of his kind."

Footnote

[1] Walcott *Sea Grapes*. London: Jonathan Cape, 1976. All subsequent pagination refers to this
edition.

DISPLACED PERSON

Edith Oliver

A retired Trinidadian teacher, Albert Jordan, in Port of Spain, is the hero of
Derek Walcott's *Remembrance*, lately at the Public. He is a sardonic, humorous old
man, bored and fed up, an "anachronism" in independent Trinidad, his head (and
heart) crammed with English poetry, and still grief-stricken at the death of his elder
son in a riot years before, when a British policeman's gun went off accidentally. A
black man unable to feel a part of the black world, Jordan is yet too wise to feel at
home in the British tradition. He is not only a teacher but a celebrated writer of
poems and short stories, and when the play opens he is seated at a table being
interviewed by a young reporter from a local paper who is tape-recording his
reminiscences and a few of his autobiographical stories. The recording is the point of
departure for the action, and as it progresses we see a younger Jordan in the
classroom drilling Gray's "Elegy," line by line, into the heads of his frisky, heckling
students. We see him returning home late at night, arm in arm with his oldest
friend, the editor of the reporter's paper, both of them drunk and singing a calypso
song about Adolf Hitler and the conquest of Germany; we see him with his
marvellous wife, who never allows her justified impatience with him to break
through; we see him with his younger son, a Pop artist who paints a large American
flag on the roof of the family house and then refuses to sell the roof (and the house)
to a brash Yankee art prospector. The final story in the first act is set in the nineteen-
forties, when Jordan falls in love with an English Wren stationed in Port of Spain
and then, unable to face the consequences of his dreams, runs away when she agrees
to marry him. In the second act, the stories and reminiscences are over. A young
white American dancer, broke and down on her luck, has sought refuge and found it
with the Jordans. Her resemblance to the Wren (both parts were very well played by
Laurie Kennedy) brings a lot of old feelings to the boil, and there is a resolution of
sorts.

Remembrance is a loosely constructed play (and none the worse for that), slowing
and darkening as it proceeds. Its chief pleasures lie in its details and its lines. Mr.
Walcott is a poet, and his writing is of a quality we seldom hear in the theatre. As
Jordan, Roscoe Lee Browne captured the full anguish and wit of this exasperating,
inspired man. Cynthia Belgrave, as was to be expected, was marvellous as the

marvellous wife, and Earle Hyman, Frankie Faison, Lou Ferguson, and Gil Rogers were fine, too, as editor, son, reporter, and Yankee, respectively. Scenery by Wynn P. Thomas, costumes by Judy Dearing, and lighting by Spencer Mosse — all commendable.

REMEMBRANCE

Mark McWatt

Stage One's record production in Barbados of Derek Walcott's play *Remembrance* (Queen's Park Steel Shed), was one of those rare and fortunate theatrical events where words and plot leap into life and the playwright's vision becomes the living experience of the audience.

Remembrance, the play itself, is the product of a Walcott who must surely be at the peak of his powers of theatrical invention and stagecraft. It is a wonderfully well-written play, which presents the reminiscences of Albert Perez Jordan, the central character, an ageing retired schoolmaster whom we have all met at some time or another and whose conflict of values many of us still carry around inside, with varying degrees of reluctance.

It is typical of this most recent phase of Walcott's career as playwright that we should have the sense that the action on stage is somehow central to our experience as West Indians. Underlying the play and its conflict of values is our whole bitter past, and yet the play is not bitter but rather haunting, and frequently very funny.

As played by Michael Gilkes, Jordan is a towering figure whose memories, values and inner contradictions radiate outward from the storm-centre of his presence on stage to affect/infect all the other characters as well as the audience. The play is really Jordan's statement, the enactment of his processes of memory as we shift backwards in time. The importance of Jordan's memory becomes clear as we see the central conflict of his life unfolding as he re-enacts the substance of his earlier life, largely contained in his two "short-stories" — *Barrley and the Roof* and *My War Effort*.

Barrley and the Roof portrays his son Frederick's individual integrity as he resists the offer of Barrley, American tourist and culture-collector (a Walcott cliché played wonderfully by Desmond Bourne) to buy him out. This is a vindication of the positive values taught and held by Jordan. *My War Effort*, on the other hand explores the negative legacy of Jordan's colonial upbringing — the racial inferiority complex that prevents him from returning the love of the English woman who offers her heart to him. A third crucial event in the past is the death of Jordan's first son who was shot at a black-power demonstration. Jordan is haunted by the idea that his "Uncle Tom" values might have driven this son to his fatal extremity.

The complexity of the layers of time and memory in the play renders the part of

Jordan an extremely demanding one, hence it was most satisfying to see Michael Gilkes' Jordan move easily between the various time zones carrying with him the authority, the wit and the curious wisdom that the character acquires in the play.

In this the actor is aided enormously by the symbolism of the set: a huge, handless grandfather clock brooded over the stage and was also the central spider in an enormous web that separated off a raised portion at the rear of the stage which represented the past. Players actually passed through the body of the grandfather clock into this symbolic space. It is difficult to imagine the Steel Shed used more effectively as a theatre space. Everything about the theatrical aspect of the play seemed to underline the fact that Stage One is managing to bring a new, understated technical and professional expertise to Barbadian theatre. Director, Earl Warner's interpretation of the play emphasises the major themes of time and memory and the central conflict of values, but it also communicates the playwright's peripheral subtleties of language and humour which lend an ornamental sparkle throughout the length of the play. The movement of players onto and off the stage was functional but with sufficient variety of pace and direction to avoid monotony, and the lighting was superb.

It was inevitable that the character of Jordan should dominate, but the other actors were nevertheless more than equal to their parts. Cynthia Wilson, as Mabel Jordan(the Xantippe to his Socrates) was, as always, entirely competent — as she quarreled with her husband,worried about him, taunted him, ran away from and returned to him and stoutly defended him from the disparagements of their son Frederick.

One small complaint about Cynthia Wilson's portrayal: Like the Roman God Vulcan, she walked with a limp for part of the performance — that limp seemed about as relevant to the business of the play as is the Roman God Vulcan to this review. Such is the versatility and range of Clairmont Taitt as an actor that although he played the two parts of Ezra Pilgrim, the newspaper editor, and the young interviewer of Jordan (in which roles he was the perfect foil for the baroque reminiscences and self-depreciations of Jordan) we nevertheless felt that he could have played several more roles without much additional effort.

Rachel Ennevor, on the other hand was working so hard to preserve the necessary distinction between the two roles she played that she seemed to overdo the English woman's reserve with the result that that particular scene seemed somewhat slow and faltering. As Anna Herschel she was bright and convincing. On the whole, however, I think she did marvellously for a first-time actress.

In the end the individual efforts of the actors — apart from Gilkes as Jordan — assumed less importance because of the overwhelming powerful effect of the evening's performance as a whole. The play managed to achieve a subtle balance of values and emphases among all its conflicting elements: colonial past and revolutionary present, art and political necessity, self-accusation and self-acceptance. And in that balance lies perhaps the peculiar truth about our present situation in this region — the privilege and panic of being West Indian.

WHITE MAN, BLACK MAN

Christopher Gunness

Christopher Gunness talks to Derek Walcott about his latest play,
Pantomime, which ran for 12 nights at the Little Carib Theatre.

At first, this two-act play appears to be some sort of theatrical allegory representing
the age-old debate on colonialism; a sort of metaphor, symbolic of the cultural, social
and political interactions of the white and the black man. But the playwright is quick
to point out that this was not his primary interest, says Derek Walcott: "It is an
entirely human drama between two people and though there are infinite resonances
that spring from their conflict, these did not interest me directly." The play, then, is
primarily about the interaction of a white and a black man; any other ideas apparent
are incidental.

The plot is simple. Harry Trewe, a white hotelier in Tobago, is planning a
pantomime to attract visitors to his nearly defunct guest house, The Castaway. He is
quickly frustrated by Jackson, his man-servant, who baits him in opposing all his
well-intentioned ideas for the performance. As the conflict progresses though, a
darker atmosphere clouds the stage and we realise that Jackson has a profound motive
for opposing Trewe and his ideas. Through the conflict, Jackson brings Trewe to self-
knowledge. He sees further and further into Trewe, dragging his old inhibitions to
the surface and in forcing him to recognise them, he cleanses him of them. By the
end, the wound is healed; the conflict is resolved and the pantomime can go ahead.

Maurice Brash and Wilbert Holder handle with great control the complex interaction of Trewe and Jackson. This is how Derek Walcott describes that interaction:
"There is that stolid facade, that mask of the Englishman, that wall behind which
there is much horror and fear and trembling. The cracks appear and it is where these
cracks appear that Jackson darts in and widens. The play is about Jackson besieging
and darting in and out until the whole thing crumbles, the wall is broken down and
we look into his room and see Trewe naked and exposed. This is how confessional
psychodrama works."

Maurice Brash captures the vulnerability of Trewe. At first we see nothing of
Trewe but the superficial wall that shields the raw nerve ends which Jackson strives to

290

locate. Gradually, Maurice Brash allows the "cracks to appear" and brings out the delicate frailty that lies behind Trewe's "stiff upper lip" approach to life. As the catharsis looms and Jackson batters the final bricks in the wall, Maurice Brash reveals the disturbing truth of Trewe's afflictions in an overwhelming climax speech. He has brought forward every ounce of character that the playwright gave him in a well graded development of his character.

Wilbert Holder embodies the cynical and very intelligent healing energies of Jackson that work on Trewe. "The kind of energy," says Walcott, "which looks coarse and unsophisticated and may be, but which has at its source a very revitalising element. It is an energy which cannot be bossed or put down, the Creole energy." Wilbert Holder brings out these "Creole energies" in the vital delivery of his stinging punchlines that eventually batter Trewe into recognising the root of his problems. The script gives him every opportunity to lash Trewe with a mercilessly biting humour; these opportunities he uses in a very energetic and imaginative way. Wilbert Holder harnesses all his energies and crams them magnificently into Jackson, the pillar of strength that redeems Harry Trewe.

The play itself has a marvellous feeling of wholeness. And this is not surprising when one considers the way it came to Derek Walcott. He was in Tobago, and suddenly in one creative gush that lasted a couple of days, it was written. Says Walcott: "I had been living in Tobago for a long time and it was a lot to do with the experience of being there in Tobago, looking around and seeing the situation there. It must have been gathering inside me. I got up in the middle of one night and for about two or three days the play just came. And what, for me is remarkable, is that it cleared its own obstacles as it progressed. The nearer a play gets to this, the greater its chances of being whole, being one piece."

At the start of the play, the atmosphere is made light and by the quick verbal exchanges that flash brilliantly between the two characters. But a dark shadow gathers over the action and the emotional pitch intensifies as more of Trewe is revealed. Unfortunately though, this tension is never dissolved; the ending, with which Walcott is not satisfied, does not show a clear enough picture of what has come out of this conflict. The audience is left wondering, "where exactly has the resolution of this conflict taken us?"

MYTH AND REALITY IN CARIBBEAN NARRATIVE: DEREK WALCOTT'S *PANTOMIME*

Patrick Taylor

The history of slavery, colonialism and imperialism and the struggle to overthrow these forms of exploitation and domination are recurring themes both in Derek Walcott's works and in Caribbean life and literature in general. According to Selwyn Cudjoe, in his book *Resistance and Caribbean Literature,* the Caribbean writer plunges into the archetypal recollections of the community in order to recapture the nobility of man's struggle against oppression. [1] But the Caribbean writer today who is committed to his people must avoid the pitfalls of ethnic or national chauvinism. As Frantz Fanon argues throughout his work, it is not enough to replace the colonial myths with new myths of the Golden Age.[2] Derek Walcott's *Pantomime* presents us with a similar challenge. From the point of view of liberation, what is important is the social appropriation of history and tradition in an authentic openness to reality, an openness that recognizes that reality is generated and actualized in human social activity.

The narrative structure of literature orders human activity over time in terms of a culturally meaningful plot. Disparate and contradictory social events are shaped into meaningful wholes on the basis of which we can understand the human world and act on it. Narrative in this sense includes not only the novel or short story, but also any genre of social discourse ordered in terms of a unifying plot: drama, some types of poetry, even community legends and living rituals are thus forms of narrative.[3]

Two fundamental types of narratives, however, must be distinguished: mythical and liberating narrative. It is the mythical core in any text that establishes its basic plot or narrative unity. Such core myths draw on the archetypal patterns of a culture or society in order to render meaningful new, contradictory lived experiences. Myth provides a cultural order to reality and informs human activity. At the same time, this cultural order is transformed as human activity opens up new realms of experience which its mythical structures must encompass. A problem occurs, however, if the mythical form of a work so dominates the narrative totality that the text becomes dependent on a closed, past-oriented approach to tradition. Such narrative is vulnerable to ideological appropriation, wherein myth functions to legitimate the status of particular classes or groups in society. Because it cannot be universalized, mythical narrative may be used either to defend an oppressive status quo, or to justify a rival group destined itself to become the agent of domination. One need only think of Voodoo, which once unified the Haitian people against slavery but then quickly became a tool manipulated by new élites.

Liberating narrative, too, must order and make meaningful new experiences of reality in terms of a cultural tradition. The history of the thoughts and actions of ordinary people are a vital part of it. Liberating narrative makes a decisive break with mythical narrative, however, when it goes radically beyond the latter to assert the fundamentally historical character of the human condition. It attacks mythical and ideological categories for sustaining oppressive situations which restrict and hide the reality of human freedom. Liberating narrative grounds itself in the history of lived freedom, in the story of individuals and groups pushing up from below, as Auerbach puts it, to reveal the ambiguity and multi-layeredness of socially constructed reality.[4] It lifts us out of our closed realms to bring us into universal history, insisting on the fundamental unity, even in diversity, of all humanity. Sustained by the ever-changing activity of men, such narrative resists the illusions of a permanent Golden Age, and the ideologies founded on such fantasies.

In the play *Pantomime* Derek Walcott takes that old but enduring European myth of Crusoe and Friday (Prospero and Caliban, if you like) and transforms it to bring Caribbean man to a true confrontation with his freedom in history. Mythical narrative is re-created in terms of liberating narrative. We are presented with the story of Harry, a white expatriate guest-house owner, and Jackson, his black ex-calypsonian factotum, in post-colonial Tobago, Crusoe's island. The plot revolves around a rehearsal of a Pantomime of the Crusoe-Friday myth with which Harry plans to entertain his European and North American guests. He asks Jackson to participate as Friday. From the beginning a parallel is established between the myth and the Caribbean social context which it legitimates. Harry is the new Crusoe; Jackson is his servant. At one point in the play, Jackson recalls the history of this servitude:

> For three hundred years I served you. Three hundred years I served you breakfast in . . . in my white jacket on a white veranda, boss, bwana, effendi, bacra, sahib . . . in that sun that never set on your empire I was your shadow, I did what you did, boss, bwana, effendi, bacra, sahib . . . that was my Pantomime. Every movement you made, your shadow copied . . . and you smiled at me as a child does smile at his shadow's helpless obedience, boss, bwana, effendi, bacra, sahib, Mr. Crusoe.[5]

Saved from the ravages of his natural life, Defoe's trembling savage bowed down on the sand and placed his master's foot upon his head.[6] This was the token of submission that the non-European world was supposed to have offered, and it was used to justify Europe's international expansion. The myth was and is the core of an ideology keeping slaves, peasants and workers in their set place. It has endured for more than three hundred years.

At the base of the colonial pyramid, Caribbean people fought to escape Crusoe's tyranny and so to maintain traditional cultural and social systems. Many institutions were disrupted, however, by the genocidal activities of the colonizers and by the vagaries of the middle passage. Those cultural forms that threatened the slave system were systematically attacked by the masters. The consequence of this was a tendency towards the adoption of the master's culture and language, the culture and language of work. If he were to survive and perhaps even rise to the level of driver or overseer, the slave had to deny his cultural self. The black man became the white man's shadow. The colonizer transformed the colonized into an animal-like inferior. The colonized tried to overcome this degradation by striving for the white ideal. This is the monkey trap in which Walcott's Makak finds himself in *Dream on Monkey Mountain*.[7] As Walcott states in his poem "Crusoe's Journal:"

> like Christofer he bears
> in speech mnemonic as a missionary's
> the Word to savages,
> its shape an earthen, water-bearing vessel's
> whose sprinkling alters us
> into good Fridays who recite His praise,
> parroting our master's
> style and voice, we make his language ours,
> converted cannibals
> we learn with him to eat the flesh of Christ.[8]

There can be no denying the importance of the trauma of colonization and enslavement. As Nathan Wachtel shows in his study of the Spanish conquest of Central and South America, this psychic trauma is still re-enacted and suffered today.[9] It has influenced all subsequent cultural orientation. Either one tries to cope by giving up one's traditional values and customs, or one preserves or recaptures one's ancestral culture in opposition to the dominant culture. Jackson could choose to accept Crusoe's vision of the servant, thus seeing himself as a cannibal from a race of backward sub-humans. In this case, he would either remain in his lost state, or like the good slave Friday, triumph over himself and adopt the master's values. It is the latter route that the character Jane ultimately follows in Herbert G. de Lisser's early Jamaican novel.[10] The irony, of course, is that the converted cannibal eats not only the flesh of Christ, but the body and blood of his own self and people.

Walcott's Jackson knows this. He is neither Jane nor a good Friday. Enlightened by the consciousness of the post-colonial era, he will not accept the role of shadow.

That is why he must kill Harry's parrot, which, moreover, is in the habit of ceaselessly calling out what cannot be German in a colonial context: "Heinegger! . . . Heinegger!" Harry, "liberal" that he is, has some sympathy for Jackson's position and thus suggests that the Pantomime should be a satire on the master-slave relationship and its black-white, labour-management variations: Jackson, the servant, is to play Crusoe. Jackson finds this approach much more attractive than the classical interpretation. He tells Harry what to say in his role as Friday and improvises a calypso melody on Crusoe, climaxing with the words *"But one day things bound to go in reverse, / with Crusoe the slave and Friday the boss"* (p. 117). Playing the role of black Crusoe, Jackson paddles his canoe, mimes a shipwreck and then proceeds to teach his white slave an African language.

Jackson's attempt to recapture his African tradition represents the choice of an African heritage in the face of colonial culture and mental domination. Like Aimé Césaire, he utters the African word and makes regal the canoe traversing the foaming waves. In one form or another, this is the choice that most Caribbean writers make today. The search for a tradition in which to be rooted leads back to a pre-colonial time, the cyclical time of ancestral myths. [11] The search encounters primal narratives and the transformations they have undergone as slaves. Maroons and their descendents attempted to preserve their cultural orientation to the world despite the master's onslaught. "The recognition of an ancestral relationship with the folk or aboriginal culture," Edward Brathwaite writes, "involves the artist and participant in a journey into the past and hinterland which is at the same time a movement of possession into present and future." [12] This is the journey that black Crusoe makes.

The metamorphosis from Friday to Crusoe is fraught with a double irony, however, which does not escape Jackson. He uses the image of a child's shadow to describe the parrot-like servant. The child cannot get rid of the shadow, and it is eventually the "black magic of the shadow" that starts to dominate the child; it is the servant that starts "dominating the master" (p. 113). The inversion and Africanization of the classical Crusoe myth is the servant's way of taking control over the master and the master's version of history. In fact, throughout the play instances of Jackson taking control are presented. The servant tells the master what to say, orders him to put on his clothes and so forth. But a servant giving orders does not a master make. The servant "dominates" the master, but he is still the servant. The servant remains bound by the white power structure, economic reality and ideology. Even the assertion of an alternative "classical" African Crusoe, dwelling in the Golden Age of *Guiné,* is a reaction to the dominant white ideology and its traumatic impact. The African myth is determined by its opposition to the hegemony of the European myth. This is the realization that Makak comes to in *Dream on Monkey Mountain.* The romantic appeal to the black Golden Age is a form of narcissism found in many *négritude* writers, but sharply denounced by Caribbean thinkers like Fanon.[13] Simply to juxtapose African mythical narrative to European mythical narrative is to fail to confront the totality of contemporary Caribbean reality. Walcott refuses to be part of the creation of a new myth, and for this his work is often criticized. The return to the past, to the origin, though necessary, must be incorporated into the critique of contemporary ideological and mythical structures. It must occur by means of liberating narrative rather than mythical narrative.

Jackson acts the role of black Crusoe, but never falls into the deception of identifying himself with that role. He knows that if Harry carries out his threat to commit suicide by jumping off the edge of the cliff, he, the servant, will be charged with murder. The white rulers may have departed now that Crusoe's island is independent, but they are still very much present. The black Crusoes are their agents, their neo-colonial shadows; the reversal is only an appearance. "The national middle class," Fanon argues, "will have nothing better to do than to take on the role of manager of Western enterprise, and it will in practice set up its country as the brothel of Europe."[14] White Crusoe knows that he can keep the colonized under control today if he allows them the semblance of cultural identity and political power. Walcott makes this point forcefully in *The Star-Apple Kingdom:*

> One morning the Caribbean was cut up
> by seven prime ministers who bought the sea in bolts—
> . . .
> who sold it at a markup to the conglomerates,
> the same conglomerates who had rented the water spouts
> for ninety-nine years in exchange for fifty ships,
> who retailed it in turn to the ministers
> with only one bank account, who then resold it
> in ads for the Caribbean Economic Community,
> till everyone owned a little piece of the sea,
> from which some made saris, some made bandannas,
> the rest was offered on trays to white cruise ships
> taller than the post office; then the dogfights
> began in the cabinets as to who had first sold
> the archipelago for this chain store of islands.[15]

The alternative to the appeal to mythical narrative is the creative encounter with history that is the task of liberating narrative. If mythical narrative is "classical" in both its European and African versions, liberating narrative is the authentic Creole appropriation of the classical traditions. Both Harry and Jackson are actors, even though they play their roles very differently. Because acting was his profession in England, Harry calls himself a "classical" actor. Here, in Tobago, he has to play Hotel Manager in the new script of life, and he asserts his intention to play this role "to the hilt" (p. 108). In England he was a poor actor, however, and now in Tobago he has trouble playing his social role. Nevertheless, he continues to identify himself with his role, and when the crunch comes, he sees himself as master.

Jackson is very different. As a former calypso singer, he too is an actor. However, he never identifies himself with the role he is playing. He refuses to act the role of Friday, and he does not imprison himself in a mythical black Crusoe. Most important of all, though he has chosen to play the role of servant in the guest-house, he knows that he is more than a servant, that he is a person, a free agent, who cannot be cornered into one particular role. To use Peter Berger's language, he is "ecstatic:" he is able to step out of socially defined roles and then re-enter them, without confusing self and role.[16] This is why Jackson says with complete self-consciousness:

> You see, two of we both acting a role here we ain't really believe in, you
> know. I ent think you strong enough to give people orders, and I know I
> ain't the kind who like taking *them*. So both of we doesn't have to
> *improvise* so much as *exaggerate*. We faking, faking all the time. But, man
> to man, I mean . . . that could be something else. Right, Mr. Trewe?
> (p. 138)

Harry Trewe has been playing what he calls a "man to man" game with Jackson, but he does not go beyond the surface roles to respect the man in Jackson. Jackson, however, knows who he is, and demands recognition.

In one sense Jackson resembles the Quashee stereotype: the smiling slave who feigns stupidity in order to dupe the master. As Harry notes, he is a "stage nigger": behind his mispronounced words, his smiling face and long toilet ritual lies a "bloody dagger" (pp. 139-40). However Jackson plays the Quashee role the way Hamlet plays madness. It is done consciously, with distance, in the interest of truth. Jackson's ultimate goal is not to deceive Harry, but to cut through the illusions of racial domination.

Paradoxically, it is this self-consciousness that ultimately makes Jackson the master in reality. This is the significance of the Creole appropriation of the Crusoe legend. Despite Harry's objections, Jackson continues to play Crusoe's role in the Panto-mime, and he does not do it the way Harry wants him to. The distinction between "Creole" and "classical" acting which Jackson makes in jest begins to take on significance when we associate Jackson's self-consciousness with Creole acting, and Harry's mystifications with classical. Walcott's Crusoe has both a classical and a Creole side. Harry interprets Crusoe romantically in terms of his own anguish and loneliness: classical Crusoe is a castaway. Jackson interprets Crusoe historically in terms of the artist's creative appropriation of his particular situation: Creole Crusoe is a craftsman.[17] Harry's Crusoe is a lonely alienated man, far from his home and family, Adam without Eve in Paradise. Jackson first mimes a classical black Crusoe in an equally romantic vein. However, Jackson goes beyond classical Crusoe to make manifest the Creole Crusoe. He ridicules Harry's language and imagery, breaking through its melancholia, demanding that a goat be added to the set. Crusoe must face reality, he must kill the goat for clothes, build a hut, achieve something. He does not despair, but faithfully encounters the world knowing that some day a sail will appear. This is the way that Jackson himself faces reality. For him the story of Robinson Crusoe is history, "the history of imperialism" (p. 125). History cannot be returned to a pre-colonial garden. It must be embraced faithfully and creatively. The Creole Crusoe is the liberated Friday. Harry objects to Jackson's emphasis on imperialism and black culture and experience. They are rehearsing a Pantomime, not a play, for the purpose of entertainment, not of creating art. Art, says Harry, "is a kind of crime in this society," it makes people "think too much" (p. 125). But Jackson is interested in bringing truth to human experience. He is interested in recovering the past in all of its multifaceted and ambivalent dimensions in order to create out of it a new history. Jackson's story is that of liberating narrative, not of myth. It is an affront only to those who refuse to think.

If Harry is the melancholic Crusoe lacking both faith and creativity, Jackson's Crusoe can help Harry reconquer himself. A final Pantomime is acted out in which Harry relives the traumatic death of his son and subsequent divorce from his wife. Jackson plays the role of Ellen, Harry's wife, allowing Harry to voice his resentment against her for killing his son in a car accident. In this way, Harry's repressed history unfolds. Ellen too was an actor, but she always played the dominant role. She played Crusoe and made an idiot out of her husband, who played Friday. It becomes evident that Harry's sentiments of mastery are attempts to cover up his own inferiority complex, loneliness and impotence. But Jackson, almost like a psycho-analyst, breaks through the transference to call Crusoe back to reality: Crusoe must get up to face the next day again, "man must live." And it is Friday's naked footprint, says Jackson, that is the mark of Crusoe's salvation (p. 164). Friday brings Crusoe back into reality; Jackson makes Harry confront history. The play closes with Jackson's last words: "Starting from Friday, Robinson, we could talk 'bout a raise?" (p. 170). The multiplicity of meanings in this question, the double meanings of "Friday" and "raise," suggest not that Jackson is merely a servant asking for a salary increase, but that Friday, all Fridays, demand that their statuses be raised; they demand recognition.

Role-playing brings about a significant change in Harry as he begins to under-stand himself and address Jackson with respect, as Mr. Phillip. Any member of the audience or reader of the play, whether Friday's progeny or Crusoe's, is likewise brought into a relation with history. The mythical form, the Prospero-Caliban archetype, is transformed by the content of the play, the reality of man in history. *Pantomime* is a mimesis or creative imitation of a social drama structured in terms of mimicry. Walcott's play takes this Pantomime form (the Crusoe drama) as its content and opens it to the possibilities of liberating narrative. We are challenged to appropri-ate the text in terms of our own reality, in terms of the faithful overthrow of myth, in terms, we might want to add, of the content of neo-colonialism *today*.

Harry, at his weakest point, ridiculed by his learned Friday, utters in desperation when Jackson kills his parrot:

> You people create nothing. You imitate everything. It's all been done
> before, you see, Jackson. The parrot. Think that's something? It's from
> *The Seagull*. It's from *Miss Julie*. You can't ever be original, boy. That's the
> trouble with shadows, right? They can't think for themselves. (p. 156)

In one powerful blow, Walcott takes a swipe at his detractors both at home in the West Indies, and in the metropolitan countries, for this is a criticism often leveled at

Walcott himself. Coming as it does from Harry, we realize the prejudice underpinning it: two worlds, black and white; two classical stories, ours and yours. The structure of "creole acting," that is, of liberating narrative, is ignored. Art makes people think, Harry had objected, and who would want people to think? The paradox of art for Walcott is that everything is imitation, and nothing is imitation. Not only is this the paradox of Walcott's own personal background, it is also the paradox of man's universality and historicity; it is only by confronting both terms in their unity that we truly begin to enter the realm of human reality.

Footnotes

[1] Selwyn Cudjoe, *Resistance and Caribbean Literature* (Athens: Ohio University Press; 1980), pp. 257-60.

[2] See in particular Fanon's critique of the national bourgeoisie in chapter three of *The Wretched of the Earth* trans. Constance Farrington (New York: Grove Press, 1968).

[3] See Victor Turner, "Social Dramas and Stories About Them, in *On Narrative* ed. W.J.T.Mitchell (Chicago and London: University of Chicago Press, 1981), particularly pp. 154, 163-64.

[4] Erich Auerbach, *Mimesis: The Representation of Reality in Western Literature,* trans. Willard Trask (New York: Anchor-Doubleday, 1957), p. 18.

[5] *Remembrance and Pantomime: Two Plays* (New York: Farrar, Straus and Giroux, 1980), p. 112. Further references are incorporated in the text.

[6] Daniel Defoe, *Robinson Crusoe* (1719; Harmondsworth: Penguin, 1965), p. 207.

[7] *Dream on Monkey Mountain and Other Plays* (New York: Farrar, Straus and Giroux, 1970).

[8] *The Castaway and Other Poems* (London: Jonathan Cape, 1969), p. 51

[9] Nathan Wachtel, *The Vision of The Vanquished: The Spanish Conquest of Peru through Indian Eyes, 1530-1570,* trans. Ben and Siân Reynolds (Hassocks, Sussex: Harvester Press, 1977), particularly part one and part two, section three.

[10] Herbert G. de Lisser, *Jane 's Career: A Story of Jamaica* (1914; London: Heinemann, 1971).

[11] Bonnie Barthold's *Black Time: Fiction of Africa, the Caribbean and the United States* (New Haven and London: Yale University Press, 1981), tries to revive the idea of "black time," arguing that black writers celebrate a cyclical, mythic pre-Western concept of time which she dualistically opposes to Western "historical" time.

[12] "Timehri," in *Is Massa Day Dead: Black Moods in the Caribbean,* ed. Orde Coombs (New York: Anchor Doubleday, 1974), p. 42.

[13] In *Black Skin, White Masks,* trans. Charles Lam Markmann (New York: Grove Press, 1967), for example, Fanon states that "There is no Negro Mission" (p. 228).

[14] *The Wretched of the Earth,* p. 154.

[15] *The Star-Apple Kingdom* (New York: Farrar, Straus and Giroux, 1979), p. 53.

[16] *Invitation to Sociology: A Humanistic Perspective* (New York: Anchor-Doubleday, 1963), p. 136.

[17] This liberating sense of "Creole" should be distinguished from the aesthetic sense of "Creole" found in Edward Brathwaite's *The Development of Creole Society in Jamaica 1770-1820* (Oxford: Clarendon Press, 1971). pp. 306-11. Though for Brathwaite Creole brings together the dualism of African and European heritages in the framework of popular culture, there is no historical or liberating consciousness necessarily implied in this process. For Brathwaite Creole culture becomes just another form of mythical narrative.

POEMS OF CARIBBEAN WOUNDS

Benjamin DeMott

Derek Walcott's superb new collection [*The Star-Apple Kingdom*] is described by its publishers as an "odyssey," and justly. The book opens with a long narrative about a poor mulatto sailor in flight northward from Trinidad, closes with the title poem, which dramatizes revolutionary movements of mind and feeling in Jamaica, and includes several shorter pieces set in island villages in St. Croix and elsewhere. The only items remote from the Caribbean circuit are a salute to Joseph Brodsky and a memorial to Robert Lowell.

The chief preoccupation, though, isn't peregrination, but power — or rather power and its undoings, actual and imagined, temporary and permanent. And contemporary political realities — the developed nations versus the third world — are frequently in sight. The poet, who was born in St. Lucia, educated in Jamaica and now lives in Trinidad, knows the developed nations through their deeds, their tourists and their students (he has taught at Yale and Columbia). And glimpses of their leaders turn up repeatedly in this book, as for example in the title poem, which in one satiric section portrays conglomerate managers cutting deals through the Caribbean Economic Community, buying the sea in bolts, reselling it in ads:

> . . . till everyone owned a little piece of the sea,
> from which some made saris, some made bandannas;
> the rest was offered on trays to white cruise ships
> taller than the post office; then the dogfights
> began in the cabinets as to who had first sold
> the archipelago for this chain store of islands. (p. 53)

But the historico-political context of *The Star-Apple Kingdom* is by no means narrow. The exploitative masters who populate these poems are a various lot — slave-ship captains and kingpin admirals, as well as capitalist tycoons and representatives of the classic 19th-century imperialist cultures. (The most fascinating of the imperialists is a Conradian missionary-soldier who appears in an extraordinary narrative called "Koenig of the River.") And the causes of the masters' undoings are as various as the characters themselves. They include not just mortality, inner sickening at personal corruption and revolution, but also, in one key poem, the discovery of the possibility of a nonmanipulative code of value.

That poem is called "Egypt, Tobago," the title carrying a suggestion of the interchangeability of the victimized quarters of this earth, Trinidad, the Middle East, wherever. The central figure is Shakespeare's truant Antony. The time is just before Antony's huge defeat — the loss of all for love. Beside the hero, on a "fierce shore," Cleopatra sleeps, and in the opening lines — as in Shakespeare's play — bawdy and elevation coexist, coition as combat is among the imperial themes, and the atmosphere is drenched with sexuality:

> Her salt marsh dries in the heat
> where he foundered
> without armour.
> He exchanged an empire for her beads of sweat. . . .

But swiftly the focus shifts to the Queen's slumber, her helpless trust. The authority of her silence, as of that of the silent sand and sky, is set over against the hum and buzz of standard imperial ego. And the poem's ultimate achievement is the creation of an experience of heroic suspension, an interval during which exploitative power is immobilized by a perception of its own emptiness and by an intimation of a new way of inhabiting the world and time:

> All-humbling sleep, whose peace
> is sweet as death,
> whose silence has
> all the sea's weight and volubility,
>
> who swings this globe by a hair's trembling breath.
>
> Shattered and wild and
> palm-crowned Antony,
> rusting in Egypt,
> ready to lose the world,
> to Actium and sand,
>
> everything else
> is vanity, but this tenderness
> for a woman not his mistress
> but his sleeping child.
>
> The sky is cloudless. The afternoon is mild.

Here, and throughout *The Star-Apple Kingdom,* the impression is of a subject known to its marrow, explored in microcosm and macrocosm, past and present, both for its political bearings and for the light it casts on the moral development of our kind. And that impression is confirmed by a glance at Walcott's earlier books. The present work is a fifth volume by a poet whose feeling for English was hailed nearly two decades ago by Robert Graves. Poems on the building and undermining of empire that Walcott published in the 50's — views, for instance, of African children singing "Rule, Britannia" — stand in a direct line with such larger-scaled efforts as "Koenig." The vision of revolution animating portions of *The Star-Apple Kingdom* is rooted in the more impassive accountings, in the poets earliest work, of the wounds of Caribbean shack towns. And the brilliance with which native dialects are here transformed into instruments of public range, even grandeur, owes much to the rather more casual experiments with popular speech that he began long ago. (It is fair to add that a sin visible at the start of this career — a taste for portentousness — is still apparent; witness these lines: "Like neon lasers shot across the bars / discos blast out the music of the spheres,/ and, one by one, science infects the stars.")

It is scripture nowadays that political poetry is almost invariably smutched by highmindedness, phony commitment and detachable sentiment. But *The Star-Apple Kingdom* seems to me utterly free of such pollutions. In skies this high, with contexts of thought and feeling this rich, self-righteousness is a flea — it wouldn't be noticed if it were there. Nor does the poet's embattlement ever come across as a matter of contentious opinion; it is first of all a charge on the language, a stirring muscularity in the verse. Walcott's struggle with the dominating mad masters who pack it in these poems packs his line with fury. A ceaseless energy conversion is in process, seemingly — larger-than-life physical force becoming verbal force and producing in the end verse which, while densely particularized and personally accented, is also spacious as a tide, irresistible, Elizabethan.

And, far more important than any of this, the poet's conception of himself as spokesman is accompanied by an ability to imagine believably comprehensive voices, tuned to bottom dog and visionary alike. The narrator of the opening poem, "The Schooner *Flight,*" is a crewman-scribbler who bears the generic name Shabine and has a marvelously flexible voice. Listen, for example, to this passage on a sunrise encounter:

> Man, I brisk in the galley first thing next dawn,
> brewing li'l coffee; fog coil from the sea
> like the kettle steaming when I put it down
> slow, slow, 'cause I couldn't believe what I see: . . .
> We float through a rustling forest of ships
> with sails dry like paper, behind the glass
> I saw men with rusty eyeholes like cannons,
> and wherever their half-naked crews cross the sun,
> right through their tissue, you traced their bones
> like leaves against the sunlight; frigates, barkentines,

> the backward-moving current swept them on,
> and high on their decks I saw great admirals,
> Rodney, Nelson, de Grasse, I heard the hoarse orders
> they gave those Shabines, and that forest
> of masts sail right through the *Flight*,
> and all you could hear was the ghostly sound
> of waves rustling like grass in a low wind
> and the hissing weeds they trailed from the stern;
> slowly they heaved past from east-to-west
> like this round world was some cranked water wheel,
> every ship pouring like a wooden bucket
> dredged from the deep; my memory revolve
> on all sailors before me, then the sun
> heat the horizon's ring and they was mist. (pp. 10-11)

"The line comes," Charles Olson says, "from the breath, from the breathing of the man who writes, at the moment that he writes." But before "The Schooner *Flight*" is finished the line comes, as I hear it, from the breathing of the man conjoined with breathings of the common wind — right-reasoned longings for justice, aspirations to solidarity that are shared. *The Star-Apple Kingdom* marks, in other words, the return, after an absence, of a moving public speech to poetry in English. And that places it with the headiest and rarest kinds of poetic experience — fruitful to people who practice the art and to all the rest of us, too.

THE LANGUAGE OF EXILE

Seamus Heaney

A poet appeases his original needs by learning to make works that seem to be all his own work — Yeats at the stage of *The Wind among the Reeds*. Then begins that bothersome and and exhilarating second need, to go beyond what he has mastered of himself, take on the otherness of the world and take it into works that remain his own yet offer rights-of-way to everybody else: the kind of understanding and composure Yeats had won by the time he published *The Wild Swans at Coole*. Or the kind of sumptuous authority which Derek Walcott displays in *The Star-Apple Kingdom*.

"The Schooner *Flight*," the long poem at the start of the book, is epoch-making. All that Walcott knew in his bones and plied in his thought before this moves like a long swell of energy under its fluent verse which sails, well rigged and richly cargoed, into the needy future. I imagine he has done for the Caribbean what Synge did for Ireland, found a language woven out of dialect and literature, neither folksy nor condescending, a singular idiom evolved out of one man's inherited divisions and obsessions that allows an older life to exult in itself yet at the same time keeps the cool of "the new." A few years ago, in the turbulent and beautiful essay which prefaced his collection of plays, *Dream on Monkey Mountain*, Walcott wrote out of and about the hunger for a proper form, for an instrument to bleed off the accumulated humors of his peculiar colonial ague. He has now found that instrument and wields it with rare confidence:

> You ever look up from some lonely beach
> and see a far schooner? Well, when I write
> this poem, each phrase go be soaked in salt;
> I go draw and knot every line as tight
> as ropes in this rigging; in simple speech
> my common language go be the wind,
> my pages the sails of the schooner *Flight.* (p. 5)

The speaker fixes his language in terms that recall Walcott's description of an ideal troupe of actors, "sinewy, tuned, elate," and the language works for him as a well-disciplined troupe works for the dramatist. It is not for subjective lyric effects but for

304

what James Wright has called "the poetry of a grown man" and the man has grown to that definitive stage which Yeats called "the finished man among his enemies."

For those awakening to the nightmare of history, revenge —'Walcott has conceded — can be a kind of vision, yet he himself is not vengeful. Nor is he simply a patient singer of the tears of things. His intelligence is fierce but it is literary. He assumes that art is a power and to be visited by it is to be endangered, but he also knows that works of art endanger nobody else, that they are benign. From the beginning he has never simplified or sold short. Africa and England beat messages along his blood. The humanist voices of his education and the voices from his elemental inarticulate place keep insisting on their full claims, pulling him in two different directions. He always had the capacity to write with the elegance of a Larkin and make himself a ventriloquist's doll to the English tradition which he inherited, though that of course would have been an attenuation of his gifts, for he also has the capacity to write with the murky voluptuousness of a Neruda and make himself a romantic tongue, licking poetic good things off his islands. He did neither, but made a theme of the choice and the impossibility of choosing. And now he has embodied the theme in the person of Shabine, the poor mulatto sailor of the *Flight*, a kind of democratic West Indian Ulysses, his mind full of wind and poetry and women. Indeed, when Walcott lets the sea-breeze freshen in his imagination, the result is a poetry as spacious and heart-lifting as the sea-weather at the opening of Joyce's *Ulysses*, a poetry that comes from no easy evocation of mood but from stored sensations of the actual:

> In idle August, while the sea soft,
> and leaves of brown islands stick to the rim
> of this Caribbean, I blow out the light
> by the dreamless face of Maria Concepcion
> to ship as a seaman on the schooner *Flight*.
> Out in the yard turning gray in the dawn,
> I stood like a stone and nothing else move
> but the cold sea rippling like galvanize
> and the nail holes of stars in the sky roof,
> till a wind start to interfere with the trees. (p. 3)

It is a sign of Walcott's mastery that his fidelity to the genius of English now leads him not away from but right into the quick of West Indian speech. When he wrote these opening lines, how conscious was he of another morning departure, another allegorical early-riser? The murmur of Malvern is under that writing for surely it returns to an origin in *Piers Plowman:*

> In summer season, when soft was the sun,
> I rigged myself up in a long robe, rough like a sheep's,
> With skirts hanging like a hermit's, unholy of works,
> Went wide in this world, wonders to hear.

> But on a May morning, on Malvern Hills,
> A marvel befel me —— magic it seemed.
> I was weary of wandering and went for a rest
> Under a broad bank, by a brook's side;
> And as I lay lolling, looking at the water,
> I slid into a sleep . . .

The whole passage could stand as an epigraph to the book insofar as it is at once speech and melody, amorous of the landscape, matter of fact but capable of modulation to the visionary. Walcott's glamorous, voluble Caribbean harbors recall Langland's field full of folk. Love and anger inspire both writers, and both manage, in Eliot's phrase, to fuse the most ancient and most civilized mentality. The best poems in *The Star-Apple Kingdom* are dream visions; the high moments are hallucinatory, cathartic, redemptive even. Here, for example, is a passage from "Koenig of the River," where Koenig appears on his shallop like some Dantesque shade arisen out of the imperial dream, being forced to relive it in order to comprehend it:

> Around the bend the river poured its silver
> like some remorseful mine, giving and giving
> everything green and white: white sky, white
> water, and the dull green like a drumbeat
> of the slow-sliding forest, the green heat;
> then, on some sandbar, a mirage ahead:
> fabric of muslin sails, spiderweb rigging,
> a schooner, foundered on black river mud,
> was rising slowly up from the riverbed,
> and a top-hatted native reading an inverted newspaper
> "Where's our Queen?" Koenig shouted.
> "Where's our Kaiser?"
>   The nigger disappeared.
> Koenig felt that he himself was being read
> like the newspaper or a hundred-year-old novel.
> "The Queen dead! Kaiser dead!" the voices shouted.
> And it flashed through him those trunks were not wood
> but that the ghosts of slaughtered Indians stood
> there in the mangroves, their eyes like fireflies
> in the green dark, and that like hummingbirds
> they sailed rather than ran between the trees.
> The river carried him past his shouted words.
> The schooner had gone down without a trace.
> "There was a time when we ruled everything,"
> Koenig sang to his corrugated white reflection. (pp. 44-45)

There is a magnificence and pride about this art — specifically the art, not specially the politics — that rebukes that old British notion of "commonwealth literature." Walcott possesses English more deeply and sonorously than most of the English themselves. Except for Ted Hughes, I can think of nobody now writing with such imperious linguistic gifts. And in spite of the sheen off those lines, I suspect he is not so much interested in the "finish" of his work as in its drive. He has written lyrics of memorable grace — "In a Green Night" and "Coral" come to mind as two different kinds of excellence — and his deliberately designed early sonnet sequence "Tales of the Islands" guaranteed the possibility of these latest monologues and narratives. His work for the stage has paid into his address to the poetry until the latter now moves itself and us in a way that Osip Mandelstam would certainly have approved. In his "Conversation about Dante'" Mandelstam wrote:

> The quality of poetry is decided by the speed and decisiveness with which it embodies its schemes and commands in diction, the instrumentless, lexical, purely quantitative verbal matter. One must traverse the full width of a river crammed with Chinese junks moving simultaneously in different directions — this is how the meaning of poetic discourse is created. The meaning, its itinerary, cannot be reconstructed by interrogating the boatmen: they will not be able to tell how and why we were skipping from junk to junk.

Something of that unpredictable, resourceful, and expeditionary motion keeps the title poem going. "The Star-Apple Kingdom" is discursive and meditative, a dive into the cultural and political matter of post-colonial Jamaica, yet the mode of the poem could hardly be described as either meditative or discursive. Again, there is a dream-heavy thing at work, as if the years of analysis and commitment to proper thinking and action resolved themselves for the poet into a sound halfway between sobbing and sighing. The poem does not have the pure windfall grace of "The Schooner Flight"— in places it sags into "writing" — but its pitch and boldness make a lovely orchestration of the music of what happens:

> What was the Caribbean? A green pond mantling
> behind the Great House columns of Whitehall,
> behind the Greek façades of Washington,
> with bloated frogs squatting on lily pads
> like islands, islands that coupled as sadly as turtles
> engendering islets, as the turtle of Cuba
> mounting Jamaica engendered the Caymans, as, behind
> the hammerhead turtle of Haiti-San Domingo
> trailed the little turtles from Tortuga to Tobago;
> he followed the bobbing trek of the turtles
> leaving America for the open Atlantic,
> felt his own flesh loaded like the pregnant beaches

with their moon-guarded eggs—they yearned for Africa,
they were lemmings drawn by magnetic memory
to an older death, to broader beaches
where the coughing of lions was dumbed by breakers.
Yes, he could understand their natural direction
but they would drown, sea eagles circling them,
and the languor of frigates that do not beat wings . . .

Walcott's poetry has passed the stage of self-questioning, self-exposure, self-healing to become a common resource. He is no propagandist. What he would propagate is magnanimity and courage and I am sure that he would agree with Hopkin's affirmation that feeling, and in particular love, is the great power and spring of verse. This book is awash with love of people and places and language: love as knowledge, love as longing, love as consummation, at one time the Sermon on the Mount, at another *Antony and Cleopatra:*

He lies like a copper palm
tree at three in the afternoon
by a hot sea
and a river, in Egypt, Tobago.

Her salt marsh dries in the heat
where he foundered
without armor.
He exchanged an empire for her beads of sweat.

the uproar of arenas,
the changing surf
of senators, for
this silent ceiling over silent sand —

this grizzled bear, whose fur,
moulting, is silvered —
for this quick fox with her
sweet stench. . .
("Egypt, Tobago" p. 30)

There is something risky about such large appropriations, but they are legitimate because Walcott's Caribbean and Cleopatra's Nile have the same sweltering awareness of the cynicism and brutality of political adventurers. He is not going beyond the field of his own imagery, he is appropriating Shakespeare, not expropriating him — the unkindest post-colonial cut of all.

Conscious maker that he is, Derek Walcott is certainly aware that the whirligig of time has brought in such revenges which turn out to be more ironies than revenges.

His sense of options and traditions is highly developed and his deliberate progress as a writer has not ended. Much that he inherited as inchoate communal plight has been voiced, especially in the dramatic modes of this volume, yet I am not sure that he won't return inwards to the self, to refine the rhetoric. "Forest of Europe," the poem dedicated to Joseph Brodsky, is aimed at the center of Walcott's themes — language, exile, art — and is written with the surge of ambition that marks him as a major voice. But I feel that the willful shaping intelligence has got too much of the upper hand in the poem, that the thrill of addressing a heroic comrade in the art has forced the note. I rejoice in everything the poem says — "what's poetry, if it is worth its salt, /but a phrase men can pass from hand to mouth?" (p. 40) — yet the poem is not securely in possession of its tone. Which could never be said of Shabine, who deals with the big themes in his own nonchalant way:

> I met History once, but he ain't recognize me
> a parchment Creole, with warts
> like an old sea bottle, crawling like a crab
> through the holes of shadow cast by the net
> of a grille balcony; cream linen, cream hat.
> I confront him and shout, "Sir, is Shabine!
> They say I'se your grandson. You remember Grandma,
> your black cook, at all?" The bitch hawk and spat.
> A spit like that worth any number of words.
> But that's all them bastards have left us: words. (pp. 8-9)

D.
"A SIMPLE FLAME"
(1980 -)

DEREK WALCOTT: CONTEMPORARY

Calvin Bedient

Something like genius, like a convicting and convincing necessity, woke in "The Schooner *Flight*," the long lead poem in Derek Walcott's last volume, *The Star-Apple Kingdom* (1979). And the rest of the book did not much let one down. *The Fortunate Traveller*, by contrast, shows more gift than genius. Walcott's characteristic strength remains a combination of facility and passion but the proportions are not quite right. I miss in the new book a near approach to the "necessary and unalterable" — the qualities Proust located in "the beauty of landscapes or of great works of art," things more genuine than ourselves. The assured diction and tone, the limber eloquence, the varied metrical craft, the auditory imagination perhaps second in consummate concentration only to Geoffrey Hill's (if also now and then to Seamus Heaney's), the visual imagination clear as air and almost as surprisingly detailed as space, the cultural sensitivity acute as anyone's, plus the usual sheaf of personal griefs — these continue to engross. But the volume makes one long to find the facility forgotten, surpassed in some awful absorption. (This nearly happens, to be sure, in "Wales" and perhaps does in "Jean Rhys.")

Here Walcott is a rolling stone, not a landscape of a mind. He suffers the twentieth-century dislocation. He lacks authority. He whiffles; his uprootedness is sometimes indulged. He seems to write, now and again, on whim, nostalgic for a home in poetry but finding none — not even (in a beautiful phrase from *Sea Grapes*, his volume of 1976) "the river's startled flowing."

Restless incertitude is conspicuous — as are starts away from it — in the first five poems, all on America. Here Walcott roams the East Coast as if looking for an America to call home. (Born in St. Lucia and imprinted as a Trinidadian, he has taught recently at Harvard and Columbia.) Now, Walcott is welcome to America; she could use a poet who would see her; she is tired of those lovers who keep her up all night talking about themselves. But his gifts of observation, his mimicry of some of our poets, and his home-need do not turn the trick. Except in the South he's too eager to please and be pleased. His citizenship is would-be, griefless and untried.

Besides, his mimicry of Robert Lowell and Elizabeth Bishop is soft. "Upstate"

313

copies the latter's offhand unfoldment: "A knife blade of cold air keeps prying/ the bus window open.... The door to the john/ keeps banging. There're a few of us: /a stale-drunk or stoned woman in torn jeans," and so on. But the poem devolves from the precarious Bishop model and misses her sort of sliding, infinitely gentle cohesion. It slithers, rather, to "I am falling in love with America":

> I will knock at the widowed door
> of one of these villages
> where she will admit me like a broad meadow,
> like a blue space between mountains,
> and holding her arms at the broken elbows
> brush the dank hair from a forehead
> as warm as bread or as a homecoming. (pp. 5-6)

As Allen Grossman notes in *Against Our Vanishing,* Bishop's "management of perception" in the absence of decisions about "how we know" and "what there is" "excites admiration at the point where it expresses the consequences for sentiment of the relentless focus which she everywhere practices." In "Upstate" the descriptive discipline relents, giving way to the "rush" of a romantic homecoming.

For all five poems, grouped under the section title "North," the ideal reader would be the kind of "consumer" described by Theodor W. Adorno in his *Introduction to the Sociology of Music*: one for whom "the unfoldment of a composition does not matter," for whom "the structure of hearing is atomistic: the type lies in wait for specific elements, for supposedly beautiful melodies, for grandiose moments." How else read "Old New England," with its shudderingly perfect bits:

> and railway lines are arrowing to the far
> mountainwide absence of the Iroquois. (p. 3)

Why complain that Walcott is not in fact a New England poet, that the "our" in "The crest of our conviction grows as loud/ as the spring oaks" or "our sons home from the East" is ersatz when most American poets would sell their convictionless souls to be able to write like this? Still the poem is excessively written in proportion to what it has to say—is virtuosic merely. It reads like a smooth dream of phrases that not even Vietnam ("our sons home from the East") can wake up. In a way that is its point, but the poet's hunger to absorb New England, and Robert Lowell, places him curiously inside the dream, insulated there, enjoying it.

If Walcott is free for this maundering it's because he's in the strictest sense Contemporary. Back in his great poem "The Schooner *Flight*" he sailed, so it seemed, by the last breath of Romantic quest, one grown refreshingly tropical. He proved one of those poets (the great example is Shakespeare) whose country has emerged out of the shell of the blind elements as a thing preternaturally comely and kind, a blood-warm goddess. She was the Maria Concepcion who

> . . . was all my thought
> watching the sea heaving up and down
> as the port side of dories, schooners, and yachts
> was painted afresh by the strokes of the sun
> signing her name with every reflection
> I knew when dark-haired evening put on
> her bright silk at sunset, and, folding the sea,
> sidled under the sheet with her starry laugh,
> that there'd be no rest, there'd be no forgetting.
> (*The Star-Apple Kingdom*, p. 4)

Through his persona Shabine, both fabulous and human, and the wakeful naiveté of unabashed yearning — "The bowsprit, the arrow, the longing, the lunging heart —/ the flight to a target whose aim we'll never know" — the poet pushed passion to its utmost cathartic emergence and expression. That was yesterday. Today, his heart as perplexed as it is full, he's back in the modern world, where "the mania/ of history veils even the clearest air,/ The sickly sweet taste of ash, of something burning." (*The Star-Apple Kingdom*, p. 14)

This is no pose. It is felt as debility, not nobility. Walcott's mind says it may be over, the human adventure. He's Contemporary in that he doesn't know what to do with his humanness, regret or refine it (it's too late to rejoice in it). Neither does he know how to use it for his own or others' good. Contemporary in that for him everything is tentative, in transit. Contemporary, too, in his disconnection. True, he's far from free, despite wishing, of his Caribbean origins, his "white" and "black" racial inheritances, the stateliness of *their* English and the dandelion tea of *their* dialect, friendship and family, the poetry of sea grapes, sea almonds, and the indigo sea. . . . Still he's unsure of who he is, an unfinished man.

Although a few have managed to make tentativeness and transitiveness a cause — William Carlos Williams for instance, early on — for others the Contemporary is a diffuse, deadening fate, life without a fuse. It was so for Lowell, it is so for Ashbery. How like Lowell is Walcott when writing of his two divorces, particularly (in "Store Bay") the second:

> I still lug my house on my back —
> a mottled, brown shoulder bag
> like a turtle's —
> to the shadow of a rock,
> quivering from sunstroke
> and my second divorce. (p. 81)

Defensively the last line comes as if an afterthought and modestly, for nowadays what's more banal than personal crisis? It highlights "the house on my back" as the poignant emblem of two generations. (Walcott was born in 1930, a few years before the peripatetic Bishop published *North and South*, titular parent to the geographical

divisions of *The Fortunate Traveller.)* The sense of a lonely laboring, of shock, of
scarifying repetition, the homelessness, the transiency build to a wish for utter
disconnection:

> I unplug the hotel lamp and lie in bed,
> my head full of black surf.
> I envy the octopus with ink for blood,
> his dangling, disconnected wires
> adrift, unmarried. (p. 83)

Lug and unplug: the whole plot in an ugly rhyme. "On fading sand," he has earlier
said, "I pass/ a mackerel that leapt from its element,/ trying to be different —/ its eye
a golden ring,/ married to nothing" (p. 82). Evidently the effort to be a poet, to
transform immediate into reflective emotion, golden, unmarried, contributed to the
divorce, a divorce not complete enough since blood not ink flows in the poet's veins.
The Contemporary poet knows too well the brief route back from every dream:

> To the thud of reggaes
> from a concrete gazebo,
> a yellow glass-bottom launch,
> trailing weed from its jaws,
> sharks in from the coral gardens
> for the next shoal of picnickers. (p. 81)

"Change me, my sign," Walcott asks in the poem about his first divorce "The Hotel
Normandie Pool," "to someone I can bear."
     The "High Moderns," to quote Grossman again, could still aspire to "central and
gigantic utterance." Pound, Eliot, Stevens, and even Yeats had themes they thought
crucial and beneficial to many, timely, essential. In the main they thought they had
something more "important" to write about than their divorces or breakdowns — or
they boldly took from these the pulse of their civilization. For them the poet was not
the private man in the public eye but impersonal man disclosing the verbs and nouns
of being. Their advocacy of impersonality was not modesty but a passion to haul in
their verbal nets all reality; it was a passion to heal.
     With the Contemporaries the trick is rather to extricate from the confusion and
disconnections of their always provisional lives a socially valid part of themselves,
someone they can accept and like. How try for the total picture when the paint is still
wet on their faces, burning their eyes? For them history has become maniacal and just
to have the assurance of an "I" in the great deliquescence of the "We" is task enough,
or so it seems.
     The Contemporary is the weakening of the will to form, as despair of an overall
purpose is communicated from life to the poem. Vigorous evolution becomes obso-
lete when the launch is already returning (you knew it would) trailing weed from its
inoperable jaws. Here is a serious dilemma. We want art to be truthful but not to

drain our energy. Form is its means of quickening us. What for the Contemporary is left of structural refinements of hearing, formal ambush, architectonic mystery and economy?

The soul, as Whitehead said, consists of discovery, and discovery must remain the principle, or faith, governing art. There's no totally satisfactory alternative, in art, to a religious concentration: to a divination that coincides with the labor of design. "Store Bay" discovers the self-punishing desire for disconnection. The end is not given entire in the beginning but is a depth that the opening line, like a plumb-string, enters cold. Too much of the longer "Hotel Normandie Pool" is strung out along the surface. The poet himself talks on and then a towel-draped Ovid at poolside talks on, exile consoling exile.

Yet politics, too, is a way of quickening form and if Walcott in his post-colonial loneliness, his need to invent an identity, illustrates the Contemporary (without performing it in mock-fever, like John Ashbery or W. S. Graham), he has the advantage of a troubled patrimony, one that, when it riles him, rouses his idle deracinated abilities. His wandering and memory of Dachau and the passport of his perfect English may make him "international" — Delmore Schwartz's label for T. S. Eliot (who however ventured beyond internationalism to divinity, as a would-be isolate and ascetic) — but he remains bound in a way to the Caribbean, in a marriage all blows and departures. And in his politics he finds the privileged, pivotal point of the Contemporary, gaining purpose from, precisely, tentativeness and disconnection, turning in accusation against their source. (What a relief as the satirist, renouncing helplessness and assuming mastery, puts Power at the mercy of his pen.)

What ails the West Indies is (it seems) the Contemporary blight itself, a want of confidence and self-release. On these former colonies the various groups of people either wrangle or keep to themselves. Or so V.S. Naipaul found when, revisiting the islands in 1960, after years of expatriation, he made this summary:

> For seven months I had been travelling through territories which, unimportant except to themselves, and faced with every sort of problem, were exhausting their energies in petty power squabbles and the maintaining of the petty prejudices of petty societies. I had seen how deep in nearly every West Indian, high and low, were the prejudices of race; how often these prejudices were rooted in self-contempt; and how much important action they prompted. Everyone spoke of nation and nationalism but no one was willing to surrender the privileges or even the separateness of his group. (*The Middle Passage*, p. 230)

Naipaul himself, as here in *The Middle Passage* (1962) and in his remorseless novel *Guerrillas* (1976), has been deliberately the sort of writer the West Indian — insecure and resisting satire — needs, one who will "tell him who he is and where he stands." And Walcott, starting from scratch and anger, has singlehandedly created a mature West Indian branch of English poetry.[1]

Toward this end he has had to hand not only his beautiful formal English but what

Naipaul calls the "lively and inventive Trinidad dialect," which he yet uses sparingly. It can be no small privilege and excitement to "represent" in "English" poetry the language of calypso and by way of identifying the collectivity that authenticates him as a poet with a people. Shabine's radiantly aggressive idiolect, at once racy and majestic, models what it means to be a self-made individual. In his new poem "The Spoiler's Return" Walcott lashes the Trinidadians in something closer, perhaps, to their own tongue (while avoiding the barbarousness endemic in dialect literature). Satire delights in this idiom with its jazzy resistance to the genteel:

> The shark, racing the shadow of the shark
> across clear coral rocks, does make them dark —
> that is my premonition of the scene
> of what passing over this Caribbean.
> Is crab climbing crab-back, in a crab-quarrel,
> and going round and round in the same barrel,
> is sharks with shirt-jacs, sharks with well-pressed fins,
> ripping we small fry off with razor grins;
> nothing ain't change but color and attire,
> so back me up, Old Brigade of Satire,
> back me up, Martial, Juvenal, and Pope
> (to hang theirself I giving plenty rope). . . . (p. 54)

And later: "all you go bawl out, 'Spoils, things ain't so bad,'/ This ain't the Dark Age, is just Trinidad,/ is human nature, Spoiler, after all,/ it ain't big genocide, is just bohbol" (pp. 55-56).

Light and glittering, perhaps two out of every three couplets cut. Certainly the form, with its flourishes, means to intimidate and the couplets with their slip-nooses of rhyme would bag evil. But the social grief is enormous: ". . . all Power has/ made the sky shit and vermin of the stars" neglects to laugh. Spoiler "feel to bawl/ 'area of darkness' with V. S. Nightfall" and finally he quits: he goes back to Hell — "One thing with Hell, at least it organize/ in soaring circles . . ." (p. 56, 58, 59). Satire may imply an imperious unforgiveness that itself seems to affirm rational man. But who's listening? The rude rousing revenge sours. The poem disturbs satire with pathos. In an unkindest cut that cuts both ways, it shuts up in despair.

"The Spoiler's Return" is a razzle-dazzle but, after its kind, it rambles. "The Liberator" shows more securely what political purpose can do for poetic form. Here satire succeeds to irony in a justice almost bleedingly deep. The poem risks a sympathetic inwardness with the will-rot of Antillean cultures as well as protests against it. In a Venezuelan jungle the guerrilla followers of a certain Sonora "bawl for their mudder and their children haunt them./ They dream of mattresses, even those in prison" (p. 51). "We was going so good," sums up Sonora. "But then, they get tired" (p. 52). If he can say no more neither can Walcott, who's in the sticky position of sounding detached and English, untested: it's Sonora who suffered, who was there. No wonder Walcott lets the sweated dialect take over:

> In a blue bar at the crossroads, before you turn
> into Valencia or Grande, Castilian bequests,
> in back of that bar, cool and dark as prison,
> where a sunbeam dances through brown rum-bottles
> like a firefly through a thicket of cocoa,
> like an army torch looking for a guerrilla,
> the guerrilla with the gouged Spanish face named
> Sonora again climbs the track through wild bananas,
> sweat glued to his face like a hot cloth
> under the barber's hand. The jungle is steam.
> He would like to plunge his hands in those clouds
> on the next range. From Grande to Valencia
> the blue-green plain below breaks through the leaves.
> "Adios, then," said Estenzia. He went downhill
> And the army find him. The world keep the same. . . . (p. 51)

Reasserting itself at the end, where the opening lines are repeated with a difference, the standard English is tantamount to the majestic clouds on the next range, into which the likes of Sonora will never plunge their hands. But meanwhile English words have talked and a man different from the poet and his readers has emerged and become more important than the correct words. (His words are in the context the correct ones.) If he sounds clownish when he says, "A fly, big like a bee, dance on my rifle barrel/ like he knew who was holding it already dead," he speaks with a representative liveliness that has its own dignity and his mimetic enfranchisement is not unrelated to a possible political one—one that "a loss of heredity," as the last line of the poem somewhat fecklessly notes, "needs to create."

Hovering within the poem is the old complaint of the best laid plans of mice and men. The flesh is weak, heroism hard, we know that. But the poem gently exceeds a specific cultural malaise without diminishing it. Walcott may lack the ideologue's assurance of where to fix the blame, but here nothing is forgotten or excused or absolved.

The long title poem, ambitiously scaled to an international betrayal of the poor, is less happy, if in its tone and procedure wonderfully hush-hush:

> We are roaches,
> riddling the state cabinets, entering the dark holes
> of power, carapaced in topcoats,
> scuttling around columns, signalling for taxis,
> with frantic antennae, to other huddles with roaches;
> we infect with optimism, and when
> the cabinets crack, we are the first
> to scuttle, radiating separately
> back to Geneva, Bonn, Washington, London. (p. 90)

Queerly the speaker knows his own evil to a "t" — he even privately rehearses "the ecstasies of starvation," mimicking his victims. Who, exactly, does he represent? And why emphasize "white" evil as in "The heart of darkness is not Africa./ The heart of darkness is the core of fire/ in the white center of the holocaust . . . / the tinkling nickel instrument on the white altar" (pp. 93-94), as if Conrad had been wrong to locate it in everyone? Improbably the speaker foresees at the end his own nemesis: "through thin stalks,/ the smoking stubble, stalks/ grasshopper: third horseman,/ the leather-helmed locust" (p. 97), and this also seems too convenient. A brilliantly scary Third World political cartoon of The Man, the poem perhaps errs in endowing the speaker — that beetle-like criminal — with the poet's own blazing conscience: a poetic economy that falsifies.

"The Season of Phantasmal Peace," which follows it, is its sentimental obverse, a fable of "all the nations of birds" lifting together "the huge net of the shadows of this earth/ in multitudinous dialects" and flying it at a seasonless height invisible to those "wingless ones/ below them who shared dark holes in windows and in houses." In this precious fantasy men can't see the net of shadows except as light "at evening on the side of a hill/ in yellow October," and, to add to the confusion, the "season" of this "seasonless" Love "lasted one moment . . . / but, for such as our earth is now, it lasted long" (pp. 98-99). These conundrums are idle. The poem is effectively counter-political, distracting the reader from actual conditions. (Anyway this earthling would like the shadows, at least those "of long pines down trackless slopes," left where they belong.)

Even in political poetry the muse must be with you, your wits about you. But suppose Walcott were always to get it right, still you would want him on call for other things. If his exile's loose-endedness is a problem, heterogeneity is with him a grace, almost a way. (Even among the four political poems just examined the range of tone is unusual.) His powers long to travel and his sensibility enlarges everything to its widest limits.

At the level of style alone Walcott offers God's plenty. In addition to the aphoristic pentameter of the Spoiler, all tang, you find in *The Fortunate Traveller* morally exhausted hexameters:

> Under the blue sky of winter in Virginia
> the brick chimneys flute white smoke through skeletal
>   lindens,
> as a spaniel churns up a pyre of blood-rusted leaves;
> there is no memorial here to their Treblinka —
> as a van delivers from the ovens loaves
> as warm as flesh, its brakes jaggedly screech
> like the square wheel of a swastika. . . .
>   ("North and South," p. 14)

You find trimeters packed with word-painting and word-music:

> The edge-erasing mist

through which the sun was splayed
in radials has grayed
the harbor's amethyst. . . .
("A Sea Change," p. 19)

And maybe a dozen other manners. If so much versatility produces misgivings (it suggests a talent of easy virtue), the happier view is that Walcott is the sort of poet, very rare, in whom the accumulated resources of a tradition break on the present like a brilliant surf.

When you think of the volume as a whole you may miss purpose like a "tightened bow" but feel ready to scrap with anyone who wanted to take from you, say, "Early Pompeian," "Hurucan," "Wales," or "Jean Rhys," various though their subjects and treatments are and though only the last two are free of faults. One would miss in the first the delicate appreciation of the deepening and quickening of womanhood, the monstrous size of the father's grief over the stillbirth, and the demonic metaphors that, hurtingly inspired, wrest for their tenors the last affective truths. Or from "Hurucan" numerous descriptions of the furious storm, which proves "havoc, reminder, ancestor,/ and, when morning enters, pale/ as an insurance broker,/ god."

What have these poems, the first slowly traversing grief, the other all reportorial frenzy, a race to keep up with the hurricane, in common with the tidy, dignified "Wales," except a seizing craft and a demonic intensity of metaphor? "Wales" is peaceful and exciting, as classic art has always been. Patient, impersonal, remote, it reads like an inspired aside in some divine annal of the earth. The muse of history herself might be bemused by this concentrated yet casual evocation of a landscape saturated in past times:

Those white flecks cropping the ridges of Snowdon
will thicken their fleece and come wintering down
through the gap between alliterative hills,
through the caesura that let in the Legions,
past the dark disfigured mouths of the chapels,
till a white silence comes to green-throated Wales. (p. 87)

How assured each syllable is, validated by a usage that feels both old and young as the hills. (Among other felicities it is right that the short flinty *i* should not relent till the "white silence comes to green-throated Wales.") The authority of the writing seems uncanny, since Walcott can only have visited the country. It is with a ferreting genius that this Caribbean deprived of history goes after its insignia in other lands. In Wales he can feel even in the bones of the conqueror's language, which happens also to be his, a deep resistance to modernity:

A plump raven, Plantagenet, unfurls its heraldic
caw over walls that held the cult of the horse.
In blackened cottages with their stony hatred

of industrial fires, a language is shared
like bread to the mouth, white flocks to dark byres. (p. 87)

All three poems reflect, however differently, an imminent or actual "loss of heredity." (The rumor of this runs wild throughout the volume.) Jean Rhys has the same intelligence. A child when the nineteenth century was "beginning to groan sideways from the ax stroke!" she developed, like Sonora, a need to create, or so Walcott imagines in his beautiful poem on her Dominican childhood, where photographs mottled "like the left hand of some spinster aunt" place her among "bone-collared gentlemen/ with spiked mustaches/ and their wives embayed in the wicker-work/ armchairs" (p. 45). In the "furnace of boredom after church" (for the photographs are quickened into cinematic biography) "A maiden aunt canoes through lilies of clouds/ in a Carib hammock, to a hymn's metronome" while the child "sees the hills dip and straighten with each lurch" (p. 46). She will become, this girl whose senses are sharpened by "the cement grindstone of the afternoon," a writer about women whose every waking moment — in Paris, in London — seems a lurch. (Often they are left in one.) But back before the mania of history, when "grace was common as malaria," this fierce writer foresaw, from a lion-footed couch, her own hard salvation, such as it was: her calling as a writer.

. . . the gas lanterns' hiss on the veranda
drew the aunts out like moths
doomed to be pressed in a book, to fall
into the brown oblivion of an album,
embroiderers of silence
for whom the arches of the Thames,
Parliament's needles,
and the petit-point reflections of London Bridge
fade on the hammock cushions from the sun,
where one night
a child stares at the windless candle flame
from the corner of a lion-footed couch
at the erect white light,
her right hand married to *Jane Eyre*
forseeing that her own white wedding dress
will be white paper. (p. 47)

One notices the sureness and seductive power of the detail and, increasingly, of the pacing. Admirable too is the unforced biographical allusion (Rhys was to know a very different London from the souvenir scenes fading on the cushions and to write the story of the first Mrs. Rochester, mad and Creole, in *Wide Sargasso Sea*). And the contrast between the "brown oblivion" of the spinster aunts and the white-paper wedding dress is poignantly complex (since writing is both sexual and abstinent, the page an eternal union and virginal). Besides dowering Rhys's parched sensibility with his own lush and delicate range of impressions, with this poem, so different from the others, Walcott at once fixes and graces her, and implicitly himself, with the myth of what Grahame Greene called the "fatal moment." Here the accidents and irrelations of a Sunday afternoon transcend themselves, becoming the provocation of a marriage and a destiny. The gentle, Proustian movement of the poem, the syntax branching and branching as if desiring never to break with the moment, first conceals then delivers the inexorable. Even the solecism of the recurring "at" (in "at the erect white light") is suitably riveting. The structure is not ambitious but (in both senses) holds. As writing, we are given to understand, holds every writer — in a curiously alert fascination and a marriage with the muse that is too like celibacy to be altogether happy: at best a privileged loneliness.

"Jean Rhys" is contemporary in the sense most poetry is — it is written as if from a tragically privileged position within time, not an inhumanly privileged one outside it. Beyond that it's Contemporary in the peculiar sense intended in this review: it faces on time not as what coheres but as what disperses, not as what can be mastered but as what must be endured. This, too, is old. What is new is the nakedness with which it is suffered.

Footnote

[1] Andrew Salkey's anthology, *Breaklight* (1971), like his own long poem *Jamaica* (1973), seems designed to make the Caribbeans feel good, indeed a little righteous, about being Caribbean, and heady with their future ("Culture come when you buck up/on you'self"). Walcott, with his comparatively international intellect, his assimilation of English poetry, and his peculiarly strong sense of Contemporary loneliness, stands apart. He "participates in the celebration of a West Indian consciousness that has evolved from an unlikely history and from an insular separateness," as Lloyd W. Brown puts it in *West Indian Poetry*, but "his much greater emphasis on the persistence of individual separation tempers his perception of a communal or regional identity." So does his analysis "of the . . . tensions . . . between the moral and emotional promise of a communally perceived ideal and the human failings which blunt that promise."

ONE WALCOTT, AND HE WOULD BE MASTER

Richard Dwyer

The publication of Derek Walcott's new book of verse, *The Fortunate Traveller,* (Farrar, Straus & Giroux Inc., 1982) has brought forth a number of thoughtful retrospective reviews of his lifework. Those by Helen Vendler in the *New York Review of Books,* entitled "Poet of Two Worlds," and by Denis Donoghue in the *New York Times Book Review,* called "The Two Sides of Derek Walcott," are among the best, as well as being symptomatic of how close commentary on Walcott is to depositing a cliché. Their titles tell most of the story. Walcott is seen as living a kind of schizoid life, divided between the allegiance of much of his verse to British literature, the classics, and now, American culture, while his plays cling to the accents of Trinidad and aspire to give his region's people the heroes that V.S. Naipaul claims they deny themselves. Variants on this assessment, particularly among Caribbean writers, see Walcott divided into the personae of Exile and Castaway, and expressing both essential rootlessness and anguished racination, or they pit his squinting celebration of the islands against Naipaul's transcendant cynicism. Real experts at this game go on to attribute the contrast to the relatively greater security of the descendants of plantation slaves on the one hand and anxiety of the more recent East Indian economic immigrants on the other.

While all of this is true, it needs qualification if Walcott's full stature, or at least the one he hopes for, is to be appreciated, particularly in the Caribbean. One obstacle to a larger assessment is Walcott himself, who has endlessly abetted this split image from the time of his very earliest poems. Witness the well-known lines of "A Far Cry from Africa": "How choose/Between this Africa and the English tongue I love?/Betray them both or give back what they give?" In the language of the *Norton Anthology of English Literature,* Walcott explores the anxieties and opportunities of Third World status, according to his critics. It is true that he encourages this impression by complaining of the pains and pleasures of exile—or at least sojourns abroad. And he acknowledges the discontents of racination: "I am growing hoarse/from repeating the praise/of the ape and the ass,/the enslaved, the indentured,/who are nothing" ("At Last" — *Sea Grapes,* p. 79).

The limitless Caribbean seascapes are as beautiful as they are boring; "There is too much nothing here." And he hates colonial history—his own version of the night-mare from which Joyce's Stephen Dedalus was trying to escape. He hates the squalor of the slums of empire, and, above all, he hates the local "Mimic Men"—the vulgar imitators of power politics, cheap exploiters of Third World dreams, tawdry sellouts to coin of a dozen overseas origins: "that new race of dung beetles, frock-coated,/ iridescent/ crawling over the people" ("Hic Jacet" — *The Gulf*, p. 110)). His other gestures toward the image of his own bifurcation are manifold, ranging from the titles of his early books, like *The Castaway* (1965) and *The Gulf* (1969) to the organization of the latest volume into the sections "North, South, North." Now, at least financially secure, he would make his own qualification as to the meaning of his dual nature, in an interview with the Trinidad *Express* (3/14/82), by saying that "I think I have achieved a *balance* between being in the United States and Trinidad."

But all of this is merely to make an arbitrary division of his subject matter, topics, themes, and essential imagery into two piles and to miss the fundamental distinction between all of that on the one hand, and on the other, his self-conception as an artist. This is the new distinction I would make as a contribution toward placing him among the company of his real peers and reinterpreting the meaning of those "two worlds."

The evidence for a rereading is everywhere in his books, if we can get beyond the idea that he is one more victim of empire, another of Frantz Fanon's psychiatric casualties, mooning like Caliban about his island, pursued by patronizing cries of "O, brave Third World!" Absolutely central to the evidence is his book *Another Life* (1973). This masterpiece is his equivalent both of Wordsworth's *Prelude* and Joyce's *A Portrait of the Artist as a Young Man*. It is a spiritual autobiography narrating the growth of the poet's mind. From the epigraph to the first section, "The Divided Child," commentators have drawn one of the chief images of his situation. But a full citation of the passage that he takes from André Malraux's *Psychology of Art* will show that it has been narrowly interpreted to yield a colonial, rather than a human, message: "An old story goes that Cimabue was struck with admiration when he saw the shepherd boy, Giotto, sketching sheep. But, according to the true biographies, it is never the sheep that inspire a Giotto with the love of painting: but, rather, his first sight of the paintings of such a man as Cimabue. What makes the artist is the circumstance that in his youth he was more deeply moved by the sight of the works of art than by that of the things which they portray."

There is the heart of the matter: works of art versus the things of this world. This crucial passage speaks of the division felt by everyone, from the islands of the Aegean, the North Sea, or the Caribbean. who strives to add to the real world into which he was fortuitously born another ideal world of art and civilization, chosen by vocation. The contrast is not simply between one culture and another, but between everyday life and the life of the imagination as cultivated by centuries of artistic tradition.

For us, the principal component of this tradition is the place of excellence in its ideology. The hierarchical structure of earlier Europe permitted, as a consequence of the concentration of surplus wealth in the hands of a small class of aristocrats, the elaboration of a self-justifying idea of excellence through many aspects of that society. From the notion of excellent people who deserve their privileges, the concept is easily broadened to include the works made for them and eventually the makers of those works; although it took a Petrarch to assert the "nobility" of the poet's calling.

From its adherents, the tradition demands extreme craftsmanship, in contrast to the products of popular, mass, or provincial culture, as well as allegiance to a standard language and its decorums, a vast arcana of knowledge gleaned from Greco-Roman and Judeo-Christian traditions, and a deep anxiety about belonging to the Happy, Fit, Chosen Few. I think it is clear that Walcott has elected himself to this elite and that his explicit statements constitute as much of a claim to membership as his poetry reflects that club's benefits and liabilities.

For one thing, in the *Express* interview just cited, Walcott praises the colonial system of education and its adherence to a standard language. "Art is not democratic, art is hierarchical, and all artists know that. They know that it takes all your life to achieve some level where you can be among your peers. But if immediately your peers are made to be the illiterate, or the people who feel education is restricted entirely to self-expression without craft, then society is in danger. It is in more danger than it is from terrorists and revolutionaries. . .The whole process of civilization is cyclical. The good civilization absorbs a certain amount, like the Greeks. Empires are smart enough to steal from the people they conquer. They steal the best things. And the people who have been conquered should have enough sense to steal back." Most recently, in an excerpt from his forthcoming autobiography, *American Without America*, printed in *Antaeus* (Spring/Summer, 1982), Walcott gives a glimpse of his feverish search for the best things a St. Lucian student could steal:

> What names, what objects do I remember from that time? The brown-covered *Penguin Series of Modern Painters:* Stanley Spencer, Frances Hodgkins, Paul Nash, Ben Nicholson; the pocket-sized Dent edition of Thomas's *Death and Entrances,* the Eliot recordings of *Four Quartets,* dropped names like Graham Sutherland, and Carola and Ben Fleming's and Harry's reminiscences of ICA student days. and Harry's self-belittling anecdote of how he had once heard that Augustus John was aboard a cruise ship and he had rushed up to see him with a pile of canvases and how John, agreeing to look at them, had glared back and said. "You can't paint, but I admire your brass!," *BIM* magazine, Henry Swanzy's Caribbean Voices programme, *Caribbean Quarterly,* and the first West Indian novels, *New Day* and *A Morning at the Office.* Once Mittelholzer had sat in our drawing room and warned me to give up writing verse-tragedies, because "they" would never take them.

What these passages indicate is both the range and variety of the matter of his vocation — not two worlds but many — and the deep division between that artistic vocation and the illiterate victims who neglect the master's lesson in stealing. In addition to these explicit statements, I would turn now to the poetic fruits of his vocation, especially as they reveal the self-concept of the journeyman bard. Elsewhere in *Another Life,* that pivotal book reveals the Wordsworthian echos that lifted the young poet to a sentimental ecstasy:

About the August of my fourteenth year
I lost myself somewhere above a valley. . .
and I dissolved into a trance.
I was seized by a pity more profound
than my young body could bear, I climbed
with the labouring smoke,
I drowned in labouring breakers of bright cloud,
then uncontrollably I began to weep
inwardly, without tears, with a serene extinction of all
sense. . . (p. 42-43)

That is the language of someone toiling in what Harold Bloom would call an extreme "anxiety of influence," Oedipally wrestling Wordsworth to the ground in a rite of poetic passage that will qualify him for admission to the Visionary Company of poets on Fortune's Hill. This child is divided between real hills—whether cactus-strewn in St. Lucia or gorse-covered in Westmoreland, and the ideal peaks that poets have ascended since Parnassus.

Later on, the youth tells of his First Love. Here, the tale tastes more like Joyce than Wordsworth, and ventures into that self-conscious estheticization of the erotic experience, as he describes a walk with a girl already passing into metaphor:

And which of them in time would be betrayed
was never questioned by that poetry
which breathed within the evening naturally,
but by the noble treachery of art
that looks for fear when it is least afraid,
that coldly takes the pulse-beat of the heart
in happiness; that praised its need to die
to the bright candour of the evening sky,
that preferred love to immortality;
so every step increased that subtlety
which hoped that their two bodies could be made
one body of immortal metaphor.
The hand she held already had betrayed
them by its longing for describing her. (p. 94)

Poor Anna in this passage was of course not content with joining the poetic company of Beatrice, Laura, Stella, and Idea. Complaining that she was, on the contrary, "as simple as salt," she left the poet to his guilty fictionizing. But we can take both of these episodes as clear testimony that we have on our hands a classic poet, divided between the world of muddy hills and freckled girls and those rarer realms of literary transformation.

For such an artist, as it was for Joyce, physical exile could only be a life sentence to the imaginative re-creation of reality into the meaningful categories of western

art. That art has many voices and vocabularies. It should not be surprising that a
writer with such rich and varied experience as Walcott should use a great range of
them in his creation. *The Fortunate Traveller* shows many of them at work, and it
would be a profound mistake to reduce them to two. In addition to the elementary
distinction between the voices of calypso and Jacobean tragedy that the reviewers
have detected here, we can hear, for example, the precious accents of Wallace
Stevens:

> The sun dries the avenue's pumice façade
> delicately as a girl tamps tissue on her cheek;
> the asphalt shines like a silk hat,
> the fountains trot like percherons round the Met,
> clip, clop, clip, clop in Belle Epoque Manhattan,
> as gutters part their lips to the spring rain—
> ("Piano Practice," p. 9)

And we can thrill in the presence of Robert Lowell's Yankee agonies:

> A white church spire whistles into space
> like a swordfish, a rocket pierces heaven
> as the thawed springs in icy chevrons race
> down hillsides and Old Glories flail
> the crosses of green farm boys back from 'Nam.
> ("Old New England," p. 3)

And we behold William Carlos William's sturdy images:

> No billboard model
> but a woman, gaunt,
> in a freckled print,
> some bony aunt
> whose man broke down at the steel mill,
> whose daughter chews wild grain in some commune in
> Arizona,
> whose son is a wreath of dried corn
> nailed to the door;
> ("American Muse," p. 7)

While an unsympathetic reviewer might lump all this together as derivative, I
think for Walcott these echoes constitute the array of coin in which the journeyman
poet pays tribute to his peers.

Leaving behind this miscellaneous evidence of Walcott's self-conception, I would
turn now to a single poem from *The Fortunate Traveller* to make a more analytical
case. Reviewers have tended to focus on the same poems, and none of us will attempt

to unravel the persona and telegraphic drama of the book's title poem. For my special purposes, "The Hotel Normandie Pool" will do nicely

To begin with, this eight-page poem is about writing poetry, one sure and perhaps telling theme of the greatest poets. Its occasion is a visit to Port of Spain, Trinidad, and some reveries during the composition of a poem at poolside. In images that play with fluidity, reflection, surface and shadow, the poem is thematically autobiographical: "For this my fiftieth year, /I muttered to the ribbon-medalled water, /Change me, my sign, to someone I can bear" (p. 64). Such narcissism leads the poet to Aquarian reflections on himself, his swimming daughters, the career of Ovid, the problem of exile, the springs and uses of poetry.

The four-page second section rehearses an envisioned visit of the shade of Ovid to the pool. That Master recalls his own exile from Rome, daughter, language, and origin to the Gothic frontier town of Tomis on the Black Sea. The consolation offered by this spirit is that exile made his verses better, "till, on a tablet smooth as the pool's skin,/I made reflections that, in many ways,/were even stronger than their origin" (p. 68). In the contrast between the Romans, mocking his slavish rhyme, and the slaves, who scorned his love of Roman structures, we can feel the tension of Walcott's own two readerships, north and south. But, as he insists in self-defense, art obeys its own order. Finally, in answer to the writer's question, Ovid's echo ripples: "Why here, of all places,/a small, suburban tropical hotel/its pool pitched to a Mediterranean blue/its palms rusting in their concrete oasis?/Because to make my image flatters you" (p. 69).

The final section, one page long, recalls us to the reality that poets share with the rest of us: "no laurel, but the scant applause/ of one dry, scraping palm tree." The poem ends in an image repeated frequently in Walcott's best work: Sunset, never supposed to fall on the outposts of Empire, now brings with it repose, closure, speechlessness, "Suspension of every image and its voice./The mangoes pitch from their green dark like meteors./The fruit bat swings on its branch, a tongueless bell" (p. 70). Self-conscious of self-flattery, Walcott nevertheless associates himself on several levels with the classic poet-exile, Ovid, the *magister.* Is there any verity in this vanity? Some.

There is growing acceptance on the part of the machinery of literary production that Derek Walcott belongs with the best. When Philip Larkin put together the *Oxford Book of Twentieth Century English Verse* in 1965, he broke his own rules in order to include Walcott, who at that time had published a single volume. Although Larkin excluded poems by American and Commonwealth writers, Walcott gets almost six pages — one more than was allotted to his contemporary Ted Hughes. Richard Ellmann's *Norton Anthology of Modern Poetry* also makes room for, to my thinking, an idiosyncratic little selection of five poems. Now that Walcott has been admitted to the company of Boston University and has received the prestigious and lucrative award of the MacArthur Foundation, he is accumulating the trappings that should qualify him for the company of his peers: The next *Oxford Book of Modern Verse* — the last was edited by W. B. Yeats in 1935 — and the next *Oxford Book of English Verse,* which hasn't been redone since Sir Arthur Quiller-Couch's edition of 1900. If he continues to sharpen his aim at excellence and eludes the snares of success and notoriety, Derek Walcott, the journeyman, may yet make Master.

HEIR APPARENT

Sven Birkerts

Midsummer by Derek Walcott

Last October 17, in one of the more unlikely ceremonial moments in the world of poetry, Derek Walcott mounted the high pulpit in New York's Cathedral Church of St. John the Divine to read his "Eulogy for W. H. Auden" (TNR, November 21, 1983). The event was part of a week-long commemoration of the tenth anniversary of Auden's death. What could have been a greater study in contrasts — a powerfully knit black poet from the Caribbean declaiming lines to honor the whey-faced and rumpled don of English-language letters? And what could have been more appropriate? If poets are, by definition, suitors of the Muse, then these two have been, in our age, among her special favorites. They have perceived more than others that she is a woman with a past.

Walcott has been writing poetry for some four decades now. He apprenticed himself to the English tradition and has never strayed far from the declamatory lyrical line. His mentors, the voices that one hears running as a weft through his lines, include the Elizabethans and Jacobeans, Wordsworth, Tennyson, Yeats, Hardy, and Robert Lowell (who himself sought to incorporate that tradition into his work). Reverberating against this diction one hears the local influences, the dialect phrases and constructions of the Caribbean. The whole heritage is there, but it is quickened and jazzed — and entirely unique.

In the crisis-ridden decades of the 1950s and 1960s, when poets took up various cudgels — for free verse, projectivism, beat prosody, confessionalism, a return to American roots, and so on— Walcott's work was little heeded. He was always to one side of the current excitement. But power and craft like his could not be kept off the stage forever, no more than poetry could keep going without its central sustenance: metric structure. In the last ten years, as the productions of our tenured poets have proved increasingly feeble and enervated, Walcott has moved forward to claim his rightful place. *The Star-Apple Kingdom* (1979) and *The Fortunate Traveller* (1981) were both major collections. The poet had found a way to fuse the diction of his masters with his own energetic and sensuous idiom. Now in *Midsummer*, with all the grace and gall of a writer at his prime, he has essayed the most hazardous of ventures.

Midsummer is a fifty-four-poem sequence that was written over the course of two summers in Trinidad. We don't need a calculator to figure out that's about a poem every other day — and these are solid seventeen-to-thirty line compositions. Poets have been known to compose at such a rate — think of Byron, Neruda, Berryman, or Lowell in his *Notebooks* period — but it is hardly common practice. The risks are so obvious: repetition, slackness, the stretching of material. But Walcott has taken them on for a shot at the rewards — velocity, immediacy, and freshness. And he has upped the ante by avoiding dramatic progression or continuity of subject. These are the meditations of a middle-aged prodigal son, nothing more. The intent is evident. By taking away drama, subject, and any sort of finishing varnish, Walcott is forcing the full weight of scrutiny onto the lines. The poetry has nothing to hide behind — no tricks, no feints. It's an all-or-nothing gamble, and it succeeds.

Poetry in recent years has become more and more bound up with the magazine industry. A poet puts out twenty or thirty separate "pieces" and then collects them into a book. The ancient tribal song has been groomed and pomaded until it looks like a whisper. *Midsummer,* ragged-edged and robust, is anything but a magazine book. Its lines are like the links of a chain saw moving through the broad trunk of a life. We are to look at the cloven bole, its rings, whorls, and irregularities. Connections and links have not been engineered — they are implicit and organic. If there are chips and splinters, so be it. Walcott would have it no other way. Here is his own metaphor:

> . . . My palms have been sliced by the twine
> of the craft I have pulled at for more than forty years.
> My Ionia is the smell of burnt grass, the scorched handle
> of a cistern in August squeaking to rusty islands;
> the lines I love have all their knots left in
> — XXV

Midsummer: boredom, stasis, the harsh afternoon glare of self-assessment. Midsummer equals mid-career, middle age, Dante's "*mezzo del cammin di nostra vita.* . . ." The only real narrative prop that we have for any of these numbered poems is given in the first. The poet, comfortably identified with the "I" of the speaking voice, is returning by air to his old island home. The plane descends over "pages of earth . . . canefields set in stanzas," and as the wheels touch the tarmac he exclaims:

> It comes too fast, this shelving sense of home —
> canes rushing the wing, a fence; a world that still stands as
> the trundling tires keep shaking and shaking the heart.

Walcott has the Ovidian gift; his compressions, associations, and transformations appear effortless. So, in this poem, the jet is likened to a silverfish that "bores . . . through volumes of cloud," clouds are linked to the coral shapes below, and both become "pages in a damp culture that come apart." As the clouds part to reveal the island, while the jet's shadow ripples over the jungle "as steadily as a minnow," Walcott suddenly wrenches open the frame to apostrophize a fellow poet:

> ... Our sunlight is shared by Rome
> and your white paper, Joseph. Here, as everywhere else,
> it is the same age. In cities, in settlements of mud,
> light has never had epochs.

But two lines later he is back, noting "steeples so tiny you couldn't hear their bells." Space and time are like baker's dough to this man; he kneads, stretches and punches them as he sees fit. Nor is he afraid to hook a thought to its prompting detail, however unlikely the connection. His faith in the elasticity of the metered line is complete.

The poems that follow are no less various in their internal composition. Though mainly grounded in the Caribbean, and attentive to local detail, they are as diverse as Walcott's own nature. There are passages of intense expressionistic observation —

> ... Monotonous lurid bushes
> brush the damp clouds with ideograms of buzzards
> over the Chinese groceries. . .
> —VI

side by side with solemn brooding —

> I can sense it coming from far, too, Maman, the tide
> since day has passed its turn . . .
> —XV

and sudden celebratory surges —

> ... Midsummer bursts
> out of its body, and its poems come unwarranted,
> as when, hearing what sounds like rain, we startle a place
> where a waterfall crashes down rocks. Abounding grace!
> —VIII

The range is restricted only by the circumstances of compressed composition and the psyche's inevitable recurrences.

The visual is one strong component in Walcott's work. He has a painter's eye for shape and color value and a strong sense of proportion. Descriptive elements in the poem are arranged as if words and their sounds were equivalent to pigments:

> Gnats drill little holes around a saw-toothed cactus,
> a furnace has curled the knives of the oleander,

> and a branch of the logwood blurs with wild characters.
> A stone house waits on the steps. Its white porch blazes.
> —XXV

This structure and detail-oriented instinct can be said to represent Walcott's objective pole. But the subjective counterpart is there in equal portion. Sharply etched descriptions give way to dark surges, upright consonants lean over like palms in a storm. At times Walcott will flash back and forth between the two poles, at other times he will force them into fusion. These are his supreme moments — when he modulates into passionate declaration:

> O Christ, my craft, and the long time it is taking!
> Sometimes the flash is seen, a sudden exultation
> of lightning fixing earth in its place; the asphalt's skin
> smells freshly of childhood in the drying rain.
> Then I believe that it is still possible, the happiness
> of truth. . . .
> —XIII

If nothing is rarer in poetry than this note, it is because nothing is riskier. Full-throated ease is something our culture has unlearned.

It is impossible, of course, to give a fair account of a cycle like this. Walcott is trying to fix, in sharp, living lines, the particular texture of his inner life during the course of two summers. The ambition carries certain hazards in its train. A certain monotony, for one thing. Reading the undifferentiated stanzas from start to finish can be like wandering around in a rain forest. There is something almost vegetal in the proliferation of Walcott's lines. How can anyone produce so many naturally flexed hexameters so quickly?

Walcott is not, of course, blind to the repetitious nature of his project — he wants it to be that way. He tests the constraints of subject that seem to inhere in metric verse, but he does so from within. Like Cézanne, who painted hill after hill because hills were not what he was interested in, Walcott writes poem after poem with little differentiation of subject. His settings and descriptions are, in a sense, pretexts. He would like to throw out as much as possible in order to clear a path to his real subject: language becoming poetry.

Poetry, like speech, is a complex connivance of sound and sense. The lyrical ideal is a condition in which the two are seamlessly joined. Or, better yet, a condition in which it becomes clear that sound is a kind of sense, and vice versa. For as sense is proper to the mind, so sound is to the heart. And the heart, as great lyric poets have always known, is the tribunal before which reason lays its spoils. "To betray philosophy," writes Walcott, "is the gentle treason / of poets. . . ." He is reducing, or eliminating as much as possible, the ostensible subject of the poem, so that the plaiting movement of sound and sense can show itself. This is not an evasion of subject so much as a deeper perception of the poet's function.

Walcott is re-establishing the sound, the music, as a connection to felt and perceived experience. When he writes:

> The oak inns creak in their joints as light declines
> from the ale-coloured skies of Warwickshire.
> Autumn has blown the froth from the foaming orchards,
> so white-haired regulars draw chairs nearer the grate
> to spit on logs that crackle into leaves of fire.
> —XXXVI

he is promoting the status of sound as meaning and is arguing against the notion that meaning is some kind of detachable content. The treason of poets is to believe that sonorousness and rhythmic emphasis establish a body circuit through experience that reason alone cannot achieve.

Walcott writes a strongly accented, densely packed line that seldom slackens and yet never loses conversational intimacy. He works in form, but he is not formal. His agitated phonetic surfaces can at times recall Lowell's, but the two are quite different. In Lowell, one feels the torque of mind; in Walcott, the senses predominate. And Walcott's lines ring with a spontaneity that Lowell's often lack:

> White sanderlings race the withdrawing surf to pick,
> with wink-quick stabs, the shellfish between the pebbles.
> —XLVIII

There is not a single forced emphasis. The lines are at once mimetic — the "withdrawing surf" is perfectly off-set by the "wink-quick" beaks — and perfectly natural.

Though Walcott is very much aware of the assaults that modernism has waged upon the metric line, he has elected to work with its possibilities. In part this is a matter of temperament. But there is also the matter of the poet's unique relation to the English language. He acquired in the Caribbean an English very different from that spoken by his counterparts in England and America. Not only is the region a linguistic seed-bed, with every kind of pidgin and dialect, but successive waves of colonization (and oppression) have left phenocrysts of all descriptions. As Walcott said in a recent interview in *The Threepenny Review:*

> . . . it's very hard for people to understand my love of the Jacobean —
> it's not from a distance. If you hear a guy from Barbados, or Jamaica,
> speaking English, and you listen to that speech, you hear seventeenth-
> century constructions. I once heard in *Henry V* a soldier speaking in a
> Yorkshire dialect and it sounded like pure Barbadian speech.

Walcott's traditional metric is more than a simple act of homage to the past — it is the most expeditious way for him to organize his complex linguistic heritage. Controlled by a firm structure, each element of that heritage can declare itself. And the various distinctions, as anyone in the third world can testify, are not just historical; they are political as well:

> for so much here is the Empire envied and hated
> that whether one chooses to say *"ven-thes"* or *"ven-ces"*
> involves the class struggle as well. . . .
> —XLIII

There is no one writing in English at present who can join power with delicacy the way Walcott can. He is the outsider, the poet from the periphery, but it may be time to center the compass at his position and draw the circle again.

THE PAINTER AS POET: DEREK WALCOTT'S *MIDSUMMER*

Robert Bensen

An island of obsessive beauty, a people impoverished but rich in their cultural heritage from Africa and Europe, and a lifetime to celebrate them in art: these gifts had been given the young Derek Walcott, who swore with his friend Dunstan St. Omer not to leave St. Lucia before they had put the island on canvas and in words — every ravine, inlet, mangrove swamp and hill track.[1]

Walcott had been drawn to art early by being "more deeply moved by the sight of works of art than by that of the things which they portray," as Malraux wrote of Giotto. Walcott used Malraux's anecdote as an epigraph in *Another Life*, in which he wrote of his discovering art as if he were Saul, blinded with revelation of the true religion *(AL*, p. 1). His will alone could "transfigure" the mountain shacks of the poor into a "cinquecento fragment in gilt frame" *(AL, p.* 4). He felt the power of art to recreate the world, to transcend the poverty of those shacks, to redeem his dispossessed people and their history. The task was as immense as that of Adam standing before his unnamed world, though Walcott had this advantage: in the books of his father's library, he had inherited the work of centuries of European masters.

The West Indian reverence for ancestors became for Walcott a need to assimilate tradition, to assume its features, to make it part of his visual vocabulary. He believed that his knowledge of tradition would augment his treatment of the island's water-color seas, its vegetation ripe for oils. But where St. Omer painted "with the linear elation of an eel," Walcott's own hand was "crabbed by that style,/this epoch, that school/or the next" *(AL, p.* 59). Tradition proved too powerful a master; he was its sunstruck Caliban.

His gift emerged instead in the multiple facets of metaphor, in language as physical as what it described. Horace's critical observation, *ut pictura poesis,* Walcott made into a conduit for painting to nourish his poetry, in the character of his imagemaking, his visual imagination, as well as in his sense of line and composition. Painting pervades his use of metaphor, as in this imagistic Moebius strip in which art and life imitate each other endlessly: "the hills stippled with violet/ as if they had seen Pissarro," or in this rendering of a seascape as still life: "A peel of lemon sand/curled like a rind across the sea's blue dish" *(AL* p. 74; pp. 65-6).

The connection between poet and painter in Walcott lies deeper than eye-level, being rooted in his early, most basic experience of the world. *Another Life* is the autobiography of his life as a young artist, an intimate Odyssey in which he first experiences the primal facts of life and death through art. He undertakes the conventional epic journey to the underworld, the land of the dead, which he finds in books of paintings by the European masters:

> I learnt their strict necrology of dead kings,
> bones freckling the rushes of damp tombs,
> the light-furred luminous world of Claude,
> their ruined temples, and in drizzling twilights, Turner.
> (—*AL,* p. 44)

Among the relics of art, he recognizes his father, who is not his natural father (also a painter, but who had died young) and not the liturgical Our-Father-who-art-in-heaven, but "Our father,/who floated in the vaults of Michelangelo" *(AL, p. 44)*. His spiritual father could be accessible only through art, wherein Walcott collects his true heritage and recognizes his future.

> it was then
>   that he fell in love, having no care
> for truth,
>   that he could enter the doorway of a triptych,
> that he believed
>   those three stiff horsemen cantering past a rock,
>   towards jewelled cities on a cracked horizon,
>   that the lances of Uccello shivered him,
>   like Saul, unhorsed,
> that he fell in love with art,
>   and life began.
> (—*AL,* p. 44)

If European art was a reliquary, it was also a revelation. He fell in love with its power over him and with the power it places in the hands of the very few.

Ars longa, vita brevis. Those chosen by the Muse must devote their lives to the practice of her art; there is no other way. In Walcott's Caribbean, the artist, the storyteller, the poet, the *raconteur, houngan,* or priest; all exercise power over domains beyond the ken of the uninitiated — the past, the future, the dead, the fortunes and misfortunes of the living. The monumental certainty of vocation in Walcott's poetry comes out of a selfhood that is forged in a culture rather more distant from that of the United States than has been generally recognized in this country. Certainly the

magnitude of his appropriation of European traditions in art and literature for his
life-long effort to make poetry and painting "cohere" and ultimately "ignite" suggests
the primal role of the artist as a tribal, and Promethean, fire-starter, on whom the
survival of his people depends *(AL,* p. 58-9).

Painting has always been at the heart of Walcott's poetry, as central as St. Omer's
altarpiece is to the Roseau Valley in "St. Lucie," in which the painting reflects the life
of the valley that surrounds it.[2] The preoccupation with painting in the autobio-
graphic mode of *Another Life* moves toward self-portraiture in *Midsummer.* [3] In the
former volume, painting is the occasion for the high drama of self-discovery, as the
author recounts his enthusiasm and disappointment as a young painter. After thirty
years of devotion to both arts, the episodic narrative of the young painter continues in
Midsummer in poems frequently conceived and composed as verbal paintings —
portraits, landscapes, seascapes, studies and sketches. Painting informs many of the
poems directly as subject ("Gauguin" XIX and "Watteau" XX), as a source of
imagery, in the handling of qualities of light and color, and in the range of themes.
Painting prompts his intense scrutiny of his motives for art, of large historical
questions about the relationship between art and power, and of the value of art in the
confrontation of human mortality.

I

Midsummer is the poet's sketchbook, the artist's diary, running the course of one
year from summer to summer. It is less a recording or a chronology than it is a
clearing of vision, an arrangement of things in their true significance, which is what
both painter and poet mean by composition:

> Through the stunned afternoon, when it's too hot to think
> and the muse of this inland ocean still waits for a name,
> and from the salt, dark room, the tight horizon line
> catches nothing, I wait. Chairs sweat. Paper crumples the
> floor.
> A lizard gasps on the wall. The sea glares like zinc.
> Then, in the door light: not Nike loosening her sandal,
> but a girl slapping sand from her foot, one hand on the frame.
> (— XXV)

Light, its movements and textures and intensities and absence, is all. It glazes the
brilliant seascape and shades the room, both of which the poet has carefully prepared
as ground for the figure of one of his daughters, or the nameless muse herself, coming
in from the beach. She is also the artist's model, her silhouette balanced momentarily
in one long line that is backlit by the previous line. Her image is both painterly and
sculptural, classical and modern. She is not Nike, but she assumes her pose *à la* Degas,
which Walcott alters both toward the Baroque by her hand's bracing against the
frame, and toward a sly Post-Modernist pun, as the frame itself is framed within the

poetic image. The loving portrait is in part the work of a bored father with nothing to do but wait for his daughter and her everyday grace. It is also the work of a poet with a painter's eye for nuances of light and composition, for the suggestion of the figure's weight, balance and form in the girl's gesture. Her very being, in its simplicity, answers the poet's masked self-portrait which begins the poem ("The sun has fired my face to terra-cotta") and the Faustian promise of the surf that he

> . . . shall see transparent Helen pass like a candle
> flame in sunlight, weightless as woodsmoke that hazes
> the sand with no shadow.
> (— XXV)

The girl is neither mask nor spirit. She is just what the poet had been fishing for with the horizon line, a well-made pun on his own poetic line. Until she enters, his lines have caught nothing of moment, merely the momentary, the static objects at hand which, lacking her presence, fail to cohere into composition. The setting needs her, the poetic line needs her, the artist needs her—indeed, her coming allows time, which had nearly ceased in the poet's torpor, to resume. She is no more than a sketch, but those quick, bold strokes of the pen bear the emotional weight of the poem.

Where the young painter in *Another Life* wanted to surround his island's shacks with a gilt frame, the seasoned master in *Midsummer* concludes that "the frame of human happiness is time," knowing that the frame of time is art. At the beginning of *Another Life,* line after line calls back the moment when light failed and his drawing was done, and his future as a painter seemed assured. The poet stitches his lines into a verbal net that pulls the moment back and holds it, briefly: "I begin here again,/begin until this ocean's/a shut book . . . . /Begin with twilight . . . " (*AL*, p. 3).

In *Midsummer,* time has entered the very lines, extending their duration, becoming part of the artist's gesture. The apparent ease with which the girl in the doorway is fixed in portraiture lies in the grace of the poetic line swelling beyond the surface tension of iambic pentameter, the measure most conformable to English phrasing and rhythm. Walcott uses that meter elsewhere in poetry and verse plays with Elizabethan richness and Jacobean wit. But in *Midsummer* he takes deep draughts of the warm Caribbean air and his line lengthens with the amplitude of his West Indian English. It lengthens as the fecund Caribbean crowds into his field of vision. The poems press toward the white margin like a sea of words at high tide. And because time moves slowly in the tropics, the line takes longer to ripen, all motion slows but that of the mind and the mind's eye:

> Something primal in our spine makes the child swing
> from the gnarled trapeze of a sea-almond branch.
> I have been comparing the sea-almond's shapes to the
>   suffering
> in Van Gogh's orchards. And that, too, is primal. A bunch

of sea grapes hangs over the calm sea. . .
(—XXVIII)

Here is the poet at ease, on holiday with his daughters, getting a few lines down in his sketchbook, perhaps for *Midsummer's* cover painting of the sea-almond tree, as well as for the poem. The long lines might read as prose, did not the end-rhymes staple the aural canvas taut for the internal Pointillism of vowels and consonants, which register on the ear as a patterned aura around the shape of the child. The long vowels in *primal, spine,* and *child* establish a declarative line that anchors the precarious *swing* as firmly as the baroque branch anchors the child in the second line, with its clustered consonants twisting around the darker *e*'s and *a*'s. The initial long *i*'s, the firm open tones of the poet's meditative mind-set, prepare the ear for the stroke of the ideogrammatic I, the body's slender stalk from which the poem's speculative intelligence will branch.

Comparing the sea-almond's shape to that of Van Gogh's olive trees is neither pretentious nor an idle exercise of Postcolonial wit. Rather, he is asserting the validity of his experience and culture in that island which is "known . . . for making nothing" (I). In his youth, he had imagined the landscape transformed into fourteenth century pastoral in a gilt frame, but now the frame is gone, the European manner is gone, and the tree itself as an image of suffering is at issue. And the issue is resolved instantly and certainly.

The poet resumes his composition of the landscape by noticing the bunch of sea grapes. He outlines the arrangement of things on the beach and out on the reef, a still ground against which the most minute movements register on the surveying eye, as in a painting so lifelike the viewer thinks something moved:

Noon jerks toward its rigid, inert center.
Sunbathers broil on their grid. . . .
In the thatched beach bar, a clock tests its stiff elbow
every minute and, outside, an even older iguana
climbs hand over claw, as unloved as Quasimodo,
into his belfry of shade, swaying there. . .
(— XXVIII)

The day's heat brings the human figures, the lizard and clock all near the melting point of Daliesque surrealism, but Walcott has them all hold their poses timelessly on a day as infinitely repeatable as any other in the tropics.

But the poet is not to be self-hypnotized by his own idyll.

. . . When a
cloud darkens, my terror caused it. Lizzie and Anna
lie idling on different rafts, their shadows under them.
The curled swell has the clarity of lime.
In two more days my daughters will go home.

> The frame of human happiness is time,
> the child's swing slackens to a metronome.
> Happiness sparkles on the sea like soda.
> (— XXVIII)

Isolate the last line, and it's pure corn, tacked onto a perfectly good final quatrain, and a violation of Pound's dictum not to turn abstractions into symbols such as "dim lands of peace." But it is also the perfect grace note to the sombre intimation of mortality in the beat of the child's swing, a serendipitous dance on the graver, epigrammatic, "The frame of human happiness is time." The line effervesces just as the poet almost submits to Time and Fate; it freshens like a late afternoon breeze; it gently declines to fret; it insists that for the moment at least, the poet of exile and rootlessness look no further.

II

But the sparkle dissipates, the sun declines a few degrees, the moment with its tranquility passes, and the sequence resumes on the next page. Walcott's calm is the eye of the hurricane, the moment before "that thundercloud breaks from its hawsers" (XXVI), or the morning after "a storm has wrecked the island" (XLIX). The West Indian poet must either master or submit to the extremes of his region's nature as well as its history. Walcott's powers are always sustained by the immediate, the local, firmly grounded as a lightning rod driven into the earth to pull divine flame from the sky:

> . . . Christ, my craft, and the long time it is taking!
> Sometimes the flash is seen, a sudden exultation
> of lightning fixing earth in its place; the asphalt's skin
> smells freshly of childhood in the drying rain.
> (— XIII)

Art is long, life short: the labor continues, work accumulates, the lines increase stroke by stroke their store of reality. His work bears nothing of the self-cancelling exercises in syntax that are the other side of modernism. *Midsummer* is studded with brief self-portraits of the poet as laborer, working his physical and metaphoric lines:

> My palms have been sliced by the twine
> of the craft I have pulled at for more than forty years. . . .
> The lines I love have all their knots left in.
> (— XXV)

The West Indian sailor-fisherman must keep his nets mended or he catches nothing. The knots give a sure grip on the experience that is the object of the poet's handiwork. Walcott's line can thin out to a watercolor wash, or thicken into impasto, to such density that the nouns stuck in the verbiage pull the syntax to a halt: "Mud. Clods. The sucking heel of the rain-flinger" (XXXV). Halfway between Homer and Heaney, the thick, clotted monosyllables ballast the agile feminine ending: from dull earth springs the mythic god. His lines have a muscular energy that confirms the self-portraits of the poet as Herculean laborer, doomed to pull the full weight of his memory in his wake:

> I drag, as on a chain behind me, laterite landscapes —
> . . . I pull the voices
> of children behind me.
> (— XLVIV)

Or, as a tailor, an important occupation in the Caribbean, remembering his mother treadling at her Singer:

> I stitch her lines to mine now with the same machine.
> (— XVII)

Or, as the painter at once glorifying his subject and laboring to provide through art an antidote to the destruction of history:

> A radiant summer, so fierce it turns yellow
> like the haze before a holocaust. Like a general,
> I arrange lines that must increase its radiance, work
> that will ripen with peace, like a gold-framed meadow
> in Breughel or Pissarro.
> (— VIII)

Yeats' conception of things falling apart from a failing center pervades *Midsummer*—the island wrecked by storm, clouds as "pages in a damp culture that come apart," the poet's exile from his family — though in the West Indies that may all be business as usual. The fisherman and tailor keep mending, and the poet, like the painter, composes his lines to harness the sun and harvest the parched, intractable fields.

III

> I can sense it coming from far, too, Maman, the tide
> since day has passed its turn, but I still note
> that as a white gull flashes over the sea, its underside
> catches the green, and I promise to use it later.
> (— XV)

Sensing the approach of death, the poet persists in recording the minute truths of his experience, storing his sensory impressions to use later in a painting. There is no diminishing of ambition, just the recognition that of the thousands, perhaps millions of seagulls he has surely seen, he is just now noticing how its belly reflects the ocean. In *Another Life*, the young artist was awakened through painting to the power of death. His tropical paradise admits death, breeds it as rapidly as life, awaits its stroke as the poet and his mother anticipate the inevitable tide. Death gives meaning to his life's work, though such a tidy consolation seems remote in *Midsummer*. Momentarily one can cherish the memory of "clean, scoured things that . . . /the sea has whitened, chaste":

> A yard, an old brown man with a mustache
> like a general's, a boy drawing castor-oil leaves in
> great detail, hoping to be another Albrecht Dürer.
> I have cherished these better than coherence
> as the same tide for us both, Maman, comes nearer. . . .
> (— XV)

But the emotional tide of the poetic sequence will not settle into nostalgia, as, in the following poem, the poet looks beyond the individual death toward the massive symmetries of metropolis and necropolis, and asks, "So what shall we do for the dead . . . ?" (XVI). The imagination that returns the things of this life is futile in supposing that the dead "share the immense, inaudible pulse/ of the clock-shaped earth." Our treasured memorabilia they cannot see, and natural beauty means nothing to those suspended outside of time, neither grim nor beatific, who on the shore "wait neither to end nor begin." The echo of Milton's "They also serve who only stand and wait" (Sonnet XIX) focusses the problem in both poems: the value of human effort in the face of death. Walcott asks, "What use is any labor we/ accept?" He does not, like Hercules, gain life thereby, or like Milton, an afterlife in paradise. It is the question the artist asks of his vocation, and while it is not answered as a theologian or philosopher might, neither is it dismissed. It broods above the progress of *Midsummer* from the moment the clouds part in the first poem. If we are incapable of imagining our end, what use is the imagination? What use is the life devoted to it, and why spend years in its cultivation? Why labor only to grow, as the poet laments, "more skillful" and "more dissatisfied?" (IX).

The issue of the efficacy of art is enlarged by the sense of the artist's diminishing power to affect the outcome of humanity's large struggles. Walcott's helplessness in the face of tyranny, poverty, and hightech weaponry is fixed in an emblematic triptych:

> . . . The stalled cars are as frozen
> as the faces of cloaked queues on a Warsaw street,
> or the hands of black derelicts flexing over a fire-
> barrel under the El; above, the punctured sky

> is needled by rockets that keep both Empires high.
> (— XLII)

The imperial power-junkies rule both skies with absolute despair. It may be too late, certainly too late to establish even a lopsided equation between the potential for absolute destruction and the value of art. The poem ends with a vision of a city bombed back almost to the Stone Age. For the origin of such despair, Walcott turns back to the beginnings of modern warfare and modern art in the late nineteenth century.

Impressionism, the beginning of modernity in art, accomplished by isolating the momentary effects of light, made possible the fragmentation of space and obliteration of form that was to come, and the meaning of art increasingly lay in its surface, its superficiality:

> art was *une tranche de vie*, cheese or home-baked bread —
> light, in their view, was the best that time offered.
> The eye was the only truth, and whatever traverses
> the retina fades when it darkens; the depth of *nature morte*
> was that death itself is only another surface
> like the canvas, since painting cannot capture thought.
> (— XVIII)

The Impressionist surface is lovely, capable of *joie de vivre* and nostalgia, but death arrived on a much grander scale than the painters of "bustled skirts, boating parties, zinc-white strokes on water" could handle, and they retreated into abstraction.

> Then, like dried-up tubes, the coiled soldiers
> piled up on the Somme, and Verdun. And the dead
> less real than a spray burst of chrysanthemums,
> the identical carmine for still life and for the slaughter
> of youth. They were right—everything becomes
> its idea to the painter with easel rifled on his shoulders.
> (— XVIII)

The image of the painter is borrowed from the more confident days of *Another Life*, when painting was a disciplined act of love:

> Gregorias, the easel rifled on his shoulder, marching
> towards an Atlantic flashing tinfoil,
> singing "O Paradiso"
> till the Western breakers laboured to that music,
> his canvas crucified against a tree.
> (— *AL, p. 52*)

Gregorias is marching off to his Passion, his holy war. In *Midsummer,* the painter retains the posture, but the soldiering is ambivalent, a mimicking of the real soldier going off to nearly certain death, and the pure motive of art for art's sake is sullied by the carnage it can represent, but not prevent, with generous amounts of carmine.

The bitterly sardonic tone of "They were right," about coolly abstracting from harsh reality its Platonic idea, updates Auden's famous line, "About suffering they were never wrong,/The Old Masters."[4] The farmer plows and the galleon sails while Icarus drowns unnoticed by all except the artist, who sees all and understands all and tells all. But Walcott's artist is also right: art is abstraction. To create art = to paint pictures = to write poems. Between infinitive and object, between the making and the made, the triggering subject cannot intrude, merely follow appended by a preposition: to paint a picture *of,* to write poems *about.* The artist is removed from his subject by the very act of creating. The challenge is to connect himself to his subject through the art, even if the subject is oneself: "I cannot connect these lines with the lines on my face" (III). How much more difficult then it must be to connect with matters of conscience. His bitter acknowledgement of the rectitude of those for whom death "is only another surface/like the canvas" underscores his deepest doubts about his vocation, which he had begun with the greatest exuberance: "I felt that/the gift of poetry had made me one of the chosen,/that all experience was kindling to the fire of the Muse" (XLI). To be one on whom nothing is lost is almost to lose oneself to that Apollonian as well as Hebraic flame. The burning of the chosen one is of course double-edged in a poem about Hitler's death camps. The ultimate question in that poem parallels Walcott's earlier question in XVI about the value of labor in the face of death.

> . . . But had I known then
> that the fronds of my island were harrows, its sand the ash
> of the distant camps, would I have broken my pen
> because this century's pastorals were being written
> by the chimneys of Dachau, of Auschwitz, of Sachsenhausen?
> (— XLI)

The rhyme of the last, prolific camp with *pen* and *written* tightens the sense of complicity of the artist, now self-accused. The syllables mount like the dreaded piles of human kindling.

IV

Where Auden's subject in "Musée des Beaux Arts" was the single tragedy that fails to touch the common lives of men, Walcott reverses the proportion: how mass suffering fails to touch the artist absorbed in his work. We expect the artist to be a seismograph of his culture and register its shock. According to Pasternak, "The more self-contained the individuality from which the life derives, the more collective . . . is its story. In a genius the domain of the subconscious . . . is composed of all that is happening to his readers."[5] If what is happening in the world is unprecedented destruction, and if the scale of threatened destruction multiplies astronomically over half a century, the artist's imagination can no longer draw vitally from the collective life and his choice of subject becomes amoral: whether to paint the casualty or the chrysanthemum makes no difference to the dead.

Randall Jarrell diagnosed the malady afflicting modern poets who "no longer have the heart to write about what is most terrible in the world of the present: the bombs waiting beside the rockets, the hundreds of millions staring into the temporary shelter of their television sets."[6]

The paralysis of the artist is perhaps an accurate reflection of a world trapped by its own defense systems. The artist, if we take *Midsummer* at face value, needs to confront the terror, to risk incinerating the will and drowning out the muse's call. In the poem about the death camps, though forty years after the fact, their impact raises the question of whether the poet would have continued to write had he known of their horror.

The question is not rhetorical, even if it comes late, because it is really a question of faith and sustenance. That the poem has been written is the answer to its own question. Art turns out to be not for its own sake but for the sake of the artist, turns out to be his way of sustaining faith that there is more to life than dying, the faith that allows him to move into the unknown territory of his work.

Those, like Rimbaud, who lose that faith, quit and go on living in spiritual if not physical exile, or quit living altogether. In the last poem of *Midsummer* Walcott writes of the boyhood "faith I betrayed, or the faith that betrayed me" (LIV), the "distracting signs" of which rise before him out of the landscape. He wonders where is "the heaven I worship with no faith in heaven," and in that paradox is the strength to persevere, to create what he began by celebrating. The portrait of the poet and painter as the ambivalent, troubled, yet titanic creator is completed in the final lines of the book. As he had in the first poems of the book, he addresses the Russian poet Joseph Brodsky, who epitomizes the artist exiled from the land that sustains his art:

> Ah, Joseph, though no man ever dies in his own country,
> the grateful grass will grow thick from his heart.
> (— LIV)

The poet's metaphorical recreation of his world is not complete until his body physically joins its nature to that larger nature, which in life it could never completely align with.

Art is the way to explore that misalignment, to draw the figure it makes upon the human spirit. That is where painting and poetry meet in Walcott's work. A line is made by a point of no dimension moving in one unchanging direction. That ideal line can scarcely exist in painting, and not merely because the point of a brush is at least as thick as one sable hair. The painter works in areas of paint, and the line is defined by their misalignment, becoming a record of their disjuncture. Walcott's poetic line is similarly shaped as a record of the disjointedness of his experience in the world. The true artist is the maker — poet or painter — whose line is the seam joining the world together, composing it as fast as our collective despair keeps letting it fall from our grasp.

Footnotes

[1] Derek Walcott, *Another Life* (New York: Farrar, Straus and Giroux, 1973), p. 52. Cited as *AL*. Walcott has frequently written of the West Indian writer's need to resist the tendency to sentimentalize poverty and lapse into the romantic cliché that the beauty of the Caribbean can inspire. Nevertheless his elemental response to that beauty is awe: "The beauty is overwhelming, it really is. It's not a used beauty, there are no houses; it's not a known beauty, and so the privilege of just looking at these places and seeing their totally uncorrupted existence remains an Adamic experience" ["An Interview with Derek Walcott," conducted by Edward Hirsch, *Contemporary Literature* XX:3 (1979), 283].

[2] *Sea Grapes* (New York: Farrar, Straus and Giroux, 1976), p. 46. "The chapel, as the pivot of this valley,/ round which whatever is rooted loosely turns . . . / draws all to it, to the altar/ and the massive altarpiece. . . . "

[3] *Midsummer* (New York: Farrar, Straus and Giroux, 1984). Poems from *Midsummer* are cited in the text by their Roman numeral.

[4] *Collected Poems* (New York: Random House, 1976), p. 146.

[5] Boris Pasternak, *Safe Conduct*, trans. Beatrice Scott (New York: New Directions, 1958), pp. 26-7.

[6] "Fifty Years of American Poetry," *The Third Book of Criticism* (New York: Farrar, Straus and Giroux, 1969), pp. 332-3.

THE POETRY OF DEREK WALCOTT

Peter Balakian

Collected Poems: 1948-1984, by Derek Walcott

It may seem audacious for a young poet to liken his situation to that of St. John on Patmos receiving revelation, yet Derek Walcott's early poem "As John to Patmos" is an *ars poetica* and a written vow. This early (the poem was written when the poet was in his twenties) he expresses his sacred sense of vocation and his moral and aesthetic commitment to his native realm — his island, St. Lucia, and the entire Caribbean archipelago: "So I shall voyage no more from home; / may I speak here. / This island is heaven." After evoking the island's almost mystical landscape, he consecrates his need "To praise love long, the living and the brown dead" (p. 5). While the early poems included in *Collected Poems* are more modest in their intentions and less complex in their metaphorical richness than what will follow, there is still a remarkable maturity and confidence in them. (It is astonishing to realize that "Prelude" was written by a poet in his teens.) These poems allow us to see the young poet developing the idiom and grappling with the problems that will come to define his life's work and his distinctive sensibility.

Derek Walcott's *Collected Poems: 1948-1984* is a large Selected Poems of over 500 pages and includes work from all of his books, beginning with *In a Green Night: Poems 1948-1960*, which was first published in England by Jonathan Cape in 1962. Because 1948 marks the public beginning of Walcott's career (his first book, *25 Poems*, was published in that year), this new collection enables the reader to gain a sense of this major poet's growth and evolution. And, because all of his books prior to *Sea Grapes* (1976) are out of print, *Collected Poems* makes available the entirety of Walcott's book length poem, *Another Life* (1973), and many other important poems from the first half of his career.

The poems from his early books, *In a Green Night, Selected Poems* (1964), and *The Castaway and Other Poems* (1965) reveal his mystic sense of place and a lush imagination which is always poised against a high eloquence. In an extraordinary early poem, "Origins," he is already able to create a language that can contain one of his major concerns — the creation myth of his native place. His ability to discover the sources of a hitherto unnamed place puts him in the company of the lyrical epic poets of the Western hemisphere, especially Whitman and Neruda. Walcott's Adamic ability to embody rhythmically and metaphorically the natural history of his world and transform it into culture-making language is what Emerson called Naming in the highest poetic fashion. "Origins" is a prologue to poems like "The Sea Is History," "Schooner *Flight*," "The Star-Apple Kingdom," "Sainte Lucie," and his book-length epic, *Another Life*. In "Origins," as in these later poems, Walcott is able to find in the cosmogonic conditions of his landscape a protean identity as a man and an epic consciousness for his culture. The warm Caribbean waters become an amniotic bath for this poet whose memory encompasses, at once, phylogeny and ontogeny. "In my warm, malarial bush-bath, / The wet leaves leeched to my flesh. An infant Moses, / I dreamed of dying, I saw / Paradise as columns of lilies and wheat-headed angels" (p. 12). Out of the Proustian remembrances of his childhood and his deeper racial memory comes a force of imagination in a surging rhythm that defines what he refers to as "the mind, among sea-wrack, see[ing] its mythopoetic coast":

> *O clear, brown tongue of the sun-warmed, sun-wooded*
> > *Troumassee*
> *of laundresses and old leaves, and winds that buried their old*
> *songs in archives of bamboo and wild plantain, their white sails*
> *bleached and beaten on dry stone, the handkerchiefs of adieux*
> *and ba-bye! O sea, leaving your villages of cracked mud. . . .*
> (p. 13)

The selections from *In a Green Night* (1962) show us Walcott's various formal virtuosities. His rhyming quatrains of iambic tetrameter in poems like "Pocomania" and "In a Green Night," or his sonnet sequence, "Tales of the Islands," reveal his ability to mine traditional forms of English poetry without ever compromising his passionate energy or his language's inner music. One senses that the vestiges of form are in the deeper structures of so many of Walcott's later, freer poems. For example, the inner cohesion of the lyrical epic, *Another Life*, is in part created by the delicate balance between Walcott's eruptive imagination and the harnessing control of his tradition-bound intellect.

Other poems from the 1962 collection, such as "A Far Cry from Africa," "Ruins of a Great House," "Two Poems on the Passing of an Empire," show Walcott beginning to wrestle with the complex identity that will unfold in his later books — his irreconcilable and pluralistic cultural situation as a transplanted African in a colonial English society. Perhaps he sums up his life's dilemma when he cries out at the close of "A Far Cry from Africa":

> I who am poisoned with the blood of both,
> Where shall I turn, divided to the vein?
> I who have cursed

> The drunken officer of British rule, how choose
> Between this Africa and the English tongue I love?
> Betray them both, or give back what they give?
> How can I face such slaughter and be cool?
> How can I turn from Africa and live?
> (p. 18)

For his ability to embrace his Black West Indian identity and to accept, with the ingenuity of an artist, the language of his inherited culture accounts for much of the genius and richness of his idiom. Using the English tongue he loves does not preclude his moral outrage at the crimes that the Empire has committed against his people. He hears in the mansion of English culture a death-rattle in each room. In "Ruins of a Great House" he sees clearly "Hawkins, Walter Raleigh, Drake, / [as] Ancestral murderers and poets," and confesses that his "eyes burned from the ashen prose of Donne" (p. 20). Knowing his love affair with English literature, one senses the complexity of Walcott's mind.

For the most part the poems from *The Gulf* (1970) are more personal than the earlier work and bear the imprint of some of Lowell's tone and mood in *Life Studies* and *For the Union Dead*. Travelling between the West Indies and the States, Walcott has acquired a new sense of North-South tension. With his Juvenalian eye, he observes another empire in the midst of its internal conflicts and violence. In the title poem, a flight over Texas provokes his vision of America as "detached, divided states, whose slaughter / darkens each summer now, as one by one, / the smoke of bursting ghettos clouds the glass" (p. 106). In "Elegy," written on the night of Robert Kennedy's assassination, Walcott's sober view of America ends with his recasting of that famous American couple of Grant Wood's "American Gothic": they stand "like Calvin's saints, waspish, pragmatic, poor, / gripping the devil's pitchfork / stare[ing] rigidly towards the immortal wheat" (p. 110).

In *The Gulf* and *The Castaway and Other Poems* (1965). Walcott's luxuriant images and tropes have become so rooted in his nature — in his pathological relationship to the world — that sight and insight, sensory perception and meta-phorical meaning merge. In "The Flock," a stunning poem that opens *The Castaway*, his reflection on the imagination and the creative process begins with an image of birds migrating south: "The grip of winter tightening, its thinned / volleys of blue-wing teal and mallard fly / from the longbows of reeds bent by the wind, / arrows of yearning for our different sky" (p. 77). Before the poem is over the birds have become part of the imagination's topography without ever losing their naturalistic authentic-ity — natural fact and metaphor remain one.

Another Life (1972), written between 1965 and 1972, is an extraordinary leap forward in the evolution of Walcott's work. He has, in this poem of four books and twenty-three sections, "sung," in the epic meaning of the word, a life's story into a mythic journey. Beginning the poem in the middle of his life's journey, he exclaims near the end of the poem, "a man lives half of life, / the second half is memory" (p. 243). And the memory in this poem is that of a collective mind and an intimately

personal one. The texture, color, tone of the poet's childhood on St. Lucia and his
rites of initiation into manhood and art are matched by a language so rich and
sensuous that one feels in it that rare balance between the personal life and the fully
metaphorical meaning of that life. Consequently, the poem is balanced between its
narrative elements — the people, places and events that have shaped the poet's life
(his mother's house, the local townsfolk who become his heroes, his soul-mate the
drunken painter Gregorias, his discovery of his history, his metaphorical marriage) —
and the lyrical transfigurations of those elements. The poem is at once a paen to the
culture of his island and the history of the Caribbean and a dramatization of the
morphology of the poet's mind. In his double culture and his divided self, he sees the
music of language, the basis of metaphor, and the moral meaning of poetry. For all of
the immensely cultured intellect in this poem (I cannot think of a poet who uses the
history of Western painting as brilliantly as he does here), there is never anything
effete or rarified in the Stevensian sense. He has managed to do what a modern epic
poet must do: encompass history, myth, culture, and the personal life with the realm
of aesthetic vision. Some of these passages illustrate what I mean.

His sacramental sense of culture, landscape, and history:

> At every first communion, the moon
> would lend her lace to a barefooted town
> christened, married, and buried in borrowed white,
> in fretwork borders of carpenter's Gothic
> in mansard bonnets, pleated jalousies,
> when, with her laces laid aside,
> she was a servant, her sign
> a dry park of disconsolate palms, like brooms,
> planted by the seventh Edward, Prince of Wales. . . .
> (p. 152)

In his love celebration, the blood of nature becomes the blood of sacrament:

> And a vein opened in the earth,
> its drops congealing into plum,
> sorrel, and berry,
> the year bleeding again, Noel, Noel,
> blood for the bloodless birth,
> blood deepening the poinsettia's Roman blades
> after the Festival of the Innocents.
> (p. 231)

This historical burden of his people:

> The bones of our Hebraic faith were scattered
> over such a desert, burnt and brackened gorse,

their war was over, it had not been
the formal tapestry bled white by decorum,
it had infected language,
gloria Dei and the glory of
the Jacobean Bible were the same. The shoes
of cherubs piled in pyramids
outside the Aryan ovens.
(p. 246)

The exuberant drunkenness of the young poet and his painter friend:

while the black, black-sweatered, horn-soled fisherman drank
their *l'absinthe* in sand back yards standing up,
on the clear beer of sunrise,
on cheap, tannic Canaries muscatel,
on glue, on linseed oil, on kerosene,
as Van Gogh's shadow rippling on a cornfield,
on Cézanne's boots grinding the stones of Aix
to shales of slate, ochre, and Vigie blue,
on Gauguin's hand shaking the gin-coloured dew
from the umbrella yams,
garrulous, all day, sun-struck. . . .
(p. 193)

Sea Grapes (1976) is in certain obvious ways a quieter and more austere book. After the outpouring of the long poem, it is as if Walcott were forced to retreat in order to examine the troubles of his present life. Poems like "Sea Grapes," "The Fist," "Winding Up," and "Love after Love" deal with the tensions between the passionate life of love and poetry and his responsibilities to his domestic life and his solitary self. Nevertheless, the one long poem, "Sainte Lucie," shows us that he is never too far from his tribal self. This five-part poem, which is a kind of psalm to his island, is a mixture of French Creole and even a Creole song, touches of a vernacular speech, and Walcott's inimitable eloquence. In a way the poem looks forward to the continuing epic impulse that defines *The Star-Apple Kingdom* (1979).

Coming to *The Star-Apple Kingdom* after the poems that have preceded it, one becomes aware not only of Walcott's genius but of his stature as a major poet. His ability to renew himself, to revitalize his imagination, to rediscover the myth of his life and his culture, places him among the greatest poets of our century — Yeats, Neruda, Rilke, William, Elytis, for example — poets who write out of their obsessions without repeating themselves. Two of his most powerful poems, "The Schooner *Flight*" and "The Star-Apple Kingdom," reveal Walcott's seemingly inexhaustible resources. In "The Schooner *Flight*," he unites beautifully a vernacular tradition, with his high eloquence, so that the reader believes that his persona, Shabine, is both a common man and a speaker of poetry. Shabine, who is trying to escape the woes of his life by fleeing his island as a castaway, is able to sustain a tone that is both autobiographical and mythic. "I'm just a red nigger who love the sea, / I had a sound colonial education, / I have Dutch, nigger, and English in me, / and either I'm nobody, or I'm a nation" (p. 346). He becomes a kind of underwater Isaiah whose vision encompasses his people's history. He sees what it was to be a "colonial nigger," and as the rhythms of the sea provoke Shabine's inner eye ("I had no nation . . . but the imagination"), he relives the middle passage, sees the corruption of the imperialist businessman and ministers, and as an angry prophet cries out: "I shall scatter your lives like a handful of sand, / I who have no weapon but poetry and / the lances of palms and the sea's shining shield!" (p. 358).

The language of the title poem, which is set in Jamaica, is able to hold in tension the pastoral munificence of the colonial world and its morally rotten underpinnings:

> Strange, that the rancour of hatred hid in that dream
> of slow rivers and lily-like parasols, in snaps
> of fine old colonial families, curled at the edge
> not from age or from fire or the chemicals, no, not at all,
> but because, off at its edges, innocently excluded
> stood the groom, the cattle boy, the housemaid, the
>   gardeners,
> the tenants, the good Negroes down in the village,
> their mouths in the locked jaw of a silent scream.
> (p. 348)

As he recounts the history of the Caribbean, he sees the islands as beads on the rosary — and through this ingenious sacramental conceit he leads us back into history (the Conquistadors, "the empires of tobacco, sugar, and bananas," "the footbath of dictators, Trujillo, Machado," "the alphabet soup of CIA, PNP, OPEC"). But, as so often happens in Walcott's poems, the journey into the darkness of history enables him to validate his identity as a West Indian Black man so that he can "sleep the sleep that wipes out history" and envision, once again, another version of Genesis — what becomes for him almost an imaginative ritual allowing him to reclaim his people's strength. He imagines his "history-orphaned islands" from Cuba to Tobago as turtles coupling, and finds the history of his race in one black woman who sees "the creak of light" that divided the world between "rich and poor," "North and South," "black and white," "between two Americas," as she hears the transcendent silence of the beginning in the "white, silent roar / of the old water wheel in the star-apple kingdom" (p. 395).

Since the ten poems in *The Star-Apple Kingdom* (only eight are reprinted here) comprise a sustained book-length poem, it would seem hard to surpass such an effort in a short period of time. However, *The Fortunate Traveler* (1981) is again a surge forward — another poetic renewal. The book shows Walcott's various selves: an exiled poet writing with ambivalent passion about the North, the Augustan satirist writing in a comic vernacular in "The Spoiler's Return," and the elegist enlarging his familiar theme of exile into a modern vision.

In one of the magnificent poems of the collection, "North and South," the poet confesses his identity as a "colonial upstart at the end of an empire, / a single, circling, homeless satellite." He becomes a modern exiled poet with a global vision of what empire means as he hears "its gutteral death rattle in the shoal / of the legions' withdrawing roar, from the raj, / from the Reich, and see[s] the full moon again / like a white flag rising over Fort Charlotte" (p. 405). Like Ellison's Invisible Man or Wright's Bigger Thomas, Walcott finds himself a deracinated Black man wandering through the snowy surreal white streets of the urban North (Manhattan). He is enervated by how far he is from the "salt freshness" of his "raw" culture, and tired of the decadence of America and Europe with its "literature . . . an old couch stuffed with fleas" (p. 407). As the poem shifts to a winter Virginia landscape (amplifying the double meaning of North and South), the poet identifies himself as a slave, and as he imagines that a blue-eyed, red-haired aunt of his might be part Jewish, he makes a pact with all the oppressed peoples of the world and would rather have "the privilege / to be yet another of the races they fear and hate / instead of one of the haters and the afraid" (p. 408).

He extends this human empathy even further in the title poem. His self-effacing and poignant use of the famous refrain of St. Paul in Corinthians, *"and have not charity,"* is the poem's hymning refrain; it serves as a benediction and an admonition. The poem is borne out of the poet's painful sense of the fissure between the need for a religious ethos and the absence of any moral order in our time. With his savage wit he recasts history so that "After Dachau" supplants "Anno Domini." As he contemplates the 10,000,000 people starving on the earth and the 765,000 skeletons in Somalia, that horseman of the apocalypse — famine — "the leather-helmed locust" stalks his imagination. The beast that Yeats saw "slouching toward Bethlehem" is now among us as Walcott looks at the twentieth century to see "The heart of darkness is the core of fire / in the white center of the holocaust" (p. 461). The poem reminds us of the meaning of *caritas* and the fact that all reform must begin in the human heart. For all the moral advocacy in this poem, Walcott never strays from the richness of his metaphor or collapses his poetic eloquence for the sake of a message. This is the kind of political poem that only a master can write.

The *Collected Poems* concludes with a selection of thirty poems from his most recent book, *Midsummer* (1984). The collection is comprised of fifty-four short lyric poems, which in their diary-like tone give the sense of a poet charting his preoccupations during the course of a year. Since the collection is a kind of book-length poem, I wish the entire book had been republished. In a certain sense, this is Walcott's most American book (although its personal tone is always ballasted by his sumptuous imagination). Here, he appears more at home in his exile, a cosmopolitan poet absorbing the pulse of many cultures; he exclaims "this is the lot of all wanderers, this is their fate, / that the more they wander, the more the world grows wide" (p. 474). He becomes the poet as ethnographer and we see him in the pensiones, hotels, motels, and inns of Rome, New York, Warwickshire, Boston, and even having a nightmarish vision of nuclear winter in Chicago. He has also found a more personal idiom for writing about one of his passions — painting.

His lyrical ruminations on Watteau, Gaughin, Van Gogh, and Chardin show us how Walcott's rich imagination continues to be informed by texture, tone, gradation of color, hard and soft lines, and shifting perspectives — and how much the art of Gregorias's friend is a love-affair with the world. In concluding, it is fitting to mention Walcott's love poems. For they are as full-bodied, erotic, compassionate, personal and mythic at once, as any love poems written in English in this century. "Bleeker Street, Summer," "Goats and Monkeys," the epithalamion in *Another Life*, "Egypt, Tobago," "Europa," and the astounding poem about his still-born daughter, "Early Pompeian," are poems that embody another dimension of *caritas*.

It is difficult to think of a poet in our century who — without ever betraying his native sources — has so organically assimilated the evolution of English literature from the Renaissance to the present, who has absorbed the Classical and Judeo-Christian past, and who has mined the history of Western painting as Walcott has. Throughout his entire body of work he has managed to hold in balance his passionate moral concerns with the ideal of art. By his fifty-fifth year Derek Walcott has made his culture, history, and sociology into a myth for our age and into an epic song that has already taken its place in the history of Western literature.

DIVIDED CHILD

J.D. McClatchy

Collected Poems 1948-1984 by Derek Walcott

At the recent International PEN Congress in New York, as part of a panel considering "Alienation and the State," Derek Walcott spoke of having been born on an island, St. Lucia, with no ruins, no museum, no dates. "It was," he said, "a country without a history." The task he set himself as a young poet was not to discover his history but to create one, and to make it out of himself, out of his circumstances and his birthright.

Can it be coincidental that the title of his second collection is *The Castaway* and that a recurrent figure in his early work is Robinson Crusoe? Walcott himself was never at home on his island. He has called himself a "divided child" — a black with a white grandfather; a colonial schoolboy who sang the verse of "Rule Britannia" that goes "Britons never, never shall be slaves"; part of the educated middle class in a backwater of poverty, and raised as a Methodist in a Catholic country. In sum, the self-conscious outsider in his tiny paradise.

These contradictions, when they are dramatized or when they are suppressed, animate the poems he wrote until 1970. One of his best-known early poems, "A Far Cry from Africa," ends with a series of questions he will not be able to answer for many more years. What seems a historical dilemma is actually a quarrel with the self:

> I who am poisoned with the blood of both,
> Where shall I turn, divided to the vein?
> I who have cursed
> The drunken officer of British rule, how choose
> Between this Africa and the English tongue I love?
> Betray them both, or give back what they give?
> How can I face such slaughter and be cool?
> How can I turn from Africa and live?
> (p. 18)

It is not just the rhetorical authority or the charged estrangements of his subsequent books that make these early poems seem, especially in this retrospective collection, so stiff and unconvincing. They are — for a good reason but to no good effect — deliberately derivative, defiantly literary. From the start, his language and its literature were an available history, a means of composing the self. Actually, Walcott grew up with three languages — French Creole, English Creole, and English. Though he mostly reserved patois for his plays, he has incorporated it into his poems, and some readers have objected. Helen Vendler, for instance, has criticized Walcott's poems in dialect as damp matches, and insists that "mixed diction has yet to validate itself as a literary resource with aesthetic power."

I think Vendler is wrong, and so would readers of Dante and Burns, or of such contemporaries as Tony Harrison in England or Tom Paulin in Ireland. But the real point is that all poetry is written in dialect. As Craig Raine wryly notes, "most bad poetry is written in the dialect of the previous age." Our best poets have created their own. Though we use the term "style" because we more often read than listen to poems, dialect would just as likely describe an Ashbery or a Plath poem whose distinctive accents are unmistakable. Walcott too is a poet who wants to be both read and listened to. His style could be called English speech with a West Indian inflection; or, as he himself might describe it, he thinks in one language and moves in another. Even his "standard" poems have a peculiar loping quality to their lines, a slower rhythm than those of his peers.

Walcott was probably attracted to patois for two reasons. First, at the level of diction and metaphor, as he once told an interviewer, because "the things I saw around me were being named by people in a new language." Second, at the level of gesture and tone, because he associates patois with a native theatricalism: "My society loves rhetoric, performance, panache, melodrama, carnival, dressing up, playing roles. Thank God I was born in it, which made me love live and artificial theater." Walcott tends to use dialect precisely when he wants these extravagant effects; in fact, "artificial theater" is as good a name for it as any. At its worst, it is picturesque. At its best, it can be subversive, upsetting political and cultural habits. And some of his best sustained poems use it. "The Schooner *Flight*" is one. "Either I'm nobody, or I'm a nation," boasts the poem's hero, a mulatto sailor named Shabine, a Caribbean Ulysses. The mixed diction of Walcott's poems eloquently expresses his mixed state, without indulging in either ethnic chic or imperial drag. Here is his gift of tongues, which enables him to speak with intimacy and power.

The dialect he most often used in his apprentice work, however, was the florid grandiloquence of Yeats, Eliot, Dylan Thomas. The experience in, and of, his first few books is largely literary. This was an act both of homage and of assimilation. West Indian literature — its "postcard poetry" and limp tract-novels — simply didn't exist for him, and English literature was his birthright. "Either man is a myth or a piece of dirt," he once said. "Roman, Greek, African, all mine, veined in me, more alive than marble, bleeding and drying up. Literature reopens wounds more deeply than history does. It also releases the force of joy." But in such borrowed robes, his early work is, to use a phrase of his own devising, "fireless and average." Not until his book-length poem *Another Life* in 1973, when he turned his manner into his subject matter, did Walcott use literary history to tap a responding strength in himself.

The poem is the centerpiece of this *Collected Poems,* and remains central in
Walcott's career. It is also one of the best long (there are over 4,000 lines) autobiographical poems in English, with the narrative sweep, the lavish layering of details,
and the mythic resonance of a certain classic. His story is a simple and traditional one,
the growth-of-the-poet's-mind, how "he fell in love with art,/and life began." Love
and art are entwined initiations: at the same time he is learning from his painter-
mentor Gregorias, he is falling in love with Anna. Because he turns to art as "Another
Life," he turns too toward the body and toward the landscape. Walcott is a poet of
vivid sensual and celebratory power, as when he describes Anna:

> For one late afternoon, when again she stood
> in the door of a twilight always left ajar,
> when dusk had softened the first bulb
> the colour of the first weak star,
> I asked her, "Choose,"
> the amazed dusk held its breath,
> the earth's pulse staggered,
> she nodded, and that nod
> married earth with lightning.
> And now we were the first guests of the earth
> and everything stood still for us to name.
> Against the blades of palms and yellow sand,
> I hear that open laugh,
> I see her stride
> as ruthless as that flax-bright harvester
> Judith, with Holofernes' lantern in her hand.
> (p. 230-231)

He knows enough to be rueful: "The hand she held already had betrayed / them by its
longing for describing her." The tropical landscape also becomes text:

> But drunkenly, or secretly, we swore,
> disciples of that astigmatic saint,
> that we would never leave the island
> until we had put down, in paint, in words,
> as palmists learn the network of a hand,
> all of its sunken, leaf-choked ravines,
> every neglected, self-pitying inlet
> muttering in brackish dialect, the ropes of mangroves
> from which old soldier crabs slipped
> surrendering to slush,
> each ochre track seeking some hilltop and
> losing itself in an unfinished phrase,
> under sand shipyards where the burnt-out palms

> inverted the design of unrigged schooners,
> entering forests, boiling with life,
> *goyave, corrosol, bois-canot, sapotille.*
> (p. 194)

His sense of vocation *is* his identity, and what we watch evolving is a personal story of nationalistic dimensions ("a man no more/but the fervour and intelligence/of a whole country"), as well as a major heroic myth with its traditional motifs. The infernal past in Walcott's version is the great fire that destroyed Castries, the capital of St. Lucia, in 1948, the year from which Walcott counts his poetic career. In *Another Life* he calls it his "ruined Ilion." As in Dante, the protagonist is instructed by a master-artist, and inspired by a beloved. And the traditional epic tasks — a reconciliation with the fathers and the founding of a new city — are taken up in a new way. It is the example of a painter named Gregorias on which the young poet-hero models himself. (In reality, "Gregorias" was Harry Simmons, and his untimely suicide becomes the "stroke" that ends the poem on a troubled note.)[1] In the mature work of the past decade, it is Robert Lowell who has been Walcott's model. One poem not included in this *Collected* is "R.T.S.L.," Walcott's elegy for Lowell, but his influence is everywhere apparent in Walcott's three most recent books, *The Star-Apple Kingdom (1979), The Fortunate Traveller* (1981), and *Midsummer* (1984). Like Lowell, Walcott's mode has in these books shifted from the mythological to the historical, from fictions to facts, and his voice has gotten more clipped and severe. There are times when the influence is almost too direct, as in "Old New England," where he paces off Lowell's own territory:

> Black clippers, tarred with whales' blood, fold their sails
> entering New Bedford, New London, New Haven.
> A white church spire whistles into space
> like a swordfish, a rocket pierces heaven
> as the thawed springs in icy chevrons race
> down hillsides and Old Glories flail
> the crosses of green farm boys back from 'Nam .
> Seasons are measured still by the same
> span of the veined leaf and the veined body
> whenever the spring wind startles an uproar
> of marching oaks with memories of a war
> that peeled whole counties from the calendar.
> (p. 399)

At other times the influence is more diffused, as in *Midsummer's* diaristic sequence of poems, a format that controls the dynamics of fact and tone.

Nearly half of the 54 poems that make up *Midsummer* have been left out of this new edition. Though what remains shines with a renewed brilliance, it's like seeing stills from a film. In its original edition, *The Fortunate Traveller* is divided into three parts — North, South, North — to reflect the poet's displacements, his temperamental and intellectual affinities, his second thoughts. But that arrangement is lost in the *Collected's* curtailments.

Some poets gain by being read in bulk like this. I don't think Walcott does. Not only do I miss the deleted poems, I miss the wait between the books, the surprise at new turns and risks, the involvement of an entire book. This *Collected Poems*, then, is not the best way — nor should it be the first way — to read Walcott. It is fine to have *Another Life* readily available again, and the selection from recent books will be sufficient to impress any newcomer. There are poems here — "The Sea Is History," "Egypt, Tobago," "The Star-Apple Kingdom," "North and South," "Beachhead," "Europa," "The Hotel Normandie Pool," and all of *Midsummer* — that continue to dazzle, and would likely be in anyone's anthology, not just in Walcott's own.

That these poems are bunched toward the end of this book is only a sign of Walcott's increasing mastery. His style now has a range and a grave radiance that transfigure the smallest detail. And though his poems are built up from details, they have challenged their own fluency by addressing the large intractable problems of modern history—exile, injustice, the lurid terrorisms of the mind, the ordinary treasons of the heart. If art remains his focus and refreshment, sometimes too exclusively, it is because he sees art as that place where the dilemmas of a life have been most urgently portrayed. And it is his warrant for transcendence. Implicit even in his poems of evocative description or political commentary is a nearly sacramental view of human life. A coil of traffic, a cat's eye, the baptistery doors — anything may suggest a vision beyond the image. In this conclusion to "The Season of Phantasmal Peace," it is a flight of birds, a passage of light:

> it was the light
> that you will see at evening on the side of a hill
> in yellow October, and no one hearing knew
> what change had brought into the raven's cawing,
> the killdeer's screech, the ember-circling chough
> such an immense, soundless, and high concern
> for the fields and cities where the birds belong,
> except it was their seasonal passing, Love,
> made seasonless, or, from the high privilege of their birth,
> something brighter than pity for the wingless ones
> below them who shared dark holes in windows and in houses,
> and higher they lifted the net with soundless voices
> above all change, betrayals of falling suns,
> and this season lasted one moment, like the pause
> between dusk and darkness, between fury and peace,
> but, for such as our earth is now, it lasted long.
> (p. 464-465)

Footnote

[1] Actually "Gregorias" was Walcott's friend Dunstan St. Omer. Simmons was Walcott's inspirational mentor. (Ed.)

THE COLLECTED POEMS AND *THREE PLAYS* OF DEREK WALCOTT

Bruce King

Although less puzzling and profound than Geoffrey Hill, less innovative and less indicative of contemporary attitudes than John Ashbery, Derek Walcott is a significant voice of our time, the voice of the ex-colonial who transforms the English and European culture he has inherited and consequently redefines the map of tradition. We are used to such writers as Beckett and Nabokov, who appear to develop best in a foreign language, but Walcott represents a phenomenon less discussed, the artist on the margins of a culture who in mastering it becomes its master. Despite a New World perspective, he does not develop from the American tradition with its transcendentalism, physicality, immediacy, free verse, and open form. Except for Robert Lowell his models are primarily British, classical, or European. He is, along with Hill and Tony Harrison, the obvious current heir to the traditions of English poetry. Like many of the best poets from Marlowe to Eliot, he is also an excellent dramatist; he has been actively involved in the theater, although his role in the creation of serious West Indian theater is still largely unknown to those outside the region.

Collected Poems: 1948-1984 emphasizes universal themes and a myth of Walcott's life, to the neglect of more topical, argumentative poems which he has not republished. The earliest poem here is "Prelude" from 1948, which predicts his future. Already at the age of eighteen, Walcott treats his youth as material for a future autobiography. He is like a tree which while rooted grows, taking on further layers around an inner core of the self. Walcott's concern has been to understand what he is, and how he has been made by his family, his community, and his life. His poems, like those of Yeats, are a continual dramatic reforming in public of himself and his identity. Alongside poems about family, friends, loves, and a generation attempting to be artists, are poems concerned with his estrangement—as a Brown, English-speaking, Anglicized, Methodist-raised Protestant (with two English grandparents) —from the black, patois-speaking, French Catholic-voodoo culture of St. Lucia. The decision to become an artist, and subsequently an English-language poet, working in the tradition of European art and poetry, is central to his work. It is his vocation and overriding purpose in life, although by its very nature it must further distance him from the local community and life he celebrates. Essentially he will tell the same story, adding disillusionments, divorces, exile, nostalgia, a larger body of acquaintances and places, along with such recent concerns as awareness that he is aging and is threatened by the approach of death.

The ex-colonial is haunted more than others by the need for roots, for a society with which to identify. A continuing tension in the *Collected Poems* exists between the desire to win the white goddess of European poetry and an awareness that the Americas should be a new start. Walcott's thought is filled with discontinuities resulting from his dual racial and cultural heritage; he is both a castaway Robinson Crusoe and an Adam. The master of European verse forms will suddenly erupt into dialect or even patois. For Walcott, European art, particularly poetry, is a means to redeem the inarticulate and unformed society into which he was born, creating the self in the process of writing about the problems of being a Caribbean poet. If Walcott the poet is aspirant to Malraux's international museum without walls, he is also consciously in the tradition of Whitman, Neruda, St. John Perse, and others who asked what new world poetry might be. Many of the early *Collected Poems* —"A Far Cry from Africa" ("how choose / Between this Africa and the English tongue I love?"), "Ruins of a Great House" ("Albion too was once / A colony like ours") — attempt to see both sides of his racial heritage. The problem was how to become a poet where there were no worthwhile poets previously.

The very stance Walcott takes as artist creates a distance of otherness even as he proclaims himself spokesman for the majority. The early *In a Green Night (1962)* with its Marvellian ironies about the island is followed by *The Castaway (1965)* and "Crusoe's Island":

> At dusk, when they return
> For vespers, every dress
> Touched by the sun will burn
> A seraph's, an angel's,
> And nothing I can learn
> From art or loneliness
> Can bless them as the bell's
> Transfiguring tongue can bless.
> (p. 72)

Walcott's volumes after *The Castaway* note his increasing alienation from the actual society of St. Lucia while presenting him as part of Caribbean history, whether representative of a group of artists, a generation discovering West Indianness, or the alienated, nonconforming "red" among blacks and whites.

Each of Walcott's books of poems has a title suggestive of some inner unity and they appear to grow one from another. *The Gulf (1969)* includes poems representative of The Gulf between North America and the Caribbean, the exile and the native, the poet and the masses, Walcott's youthful hopes and his middle age. The titles of the poems are themselves indicative of alienation, disillusionment, and experience: "Mass Man," "Exile," "Blues," "Love in the Valley," "Nearing Forty." The feeling of being part of a community of Caribbean writers who, having to leave the region in order to survive, became estranged from the lands they write about is forcefully expressed in "Homecoming: Anse La Raye," dedicated to the fine St. Lucian novelist Garth St. Omer, who lives and teaches in California:

> for once, like them,
> you wanted no career
> but this sheer light, this clear,
> infinite, boring, paradisal sea,
> but hoped it would mean something to declare
> today, I am your poet, yours,
> all this you knew,
> but never guessed you'd come
> to know there are homecomings without home.
> (p. 128)

In *The Gulf* Walcott, fighting against back-to-Africa nostalgia and the Caribbean self-burdening obsession with history, particularly African slavery, claims a collective amnesia for the inhabitants of the New World who he feels have lost their ties to Africa, India, and Europe.

As shown by the 152-page autobiographical epic *Another Life* (1973), being a poet was part of a larger rebellion against a philistine colonial society that imported its high culture from England. In his teens Walcott belonged to a small group intent on living more fully while giving St. Lucia such arts as painting, poetry, and drama based on local subject matter:

> But drunkenly, or secretly, we swore,
> disciples of that astigmatic saint,
> that we would never leave the island
> until we had put down, in paint, in words,
> as palmists learn the network of a hand,
> all of its sunken, leaf-choked ravines,
> every neglected, self-pitying inlet
> muttering in brackish dialect, the ropes of mangroves
> from which old soldier crabs slipped
> surrendering to slush,
> each ochre track seeking some hilltop and
> losing itself in an unfinished phrase. . .
> (p. 194)

Partly a Caribbean "Portrait of the Brown Artist as a Young Man," *Another Life* mythologizes a generation of artists who discovered the West Indies, opposed the Philistines, and through creativity, sex, and love lived fully, memorably. As well as a virtuoso display in its range of verse forms, the poem is a magnificent tribute to an era when three friends, white, brown, and black, could share the excitement of discovering themselves and culture; it celebrates the heroic in a society which, according to Naipaul, has "denied itself heroes." While Walcott does not sentimentalize the racial prejudice and class divisions that existed, he complains that independence has not improved the position of the common worker or the artist. He encloses "in this circle of hell" the ministers of culture "who explain to the peasant why he is African" and why Third World "artists die / by their own hands."

His usual highly complex, incantatory, Dylan Thomas-influenced style changed in the mid-1970s, for a time becoming surprisingly taut, angry, with metaphor compressed into what appears to be plain speech. As he wrote in *Sea Grapes* (1976) more directly about local issues and learned to trust his voice, the language of the verse also was transformed, coming closer to dialect and pidgin. The five great "Sainte Lucie" poems exploit a wide variety of language, moving from Latin through various registers of English to patois.

His poems from *Sea Grapes* onward imply that he was forced from the Caribbean he loves because of his opposition to the older nationalist demand for a folk culture and the militant left identification with the urban, proletarian masses. He views the former as reactionary, an attempt to create an artificial national culture; he criticizes Black Power and Marxists for importing foreign ideologies into the Caribbean and, instead of supporting the region's artists, glorifying illiteracy. Walcott's later poetry and plays often return to the irony that national independence has not changed the condition of the "red man" who, formerly a victim of intolerance by whites, is now discriminated against by blacks. The troupe of the Trinidad Basement Theatre, which he founded, the most important theater in the West Indies, nearly broke up because Walcott wrote major parts for white actors.

As his writing becomes increasingly autobiographical, it is also more politically conscious and committed to a liberal humanism. In *The Star Apple Kingdom* (1979), "The Schooner *Flight*," an extended poem in eleven parts, projects autobiography onto a story of "a rusty head sailor with sea-green eyes / that they nickname Shabine, the patois for / any red nigger," who travels through the Caribbean to escape both local black power politicians and his women. The poem laments the shortlived West Indian Federation (1958-1962) with its concept of a Caribbean union, which the politicians destroyed to raise themselves to local power: "I am satisfied / if my hand gave voice to one people's grief." The great "Forest of Europe," dedicated to Joseph Brodsky, alludes to the life of and echoes lines from the Russian poet Osip Mandelstam, and finds analogies between oppression in America, the Caribbean, and Russia. The "Long Trail of Tears" of the Indians from Alabama to Oklahoma, where Brodsky and Walcott were staying, is "a Gulag Archipelago / under this ice." Many of the topical poems omitted in the *Collected Poems,* such as "Parades, Parades" on Papa Doc's Haiti, show that the analogy between exiled West Indian and Russian poets has more basis in fact than might at first be apparent. Walcott's claim, however, is that tyranny and oppression are common to human history—as witnessed by slavery, the destruction of the American Indians, and Nazi extermination of European Jewry—and that true poets speak against such regimes. The poets are united in telling the truth about oppression, celebrating the survival of the human spirit, and being committed to poetry:

> The tourist archipelagoes of my South
> are prisons too, corruptible, and though
> there is no harder prison than writing verse,
> what's poetry, if it is worth its salt,
> but a phrase men can pass from hand to mouth?
> ("Forest of Europe" — *Star-Apple Kingdom,* p, 40)

"Forest of Europe" concludes, in Horatian fashion, with the two poets, Walcott and Brodsky, snowed in and sitting around a fire: "exchanging gutturals in this winter cave / of a brown cottage, while in drifts outside / mastodons force their systems through the snow." The parallel is to Richard Lovelace and Cotton at the conclusion of Lovelace's "The Grasse-hopper," where the two poets exchange friendship over drink, during the winter of Cromwell's oppressive regime. To read Walcott's verse is to become aware of the worth to an artist of a sense of vocation and tradition. Poets are a brotherhood, learning from each other their craft, their truths, and how to survive. Many poems are addressed to writers and create an international, interracial community defined by a mutual concern with literature, especially poetry.

The Fortunate Traveller (1981) includes a magnificent meditation on differences between "North and South," in which, seeing parallels between the diaspora of the Jews and blacks, Walcott wonders if he is possibly part Jew, and notes that even now in small-town Virginia the cashier avoids a black man's hand. It is an irony of his later work that the "red man" fleeing black dominance should in the United States find himself regarded as black and that he should see himself as similar to the black American entertainers of the past. Several poems refer to and imitate American poetry and art as an alien culture about which Walcott has feelings of ambivalence; Robert Lowell is particularly an influence on these poems. While the North is indifferent to human suffering, except as "compassionate fodder for the travel book," Walcott too is guilty of using the South as "literary material." He observes a world that lacks charity (in the Christian sense of love) and imagines the South in apocalyptical terms: "third horseman, / the leather-helmed locust." While the globe cracks "like a begging bowl," the North destroys its surplus grain. In the concluding poem there is a vision of a "season of phantasmal peace" where

> . . .all the nations of birds lifted together
> the huge net of the shadows of this earth
> in multitudinous dialects, twittering tongues,
> stitching and crossing it . . .
> and this season lasted one moment, like the pause

between dusk and darkness, between fury and peace
but, for such as our earth is now, it lasted long.
(pp. 464-465)

In *Midsummer* (1984), a powerful linked sequence of fifty-four poems in long
Virgilian lines, Walcott, returning to the tropics, compares his memories to what he
has become. "And this is the lot of all wanderers, this is their fate, / that the more they
wander, the more the world grows wide." In these later works he asserts the European
side of his racial and artistic heritage: "I am Watteau's wild oats." He admits "all your
work was really an effort to appease / the past, a need to be admitted among your
peers." But "You were distressed by your habitat, you shall not find peace / till you
and your origins reconcile"; "The midsummer sea, the hot pitch road, this grass, these
shacks that made me."

Walcott's exploration of the white, European colonial heritage of the Caribbean
continues in *The Last Carnival* (1983), one of his recently published *Three Plays*
(1986), a radical revision of his earlier, unpublished *In a Fine Castle* (1970). In the
earlier version, Brown, a reporter, rejects his radical black nationalist girlfriend and
separates, after a brief love affair, from the guilt-stricken daughter of an elite white
colonial family. As among both the blacks and whites he finds intolerance and pride,
he is unable to commit himself to either; while the whites flee the country the black
strikers march with their banners ignoring him. *The Last Carnival* uses a similar
situation as a reporter investigates a formerly important white family and falls in love
with Clodia, the guilt-ridden daughter; but the story has been enriched by giving a
central position to Agatha Willet, an English governess of working-class socialist
background, who has taught the black maids and local children parliamentary rights
and revolutionary ideals. If the la Fontaine family represents the continental cultural
heritage—Victor is a painter in the French tradition—ignored after independence,
Agatha illustrates Trinidad's British political inheritance. Contrasted to the now
powerless family is a failed black power revolution (alluding to an actual attempted
uprising in Trinidad during 1970 against the black government), the leaders of which
are being hunted by troops. Sydney, who as a child listened to Agatha, returns to the
la Fontaine house seeking a horse with which to escape and is helped by Clodia, who
regards him as a brother. The play covers a time span of twenty-two years, from 1948
to 1970; after the war Trinidad seemed a paradise to Agatha in comparison to
England, but in 1970 the British are being evacuated from the island. The play ends
with a feeling of uprooted displacement. All is carnival. Clodia tells Brown, "Find a
cause and love it. Die for it like Sydney."

Walcott's early historical, heroic, nationalist drama of the West Indian Federation
period was followed by folk plays, and then international, ritualistic, avant-garde
theater. *Dream on Monkey Mountain* (1970) mixes Genet, Soyinka, Fanon, and Peter
Brook. As Walcott moved from experimentalism to a more mainstream version of
total theater, he had an international audience in mind in such plays as *The Joker of
Seville* (1974) and *O Babylon!* (1976). In contrast to the high theatricality of *Dream
on Monkey Mountain, Joker of Seville*, and *Pantomime* (1977), *Three Plays* belongs to a

new phase of withdrawn, introspective, more traditional drama, directly rooted in Walcott's life and focused on the social realities of the postcolonial West Indies.

A Branch of the Blue Nile (1985) tests the applicability of European art and ambitions to West Indian society. As a fledgling West Indian theater company rehearses *Antony and Cleopatra,* tension develops between the white director returned from England, a black West Indian actor who studied in New York, and Christopher, a married Trinidadian who writes plays in dialect and sleeps with Sheila, the Cleopatra. The rehearsal of the play is applicable to West Indian society: "If there's disorder here, in this little world, no trust, no center, no authority, then lunacy is correct, we're wasting time. What is wrong in here is what's wrong with this country. Our country. And if, outside, there's mismanagement and madness, we must not go mad" (p. 223). When one actor argues that the attempt to make them into a better theater company has only led to contempt for Trinidad and hallucinations of fame, the speech is a *tirade;* European conventions give form to local feelings. A theme of *A Branch of the Blue Nile* is the use and misuse of talent, especially in the arts. Sheila, both hurt by Christopher and fearing her ambitions, retreats to a fundamentalist religious group. The title of the play comes from her explanation of why she gave up playing Cleopatra and quit the theater for the church: " 'cause the Caroni isn't a branch of the river Nile, / and Trinidad isn't Egypt, except at Carnival, / so the world sniggers when I speak her lines" (p. 285). But discovering that her talent as an actress is wasted as a gospel singer, Sheila returns to the struggling theater company.

Walcott argues the need to learn from and meet international standards, but the sources of his creativity are personal and West Indian experience. The autobiographical impulses in his poetry are paralleled by the return home at the end of *Dream on Monkey Mountain,* the affirmation of the calypso tradition in *Pantomime,* Brown's search for the white part of his heritage in *The Last Carnival,* and, even, in *A Branch of the Blue Nile,* the symbolism of method acting techniques, with their insistence upon using the actor's personal experience. Walcott's poetry is filled with returns home, which result in a further awareness of how far he has evolved from his roots.

A nostalgia for the past, for a simpler, less monied, rural Caribbean society is the basis of *Beef, No Chicken* (1981), the only farce Walcott has published; its themes include being true to the values with which one was raised and fear that development and modernization will Americanize the environment, bringing, along with new wealth, a radical increase of economic and spiritual corruption. As in many works of Third World literature, the building of a road, linking a provincial village to the capital, is symbolic of social change; here the owner of an absurd old-time combined restaurant-garage refuses to accept bribes to allow planning permission for the road that threatens his quiet way of life. *Beef, No Chicken* shows Walcott's awareness that the colonial culture in which he was raised is rapidly disappearing.

Although Walcott is widely recognized as one of the best poets and dramatists of our time, his work falls outside present critical discussion. We are not used to a Third World writer who both loves his native land and thanks his colonial education for the tools to express himself. Of the poets who have continued within the traditions of English prosody and stanzaic forms while progressively incorporating the lessons of modern and world literature, perhaps only Geoffrey Hill has more power and range; but where Hill obviously writes obscure, profound verse, Walcott gives an impression of simplicity, and when found to be difficult and puzzling is incorrectly said to be imprecise. He is a complex poet whose work rapidly moves from the particular to the universal, who often is similar to Pasternak and the Russian modernists in the multiplicity of significance of his metaphors, and whose use of such commonplace images as sky, water, earth, south, and north constitutes an elaborate system of private symbols. Perhaps because the fullness of his technique makes an accurate description of his style difficult, there has not been much sustained comment on his work. As Walcott, Soyinka, and other "barbarians" from the former colonies take over the imperial literatures, English studies must undergo a far more serious revolution than that represented by current arguments about theory.

WARNER'S
BEEF, NO CHICKEN
AN INSPIRED PRODUCTION

Judy Stone

More by chance than design, I recently found myself in Barbados during the run of Stage One's latest production, Derek Walcott's comedy "Beef, No Chicken", which featured Trinidad's Errol Jones in the lead role. Errol first created the character of Otto Hogan for the Trinidad Theatre Workshop premiere of this comedy at the Little Carib, back in 1981. It was not one of the Workshop's most scintillating productions.

Ever since the role of director came to prominence in the theatre, early in this century, there has been controversy over whether it is the talent of the director or of the actors that most influences the quality of the finished production. In the developed countries with intensive theatre activity, critical opinion on the subject seems to roll in fashionable waves from one view to the other over the decades. My present reading, for instance, suggests that in England recently there has been, at least in theory, a movement away from the director's piece to the actor's piece. The point is not that one or the other talent is less necessary — a high quality production depends on high quality input in every sphere, including script and design. But in my own experience a strong director can stage a satisfying production even when the cast is second rate, while a more gifted actor may give a second-rate performance when guided by mediocre direction.

I have seen two or more productions, under different directors, of quite a number of plays, amongst which I can count Douglas Archibald's "The Rose Slip"; Errol John's "Moon on a Rainbow Shawl"; Raoul Pantin's "Hatuey"; Trevor Rhone's "Old Story Time"; Eric Roach's "Belle Fanto"; Derek Walcott's "Ti-Jean" and "Dream on Monkey Mountain" and "Pantomine", and several works of Shakespeare. In every case it has seemed to me that the calibre of the director is what, in the end, has made or marred the production.

That first Workshop production of "Beef, No Chicken", under the somewhat pedestrian direction of Cecil Gray, left me convinced that the playwright had tried an experiment — that hadn't worked. The plot meandered without point, the situation was so ludicrously far-fetched as to be beyond credibility, the humour so forced it fell flat. The production was further vitiated by some abysmally lifeless performances, and even the solid work by the Workshop stalwarts offered little that was fresh enough to offset the tedium. With the memory of this off-putting production in mind, it was more in the spirit of research than with any great enthusiasm that I arranged to take in the Stage One production at the Queen's Park Steel Shed. (Barbados, incidentally, has three fine theatre buildings, any one of which is enough to make a Trinidad theatre person green with envy.)

I should have known better. Even though here in Trinidad we have seen Earl Warner work only with more serious drama ("Like Them That Dream", "Sufferer's Song", "Woza Albert"), not comedy, we already recognised him as one of the most inspired directors in the Caribbean, and under Earl's deft touch Stage One's "Beef, No Chicken" sprang to glorious life. To be fair, since the Trinidad run Derek Walcott had done some serious rewriting to produce a more coherent — and funnier—script, and then Earl waded in with his cutting scissors to shape a tauter production.

The result revealed one of Derek's most accessible works, genuinely a "hilarious comedy" as advertised, but layered with the small personal tragedies that are concomitant with progress. Far from being pointless, the production drove home a clear statement to every one of us in these developing societies; and what had seemed ludicrous was now presented with its own inner logic so consistently intact as to be entirely credible on its own terms. No wonder Earl was able to open his programme note with the following sympathetic paragraph:

> It is a delicate process to take a tragic situation and shape from it a
> hilarious comedy without crudity and insensitivity to the subject matter.
> The success of this comedy as literature and theatre testifies to the power
> of Walcott's acute and masterful craft.
>
> The play is a kaiso, a seriocomic ballad on a real social experience. Yet,
> finally, the pathos within the given situations is never lost, and the
> ambivalence of progress is illuminated.

And perhaps the vital difference between the two directorial approaches was that Cecil Gray strove to emphasise the comedy, and play down the tragedy, while Earl Warner never lost sight of the tragedy, and the comedy as a result was all the richer and more poignant.

The catalyst for the action of the play is the opening of a new highway in Couva, which threatens the livelihood of Otto, his sister Euphony and his niece Drusilla, as it threatens the roti-eatery (cum-mechanic-shop) that they run. It is the antics of these three, as they try according to their individual reactions to avert or surmount or harness progress, that provide most of the action and comedy of the piece.

Stage One counts among its members several major talents, and its first President and Artistic Director, writer-director Michael Gilkes, virtually stole the show as

Euphony's reserved fiance, school-master Eldridge Franco. When he first appeared on stage, strutting with hump-shoulders and craned neck, a questing jaw and quixotically rolling eyes, in an interpretation of the role that bordered on farcical caricature, I doubted he could carry it through successfully. But he did, triumphantly, with enough depth and occasional sanity in his engaging lunacy to create a wholly convincing character. So riveting was Michael's performance, it was fortunate that Errol Jones was there to balance the cast with a strong but well-controlled Otto.

The rest of the Stage One cast was generally less powerful and accomplished, but worked with a will. I found it interesting that all four actresses, while working with a very sure sense of character, projected less personality than the Workshop's quartet (which comprised Theresa Awai, Sonya Moze, Jerline Quamina and Brenda Shillingford, a high-powered list), while the Stage One councillors, headed by veteran Clairmonte Taitt as the mayor, bristled with personality, contrived or otherwise and despite some fairly green work, in startling contrast to the dreary council meetings of the Workshop version.

The entire Stage One cast contributed to a vibrant swiftly-moving production that didn't let up until the last fifteen minutes or so — an end clearly over-written and under-rehearsed — but by that time the audience, which had been literally leaping out of its seat in spontaneous appreciation, would have forgiven anything.

One last comment. Credit to the director and cast in this Stage One production speaks for itself—but is still spelled out in the programme. As is credit for innumerable other functions from technicians, set construction and costumes to front-of house, programmes and publicity. It is incomprehensible to me that no credit is given either for the superb set design, or for the lighting design.

I assume, perhaps incorrectly, that it is again Earl Warner who deserves that credit. As another theatre practitioner remarked to me, the omission of these essential credits is symptomatic of certain hangover attitudes from the past in Caribbean theatre. We have to remember that the quality of the final production depends on the quality of input in every sphere, even if it is the director's hand that leaves the clearest mark.

THE LAST CARNIVAL

Earl Lovelace

When Agatha Willet (Fran McDormand) the young English governess arrives in Trinidad to take care of Victor De La Fontaine's two children whose mother is dead, she sets up a not so subtle contest between Victor and his brother Oswald who both want to impress her, a contest in which each brother attempts to rationalise his existence. It is by this means that we enter the lives of the De La Fontaines, a French Creole family, settled on their Santa Rosa Estate with their silent black maid (Joy Maitland) and their faithful house servant, George (Fred Hope) as they live out what may be seen as their history in this island.

On the one hand there is Oswald (Maurice Brash). He has remained on the estate, his island, as a planter. In him we see a man with no real passion for anything, one who is content to endure his life, a little aloof from his fellow French creoles, to drink his rum and to enjoy his carnival. He gives no suggestion of having any ambition to venture out of his privilege or plantation; but, there is a pathos about Oswald, an absence within him that he mourns with a silent cry of pain for the loss of something never embraced; for though Oswald gives the impression of being uncultured, indeed, wants to give it, we glimpse in Oswald the possession of a soul. It should be said right here that Maurice Brash rises to the challenge of portraying this Oswald and succeeds to the degree that, not only are we touched by Oswald, we want him to be saved.

Victor (Cotter Smith) the other brother, has lived and studied in Paris and is more grossly, more demonically cultured than Oswald. Art is his life, so his life, we think, is about something; but the more closely we view Victor the more do we see sterility. Victor really has no life; his life has become his artist's pain. He refuses to enter into the world around him, yet he is naive and, arrogant is not the word, foolish enough to believe that he can in any meaningful way influence its ideas of culture.

But even as we are concerned about the brothers, it is Miss Willet that engages our attention. We feel in Miss Willet a spirit and a truth and a searching and a potential on her own for a fuller, a more real life than is lived by the brothers. We believe that Miss Willet has the gifts to unlock the clear potential in the brothers, to make them face the reality of their living, to extend themselves beyond their privilege and their plantation. It is in this relationship that the central tension of the play resides. Will

Agatha change them? Will Victor marry her? Or will Oswald get up enough spunk and claim her for himself?

Though we feel she herself would like to marry Victor, she is a better complement to Oswald, but Victor is a possessive, domineering, suicidal being who already views her as his property. To him she is someone to perform before, to torment with claims of his pain, to admire his work and to listen to his self-deprecation. Agatha Willet tries, but she doesn't change the brothers; it is she who is changed, and when she is, it is with a strict hygienic unfeeling more gross in its way than that of the brothers.

She resents this change in herself, she resents the brothers for what they have done to her, but she remains to watch the island's independence, its flag lifted as Victor cynically observes its air force with its single plane, to applaud Oswald batting at the cricket match, to drink wine, the same brand, for Independence has not changed them, and when Victor observes of the Blacks, "It is their turn now," it is as if he is talking about people on another planet.

It will take the Black Power uprisings and the burning down of their Santa Rosa Estate to bring the De La Fontaines into the reality that had lived for two hundred years on their doorstep a million miles away. Now for the first time Black people as a force, as a potential for power, enter their lives in the persons of George (Fred Hope), Sydney, George's nephew the Black power militant and Brown, the journalist. Victor by this time is dead, Oswald is old and settled in his ways, and it is really the children, Tony and Clodia, who have by now become adults who must now respond to this new situation.

Sadly, Tony shows more bewilderment than resolution. Indeed, his character seems to fall apart and he has nothing to offer to the situation except to follow the advice of his uncle Oswald which is to run to safety. This running will be done well: women first: Clodia must leave first, the men will follow.

But Clodia has jumped up with Invaders while the riot raged, got spat upon and now comes to their house in Port of Spain to offer Sydney, the Black Power militant (Charles Applewhaite) her horse (he used to ride it as a boy on the Estate and get beaten by George for doing so) by which means he would escape to the hills.

She meets Brown (Errol Roberts), at her home and establishes a most unconvincing relationship with him and very soon is offering herself to him; but Brown, the journalist, the cool dude, is unprepared to accept her offer of herself; he simply wants "to hold her hand", and the young woman, with nowhere to turn, believes the best she can do is to follow family instructions and go to the safe haven, France.

As she is leaving she tells Brown, "I love this island and I am leaving it. You hate it and you are staying."

This kind of statement is one example of the easy lines Walcott offers instead of getting into the truth that lies in the guts of the play. There is a stronger, a more fundamental truth in Clodia's attitude to the island, that has nothing to do with loving or hating. She belongs to it, by birth, by culture, by all that makes a native native of a place. Where as member of a new generation, she is an advance on the old, is in her acceptance and understanding of a truth that the others have been blind to: that France, the home of her forefathers, is not her home; Trinidad is, and she cannot ignore it and pretend herself the possessor of a superior culture like her father Victor not exist with her heart a silent cry of pain, like uncle Oswald.

My criticism of the play is that it fails to press home, indeed plunge into, those truths that are there within the fabric of the play, and that the writer, out of indulgence presents incomplete characterisation and "tough" statements to serve more unimportant points in the play.

The Black Power militant suffers, Brown suffers, Clodia herself is not properly developed and the use of the American actor and actress robs us in this play of the opportunity of seeing native talents deal with their own important story.

Even so, I would contend that "The Last Carnival" is a strong and textured play which is saying important things about people and relations and for me one of its achievements is bringing out from their privilege and plantation — to be involved in something, a life, bigger and fuller — our French Creole brethren. This will not be done with any now-for-now hypocritical cry of "All ah we is One"; but if a play can make us see them and make us see ourselves, weak, fallible, foolish, in pain and now and again magnificent and human we can move towards a life.

"The Last Carnival" can achieve this and that is why Walcott must see that in a play of such genuine artistic and social potential we cannot accept the easy state- ments, no matter how tough they sound and even though we may sometimes understand what generates them.

I am convinced that "The Last Carnival" deserves a more comprehensive and comprehensible Brown; like the play itself, Brown contains too much potential to be so limp. Brown, after all, is the new Black Walcott's cosmos, and while he is a journalist and therefore ferrying between the news and the newsroom, he suggests a power more sophisticated and responsible than the servant's power gloried in by George or the unfocussed and unreal rage Walcott imposes upon his Black Power radical, Sidney. Walcott places Brown in the position to offer Clodia a hope, but Walcott's Brown lacks passion, he lacks guts, he lacks decisiveness. Brown, desiring Clodia (within the framework of their five minute romance) wants only to hold her hand, that is enough for him, he tells her, while she is prepared to offer her whole self.

What is wrong with Brown? Firstly, the situation; and then Brown needs time to deal with the emotional demands of his new status; yet, while his diffidence is agonising for those of us who want to see a more affirming Brown, it would be disastrous to have Brown rush hot and sweaty to embrace Clodia. Brown says he believes in nothing. It is more complex than that, and the play must take us into the guts of that complexity. Maybe the problem is that Brown is made to appear to stand for too many different Blacks, when Brown, after all, is Brown.

Even with his inadequacies, Brown as a character, offers a caution that we need to heed: that the Browns, no matter what their power or potential, when they lack guts, decisiveness, when they lack heart and are too cute, are not able to offer anything and are impotent to receive love; but who is giving love? Clodia is waiting for the plane and the others are packed and waiting.

It is Miss Willet that offers the truest and most potent symbol of the play and with Oswald the most satisfying character. Miss Willet is the island to whom the De La

Fontaines despite their usage of her, do not make any commitment. Even as we see this I believe Walcott wants us to see something more: that all of us, in our ways and possibly for other reasons, have used her without making that commitment that we owe her. We may argue as to the reasons for our various attitudes. The play demonstrates poignantly the island's loneliness and all our loss.

ON EUROCENTRIC CRITICAL THEORY:
Some Paradigms From The Texts And Sub-Texts Of Post-Colonial Writing

Biodun Jeyifo

As quiet as it is kept, the realisation is gaining wide currency in literary circles around the world that the volume of writing now coming from the non-Western, Third World countries far outstrips that emanating from the "First World". More-over, it is also increasingly being recognized that this vast harvest, this cornucopia from the Third World contains some of the most interesting and innovative writing in contemporary literature. Think about it: if, with "Anglophone", "Francophone" or "Lusophone" writing from the non-Western world you include writing in the most prominent literary languages of the Third World say, Arabic, Bengali, Chinese, Urdu, Gujerati, Swahili and Amharic, you can begin to get a grasp of the shifts in the densities and concentrations of the literary map of the world. But parallel to this phenomenal reconfiguration of the global balance of forces in the production of literature is the view also prevalent throughout the world, that the most penetrating, the most seminal criticism, metacriticism or "theory" is coming from the metropolitan centres in Europe and America. Just how prevalent this view of a new international division of labour in the world of literature and criticism has become is afforded by a recent short but thought provoking article in no less a publication than *The Chronicle of Higher Education,* written by W.J.T. Mitchell (April 19, 1989). Mr. Mitchell is a professor of English at the University of Chicago and moreover, is editor of *Critical Inquiry,* one of the most influential academic journals of contemporary criticism and literary theory in the En-glish-speaking world. Let me quote some salient observations from the article:

> The most important new literature is emerging from the colonies —
> regions and peoples that have been economically or militarily dominated

376

in the past — while the most provocative new literary criticism is emanating from the imperial centres that once dominated them — the industrial
nations of Europe and America.

Horace noted long ago that the transfer of empire from Greece to
Rome (the *translatio imperii*) was accompanied by a transfer of culture
and learning (a *translatio studii*). Today the cultural transfer is no longer
one-way. But what is the nature of "the transference going on between the
declining imperial power and their former colonies, and between contemporary literature and criticism?

Professor Mitchell's views and positions in this important article come from the
liberal critical vanguardism of the American literary establishment, one that is particularly responsive to new currents, new directions from the "non-canonical" traditions of both literature and criticism. Moreover, Professor Mitchell advances the view
in this article that powerful and increasingly desperate and hysterical neo-conservative
critics and scholars are up in arms against the "reconceptualizations" and
"reconfigurations" now emerging in the world of literature and criticism and that an
alliance, "a positive, collaborative relationship between post-imperial criticism and
post-colonial literature" might be needed to stave off this projected neoconservative
redoubt. This is an important, weighty observation and I would like to frame my
reflections in this short essay around what I perceive to be its many ramifications.

The call of Professor Mitchell in this article for collaboration and solidarity
between "post-colonial literature" and "post-imperial criticism" no doubt comes
from a genuine, enlightened solicitude which relates itself to serious areas of cultural
politics, even if the designated terms and entities of the collaboration — "post-
colonial literature" and "post-imperial criticism" — are not so unproblematic [But
more on this later]. The journal which Mr. Mitchell edits has been an important
forum for important interrogations of canonical orthodoxies and exclusionary critical
practices which ignore texts and traditions other than the hegemonic literary production and critical discourses of Europe and America. One can only wish that more
journals and institutions would, like the one Mr. Mitchell directs, and which are
strategically located in the apparatus of theoretical inquiry and critical discourse, be
more responsive to, or even be more aware of developments and trends beyond the
concerns and obsessions of a self-cocooned Western canonical enclave.

But it must be recognized that the solicitude and enthusiasms of many Western
critics and scholars for non-Western, post-colonial literature, have behind them a
problematic history which is encapsulated by that troubled, loaded buzz word
"Eurocentrism". For if Eurocentrism has often expressed itself, in different forms of
cultural racism, as a denial of, a supercilious condescension towards non-Western
literary traditions, it is also often conversely expressed as a generous solicitude, an
authenticating embrace which confers what it deems a badge of authenticity, for the
non-Western text, writer or whole literary traditions, only to be accosted with charges
of paternalism and subtle forms of prejudice and will-to-domination.

At this late stage of the history of debates over imperialism and its discontents, one states the obvious by pointing out that Eurocentrism is a vast cultural and intellectual phenomenon which subsumes its more local and particular expressions in literary criticism, and now "theory". The work of contemporary writers like Aimé Césaire (*Discourse on Colonialism*), Eric R. Wolf (*Europe and the People Without History*), Edward Said (*Orientalism*), Johannes Fabian (*Time and the Other*) and Talal Asad (*Anthropology and the Colonial Encounter*), among others, show the dispersal of the phenomenon among disparate disciplines and fields of inquiry. All of which goes to demonstrate that without having the models and standards of the exacting scholarship and broad, capacious vision of these scholars in mind, one enters the terrain of discourse and counter-discourse on Eurocentrism at the risk of gross simplifications and unsuspected discursive traps. And need I add that this last observation is intended not only as a general cautionary nudge to literary criticism, which often purposes itself as a substitute for all of critical thought, but also as a reminder to myself about the lurking pitfalls of *this* discursive terrain.

It will thus be readily appreciated that I have chosen to approach the subject in this essay by way of a calculated detour through the discourses on Eurocentrism embedded in some selected literary texts. In such contexts a host of textual strategies and rhetorical mediations absorb and defamiliarize the tensions and sensitivities that discussions of Eurocentrism almost always generate. In particular I have chosen two texts of Derek Walcott, *Dream on Monkey Mountain* and *Pantomime* as paradigmatic deconstructions of the two types of Eurocentrism broadly hinted at above: the Eurocentrism which withholds, which excludes, which disdains; and that which embraces, invites, gives.

The distance covered in contemporary post-colonial writing in the debunking, the demythologization of Eurocentric claims to the embodiment of absolute Truth or Knowledge, especially of non-European peoples and societies, is, I believe, provided by the paradigmatic move in the dramaturgy of Derek Walcott from *Dream on Monkey Mountain* (1967) to *Pantomime* (1978) concerning the respective emblematic explorations in these two plays of the response of the "native" as the object of Eurocentric discursive, signifying and explanatory systems. A savage, iconoclastic, mythoclastic assault on the ethical-universal postulates of the Western intellectual traditions, and specifically the objective, positivist human sciences (like jurisprudence) marks what we may identify as the epistemological theme of these plays, where "theme" is an inaccurate, inadequate conceptual representation of these aspects of both Walcott's dramaturgy and a host of other post-colonial writers, from Achebe to Coetzee, from Soyinka to Rushdie, from Mariama Ba to Ama Ata Aidoo. We see this common iconoclastic impulse particularly in the characters of Corporal Lestrade and Moustique in *Dream on Monkey Mountain* and Jackson Philip in *Pantomime*. What powers this impulse is the thinking that "white" domination is not only political and socio-economic, it is also, or aspires to total effectivity in the naming of things, in signifying and explanatory systems; in other words, it seeks to be an *epistemic* order of control and manipulation. Corporal Lestrade and Jackson Philip in particular deploy a surfeit of brilliant, witty conceits and tropes to debunk this epistemic, nomenclatural hegemony. But there are important, even decisive departures in the respective overall demythologizing impulse and postures of these two plays, and it is this pattern of differentiation which commends them as suggestive paradigms for the debates on Eurocentrism and critical theory.

Between Corporal Lestrade and Moustique in *Dream on Monkey Mountain* what we encounter is the "native" who, having rejected both Eurocentric discursive colonization *and* autonomous indigenous epistemologies and ritual beliefs, can only lapse into a desperate cynicism, charlatanism, and in the case of Moustique, a convenient opportunism. The powerful "healing" dream scene of Act One of the play renders this aspect of Moustique's vocation as an "explainer", who, despising both the colonizer and the colonized and their respective panoply of signification, appeals to a Transcendent, omniscient Spirit [God] outside, beyond and above the contest, a Spirit in whom Moustique does not believe but only deploys in order to manipulate the colonized "native" population:

> MOUSTIQUE
> Ah, ah you see, all you.
> Ain't white priest come and nothing happen?
> Ain't white doctor come and was agony still?
> Ain't you take bush medicine, and no sweat break?
> White medicine, bush medicine,
> not one of them work!
> White prayers, black prayers,
> and still no deliverance!
> And who heal the man?
> Makak! Makak!
> All your deliverance lie in this man.
> The man is God's messenger
> So, further the cause, brothers and sisters.
> [He opens his haversack and holds it before him]
> Further the cause,
> Drop what you have in there...
> God's work must be done,
> and like Saint Peter self,
> Moustique, that's me,
> is Secretary-Treasurer
> (p. 251)

The logic of this cynically opportunist, self-cancelling, double assault on both Eurocentric epistemologies and signifying systems *and* the countermanding nativist response reaches its most brilliant, relentless articulation in the famous Apotheosis scene of the play [Scene Three, Part Two]. Walcott indisputably wrote this magnificent cautionary allegorization of the natives' revenge against what Gayatri Spivak has theorized as the totalizing "epistemic violence" of imperialism with the spirit of Bandung active in his creative consciousness, the heady spirit in the Fifties and Sixties of "emergent" Africa and Asia coming into their own and settling scores with their former colonial overlords. The allegorical power of the scene derives, I think, from Walcott's frank, unflinching engagement with the violence of Eurocentric signifying practices and explanatory systems, in their imbrication in the objective of imperialistic domination. It is indeed useful to note that Walcott has the following quote from Sartre's famous Introduction to Fanon's *The Wretched of the Earth* as an epigraph to Part Two of *Dream on Monkey Mountain,* the movement of the dramatic action of the play which brings the nihilistic confrontation with Eurocentrism to a head:

> Let us add, for certain other carefully selected unfortunates, that other witchery of which I have already spoken: Western culture. If I were them, you may say, I'd prefer my mumbo-jumbo to their Acropolis. Very good: you've grasped the situation. But not altogether, because you aren't them — or not yet. Otherwise you would know that they can't choose; they must have both. Two worlds; that makes two bewitchings; they dance all night and at dawn they crowd into the churches to hear Mass; each day the split widens. Our enemy betrays his brothers and becomes our accomplice; his brothers do the same thing. The status of "native" is a nervous condition introduced and maintained by the settler among colonized people with their consent.

Only against the background of this phantasmic but deadly serious agonistic encounter does the arraignment and trial of the whole of "Western culture" in this scene make "sense", a "sense", a logic which in fact was later to be acted out by Idi Amin in his gratuitous antics against some of the most resonant colonialist symbols and tropes of Eurocentrism such as the famous enactment in which he was borne aloft in a litter by four white men, this as a parodistic signification on the "White man's burden". It is, I think, necessary to quote from the scene at some length:

> [All have assembled. The CORPORAL steps forward, then addresses
> MAKAK]
> CORPORAL
> Inventor of history! [Kisses MAKAK's foot]
> MAKAK
> I am only a shadow.
> CORPORAL
> Shh. Quiet, my prince.
> MAKAK
> A hollow God. A phantom.
> CORPORAL
> Wives, warriors, chieftains! The law takes no sides, it changes the
> complexion of things. History is without pardon, justice hawk-swift, but
> mercy everlasting. We have prisoners and traitors, and they must be
> judged swiftly. The law of a country is the law of that country. Roman

law, my friends, is not tribal law.Tribal law,in conclusion, is not Roman
law. Therefore, wherever we are, let us have justice. We have no time for
patient reforms. Mindless as the hawk, impetuous as lions, as dried of
compassion as the bowels of a jackal. Elsewhere, the swiftness of justice
is barbarously slow, but our progress cannot stop to think. In a short
while, the prisoners shall be summoned, so prepare them, Basil and
Pamphilion. First, the accused, and after them, the tributes.
[The prisoners are presented]
Read them, Basil!
BASIL
They are Noah, but not the son of Ham, Aristotle, I'm skipping a bit,
Abraham Lincoln, Alexander of Macedon, Shakespeare, I can cite
relevant texts, Plato, Copernicus, Galileo and perhaps Ptolemy,
Christopher Marlowe, Robert E. Lee, Sir John Hawkins, Sir Francis
Drake, The Phantom, Mandrake the Magician [The TRIBES are
laughing] It's not funny, my Lords, Tarzan, Dante, Sir Cecil Rhodes,
William Wilberforce, the unidentified author of The Song of Solomon,
Lorenzo de Medici, Florence Nightingale, Al Jolson, Horatio Nelson,
and, but why go on? Their crime, whatever their plea, whatever
extenuation of circumstances, whether of genius or geography, is that
they are indubitably, with the possible exception of Alexandre Dumas,
Sr. and Jr., and Alexis, I think it is Pushkin, white. Some are dead and
cannot speak for themselves, but a drop of milk is enough to condemn
them, to banish them from the archives of the bo-leaf and the papyrus,
from the waxen tablet and the tribal stone. For you, my Lords, are
shapers of history. We await your judgement, O tribes.
TRIBES
Hang them!
(p. 310-312)

"Their crime, whatever their plea, whatever extenuation of circumstances,
whether of genius or geography, is that they are indubitably . . . white". The utter
seriousness, the implacable, crystalline logic of this absurd arraignment —
Shakespeare and Al Jolson, Galileo and the KKK — can only be grasped if we pluck
from its dispersal in disparate semiotic contexts and significatory locations the coding
and re-codings of "white" as the unmarked marker, "white" fetishized as ultimate
repository of Beauty, Reality, Value: "Whites Only", "Honorary Whites" (a term
officially accorded the Japanese in South Africa, but not other Asian national groups
like the Chinese and Indians), the white-robed and hooded "Knights of Klu-Klux-
Klan", the white anthropomorphic iconography of divinity and sainthood in Christianity, white bleaching creams. All these interfuse with more specifically *epistemological* coordinates: Western "white" civilization *racialized* (and not only by the Nazis)
and encoded as the ultimate marker of Truth, Knowledge, Rationality in the elaborate constructs of "the great chain of being", as Arthur O. Lovejoy informs us in his

famous treatise of that title. Derek Walcott is barely in control of the relentlessly
parodistic smashing of icon and fetishes in this play, given the utter negativity of the
epistemic revolt, itself a response to the unstinting negation projected by *this* particular paradigm of a Eurocentrism which withholds and excludes absolutely. At the end
of it all, Makak has exorcised the demons and phantoms of his bewitched, schizophrenic subjectivity; but he does so away in the mountains to which he now
withdraws completely, into a private space of subjectivist autarky. He cannot be the
"King of Africa", the "Conquering Lion of Judah" of his dreams since he has seen
how hollow that turns out to be in a world never quite free of both Eurocentric
"epistemic violence" and the giddy paroxyms of nihilistic revolt and manipulation
which it engenders: *aut caesar, aut nihil.*

Although it has a much smaller cast of characters, *Pantomime* encapsulates a much
more engrossing and dialectical frame of referents of epistemic Eurocentrism and its
demythologization than *Dream on Monkey Mountain.* The dramaturgic "trick" employed to achieve this seems derived from the principles of dramatic form and
performance styles developed by Athol Fugard and the South African anti-apartheid
theatrical movement of Barney Simon, John Kani, Winston Ntshona, the Market
Theatre and others; small casts of two or three characters constantly changing roles,
constantly constructing and deconstructing, totalizing and detotalizing social wholes,
social macrocosms and their fragments and microcosms. A "perfect" formalistic
vehicle for a drama which seeks the epistemic deconstruction of the texts and signs of
Eurocentrism.

The figural, metaphoric strategy which establishes *Pantomime* as a decisively
different paradigm of epistemic demythologization than *Dream on Monkey Mountain*
is that the "text" deployed in this play has been devised out of Defoe's *Robinson
Crusoe,* a classic "megatext" of Eurocentrism. Moreover, the roles are now reversed, a
reversal significantly voluntarily proposed and *demanded* by the white character,
Harry Trewe, a retired British actor who has removed himself from personal, domestic and professional disasters and decline in Britain to the island of Tobago in the
Caribbean. Here he establishes the "Castaway Guest House" and hires a retired
Trinidadian calypsonian and carnival maestro, Jackson Philip, as his "factotum". So
as to draw guests to his decrepit establishment, Trewe devises an improvisational
script reversing the roles, the identities, the figural binarisms of Defoe's classic text:
the white Trewe will play Friday; the black Philip will play Crusoe. But Harry
Trewe's project comes only partly out of business calculations; he is also a liberal, a
progressive who insists on the edifying potentiality of such an entertainment for both
the white tourists to the island and the local black Creole community:

> JACKSON
> That is white-man fighting. Anyway, Mr. Trewe, I feel the fun finish; I
> would like, with your permission, to get up now and fix up the sun
> deck. 'Cause when rain fall . . .
> HARRY
> Forget the sun deck. I'd say, Jackson, that we've come closer to a mutual

respect, and that things need not get that hostile. Sit, and let me explain what I had in mind.

JACKSON

I take it that's an order?

HARRY

You want it to be an order? Okay, it's an order.

JACKSON

It didn't sound like no order.

HARRY

Look, I'm a liberal, Jackson. I've done the whole routine. Aldermaston, Suez, Ban the Bomb, Burn the Bra, Pity the Poor Pakis, et cetera. I've even tried jumping up to the steel band at Notting Hill Gate, and I'd no idea I'd wind up in this ironic position of giving orders, but if the new script I've been given says: HARRY TREWE, HOTEL MANAGER, then I'm going to play Harry Trewe, Hotel Manager, to the hilt, damnit. So *sit* down! Please. Oh, goddamnit, *sit . . . down . . .*

(Jackson sits. Nods)

Good. Relax. Smoke. Have a cup of tepid coffee. I sat up from about three this morning, working out this whole skit in my head.

(Pause)

Mind putting that hat on for a second, it will help my point. Come on. It'll make things clearer.

(He gives Jackson the goatskin hat. Jackson, after a pause, puts it on)

JACKSON

I'll take that cigarette.

(Harry hands over a cigarette)

HARRY

They've seen that stuff, time after time. Limbo, dancing girls, fire-eating . . .

JACKSON

Light.

HARRY

Oh, sorry.

(He lights Jackson's cigarette)

JACKSON

I listening.

HARRY

We could turn this little place right here into a little cabaret, with some very witty acts. Build up the right audience. Get an edge on the others. So, I thought. Suppose I get this material down to two people. Me and . . . well, me and somebody else. Robinson Crusoe and Man Friday. We could work up a good satire, you know, on the master-servant — no offense — relationship. Labour-management, white-black, and so on . . . Making some trenchant points about topical things, you know.

Add that show to the special dinner for the price of one ticket . . .
(p. 107-109)

Things do not, of course, work out the way. Trewe's script envisions a revision of
Robinson Crusoe. For one thing, Trewe's revision does not go far enough for Philip.
Philip renames Friday Thursday. He renames all the props and paraphernalia of
survival and "civilization" that master and servant, colonizer and colonized have to
share. And he disagrees violently with Trewe over what spiritual qualities sustained
Crusoe on the island and allows him to establish dominion over it, its flora and fauna,
and Friday. The twists and turns, the explosive negative racial and cultural material
thrown up by this encounter are made bearable and commensurable only by the
powerfully enabling and metaphorically suggestive fact that both men have been
actors, performers, entertainers. The performance idioms of the English music hall
and the Trinidadian calypsonian carnival become vehicles of thorough going textual
revisions of Defoe's classic novel and deconstructive assault on a vast array of cultural
systems and codes which have defined the encounter of the colonizer and the
colonized. At the end of it all, Trewe finds that the "pantomime" cannot be played
innocently; there is too much at stake:

> HARRY
> Look, I'm sorry to interrupt you again, Jackson, but as I — you know
> — was watching you, I realized it's much more profound than that; that
> it could get offensive. We're trying to do something light, just a little
> pantomime, a little satire, a little picong. But if you take this thing
> seriously, we might commit Art, which is a kind of crime in this
> society . . . I mean, there'd be a lot of things there that people . . . well,
> it would make them think too much, and well, we don't want that . . .
> we just want a little . . . entertainment.
> JACKSON
> How do you mean, Mr. Trewe?
> HARRY
> Well, I mean if you . . . well, I mean. If you did the whole thing in
> reverse . . . I mean, okay, well, all right . . . you've got this black
> man . . . no, no . . . all right. You've got this man who is black,
> Robinson Crusoe, and he discovers this island on which there is this
> white cannibal, all right?
> JACKSON
> Yes. That is, after he has killed the goat . . .
> HARRY
> Yes, I know, I know. After he has killed the goat and made a . . . the hat,
> the parasol, and all of that . . . and, anyway, he comes across this man
> called Friday.
> JACKSON
> How do you know I mightn't choose to call him Thursday? Do I have

to copy every . . . I mean, are we improvising?

HARRY

All right, so it's Thursday. He comes across this naked white cannibal called Thursday, you know. And then look at what would happen. He would have to start to . . . well, he'd have to, sorry . . . This cannibal, who is a Christian, would have to start unlearning his Christianity. He would have to be taught . . . I mean . . . he'd have to be taught by this — African . . . that everything was wrong, that what he was doing . . . I mean, for nearly two thousand years . . . was wrong. That his civilization, his culture, his whatever, was . . . *horrible*. Was all . . . wrong. Barbarous, I mean, you know. And Crusoe would then have to teach him things like, you know, about . . . Africa, his gods, patamba, and so on . . . and it would get very, very complicated, and I suppose ultimately it would be very boring, and what we'd have on our hands would be . . . would be a play and not a little pantomime . . .

JACKSON

I'm too ambitious?

HARRY

No, no, the whole thing would have to be reversed; white would become black, you know . . .

JACKSON

(Smiling)

You see, Mr. Trewe, I don't see anything wrong with that, up to now.

HARRY

Well, I do. It's not the sort of thing I want, and I think you'd better clean up, and I'm going inside, and when I come back I'd like this whole place just as it was. I mean, just before everything started.

JACKSON

You mean you'd like it returned to its primal state? Natural? Before Crusoe finds Thursday? But, you see, that is not history. That is not the world.

HARRY

No, no. I don't give an Eskimo's fart about the world, Jackson. I just want this little place here *cleaned. up,* and I'd like you to get back to fixing the sun deck. Let's forget the whole matter. Righto. Excuse me.

(p. 125-27)

The play however does not end on this note of a return to a "colonial" *status quo ante,* at least on the individual, person-to-person, existential level. Indeed, Trewe and Philip both ultimately abandon completely the distance, formality and protocols of employer and employee, "white" and "black", English and Creole that had prevented them from playing the revised text of *Robinson Crusoe* to the bitter end. And that is precisely the "point" of this play (is it?): There is a history of Eurocentrism; Eurocentrism is also *in* history, including significantly, present history; we can neither innocently re-enact the text(s) of the "old" history, nor shake the texts of the "new" history completely free of the old texts. I think Walcott is suggesting that if this is the case, the point is not to lapse into despair or mutual isolation but to find the integrity to acknowledge the violence of that history. All the same, it is significant that both Trewe and Philip (and Walcott) back off from a complete engagement with the logic and dynamics of the *power,* or more appropriately, the will-to-power, that inheres in both the constructions of Eurocentrism and the deconstructions of oppositional nativist texts, codes and languages.

The two paradigms of the interrogation and contestation of Eurocentrism that we see in *Dream on Monkey Mountain* and *Pantomime* do not by any means exhaust the range of the literary exploration of epistemologies and discourses of colonization and decolonization in contemporary post-colonial writing. Where do we, for instance, place Achebe's *Arrow of God?* Ezeulu instantly recognizes the connection between the new religion, the new teaching and the incipient reconfigurations of power relationships generated by the new colonialism and its peculiar regime of peripheral, *administrative* capitalism (as distinct from the *settler* capitalism of colonialism in other parts of Africa). Ezeulu decides to send one son into tutelage of the new "teaching", to be on the safe side. But Ezeulu loses both ways: the new colonialism completely marginalises the great store of knowledge and wisdom that Ezeulu's priestly vocation and function draw upon (including lunar observations and calendrical calculations); it also presents him with a son, who having served his tutelage, comes with a dislocated subjectivity, an alien "soul". And where also, for another important text, do we place J.M. Coetzee's *Waiting for the Barbarians?* The protagonist, the Magistrate, is a scion of a humane, skeptical, courageous and conscientized rationalism. As he contemplates the present history of (a particular) Empire running to its conclusion, he also ruminates on History. He does this by trying to unravel the message or meaning of the cryptic scripts and writing that his excavations of the ruins of a previous empire have thrown up. Yes, he muses, the "barbarians" will outlast "us", defeat "us" (we deserve defeat); but will "they" have the capacity and the inclination to understand or interpret "us" the way we have done "our" predecessors? One wonders what Ezeulu and the Magistrate would have had to say to each other if the accidents or contingencies of history or literary creation had brought such types into direct contact.

I see the value of these two paradigms as indicating some *sub- texts* for critical theory's engagement of Eurocentrism. One can only indicate these in a very general, condensed and schematic fashion here. First, *Dream on Monkey Mountain* suggests a nativist moralism in which the rejection of "Europe" and Eurocentrism is taken to its extreme limit. It is perhaps not unfair to see this as analogous to certain forms of the "Black Aesthetic" rubric of the Sixties and early Seventies in the United States, and certain expressions of the "decolonization" poetics in Africa in the Seventies and early Eighties, especially that associated with Chinweizu, Madubuike and Jemie in their famous (or notorious) book, *Toward the De-colonization of African Literature.* The underlying impulse here is a total change of nomenclature, models, inspiration; the call for an autochthonous, pristine, originary aesthetic is so total that *any* trace or influence of European techniques and forms in literature, and any European critics and schools in literary criticism is condemned *ad initio*. I think *Dream on Monkey Mountain* effectively dramatizes the falsity and pitfalls of the "decolonization" claimed by this form of nativism.

Pantomime, I think, implies a radical relativism in its complete deconstruction of both Eurocentrism and nativism; this evidently recalls certain forms of post-structuralist and deconstructivist assault on essentialism and the "metaphysics of presence" in the canons, and the celebration of indeterminacy. As analogically dramatised in *Pantomime* this position invites its own "deconstruction" and interrogation: what is the value of a radical relativism which carries out a necessary demythologization of essentialized Eurocentrism and nativism but evades or occludes the violence of the power relations between them by tacitly assuming an equivalence of either actual power consolidation between them, or the will-to-power of their pundits and adherents? Let us reinscribe this interrogation into its concrete articulation in the global balance of forces of world literature study at the present time: what differentiated consolidations and sedimentation of power do we encounter in the world of global institutional cultural politics between, say, Derrida, de Man and the Euro-American deconstructors and post-structuralists on the one hand, and Chinweizu and his "decolonizing" nativists on the other?

TRINIDADIAN HETEROGLOSSIA:
A Bakhtinian View of Derek Walcott's Play
A Branch of the Blue Nile

Stephen P. Breslow

Multiple voices form the central fabric of drama. Variable speech patterns and intonations, differing uses of standard, slang, and dialectal language create, from a purely textual point of view, the chief differentiating features of dramatic dialogue. Bakhtinian theory, especially evident in *The Dialogic Imagination,* contains a vast number of insights into the "polyglotic" and "heteroglotic" nature of the modern novel. Although Bakhtin reserves the majority of his notions for criticism of the novel, many of them would apply equally, if not more pointedly, to drama.

Occasionally Bakhtin makes excellent use of examples from the history of drama; for example, he cites the "heteroglotic" nature of the *commedia dell'arte:* "In the *commedia dell'arte* Italian dialects were knit together with the specific types and masks of the comedy. In this respect one might even call the *commedia dell'arte* a comedy of dialects. It was an intentional dialectological hybrid" (DI, 82).[1] This example emerges out of a discussion in which he announces his central critical insight: "In the process of literary creation, languages interanimate each other and objectify precisely that side of one's own (and of the other's) language *that pertains to its world view* [Bakhtin's italics], its inner form, the axiologically accentuated system inherent in it" (62).

A Branch of the Blue Nile, the most recent published play by Derek Walcott, the St. Lucian-born poet and playwright, wonderfully exemplifies Bakhtin's notion of "heteroglossia." In the play Walcott draws upon his rich African, patois, French, English, and classical Latin linguistic legacy, his St. Lucian and Trinidadian heritage, and his long experience in the United States, to bring his mastery of heteroglotic language to a peak. He continues the sort of black/white, colonizer/colonized cultural reversals that he played with in his earlier drama, *Pantomime,* by means of his Crusoe/

Friday role shifts. He also compounds his fascination with the Antony and Cleopatra legend, which configured several of his major poems, such as "Egypt, Tobago." Intertextual and intercultural references, woven through much of Walcott's poetry and drama, multiply exponentially in A *Branch of the Blue Nile*.

From the beginning of the play, and arching over its entirety, looms the voice of Shakespeare. Walcott's characters are the actors and the director of a Trinidadian production of *Antony and Cleopatra*. As they are knitting together their Shakespearean lines, they themselves are interwoven into a complex cloth of "real life" interrelationships, many of them mirroring the characterizations and meanings inherent in Shakespeare's drama. The play opens as Sheila, playing Cleopatra, is enacting the queen's final scene: "Give me my robe, put on my crown, I have / Immortal longings in me: now no more, / The juice of Egypt's grape shall moist this lip" (213).[2] Harvey, the aging English "queen" director (there are strong hints he is a homosexual), immediately rejoins with a bit of directorial advice regarding her performance: "What's all this sexual hesitation, Sheila? You know how sensual his corpse is to her?"

Walcott's stage, then, from the outset reverberates with reflexive consciousness of itself. From this point forward Walcott delights in masterful interanimation of Shakespeare's text: his actors' reproduction of Shakespeare's play, their own personal responses to the bard, their playing with his text, and their "real life," interpersonal texts that form the basis of Walcott s overall dramatic action. Two more series of these combinations compound the intertextuality when the characters read parts of Chris's (one of the actors) texts, three "plays" he has written: one a simple-minded pastoral farce, another a symbolic representation of these same actors' "real life" relationships, and the third a word-for-word tape recorder transcription of their conversational and rehearsed lines onstage preliminary to performance. Walcott herein clearly displays a postmodern sensibility: the text within the text within the text. However, he shies away from any "avant-garde" break with the traditional boundary of the proscenium arch, as achieved by such dramatic figures as Pirandello's eponymous "six characters," who interact directly with the audience. Walcott's play remains "onstage, ' yet it greatly enlarges the number of purely heteroglotic, interanimating dramatic "languages" commonly found in contemporary plays.

Soon after the play's outset, Harvey directs Sheila/Cleopatra to "play what you feel about Chris, not Antony" (213). Harvey's suggestion emerges from his training in method acting; in addition, he is playing on what he knows is going on behind the scenes: Sheila s affair with Chris. It is at this early juncture that we can already assess the deeply cutting conflicts that brew at the interfaces of the play's various "languages." Harvey's directorial remark rapidly interanimates Sheila's played version of Shakespeare's Cleopatra and identifies the play as a hybrid seriocomedy; the dialogue is too violent, too cutting, for it to be read as light, parodic comedy. Harvey's suggestion strays toward improper use of his directorial power, and Sheila is clearly in the right to tell him, "Just leave my private life out of this, please" (213). Sheila may well feel as Shakespeare's colonial queen felt when she expressed, at the end of her tragedy, that she deeply resented the idea that her play (that is, the story of her life) would be comically performed in Rome, the imperial capital, where "the quick comedians / Extemporally will stage us" (5.2.216-17).[3]

Unfortunately, as Walcott repeatedly reveals, there does not appear to be any way for these characters to separate their private lives from their professional acting roles. The two realms are inextricably mixed, and their multiple interactions form the central action and meaning of the play. Even on the most minute linguistic level, when Walcott's actors unavoidably interject their Trinidadian accents into Shakespeare's text — when Chris, for example, blurts "Your Lord? No. He gone out" (214) — Trinidadian and Shakespearean "languages" are comically interwoven. This commingling of the performer's natural language with the language of the staged text adopts even further import, when we perceive it in extended cultural and political terms: the postcolonial, former slave society struggling to reenact the masterpieces of the colonizer's culture, and the postcolonials chastising each other for not getting the masterpiece "right."

The Trinidadian actors strike back, however, with their parody of Harvey's Americanisms, in particular his perpetual use of the term *whatever*. Gavin's satiric jibes are pointed at the director: "Would one of you care to ask Mr. Strasberg here what he means by 'whatever?'"; and later, "I'm going to be acting whatever, Chris, you hear. You ready?" (215). Gavin, the craftiest parodist of the troupe, parries with Harvey when he assumes the role of the victimized plantation slave: "You'se a hard taskmaster, Mistuh Harvey sur, you'se going make this po' nigger tote your arse across the desert, you'se pitiless as that burning sun, Mistuh Harvey. Why? Why'?" (221). Harvey, with the arch finesse of his years on the North American stage, and his practiced position as a white among blacks, plays right into Gavin's game without missing a stroke: "Whah? Whah? I'se pitiless 'cause I can't trist you house niggers, 'cause I leave you to polish the silver back in the pantry and you fucked the help, you been inter-fering. And you knows mah punishment for house niggers, boy?' Gavin foolishly continues the game and gets hit harder than he expected. He asks Harvey, in his role as plantation overseer, "[Whining, pulling at Harvey's trousers] No, Mistuh Harvey, what is it?" But Harvey suddenly shifts context on Gavin with his masterful, cynical, and politically loaded rejoinder: "They gits to be on television. They gits to be third detectives in a police series. They gits to do serious theatre in a side alley, in Noo Yawk. So git up. Git up!"

Overall, this parodic technique exemplifies Bakhtin's view of linguistic interanimation, present in Roman times in writers such as Lucian and in medieval *parodia sacra*. In such parodies writers would take a "serious" text — Homer, for example, or the Bible — and ridicule it by inserting alternate, comical words, lines, and situations. The seriocomic form, thus born, was responsible, according to Bakhtin, for the rise of the novel and the demise of traditional "serious" forms such as the epic. In Walcott's play the "serious" text is supplied by Shakespeare's *Antony and Cleopatra*, yet often the parodying form shifts to another "language," such as the speech of the southern U.S. plantation black cited above. With a Bakhtinian perspective, we can more easily discern Walcott's textual shifts and their dramatic implications: the distinction between his reasonably harmless actor's jokes and the deeper truth and fate of their lives. The predictable, ritualistic "agon" of the stage rehearsal frequently disintegrates into a variety of sobering, "real life" conflicts that plague the various members of the troupe.

Sheila, playing Cleopatra, has the dimensions of a star, but her aspirations to "make it big in the States" are jeopardized by her provincial location and her cumbersome affair with the married actor Chris (a situation that echoes the historical tragedy of Antony, Cleopatra, and Antony's wives Fulvia and Octavia). One might be tempted to read Walcott's play as simply a "heteroglotic" parody of Shakespeare, if *A Branch of the Blue Nile* did not have its own tragic dimensions. The separate intrusions of real life into the rehearsal text become more and more numerous and disruptive until both their performance of Shakespeare and the actors' psyches unravel completely.

Sheila bows out, as it were, and bequeaths her throne to Marilyn, another actress who is less talented and less idealistic but more ambitious. Sheila undergoes a religious conversion, quits the stage, and hands the part of Cleopatra over to Marilyn. She abandons the theatrical tent for God's temple, and Walcott litters his text with frequent interanimated comments between the two worlds, the secular and the divine. Still, dramatic language in general, for Walcott, clearly remains the centering force of what might be seen as an example of Bakhtin's notions of the "centrifugal" and "centripetal" tendencies of language. With only a couple of short scenes between Sheila and her newfound mentor, Brother John, Walcott provides just enough dialogue to parody the superficiality and hypocrisy of fundamentalist religious sects. In a brilliantly crafted "benediction" at her temple, a speech which reeks of double meaning — she hears "the voice of William Blake in the fields" (265) — Sheila bares her naturally talented poetic and theatrical soul to the massed congregation, which is clearly impressed by the "style" and passion of her eulogy, although not its moral content.

We are soon back "onstage," however, with Marilyn's performance as Cleopatra and with Harvey's new "dialectal" version of Shakespeare's text. The director decides to interweave the local, dialectal intonations of one of Chris's plays with *Antony and Cleopatra*. The result is exceedingly amusing and certainly would rival the heteroglotic interanimation and wit of the finest *commedia dell'arte* productions. Marilyn plays her traditional Shakespearean text straight, but Gavin, playing Shakespeare's clown, gives a hilarious Trinidadian, dialectal takeoff on the great play by the imperial bard:

MARILYN/CLEOPATRA: Hast thou the pretty worm of Nilus there,
      that kills and pains not?
GAVIN/CLOWN: MAdam, I have him, but 'tain't go be me who go
      ask you handle him, because one nip from this
      small fellow and Basil is your husband; this little
      person will make the marriage, in poison and in
      person, but the brides who go to that bed don't
      ever get up.
MARILYN/CLEOPATRA: Remember'st thou any that have died on't?

GAVIN/CLOWN Too many, lady. Male and she-male, sure. Yesterday
                self sold me a sample: a straightforward lady that
                butter couldn't melt in she mouth but a little
                crooked with the truth, which is just natural for
                any Adam's wife, fainted forever from giving it a
                little suck, with as much pain as joy. That's an
                excellent endorsement of the worm; but the man
                who believe everything he hear ain't go be saved by
                half of what men do. I sound like I ain't sure 'cause
                this worm is a funny worm. (262-3)

Bakhtin, in *The Dialogic Imagination,* makes an important observation on parodic texts: "Each separate element in it [parodic language] — parodic dialogue, scenes from everyday life, bucolic humor, etc. — is presented as if it were a fragment of some kind of unified whole" (59-60). Walcott's text revels with many of these "whole" subtexts. Above, we have seen Gavin as the clown speaking *entirely,* although in the context of a Shakespearean play, in colloquial Trinidadian dialect. Marilyn, and Sheila before her, perform "whole" authentic segments of the Shakespearean text. Harvey, in his directorial parodies, gives, in the previously quoted piece of dialogue, a "whole" microcosmic version of the plantation slave driver and then shifts into a parody of the cynical producer, retaining a decadent Southern drawl over the acrid utterances of a burnt-out urbanite. Theater, even more than the novel, depends on, and abounds in, such "speech-genres."[4] Dramatic parody would become indecipherable if these speech units were reduced to much smaller proportions, however; the audience would fail to follow them. In poetry, linguistic parody can succeed more easily word after word, not just passage after passage, since the reading audience has the written text to study. Walcott complicates his intertextual parody in *A Branch of the Blue Nile* probably as densely as is possible without utterly losing his aural audience.

The play continues, from beginning to end, to display a plethora of interanimated texts. Once the Trinidadian troupe, with Marilyn as Cleopatra, finally performs Shakespeare, the performance is marred by a ludicrous mistake of scenery when one of Chris's sets is pushed onto the stage: it is painted with banana trees instead of the proper Egyptian set. Later Gavin reads the local critic's notice of their performance, which rips Harvey, the director, for allowing such an error to occur but which obsequiously lavishes the hyperbolic praise of a fawning critic on Marilyn's performance. Walcott here is parodying the excessive — and all too typical — language of newspaper criticism.

As the play moves toward conclusion, Walcott inserts several long, truthful, self-revealing speeches: Gavin's rehearsal of his previous humiliation as a black actor trying to make it in New York; Sheila's paroxysm of shame from allowing herself to have an affair with Chris, a married man (a scene which catapults her into religious conversion); and Chris's angry outburst at all the others for failing to understand the essential linguistic/political paradoxes which compromise all of them as postcolonials with a hybrid language and culture. Chris quits the troupe to open a restaurant in Barbados, which he names "A Branch of the Blue Nile." Later, when he returns to Trinidad, he discusses the title of his restaurant and reveals its symbolic allusion to Cleopatra's river and to his earlier angry statements about the frustrating paradox of black, postcolonial culture adopting, mimicking, and twisting white (instead of blue) cultural and linguistic forms. The irony of his position cuts many ways, however, because he has come back, like Antony to Octavia, to his white wife; yet he returns again to Trinidad, still pining with love for Sheila, to lure her away from the fundamentalist church. His tool? None other than another play he has written specifically for Sheila in a central role. He confronts her with his script and recites her part for her in an attempt to seduce her back to the stage. She does visit their original theater space, but for her it is, alas, too late: Chris has returned to Barbados; Marilyn has gone on to a career in New York; Harvey has departed to London, where he dies from a sudden disease, possibly AIDS. Sheila is left onstage with the ultimate parodic mimicry: the play by Chris which is an exact playback (from a tape recorder which he had let run during their earlier rehearsals), performed by a foolishly frolicking couple, Iris and Wilfred. The play ends, in another characteristically Shakespearean form, with an appearance by a "fool" character, Phil, who gives the play closure with his scatterbrained but deeply wise exhortation to Sheila, as a talented but uncertain actress: "Continue. Do your work." The serious implications of Walcott's drama finally catch up with and triumph over the play's comic elements.

Walcott has said (at a recent conference in Florida) that North American society contains a multitude of cultural/linguistic hybrids but that its theater is unfortunately lacking — if he were to use Bakhtin's terms — in "interanimated, heteroglotic hybrids." *A Branch of the Blue Nile* brilliantly begins to fill this gap. It wonderfully fulfills many of Bakhtin's concepts of "parodic heteroglossia," a multitude of linguistic shifts that demonstrate a seriocomic imagination, that mix low and high forms, and that strive to renew the established literary tongue "by drawing on the fundamental elements of folk language" (*DI,* 49).

Footnotes

[1] M.M. Bakhtin, *The Dialogic Imagination,* Michael Holquist, ed., Caryl Emerson and Michael Holquist, trs., Austin, University of Texas Press, 1981. Where needed for clairty, the abbreviation *DI* is used in subsequent citations.

[2] Derek Walcott, *A Branch of the Blue Nile,* in his *Three Plays,* New York, Farrar, Straus & Giroux, 1986. For a review, see *WLT* 61:1 (Winter 1987), p. 147. On Walcott, see also *WLT* 51:4 (Autumn 1977), pp. 580-81, and 56:1 (Winter 1982), pp. 51-53.

[3] William Shakespeare, *Antony and Cleopatra,* in *William Shakespeare: The Complete Works,* Baltimore, Penguin, 1969.

[4] M.M. Bakhtin, *Speech Genres and Other Late Essays.* Caryl Emerson and Michael Holquist, eds., Vern W. McGee, tr., Austin, University of Texas Press, 1986. See especially pp. 60-102.

REVIEW OF
THE ARKANSAS TESTAMENT

Vernon Shetley

Perhaps in some future emblem book or dictionary of the poetic condition, Derek Walcott might stand as the sign for "Affluence." Walcott's gift for language — his seductive and precise metrical sense, his effortless production of telling metaphor — has been remarked from the beginning of his career. But beyond this easy mastery of the medium, Walcott has also been given a genuine, unavoidable subject. As a native of the West Indies, of mixed blood, the great themes of race, colonialism, and exile have pressed themselves upon him with an urgency unlike anything an American poet might feel for what he or she chose to write about. The great, sorrowing question of today's poetry, Harold Bloom has remarked, is "Why is there no subject?" But for Walcott, the very act of writing poetry must inevitably activate a complex of experience in which issues of the utmost contemporary importance lie entangled.

Of course, it is paradoxical to refer to Walcott as a representative of affluence; coming to the English tradition from a colonial margin, coming to America, an economic center, from Trinidad, a Third World outpost, inhabiting American society as an outsider by both race and origin, Walcott would seem the very type of the dispossessed, materially and culturally. And yet the impression one acquires from the writing is that of an enormous, bountiful profusion, of both perception and expression. The rhetorical excess that frequently marred the early work has long since been tamed; *The Arkansas Testament* for the most part works the personal, reflective vein Walcott has been mining in his last several collections. Even given this predominantly lyric focus, however, the full range of Walcott's oratory comes into play; the most mundane observations, even when recorded in a syncopated, jogging meter, take on a certain magnificence:

> That terra-cotta waitress,
> elbows out, seems to brood
> on her own shape, her irises
> now slate, now hazel-hued

as pebbles in the shallows
of sunlit river D'Oree;
her ears, curled jars, enclose
small talk and cutlery.

From the red clay of Piaille
this cool carafe was made;
a raw, unfinished people
there ply the potter's trade;

and on his cedar shelf is
jar after jar like this —
maternal at the pelvis
yet girlish at the wrist.
("The Villa Restaurant," p. 25)

For Walcott, the entire world is poetry; of their own accord things shape themselves into verse, and so arises Walcott's trademark metaphor, repeated to the point of being an obtrusive mannerism, in which the natural world is likened to writing: "The seaweed's Cyrillics / are your life's shorthand, the sandpiper's footmarks / your dashes and hyphens," "The surf will smooth the sand's page," "A sandpiper signs / the margin of a beach." In Walcott's universe the reader seems all but overwhelmed by a wealth of sensory experience and linguistic resource.

Though Robert Lowell is the American poet whose influence is most legible in Walcott's recent work, one might suggest James Merrill as a more apt comparison. On the surface, Merrill, scion of a Wall Street fortune and a good WASP name, could not differ more from Walcott. In the work of both, however, there operates a gift for meter and phrase-making that threatens to turn the whole world, easily and effortlessly, into poetry; both poets are prone to revel in the excess of language over matter, form over content, creating dense surfaces that resist being read through to an underlying narrative or description. Merrill, however, in the course of his career has grown suspicious of his own facility, and so a leading theme of his poetry has become the fear that words betray the poet by their very subservience to his will. Perhaps because Walcott had actively to choose a commitment to the English tradition, rather than receiving it as a birthright, he has been the more reluctant to let it go, or to exercise irony at its expense. Any individual poem by Walcott is impressive and persuasive; in quantity (and Walcott is quite prolific) his ability simply to turn out magnificent poetry provokes suspicion. One rarely feels the sense of struggle that seems necessary to authenticate the act of writing in the world of distractions that we all inhabit. Derek Walcott may fall just short of the highest excellence as a poet by the cruel circumstance of his being too talented for his own good.

A POEM IN HOMAGE TO AN UNWANTED MAN

D. J. R. Bruckner

In Derek Walcott's new 325-page poem, *Omeros*, the principal characters are Achille, Hector and Helen, and other characters also have names taken from the *Iliad* and *Odyssey* of Homer. Much of the action, which occurs in the Caribbean, but also in North America, Africa and Europe through many centuries, gains resonance from its references to incidents in those epics. And Mr. Walcott chose for his title the Greek version of the name Homer. But when critics call it an epic he objects.

"I do not think of it as an epic," Mr. Walcott said in a recent interview in New York. "Certainly not in the sense of epic design. Where are the battles? There are a few, I suppose. But 'epic' makes people think of great wars and great warriors. That isn't the Homer I was thinking of; I was thinking of Homer the poet of the seven seas."

For him *Omeros* is homage, meant to capture "the whole experience of the people of the Caribbean." Mr. Walcott was born in the Windward Islands 60 years ago and received his education at St. Mary's College in St. Lucia and then at the University of the West Indies in Kingston, Jamaica.

When he was 20 years old, his first play was produced in St. Lucia, and by the time he was 30 he had published two volumes of poetry, established the Trinidad Theatre Workshop and his plays were being performed throughout the Caribbean and in London.

As his fame grew, so did the time he spent abroad. In the last decade, he has spent most of each year in Boston, teaching at Boston University. Now when he returns home, he finds that the place, its people and its history overwhelm him. "I know how this is going to sound, but it is true," he said. "What drove me was duty: duty to the Caribbean light. The whole book is an act of gratitude. It is a fantastic privilege to be in a place in which limbs, features, smells, the lineaments and presence of the people are so powerful. If I could only capture, in painting or words or any way, some of the women's faces."

"I saw a 75-year-old fisherman with a chest like iron plates. There is a tremendous sensual excitement. And there is no history for the place. It's pristine. You feel like

Piero della Francesca. It's an early morning feeling. You're writing something down, but you're not really making it; it's there."

Tampering with what is there produces pangs of conscience. "One reason I don't like talking about an epic is that I think it is wrong to try to ennoble people," he said. "And just to write history is wrong. History makes similes of people, but these people are their own nouns." More precisely, they are becoming nouns in his analysis.

"I learned what a noun is, writing this book," he said. "No one is Adam. A noun is not a name you give something. It is something you watch becoming itself, and you have to have the patience to find out what it is. In the Caribbean, people come from everywhere, from Africa and Europe and the Mediterranean and the Middle East and the Orient." He himself derives from a background that is African, British and Dutch.

"There really are names like Hector and Achille in the Caribbean," he said. "Someone would see a slave and say 'he looks like a Pompey so we'll call him Pompey.' The place is full of slave names. But then we become our names. It's O.K. to be Smith. You don't own me because you call me that; I *am* Smith. There is a restless identity in the New World. The New World needs an identity without guilt or blame."

It sometimes seems he thinks the New World needs a whole new language, too, and he is supplying a great deal of it. But that, too, he credits to his home waters. It is not simply that the Creole patois of the islands changes pronunciations of many words in other tongues (the three syllables of the name Achilles, for instance, become ah-SHEEL in the Antilles), but Mr. Walcott contends that the sea itself affects the rhythm of the islanders' speech.

His use of the vernacular allows him to scatter hundreds of verbal jokes through his poems and plays. He has often been praised for his ability to fuse the classics, folklore and history and to combine the vernacular and the grand manner. And the sheer range of *Omeros* — the enormous variety of its language, verse structure and narrative techniques — makes it an epitome of all the writing done by this man, of whom the Nobel Prize-winning poet Joseph Brodsky wrote "he is the very man by whom the English language lives."

But the story began rather simply. Several years ago, Mr. Walcott was in St. Lucia "at a time when, I remember, there was a lot of rain."

"A very good friend of mine had died," he continued, "an actor, and I was thinking about that. And where this poem started was with the figure of Philoctetes, the man with the wound, alone on the beach: Philoctetes from the Greek legend and Timon of Athens as well." In Homer and in a play by Sophocles, Philoctetes was abandoned on an island by his Greek companions on the way to the Trojan war after a snake bit him, leaving him with an unhealable wound so noisome no one could stand being near him. But the gods decided the war could not be won without him, and the men who deserted him had to return and beg him, wound and all, to go to Troy. The moral questions raised by that myth give a sharp edge to some of the confrontations in Mr. Walcott's poem.

If the beginning of *Omeros* was simple, the poem soon began to grow, and eventually it "got to be like a mural, with all kinds of spaces to be filled in by action," Mr. Walcott said. His comparison of it to a picture is natural. In addition to being a poet and playwright, Mr. Walcott is a painter, an occupation he finds increasingly satisfying since "in painting you don't have to go through a process of opinion; it speaks directly and either it works or it doesn't."

In fact, he speaks of *Omeros* primarily in visual terms. He has written a number of film scripts through the years and said "the sense of cutting, the visual rhythm of films affected the structure of this book." Parts of the story, he added, he "would love to have made a film of," and he was thinking about film when he wrote them.

And, of course, he was thinking about writers: Homer and Dante, the only other poet he mentions and whom he loves for the Italian poet's love of the sea, his mastery of action in narrative and what Mr. Walcott calls "the gift of a phrase that can summarize an entire life." But he also acknowledged the influence of an unlikely trio — Rudyard Kipling, Joseph Conrad and Ernest Hemingway.

"I learned a lot in writing this poem," he said. "I did not realize how much great prose I had absorbed into my nervous verse system. When I began to write in hexameter lines and in stanzas, well the structure is there in the architecture of the best turn-of-the century prose, in Conrad and Kipling. And you find in them the wit of the paragraph; mentally, it keeps the rhythm up. "So, the solidity I felt behind me was the solidity of prose. I wanted the feel of great prose rather than of a strong verse line." He has a special affection for Hemingway because "he is the only one to let you see the Caribbean the way it is, to feel it and smell it."

"No one has written about it better," he continued. "When I was writing this book, you might say I was thinking of the two great Caribbean artists, Hemingway and Homer." But above all, he said he was thinking of the people and their islands. No character is a precise evocation of any individual he knows, but readers of his other work will recognize a few who have turned up in other poems, especially an expatriate British Army officer trying, in Mr. Walcott's words, "to expiate the historical respect" paid to European colonial representatives by the rest of the population.

Some of the most memorable, dazzling characters are birds. Sewed into a quilt that becomes the universe by an old woman — who, unlike Penelope in the *Odyssey*, does not unravel her work every night — they take flight and fill the skies of the book the way old gods filled the skies of Homer.

The origin of them is a reminder one is looking at the work of a poet, for Mr. Walcott is not a bird watcher. A friend of his gave him a pamphlet listing all the birds of the Caribbean, he said, "and there were so many it amazed me, and then I found myself thinking about the scansion in the list, the rhythm, and so, there they are."

But the greatest character is the Caribbean Sea itself. "The Caribbean is an immense ocean that just happens to have a few islands in it," Mr. Walcott said. "The people have an immense respect for it, awe of it." And his own vision of the world is shaped by waves. In fact, this summer, he said, "is the first time I had been around mountains." "I was in Colorado," he said. "At first I didn't know what bothered me about them. But then I noticed it: whole ranges of mountains, stacks of them, and they never move."

To the end, he insists that he is not an epic poet. "The happiness I feel about this book is that I didn't force classical reverberations or stretch to make associations with the classics. It is a book for people, not a conundrum for scholars. It was as if I was learning to read Homer when I was writing it."

BRINGING HIM BACK ALIVE

Mary Lefkowitz

Toward the end of his epic poem *Omeros*, Derek Walcott suddenly interrupts his rushing narrative and asks himself whether he has not "read and rewritten till literature / was guilty as History. When would the sails drop / from my eyes, when would I not hear the Trojan War / in two fishermen cursing?" he asks. "When would it stop, / the echo in the throat, insisting, 'Omeros'; / when would I enter that light beyond metaphor?" (p. 271). This apostrophe is a moving and appropriate challenge not only to the poet, but to the reader. Why are we in the present always haunted by the past, not just our past but the past of other people and peoples? Like Homer's Odysseus, we learn the answer by joining the poet on an exciting and disturbing journey "to see the cities of many men and to know their minds."

But it is the figure of the poet Homer, rather than the heroes of his poems, who serves as Derek Walcott's principal inspiration. According to ancient legend, Homer came from a humble background and had a hard and lonely life. Born the bastard son of a Greek girl living in Smyrna (modern Izmir), when he was young he traveled around the Mediterranean. But then he became blind and had to make a living as a beggar, by reciting his verse. Occasionally he was treated kindly, but more often he was driven away from the towns he visited; because he was an outsider and a hanger-on he acquired the name Homeros, "hostage." After much wandering, Homer finally died on the Aegean island of Ios, friendless and alone, unable to answer a simple riddle put to him by young fisher-boys.

It is this everyman's Homer, and not the comfortable court poet some people imagine Homer to have been, who inspires Derek Walcott's epic poem, and who records the past events that determine the lives of the people he describes — including that of Mr. Walcott himself and, ultimately, of all of us. This Homer is a Protean figure, infinitely knowledgeable but elusive, constantly changing shape. He is Omeros (his name in modern Greek) and also the old blind man "Seven Seas." Later he turns up as a sightless, homeless bargeman clutching a brown manuscript, only to be driven off the steps of St. Martin's-in-the-Fields church in London by a prim clergyman. He is the voice of the sea, (Winslow) Homer, and the Roman poet Virgil who guides the narrator (as he once guided Dante through hell in Dante's own epic, the *Commedia*) Omeros's authority comes from a curiosity and sympathy learned from isolation and suffering, and it is this lonely, painful knowledge that is his principal legacy to the characters in the epic, and through them to anyone who reads about their lives.

In the *Iliad* and the *Odyssey* Homer needed to recall only what happened before Odysseus' return from Troy, but now the poet must reflect on an older and larger world, with new wars and new continents. If his principal characters are Antillean people with Homeric names, one also meets here Roman emperors, Spanish conquistadors, Herman Melville and James Joyce. His mind ranges from the Antilles now to the Mediterranean in antiquity to the British Empire at its height to frontier America in the Indian wars to Boston and London last week or last year to an Africa buried so deep in the memories of its exiled children that only terrible trauma can bring them to think about it. This is, as Mr. Walcott says, "a reversible world." "Art is History's nostalgia."

But his new epic does not so much tell a story as explain the feelings and reflections of some inhabitants—past, present or, like Mr. Walcott himself, intermittent —of St. Lucia in the Windward Islands. Several characters have Homeric names, but their connection with their counterparts in the *Iliad* and the *Odyssey* is deliberately tenuous and evanescent.

Helen is as beautiful as her ancient namesake, but her face does not launch a thousand ships or bring on the destruction of her city. Achille, the "main man," son of an African slave, is strong and brave like Homer's Achilles. But instead of Patroclus Mr. Walcott gives him as companion the crippled Philoctete, who suffers, like his counterpart in the ancient story, from a wound that does not heal, and whose cure marks the end of the war. But, unlike his Greek namesake, Philoctete lives among men, enduring his pain. Achille also does not inflict his resentment on his friends, nor does he kill Hector, even over Helen. Hector dies as the result of his own recklessness, but the poem ends not with his funeral, but with the continuing existence of the survivors who learn to live with their memories.

When, toward the end of the poem, the narrator encounters Omeros, he complains he can no longer use the gods who dominate the action of the *Iliad* and the *Odyssey*. "Forget the gods," Omeros advises, "and read the rest." In their place Mr. Walcott puts forces even more pitiless and unpredictable than the gods of Olympus: nature, the sea, violent changes of weather, lizards and iguanas and the jungle foliage that casts debris and disorder onto the landscape. When Homer's Achilles goes down to the sea, he finds his goddess mother Thetis ready to come to his aid, but Achille must trust himself to a beautiful but unfeeling Sea-Mother *(mer-mère)* who can support or destroy him.

The gods brought order to Homer's world, but in Mr. Walcott's epic, Odysseus (and all of us who like him are exiles) must return to a home whose character has changed over time, even to the point where we can no longer recognize it. Yet these references to the ancient past, brief and insubstantial as they may seem, form the foundation of Mr. Walcott's poem. They endow his new characters and situations with heroism; they suggest that their experiences, particular as they are to specific places and present times, are also timeless and universal.

Omeros derives its extraordinary power not from suspense, for Mr. Walcott makes us aware in advance of what will happen, but from his ability to capture and express the thoughts of his characters and to re-create, with a remarkable clarity that compels the reader to follow and even to see them, the swift mutations of ideas and images in their minds.

The narrative mimics the process of thinking in several ways. Since we make associations first of all by patterns of sound, there are significant puns, like mer and mère and O-mer-os, or occasional and thus all the more arresting rhymes: "House of memories that grow / like shadows out of Allan Poe." Then there are literary reminiscences, often incomplete, mutated, congested: Achille's lonely, brooding fishing voyages acquire dimension from allusion to Joseph Conrad's "Nigger of the Narcissus" or the threatened shipwreck survivor in Winslow Homer's painting *The Gulf Stream*. And just when they are needed to punctuate the somber reflections, there are swift transitions to ordinary preoccupations or occasional bitter humor, as when we learn that the waiter struggling with his tray across the sand dunes of a seaside country club is called Lawrence.

Throughout the poem, as in the mind, there are persistent reflections on the historical events that have directly and indirectly shaped the characters' lives: the brutal attacks of the slavers on Achille's African forebears, of Europeans on Native Americans, of French warships against British when the Windward Islands were first colonized; of the impersonal, devastating shelling of armies in World War II. But Mr. Walcott recalls these scenes of death and suffering with the objective sympathy of a Homer, who tells what happened to Trojans as well as Greeks. No loss, individual or collective, is felt more keenly than any other's. The Romans enslaved the Greeks; the Southerners built Greek Revival houses and gave the slaves they mistreated Roman names. Sons are lost, or never born, alike to black and white.

In Homer's day, the only possible medium for epic narrative was poetry, with a strict metrical pattern based on the quantity of sounds. Mr. Walcott uses a rhythmic blank verse to call attention to patterns of sound, and to suggest likeness and contrast with sudden, dramatic metaphors and similes. Although the events of his story take place, as they must, in linear time, over several months, the narration moves in a spiral, replicating the circularity of human thought. The past can easily become present as we remember it: we can talk with the dead, and see them before us, and become the same age as, or even older than, our own parents. We can discover an ancestor who was killed in a war long ago, and begin to mourn for him.

The narrative of *Omeros* is exciting and memorable, despite the absence of the chases, duels and descriptions of violent deaths in the Greek epics. At the end, Helen returns to Hector; a warwounded Englishman in exile finds he can talk to his dead wife with the aid of one Ma Kilman, the wise old woman who runs an establishment called the No Pain Café and who also somehow recalls the ancient African remedy that cures old Philoctete's incurable wound. In place of action there is an increasing awareness of other people's suffering. Like Odysseus and the legendary Homer himself, everyone (including the narrator and reader) learns from his or her wandering and exile, even if it is only how better to understand what has happened.

Perhaps most surprisingly of all we discover that it is the remote past, antiquity and military history, that matters, rather than modern concerns about money or self-promotion. Mr. Walcott's epic is a significant and timely reminder that the past is not the property of those who first created it; it always matters to all of us, no matter who we are or where we were born.

CONTRIBUTORS

Alleyne, Keith: Past Attorney-General of Dominica.

Ashaolu, Albert Olu: Senior Lecturer in English, University of Ibadan.

Balakian, Peter: Professor of English, Colgate University. His poetry collections include *Father Fisheye* (1979), *Sad Days of Light* (1983) and *Reply from Wilderness Island* (1988). Author of *Theodore Roethke's Far Fields: The Evolution of His Poetry* (1989).

Baugh Edward: Professor and chairman of the Department of English, University of the West Indies, Mona, Kingston. Author of *West Indian Poetry 1900-1970: A Study in Cultural Decolonization* (1971), *Derek Walcott: Memory as Vision: 'Another Life'* (1978) and numerous articles on West Indian literature. Editor of *Critics on Caribbean Literature* (1978).

Bedient, Calvin: Professor of English, University of California at Los Angeles. Among his books are *In the Heart's Last Kingdom* (1986) and *He Do the Police in Different Voices: The Waste Land and Its Protagonist* (1987).

Bensen, Robert: Professor of English, Hartwick College. Among his poetry collections *In the Dream Museum* (1981), *Day Labor* (1985) and *The Scriptures of Venus* (1990). Editor of the anthology *One People's Grief: Literature of the West Indies* (1983).

Birkerts, Sven: Critic. Selected essays appear in his *An Artificial Wilderness: Essays on Twentieth Century Literature* (1989) and *The Electric Life: Essays on Modern Poetry* (1989), Ed. Maria Guarnashelli.

Breslow, Stephen R.: Assistant Professor of English, the University of Tampa.

Brown, Lloyd W.: Professor of Comparative Literature, the University of Southern California. Books include *Bits of Ivory: Narrative Techniques in Jane Austin's Fiction* (1973), *West Indian Poetry* (1978) and *El Dorado and Pardise: Canada and the Caribbean in Austin Clarke's Fiction* (1989). Editor of *The Black Writer in Africa and the Americas* (1973).

Bruckner, D.J.R.: Book review editor for *The New York Times Book Review*, Author of *Frederic Goudy*, in the Abrams "Masters of American Design" series (1990).

405

Collymore, Frank (1893-1980): Editor, poet, short story writer and actor. Influential editor of *Bim* and generous guide to many Caribbean writers. Books of poetry include *Thirty Poems* (1944), *Beneath the Casuarinas* (1945), *Flotsam* (1948), *Collected Poems* (1959). Author of *Barbadian Dialect* (4th ed. 1970).

Colson, Theodore: Professor of English, University of new Brunswick.

DeMott, Benjamin: Mellon Professor of English, Amherst College. Among his books are *Surviving the Seventies* (1971) and *Scholarship for Society* (1974).

Douglas-Smith, Aubrey: Former British Council Officer in Barbados.

Dwyer, Richard: Professor of English, Florida International University. Author of four volumes in American studies. Served on editorial board of *Southern Folklore Quarterly* and *Caribbean Review*.

Figueroa, John J. M.: Jamaica poet, international educator (retired) who counts Derek Walcott among his students at the University of the West Indies, Mona. Poetry collected in *Love Leaps Here* (1962) and *Ignoring Hurts* (1976).

Fox, Robert Eliot: Associate Professor of English and Director of Afro-American Literature Collection, Suffolk University. Taught at University of Ife, Nigeria 1978-1985. Author of *Conscientious Sorcerers* (1987) and *Masters of the Drum: Studies in the Rhetorics of Blackness* (in progress).

Goldstraw, Laurence: Part-time actor on Trinidad theater and film scene and member of the Trinidad Theatre Workshop from 1972-82. Roles in Walcott's *Franklin, The Charlatan, The Joker of Seville, O Babylon! Remembrance* and *The Rig*.

Grimes, John: Reviewer for the *Trinidad Guardian*.

Gunness, Christopher: I have been unable to obtain biographical information on Mr. Gunness.

Hamner, Robert: Professor of English and Humanities at Hardin-Simmons University. Fulbright Professor of American Literature at the University of Guyana 1975-76. Books include *V.S. Naipaul* (1973), *Critical Perspectives on V.S. Naipaul* (1977), *Derek Walcott* (1981) and *Joseph Conrad: Third World Perspectives* (1990).

Heaney, Seamus: Irish poet. Boylston Professor of Rhetoric and Oratory, Harvard University. Books include *Selected Poems, 1965-1975* (1980), *Preoccupations: Selected Prose 1968-1978* (1980), *Station Island* (1984) and *The Government of the Tongue* (1989).

Hirsch, Edward: American poet, short story writer and critic. Professor of English, Wayne State University. Books of poetry include *For the Sleepwalkers* (1981) and *Wild Gratitude* (1986).

Holder, G. A.: Retired Government Information Officer in Barbados. Now newspaper columnist and commentator on social and political affairs.

Ismond, Patricia: Chairman of the Department of English, University of the West

Indies, St. Augustine. Author of numerous articles on Walcott and West Indian literature.

Jeyifo, Biodun: Teacher at the University of Ibadan and Ife, now Professor of English at Cornell University. Published on Nigerian literature and African drama.

King, Bruce: International scholar. Among the places he has taught are Nigeria, New Zealand and the United States. Author or editor of books including *Introduction to Nigerian Literature* (1972), *Literatures of the World in English* (1974), *A Celebration of Black and African Writing* (1976) and *West Indian Literature* (1979).

Lefkowitz, Mary: Andrew W. Mellon Professor in the Humanities at Wellesley College. Author of *Lives of the Greek Poets* (1982) and *Women in Greek Myth* (1986).

Lovelace, Earl: Trinidadian novelist and playwright. Books include *While Gods are Falling* (1965), *The Dragon Can't Dance* (1979) *The Wine of Astonishment* (1982) and *Jestina's Calypso and Other Plays* (1984).

McClatchy, J. D.: American poet, short story writer and poetry editor for the Yale Review. Lecturer in creative writing, Princeton University. Books include his poetry *Scenes from Another Life* (1981), criticism *White Paper: On Contemporary American Poetry* (1989). He edited *Poet on Painters: Essays on the Art of Painting by Twentieth-Century Poets* (1987).

McWatt, Mark: Lecturer in English at the University of the West Indies, Cave Hill. Editor of the *Journal of West Indian Literature*. Author of many articles on West Indian Literature.

Milne, Anthony: Feature writer for *The Express*, Port of Spain, Trinidad.

"Mombara, Sule" (Horace Campbell): Lecturer in the Department of Government, University of the West Indies, St. Augustine.

Morris, Mervyn: Jamaican poet. Senior Lecturer in English at the University of the West Indies, Mona. His books of poetry include *The Pond* (1973), *On Holy Week* (1976) and *Shadow Boxing* (1979). Editor of *Seven Jamaican Poets* (1971).

Oliver, Edith: Member of the editorial staff and theater reviewer for the *The New Yorker*.

Questel, Victor: Trinidadian poet and critic. Many of his articles are on Walcott and West Indian literature.

Rae, Norman F.: Jamaican Trade Commissioner in Europe since 1981. Television host, journalist and critic. Author of articles and reviews on fine arts, performance and literature.

Ramchand, Kenneth: Trinidadian scholar. Professor of English, University of the West Indies, St. Augustine. Author of *The West Indian Novel and Its Background* (1970). Edited *West Indian Poetry: An Anthology for Schools* (1971), *West Indian Narrative: An Introductory Anthology* (1980) and *Best West Indian Stories* (1982).

Rohlehr, Gordon: Professor of English, University of the West Indies, St. Augustine. Educated Guyana, Jamaica and Birmingham University, England. Articles on Naipual, Walcott, Brathwaite, and on the West Indian Calypso, music, oral and literary traditions.

Shetley, Vernon: Assistant Professor of English, Wellesley College. Articles on Melville and on the choreography of Merce Cunningham.

Simmons, Harold (1914-1966): Saint Lucian artist, friend and mentor to Walcott.

Stone, Judy: Arts reviewer for the *Trinidad Guardian*.

Taylor, Patrick: Assistant Professor in the Division of Humanities and Canada Research Fellow at York University, Canada. Author of *The Narrative of Liberation: Perspectives on Afro-Caribbean Literature, Popular Culture, and Politics* (1989), and articles on Afro-Caribbean religion.

BIBLIOGRAPHY
Partially Annotated

I have spent more than sixteen years accumulating materials related to the works of Derek Walcott; however, there must be reviews and articles of which I am unaware and others that I have been unable to locate. Nevertheless, the listings in the following pages are fairly comprehensive, considering the widespread distribution of sources in the field of Commonwealth, Post-colonial or Third-World literature. The search is sometimes frustrating, but exciting and often very rewarding.

I have not attempted to list all the original publications of individual poems in the primary bibliography section. That information has been covered admirably in Irma Goldstraw's *Derek Walcott: An Annotated Bibliography of His Works* (1984). While Walcott's collections of poems and individual plays are too complex for brief summarization, I have partially annotated some of his critical articles, reviews and other journalistic pieces. This may assist researchers in determining whether specific items warrant first-hand inspection.

The secondary bibliography is annotated more extensively. I realize that brief notations are inadequate to the full treatment of closely argued essays, but my notes are intended only to suggest certain leading ideas.

Despite years of effort, a few of the materials listed in this bibliography have eluded my grasp. They may still exist somewhere, in some form, but even when I have obtained photocopies of a text, I often have to guess as to its original source of publication. At times erroneous publication data make it impossible to follow a lead. Some writers allude to items without providing adequate references. In some archives, materials have been clipped from publications and filed without dates, pagination or other pertinent details. In rare cases, issues are missing from microfilm reels and articles cannot be verified. For this reason, I have used the following symbol "#" to mark those entries which I have not examined personally in their original form. Each entry followed by the symbol "+" indicates that the item is anthologized in the present volume.

Primary Sources, A

Another Life. New York: Farrar, Straus & Giroux, 1973; London: Jonathan Cape, 1973.

"Another World for the Lost." Unpublished, c. 1947.

The Arkansas Testament. New York: Farrar, Straus & Giroux, 1987.

Cafe Martinique." *House and Garden* 157 (Mar. 1985): 140, 222, 224. Short story with narrator describing life of writer in Martinique, his disappointments, being passed by as he awaits the past.

The Caribbean Poetry of Derek Walcott and the Art of Romare Beardon. New York: Limited Editions Club, 1983. Selected poems by Walcott, illustrations by Beardon, introduction by Joseph Brodsky

The Castaway and Other Poems. London: Jonathan Cape, 1965.

Charlatan, Mimeograph in Caribbean Plays Series. Kingston, Jamaica: University of the West Indies, Extra-Mural Department, [1973]

Collected Poems 1948-1984. New York: Farrar, Straus & Giroux, 1986.

"Crossroads."' Unpublished, c. 1957.

"Cry for a Leader." Unpublished, c. 1949.

Dream on Monkey Mountain and Other Plays. New York: Farrar, Straus & Giroux, 1970; London: Jonathan Cape, 1972.

Drums and Colours. Caribbean Quarterly. 7. 1-2 special issue (Mar.-June 1961): 1-104.

Epitaph for the Young; a Poem in XII Cantoes. Bridgetown, Barbados: Advocate Co., 1949.

"Flight and Sanctuary."' Unpublished, c. 1949.

The Fortunate Traveller. New York: Farrar, Straus & Giroux, 1981; London: Jonathan Cape, 1982.

"Franklin, a Tale of the Islands " Unpublished, c. 1961, revised 1973.

The Gulf and Other Poems. London: Jonathan Cape, 1969; as *The Gulf: Poems.* New York: Farrar, Straus & Giroux, 1970.

Harry Dernier; a Play for Radio Production. Bridgetown, Barbados: Advocate Co., 1952.

Henri Christophe; a Chronicle in Seven Scenes . Bridgetown, Barbados: Advocate Co, 1950.

"'In a Fine Castle.'" Unpublished, 1970.

In a Green Night: Poems 1948-1960. London: Jonathan Cape, 1962.

Ione. Mona, Jamaica: University of the West Indies, Extra-Mural Department, 1957.

The Joker of Seville and O Babylon! New York: Farrar, Straus & Giroux, 1978; London: Jonathan Cape, 1979.

"Jourmard." Unpublished, [1967].

"Marie La Veau." *Trinidad and Tobago Review* "Literary Supplement" 3.6(Dec. 1979): un-numbered, entire supplement. Extract of musical play.

"The Matadors." Unpublished, c. 1947.

Midsummer. New York: Farrar, Straus & Giroux, 1984; London: Faber and Faber, 1984.

Omeros. New York: Farrar, Straus & Giroux, 1990.

Poems. Kingston, Jamaica: Kingston City Printery, [1951].

Remembrance and Pantomime. New York: Farrar, Straus & Giroux, 1980.

"Robin and Andrea." *Bim* 4.13 (July-Dec. 1950): 19-23.

Sea Grapes, London: Jonathan Cape, 1976; New York: Farrar, Straus & Giroux, 1976.

Selected Poems. New York: Farrar, Straus & Giroux, 1964.

Selected Poetry. Ed. Wayne Brown. London: Heinemann, 1981.

"Senza Alcun Sospetto." *B.B.C. Caribbean Voices Transcript No. 475,* 28 May 1950: 1-6. Based on Paolo and Francesca episode in Dante's *Inferno.*

"Simple Cornada." Unpublished, c. 1947.

The Star-Apple Kingdom. New York: Farrar, Straus & Giroux, 1979; London: Jonathan Cape, 1980.

Three Plays: The Last Carnival, Beef, No Chicken, and A Branch of the Blue Nile. New York: Farrar, Straus & Giroux, 1986.

Ti-Jean and His Brothers: A Colouring Book. Port of Spain: Paria Pub. Co., 1984. Condensed story for children. Illustrations by Stuart Hahn.

25 Poems. Bridgetown, Barbados: Advocate Co., 1949.

"The White Devil." *Sunday Guardian* 25 Dec, 1966. A short story for Christmas.

Wine of the Country. Mona, Jamaica: University of the West Indies, Extra-Mural Department, [1956].

Primary Sources, B

"About a Jamaican Playwright." *Trinidad Guardian* 23 Feb. 1966: 8. About Barry Reckford.

"Absolute Beginners." *Trinidad Guardian* 22 Sept, 1965: 17.

"Acculturation a Cautious Process." *Trinidad Guardian* 2 Dec. 1964: #.

"The Achievement of V. S. Naipaul." *Sunday Guardian* 12 Apr. 1964: 15. Consistently developing power in Naipaul's work; sees "first cause" in writer is "to re-create life."

"Across the Hair Dryer into the Deep Freeze." Rev. of *The Group*, by Mary McCarthy. *Sunday Guardian* 26 Apr. 1964: 17, 20.

"The Action is Panicky." Rev. of *I Hear Thunder*, by Samuel Selvon. *Sunday Guardian* 5 May 1963: 4.

"Actor Slade Hopkinson Gives a Farewell Interview." *Trinidad Guardian* 14 July 1965: 6.

"After the Winged Horses, What?" *Trinidad Guardian* 15 Oct. 1966: 8. Local group's support of area artists commendable, but stronger on rhetoric than on material backing.

"Alas! The Last Minute Road March Is Gone." *Trinidad Guardian* 3 Feb. 1963: 4. Loss of spontaneity as commercial enterprise takes over carnival bands.

"Alladin Sticks to Sensitive Themes." *Trinidad Guardian* 6 July 1963: 5.

"Almost Everyone Got into the Act." *Sunday Guardian* 5 Nov. 1961: 4. Rev. of art exhibit.

"American Anguish, Canadian Calm." *Trinidad Guardian* 22 July 1964: 5. Admits psychological dislike of woodcuts, etchings.

"American Artist Shows Technique on Velvet." *Trinidad Guardian* 9 Mar. 1961: 5.

"The Anarchic Tramp Is a Tragic Hero." *Sunday Guardian* 24 July 1966: 9. Viewing revival of Marx brothers' *Animal Crackers* and reading Charlie Chaplin's autobiography prompts discussion of absurd modern hero.

"Another Cautious, Lengthy Short Story." Rev. of *The Games Are Coming*, by Michael Anthony. *Sunday Guardian* 24 Nov. 1963: 10.

"Another Kind of Sentimentality." *Sunday Guardian Magazine* 12 Feb. 1967: 8. On staging realistic drama. Must confront prejudices.

"Another School for Mr. Hinkson." *Trinidad Guardian* 8 Sept. 1965: 7. On a local painter.

"Anthologies." Rev. of *Caribbean Narrative*, by O. R. Dathorne. *Sunday Guardian* 3 July 1966: 6. Laments generally low quality of West Indian verse.

"Are Calypsonians Digging Their Own Graves?" *Sunday Guardian* 23 Jan. 1966: 6.

"Art Exhibition a Triumph of Technique." *Sunday Guardian* 10 Apr. 1960: 7.

"Art Exhibition at the National Museum Confusing Bulk with Quality." *Sunday Guardian* 21 Apr. 1963: 6.

"Art in Guyana: Beware of Love Vines." *Sunday Guardian* 29 May 1966: 9. Warns writers not to "share" too publically, since it can cripple the essential loneliness of their particular duty."

"Art Makes a Restaurant Come-Back." *Trinidad Guardian* 28 June 1961: 5.

"Artist Experiments in Colour." *Trinidad Guardian* 31 May 1961: 5.

"An Artist Interprets Cricket." *Trinidad Guardian* 1 Jan. 1964: 5.

"Artist Volkoff's Works Bent Towards Fantasy." *Trinidad Guardian* 31 Jan. 1962: 5.

"Artists Need Some Assistance." *Sunday Guardian* 3 Apr. 1960: 7. Dangers in study abroad for artists in impressionable stage. Government can support without restraining individuality of local artists.

"Auntie Mame Dominates." *Trinidad Guardian* 1 Nov. 1963: 14. Rev. of Queen's Hall play production.

"Author Deserves Another Service." *Trinidad Guardian* 20 Aug. 1965: 5. Rev. of *One for the Road.*

"Award Goes to Nigerian Author." *Trinidad Guardian* 21 July 1965: 5. Jock Campbell New Statesman award to Achebe for *Things Fall Apart.*

"A Bajan Boyhood." Rev. of *Amongst Thistles and Thorns,* by A. C. Clarke. *Sunday Guardian* 5 Sept. 1965: 8, 11.

"Barbados and New World." *Sunday Guardian Magazine* 11 Dec. 1966: 7, 10, Comment on independence issue of *New World.* Character of Barbadian writers and leaders.

"Benedict Wright Talks to Derek Walcott." *Express Independence Magazine* (Trinidad), 31 Aug. 1969: 24, 27. Discusses *Franklin,* the importance of man's endurance.

"Berlin: The A. B. C. of Negritude." *Sunday Guardian* 18 Oct. 1964: 11. Writer's conference in Berlin. Democratization equalizes but also annihilates personality. Césaire argued that his use of "negritude" was nonaggressive, was "the product of European humanism," was "the wish to be one's self." Reaction to meeting established writers.

"'Best of Everything' Renews Hopes for W. I. Comedy." Rev. of play by Aubrey Adams. *Trinidad Guardian* 7 Nov. 1961: 5.

"Between Bunny Hops." *Trinidad Guardian* 15 Dec. 1965: 9. Reaction to censorship.

"Between Sand and Bright Blue Sea." *Trinidad Guardian* 28 Sept. 1966: 5. Inane art aimed at tourist taste.

"Bewildered and Betwixt Am I." *Trinidad Guardian* 2 Sept. 1964: 5. Columnist beset by aspiring writers and advice givers.

"Beyond the Backyard." *Sunday Guardian* 11 Dec. 1966: 10, 27. On treatment of middle class in West Indian drama.

"The Bible According to Huston." *Trinidad Guardian* 24 Dec. 1966: 6. On John Huston.

"Bi-Focal." *Trinidad Guardian* 16 Jan. 1967: 6.

"*Bim* Celebrates 21st Year." *Trinidad Guardian* 8 Jan. 1964: 5.

"*Bim* Editor Publishes His Poems." Rev. of *Collected Poems,* by Frank Collymore. *Sunday Guardian* 3 Jan. 1960: 4.

"Bim: Putting on the Style." Sunday Guardian 18 Sept. 1966: 6. Suggests weaknesses in recent numbers of *Bim:* layout and typography out of date, critical articles too congenial.

mourns news of cessation of publication for *Bim*. Blow to writers wishing to live among the people.

"Biographer Sees Thomas Plainly." Rev. of *The Life of Dylan Thomas,* by Constantine Fitzgibbon. *Trinidad Guardian* 30 Mar. 1966: 5.

"The Blaze of Vision That Is Stollmeyer's." *Trinidad Guardian* 28 Apr. 1960: 5.

"Bond Returns to Jamaica." Rev. of film *The Man with the Golden Gun. Sunday Guardian* 25 Apr. 1965: 15.

"Bond's Formula Still Irresistible." Rev. of film *Thunderball. Trinidad Guardian* 19 Jan. 1966: 5.

"Boscoe Holder Gifted Painter." *Trinidad Guardian* 22 Feb. 1961: 5.

"Brasher *Bim* Can Win More Friends." *Sunday Guardian* 28 Apr. 1963: 4.

"Bright Future Looms for Wheelchair Artist." *Sunday Guardian* 9 Apr. 1961: 7.

"British Art—It's Just as Dull as British Weather." *Trinidad Guardian* 12 Sept. 1961: 5.

"Brother Griffin's Exhibition, World Through a Stained Glass Window." *Sunday Guardian* 24 May 1964: 5.

"'Brutal Directness." *Trinidad Guardian* 29 June 1966: 5. On John Osborne, other subjects.

"Building a Home away from Home." *Trinidad Guardian* 20 Apr. 1966: 5. Plight of actors who need a center in which to perform, who lack local repertoire, local backing. Rich sources in West Indian fiction.

"Caligula's Horse." *Kunapipi* 11.1 (1989): 138-42. Conference on West Indian Literature, Mona, Jamaica, 1988.

"A Call for Clean Writing." *Trinidad Guardian* 22 Jan. 1964: 5. Contest rules spell censorship in Chamber of Commerce playwrights contest.

"The Caribbean: Culture or Mimicry?" *Journal of Interamerican Studies and World Affairs* 16.1 (Feb. 1974): 3-13. Presented to the University of Miami American Assembly on the United States and the Caribbean, University of Miami, Apr. 1973. Claims West Indian identity is dependent on more encompassing American geography. West Indian politicians defraud people with mimicry of power politics.+

"Carnival Spirit a Contempt for Material Treasures." *Sunday Guardian* 24 Feb. 1963: 10. Built-in obsolescence of this folk expression. The deterioration of the performance under government regulation.

"Carnival: The Theatre of the Streets." *Sunday Guardian* 9 Feb. 1964: 4. Approaches art, but lacks essential quality of "stillness" inherent in other arts.

"Castries: A Tired Phoenix . . . A Taste of Ashes." *Sunday Guardian* 12 June 1960: 5. Account of fire damage.

"Chapter of History Written in Guyana." *Trinidad Guardian* 2 June 1966: 5. Beneath restraint of artists at conference, lies common contempt and longing for "home," bred by exile.

"Cheers for an Insincere Clown." *Trinidad Guardian* 30 Jan. 1964: 5. Calypso review.

"Chen—A Sense of Impatience not of Fulfilment." *Trinidad Guardian* 30 June 1965: 6. Rev. of art exhibit.

"A Classic of Cricket." Rev. of *Beyond a Boundary*, by C. L. R. James. *New York Times Book Review* 89 (25 Mar. 1984): 1, 36-37. Book about grace of West Indian cricketers of African descent blending African prowess with Victorian codes.

"The Clown Prince of Calypso Drops a Bomb." *Sunday Guardian Magazine* 15 Jan. 1967: 4.

"A Colonial's-Eye View of the Empire." *Tri-quarterly* 65 (Winter 1986): 73-84. As disinterested observer, colonial realizes empires die and art survives. No power makes empire center of civilization.

"A Combination of Grace and Vigour." *Trinidad Guardian* 26 July 1963: 5. Rev. of art exhibit.

"Confidence, Sympathy Come First." *Trinidad Guardian* 18 Aug. 1965: 5.

"Confusing Bulk with Quality." *Sunday Guardian* 21 Apr. 1963: 6.

"'Conguerabia' Mural Decorates Forecourt." *Sunday Guardian* 3 Sept. 1961: 5. Carlisle Chang mural at Piarco Airport.

"Contemplative Is Word for His Genius." *Trinidad Guardian* 5 Oct. 1966: 5. Boris Pasternak's style, elevates ordinary to symbolic.

"Correction Please." *Trinidad Guardian* 11 May 1966: 5. Rev. of art exhibit.

"Creative Arts Summer School." *Sunday Guardian* 29 Aug. 1965: 6.

"Crisis of Conscience: Ban, Ban Caliban Is the Cry." *Sunday Guardian* 22 Aug 1965: 11. Commonwealth Arts Festival ironic in celebrating when commonwealth breaks down.

"Crocodile Dandy." Rev. of *The Daylight Moon* and *The Vernacular Republic*, by Les Murray. *The New Republic* 200.6 (6 Feb. 1989): 25-28.

"Crossroads of Sensibility." *Sunday Guardian* 1 Jan. 1967: 89. Latin, African currents in West Indies.

"Curious Mish-Mash of Style." *Trinidad Guardian* 12 Feb. 1964: 5. Rev. of Dimanche Gras.

"Dark Horses." *Sunday Guardian Magazine* 29 Jan. 1967: 4.

"Derek Walcott Looks at Off-Broadway Theatre." *Sunday Guardian* 20 Oct. 1963: 15. Appreciates importance of technical equipment, need to test plays in performance.

"Derek Walcott Talks about *The Joker of Seville*." *Carib* 4 (1986): 1-15. Comments at seminar at College of the Virgin Islands, Fall 1979. Process of adapting Tirso de Molina's *El Burlador de Sevilla* for his *The Joker of Seville*.

"Derek Walcott Visits the November Exhibition . . . and Sees Marked Progress in Styles, Technique." *Trinidad Guardian* 21 Apr. 1963: 6.

"Designing Sense Covers up for Artist's Lapses." *Sunday Guardian* 22 Oct. 1961: 7.

"Designing Sense Covers up for Artist's Lapses." *Sunday Guardian* 22 Oct. 1961: 7.

"Dialect and Dialectic." Rev. of *Moscow Is not My Mecca*, by Jan Carew. *Sunday Guardian* 22 Nov. 1964: 18.

"Did You See the Australian Ballet or Could You Afford It?" *Sunday Guardian* 25 June 1967: 10.

"A Dilemma Faces W. I. Artists." *Sunday Guardian* 12 Jan. 1964: 3. Failure to appreciate sense of the New World. Art is the contribution of new Caribbean.

"Diversity of Technique Makes for Fine Show." *Trinidad Guardian* 16 May 1962: 5.

"'Double-bill' Was a Triumph of Artifice." *Trinidad Guardian* 21 Feb. 1967: 5. Rev. of two plays.

"Down by the Old Gas Pump." *Trinidad Guardian* 12 May 1965: 5. Rev. of film *How to Murder Your Wife*.

"Drama: East Side, West Side." *Sunday Guardian* 25 Oct. 1964: 15.

Editor. *Ploughshares* 13.1 (1987): Special issue edited by Walcott. Says he intended to collect dramatic verse, but scarcity of submissions led to lyrical poems instead.

"Education through the Theatre." Rev. of *Moon on a Rainbow Shawl*, by Errol Hill. *Trinidad Guardian* 15 Jan. 1964: 4.

"'Electra' Unveils Close-Up of Horror." *Trinidad Guardian* 13 Nov. 1963: 9. Rev. of film.

"Eliza Blunts the Irony of Shaw's Point." *Sunday Guardian* 1 Jan. 1966: 6. Rev. film *My Fair Lady*.

"Encouraging Turn." *Trinidad Guardian* 29 Dec. 1965: 6. Funds for arts centre.

"Energetic Guild Comes to Town." *Trinidad Guardian* 19 May 1965: 5.

"English Artist Paints W. I. Way of Life." *Trinidad Guardian* 4 May 1961: 5.

"Enough to Gain the Title, 'Epic.'" *Trinidad Guardian* 23 Dec. 1964: 5. Rev. of film *How the West Was Won*.

"Enter Kirkley and Pitts, and a Promise is Kept." *Trinidad Guardian* 17 Dec. 1964: 4.

"Errol John—Busy Man with a Dual Career." *Sunday Guardian* 30 July 1961: 7.

"Errors and Terrors of West Indian Writing." Rev. of *Caribbean Literature*, ed. G. R. Coulthard. *Trinidad Guardian* 9 Feb. 1966: 5. Unambitious in scope, selections predictable, poorly edited text.

"Eulogy to W. H. Auden." *The New Republic* 21 Nov. 1983: 39.

"Exact Balance of Exposition, Acting." *Trinidad Guardian* 6 May 1964: 5.

"Exile & Independence." *Sunday Guardian Independence Supplement* 30 Aug. 1964: 15, 42, 47. Artist must "earn his exile, not adopt it out of desperation."

"Explorer Is in Danger of Disappearing." *Sunday Guardian* 27 Feb. 1966: 8. Touches Harris, Mais, *Bim* No. 42, Janheinz Jahn's bibliography.

"Expression.'" *Express* 24 Oct. 1971: 22-24.

"The Faces Never Meet." *Trinidad Guardian* 18 May 1966: 5. Rev. films *A Patch of Blue, The Slender Thread.*

"Farewell Exhibition One of Staggering Triviality." *Trinidad Guardian* 4 May 1962: 5.

"Fellini's Masterpiece." *Sunday Guardian* 4 Apr. 1965: 6. Rev. of film *8 1/2.*

"Fellowships." *Sunday Guardian Magazine* 15 Jan. 1967: 9. Rev. of *Foundations* by Anthony La Rose.

"Fiddle, Chac Chac and Drum Take Over." *Sunday Guardian* 26 July 1964: 4. Community concerts competitions.

"The Figure of Crusoe; on the Theme of Isolation in West Indian Writing." Unpublished typescript of lecture delivered at the University of the West Indies in the Open Lecture Series, 27 Oct. 1965. Discusses archetypal richness of Adam/ Crusoe figure.+

"Film with a Hundred Heroes." *Trinidad Guardian* 15 Sept. 1965: 7. Rev. of film on Tokyo Olympics.

"Finest Thing Is Its Rhythm." *Trinidad Guardian* 15 Apr. 1964: 5. Rev. of film *Soldier in the Rain.*

"42 Works Fetch $1,598." *Sunday Guardian* 10 Dec. 1961: 5.

"400 Years of Indian Painting on Show Today." *Trinidad Guardian* 15 Apr. 1961: 5.

"A Fracas of Words and Music." *Sunday Guardian* 27 Jan. 1963: 4. Preparation for carnival band tents.

"Fruits, Flowers and Faces. The 'Little Exhibition.'" *Trinidad Guardian* 17 May 1964: 5.

"Future of Art Promising." *Sunday Guardian* 31 Aug. 1963: "Independence Progress Supplement," supplement 26-27. Need for national theatre. "Enthusiasm for 'a national culture' . . . because of impatience and fake pride, can retard artistic development."

"The Garden Path." Rev. of *The Enigma of Arrival,* by V. 5. Naipaul. *New Republic* 13 Apr. 1987: 27-31. "Negligible as a novel and crucial as autobiography."

"Glory for 'The King and I.'" *Trinidad Guardian* 22 Nov. 1963: 5. Rev. of local production.

"Good Times, Wonderful Times: The Travels and Joys of a Touring Company." *Trinidad Theatre Workshop in a Season of Plays.* Ed. Derek Walcott. n.p.: Kingston, 1971. 1-2. Program introduction for appearance in Jamaica.

"The Great Irony.'" *Sunday Guardian* 25 Sept. 1966: 6. Devices employed by Genêt in *The Blacks* familiar to West Indians: "the masking, the ceremonial costumes, the ritual assuming of idealized roles . . . done in solemn fun."

"A Great New Novel of the West Indies." Rev. of *A House for Mr. Biswas,* by V. S. Naipaul. *Sunday Guardian* 5 Nov. 1961: 17. Naipaul's novels full of the "'pathos of understanding."

"A Great Russian Novel." Rev. of *The Gift,* by Vladimir Nabokov. *Sunday Guardian* 19 Apr. 1964: 15.

"Hail, Hail; the Gang's All Hair." *Trinidad Guardian* 20 Jan. 1965: 5. Rev. of film *A Hard Day's Night.*

"Happy New Year in September." *Trinidad Guardian* 14 Sept. 1966: 6. On artists who commit suicide, public martyrs. Replies to complaint "This country killing me,"—. . . which country doesn't?"

"Hell-bent on Being Modern." *Trinidad Guardian* 2 Feb. 1966: 5. Rev. of art exhibit.

"Here They Come, Ready or Not." *Trinidad Guardian* 26 May 1965: 5.

"The Hero Takes Snobbery Course." *Trinidad Guardian* 16 Sept. 1964: 5.

"The Hills Are Joyful Together." *Sunday Guardian* 17 Apr. 1966: 6. Rev. of film *The Sound of Music.*

"His Is the Pivotal One about Race." Rev. of *Other Leopards,* by Dennis Williams. *Sunday Guardian* 1 Dec. 1963: 22.

"His Sense of Design Is Still Strong." *Trinidad Guardian* 23 Jan. 1962: 5.

"History and Picong . . . in *The Middle Passage.*" Rev. of *The Middle Passage,* by V. S. Naipaul. *Sunday Guardian* 30 Sept. 1962: 9. Comparisons with travel writers Trollope, Froude, Kingsley, with Lamming, with satire of Joyce and Swift.+

"Identity Kit." *Trinidad Guardian* 6 Oct. 1965: 5.

"Idioms Are His Forte." *Trinidad Guardian* 26 Feb. 1964: 5. Praises short stories of Bernard Malamud.

"I Have Always Had a Psychological Aversion ..." *Trinidad Guardian* 22 July 1964: 5.

"I'm a Reporter, Says Mural Man." *Sunday Guardian* 3 Dec. 1961: 7.

"In Middle Passage: The James Version." Rev. of *The Black Jacobins,* by C. L. R. James. *Sunday Guardian* 16 Aug. 1964: 3.

"In Praise of Pesantry." *Trinidad Guardian* 18 July 1965: 9. On playwright Eric Roach.

"In Search of the Carnival Spirit." *Sunday Guardian* 13 Feb. 1965: 3. Rev. of art exhibit.

"Industry Gives $950 Boost to the Arts in Trinidad Show." *Sunday Guardian* 10 Dec. 1961: 5.

"Inside Dope on Hazards of the Literary Race." Rev. of *Archipelagoes Old and New,* by Cyril Connolly. *Sunday Guardian* 5 Apr. 1964: 11.

"Integrating the Arts." *Trinidad Guardian* 29 July 1964: 5. Carnival costumes; problem of remembering slavery.

[Interview] *Jamaica Daily News Magazine* 7 Dec. 1975: 6. Interview. Discusses staging of *The Joker of Seville* in Jamaica.

"Interview with an Actor." *Trinidad Guardian* 13 Oct. 1965: 5. Interviews Errol Jones.

"Interview with V. S. Naipaul." *Sunday Guardian* 7 Mar. 1965: 5, 7. West Indian ideals lowered by proletarian standards. Naipaul prefers label of ironist rather than satirist because satire requires too much optimism.

"Irate Marxist Waxes Wrath." *Trinidad Guardian* 27 July 1966: 5.

"Is Bad Verse Forgivable at a Certain Stage of Our Evolution?" *Sunday Guardian* 11 Sept. 1966: 5. Danger of collecting mediocrity in anthologies drawn from limited sources.

"Islands in the Limelight." *Sunday Guardian* 31 Oct 1965: 6.

"Is V. S. Naipaul an Angry Young Man?" *Trinidad Guardian* 6 Aug. 1967: 8-9. To understand Naipaul, necessary to forget his mask of despair. *The Mimic Men* saved by its style.

"It Sees History as Endeavour." *Trinidad Guardian* 29 Apr. 1964: 5. Rev. of film *The Leopard.*

"It's Our Own Kind of Artist Figure." *Sunday Guardian* 5 Feb. 1967: 11. Need for performing arts center. Difficulties of judging carnival contests.

"Jack Spector Saves a Falling 'Whittington." *Trinidad Guardian* 18 Dec. 1959: 5.

"The Joker: Closer to Continuous Theatre." *Trinidad Guardian* 22 Mar. 1975: 5. Experiments with second Port of Spain run of *Joker of Seville.* Calls for a national theatre.

"The Joker of Seville." *Caribbean Tempo* 3.1 (1975): 16-18. Duplicates "Soul Brother to 'The Joker of Seville'" (1974).

"A Journey into the Interior." *Sunday Guardian* 11 Apr. 1965: 6. On lecture by C. L. R. James.

"Joyous Nothingness about This Show." *Trinidad Guardian* 28 Nov. 1963: 5.

"Judging Standards." *Trinidad Guardian* 20 Oct. 1965: 5. Danger to provincial artist under local adulation, never knows how good he is.

"Juniors Reveal Easy Course in Techniques." *Sunday Guardian* 8 Oct. 1961: 6.

"Just the Way It Was." Rev. of *The Year in San Fernando,* by Michael Anthony. *Sunday Guardian* 14 Mar. 1965: 8.

"The Kabuki . . . Something to Give to Our Theatre." *Sunday Guardian* 16 Feb. 1964: 14. Influence of oriental theatre on modern stage. Parallels between Kabuki and West Indian culture: "our folk-lore, and dance . . . its primitive mythology, its devils, thief-heroes, old-men and witch-figures, and . . . its masks."

"Kaiso, Genius of the Folk." *Sunday Guardian* 9 Feb. 1964: 13. Sees decline of folk element in calypso.

"Keeping up with the Times." *Sunday Guardian* 21 July 1968: 6. Finds recent exhibition of expressionist paintings outdated. Obscurity not an end in itself.

"Kelshall's Selections Stand Out in South Exhibition." *Sunday Guardian* 25 Sept. 1960: 7.

"The King 'Ain' Dead Yet." *Sunday Guardian* 2 Feb. 1964: 13. Rev. of calypso tent, refers to Sparrow.

"The Knack-out." *Trinidad Guardian* 17 Aug. 1966: 7. Rev. of film *The Knack and How to Get It.*

"Kramer's Middle Passage." *Trinidad Guardian* 27 Apr. 1966: 7. Rev. of film *Ship of Fools*.

"Lame Tribute from the Arts." *Trinidad Guardian* 1 July 1964: 5. Rev. of art exhibition. Negative features of "public" art.

"'La Notte'—A New Way of Looking." *Trinidad Guardian* 13 July 1963: 5. Rev. of film *La Notte*.

"A Laventville Crookback." *Trinidad Guardian* 1 Feb. 1966: 5. Rev. of play *King Cobo*, by Freddie Kissoon.

"Leaving School." *London Magazine* 5.6 (1965): 4-14. Rich autobiographical detail of early years, influential names, events, reading matter.+

"Lent Opens with a Muffled Bang for Art Lovers." *Sunday Guardian* 19 Feb. 1961: 7.

"Let's Have the Puppets." *Trinidad Guardian* 21 July 1966: 5.

"A Likely Case of 'Squareness.'" *Trinidad Guardian* 7 Apr. 1965: 5.

"Listen! Farnsworth, the Drums Have Stopped." *Sunday Guardian* 6 Dec. 1964: 26. Rev. of film *Guns of Batasi*.

"The Little Carib Theatre Workshop." *Opus* 1.1 (Feb. 1960): 31. Article attributed to Walcott.

"Lively Camp." *Sunday Guardian* 30 Oct. 1966: 6. Rev. local production of *The Desert Song*.

"Living with Genius." Rev. of *Life with Picasso*, by Françoise Gilot and Carlton Lake. *Sunday Guardian* 16 Jan. 1966: 7.

"Local Art Headed in Confident Direction." *Sunday Guardian* 31 July 1960: 6.

"Looking on in Comfort." *Trinidad Guardian* 14 Mar. 1957: 7. Rev. local production of *Look Back in Anger*.

"Look Ma, I'm Dancing." *Trinidad Guardian* 23 June 1965: 5.

"Machine-Gun Moliere." *Trinidad Guardian* 6 May 1966: 5.

"Magic Industry." Rev. of *To Urania*, by Joseph Brodsky. *New York Review of Books* 24 Nov. 1988: 35-39.

"Magnificence and Art in the Carnival Spectacle." *Trinidad Guardian* 5 Mar. 1962: 6. Trinidad Carnival result of European and African confluences.

"Mailer by Mailer." Rev. of *The Presidential Papers* by Norman Mailer. *Sunday Guardian* 5 July 1964: 4.

"Making No Move in Tough Stance." *Trinidad Guardian* 3 Nov. 1965: 5.

"The Man Who Was Born Unlucky." Rev. of *A House for Mr Biswas* by V. S. Naipaul. *Sunday Guardian* 5 Nov. 1961: 17. Novel "enhances the ordinary and illuminates the defeat of millions like us."

"Mary, Mary, How Predictable." *Trinidad Guardian* 7 Dec. 1963: 10 .

"Master of the Ordinary." Rev. of *Philip Larkin: Collected Poems*, by Anthony Thwaite and Philip Larkin. *New York Review of Books* 1 June 1989: 37-40.

"Masterly Job, Mr. Lewis." *Sunday Guardian* 15 Apr. 1962: 6.

"Mausica Still Bogged Down." *Sunday Guardian* 12 July 1964: 4. Mausica Teacher's Training College, other local matters.

"Maybe Some Small Voice Is Buried Under Confusion." *Trinidad Guardian* 4 Aug. 1966: 7. Need for a national theatre, an outlet for country's great number of plays, actors.

"Meanings." *Savacou* 2 (1970): 45-51. Detailed account of career to *Dream on Monkey Mountain*. Attests to local, African, European, and Oriental influences.+

"Mighty Terror—A Great Matador." *Sunday Guardian* 17 Jan. 1965: 13.

"Migrant's Lot." Rev. of *Journey to an Illusion*, by Douglas Hinds. *Trinidad Guardian* 20 Oct. 1966: 8.

"Mixing the Dance and Drama." *Trinidad Guardian* 6 Dec. 1972: 5. Many roles of performing company director, on Astor Johnson's dance troupe.

"Modern Theatre." *The Daily Gleaner* (Jamaica) 25 Mar. 1957: #.

"More Appeals." *Trinidad Guardian* 22 Oct. 1966: 6. Requirements of an arts center.

"More Direction of Style Evident Among the Oils." *Trinidad Guardian* 23 May 1962: 5.

"More or Less an Anthology of Walks." *Trinidad Guardian* 5 May 1965: 5.

"More W. I. Radio Dramas Urged in Caribbean." *Sunday Guardian* 24 Jan. 1960: 5.

"Movement Marks Chase's Exhibition Abstract Art Show in Woodbrook." *Trinidad Guardian* 26 July 1961: 5.

"Mr. Naipaul's Passage to India." Rev. of *An Area of Darkness*, by V. S. Naipaul. *Sunday Guardian* 20 Sept. 1964: 2, 4. Part of necessary middle passage, a scrupulously honest self-portrait and critical analysis

"The Muse of History: An Essay." *Is Massa Day Dead?* Ed. Orde Coombs. Garden City, N Y : Doubleday, 1974. 1-28. Reprinted in *Carifesta Forum*. Ed. by John Hearne. [Kingston, Jamaica]: Carifesta, [1976]. The aesthetic of the colonial poet who masters history, language. Elated with potential in the West Indies. Topics: burden of history, Adamic poet as opposed to polemic revolutionaries, language, race, "imitation" as creation, the folk.

"The Muse of the Jungle." *Sunday Guardian* 15 Nov. 1964: 21. On Wilson Harris's *Heartland* and other Guyanese writers.

"Museum Curator in Limelight." *Trinidad Guardian* 4 May 1966: 7.

"Naipaul's New Book." Rev. of *Mr Stone and the Knights Companion*, by V. S. Naipaul. *Sunday Guardian* 7 July 1963: 15.

"Naparima Bowl Fosters South's Artistic Activity." *Trinidad Guardian* 7 July 1965: 6.

"National Theatre Is the Answer." *Trinidad Guardian* 12 Aug. 1964: 5. Characteristics of a West Indian drama form.

"Native Dancer." *Sunday Guardian Magazine* 4 Dec. 1966: 8-9. Choreography of local dance.

"Native Women under Sea-Almond Trees: Musings on Art, Life, and the Island of St. Lucia." *House and Garden* 156.8 (Aug. 1984): 114-15, 161-63. Compares present with memories upon recent visit to St. Lucia.

"Necessity of Negritude." *Trinidad Guardian* 28 Sept. 1964: 8. On Senghor, and French concepts of Negritude, surrealism, colonialism. The poetry of naming things.+

"Neo-Realism Parallel Noted in W. I. Novels." *Trinidad Guardian* 24 Apr. 1960: 7. Time to place Mittelholzer, Hearne, Selvon in setting of contemporary literature. Absorbing lessons of masters, they produce works of individual stamp.

"'Nevada' Meets All Demands." *Trinidad Guardian* 21 Sept. 1966: 5. Rev. of film *Nevada Smith.*

"New Acquisitions Add Variety to Art Gallery." *Sunday Guardian* 1 Oct. 1961: 7.

"The New British Theatre." Rev. of *Anger and Auter,* ed. John R. Taylor. *Sunday Guardian* 10 Nov. 1963: 5. Positive value of having standards challenged. Repeats need for national support of theatre.

"New Gallery Boasts of Fine Location." *Trinidad Guardian* 26 July 1962: 5.

"A New Jamaican Novelist." Rev. of *The Children of Sisyphus,* by Orlando Patterson. *Sunday Guardian* 7 May 1964: 15.

"A New Poet Jamaican." *Sunday Guardian* 20 June 1965: 6. On London publishers of West Indian literature.

"The New York I Know." *Sunday Guardian* 27 Dec. 1964: 12-13. His neighborhood, the depression of the "village."

"The Nigerian Teacher Who Became Editor." Rev. of *Wand of Noble Weed,* by O'Nuora Nzekwu. *Trinidad Guardian* 17 Nov. 1961: 5.

"Nobody Knows Their Names." *Sunday Guardian* 4 July 1965: 7. Rev. collection of essays by Third-World students.

"Nostalgia Haunts Visiting Painter." *Trinidad Guardian* 5 Jan. 1966: 5. Mentions Workshop productions of Albee's *The Zoo Story* and *The Sea at Dauphin.*

"Not So Fast, Mr. Cambridge!" *Trinidad Guardian* 31 May 1967: 4. Regardless of quality, local troupes create local audience for indigenous drama.

"Of Masks and Men." *Trinidad Guardian* 12 Oct. 1967: 8. Bitter remarks on hopelessness of "progress and culture."

"On Choosing Port of Spain." *David Frost Introduces Trinidad and Tobago.* Ed. David Frost. Andre Deutsch: London, 1975. 14-23. Tribute to city, scenes, sounds, people. Problems of lost history, "creole frame of mind," hedonism.

"On Robert Lowell." *New York Review of Books* 31 (1 Mar. 1984): 25, 28-31. Tribute, memories of friend and model. Lowell "imitated" in tradition of Renaissance masters.

"On the Beat in Trinidad." *The New York Times Magazine* 5 Oct. 1986: Sec. VI, pt.

ii, pp. 38, 40-41, 43-44. Smallness of St. Lucia compared with diversities of Port of Spain, clichés of Caribbean life.

"Opening the Road." *Sunday Guardian* 23 Oct. 1966: 6. Preparing production of Soyinka's *The Road* notes character and humor parallels with Caribbean.

"Othello." *Sunday Guardian* 23 Apr. 1967: 6.

"Othello Off and On." *Sunday Guardian* 7 May 1967: 6.

"Our Poetry in Song." *Trinidad Guardian* 9 Feb. 1964: #.

"'Our Town' Beyond Present Scope of 'The Players.'" *Sunday Guardian* 6 Dec. 1959: 7.

"Outlook for a National Theatre." *Sunday Guardian* 22 Mar. 1964: 17. Rich potential for theatre in multi-racial society, the mingling of Tagore, Lorca, Shakespeare and Noh theatre.

"Painter Chen Tries to Capture Sound." *Sunday Guardian* 1 July 1962: 4.

"Painter Leaps the Chasm Too Soon." *Sunday Guardian* 25 June 1961: 7.

"A Painter's Journal." *Trinidad Guardian* 22 Sept. 1967: 5. Guyanese painters.

"Papa's Flying Machines." Rev. of *The Glorious Flight*, by Louis Bleriot. *New York Time's Book Review* 88 (13 Nov. 1983): 37, 51.

"Parody of the Protest Formula." Rev. of *Survivors of the Crossing*, by Austin Clarke. *Sunday Guardian* 23 Aug. 1964: 4.

"Patterns of Existence." *Trinidad Guardian* 24 Mar. 1966: 7. Rev. of art exhibition.

"Patterns to Forget." *Trinidad Guardian* 22 June 1966: 5. Detects patterns of emergent forms identifiable West Indian musical drama. Choreographer must rely more on imagination. Offers elements of classic Kabuki and American musical as useful starting points.

"Permanent Art Gallery Decision Commendable One." *Sunday Guardian* 23 Apr. 1961: 7.

"Pinache." *Sunday Guardian* 18 Dec. 1966: 6.

"Playing the Old Race Game." Rev. of *The Scholar Man*, by 0. R. Dathorne. *Sunday Guardian* 29 Nov. 1964: 21.

"Please Come Better." *Express* (Trinidad) 8 June 1978: 24. Open letter of concern over Jeremy Taylor's criticism of dance company performance.

"The Poet in the Theatre." *Poetry Review* 80.4 (Winter 1990-91): 4-8. Finest tragedies propelled as much by metre and symmetry as by character and plot. Nihilism and minimalism of contemporary theatre "[have] become baroque." Poets driven from stage because meter dismissed as too artificial.

"Poetry and History, Exile, Race: Session 2—Questions and Answers." *Tri-quarterly* 65 (1986): 78-84. Panel discussion following Walcott's delivery of "A Colonial's Eye-View of the Empire" for Northwestern University symposium sponsored by *Tri-quarterly* Nov. 1984. Comments on political restraints, on culture, on the idea of "progress."

"Poetry—Enormously Complicated Art." *Trinidad Guardian* 18 June 1962: 3.

Defines poet's role: "the proprietor of the experience of the race." Current West Indian poetry "still precocious and artificial" for an unsettled society "whose languages have a protean vitality, that has not yet formalized its own syntax and accent."

"The Poetry of George Campbell." *Public Opinion* (Jamaica) 20 July 1957: 7

"The Poetry of Mr. G. Smith." *Public Opinion* (Jamaica) 27 July 1957: #.

"Popular Poets Are Now Severely Tested." *Trinidad Guardian* 14 Feb. 1960: #.

"Portrait of the Artist as a Tough Guy." *Sunday Guardian* 9 Aug. 1964: 6.

"Posthumous Papa." Rev. of *A Moveable Feast,* by Ernest Hemingway. *Sunday Guardian* 10 May 1964: 15.

"A Post Mortem." *Trinidad Guardian* 15 June 1966: 5. Laments split between drama groups which creates exclusive "clubs," discourages playwrights, causes timidity in play selection.

"Powerful Acting in 'Long Day's Journey.'" *Trinidad Guardian* 26 Nov. 1963: 5. Rev. Sidney Lumet film.

"Premature Display at Nina's Gallery." *Trinidad Guardian* 18 July 1962: 5.

"Présence Africaine." *Sunday Guardian* 12 June 1966: 15. Rev. Miriam Makeba show.

"Priestly Ends on a Note of Doom." *Sunday Guardian* 9 Jan. 1966: 11. J. B. Priestly suggests his civilization may be ending.

"Principle Must Be Questioned." *Trinidad Guardian* 2 Sept. 1965: 6. On literary and art prizes.

"Problems of a Period of Transition." *Trinidad Guardian* 10 June 1964: 5. Dislocation and exile still make artists imitate foreign standards.

"Problems of Exile." *Trinidad Guardian* 13 July 1966: 5. Need technical training for stage. Requirements of carnival and stage different.

"Professional vs.the Amateur." *Trinidad Guardian* 12 Jan. 1966: 5.

"The Prospect of a National Theatre." *Sunday Guardian* 6 Mar. 1966: 6. Many unsuccessful plans for national arts centre. No qualified personnel to supervise centre. Need scholarships for training professionals.

"Provincial Critic or Sunday Serenade." *Sunday Guardian* 6 Nov. 1966: 1.

"'Psychological House,' Like a Clover-leaf in Concrete." *Sunday Guardian* 22 May 1960: 5. Innovative architectural design.

"Pulpit to Stage." Rev. of *Blues for Mr. Charlie,* by James Baldwin. *Sunday Guardian* 27 Dec. 1964: 13, 17. Has refined anger, recrimination, despair into something pure and articulate.

"Pyrrhic Victories." *Trinidad Guardian* 11 Feb. 1967: 6. Rev. of local art exhibit.

"A Quiet Look Back Over the Year." *Trinidad Guardian* 31 Dec. 1966: 8.

"Reflections on the November Exhibition." *Sunday Guardian* 13 Nov. 1960: 7. Profound sources of art in South American culture ignored in favor of European tradition.

"Refreshing Art Show Today." *Trinidad Guardian* 11 July 1961: 5.

"Regular Old Comedy.'" *Sunday Guardian* 30 May 1965: 6. Rev. local production of "The Irregular Verb, To Love."

"Requiem for an Augustan Legend." *Trinidad Guardian* 11 Dec. 1963: 5. This "Focus on the Arts" feature becomes a regular Wednesday column.

"Review of Art Exhibition." *Sunday Guardian* 20 Nov. 1966: 6. What critic seeks in painting. Anthropologist finds ethnic mixture, melting pot, egalitarianism, joy. Local critic sees confusion, uncertainty, mechanical imitation.

"A Review of a Shakespeare Exhibition.'" *Sunday Guardian* 19 Apr. 1964: 15.

"Rice Is Bitter." Rev. of *Old Thom's Harvest,* by Lauchmonen. *Sunday Guardian* 11 July 1965: 8.

"'Rights of Passage' Drama in Itself." *Trinidad Guardian* 25 Apr. 1973: 5. Brathwaite's trilogy has theatrical qualities: compressed island dialect spoken, swift character delineation, music in speech rhythms.

"St. Lucian Writer, St. Lucian Painter." *Public Opinion* (Jamaica) 3 May 1958: #. Autobiographical sketch. Duplicates "West Indies Festival of Arts, 1958."

"The Same Zing but Different." *Trinidad Guardian* 12 June 1965: 5. Rev. local variety show.

"S[angre] Grande Tonight; Broadway Next." *Trinidad Guardian* 27 Jan. 1965: 5. On Errol Hill.

"Scenes of Provincial Life." *Trinidad Guardian* 22 Dec. 1965: 6. Rev. of art exhibition.

"Schoolgirl Artists Display High Standard of Painting." *Trinidad Guardian* 26 May 1960: 11

"Sculpture on Show—This Time It's by Pt. Fortin Artists." *Trinidad Guardian* 27 Sept. 1961: 5.

"'Seance' Vibrates but Not with Artificial Terror." *Sunday Guardian* 23 May 1965: 6. Rev. of film *Seance on a Wet Afternoon.*

"The Season Opens 'With Love.'" *Trinidad Guardian* 9 June 1965: 5.

"A Self-Interview Raises Questions of Identity." *Sunday Guardian* 16 Oct. 1966: 7. Claims West Indian rather than national identity. Rich mixtures of Caribbean theatre is what gives it force.

"Selvon Has Returned to the Old Form." Rev. of *The Housing Lark,* by Samuel Selvon. *Sunday Guardian* 27 June 1965: 7.

"Sentimental Journey." *Sunday Guardian* 15 Aug. 1965: 7. Rev. of *Bim* #41.

"'Seven Year Itch' Not up to Scratch." *Trinidad Guardian* 14 Nov. 1959: 5. Rev. local production.

"Sex Plus Art Is Big Business." *Trinidad Guardian* 26 Aug. 1964: 5.

"Short of a Miracle." *Trinidad Guardian* 18 Mar. 1964: 5.

"Sir Laurence Omits the Vulgarities." *Sunday Guardian* 23 Feb. 1964: 4. Rev. of film *The Entertainer.*

"Small Town Othello." *Trinidad Guardian* 10 Nov. 1965: 7.

"Soarings among the Jolts." *Trinidad Guardian* 17 Feb. 1965: S. On Frank Collymore and *Bim.*

"Society and the Artist." *Public Opinion* (Jamaica) 4 May 1957: 7. +

"Some African Voices." Rev. of *Modern Poetry from Africa,* ed. Gerald Moore and Ulli Beier. *Sunday Guardian* 22 Dec. 1963: 15.

"Some Jamaican Poets-1." *Public Opinion* (Jamaica) 3 Aug. 1957: 7.

"Some Jamaican Poets-2." *Public Opinion* (Jamaica) 10 Aug. 1957: 7.

"Some West Indian Poets." *London Magazine* 5 (Sept. 1965): 15-30. Climate for poetry not encouraging, leads some to exile. Challenge for new poets to find tone without being distant, to invent natural form of expression. Through appreciating richer expressiveness of spontaneous dialect, is not willing to sacrifice the syntactical power of English. "That dramatic ambivalence is part of what it means to be a West Indian now."

"Soul Brother to 'The Joker of Seville.'" *Trinidad Guardian* 6 Nov. 1974: 4. Recounts commissioning of play. Affinities between modern Trinidad and 16th century Spain of Tirso de Molina. On adaptation of classic work. "Shakespeare creolized classic theatre as much as any Third World writer who re-invents" universal legends.

"The Southern Art Society's Exhibition from South Moves to P. O. S." *Trinidad Guardian* 7 July 1965: 6.

"Sparrowdrama!" *Trinidad Guardian* 2 Mar. 1966: 5.

"Spate of Anthologies Coming Up." *Trinidad Guardian* 11 Nov. 1964: 5.

"Spiritual Purpose Lacking." *Sunday Guardian* 5 Jan. 1964: 3. Difficulty with diverse languages, dialects and cultures of West Indies. Collapse of Federation left no common spiritual bond: made artist "more pathetically isolated, although more important to his 'nation.'" Need training center for artists, performers.

"Spreading Our Culture Abroad." *Sunday Guardian* 8 Nov. 1964 18. Valid criticism of different kinds of theatre requires mature knowledge.

"Still Struggling with Expressionism." *Sunday Guardian* 28 Feb. 1965: 7.

"A Story of Seductions." *Trinidad Guardian* 19 Feb. 1964: 5. Rev. of Roger Vadim film *Les Liaisons Dangereuses* in Port of Spain.

"A Summing Up." *Sunday Guardian* 2 Aug. 1964: 6. Prime Minister's Community Concerts Competition.

"Survivor in Comeback with Drama in Verse." *Trinidad Guardian* 9 Sept. 1964: 5. Rev. of Austin Clarke play, "Road to Glory."

"Sybil Atteck Breaks Through to New Style." *Trinidad Guardian* 21 Nov. 1963: 5.

"Take the Money and Write." *The New York Times* 3 Nov. 1991, late ed., sec.4: 15. Discusses literary prizes. Though valuable, may influence author to sell self.

"Taming the Nightmare." Rev. *An American Dream*, by Norman Mailer. *Sunday Guardian* 12 Sept. 1965: 15.

"Techniques of South's Artists." *Sunday Guardian* 13 June 1965: 6.

"Tension Explodes into Hysterical Giggling." *Sunday Guardian* 10 May 1964: 15. Rev. of film *Dr. Strangelove*.

"Texaco's Show Paced Fine Year of Art." *Sunday Guardian* 1 Jan. 1961: 10.

"That's the True Soul Music." *Trinidad Guardian* 3 Dec. 1968: 7. Rev. of performance of Grand African Ballet.

"Theatre and the Tents in Trinidad." *Tapia* 7.2 (9 Jan. 1977): 6-7. Views calypso as possible musical drama. Sparrow's enactment of "Ten to One Is Murder" has quality of drama; most others fail: structural banality, jaded rhymes, outworn sexual metaphors, poor verse. Sees his *Charlatan* as domestic farce despite its setting in carnival.

"The Theatre of Abuse." Rev. of *Four Black Revolutionary Plays*, by LeRoi Jones. *Sunday Guardian* 3 Jan. 1965: 4.

"There's Ample Room for a Theatre." *Trinidad Guardian* 16 Dec. 1964: 5.

"This Exhibition Is Premature." *Trinidad Guardian* 23 Aug. 1962: 6.

"This Time, Paradise Is St. Lucia." Rev. of *Orchids on the Calabash Tree*, by George Eggleston. *Sunday Guardian* 8 Dec. 1963: 14.

"Time to Separate Politics from Good Verse." Rev. of *Caribbean Literature*, ed. G. R. Coulthard. *Trinidad Guardian* 17 Mar. 1966: 5.

"Timidity and the Sweet South." *Trinidad Guardian* 7 May 1966: 5.

"A Tireless Worker for W. I. Writing." Trinidad Guardian 26 Jan. 1966: 5. Tributes to Edna Manley, Frank Collymore, A. J. Seymour.

"To Africa, with Love." Rev. of *A Kind of Homecoming*, by E. R. Braithwaite. *Sunday Guardian* 22 July 1962: 7.

"To Boo, or Not to Boo." *Trinidad Guardian* 14 Apr. 1965: 5. Review of film, *The Train*.

"Too Early Mr. Clarke." *Sunday Guardian* 31 July 1966: 13. Rev. of art exhibition.

"Too Much of the Wrong Subject." Rev. of *Poems of Resistance*, by Martin Carter. *Sunday Guardian* 14 June 1964: 6.

"Top Painters Featured in Pioneer Art Gallery." *Trinidad Guardian* 18 Aug. 1961: 5.

"Tracking Mr. Wilson Harris." *Sunday Guardian* 24 Apr. 1966: 5. Reviews C. L. R. James' lecture, then the vision and language of Jamaica's Rastafarians.

"Tradition Is Upheld—So the Show Goes On." *Trinidad Guardian* 5 Aug. 1964: 5.

"Tribal Flutes." Rev. of *Rights of Passage*, by Edward Brathwaite. *Sunday Guardian* 19 Mar. 1967: 2. Uses music to analyse structure. Sees parallels with other poets.+

"Tribute to a Master." *Sunday Guardian* 15 May 1966: 9. The influence of Harold Simmons.

"Trinidadian, 12 a Winning Painter." *Sunday Guardian* 7 Aug. 1960: 7.

"Trinidadians Impress New York." *Sunday Guardian* 28 Jan. 1962: 4.

"Trinidad's 1st Repertory Season Opens Next Month." *Sunday Guardian* 11 Sept. 1966: 6. Announces opening of season in "Basement Theatre" in Bretton Hall Hotel: bill includes *The Blacks, The Road, Bell Fanto.*

"T. S. Eliot—Master of an Age." *Sunday Guardian* 10 Jan. 1965: 3.

"Tussaud, with Love." *Sunday Guardian* 15 Oct. 1967: 6. Rev. film of Braithwaite's *To Sir with Love.*

"'Twelfth Night' Is Praiseworthy." *Sunday Guardian* 10 July 1960: 5. Rev. local production.

"A Twenty-One-Year Struggle." *Trinidad Guardian* 2 June 1965: 5. Rev. of art exhibit.

"Two Revivals Coming Up." *Trinidad Guardian* 15 July 1964: 5.

"Under the Influence." *Sunday Guardian* 6 Sept. 1964: 18. Rev. of Henri Telfer art exhibit in Port of Spain.

"Via the Billboards." *Trinidad Guardian* 5 Feb. 1964: 5. Self-expression paralyzed when institutions interfere with art in name of protection.

"Victims of the Cold War." *Trinidad Guardian* 25 May 1966: 5. Rev. of film *The Spy Who Came in from the Cold.*

"Viewing." *Sunday Guardian* 17 Oct. 1965: 14. Rev. of Commonwealth literature, films, theatre.

"Village Theatre: A Summing Up." *Sunday Guardian* 2 Aug. 1964: 7. Need research into Chinese classical theatre, Indian epic theatre and African dance in order for adaptation into indigenous theatre.

"Village Theatre: It's the kind of War I Like." *Sunday Guardian* 19 July 1964: 15. Local theatre competitions.

"Vintage Mittelholzer." Rev. of *Morning at the Office*, by Edgar Mittelholzer. *Sunday Guardian* 21 June 1964: 15.

"Vintage Year for Calypso." *Trinidad Guardian* 16 Feb. 1966: 6.

"Violent Gestures in 'Sharpeville.'" *Sunday Guardian* 17 July 1960: 7.

"Voices, Old and New." *Trinidad Guardian* 19 Aug. 1964: 5. Morgue of BBC's "Caribbean Voices" program and back numbers of *Bim* repositories of West Indian literary movement. Influences of Senghor and Césaire.

"Voices: Will They Grow Louder, or Ebb into a Whisper?" *Sunday Guardian Magazine* 20 Feb. 1966: 8-9. *Voices* literary magazine edited by Clifford Sealey.

"West Indian Art Today." *Sunday Guardian Magazine* 8 May 1966: 8.

"The West Indian Attitude to Crickett." Rev. of *Beyond a Boundary*, by C. L. R. James. *Sunday Guardian* 28 July 1963: 14.

"West Indian Dance, Dancers." *Sunday Guardian Magazine* 4 June 1967: 8.

"W. I. Writers Must Risk Talent." *Trinidad Guardian* 6 June 1963: 8. Dangers of pseudo-folk art and futile competition with European literature. Need creative response to spoken, evolving language—experimentation.

"West Indian Writers." *Times Literary Supplement* 23 May 1952: 348. Attributed to Walcott. Discusses conditions favoring growth of West Indian literature. Intelligentsia exists, publication outlets. Problems of audience, exile, lack of established culture.

"What the Lower House Demands." *Trinidad Guardian* 6 July 1966: 5. Rev. of film *The Married Woman*. "Pit" audience must be respected; art-theatre can reach variety of tastes. Liveliness, "even the right vulgarity," are gifts of "entertainer geniuses from Shakespeare to Fellini."

"What the Twilight Says: An Overture." Introduction. *Dream on Monkey Mountain and Other Plays*, by Walcott. New York: Farrar, Straus and Giroux, 1970. 3-40. Aspirations, fears, reminiscences of development from colonial childhood to maturity. Topics range from colonialism and race relations to theories of language and aesthetics.

"When Is a Primitive Not a Primitive?" *Trinidad Guardian* 16 Aug. 1961: 5.

"Where Do They Get Their Style?" *Trinidad Guardian* 21 Apr. 1965: 5. Comments on Mittelholzer, Reid, Selvon, Lamming, Harris, Naipaul, Carew, and others.

"Where Exuberance Triumphs." *Times* 8 Oct. 1968: 17. Vulgar as exuberance may seem, it is life celebrating life.

"Whistler Brings His Art to P. O. S." *Trinidad Guardian* 5 May 1961: 5.

"Who's Afraid of Noel Coward?" *Trinidad Guardian* 8 July 1964: 5. *Blithe Spirit* to be staged.

"Why Do Chekhov Here?" *Sunday Guardian* 29 June 1975: 7. Affinities between Chekhov and West Indian styles. "Our manner is energised by flamboyance, by the self-dramatising flourish." Chekhov's provincials and their history are recognizable.

"Why Does This West Indian Writer Have to Be Vulgar?" *Trinidad Guardian* 23 Nov. 1961: 5.

"Why Is Our Theatre So Tame?" *Sunday Guardian* 30 Apr. 1967: 8. Novels outdistancing local theatre. Playwrights must transcend the easy, established methods, the stereotypes.

"Why This Astigmatism toward the Workshop's White Actors?" *Trinidad Guardian* 19 Apr. 1973: 5. Commends performers whose skills seem to be ignored by commentators.

"Why We Do Shakespeare Badly." *Sunday Guardian* 8 Mar. 1964: 17.

"Work of Exciting Contrasts—But No Coherence." *Trinidad Guardian* 30 Jan. 1962: 5.

"A Work of Passion, but Still Valuable." *Sunday Guardian* 11 June 1961: 5.

"A World in Twilight." *Trinidad Guardian* 7 May 1965: 7. On Mittelholzer.

"Writer's Cramp on Stage." *Trinidad Guardian* 8 June 1966: 5. Need permanent theatre, a national company.

"Writing for Children." *Sunday Guardian Magazine* 23 Jan. 1966: 2. Part I of III parts. Great potential in children's books virtually ignored by poets and novelists.

"Writing for Children." *Sunday Guardian Magazine* 6 Feb. 1966: 28-29. Part II of III parts. Discusses project of Education Department of the University of the West Indies.

"Writing for Children." *Sunday Guardian Magazine* 13 Feb. 1966: 3. Part III of III parts. Teaching methods.

"*Year Book* Reflects a Big Advance." *Trinidad Guardian* 23 Mar. 1966: 5. Rev. Trinidad and Tobago Society of Architect's *Year Book 1965-1966*.

"Young Artist's Work Reveals Struggle." *Sunday Guardian* 17 July 1960: 7.

"Young Painters Show Maturity." *Trinidad Guardian* 10 Aug. 1961: 5.

"Young Trinidadian Poets." Rev. of *The Flaming Circle*, by Jagdip Maraj. *Sunday Guardian* 19 June 1966: 5. After tortuous search through other voices, "the poet by acquiring all of these demons, becomes himself."

Secondary Sources

Absher, Tom "World Enough and Time." Rev. of *The Star-Apple Kingdom*. *Ploughshares* 6.4 (1981): 228-32. Long, lyrical poem includes political issues besides private and domestic, without declaiming a cause.

Adekoya, Segun. "Between Beasthood and Godhead: An Inquiry into the Definition of Man." *The Literary Half-Yearly (Mysore)* 28.1 (Jan.1987): 53-60. Duplicates "*Malcochon* and the Definition of Man." Walcott "breaks down all absolutes and ideologies and organizes them back into coherent" patterns which enhance life without blind acceptance.

_____. "*Malcochon* and the Definition of Man." *World Literature Written in English* 27.1 (Spring 1987): 62-67. Paradox used to unify life in face of terror, suffering, impossible absolutes and ideologies. *Malcochon* best defines Walcott's concept of man.

Agren, Johanna. "West Indian Poet Derek Walcott Is Named Nobel Laureate for Literature." *Fort Worth Star-Telegram* 9 Oct. 1992: 19A.

_____. "West Indian Poet Wins Nobel." *Austin American Statesman* 9 Oct. 1992: A6.

Aiyejina, Funso. "Derek Walcott and the West Indian Dream and Veneration of Africa." *The Literary Half-Yearly* 26.1 (Jan. 1985): 180-93. Dreams of Africa used in *Dream on* Monkey Mountain and O Babylon! to elucidate West Indian psyche.

_____. "Derek Walcott: The Poet as a Federated Consciousness." *World Literature Written in English* 27.1 (Spring 1987): 67-80. After failure of political federation, left to artists and writers to articulate complex cultural federation.

Alcock, Peter. "'. . . Some deep, amnesiac blow': Amnesia in the Poetic Development of Derek Walcott." *SPAN* 21 (1985): 75-95. Uses of "amnesia" and "nothingness" up through *Another Life*.

Alleyne, Keith. Rev. of *Epitaph for the Young*. *Bim* 3.11 [1949]: 267-72. Poem is allegorical, full of traditional influences.+

Alvarez, A. Rev. of *The Castaway*. *Sunday Observer* (London) 24 Oct. 1965: 27.

Andrews, Lyman. Rev. of *Sea Grapes*. *Sunday Times* 11 July 1976: 35.

Angustus, Earl. "In a Fine Castle." Rev. of *In a Fine Castle*. *Express* 7 Nov. 1971: 17, 30. Theme is changelessness of Negro-Saxon personality according to Walcott's psychology.

Anthony, Michael. "Writers Spell out Way to Go." *Sunday Guardian* 24 Sept. 1972: 10. Artists at "Carifesta '72" in Guyana.

Anthony, Patrick. "The Silent Revolution." *Caribbean Contact* 5.5 (Aug. 1977): 10-11. Biographical on Dunstan St. Omer, and St. Lucian references which appear in such works as *Another Life*.

"The Arts." *Moko* 23 (27 Feb. 1970): 4. Defends truncated t.v. production of *Dream on Monkey Mountain*. Projects conflicts of Caribbean society.

Asein, Samuel Omo. "Derek Walcott and the Great Tradition." *The Literary Criterion* (Mysore) 16.2 (1981): 18-30.

_____. "Derek Walcott: The Man and His Ideas." *The Literary Half-Yearly* 17.2 (1976): 59-79. Themes develop progressively from problems of coming of age to existential predicament of the New World Negro. Man's dignity determined by degree of success in "reconciling himself with his world without compromising the essentials of his being.

_____. "Drama, the Church and the Nation in the Caribbean." *The Literary Half-Yearly* 26.1 (Jan. 1985): 149-62.

_____. "Walcott's Jamaica Years." *The Literary Half-Yearly* 21.2 (1980): 23-41. Account of 1950-57. Involvement in campus journalism, drama, art, contact with West Indian personalities and early experience as teacher shaped Walcott's development.

_____. "West Indian Poetry in English, 1900-1970: A Selective Bibliography." *Black Images* 1.2 (Summer 1972): 12-15.

Ashaolu, Albert Olu. "Allegory in *Ti Jean and and His Brothers*." *World Literature Written in English* 16.1 (Apr. 1977): 203-11. Examines six levels of allegory: artistic, historical, political, moral, Christian, social.+

"At a Private Viewing." *Trinidad Guardian* 10 July 1982: #. Announces art show.

Atlas, James. "Derek Walcott: Poet of Two Worlds." *New York Times Magazine* 23 May 1982: 32-38.

"An Award for Derek Walcott." *Caribbean Contact* 5.9 (Jan. 1978): 9. Guggenheim award for 1977; contains Chronological data on recent activities.

Bagchee, Shyamal. "Derek Walcott and the 'Power of Provincialism.'" *World Literature Written in English* 27.1 (Spring 1987): 80-86. Disclosure of provincial self positive, necessary act for universal poet.

———. "Derek Walcott's 'Metamorphoses': An Interpretation." *CHIMO: Newsletter of Canadian ACLALS* 4 (Fall 1984): 31-35.

Baker, J. S. "Canvas too Large for Walcott's Brush." *Trinidad Guardian* 30 Nov. 1954: 10.

Balakian, Peter. "The Poetry of Derek Walcott." Rev. of *Collected Poems*. *Poetry* 148.3 (June 1986): 169-77. Walcott has "organically assimilated the evolution of English literature . . . absorbed the Classical and Judeo-Christian past . . mined the history of Western Painting."+

Baptiste, Owen. "The Music of the Caribbean." *People* 1.9 (Apr. 1976): 5. Mentions Walcott/Galt McDermot music in *O Babylon!*

Barker, Thomas and Charles Dameron. "The Twilight and the God: Two Long Poems of Walcott and Soyinka." *Association of Commonwealth Literature and Language Studies Bulletin* (Mysore) 5.3 (Dec. 1980): 51-61.

Barnes, Bob. "'Dream' for TTT." *Trinidad Guardian* 12 Feb. 1970: 5. Trinidad showing of N. B. C. adaptation of *Dream on Monkey Mountain.*

Barnes, Clive. "Racial Allegory: The 'Dream on Monkey Mountain' Presented." Rev. of *Dream on Monkey Mountain. New York Times* 15 Mar. 1971: 52. Compares character Basil to *Peer Gynt's* button molder.

———. Rev. of *Ti-Jean and His Brothers. New York Times* 28 July 1972: 20. Shakespeare Theatre Festival production.

Baugh, Edward. "Derek Walcott." *Fifty Caribbean Writers*. Ed. Daryl Cumber Dance. New York: Greenwood Press, 1986. 462-73.

———. *Derek Walcott: Memory as Vision: Another Life*. London: Longman, 1978. Impact of memory (history). Influence of childhood friends and tradition. Substantiates factual world underlying poem. Finds rich variety of moods, masterful handling of ideal and ordinary.

———. "Exiles, Guerrillas and Visions of Eden." *Queen's Quarterly* 84.2 (Summer 1977): 273-86. Balanced, affirmative spirit grows in Walcott.

———. "Metaphor and Plainness in the Poetry of Derek Walcott." *The Literary Half-Yearly* 11.2 (1970): 47-58. Expressive tension created by metaphors is a concentrating force in poetry through *The Gulf.*

———. "Painters and Painting in 'Another Life.'" *Caribbean Quarterly* 26.1-2 (Mar.-June 1980): 83-93. Art imagery complements historical allusions, significant in complex subject and texture of this layered poem.+

———. "The Poem as Autobiographical Novel: Derek Walcott's 'Another Life' in Relation to Wordsworth's 'Prelude' and Joyce's 'Portrait.'" *Awakened Conscience: Studies in Commonwealth Literature*. Ed. C. D. Narasimhaiah. New

Delhi: Sterling Publishers, Ltd., 1978. 226-35.

———. Rev. of *Another Life*. *Caribbean Quarterly* 21.3 (Sept. 1975): 58-59.

———. Rev. of *Another Life*. *Queen's Quarterly* 81.2 (Summer 1974): 317-18. Real and ideal dramatized. Proves possibility of still writing "grandly and well."

———. Rev. of *The Star-Apple Kingdom*. *Queen's Quarterly* 87 (Autumn 1980): 470-73. Idealized narrator may be based on Manley of Jamaica. Before Marquez, Walcott conceived simultaneity of history.

———. "Ripening With Walcott." *Caribbean Quarterly* 23.2-3 (June-Sept. 1977): 84-90. Breadth of vision in *Sea Grapes* is rooted in personal experience.+

———. "Towards a West Indian Criticism." *Caribbean Quarterly* 14 (Mar.-June 1968): 140-44. Background to criticism.

———. "West Indian Poetry 1900-1970." *Pamphlet No. 1*. Kingston: Savacou Pub., Ltd. n.d: #.

———. "The West Indian Writer and His quarrel with History." *Tapia* 7.8 (20 Feb. 1977): 6-7. Argues the extent to which history matters in West Indian literature despite Walcott's complex denial of the past.

Beaufort, John. "Walcott Serves up Rewarding Reversal of Servant/Master." Rev. of *Pantomime*, by Walcott. *The Christian Science Monitor* 2 Jan. 1987: 28.

Beckman, Susan. "The Mulatto of Style: Language in Derek Walcott's Drama." *Canadian Drama* 6 (Spring 1960): 71-89. Artistic and physical schizophrenia leads to new poetic idiom in poetry and drama, to shaping the language of a race and creating an intellectual mask.

Bedient, Calvin "'Derek Walcott, Contemporary." *Parnassus* 9.2 (Fall-Winter 1981): 31-44. Excessively written for content. Recent voice bardic, prophetic.+

Benfey, Christopher. "Coming Home." Rev. of *Omeros*. *New Republic* 203 (29 Oct. 1990): 36-39.

Bensen, Robert. "The New World Poetry of Derek Walcott." *Concerning Poetry* 16.2 (1984): 29-42.

———. "The Painter as Poet: Derek Walcott's *Midsummer*." *The Literary Review* 29.3 (Spring 1986): 257-68. Painting as subject, source of imagery. It governs use of light and color, range of themes.+

Berger, Joseph. "Encounters with Liberty." *New York Times* 18 May 1986: 102. Walcott comments on first impressions of Statue of Liberty.

Berman, Paul. "Theatre." *The Nation* 240 (13 Apr. 1985): 443-44. Rev. Brooklyn performance of *Pantomime*. Trifle long, contrived, but witty and well performed.

"A Big Payoff for Brilliance." *Ebony* 37 (Dec. 1981): 77-78, 82. Walcott recipient of MacArthur Foundation award.

Birkerts, Sven. "Heir Apparent." Rev. of *Midsummer*. *New Republic* 190 (23 Jan. 1984): 31-33. Sees uniqueness in Walcott's blend of Western tradition and Caribbean influences.+

————. "V. S. Naipaul and Derek Walcott: A Multiplicity of Truths." *New Boston Review* (Aug.-Sept. 1980): 19-21.

"Black Poet Is Accused of Sex Harassment at Harvard." *Jet* 62 (28 June 1982): 23. Account of charge lodged by coed.

Bloom, Harold. Rev. of *Sea Grapes. New Republic* 20 Nov. 1976: 23.

Bousquet, Earl. "Walcott: An Award Winner's Homecoming." *Caribbean Contact* 16.4 (Sept. 1988): 14. First Commonwealth citizen outside Britain to be awarded annual Queen's Gold Medal for Poetry.

Boxill, Anthony. "The Conteur as Mythmaker in Derek Walcott's *Malcochon, or the Six in the Rain.*" *Commonwealth* 13.2 (Spring 1991): 1-7. "By juxtaposing man with nature . . . Creole world with the European . . . [Walcott and Conteur] have in a truly revolutionary way rejected conventional linear history for a more creative history."

Brathwaite, Anthony. Rev. of *The Fortunate Traveller. Bajan* (May 1982): 46.

Brathwaite, Edward. "Edward Brathwaite Looks at Walcott's *In a Green Night.*" *The Voice of St. Lucia* 13 Apr. 1963: 4.#

————. "The House in the West Indian Novel." *Tapia* 7.26 (3 July 1977): 5-7. Walcott, among others, sets plays out of doors, people without protective housing.

————. Rev. of *The Castaway. Bim* 11.42 (Jan.-June 1966): 139-41. Walcott's acceptance of inherited dichotomy, his rare balance.

————. "Themes from the Caribbean." *Times Educational Supplement* 6 Sept. 1968: 396. Defines problems of writing in West Indies.

————. "Timehri." *Savacou* 1.2 (Sept. 1970): 35-44. Mentions Walcott, among others.

Breiner, Lawrence. "Lyric and Autobiography in West Indian Literature." *Journal of West Indian Literature* 3.1 (Jan. 1983): 3-15. Autobiographical influence evident in prose, long poem and lyric reflects intimacy between West Indian writers and their society.

————. "Tradition, Society, the Figure of the Poet." *Caribbean Quarterly* 26 (Mar.-June 1980): 1-12.

Breslin, Paul. "'I Met History Once, but He Ain't Recognize Me': The Poetry of Derek Walcott." *Tri-quarterly* 68 (Winter 1987): 168-83.

————. Rev. of *Midsummer. Poetry* 145 (Dec. 1984): 173-74.

Breslow, Stephen P. "Trinidadian Heteroglossia: A Bakhtinian View of Derek Walcott's Play *A Branch of the Blue Nile.*" *World Literature Today* 63.1 (Winter 1989): 36-39. Draws from African, patois, French, English, classical Latin legacy and experience of St. Lucia, Trinidad and the United States. Play "reverberates with reflexive consciousness of itself."+

Brodsky, Joseph. "On Derek Walcott." *New York Review of Books* 30.17 (10 Nov. 1983): 39-41. Mixture of Walcott's heritage "gives us a sense of infinity embodied in the language."

_____. "The Sound of the Tide." *Less Than One: Selected Essays.* Farrar, Straus & Giroux, 1986. Walcott turns to advantage colonial writer's position on fringe of imperial culture and language.

Bromell, Nicholas. Rev. of *The Fortunate Traveller. New Boston Review* 7.2 (Apr. 1982): 12-13.

Brown, Lloyd. "Caribbean Castaway New World Odyssey: Derek Walcott's Poetry." *Journal of Commonwealth Literature* 11.2 (Dec. 1976): 149- 59. New World as dream and corrupted reality. Poet's role.

_____. "Dreamers and Slaves—The Ethos of Revolution in Walcott and Leroi Jones." *Caribbean Quarterly* 17.3-4 (Sept.-Dec. 1971): 36-44. Parallels between works by Jones and Walcott reveal pan-African links.+

_____. "The Isolated Self in West Indian Fiction.'" *Caribbean Quarterly* 23.2-3 (June-Sept. 1977): 54-65. Theme in Walcott mentioned in passing.

_____. "The Personal Odyssey of Derek Walcott." *West Indian Poetry.* Ed. Lloyd Brown. Boston: Twayne, 1978. 118-38. Argues for elements of West Indian tradition; Walcott's private self becomes metaphor for Caribbean and universal implications.

_____. "The Revolutionary Dream of Walcott's Makak." *Critics on Caribbean Literature.* Ed. Edward Baugh. London: George Allen and Unwin, Ltd., 1978. 58-62.

Brown, Robert and Cheryl Johnson. "Thinking Poetry: An Interview with Derek Walcott." *The Cream City Review* 14.2 (Winter 1990): 209-33. Has no concern regarding originality or influences. *Omeros* not sequel to Homeric epics. Values meter and rhyme over egocentric free verse.

Brown, Stewart, Ed. *The Art of Derek Walcott.* Chester Springs, PA.: Dufour Editions, Inc., 1991. Collection of essays addresses apprentice works and individual volumes through *Omeros.*

_____. "Bread That Will Last." Rev. of *The Star-Apple Kingdom. The Literary Half-Yearly* 26.1 (Jan. 1985): 194-96.

_____. "Derek Walcott: The Poems." *A Handbook for the Teaching of Caribbean Literature.* Ed. David Dabydeen. London: Heinemann, 1988. 96-103.

_____. "Spoiler, Walcott's People's Patriot." *Wasafiri* 9 (Winter 1988-89): 10-15. Voice of the narrator in "Spoiler" from *The Fortunate Traveller.* Appearance of the "patriot" and social criticism of Walcott's poetry.

_____. "Walcott's Fortunate Traveller: A Portrait in Exile." *Carib* (Kingston, Jamaica) 5 (Winter 1989-90): 1-18.

Brown, Wayne. "Caribbean Booktalk: Derek Walcott—his Poetry and His People." *Caribbean Affairs* 1.3 (July-Sept. 1988): 174-93. Analysis of *The Arkansas Testament.* Makes connections between text and Naipaul's *The Enigma of Arrival.*

_____. Introduction. *Selected Poems,* by Walcott. London: Heinemann, 1980.

_____. "W. I. Literature of the Past Year." *Sunday Guardian* (Trinidad) 30 Aug. 1970: 5. Mentions *The Gulf.*

Bruckner, D. J. R. "A Poem in Homage to an Unwanted Man." Rev. of *Omeros. New York Times* 9 Oct. 1990: 13, 17. Article also published in separate edition as "The Poet Who Fused Folklore, Homer and Hemingway."+

Burt, John. "On Derek Walcott." Rev. of *The Arkansas Testament. Partisan Review* 56.4 (Fall 1989): 668-71.

Burton, Richard D. E. "Derek Walcott and the Medusa of History." *Caliban* 3 (1980): 3-48. Creation of a creole culture re-humanizes in wake of plantation society. Neither popular nor populist, avoids propaganda.

C., L. "Actors Score with Comedy and Drama." *Trinidad Guardian* 24 Jan. 1964: 7. Rev. Little Carib Theatre production of Ionesco's *The Lesson* and Walcott's *Malcochon.*

_____. "Basement Develops New Touch!" *Trinidad Guardian* 22 Oct. 1966: 5. Rev. Workshop production of John's *Belle Fanto.*

Campbell, Ralph. "The Birth of Professional Theatre in Trinidad." *Sunday Guardian* 22 July 1973: 4 Inadequacies of professional theater in Trinidad.

Carr, Bill [William]. "The Clear-Eyed Muse." *Sunday Gleaner* (Jamaica) 20 Jan. 1963: 14, 20. Radio broadcast discussion of *In a Green Night.* Imagination above propaganda, rigorous and compassionate.

_____. "The Significance of Derek Walcott." *Public Opinion* (Jamaica) 28 Feb. 1964: 8, 9, 14. Background of "colonialist" poetry. Need voice of "forged personal instrument," that uses experience poetically, not as "historical or idiosyncratic exercise.'"

Carruth, Hayden. "Poets on the Fringe." Rev. of *The Star-Apple Kingdom. Harpers* 260 (Jan. 1980): 80-81.

Cavan, Romilly. Rev. of *Dream on Monkey Mountain. Books and Bookmen* Apr. 1972: 60.

Chamberlin, J. E. Rev. of *Sea Grapes. The Hudson Review* 30 (Spring 1977): 112-14.

Chism, Olin. "Caribbean Poet Walcott Wins Nobel for Literature." *The Dallas Morning News* 9 Oct. 1992: 1A, 8A.

Christian, Lawrence. Rev. of *In a Fine Castle. Los Angeles Herald Examiner* 13 May 1972: #.

Ciccarelli, Sharon L. "Reflections Before and After Carnival: An Interview with Derek Walcott." *Chant of Saints.* Ed. Michael S. Harper and Robert B. Stepto. Urbana: University of Illinois Press, 1979. 296-309. Artist rooted in lower class needs support from rich to survive in stratified Trinidad. Advantages in linguistic duality.

Clarke, Le Roy. "*Marie La Veau*—An Artificial Resurrection." *Express* (Trinidad) 18 June 1980: 24,25. A failure, blasphemous, exploitative spectacle for tourism.

Clurman, Harold. "Theatre." *The Nation* 212 (3 May 1971): 572. Negro Ensemble Co. production of *Dream on Monkey Mountain*.

Cluysenaar, A. Rev. of *Another Life. Stand* (Newcastle) 15.1 n.d.#: 66.

Coe, Richard N. "Poetry and the Child-Self: Lyric and the Epic in the Autobiographical Mode." *Research in African Literatures* 12.2 (1985): 47-93. Passing reference to Walcott's persona in *Another Life* (82-84).

"Coed Complaint." *Time* 119 (14 June 1982): 81.

Coke, Lloyd. "Walcott's Mad Innocents: Theatre Review." *Savacou* 5 (June 1971): 121-24. Walcott a "fusionist." Production details for performances of *Ti-Jean* and *Dream*.

Collier, Gordon. "Artistic Autonomy and Cultural Allegiance: Aspects of the Walcott-Brathwaite Debate Re-examined." *The Literary Half-Yearly* (Mysore) 20.1 (Jan. 1979): 93-105. Basis of conflicting responses to Walcott and Brathwaite "incompatibility between the demands imposed by aesthetic design and social responsibility."

_____. "Edward Kamau Brathwaite und das Selbstverständnis der Schwarzen in der Englischsprachegen Karibik." *Black Literature*. Ed. Eckhard Breitinger. Munchen: Wilhelm Fink Verlag, 1979. 214-54. Walcott discussed pp. 232-38.

Collymore, Frank A. "An Introduction to the Poetry of Derek Walcott." *Bim* 3.10 (June 1949): 125-32. *25 Poems* work of accomplished poet.+

_____. Rev. of *Poems. Bim* 4.15 ([Dec. 1951]): 224-27. Tension between influences of Dylan Thomas and W. H. Auden, leaning toward Auden.

"Colourful Presentation of Walcott's *Dream*." *Trinidad Guardian* 27 July 1981: 15.

Colson, Theodore. "Derek Walcott's Plays: Outrage and Compassion." *World Literature Written in English* 12.1 (Apr. 1973): 80-96. Walcott is voice of white, black and mixed races. Analysis of *Ti-Jean, Malcochon, Dream*.+

Cooke, Michael G. "History in E. K. Brathwaite and Derek Walcott: Panel Discussion." *The Common Wealth of Letters* 1.1 (June 1989): 3-14. Panel moderated by Cooke: Walcott, Brathwaite and Joan Dayan. Caught between the Marxist and Christian-capitalist lies, Caribbean writer resorts to imaginative powers.

Cooper, Carolyn. "A Language Beyond Mimicry: Language as Metaphor and Meaning in Derek Walcott's Oeuvre." *The Literary Half-Yearly* 26.1 (Jan. 1985): 23-40. Linguistic heterogeneity poses value questions for creative writer.

Cordua, Carla. "Walcott, El Afrosajon." *Caribbean Studies* 22.3-4 (July-Dec. 1989): 87-89. Places Walcott in line of European influenced writers of Caribbean and Latin America.

Crawford, Robert. "Homing." Rev. of *Omeros. Poetry Review* 80.4 (Winter 1990-91): 9. "An exile's examination of home and displacement."

Crossley-Holland, Kevin. "Small-Scale Skills." Rev. of *The Fortunate Traveller. Times*

Educational Supplement 6 Aug. 1982: 20. Current poets lack authoritative voices.

"A Crystal of Ambiguities." Rev. of *Another Life*. *Sunday Gleaner* (Jamaica) 30 Sept. 1973: 23.

Curtis, Tony. Rev. of *The Fortunate Traveler*. *Poetry Wales* 18 (1982): 127-31. Prolific changes of focus. Straining to define contemporary situation in classical terms.

D'Aguiar, Fred. "Fragrant Creole." Rev. of *The Arkansas Testament*. *Poetry Review* 78.1 (1988): 16-17.

_____. "Lines with Their Knots Left in: Third World Poems by Edward Kamau Brathwaite and *Midsummer* by Derek Walcott." *Wasafiri* 1.2 (Spring 1985): 37-38.

Daizal, R. Samad. "Cultural Imperatives in Derek Walcott's *Dream on Monkey Mountain*." *Commonwealth Essays and Studies* 13 (Spring 1991): 8-21.

Dasenbrock, Reed Way. Rev. of *The Arkansas Testament*. *World Literature Today* 62.2 (Spring 1988): 327.

_____. "Trinidad." Rev. of *Collected Poems*. *World Literature Today* 60.3 (Summer 1986): 512-13. Collection marks major status of Walcott.

_____. "Trinidad." Rev. of *Three Plays*. *World Literature Today* 61.1 (Winter 1987): 147.

Dathorne, O. R. *Dark Ancestors*. Baton Rouge: Louisiana State U. P., 1980. For Walcott, "it seems that poetry will remain a fashionable literary ailment, voluntarily contracted."

Davis, Dick. Rev. of *The Fortunate Traveller*. *The Listener* 6 May 1982: 26.

_____. Rev. of *The Star-Apple Kingdom*. *The Listener* 5 June 1980: 729. Fluid and supple, moments of great power, "rhetoric balanced by sad sanity."

Dawes, Neville. *Prolegomena to Caribbean Literature*. [Kingston]: Institute of Jamaica, 1977. Discusses Walcott's treatment of Africa.

Dayan, Joan. "Caribbean Cannibals and Whores." *Raritan—Quarterly Review* 9 (1989): 45-67. In order to present the "cultural reality of women writing, the obstacles they face . . . new female voices, very recent, and nearly nonexistent in Haiti," Dayan first accounts for colonial stereotypes in Caribbean male writers: René Depestre, Derek Walcott.

"Death of Our Dodos in *The Last Carnival*: A Play of Rare Quality Camps in an Unlovely Tent." *Trinidad Guardian* 15 July 1982: 18.

De Lima, Clara Rosa. "'All That's Wrong with Our Performing Arts Centers." *People* 4.5 (Dec. 1978): 14, 16. Itemizes inadequacies of performance halls around Port of Spain.

_____. "Walcott's Drama in the Rain Something to Remember." *Sunday Guardian* 12 Aug. 1984: 14. Production of Walcott's unpublished "The Haitian Earth."

Demos, John. Rev. of *Another Life. Library Journal* 97 (15 Nov. 1972): 3717.

_____. Rev. of *The Gulf. Library Journal* 95 (15 Apr. 1970): 1487.

De Mott, Benjamin. "Poems of Caribbean Wounds." Rev. of *The Star-Apple King-dom. The New York Review of Books* 13 May 1979: 11, 30. Absence of Political "highmindedness;" muscularity of verse, "a ceaseless energy conversion is in process."+

"Derek Back in the Spotlight.'" *Express* (Trinidad) 21 May 1978: 5.

"Derek Play for St. Lucia." *Sunday Guardian* 15 June 1980: 21. Rev. production of *Pantomime.*

"Derek Walcott." Rev. of *In a Green Night. Daily Gleaner* (Jamaica) 2 Aug. 1962: #.

"Derek Walcott Gets Fellowship." *The Voice of St. Lucia* 4 Oct. 1958: 1. Reports Rockefeller grant, Walcott's growing reputation.

"Derek Walcott Hailed." *Trinidad Guardian* 25 Jan. 1980: 8. On occasion of Walcott's 50th birthday, his plays being produced in London, Cave Hill and Port of Spain.

"Derek Walcott, Poet and Dramatist." *Bajan* (Jan. 1970): 4-6.

"Derek Walcott Wins Campbell Prize." *Trinidad Guardian* 25 Dec. 1974: 1. Award for *Another Life.*

"Derek Walcott Wins Top Writer's Prize." *Express* (Trinidad) 26 July 1979: 23.

"Derek Walcott's 'A Branch of the Blue Nile' Is Gripping as a Cricket Test Match." Rev. of *A Branch of the Blue Nile.*" *Trinidad Guardian* 10 Nov. 1983: 25.

"Derek Walcott's Basement Theatre." *Trinidad Guardian* 4 Nov. 1966: 12. Rev. of three plays finds *The Road* more successful than performances of *The Blacks* and *Belle Fanto.* Decries lack of criticism from public.

"Derek Walcott's Play Is Poetic Drama." *Trinidad Guardian* 12 Aug. 1954: #.

Devlin, Diana. "Plays in Print." Rev. of *Remembrance and Pantomime. Drama* 139 (1981): 55.

Dickey, James. Rev. of *Selected Poems. New York Times Book Review.* 13 Sept. 1964: 44.

_____. "The Worlds of a Cosmic Castaway. Rev. of *Collected Poems. New York Times Book Review* 91 (2 Feb. 1986): 8.

Dobbs, Kildare. "An Outstanding Poet of This Generation." *Toronto Star* 19 May 1973: #.

Dockray, Brian. "A Most Significant Musical Contribution." Rev. of *Ti-Jean and His Brothers. Trinidad Guardian* 27 June 1970: 5.

Donoghue, Denis. "Metaphorical Duality." Rev. of *The Fortunate Traveller. New York Times Book Review* 87 (21 Feb. 1982): 41.

_____. "Themes from Derek Walcott." Rev. of *Sea Grapes. Parnassus* 6 (1977): 88-100. Finds too much rhetoric and overwriting.

_____. "The Two Sides of Derek Walcott." Rev. of *The Fortunate Traveller. New York Times Book Review* 86 (3 Jan. 1982): 5.

_____. "Waiting for the End." Rev. of *The Gulf. New York Review of Books* 16 (6 May 1971): 27. Suffers from dual weight of his own and his people's burden, grandiose.

Dorant, St. Claire. "Tears of Dismay for Theatre." *Trinidad Guardian* 5 June 1982: 10. Necessity of national theatre.

_____. "Theatre Plays Vital Role." *Trinidad Guardian* 8 June 1982: 11.

Douglas-Smith, Aubrey. Rev. of *Henri Christophe. Bim* 3.12 [June 1950]: 349-53. Focuses on historical element; Christophe's more tragic than Toussaint's fate.+

Dove, Rita. "Either I'm Nobody or I'm a Nation." *Parnassus* 14.1 (1987): 49-76. Extended overview of Walcott's career through review of *Collected Poems.* Regrets apparently diminished power in later works.

Drayton, Arthur D. "The European Factor in West Indian Literature." The *The Literary Half-Yearly* 11.1 (1970): 71-95. Surveys literary scene. Fears Walcott's balanced, humanistic voice will be smothered by extremists using literature as weapon in racial struggle.

Drayton, Kathleen. "A Dream to Change the World." *Caribbean Contact* 7. 11 (Mar. 1980): 15.

"Dream Gets Top U. S. Award." *Trinidad Guardian* 29 May 1971:9. Obie award for best foreign play of year: *Dream.*

"Dream in Patois." *Express* (Trinidad) 8 Sept. 1982: #. Celebrates Creole Day in Dominica.

"'Dream on Monkey Mountain' Called the Best in W. I." *Sunday Guardian* 14 Jan. 1968: 6.

Dwyer, Richard. "One Walcott: And He Would be Be Master." *Caribbean Review* 11.4 (1982): 14, 36-37. Reviews *The Fortunate Traveller* and discusses Walcott's mounting reputation.+

Eagleton, Terry. "Pleanty of Life." Rev. of *Midsummer. Times Literary Supplement* 9 Nov. 1984: 1290.

_____. "'Poetry Chronicle." Rev. of *Collected Poems, Stand Magazine* 29.1 (1988): 65-67. Review of several poetry collections.

"Ebony Book Shelf." Rev. of *The Fortunate Traveller. Ebony* 37.6 (Apr. 1982): 23.

Eder, Richard. "Stage, Walcott's 'Remembrance,' Tale of Trinidad." Rev. of *Remembrance. New York Times* 10 May 1979: 18. Play becomes heavier, tedious in later moments.

"Editor's Choice." Rev. of *Omeros. The New York Times* 2 Dec. 1990: 81. Cited as one of best books of 1990. Poem "makes us realize that history, all of it, belongs to us."

Edwards, Thomas R. Rev. of *Another life. New York Review of Books* 21 (13 June 1974): 38-39.

Elliott, George P. "Poetry Chronicle." Rev. of *Selected Poems. Hudson Review* 17.3 (Autumn 1964): 456-57. Voice sustained too long on high level.

Enright, D.J. "Frank Incense." Rev. of *The Arkansas Testament. New Republic* 197.18 (2 Nov. 1987): 46-47.

Evans, S. Marsden. "Karl Broodhagen, Scenes from *Henri Christophe* and *The Importance of Being Earnest.*" *Bim* 5.17 (Dec. 1952); (facing 40), 41. Photographs reproduced.

Fabre, Michel. "'Adam's Task of Giving Things Their Name': The Poetry of Derek Walcott." *New Letters* 41.1 (Fall 1974): 91-107. Dialectical development of folk and traditional elements in poetry.

_____. "The Poetical Journey of Derek Walcott." *Commonwealth Literature and the Modern World.* Papers delivered at conference, University of Liege, Apr. 2-5. Ed. Hena Maes-Jelinek. Brussels: Didier, 1974. 61-67. Evolved from "the wary self-affirmation . . . to open-hearted self-evaluation." His poetic language in *Dream* and *Another Life* at one with that of his people.

Fahey, James. Rev. of *Another Life. Best Sellers* 15 Aug. 1973: 225-26.

Falck, Colin. Rev. of *The Gulf. The New Review* (June 1975): 70.

_____. Rev. of *Sea Grapes. The New Review* (July 1976): 56.

Falcon, John. "The Spiritual Agony of an Old Coal-Burner." Rev. of *Dream on Monkey Mountain. Trinidad Guardian* 5 Aug. 1974: 5.

Feaver, Vicki. "An Island and Its Noises." *Times Literary Supplement* 8 Aug. 1980: 903.

Fido, Elaine. "Images of Dream: Walcott, Soyinka, and Genêt." *African Theatre Review* 1.1 (Apr. 1985): 99-114. Elements of Genêt's *The Blacks* in Walcott's *Dream on Monkey Mountain* and Soyinka's *The Road.*

_____. "Value Judgments on Art and the Question of Macho Attitudes: The Case of Derek Walcott." *The Journal of Commonwealth Literature* 21.1 (1986): 109-19. Despite Walcott's intelligence, originality and anger in treating racism, colonialism and the plight of the poor, "his treatment of women is full of clichés, stereotypes and negativity."

_____. "Walcott and Sexual Politics: Macho Conventions Shape the Moon." *The Literary Half-Yearly* 26.1 (Jan. 1985): 43-60. Walcott's depiction of women, symbolic, mythical patterns in Caribbean and more universal cultural perceptions of women.

Fido, Martin *"Creolization vs. Colonization."* Paper mimeographed at Univ. of the West Indies, 11 Nov. 1979: Examines Walcott, Brathwaite and others as to degree of creolization and cultural fusion in recent West Indian literature.

Figueroa, John. "Derek Walcott: A Brief Introduction to His Work." *Poetry Wales* 16.2 (Autumn 1980): 52-63. Draws connections between Walcott's colonial island and Welsh past.

_____. "Derek Walcott's 'Poopa' Da Was a Fete!' and Evan Jones's 'Lament of the Banana Man.'" *Critics on Caribbean Literature.* Ed. Edward Baugh. London: George Allen and Unwin, Ltd., 1978. 149-52.

_____. "Dialect as Narrative." Rev. of *The Star-Apple Kingdom. London Magazine* 21.2-3 (Apr.-May 1981): 115-18.

_____. "A Note on Derek Walcott's Concern with Nothing." *Revista Interamericana Review* 4.3 (Fall 1974): 422-28. Traces theme from *Green Night* through *Another Life.* Coping with "nothingness" is ultimately necessary aspect of "real knowledge" of self, environment, history, the future.

_____. Rev. of *Another Life. Bim* 15.58 (June 1975): 160-70. Mythical and linguistic aspects of Walcott's style.

_____. Rev of *Another Life. Caribbean Review* 7.1 (Jan. -Mar. 1975): 30-31.

_____. Rev. of *In a Green Night. Caribbean Quarterly* 8.4 (Dec. 1962): 67-69. Strands of Walcott's heritage converge advantageously.

_____. "Sea Memories." Rev. of *Midsummer. London Magazine* 24.9-10 (Jan. 1985): 128-30.

_____. "Some Subtleties of the Isle: A Commentary on Certain Aspects of Derek Walcott's Sonnet Sequence, *Tales of the Islands." World Literature Written in English* 15.1 (Apr. 1976): 190-228. Thematic and structural study of difficulties converted to strength.+

"Five-Island Tour." *Sunday Guardian* 3 Nov. 1968: 11. Describes return of Theatre Workshop troupe from tour with *Belle Fanto* and *Dream.*

Fleming, Carrol B. "Plays and Poems of Derek Walcott: Singing the True Caribbean." *Americas* 34.3 (May-June 1982): 8-11.

Fletcher, C. Rev. of *Sea Grapes. Booklist* 72 (15 July 1976): 1568.

Flint, R. W. "Midsummer." Rev. of *Midsummer. New York Times Book Review* 89 (8 Apr. 1984): 14. Rambling, restful collection of "sonnets." West Indian better than Boston pieces.

Forbes, Peter. "Far and Feverish." Rev. of *Collected Poems 1948-1984. Poetry Review* 76.3 (Oct. 1986): 14-16. Utilizes array of touchstones, talismans, archetypes, images to transcend language.

Forde, A. N. Rev. of *In a Green Night. Bim* 9.36 (Jan.-June 1963): 288-90. Models must come from outside area. "A West Indian Poetry will only emerge when we attain the self-respect that comes with being practitioners equal in sensitivity and purpose with any other poets practising in the English tongue." Walcott has properly entered international company of poets.

"Four Blacks to Share in $4 Million Grant." *Jet* 60 (4 June 1981): 55. MacArthur Foundation award.

Fox, Robert Elliot. "Big Night Music: Derek Walcott's *Dream on Monkey Mountain* and 'The Splendours of Imagination.'" *Journal of Commonwealth Literature* 17.1 (1982): 16-27. Makak mythological, his dream, the work and the world merge at crossroads of imagination.+

_____. "Derek Walcott: History as Dis-ease." *The Literary Half-Yearly* 26.1 (Jan. 1985): 105-17 History as informing image.

Fraser, Fitzroy. "Jamaica Government Moves to Aid Artists." *Sunday Guardian* (Trinidad) 18 Sept. 1960: 7.

"From All Quarters." *Sunday Guardian* 2 July 1967: 6. Itinerary for Workshop Caribbean tour.

Fulchino, Stephen A. Rev. of *Three Plays: The Last Carnival; Beef, No Chicken; A Branch of the Blue Nile. Library Journal* 111 (1 Sept. 1986): 211.

Fuller, Roy. Rev. of "Senza Alcun Sospetto." *B.B.C. Caribbean Voices Transcript No. 475 (Epilogue)* 28 May 1950: 2. Review of broadcast.

_____. Rev. of *The Gulf. London Magazine* 9.8 (Nov. 1969): 89-90. Theme is journey from and back to provincialism. Some syntactical clumsiness and unnecessary obscurity.

Funsten, Kenneth. Rev. of *Midsummer. Los Angeles Times Book Review* 21 Apr. 1985: 4.

Furbank, P. N. "New Poetry." Rev. of *In a Green Night. Listener* 68.1736 (5 July 1962): 33. Hears echoes of Villion, Dante, Catullus, metaphysicals, Sitwell, Thomas, Browne, Donne, Shakespeare.

Fure, Rob. Rev. of *The Star-Apple Kingdom. Library Journal* 104 (15 June 1979): 1342. An "imagination gone into an obscure and private place."

Gamerman, Amy. "Trinidadian Poet Derek Walcott Wins Nobel." *The Wall Street Journal* 9 Oct. 1992: A10. Mentions new play *The Odyssey.*

Garfitt, Roger. "Resisting the Classics." Rev. of *The Fortunate Traveller. Times Literary Supplement* 24 Sept. 1982: 1041.

_____. Rev. of *Another Life. London Magazine* 13.5 (Dec. 1973-Jan. 1974): 124-27. Exploration, rediscovery, reconciliation, impressive in its concealed organization.

Garrison, Joseph. Rev. of *Sea Grapes. Library Journal* 101 (Aug. 1976): 1641.

Garuba, Harry. "'Derek Walcott and Wole Soyinka." *The Literary Half-Yearly* 26.1 (Jan. 1985): 63-79. While Soyinka delves into myth of Ogun, Walcott explores subconscious. Similarities in imagery, theme, techniques, style and ideological positions as well as biographical parallels.

Gates, Henry Louis. Jr. "Metaphorical Duality." *New York Times Book Review* 87 (21 Feb. 1982): 41. Letter criticizing Donoghue's review of The Fortunate Traveller.

Gibbons, Rawle. Rev. of *O Babylon! Kairi* (1976): 12-13. Roles of each character. Focus on individual affirmation, neglects deeper exploration of Rastafari meaning and reggae moods.

Gibbons, Reginald, Michael Harper, Walcott, et al. "The Writer in Our World, A Symposium: Roundtable." *Tri-Quarterly* 65 (1986): 277-309. Discussion of various topics: writer's responsibilities, cultural suppression, aesthetics.

Gilboy, Thomas J. Rev. of *Sea Grapes. Best Sellers* (Dec. 1976): 305.

Gilkes, Michael. Rev. of *Midsummer. Caribbean Contact* (Mar. 1985): 15. Increased awareness of superpower relations with Third World.

_____. "The Theatrical into Theatre." Rev. of *Theatrical into Theatre*, by Kole Omotoso. *Caribbean Contact* 10.12 (Apr. 1983): 6-7.

Goldstraw, Irma E. *Derek Walcott: A Bibliography of Published Poems with Dates of Publication and Variant Versions 1944-1979*. St. Augustine, Trinidad: University of the West Indies Research and Publication Committee, 1979.

_____. *Derek Walcott: An Annotated Bibliography of His Works*. New York: Garland, 1984. Thorough listing of primary publications to 1984.

Gonzalez, Anson. "Walcott's 'Laventville.'" *The New Voices* 10.19 (Mar. 1982): 39-44. Close reading of poem published in *The Castaway*: cerebral, complicated rhyme, heavy alliteration.

Goodman, Henry. "Carnival with a Calypso Beat." Rev. of *Charlatan*. *The Wall Street Journal* 4 June 1974: 20. Produced in Los Angeles at Mark Taper Forum.

_____. "Charlatan Scores in Los Angeles." Rev. of *Charalatan*. *Sunday Guardian* 16 June 1974: 6. Reprint of article "Carnival with a Calypso Beat."

Goodman, Walter. "The Stage: 'Pantomime' Play by Derek Walcott." *The New York Times* 17 Dec. 1986: Sec. 37, p. 25. Performance at the Hudson Guild Theatre Dec. 1986.

Gordon, William. "Rich Drama of Walcott's *Last Carnival*." *Trinidad Guardian* 2 Aug. 1982: 19.

_____. "The Time Has Come, D. Walcott Said to Speak of Many Things" [sic.]. *Trinidad Guardian* 26 Mar. 1982: 18.

Gowda, H. H. Anniah. "History of Derek Walcott's Voice: Study in Poetry." *Literary Half-Yearly* 24.1 (Jan. 1983): 36-45. Reprinted also in 26.1 (1985): 92-101. Brathwaite and Walcott examples of poets using English as a world language. Walcott borrowed from Europe then evolved into Caribbean writer.

Gray, Cecil. "Folk Themes in West Indian Drama." *Caribbean Quarterly* 14.1-2 (Mar.-June 1968): 102-9. Sees five general categories of Folk play according to social setting and time. Walcott has several in category of "Peasant and Rural Folk Life," two "Historical Plays."

Gray, Paul. "Bard of the Island Life." *Time* 140 (19 Oct. 1992): 65. Nobel Prize for literature, 1992.

_____. "The Fortunate Traveller." Rev. of *The Fortunate Traveller*. *Time* 119 (15 Mar. 1982): 83.

Grecco, Stephen. Rev. of *Remembrance and Pantomime*. *World Literature Today* 55.3 (Summer 1981): 521.

Griffith, Lynne. Rev. of *The Castaway*. *Art and Man* (June 1969): 15-19.

Grimes, John. "'Company of Players' Wins Praise for 'Ione.'" Rev. of *Ione*. *Trinidad Guardian* 9 Nov. 1957: [n.p.]. Review finds production melodramatic, but good acting.+

Guillory, Daniel L. Rev. of *The Arkansas Testament*. *Library Journal* 112.17 (15 Oct. 1987): 84.

_____. Rev. of *Collected Poems 1948-1984*. *Library Journal* 111 (15 Feb. 1986): 184-5.

_____. Rev. of *Midsummer*. *Library Journal* 109 (Jan. 1984): 97.

"Guinness Award for a W. I. Poet." *Trinidad Guardian* 27 Nov. 1961: 5. Announces Walcott's prize for "A Sea Chanty."

Gunness, Christopher. "White Man, Black Man." *People* 3.26 (June 1978): 14, 51-52. Rev. and discussion with Walcott about *Pantomime* production in Trinidad.+

H., S. "Ti-Jean and His Brothers." *Public Opinion* (Jamaica) 29 Nov. 1958: n.p#. Newspaper to finance Workshop production of *Ti-Jean* in Kingston.

Hackett, Winston. "Identity in the Poetry of Walcott." *Moko* 8 (14 Feb. 1969): 2. Unresolved ambiguities persist in *Green Night* and *Castaway*.

Hamner, Robert D. "The Art of Chiaroscuro-Caliban Confronts the White World." *International Literature in English: Essays on the Major Writers*. Ed. Robert Ross. New York: Garland, 1991. 703-16. Device of chiaroscuro lends dimensions to poetry and drama.

_____. "Aspects of National Character in V. S. Naipaul and Derek Walcott." *Language and Literature: ACLALS Proceedings*. Ed. Satendra Nandan. Suva, Fiji: University of the South Pacific, 1983. 179-88.

_____. "Caliban Agonistes: Stages of Cultural Development in Plays of Derek Walcott." *The Literary Half-Yearly* 26.1 (Jan. 1985): 120-31. Means by which West Indian background yields artistic and social themes.

_____. "Conversation with Derek Walcott." *World Literature Written in English* 16.2 (Nov. 1977): 409-20 Interview on theatre, nature of poetry, criticism in Trinidad.

_____. "Derek A. Walcott." *Magill's Critical Survey of Drama: English Language Series*. Ed. Frank N. Magill. Englewood Cliffs: Salem Press, 1985. 1997-2005.

_____. "Derek A. Walcott." *Magill's Critical Survey of Poetry*. Ed. Frank N. Magill. Englewood Cliffs: Salem Press, 1982. 3001-7.

_____. *Derek Walcott*. Boston: Twayne, 1981. Assesses career to 1980.

_____. "Derek Walcott: His Works and His Critics: An Annotated Bibliography, 1947-1980." *The Journal of Commonwealth Literature* 16.1 (Aug. 1981): 142-84.

_____. "Derek Walcott's Theater of Assimilation." *West Virginia University Philological Papers* 25 (Feb. 1979): 86-93. Synthesis of cultural and artistic elements in the plays.

_____. "Derek Walcott." *Twentieth-Century Caribbean and Black African Writers*, first series. Ed. Bernth Lindfors and Rinehard Sander. Vol. 117 of *Dictionary of Literary Biography*. Detroit: Gale, 1992. 290-312.

_____. "Exorcising the Planter Devil in the Plays of Derek Walcott." *Commonwealth* 7.2 (Spring 1985): 95-102.

_____. "Mythological Aspects of Derek Walcott's Drama." *Ariel* 8.3 (July 1977): 35-58. Archetypal figures, themes, images speak to condition of modern life.

_____. "New World Burden." Rev. of *Sea Grapes. World Literature Written in English.* 16.1 (Apr. 1977): 212-14.

_____. Rev. of *Midsummer. World Literature Written in English* 23.2 (Spring 1984): 416-19.

Hanley, Charles J. "'He's the Poet Laureate of the Region." *Sunday Guardian* 22 July 1984: 8.

"Harvard Admonishes Professor." *Abilene Reporter News* 9 June 1982: 2. Account of coed's complaint.

Heaney, Seamus. "An Authentic Poetic Voice that Bridges Time, Cultures." Rev. of *Collected Poems. The Boston Globe* 9 Feb. 1986: 27-28.

_____. "The Language of Exile." Rev. of *The Star-Apple Kingdom. Parnassus* 8.1 (Fall-Winter 1979): 5-11. Respects Walcott's deliberate progress, his understanding of "options and traditions."

Hendrick, Kimmis. "Walcott's Poetic Play in L. A." Rev. of *Dream on Monkey Mountain. Christian Science Monitor* 9 Sept. 1970: 4.

Hendriks, A L. Rev. of "Epitaph for the Young." *Public Opinion* (Jamaica) 31 Dec. 1949: 6.

Henling, Wade. "Derek Walcott to Us." *Sunday Gleaner* (Jamaica) 1 Nov. 1970: 29.

Hill, Errol. *Derek Walcott* London: Macmillan, 1984. #

_____. "The Emergence of a National Drama in the West Indies." *Caribbean Quarterly* 18.4 (Dec. 1972): 9-40. Historical growth, experiments in utilizing indigeneous forms.

_____. "'Ione' Opens New Era in Jamaican Theatre." *Sunday Gleaner* 10 Mar. 1957: #. Opening Kingston production.

_____. "Is 'Man Better Man' Mr. Walcott?" *Trinidad Guardian* 3 Feb. 1965: 5. Calls Walcott to task for his role as critic.

_____. *The Trinidad Carnival, Mandate for a National Theatre.* Austin: University of Texas Press, 1972. Development of Carnival, its theatrical characteristics.

Hilton, A. "*Pantomime.*" *Express* (Trinidad) 23 Apr. 1978: 14-15. Rev. performance of play.

_____. "Walcott's World." *Catholic News* 25 June 1978: 11.

Hirsch, Edward. "The Art of Poetry." *Paris Review* 28 (Winter 1986): 197-230. Interview, 1984. Island background, "religious" experience of poetry, Trinidad theatre, personal relationships with Robert Lowell, Joseph Brodsky, Seamus Heaney.+

_____. "An Interview with Derek Walcott." *Contemporary Literature* 20 (Summer 1979): 279-92.

_____. Rev. of *Sea Grapes*. *New York Times Book Review* 31 Oct. 1976: 38.

Hodgin, John T. Rev of *Midsummer*. *Kliatt* 19.3 (Apr. 1985): 32-33.

Holder, G. A. "B. B. C.'s Broadcast of *Henri Christophe.*" *Bim* 4.14 (Jan.-June 1951): 141-42. First part indecisive, second part powerful, effective.+

Hollander, John. Rev. of *Midsummer*. *Yale Review* 74.1 (Autumn 1984): xi-xii. Fine essayistic quality with lyrical moments.

"Honour for Derek in His Prime." *Sunday Guardian* 28 Jan. 1973: 15. Honorary Doctor of Letters by University of the West Indies.

Hope, Christopher. "Colonial Outposts." Rev. of *Sea Grapes*. *London Magazine* 16.6 (Feb.-Mar. 1977): 82-83.

Hope, Fred. "Revised *Ti-Jean* Goes to Jamaica." *Trinidad Guardian* 7 Apr. 1971: 6.

Hopkinson, Slade. "'Dream on Monkey Mountain' and the Popular Response." *Caribbean Quarterly* 23.2-3 (June-Sept. 1977): 77-79. Reception of play in St. Lucia.

_____. "So the Sun Went Down." *Sunday Gleaner* (Jamaica) 15 Apr. 1956: n.p#. Prose-poetry of St. Lucian idiom in *Sea at Dauphin* clarified through dramatization on stage, in word, gesture, facial expression, intonation.

Hosein, Clyde. "Breakthrough for W. I. Writing." *Trinidad Guardian* 12 Nov. 1969: 4. N. B. C. television production of *Dream*.

_____. "The Creative Man's Two Worlds." *Trinidad Guardian* 21 Apr. 1971: 6. Commentary on Walcott's article "Meanings."

_____. "Lack of Appreciation Drives One to Madness." *Trinidad Guardian* 10 June 1971: #. Interview with Workshop actor Errol Jones.

_____. "The New Walcott: Sweeping, Involved, Audacious." Rev. of *The Gulf and Other Poems*. *Express* (Trinidad) 9 Nov. 1969: 25.

_____. "No Beating About the Bush." *Trinidad Guardian* 4 Mar. 1970: 4. Rev. of N. B. C. version of *Dream*.

_____. "See Walcott's 'Dream' on Television Tonight." *Trinidad Guardian* 14 Feb. 1970: 2.

_____. "Stormy Applause Well Deserved." Rev. of *Ti-Jean and His Brothers*. *Trinidad Guardian* 27 June 1970: 5.

_____. "*Ti-Jean* Promises a Good Performance." *Trinidad Guardian* 25 June 1970: 4.

_____. "When a Playwright's Tenacity Pays off." *Trinidad Guardian* 18 Feb. 1970: 4. Walcott signing contract with Canadian Broadcasting Corp. to produce *Ti-Jean* for radio.

Howard, Ben. "Trailways Fantasist." Rev. of *The Fortunate Traveller*. *Prairie Schooner* 51.1 (Spring 1983): 93-98. Lowell's voice prevails over Walcott's in "Old New England;" Walcott epistolary elsewhere. American themes Walcott's strength.

"How Far Are Derek Walcott and Edward Brathwaite Similar? Is It Impossible for
    the Caribbean to Choose Between the Two, if So, Which Way Should They
    Choose and Why?" *Busara* 6.1 (1974): 90-100   Ungrammatical, biased,
    misreading of Walcott and Brathwaite.

"The Importance of Derek Walcott." Rev. of *The Castaway and Other Poems. New
    World* 37 (1 Apr. 1966): 23-25.

"International Poets Read." *Trinidad Guardian* 17 Jan. 1980: 5. Walcott, Joseph
    Brodsky, Mark Strand read at Little Carib Theatre.

Ireland, Kevin. "Place and Poetic Identity." Rev. of *The Castaway. Journal of Com-
    monwealth Literature* 2 (Dec. 1966): 157-58.

"The Isle Is Full of Noises." *Variety* 307 (12 May 1982): 474. Rev. production of
    play.

Ismond, Patricia. "*Another Life*: Autobiography as Alternative History." *Journal of
    West Indian Literature* 4.1 (Jan. 1990): 41-49. Informing purpose of *An-
    other Life* is "re-searching of the personal history for an idea of human
    destiny, an order of truth . . . as an integral part of the arrival at maturity."

_____. "Breaking Myths and Maidenheads." Rev. of *The Joker of Seville. Tapia* 5.20
    (18 May 1975): 4-5, 9. Adaptation of a classic for modern stage (first of two
    parts).+

_____. "Breaking Myths and Maidenheads." Rev. of *The Joker of Seville. Tapia* 5.22
    (1 June 1975): 6-8. Liberating spirit of Don Juan's exploits (second of two
    parts).+

_____. "Naming and Homecoming: Walcott's Poetry Since *Another Life*." The
    Literary Half-Yearly 26.1 (Jan. 1985): 3-19. Naming definitive for
    Walcott's New World identity. Theme heightened since *Another Life.*

_____. "North and South—A Look at Walcott's *Midsummer*." *Kunapipi* 8.2
    (1986): 77-85. Walcott not becoming detached. Continues political con-
    cerns, including geopolitical relations.

_____. "North and South: A Look at Derek Walcott's *Midsummer*." *World Litera-
    ture Written in English* 27.1 (Spring 1987): 86-93. Heightened awareness of
    Third World relations to superpowers since Walcott moved to United
    States. Reprint of article in *Kunapipi.*

_____. "Self-Portrait of an Island: St. Lucia through the Eyes of Its Writers."
    Journal of West Indian Literature 1.1 (Oct. 1986): 59-73.

_____. "The St. Lucian Background in Garth St. Omer and Derek Walcott."
    Caribbean Quarterly 28.1-2 (Mar.-June 1982): 32-43. Links "private orien-
    tation" of two writers to influences of native island.

_____."Walcott versus Brathwaite." *Caribbean Quarterly* 17.3-4 (Dec. 1971): 54-
    71. Exposition of relative positions; Brathwaite as folk poet and Walcott as
    Eurocentric traditionalist. Walcott is superior craftsman.+

_____. "Walcott's Later Drama: From 'Joker' to 'Remembrance.'" *Ariel* 16.3 (July
    1985): 89-101. *Remembrance* and *Pantomime* show technical innovation

and shift to themes of post-independence. Jackson Philip prototype of new Caribbean man.

———. "Walcott's *Omeros*—a Complex, Ambitious Work." *Caribbean Contact* 18.5 (Mar.-Apr. 1991): 10-11. Major achievement informed more by lyric than by epic muse.

———. "West Indian Literature as an Expression of National Cultures: The Literature of St. Lucia." *World Literature Written in English* 29.2 (Autumn 1989): 104-15. Despite shared experience common to West Indies, each writer reflects particulars of his nation's background. Case study of Derek Walcott and Garth St. Omer shows how St. Lucia informs their works.

Izevbaye, D. S. "The Exile and the Prodigal: Derek Walcott as West Indian Poet." *Caribbean Quarterly* 26.1-2 (Mar.-June 1980): 70-82. Career reflects cultivation of birthplace, place of work, fact of being West Indian. Profound faith in being "provincial" poet.

Jacob, John. Rev. of *Sea Grapes*. *Booklist* 74 (15 Oct. 1977): 352.

Jacobs, Carl. "At 35 Walcott Is Something of a Phenomenon." *Sunday Guardian* 15 May 1966: 9. Biographical sketch.

———. "Bajans Are Still Very Insular and Prejudiced." *Sunday Guardian* 23 July 1967: 5. Interviews Walcott on Workshop repertoire, financing.

———. Interview with Walcott. *Sunday Guardian* 23 July 1967: 5. Interviews Walcott concerning *Dream on Monkey Mountain*.#

———. "Spiritual Crippling from an Absence of Vision." *Sunday Guardian* 31 Aug. 1974: 30. Interview.

———. "Theatre Workshop Presents Two One-Act Plays." *Trinidad Guardian Nation* 14 Jan. 1964: 5. Twinbill—Ionesco's *The Lesson* and Walcott's *Malcochon*, Jan. 22-23 at Little Carib Theatre.

———. "There's No Bitterness in Our Literature." *Sunday Guardian* 22 May 1966: 9. Interview. Positive aspects of writing in Caribbean. On sources of poetic ideas.

Jahn, Janheinz. "The Contribution of the West Indies to Poetry." *Bim* 6.21 (Dec. 1954): 16-22. Distinguishing element is black component. Compares African and West Indian characteristics.

James, C. L. R. "Here's a Poet Who Sees the Real West Indies." Rev. of *In a Green Night*. *Sunday Guardian* 6 May 1962: 5. Whether a West Indian literature exists, area writers are adding to wealth of English-speaking peoples.

James, John. Rev. of *Beef, No Chicken*. *Times Educational Supplement* 31 Mar. 1989: 25. Performance at Shaw Theatre, London.

James, Louis. "Caribbean Poetry in English—Some Problems." *Savacou* 2 (1970): 78-86. Problems of writing in West Indies. Emphasis on Brathwaite and Walcott contributions.

———. "Landscape Locked in Amber." Rev. of *Another Life*. *Commonwealth Newsletter* 6 (1974): 14-15. Homage to mentor and friend is most directly visual poetry to date, showing painter's concern with light and texture.

James, Sybil L. "Aspects of Symbolism in Derek Walcott's *Dream on Monkey Mountain.*" *The Literary Half-Yearly* 26.1 (Jan. 1985): 82-90. Makak symbolizes spiritual and emotional entrapment of black man imitating whites. Ape figure positive in that primitive innocence must be achieved before man may escape blind mimicry.

Jenkin, Veronika. "Drums and Colours." *Bim* 7.27 (July-Dec. 1958): 183-84. Rev. of performance.

Jenkins, Alan. Rev. of *The Fortunate Traveller. Encounter* 59.5 (Nov. 1982): 62-63. Excessive rhetoric, verbal laxity, ideological posturing.

Jenkins, Paul. Rev. of *The Arkansas Testament. The Massachusetts Review* 29.1 (Spring 1988): 128-32. Walcott "appropriates 'foreign' and 'indigenous'— and mixes . . . until they will not be separated."

Jepson, John. "Oh, How We Missed June Nathaniel's Singing . . ." *People* 5.11 (June 1980): 82. Rev. Toronto production of *The Joker of Seville.*

Jeyifo, Biodun. "On Eurocentric Critical Theory: Some Paradigms from the Texts and Sub-Texts of Post-Colonial Writing." *Kunapipi* 11.1 (1989): 107-18. Walcott's dramaturgy from *Dream on Monkey Mountain* to *Pantomime* is paradigm of "distance covered in contemporary post-colonial writing in the debunking, the demythologization of Eurocentric claims to the embodiment of absolute truth or knowledge."+

Johnson, Geoffrey. Rev. of *In a Green Night. Twentieth Century* (Summer 1962): 190.

_____. "Three Notables and a Newcomer." Rev. of *In a Green Night. Poetry Review* 53.4 (Autumn 1962): 254.

Johnson, Lee. "Walcott's 'Another Life:' Rich and Complex." *Jamaica Daily News* 17 Feb. 1974: 5.

"'Joker of Seville' to Be Staged Gayelle-Style." *Sunday Guardian* 17 Nov. 1974: 7. Experiment with theatre in the round to encourage sense of audience participation.

Jones, Dennis. "Derek Walcott." *Dictionary of Literary Biography Yearbook.* Detroit: Gale Research Co., 1982. 270-78.

Jones, Katie. "The Mulatto of Style: Derek Walcott's *Collected Poems 1948-84.*" *Planet* 62 (Apr.-May 1987): 97-99.

Jones, Marylin. "A Home for Our Artists Please." *Trinidad Guardian* 9 Apr. 1975: 4. Accounts hardships of producing with inadequate funds.

_____. Roger Christiani and Glenn Forte. Production program for *Remembrance.* Normandie Hotel, Port of Spain, Trinidad, July 1979. No publication data. Pictures and information on cast, dinner theatre format.

_____. "Striking a Blow for Women's Lib." *Trinidad Guardian* 12 Dec. 1974: 4. *Joker* opens social roles of sexes.

Judson, Jerome. "Page-turners." Rev. of *Midsummer. Writer's Digest* 64 (Aug. 1984): 11.

"Kairi Comment." *Kairi* 1/75 [6th issue] (1975): Kairi Comment 3.1 [sic]. Rev. production of "The Joker of Seville." Suggests preparing musical album to accompany "'Ti-Jean and His Brothers."

Kakutani, Michiko. "Books of the Times." Rev. of *Collected Poems. New York Times* 15 Jan. 1986: 19.

Keates, Jonathan. Rev. of *The Star-Apple Kingdom. Spectator* 10 May 1980: 24.

"Keener Political Focus in *Star-Apple Kingdom*." Rev. of *The Star-Apple Kingdom. Trinidad Guardian* 3 June 1978: 9

"Keeping in Touch." Rev. of *Another Life. Times Literary Supplement* 3 Aug. 1973: 894.

Kell, R. Rev. of *The Castaway and Other Poems. Manchester Guardian* 16 Dec. 1965: 11.

Kellman, Anthony. "Derek Walcott, *The Arkansas Testament*." *Kyk-Over-Al* 39 (Dec. 1988): 90-93. Walcott's dispossessed personae and the need to transcend insularity and parochialism.

_____. "Testimony from Here and Elsewhere." *Callaloo* 12.3 (Summer 1989): 605-8. Finds *Arkansas Testament* uneven, Caribbean sections more accomplished than poems set in America.

Kennedy, X. J. Rev of *The Fortunate Traveller. New York Times Book Review* 87 (5 Dec 1982): 54.

_____. Rev. of *The Fortunate Traveller. Poetry* 141 (Mar. 1983): 353-54.

Kerr, Walter. Rev. of *Dream on Monkey Mountain. New York Times* 21 Mar. 1971: 3, sec. 2.

Khan, Naseem. "Fringe in Performance." Rev. of *O Babylon! Drama* 168 (1988): 33-34. Rev. *O Babylon!* performance in London.

"Kicking Off with the 'Blacks.'" *Trinidad Guardian* 6 Oct. 1966: 10. Workshop production of Genêt's *The Blacks.*

Killam, G. D. "A Note on the Title of *Petals of Blood*." *The Journal of Commonwealth Literature* 15.1 (1 Aug. 1980): 125-32. Line from Walcott's "The Swamp" from *Selected Poems* as source for Ngugi title.

King, Bruce. "*The Collected Poems* and *Three Plays* of Derek Walcott." *The Southern Review* 23.1 (Jan. 1987): 741-49. *Collected Poems* emphasizes universal themes and myths of Walcott's life. *Three Plays* reflects new phase of "withdrawn, introspective, more traditional drama."+

_____. "Derek Walcott: Artist and Community." *Individual and Community in Commonwealth Literature*. Ed. Daniel Massa. Msida, Malta: University Press, 1979. 84-89. Clarifies apparent contradictions in some public statements. Humanistic consciousness avoids simplistic polemics. Artist's role "to record, orchestrate and refine . . . multiform complexity as he has experienced it."

_____. Rev. of *Selected Poems. Pacific Quarterly* (Moana) 8.3 (1983): 138-40.

_____. "Walcott and the Domain of English Poetry." Rev. of *The Star-Apple Kingdom. Sewanee Review* 88.3 (1980): 63-65 "The Schooner *Flight*" influenced by Lowell.

_____. "Walcott, Brathwaite and Authenticity." *The New English Literatures—Cultural Nationalism in a Changing World.* New York: St. Martin's Press, 1980. 118-39.

King, Cameron, and Louis James. "In Solitude for Company: The Poetry of Derek Walcott." *The Islands in Between.* Ed. Louis James. London: Oxford UP, 1968: 86-99. Contradictions of life and art fundamental to Walcott's poetry.

King, C. G. O. "The Poems of Derek Walcott." *Caribbean Quarterly.* 10.3 (Sept. 1964): 3-30. "Reveals . . . That a poet's merit lies . . . in his power to grasp the elements of his own experience, and to show . . . that they are a meaningful part of the world's experience."

King, Lloyd. "Bard in the Rubbish Heap: The Problem of Walcott's Poetry." *Tapia* 5 (1 Feb. 1970): 7-8 Fundamental theme is destiny of the artist in West Indies. Limitations of the humanistic position.

_____. "Derek Walcott: The Literary Humanist in the Caribbean." *Caribbean Quarterly* 16.4 (Dec. 1970): 36-42. Duplicates his "Bard in the Rubbish Heap." Fundamental theme is destiny of the artist in West Indies. Limitations of the humanistic position.

_____. "The Ugly Intellectual?" *Tapia* 6.1 (4 Jan 1975): 2 "Laventville" in *Castaway* shows middle-class reaction to black poverty: slick, neat, role-playing.

Kinzie, Mary. Rev. of *The Fortunate Traveller. Nation* 234 (27 Feb. 1982): 247.

Knox, Bernard. "Achilles in the Caribbean." Rev. of *Omeros. The New York Review of Books* 7 Mar. 1991: 3-4.

"Lack of Resources Proved No Barrier." *Trinidad Guardian* 28 Oct. 1966: 5 Rev. Workshop production of Soyinka's *The Road.*

Lamming, George. "Two Poets with Diversity and Vitality." Rev. of *Another Life. New York Times Book Review* 6 May 1973: 36-37. Race and politics put writer on trial. Compares with Ishmael Reed (*Selected Poems 1963-1970*).

Lane, M. Travis. "At Home in Homelessness: The Poetry of Derek Walcott." *Dalhousie Review* 53.2 (Summer 1973): 325-38. Traces themes in many poems. Conflicts between public and private aspects of art.

_____. "A Different 'Growth of a Poet's Mind': Derek Walcott's *Another Life.*" *Ariel* 9 (Oct. 1978): 65-78. Walcott more rewarding and suggestive than most contemporaries. Compares Walcott with Wordsworth.

Lattimore, R. "Poetry Chronicle." Rev. of *Star-Apple Kingdom. Hudson Review* 32 (Autumn 1979): 442-43.

Lawton, David. Rev. of *The Gulf. Revista Interamericana Review* 2.2 (Summer 1972):

242-47. Compromises in preservation of spirit and feel of Caribbean in European poetic forms. Oneness of man revealed.

Lee, Robert. "The Joker of Seville." *Tapia* 5.26 (29 June 1975): 6-7. Rev. of St. Lucia performance.

Lefkowitz, Mary. "Bringing Him Back Alive." Rev. of *Omeros. New York Times Book Review* 7 Oct. 1990: 1, 34-35. Review contains comments from Walcott on *Omeros*. Influences of Homer, Dante, Conrad, Hemingway, the people of the Caribbean and of film techniques.+

Lehman, David. Rev. of *Midsummer. Washington Post* 4 Mar 1984: 11.

Leithauser, Brad. "Ancestral Rhyme." Rev. of *Omeros. New Yorker* 66.52 (11 Feb. 1991): 91-95.

Lesser, Judith. Rev. of *The Star-Apple Kingdom. Booklist* 75. 18 (15 May 1979): 1416-17.

Lieberman, Laurence. "Derek Walcott and Michael S. Harper: The Muse of History." *Unassigned Frequencies*. Ed. Laurence Lieberman. Chicago: Illinois U. P., 1973. 284-96.

_____. "New Poetry: The Muse of History." Rev. of *Another Life. Yale Review* 63 (Oct. 1973): 113-22. Walcott emerges as one of the brilliant historic mythologists of our day—has yet to synthesize the medley of styles, mannerisms, dialects.

Lindo, Archie. *The Star* 25 Nov. 1975: 4. Rev. Workshop production of *The Joker of Seville*.

Lipenga, Ken. "Okigbo and Walcott: The Quest for a Vision." *Odi* (Chichiri, Blantyre 3, Malawi) 4.1 (May 1982): 46-63. Similarities of theme and imagery because Okigbo and Walcott portray "prodigals" in quest of "poetic vision."

Livingston, James T. "Derek Walcott: Poet of the New World." 26 Nov. 1971: n. p. Unpublished typescript of conference paper, National Council of Teachers of English, Las Vegas, Nev. Learned craft and developed individual voice. Particularity of setting, universality of theme.

Lofley, Lin. "Caribbean Epic." Rev. of *Omreos. American Visions* 6 (Feb. 1991): 39. W. H. Smith Literary Award for *Omeros*.

Logan, William. "Language Against Fear." Rev. of *Sea Grapes. Poetry* 130 (July 1977): 228-29.

"London Theatre Honours Walcott." *Express* (Trinidad) 14 Feb 1980: 19. Staging of *Remembrance*.

"London Theatre Man Brought for W.I. Pageant." *The Daily Gleaner* (Jamaica) 30 Aug. 1957: #. *Remembrance*. Tyrone Guthrie to assist production of Walcott's *Drums and Colours*.

Longley, Edna. "Cooked and Raw." Rev. of *The Fortunate Traveller. New Statesman* 103:2661 (19 Mar. 1982): 19-20.

Lovelace, Earl. Rev. of "The Last Carnival." *Express* (Trinidad) 25 July 1982: 15, 18. Argues that Walcott sometimes settles for easy lines instead of probing "a stronger, a more fundamental truth" in some of the characters.+

_____. "Rude Bwoy Walcott." Rev. of *O Babylon! People* 1.2 (1975): 37-39.

_____. "Theatre and Audience." *Sunday Guardian* 1 May 1966: 7. Potential of Workshop company deserves more adequate facilities. Rev. of production of Eric Roach's *Belle Fanto*.

Lowhar, Syl. "Another Station of the Cross." Rev. of *In a Fine Castle*. *Tapia* 23 (26 Dec. 1971): 19.

_____. "'Blue Nile' a Play for the Young." *People Magazine* (1 Sept. 1985): 16. Rev. of Port of Spain production.

_____. "*Drums and Colours.*" Rev. of *Drums and Colours*. *Tapia* 3.18 (6 May 1973): 9-10.

_____. "A Struggle for Freedom." Rev. of *Ti-Jean and His Brothers*. *Tapia* 8 (9 Aug. 1970): 6.

_____. "Ti-Jean—A Mom and Son's Battle for a Better Life." *Daily Express* (Trinidad) 14 July 1970: 13.

Lownie, Wyn. "West Indian Actresses Fail to Impress Walcott." *Trinidad Guardian* 2 July 1959: 5. Discusses problems of developing local actresses. Interested in "theatre in the round." Not much local encouragement.

Lucas, John. "In Multitudinous Dialects." Rev. of *Collected Poems 1948-1984*. *New Statesman and Society* 3.86 (2 Feb. 1990): 33-34.

_____. "The Sea, the Sea." Rev. of *Omeros*. *New Statesman and Society* 3 (5 Oct. 1990): 36.

Luddy, Thomas E. Rev. of *Dream on Monkey Mountain and Other Plays*. *Library Journal* 96 (1 Jan. 1971): 97.

_____. Rev. of *Remembrance and Pantomime*. *Library Journal* 105 (1 June 1980): 1324. Poetic gifts on stage in two comedies.

Lydon, Christopher, with Derek Walcott and Seamus Heaney. "Robert Penn Warren." *Partisan Review* 53.4 (1986): 606-12. Interview. Conducted by Lydon. Walcott says Warren sticks to personal experience. Great poets make horizon part of their own experience.

Lyn, Diana. "The Concept of the Mulatto in Some Works of Derek Walcott." *Caribbean Quarterly* 26.1-2 (Mar.-June 1980): 49-67.

Lyndersay, Mark. ". . . And the Audience Make Three." *Catholic News* 30 Apr. 1978: 5. Rev. performance at Little Carib Theatre.

_____. "A Most Undramatic Season." *Trinidad and Tobago Review* 6.3 ("Back to School" issue 1982): 22-23. Poor quality of productions at annual "Drama Festival." Mentions Walcott's work on TV film "The Rig."

_____. "New York Critics Find Derek Walcott's 'Remembrance' Appealing." *People* (July 1979): 46-47.

_____. "Pantomime Is Still a Joy." *Express* (Trinidad) 14 Oct. 1980: 11.

_____. "Under Lights." Rev. of *Remembrance. Catholic News* 15 July 1979: 11.

_____. "You Want Jokes? I'll Give You Jokes." *Trinidad Guardian* 12 May 1981: 15. *Beef, No Chicken* a "sitcom" with little direction and substance.

Lyon, David. "A Human Voice on the American Condition." Rev. of *Collected Poems 1948-1984. Americas* 39.2 (Mar.-Apr. 1987): 60-62.

Mackinnon, Lachlan. "Nobody or a Nation." Rev. of *Collected Poems 1948-1984. Times Literary Supplement* 24 Oct. 1986: 1185-86.

_____. Rev. of *Remembrance. Times Literary Supplement* 27 July 1990: 800. Performance at Tricycle Theatre, London.

"Makak Symbolizes Workshop." *Trinidad Guardian* 1 Aug. 1974: 7.

Malle, Louis. Dir. *The Pursuit of Happiness* (1986): Pretty Mouse Films Producer: Louis Malle. Editor: Nancy Baker. Documentary film interview with Walcott and others.

"The Mango and the Oak." Rev. of *Omeros. The Economist* 317.7678 (27 Oct. 1990): 97-98. Poem's multiplicity of themes comes back to the "simplest of matters."

"Man of the Theatre." *New Yorker* 47 (26 June 1971): 30-31. Interview. *Dream* moves beyond racial theme. *Fine Castle* contrasts carnival and revolution.

Mariani, Paul. "Summoning the Dead: Politics and the Sublime in Contemporary English Poetry." *New England Review and Breadloaf Quarterly* 7.3 (Spring 1985): 299-314. Walcott, among others, briefly discussed. Visited by master poets of past, Walcott assumes role as witness to present.

Marowski, Daniel G. and Roger Matuz, eds. "Derek Walcott." *Contemporary Literary Criticism* 42 (1987): 414-23. Biographical sketch and survey of critical opinions directed at Walcott.

Marsh, Peter. Rev. of *In a Green Night. The Review* (Oxford) (June-July 1962): 33.

Marshall, Trevor. Rev. of *Pantomime. Bajan* (July 1980): 12-13.

Martin, Graham. "New Poetry." Rev. of *The Castaway. The Listener* 75.1928 (10 March 1966): 359. Some melodrama, prolixity, several impressive poems.

Mason, David. "Derek Walcott: Poet of the New World." *The Literary Review* 29.3 (Spring 1986): 269-75.

_____. "Poetry Chronical." Rev. of *Omeros. The Hudson Review* 44.3 (Autumn 1991): 513-15.

Mauby . "Now the Joker's Laugh is Mature and Polished." *Trinidad Guardian* 24 Oct. 1975: 4. Previews play before road engagement in Jamaica.

_____. "O Babylon, Do Mafia Play with Beach Balls " *Trinidad Guardian* 1 Apr. 1976: 4

Mazzocco, Robert. "Embracing Adversity." Rev. of *The Star-Apple Kingdom. New York Review of Books* 26.9 (31 May 1979): 34.

_____. "Three Poets." Rev. of *Selected Poems*. *New York Review of Books* 3.10 (31 Dec. 1964): 18-19.

McClatchy, J. D. "Divided Child." Rev. of *Collected Poems 1948-1984*. *The New Republic* 194.12 (24 Mar. 1986): 36-38. Walcott's "style now has a range and a grave radiance that transfigure the smallest detail."+

McCorkle, James. "Re-Mapping the New World." *Ariel* 17 (Apr. 1986): 3-14. Walcott's vision is temporal and durational in *The Fortunate Traveller* and *Midsummer*. Maps define, as new world inscribed with old.

McShine, K. L. Rev. of *Selected Poems*. *Sunday Guardian* 7 June 1964: 4.

McWatt, Mark A. "Derek Walcott: An Island Poet and His Sea Voice." *Third World Quarterly* 10.4 (1988): 1607-15. Emphasizes Caribbean context of Walcott's voice in poetry and drama.

_____. "*Remembrance*." Rev. of *Remembrance*. *Caribbean Contact* 10.8 (Dec. 1982): 11. Balanced presentation of the situation in the West Indies—colonial past and revolutionary present.+

_____. Rev. of *Dream on Monkey Mountain*. *Bulletin of Eastern Caribbean Affairs* 5.6 (Jan.-Feb. 1980): 16-20.

Melser, John. "Landmark for Local Drama and Triumph for Workshop." *Trinidad Guardian* 29 Jan. 1968: 11. Rev. local production of *Dream*.

_____. "A Similar Quality Could Be Achieved." *Trinidad Guardian* 25 Apr. 1969: 7. *Malcochon* and two other plays performed by New York Negro Ensemble Company. Such productions could work in West Indies.

_____. "We Haven't Developed Our Own Idiom in Theatre." *Trinidad Guardian* 20 May 1969: 4. Need to adapt foreign and indigenous forms in Trinidad theatre.

Mentus, Ulric. "Is There Something Called Black Art?" *Caribbean Contact* 3.11 (Feb. 1976): 7, 17. Rex Nettleford responds to questions concerning Walcott's position on problem of African longing and need to develop West Indian identity. On power politics and "hot-house'" art of cultural fairs.

_____. Rev. of *Dream on Monkey Mountain*. *Evening News* (Jamaica) 31 Jan. 1968: 5.

_____. "The Little Workshop's Mammoth Task of 5 Plays a Year." *Sunday Mirror* 8 May 1966: np. Production schedule for 1966.#

_____. "Walcott: Nobody Wants to be a West Indian." *Jamaica Daily News* 7 Dec. 1975: 5, 6, 7. Interviews Walcott.

_____. "Warhead in 'Dream' Has Not Yet Exploded." *Evening News* (Jamaica) 31 Jan. 1968: 5. Rev. of production.

_____. "Watch Out—They're Coming for the Theatre." *Caribbean Contact* 3.10 (Jan. 1976): 1. Danger of government censorship of theatre.

Meserve, Walter J. "Derek Walcott." *Contemporary Dramatists*. Ed. James Vinson. New York: St. Martin's Press, 1973. 780-83.

Mills, Therese. "Conversation with Derek Walcott." *Sunday Guardian* 20 June 1971: 10, 17. Interview with Walcott.

―――. "Don Juan Was a Stickman!" *Sunday Guardian* 18 Nov. 1973: 5. Interview. *Joker's* use of foreign and local elements.

―――. "Focus:―The Theatre Workshop." *Sunday Guardian* 23 Apr. 1967: 1. Rev. Workshop production of John's *Moon on a Rainbow Shawl.*

―――. "No 'Stardust,' Just the Polish of Hard Work." *Sunday Guardian* 23 July 1967: 6. Improvements in local theatre productions. Workshop established solid foundation.

―――. "Sell-out Crowd Enjoys 'The Joker.'" *Trinidad Guardian* 1 Jan. 1974: 3, 15.

―――. "This Is an Experiment in Courage." *Sunday Guardian* 15 Apr. 1973: 8. Some statistics on funds and attendance at Workshop production.

Milne, Anthony. "Derek Walcott." *Express* (Trinidad) 14 March 1982: 18. Interview questions Walcott's career divided between North America and the Caribbean, problems of theatre in Trinidad.+

Milner, Harry. "Lack of Voice Control." Rev. of *The Joker of Seville. Sunday Gleaner* (Jamaica) 30 Nov. 1975: 4-5.

―――. "Makak's Odyssey." *Sunday Gleaner* (Jamaica) 31 Aug. 1975: 5. Rev. of production of *Dream.*

―――. "Poet at the Crossroads." Rev. of *Poems. Sunday Gleaner* (Jamaica) 14 Oct. 1951: 4.

―――. Rev. of "The Dying Gods." *Sunday Gleaner* (Jamaica) 15 Feb. 1953: 4. Rev. production of Walcott's unpublished play.

"Mimic Men? Absurd." *Sunday Guardian* 29 Apr. 1973: 1. Report on Walcott's speech in Miami: "The Caribbean: Culture or Mimicry?"

Mombara, Sule. "'O Babylon'―Where It Went Wrong." *Caribbean Contact* 4.2 (May 1976): 15. Rev. of production. Drama breaks down over conflicting elements: European musical form, African and Rastafarian material.

"Monkey Mountain in Munich." *Trinidad Guardian* 30 Oct. 1972: 5. *Dream* carried to Germany by New York Negro Ensemble Company.

Montague, John. "Fluent Muse." Rev. of *In a Green Night. Spectator* 6992 (29 June 1962): 864.

Montenegro, David. "An Interview with Derek Walcott." *Partisan Review* 57.2 (Spring 1990): 202-14. Influence of painting on his poetry. Political nature of language. Value of feeling needed as a poet.

Moore, Gerald. *The Chosen Tongue: English Writing in the Tropical World.* New York: Harper, 1970. References to Walcott: 20-25, 28-29, 44-45.

Mootry, Maria K. "Three Caribbean Poets: Sea Imagery as an Index to Their African Consciousness." *Pan-Africanist* 1.2 (June 1971): 22-27. Césaire, Walcott, Brathwaite. Walcott rejects old Africa, turns to potentials of New World Adam.

"Moral Landscapes." Rev. of *The Gulf. Times Literary Supplement* 25 Dec. 1969: 1467. Lushness checked by deft metrical control and intelligence.

Mordecai, Pamela. "'A Crystal of Ambiguities': Metaphors for Creativity and the Art of Writing in Derek Walcott's *Another Life.*" *World Literature Written in English* 27.1 (Spring 1987): 93-105. Argues for a Caribbean artistic cognition labeled "prismatic": the "disposition to perceive and construe experience in sometimes unresolved pluralities."

Morris, Mervyn. "A crystal of Ambiguities" *Another Life.*" *Jamaica Sunday Gleaner* 1973: 23.#

_____. "Derek Walcott." *West Indian Literature.* Ed. Bruce King. London: Macmillan, 1979. 144-60, 235-37. Multiplicity of heritage permeates poetry and drama even in local scenes. Uses innate ambiguities in situations and language to advantage.

_____. "New Poetry by Brathwaite and Walcott." Rev. of *The Gulf. Sunday Gleaner* (Jamaica) 30 Nov. 1969: 4.

_____. "Walcott and the Audience for Poetry." *Caribbean Quarterly* 14.1-2 (Mar.-June 1968): 7-24. In spite of artistic sophistication, Walcott communicates with people. Notes skill through range of linguistic levels.+

Morrison, Blake. "Beach Poets." Rev. of *The Fortunate Traveller. London Review of Books* 4 (16 Sept.-6 Oct. 1982): 16.

_____. Rev. of *Midsummer. London Review of Books* 6.16 (6-19 Sept. 1984): 23.

Morsberger, Robert E. and Katherine M. Rev. of *Dream on Monkey Mountain. Books Abroad* 46.1 (Winter 1972): 172.

"Movement's Wake." Rev. of *The Castaway and Other Poems. Times Literary Supplement* 10 Feb. 1966: 104.

Murray, G. E. "Six Poets." Rev. of *The Star-Apple Kingdom. The Nation* 228.19 (19 May 1979): 578, 580.

"Naipaul, Walcott Win Rave Reviews in New York." *Express* (Trinidad) 30 May 1979: 11.

"Need for a National Theatre." *Express* (Trinidad) 8 Oct. 1969: #. N.B.C. investment in Workshop reflects on local values.

Neumark, Victoria. "Caribbean Criticism." Rev. of *Selected Poetry. Times Educational Supplement* 26 Feb. 1982: 29. Objects to "nit-picking'" introductions.

"New Walcott Play Without a Home." *Express* (Trinidad) 13 June 1982: 15.

Novick, Julius. Rev. of *Ti-Jean and His Brothers. New York Times* 6 Aug. 1972: 1, 3. Critical of melodramatic scenes and maudlin ending.

"Now St. Croix Hails Walcott's Dream." *Trinidad Guardian* 23 Oct. 1974: 4. Brief production history of *Dream on Monkey* Mountain.

Nunez, Phillip. Rev. of *In a Fine Castle. Moko* 73 (29 Oct. 1971): 12-13.

O'Hara, T. Rev. of *Another Life. Best Sellers* 15 June 1973: 134.

"O. B. E. Award for Walcott." *Trinidad Guardian* 3 Jan 1972: 1.

Oberg, Arthur. Rev. of *Sea Grapes*. *Western Humanities Review* 31 (Spring 1977): 186-89. Intent on roots and correspondences.

O'Brien, Sean. "In Terms of the Ocean." Rev. of *Omeros*. *Times Literary Supplement* 4563 (14-20 Sept. 1990): 977-78.

"O Babylon Opens in Mid March." *Sunday Guardian* 15 Feb. 1976: 6.

Ochillo, Yvonne. "Aspects of Alienation in the Poetry of Derek Walcott." *Journal of West Indian Literature* 3.2 (Sept. 1989): 39-52. Poetry reflects fragmentation, anxieties of the people. Walcott's detachment permits "vision that may impose order and beauty on the surrounding chaos."

_____. "The Power of the Poet in Walcott's *Another Life*." *Xavier Review* 8.1-2 (1988): 26-38.

Odlum, George. "Appreciation of a Walcott Poem." *The Voice of St. Lucia* 6 May 1967: 5, 8. Personal accounts of St. Lucia and his classmate, Walcott.

Olaogun, Modupe. "Sensuous Imagery in Derek Walcott's *Another Life*." *World Literature Written in English* 27.1 (Spring 1987): 106-18. Discusses style through relation of image and metaphor to meaning and structure.

Oliver, Edith. "Displaced Person." Rev. of *Remembrance*. *New Yorker* 55 (21 May 1979): 105-6. Loose structure slows and darkens effectively. Fine poetic writing. +

_____. "Once Upon a Full Moon." *New Yorker* 47.6 (27 Mar. 1971): 83-84. Rev. of *Dream on Monkey Mountain*, Negro Ensemble Company production.

_____. Rev. of *Pantomime*. *New Yorker* 62.45 (29 Dec. 1986): 78-79. Production at Hudson Guild Theater.

Owens, R. J. "West Indian Poetry." *Caribbean Quarterly* 7 (Dec. 1961): 120-27. Lack of competent criticism in Caribbean. Walcott fails in integrating diverse materials.

P, R. A. "I've Written a New Play." *Tapia* 7.19 (8 May 1977): 9. *Remembrance* played St. Croix, U. S. Virgin Islands, 23 Apr.-1 May 1977. Required staging "in the round."

_____. "Poet Walcott Blasts Trinidad on Freedom." *Caribbean Contact* 5.10 (Feb. 1978): 1. Resents pressures on writers and critics to conform.

Paddington, Bruce. "Saint Lucia: Coming Home." *Sunjet* 4 (1984): 50-53. Interview with Walcott.

Pantin, Raoul. "The Amazing 'Joker of Seville'" *Express* (Trinidad) 6 Apr. 1975: 7, 10.

_____. "Any Revolution Based on Race Is Suicidal." *Caribbean Contact* 1.8 (Aug. 1973): 14, 16. Part II of two parts (see "We Are Still Being Being Betrayed"). Interview. Relations with public. Workshop's kind of revolution. Value of craftsmanship.

_____. "Back to Africa Theme: Walcott at It Again." Rev. of *O Babylon!* *Tapia* 6.13 (28 Mar. 1976): 9, 11.

———. "The Mouse Who Roared—A Little." *Trinidad and Tobago Review* 3.3 (July [Aug.?] 1979): 23. Rev. performance of "Remembrance." Protagonist's assertions inadequate to events of Trinidad's 1970 "February Revolution."#

———. "O Babylon!" *Caribbean Contact* 4.1 (Apr. 1976): 17. *O Babylon!* translates social conditions into dramatic form. Music too delicate for physical reggae.

———. "O Babylon!" *Tapia* 6.3 (18 Jan. 1976): 10.

———. "We Are Still Being Betrayed." *Caribbean Contact* 1.7 (July 1973): 14, 16. Part I of two parts (see "Any Revolution Based on Race Is Suicidal"). Interview. On his audience, maintaining standards, and advantages of writing in Caribbean.

"*Pantomime* Returns for Third Run at Little Carib." *Express* (Trinidad) 8 Oct. 1980: 32.

"*Pantomime* Seemed to Miss Something." *Express* (Trinidad) 4 Sept. 1978: 9.

Panton, George. "The Magic of Words." Rev. of *In a Green Night*. *Sunday Gleaner* (Jamaica) 13 May 1962: #.

———. "Major Poet." Rev. of *Selected Poems*. *Sunday Gleaner* (Jamaica) 18 Oct. 1964: 4.

Parameswaran, Uma. Rev. of *Sea Grapes*. *World Literature Today* 51 (Spring 1977): 325.

Parisi, Joseph. Rev. of *Collected Poems 1948-1984*. *Booklist* 82.16 (15 Apr. 1986): 1177.

———. Rev. of *The Fortunate Traveller*. *Booklist* 78.9 (1 Jan. 1982): 582.

———. Rev. of *Midsummer*. *Booklist* 80.12 (15 Feb. 1984): 841-42.

Parker, Derek. "Radio Drama." *Drama* 140 (1981): 47. Radio production of "Remembrance" falls short of previous achievements.

Paul. "Pantomime." *Variety* 303 (17 June 1981): 90. Rev. of *Pantomime* production in Washington, D. C.

Pearce, Edward. "Theatre." Rev. of *O Babylon!* by Derek Walcott. *Encounter* 70.5 (May 1988): 76. Production at Riverside Theatre, London.

Peters, Erskine. "The Theme of Madness in the Plays of Derek Walcott." *College Language Association Journal* 32.2 (1988): 148-69.

Petrie, Phil W. Rev. of *Poems of the Caribbean*. *Black Enterprise* 12.5 (Dec. 1982): 30.

Pettingell, Phoebe. "Reconciling Disparate Worlds." Rev. of *The Fortunate Traveller*. *New Leader* 65 (3 May 1982): 14-15.

Pevear, Richard. "Caribbean Images." Rev. of *Sea Grapes*. *The Nation* 12 Feb. 1977: 185-86. Gives sense of dispersal of talent, mixed impulses.

Phelps, Karen. "'Belle Fanto' Much Too Confined." *Sunday Guardian* 17 Apr. 1966: 6. Staging play in Basement Theatre.

———. "Where Actors and Audience Share Same Level." *Trinidad Guardian* 12 Jan. 1966: 3. Intimacy of Bretton Hall Hotel basement performances of Workshop (Workshop then called "Basement Theatre").

Phillip, Neil. Rev. of *The Fortunate Traveller*. *British Book News* (July 1982): 438.

"Picking up Where 'Pieces' Left Off." *Express* (Trinidad) 20 Mar. 1973: 9. Collaboration with Astor Johnson's Repertory Dance Theatre.

"Poems of the Caribbean." *Black Enterprise* 12 (Dec. 1982): 30.

"Poet Derek Walcott gets British Poetry Honour." *Jet* 74 (18 July 1988): 24.

"Poet of the Islands." *Times Educational Supplement* 23 Jan. 1981: 21. Regarding Welsh Arts Council's International Writer's Prize to Walcott in 1980.

"Poet 'Stunned' about Winning Nobel Prize." *Abilene Reporter News* 9 Oct. 1992: 10A.

"Poet Walcott Weds Jamaican Girl." *Trinidad Guardian* 27 Aug. 1954: 1. Announces marriage to Faye Moyston.

Porter, Peter. Rev. of *Another Life*. *Sunday Observer* (London) 5 Aug. 1973: 28.

"Praise for Naipaul and Walcott." *Trinidad Guardian* 29 Dec. 1966: 9.

Pritchard, William H. Rev. of *Midsummer*. *The Hudson Review* 37.2 (Summer 1984): 331. Unmodulated verse, "a mistaken enterprise."

"Shags and Poets." Rev. of *The Gulf*. *Hudson Review* 23.3 (Autumn 1970): 569.

Procope, Monica. "Newcomers Do Well in Workshop Plays." *Barbados Advocate* 27 Mar. 1971: #.

Pybus, Rodney. Rev. of *The Arkansas Testament*. *Stand Magazine* 31 (1989): 76-7.

Questel , Victor D. "Black American Not Given a Chance." *Trinidad and Tobago Review* 5.3 (1981): 11, 12-13, 14. Second part of interview continues "I Have Moved. . ." Need for professional choreographers, critics in Caribbean.

_____. "The Blue Note of Caribbean Poetry." *Trinidad and Tobago Review* 2.5 (Jan. 1978): 7, 10, 31. Idiom and rhythms of "blues" in Brathwaite and Walcott.

_____. "Dream on Monkey Mountain." *Tapia* 4.35 (1 Sept. 1974): 2-3. Part I of IV parts (see subsequent entries under same title). Discusses political, spiritual implications of Makak beheading white apparition. Compares Noh and Brechtian methods. Makak is sum of contradictory ideas in Walcott. Circular pattern in *Dream*.

_____. "Dream on Monkey Mountain." *Tapia* 4.36 (8 Sept. 1974): 6-7, 10. Part II of IV parts (see other entries under same title).

_____. "Dream on Monkey Mountain." *Tapia* 4.37 (15 Sept. 1974): 6-7. Part III of IV parts (see other entries under same title).

_____. "Dream on Monkey Mountain." *Tapia* 4.39 (29 Sept. 1974): 5-8. Part IV of IV parts (see other entries under same title).

_____. "The Horns of Derek's Dilemma." *Tapia* 3.12 (25 Mar. 1973): 4-5. Walcott's Sisyphian martyr complex part of the paradox of his conflicting ideas.

_____. "I Have Moved Away from the Big Speech . . . Says Derek Walcott." *Trinidad and Tobago Review* 5.1 (1981): 11, 12-13, 14. Interview, part I of II. Painting scene leads to dialogue — influence of Hokusai and Hiroshige. Racial polarities in U.S. limits black actor's expectations.

_____. "Interlude for Rest or Prelude to Disaster?" *Tapia* 6.13 (28 Mar. 1976): 4, 11. Rev. of *O Babylon!* production finds action and musical score insufficiently motivated.+

_____. "List of Derek Walcott's Essays as They Appeared in *The Guardian* for the Year 1964." Unpublished typescript in the library, Univ. of the West Indies, St. Augustine, Trinidad, 1972: 23 pages.

_____. "The Little Carib Theatre (1948-1976)." *Caribbean Contact* 4 (Dec. 1976): 22. History of a theatre where Workshop has performed.

_____. "*Marie La Veau*—Disappointing, Uneven." *Trinidad and Tobago Review* 3.10 (1980): 8, 18, 21. Attempt to transcend failed West Indian Federation and spirit of isolation.

_____. "Poets Get Standing Ovation." *Sunday Guardian,* 27 Jan. 1980: 6. Poetry readings by Walcott, Joseph Brodsky, Mark Strand.

_____. "*Remembrance*: An Inspiring Elegy for the Afro-Saxon." *Trinidad Guardian* 3 July 1979: 7.

_____. "Schooner Flight from Paradise of Trinidad." Rev. of *The Star-Apple Kingdom. Trinidad Guardian* 3 Jan. 1980: 4.

_____. "Trinidad Theatre Workshop: A Bibliography." *Kairi* (1976): 53-59. Lists chronology of performances, reviews by Walcott, secondary reviews of Workshop, interviews with Walcott.

_____. "The Trinidad Theatre Workshop 1966-1967." *The Literary Half-Yearly* 26.1 (Jan. 1985): 163-79.

_____. "Walcott's Genius at One Sitting." *Trinidad Guardian* 14 July 1981: 24.

_____. "Walcott's Hack's Hired Prose: A Bibliography of Derek Walcott's Articles on Architecture, Sculpture, and Painting while a Critic for the *Trinidad Guardian*." *Kairi* (1978): 64-67.

_____. "Walcott's Major Triumph." Rev. of *Another Life. Tapia* 3.51 (23 Dec. 1973): 6-7. Part I of II part rev. Echoes of Lowell, MacNeice, Pasternak. Techniques of painter.

_____. "Walcott's Major Triumph." Rev. of *Another Life. Tapia* 3.52 (30 Dec. 1973): 6-7. Part II or II part rev. (See entry under same title).

_____. "Will Walcott Have the Last Laugh on His Joker?" *Trinidad Guardian* 6 Dec. 1974: 4. Rev. of *Joker of Seville* production. Several issues of debate raised. Role of death not worked out fully. Musical score and content enhance each other.

Quinn, Bernetta. "Two Signatures." Rev. of *The Gulf. Poetry* 119.5 (Feb. 1972): 301-2.

"R S L Fellowship for Walcott." *Trinidad Guardian* 11 May 1966: 1. Royal Society of
    Literature grant.

Rabkin, Gerald. "Black Skin and Blue Eyes." Rev. of *Dream on Monkey Mountain
    and Other Plays*. *Review: Latin American Literature and Arts* 13 (Winter
    1974): 67-70. "Successful appropriation of folk materials. . . . thematically
    complex. . . . playwright finding his distinctive voice."

Radin, Victoria. "Poetic License." Rev. of *Remembrance*. *New Statesman* 114 (18
    Sept. 1987): 26. Production at Arts Theatre, London.

Rae, Norman. "'Ione': Colourful but Academic." Rev. of *Ione*. *Daily Gleaner* (Ja-
    maica) 18 Mar. 1957: #. Play too academic, but good acting. Signs indicate
    West Indian drama becoming more than "just a collection of persons
    making conversation."+

Ramchand, Kenneth. "Derek Walcott." *An Introduction to the Study of West Indian
    Literature*. Ed. Kenneth Ramchand. London: Thomas Nelson and Sons,
    1976. 108-26. General survey of evolving career, section analyzing
    "Laventille." Argues connections between the poems, Walcott's life and the
    landscape.

_____. "Parades, Parades: Modern West Indian Poetry." *Sewanee Review* 87.1
    (Winter 1979): 96-118. Difficulty of judging variety of poetic forms. West
    Indian literature marked by its imagery and rhythm. Historical framework,
    primary attention to Walcott and Brathwaite.

_____. "Poetry Reading Held at the Little Carib Theatre to Mark Derek Walcott's
    50th Anniversary." *Trinidad and Tobago Review* 3.7 (Year End 1979): 4, 21.
    Walcott, Mark Strand and Joseph Brodsky in public readings.

_____. "Readings of Laventille." *Tapia* 5.50 (14 Dec. 1975): 67. Analysis of
    "Laventville" from *The Castaway and Other Poems*.+

_____. "The West Indies." *Literature of the World in English*. Ed. Bruce King.
    London: Routledge and Kegan Paul, 1974. 192-211, 224-25. Walcott uses
    dialect, reaches the folk, and advances regional drama.

_____. "West Indian Exiles at Home and Abroad." *Trinidad Tobago Review* 2.3
    (Dec. 1977): 13, 14, 16, 27. Walcott mentioned, 27.

Ramke, Bin. "Your Words Is English, Is a Different Tree: On Derek Walcott."
    Denver Quarterly 23.2 (1988): 90-99. Considering Walcott's chosen lan-
    guage, argues that language colonizes everyone—possesses the poet, the
    exile, the rebel.

Ramsaran, J. A. "Derek Walcott: New World Mediterranean Poet." *World Literature
    Written in English* 21.1 (Spring 1982): 133-47. Emphasizes need for West
    Indian consciousness "combining all strands originating from the Old
    World—the Mediterranean, the African and the Asian."

_____. Rev. of *The Joker of Seville*. *The Anglo-Welsh Review* 14 (1979): 173-76.

_____. "West Indian Gallery: The Works of Derek Walcott." *Black World* 24.8

(June 1975): 39-48. *Another Life* assimilates, transmutes language and literature of colonial education into new creation. Enables others to see their world.

Randall, D. Rev. of *Selected Poems*. *Negro Digest* 14 (Sept. 1965): 27.

Raphael, Lennox. "The Poet Read with a Twinkle in His Eyes." *Trinidad Guardian* 26 Oct. 1964: 7. Walcott reads poetry at Guggenheim Museum, N. Y. Introduced by Robert Lowell.

Ratiner, Steven. "In His Own Way." Rev. of *Midsummer*. *The Christian Science Monitor* 6 Apr. 1984: B9.

"A Refreshing Reading from the Master Poet." *Express* (Trinidad) 10 Mar. 1982: #.

Rev. of *Another Life*. *Booklist* 70 (1 Sept. 1973): 25.

Rev. of *Another Life*. *Choice* 10 (Sept. 1973): 986.

Rev. of *Another Life*. *Kirkus Review* 15 Oct. 1972: 1224.

Rev. of *Another Life*. *Times Literary Supplement* 3 Aug. 1973: 849.

Rev. of *Another Life*. *Virginia Quarterly Review* 50 (Winter 1974): xiv.

Rev. of *Another Life*. *Virginia Quarterly Review* 51 (Spring 1975): lviii.

Rev. of *The Arkansas Testament*. *The Virginia Quarterly Review* 64.2 (Spring 1988): 63.

Rev. of *Collected Poems 1948-1984*. *Library Journal* 112.1 (1 Jan . 1987): 59.

Rev. of *Dream on Monkey Mountain*. *Moko* 23 (27 Feb . 1970): 4. Rev. of TV version of play.

Rev. of *Dream on Monkey Mountain and Other Plays*. *Black World* 21 (Dec. 1971): 96 .

Rev. of *Dream on Monkey Mountain and Other Plays*. *Booklist* 67 (1 May 1971): 724.

Rev . of *Dream on Monkey Mountain and Other Plays*. *Choice* 8 (July-Aug. 1971): 691.

Rev. of *Dream on Monkey Mountain and Other Plays*. *Publishers Weekly* 30 Nov. 1970: 44.

Rev. of *The Fortunate Traveller*. *Ebony* 37 (Apr. 1982): 23.

Rev. of *The Fortunate Traveller*. *Express* (Trinidad) 21 Mar. 1982: 33.

Rev. of *The Fortunate Traveller*. *Kirkus Review* 49 (1 Dec. 1981): 1516. Occasionally strains framework, attempting to force too much material into a poem.

Rev. of *The Fortunate Traveller*. *New Leader* 65 (3 May 1982): 14.

Rev. of *The Fortunate Traveller*. *New York Times Book Review* 5 Dec. 1982: 54.

Rev. of *The Fortunate Traveller*. *Observer* (London) 2 May 1982: 31.

Rev. of *The Fortunate Traveller*. *People* 18 (12 July 1982): 10.

Rev. of *The Fortunate Traveller*. *Publishers Weekly* 220 (27 Nov. 1981): 76.

Rev. of *The Fortunate Traveller*. *Publishers Weekly* 222 (5 Nov. 1982): 68.

Rev. of *The Fortunate Traveller*. *Virginia Quarterly Review* 58.4 (Autumn 1982): 133.

Rev. of *The Gulf*. *Bajan* 197 (Jan. 1970): 18.

Rev. of *The Gulf. Booklist* 67 (15 Feb. 1971): 470.

Rev. of *The Gulf. Kirkus Review* 1 Apr. 1970: 438. Lyric gift, does not sustain power of moods.

Rev. of *Harry Dernier. Bim* 5.17 (Dec. 1952): 79-80.

Rev. of *Henri Christophe. Kyk-Over-Al* 3.11 (11 Oct. 1950): 73-74.

Rev. of *The Isle Is Full of Noises. The New York Times* 2 May 1982: #.

Rev. of *The Joker of Seville and O Babylon! Choice* 15 (Oct. 1978): 1056.

Rev. of *Midsummer. Publishers Weekly* 224 (9 Dec. 1983): 42.

Rev. of *Midsummer. Virginia Quarterly Review* 60.3 (Summer 1984): 90-91.

Rev. of *Omeros. American Visions* 6.1 (Feb. 1991): 39.

Rev. of *Omeros. The New York Times Book Review* 2 Dec. 1990: 81.

Rev. of *Omeros. Virginia Quarterly Review* 67.1 (Winter 1991): 27.

Rev. of *Remembrance and Pantomime. Choice* 18.3 (Nov. 1980): 399.

Rev. of *Remembrance and Pantomime. Variety* 303 (17 June 1981): 90.

Rev. of *Sea Grapes. Choice* 13 (Nov. 1976): 1144.

Rev. of *The Star-Apple Kingdom. Choice* 16.5-6 (July-Aug. 1979): 672.

Rev. of *The Star-Apple Kingdom. Kirkus Review* 47 (1 Feb. 1979): 189.

Rev. of *The Star-Apple Kingdom. The New York Times Book Review* 30 Mar. 1980: 33.

Rev. of *The Star-Apple Kingdom. Publishers Weekly* 215 (22 Jan. 1979): 357-58.

Rev. of *The Star-Apple Kingdom. Virginia Quarterly Review* 56.4 (Autumn 1980): 144.

Rich, Frank. Rev. of "Pantomime." *New York Times.* 30 May 1981: 12. Production at Kreeger Theater.

_____. "Theatre: Douglas Turner Ward Directs Premier." *New York Times* 2 May 1982: 63. Rev. production of "The Isle Is Full of Noises." Attempts to recreate history of West Indies.

Rickards, Colin. "The Caribbean's Leading Poet." Rev . of *The Castaway and Other Poems. Sunday Gleaner* (Jamaica) 2 Jan. 1966: 18.

_____. "Walcott Is Tops." *Guyana Graphic* 5 Mar. 1966: #.

Ricks, Christopher . "Authority in Poems. " Rev. of *Selected Poems. Southern Review* 5.1 (Winter 1969): 212-13.

Riel, Violette de Barovier. "Stark, Bold and Ruthless." Rev. of *Wine of the Country. Daily Gleaner* (Jamaica) 20 Aug. 1956: #. Play packed with controversy, reveals man's inhumanity.

Riley, Clayton. Rev. of *Dream on Monkey Mountain. New York Times* 4 Apr. 1971: 3. Production stars Roscoe Lee Brown at St. Mark's Theater.

Roach, Eric. "Experiment in Establishing the West Indian Theatre." Rev. of *Franklin. Trinidad Guardian* 18 Apr. 1973: 4. Mixture of poetry, prose, music reaches audience better in this play because not overly poetic. Works

466

CRITICAL PERSPECTIVES

on several levels—love element, racial crossing, decline of empire.

_____. "It Must Be an Agonizing Place to Act." *Evening News* (Trinidad) 17 Jan. 1966: #. Difficult performing conditions in Basement Theatre.

_____. "Mrs. Adams—The Heroine." *Trinidad Guardian* 19 Apr. 1967: 7. Workshop production of John's *Moon on a Rainbow Shawl* at Queen's Hall.

_____. "'Pieces of Two' Is an Experiment in Progress." *Trinidad Guardian* 28 Mar. 1973: 7. Second season of Workshop offers combination of drama, dance music and poetry.

_____. "This Fierce Satire Is Wildly Amusing." *Sunday Guardian* 9 Oct. 1966: 13. Rev. Walcott's production of Genêt's *The Blacks*.

_____. "This Musical Fuses Both Traditions of Folk Legend." Rev. of *Ti-Jean and His Brothers*. *Sunday Guardian* (Trinidad) 28 June 1970: 11.

_____. "Walcott Makes Fine Castle of Hate, Fear." Rev. of *In a Fine Castle*. *Trinidad Guardian* 1 Nov. 1971: 6.

Robertson, Nancy. "From Walcott, Startling Imagery." Rev. of *The Fortunate Traveller*. *Christian Science Monitor* 74 (19 May 1982): 17.

Rodman, Selden. "Books in Brief: 'The Star-Apple Kingdom.'" *National Review* 31.21 (25 May 1979): 694. No poet since Lowell as successful as Walcott in combining vernacular and grand manner.

_____. "Caribbean Poet of Elizabethan Richness." Rev. of *The Gulf*. *New York Times Book Review* 11 Oct. 1970: 24.

_____. "Derek Walcott." *Tongues of Fallen Angels*. Selden Rodman. New York: New Directions, 1974. 232-59. Extended personal revelations, *Dream*, spiritual revolution, third world literature.

_____. "Derek Walcott: Redefinitions." *The American Way* (Feb. 1972): 27-32. Duplicates "Derek Walcott."

_____. Rev. of *Dream on Monkey Mountain and Other Plays*. *RRI#* 1.2 (Winter 1972): 158-60.

Rohlehr, Gordon. "Afterthoughts." *Tapia* No. 23 (26 Dec. 1971): 8, 13. Sequel to "West Indian Poetry: Some Problems of Assessment." Explains his pessimistic outlook, absurd politics and rebellion. Citing Walcott, defends capacity to survive and possibility of creative action.

_____. "A Carrion Time." *Bim* 15.58 (June 1975): 92-109. Considers the continuing debate over the creative writer's relationship to society.

_____. The Carrion Time." *Tapia* 4.24 (16 June 1974): 5-8, 11. Reaction to Wayne Brown on relationship between poets and society. Mentions Walcott's disappointed calls for assistance to artists.

_____. "The Creative Writer and Society." *Tapia* 4.31 (4 Aug. 1974): 5-9. Part I of 4 on West Indian Writing, criticism in general, major writers.

_____. "The Creative Writer and Society." *Tapia* 4.32 (11 Aug. 1974): 6-7. Part 2 of 4.

_____. "The Creative Writer and Society." *Tapia* 4.33 (18 Aug.1974): 4-6. Part 3 of 4.

_____. "The Creative Writer and Society." *Tapia* 4.35 (1 Sept. 1974): 4-5, 7. Part 4 of 4.

_____. "Derek Walcott's *The Gulf and Other Poems. Black Images* 1.1 (1972): 66-69. Revision of review entitled "Withering into Truth."

_____. "Icy Intuitions." *Trinidad and Tobago Review* 2.11-12 (July-Aug. 1978): 12, 21, 26. Walcott's reaction to destructive politicians and sociologists in 1970s. Images of growth "overwhelm those of failure and dereliction."

_____. "Making Love Look More Like Despair." *Trinidad Guardian* 13 Dec. 1969: 8. Part 3 of 3. See "Withering into Truth" and "Power in Desolation."+

_____. "My strangled City." *Trinidad and Tobago Review* 2.4 (Dec. 1977): 7, 8, 33. Walcott's revolutionary poetry of the 1960s wrapped in too much imagery.

_____. "Power in Desolation." *Trinidad Guardian* 11 Dec. 1969: 17. Part 2 of 3. See "Withering into Truth" and "Making Love Look More Like Despair."+

_____. "The Problem of the Problem of Form: The Idea of an Aesthetic Continuum and Aesthetic Code-Switching in West Indian Literature." *Caribbean Quarterly* 31.1 (1985): 1-52. Ironically, restrictions of Caribbean society instill "compulsive . . . drive to realise a complex, multi-facetd flexible sense of shape." Emphasis on Walcott, pp. 24-35.

[_____.] "The Three Stages of Black Revolution: A Brief Look at Derek Walcott's *Ti-Jean and His Brothers*." *Liberation* (Trinidad) Sept. 1970: #.

_____. "West Indian Poetry: Some Problems of Assessment." *Bim* 14.54 (Jan.-June 1972): 80-88. Reprint of article from *Tapia.*

_____. "West Indian Poetry: Some Problems of Assessment." *Tapia* No. 20 (29 Aug. 1971): 11-14. Survey of recent anthologies and apparent trends in order to elucidate context of West Indian poetry. Much attention paid to musical influences.

_____. "Withering into Truth: A Review of Derek Walcott's *The Gulf* and Other Poems." *Trinidad Guardian* 10 Dec. 1969: 18. Part 1 of 3. See "Power in Desolation" and "Making Love Look More Like Despair." *Green Night* liberated area's poetry from "mindless romanticism, a weak historicism, over-rhetorical protest and sterile abstraction." Developing themes through volumes of poetry shows evidence of Walcott's growth, his ability to change.+

Ross, Alan. "Selected Books." Rev. of *The Castaway and Other Poems. The London Magazine* 5.10 (Jan. 1966): 88-91. Suggests need for clarity. Walcott not depressive in spite of dominant melancholy.

Rowell, Charles H. "An Interview with Derek Walcott." *Callaloo* 34 (Winter 1988): 80-89. Interview: advantages of colonial education. Immediacy of Jacobean sound in Caribbean language.

"Royal Society Honours Walcott." *Trinidad Guardian* 4 May 1966: 1.

Rudman, Mark. "Voluptuaries and Maximalists." Rev. of *The Arkansas Testament. New York Times Book Review* 20 Dec. 1987: 12.

Russell, Kathlyn. "Give Me Film, Says Derek Walcott." *Sunday Express* (Trinidad) 4 Sept. 1983: 31-32. Growing interest in medium of film. Anticipates showing of "The Rig," his film about impact of oil industry on rural Mayaro, Trinidad.

_____. "This Saint Lucian Theatre Proved a Natural for the Magic of Walcott." *Express* (Trinidad) 10 Aug. 1984: 14. St. Lucia production of "The Haytian Earth."

_____. "Walcott's 'Haytian Earth' Sets Pace for Arts Revival." *Express* (Trinidad) 14 Aug. 1984: 13.

_____. "Walcott's Monkey Mountain Deserves Warmer Responses." *Express* (Trinidad) 12 Mar. 1985: 23.

St. John, Oxford. "Mr. Walcott and the Myths." *West Indian Review* (Apr. 1957): 86-87. Answers Walcott's criticism of a review unfavorable to *Ione*.

_____. Rev. of *Ti-Jean and his Brothers*. *West Indian Review* 4.4 (Apr. 1959): 57.

Salkey, Andrew. "Inconsolable Songs of Our America: The Poetry of Derek Walcott." *World Literature Today* 56 (Winter 1982): 51-53. Appreciates Walcott's people-centered poetry, his "clarity and light, harmony and completeness."

[_____.]. "Juror: Derek Walcott." *World Literature Today* 51.4 (Autumn 1977): 580-81. Biography of Walcott as jurist for 1979 Neustadt International Prize for Literature.

_____. Rev. of *The Star-Apple Kingdom*. *World Literature Today* 53.3 (Summer 1979): 550. Book leaves "poet's persona in a modest perspective" and explores dichotomies.

Salter, Mary Jo. Rev. of *The Fortunate Traveller*. *New Republic* 186 (17 Mar. 1982): 38-39.

Samad, Daizal R. "Cultural Imperatives in Derek Walcott's *Dream on Monkey Mountain*." *Commonwealth* 13.2 (Spring 1991): 8-21. To counteract the "mimic" role of West Indian, Walcott pursues the "word" back to primal origins. "The West Indian may dramatize his authentic role as a New World Adam, a role plagued and blessed with a paradoxical joy and anguish."

Sanchez, Martin. "The Poetry of Carnival." *Trinidad and Tobago Review* 2.7 (Mar. 1978): 13. Discussion of "Mass Man" from Walcott's *The Gulf*.

Sardinha, C. Dennis. "Don Juan as a Source of Caribbean Humor." *Bim* 18:69 (Dec. 1985): 58-63. Both *The Joker of Seville* by Walcott and *Mister John Tenor y Yo* by Manuel Garlich portray reality of Caribbean existence using humor.

Savory, Elaine. (See Elaine Fido).

Schoenberger, Nancy. "An Interview with Nancy Schoenberger." *Threepenny Review* (Fall 1983): 16-17. After publication of *Fortunate Traveller*, Walcott speaks of exile, immediacy of Jacobean construction in Barbadian speech, predecessors and myth in his culture.

Scobie, W. I. "The West Coast Scene." Rev. of *Dream on Monkey Mountain. National Review* 22 (3 Nov. 1970): 1173-74.

Scott, Dennis. "A Joyful Joker." *Daily Gleaner* (Jamaica) 24 Nov. 1975: 26. Rev. Jamaica production of *The Joker of Seville.*

_____. "Walcott on Walcott." *Caribbean Quarterly* 14.1-2 (Mar.-June 1968): 77-82. Interview. Influences of West Indian prose. Relationship between poetry and drama.

"Selvon on Stage." *Moko* 10 (14 Mar. 1969): 3. Walcott stages "The World of Samuel Selvon." Kitchener's Kaiso music as background.

"Shakespeare Honour for Walcott." *Trinidad Guardian* 2 July 1964: 1. Invited to contribute poems in celebration of Shakespeare's 400th birthday.

Share, Donald S. Rev. of *The Fortunate Traveller. Library Journal* 106 (15 Dec. 1981): 2396.

Shetley, Vernon. Rev. of *The Arkansas Testament. Poetry* 152.2 (May 1988): 106-7. Paradox of Walcott's being representative of Western cultural affluence when he entered English tradition from colonial origin.+

Simmons, Harold. "Art Exhibition: St. Omer and Walcott." *Bim* 4.13 (Dec. 1950): 73-74. Walcott's forte, words and imagery. Desires emphasis on West Indian sensations and ideas, less imitation of tradition.

_____. "A West Indian Poet Fulfills His Promise." Rev. of 25 *Poems. Sunday Gleaner* (Jamaica) 27 Feb. [1949]: #. Arouses imagination through sensual images, elusive, profound of thought.+

Simon, John. "Folie a deux." Rev. of *Remembrance. New York Magazine* 12.21 (21 May 1979): 76-78. Fragmented, occasional poetry.

Sjöberg, Leif. "Derek Walcott, Interview with Leif Sjöberg." *The Greenfield Review* 12.1-2 (1984): 9-15. Walcott rejects racial and linguistic ambivalences in favor of an artist's personal fusion of opposites. Sees poetry as divine, myth as part of mankind.

_____. "Derek Walcott: Mellan Besatthet och Ansvar." *Artes* 1 (1983): 23-37.

_____. "A Note on Froude, Trollope and Others in Walcott's *Midsummer. The Greenfield Review* 12.1-2 (1984): 16-25. Comments on the vast allusiveness of Walcott's *Midsummer.*

_____. "On Derek Walcott." *The Greenfield Review* 12.1-2 (1984): 1-8. Brief biographical introduction to Walcott's career.

Smilowitz, Erika. "Fruits of the Soil: Botanical Metaphors in Caribbean Literature." *World Literature Written in English* 30.1 (Spring 1990): 29-36. Uses metaphors in representative regional writers to show indigenous qualities — sexual, social, political, peasant. Walcott among those cited.

Smith, Keith. "'O Babylon': An Adventure in Reggae." *People* 1.9 (Apr. 1976): 34-39. Walcott defines play as his first "real" musical; distinguishes it from *Joker.*

Smith, William J. "Inner Magic." Rev. of *Selected Poems. Harper's* 229 (Aug. 1964): 103.

Smyth, Paul. Rev. of *Another Life. Poetry* 123 (3 Dec. 1973): 171-73. Lyric passages superior, lacks overall coherence.

Solomon, Denis. "Ape and Essence: Derek Walcott's *Dream on Monkey Mountain.*" *Tapia* 7 (19 Apr. 1970): 6. Synthesis of public and private suffering achieved.

_____. "Beginning or End?" Rev. of *Franklin. Tapia* 3.16 (22 Apr. 1973): 2-3. *Ti-Jean, Dream, Castle, Franklin,* "constitute a body of work as complete and as immediately related to our contemporary situation as any society could hope."

_____. "Divided by Class, United by Bacchanal." Rev. of *Charlatan. Tapia* 3.27 (8 July 1973): 6. Play ends with classes united.

_____. "Liberation and Libido." Rev. of *The Joker of Seville. Tapia* 4.49 (8 Dec. 1974): 3.

"Songs of Theatre at the Library." *Trinidad Guardian* 5 Nov. 1974: 4. On Galt MacDermot score for *Charlatan.*

"Special Week to Honour Caribbean Writer." *Sunday Gleaner* (Jamaica) 17 Mar. 1967: 11.

Spector, Robert D. "Betwixt Tradition and Innovation." Rev. of *The Gulf. Saturday Review* 53.52 (26 Dec.1970): 25.

"Spiritual Crippling from an Absence of Vision." *Sunday Guardian, Independence Supplement* 31 Aug. 1974: 30. Interview. Walcott on low morale, government banality. Government out of touch with spiritual life of people needs change.

"Stage One to N Y." *Caribbean Contact* 12.3 (Aug. 1984): 14. Barbados' "Stage One" troupe to perform Walcott's "A Branch of the Blue Nile" at Columbia University.

"Stern and Grand as Milton." Rev. of *The Castaway and Other Poems. Sunday Gleaner* (Jamaica) 28 Nov. 1965: 3. Beneficial influence of Robert Lowell.

Stern, Frederick C. "The Formal Poetry Reading." *The Drama Review* (Fall 1991): 67-72. Account of poets reading from works. Walcott reads "Wales." Stern mentions production of Walcott's play "To Die in Grenada."

Stevenson, Anne. Rev. of *The Gulf. The Listener* 15 Jan. 1976: 61.

Stewart, Joyce. Rev. of *Plays for Today.* Ed. Dennis Scott. *Bajan* (July/Aug. 1986): 52-53. Rev. of anthology which contains *Ti-Jean and His Brothers.*

Stewart, Marion. "Walcott and Painting." *Jamaica Journal* 45 (May 1981): 56-68. Visual impact, references to artists and schools indicate self-conscious process of converting life to art.

Stitt, Peter. Rev. of *Midsummer. Georgia Review* 38 (Summer 1984): 407-9.

_____. Rev. of *The Star-Apple Kingdom. Poetry* 135 (Jan. 1980): 235-37.

Stone, Judy. "At Last, Masterpiece on the Middle Class." Rev. of *Remembrance*. *Trinidad Guardian* 13 July 1979: 4. Spare and muscular language, bears stamp of maturity.

_____. "I May Lose Derek's Friendship." *Trinidad Guardian* 15 Nov. 1983: 17. Reaction to Walcott's rejection of Trinidad actress for production of "A Branch of the Blue Nile."

_____. "National Theatre Wanted." *Trinidad and Tobago Review* 2.4 (Dec. 1977): 9, 32. Reiterates call for performing arts facility.

_____. "Walcott's Dream Wakes Up to New Life." *Trinidad Guardian* 25 Mar. 1985: 21.

_____. "Warner's *Beef, No Chicken* an Inspired Production." *Caribbean Contact* 13.1 (June 1985): 14. Review comparing separate productions of play credits director, technicians as well as performers and dramatist for making work succeed.+

_____. "What Corsbie Did to Walcott's 'Pantomime.'" *Trinidad Guardian* 5 Feb. 1981: 13. Creative director delivers powerful interpretation.

"Strong Cast for 'Ione.'" *Daily Gleaner* (Jamaica) 14 Mar. 1957: #.

Stuttaford, Genevieve. Rev. of *Collected Poems*. *Publisher's Weekly* 29 Nov. 1985: 40.

_____. Rev. of *The Fortunate Traveller*. *Publisher's Weekly* 220 (27 Nov. 1981): 76.

_____. Rev. of *Omeros*. *Publishers Weekly* 237 (25 May 1990): 46.

_____. Rev. of *The Star-Apple Kingdom*. *Publisher's Weekly* 215 (22 Jan. 1979): 357-58.

Sudama, Trevor. "Carnival: Is It a Hedonistic Mass Ritual?" *Trinidad Guardian* 17 Sept. 1967: 20-21. Response to criticism of Walcott's review of Naipaul's *Mimic Men*.

_____. "Walcott—Naipaul: The People in Our Society Can Be Likened to Migratory Birds." *Trinidad Guardian* 20 Aug. 1967: #. Answers Walcott's criticism of *Mimic Men* in *Guardian*, 6 Aug. 1967. Cynicism does not preclude involvement.

Swanzy, Henry. *B.B.C. Caribbean Voices Transcript No. 348* 20 Mar. 1949: 2. Program on Walcott's poetry.

_____. "Henri Christophe." *Public Opinion* 29 Mar. 1952: #.

_____. Rev. of "Henri Christophe." *Bim* 5.17 (1952): 75-76.

Tafari, Ikael. "Walcott's Twilight Vision." *Caribbean Contact* 17.10 (Mar. 1990): 14. Michael Gilkes directs production of *Franklin* in Port of Spain. Superlative craftsmanship undermined by Walcott's ambivalence toward imperialism.

Taylor, Jeremy. "Caught in the Dilemma of Exile." *Express* (Trinidad) 16 Apr. 1973: 15.

_____. "The Joker of Seville—Actors Give Grand Performance." *Express* (Trinidad) 4 Dec. 1974: 9, 18.

_____. "Meaningless? Chaotic? I Never Said That, Mr. Walcott." *Express* (Trinidad) 10 June 1978: 9.

_____. "New Walcott Play Highlights Next Season at the Little Carib Theatre." *Express* (Trinidad) 15 Mar. 1978: 12.

_____. "*Pantomime* Forces a Second Look at Our Culture." *Express* (Trinidad) 2 June 1978: 12.

_____. "Perhaps . . . Derek Is the Greatest." *Express* (Trinidad) 28 May 1978: 14.

_____. "'Remembrance'—a Moving, Tender Play." Rev. of *Remembrance*. *Express* (Trinidad) 6 July 1979: 13.

_____. Rev. of *The Fortunate Traveller*. *Express* (Trinidad) 4 Aug. 1982: 23.

_____. "Theatre Blooms in Trinidad." *Caribbean Contact* 8.6 (Oct. 1980): 9.

_____. "Walcott—at 50." *Caribbean Contact* 7.11 (Mar. 1980): 14. Despite refusal to support popular causes, Walcott's staying power rests on excellence of writing and "glaring obviousness of his commitment."

_____. "Walcott Mesmerizes and Dazzles Audience with His Language." *Express* (Trinidad) 21 Oct. 1974: 5.

_____. "Walcott Nudging up to Broadway." *Express* (Trinidad) 2 June 1980: 14, 15.

Taylor, Loring. "Confluente: valorile simbolice ale peisajului la Derek Walcott." *Steaua* 26.3 (#): 48-49. Survey (in Romanian) of Walcott's career and international standing. Walcott's idiom neither British nor American, "but a compromise of universal expression intelligible on a world wide scale."

Taylor, Patrick. "Myth and Reality in Caribbean Narrative: Derek Walcott's *Pantomime*." *World Literature Written in English* 26.1 (Spring 1986): 169-77. Distinguishes between mythological and liberating narrative. *Pantomime* recreates myth of Crusoe/Friday as liberating narrative.+

Teltsch, Kathleen. "Foundation to Support 21 'Geniuses' for 5 Years." *New York Times* 19 May 1981: 1, B13. Profiles MacArthur Foundation award recipients, including Walcott.

_____. "The 'Genius' Awards." *Dialogue* (Feb. 1987): 74-75. Profiles of MacArthur Foundation award recipients, including Walcott.

"The Theatre Workshop at the Crossroads." *Sunday Guardian Magazine* 29 Sept. 1968: 4. Walcott comments on public and critics, responses to staging of Genêt's *The Blacks*.

"Theatre Workshop for U. S. Drama Festival." *Tapia* 4.39 (28 July 1974): 4. Invitational performances of Workshop at White Barn Theater, Westport, Connecticut.

"Theatre Workshop to Perform in the U. S." *Trinidad Guardian* 10 June 1969: 7. Eugene O'Neill Memorial Theatre Foundation sponsors five-week visit for Workshop at annual Playwright's Conference in Waterford, Connecticut.

Thieme, John. "Alternative Histories: Narrative Modes in West Indian Literature (with particular reference to Derek Walcott and V. S. Reid)." A *Sense of Place*. Ed. Britta Olinder. The Proceedings of the Gothenburg University Congress of Commonwealth Language and Literature, Sept. 1982. Gothenburg: English Dept., Gothenburg University, 1984. 142-50. Walcott's Adamic vision goes beyond polemic and pathos of opposed causes.

———. "A Caribbean Don Juan: Derek Walcott's *Joker of* Seville." *World Literature Written in English* 23.1 (Winter 1984): 62-75.

———. "Derek Walcott: *Ti-Jean . . .* and *Dream on Monkey Mountain*." *Handbook for the Teaching of Caribbean Literature*. Ed. David Dabydeen. London: Heinemann,1988. 86-95. Pedagogical approach offers analysis, questions for discussion, suggested activities, audio-visual resources.

———. "Gnarled Sour Grapes." Rev. of *Sea Grapes. Caribbean Review* 7.4 (Oct.-Dec. 1978): 51-53. Reaction to New World is bitter-sweet; finds middle ground, doing justice to both sides of mulatto existence, and to the New World.

———. "Scheherazade as Historian: Rudy Wiebe's 'Where Is the Voice Coming From?'" *The Journal of Commonwealth Literature* 17.1 (1982): 172-81. Walcott's use of history incorporated into discussion of Wiebe.

"Thinking about Commonwealth Literature." *Sunday Guardian* 20 Dec. 1970: 10.

"Third Premier for Walcott." *Trinidad Guardian* 10 July 1982: # .

Thomas, Clara. "Commonwealth Albums: Family Resemblance in Derek Walcott's *Another Life* and Margaret Laurence's *The Diviners. World Literature Written in English* 21.2 (Summer 1982): 262-74.

Thomas, D. M. [Ned]. "The Adamic Silence." Rev. of *Sea Grapes. Times Literary Supplement* 23 July 1976: 910.

———. "Derek Walcott." *Kunapipi* 3.2 (1981): 42-47. Despite political powerlessness, Caribbean people exert power through art and culture.

———. "Derek Walcott, Caribbean Poet." *Poetry Wales* 9.1 (#): 14-24. Creates sensuous picture, master of styles from metaphysicals to Dylan Thomas, sees geography against historical background.

———. *Derek Walcott: Poet of the Islands,*. [Merthyr Tydfil]: Welsh Arts Council, 1980. Particularity of place and voice in Walcott. Analysis of three representative poems: "Ruins of a Great House," chapters 21-22 of *Another Life*, and "The Star-Apple Kingdom."

———. "Walcott, Derek (Alton)." *Commonwealth Literature*. Ed. James Vinson. Chicago: St. James Press, 1985.

Thomas, Jo. "For a Caribbean Poet, Inner Tension and Foreign Support." *New York Times* 21 Aug. 1979: 2. Walcott lives on foreign money. Banality and indifference of wealthy in Trinidad.

Thompson, John. "Old Campaigners." Rev. of *Sea Grapes. New York Review of Books* 14 Oct. 1976: 33.

Thompson, Mertel E. "Don Juan's 'Hilarious Expliots': *The Joker of Seville* on Stage."
    The Literary Half-Yearly 26.1 (Jan. 1985): 132-48. Accounts for early
    productions, characters, cultural influences in play.

Thorpe, Michael. Rev. of *Midsummer. World Literature Today* 59.1 (Winter 1985):
    151. Midsummer is midlife, metaphor for transience.

"Three Evenings with Six Poets." *Kyk-Over-Al* 3.13 (1951): 214-20.

"Ti-Jean and His Brothers—Entertainment at Its Best." *Sunday Guardian* 2 May
    1982: 23.

Tomalin, Claire. "Derek Walcott's 'Another Life.'" *New Statesman* 88 (20 Dec.
    1974): 908.

Trinidad Guardian 10 July 1982: #. Showing of 16 oils by Dr. Boodhoo based on
    Star-Apple Kingdom .

"Trinidad Theatre Workshop Stages Chekhov's 'Seagull.'" *Tapia* 5.28 (13 July
    1975): 12 .

Trueblood, Valerie. "On Derek Walcott." *The American Poetry Review* 7.3 (May-
    June 1978): 7-10. Balanced, meditative poet, seeks resolutions, blames
    angrily.

Tucker, Martin, et al. "Education by Poetry." *Confrontation* 33 (1986): 295-306.
    Interview: Walcott, Carolyn Forché, David Ignatow. Walcott misses sense
    of heritage among young writers pressured to establish unique voice.

Tuttleton, James W. "One People's Grief." Rev. of *Collected Poems 1948-1984.
    National Review* 38 (20 June 1986): 51-52. Collection reflects mythic
    figures from Adam and Odysseus to modern castaways.

"$240,000 U.S. Award for Derek Walcott." *Trinidad Guardian* 31 May 1981: 1.
    MacArthur Foundation award.

Uhrbach, Jan R. "Language and Naming in *Dream on Monkey Mountain.*" *Callaloo*
    No. 29/9.4 (Fall 1986): 578-82. Names and symbolic values in play.

Vendler, Helen. "Poet of Two Worlds." Rev. of *The Fortunate Traveller. New York
    Review of Books* 4 Mar. 1982: 23, 26-27.

"Violent Walcott Verse Play." Rev. of "Wine of the Country." *Public Opinion*
    (Jamaica) 18 Aug. 1956: 8.

Voglesang, Arthur. Rev. of *Collected Poems 1948-1984. Los Angeles Times Book
    Review* 6 Apr. 1986: 10.

Wade, Henling. "Derek Walcott to Us." *Sunday Gleaner* (Jamaica) 1 Nov. 1970: 29.
    Walcott in Jamaica for run of *In a Fine Castle.*

"Walcott Clears the Air about 'Sex' Charge." *Express* (Trinidad) 14 June 1982: 1.
    Response to Harvard coed complaint.

"Walcott, Derek (Alton)." *Current Biography* 45 (Apr. 1984): 36-39.

"Walcott Loads His Tiny Basement Bus." *Trinidad Guardian* 1 Nov. 1966: 16. Stage
    size inadequate for production of Soyinka's *The Road.*

"Walcott Plans Instant Theatre." *Trinidad Guardian* 20 Aug. 1969: 8. Following engagement at Waterford, Connecticut, Workshop interested in mobile "Arena Theatre," an alternative to National Theatre in expensive quarters.

"Walcott Presents New Play." *The Weekly Journal* (Virgin Islands) 10 Oct. 1974: 3A, 14A. Rev. production of *Dream on Monkey Mountain.*

"Walcott, Quarrelling Voices in the Playwright's Head." *Trinidad Guardian* 11 Apr. 1978: 7.

"Walcott Reads as He Opens Exhibition at Ikon." *Trinidad Guardian* 16 July 1982: 20. Isaiah Boodhoo's paintings based on *The Star-Apple Kingdom.*

"Walcott Reads at Art Exhibition." *Express* (Trinidad) 15 July 1982: 23. Isaiah Boodhoo's paintings based on *The Star-Apple Kingdom.*

"Walcott Records Success in Jamaica and New York." *Trinidad Guardian* 29 Apr. 1971: 7. Tours of *Dream* and *Ti-Jean.*

Walcott, Roderick. "The Creole Fable." *Handbook for the Production of "Ti-Jean and His Brothers."* No pub. Program notes for production of *Ti-Jean and His Brothers* in Castries, St. Lucia, Dec. 1972: 2 pages.

"Walcott Scores with the 'Joker.'" *Trinidad Guardian* 30 Nov. 1974: 9.

"Walcott Tells of Local Amateur Actors in Disguise." *Sunday Guardian* 11 July 1982: 5, 10.

"Walcott to Conduct Workshop in London." *Guyana Chronicle* 25 May 1976: 6. Workshop at Drum Arts Centre, a multi-racial arts promotion group.

"Walcott to Revive 'Joker of Seville.'" *Express* (Trinidad) 6 Mar. 1982: 11.

"Walcott Wins Second Prize at Dakar." *Sunday Guardian* 10 Apr. 1966: 3. For *In a Green Night,* at World Festival of Negro Arts.

"Walcott's 'Blue Nile' at Home in Tent Theatre." *Express* (Trinidad) 18 Aug. 1985: 8. Tent appropriate for drama about struggling West Indian theatre troupe.

"Walcott's 'Blue Nile' Is a Drama about Theatre." *Express* (Trinidad) 13 Aug. 1985: 23.

"Walcott's 'Dream' Comes to the Carib." *Trinidad Guardian* 22 July 1974: 7.

"Walcott's 'Dream' Hits New Yorkers Right in the Gut." *Express* (Trinidad) 21 Mar 1971: 23.

"Walcott's 'Dream' to Be Filmed for T.V." *Express* (Trinidad) 8 Oct. 1969: 15.

"Walcott's 'Henri Christophe' to run for Three Nights." *Trinidad Guardian* 11 Apr. 1968: 5.

"Walcott's New Play." *Caribbean Contact* 5.1 (Apr. 1977): 14. Announces *Remembrance* and Walcott's resignation from Workshop.

"Walcott's New Play at U. C. W. I. Friday." *Daily Gleaner* (Jamaica) 14 Aug. 1956: #.

"Walcott's Play Hits London Stage." *Express* (Trinidad) 15 Mar. 1980: 8.

"Walcott's Play Runs into a Picket Storm in the U. S." *Express* (Trinidad) 23 Sept. 1984: #. Actors Equity protests foreign actors in N. Y. production of *A Branch of the Blue Nile.*

Walker, Alice. Rev. of *Another Life. Village Voice* 11 Apr. 1974: 26.

Walmsley, Anne. "Dimensions of Song: A Comment on the Poetry of Derek Walcott and Edward Brathwaite." *Bim* 13 .51 (July-Dec. 1970): 152-67. Walcott worked through series of voices before finding his own.

Walsh, William. "A Life of Contradictions, a Poetry of Unities." Rev. of *The Gulf. Book World* 4.50 (13 Dec. 1970): 3. Has strength to avoid over-simplification. May prove to be best poet now writing in English.

_____. "West Indies." *Commonwealth Literature.* Ed. William Walsh. London: Oxford U. P., 1973. 46-66. General level of poetry below that of West Indian prose. Walcott the exception.

Walters, Ray. Rev. of *The Star-Apple Kingdom. New York Times Book Review* 85 (30 Mar . 1980): 33.

Warren, Rosanna. "Pilgrim's Progress." Rev. of *Collected Poems. Partisan Review* 54 .1 (1987): 157-65 . Reviews collections by John Ashbery, Stephen Spender and Walcott. "Walcott wrests an incarnational faith from the very teeth of loss."

Watts, Margaret. "The Gulf and Other Poems, by Derek Walcott." *Legon Journal of the Humanities* (Ghana) 1 (1974):131-36 .

"Welsh Honour for Walcott." *Express* (Trinidad) 7 June 1980: 16.

"West Indian Writers." *Times Literary Supplement* 23 May 1952: 348. Brief coverage of problems facing writers.

"West Indian Writers and our Past, Present and Future." *Caribbean Contact* 5.7 (Nov. 1977): 14-15. Writers comments on cultural possibilities of area. Walcott on carnival mentality.

"What Ever Happened to Walcott's Second Phase?" *Express* (Trinidad) 25 July 1982: 24-25. Conflict within Trinidad Theatre Workshop over Walcott's desire to develop on international scale.

White, J. P. "Derek Walcott: The Spirit of a Post-Elizabethan Globalist." *Green Mountains Review* NS 4.1 (Spring/Summer 1990): 13. Argues Walcott an Elizabethan "mannerist," gleaning imagery from classical, "African, European, American language and culture."

_____. "An Interview with Derek Walcott." *Green Mountains Review* NS 4.1 (Spring/Summer 1990): 14-37. Schizophrenia, excitement of emerging from slave to free mentality. Major poetic obsession is Caribbean people. Mistreatment of minorities in American theatre. *Omeros* not rewrite of *Iliad* or *Odyssey*, but combines "Homeric line and Dantesque design."

Whitwell, Stuart. Rev. of *Omeros. Booklist* 87.6 (15 Nov. 1990): 596. "Not so much a narrative as a vast Bayeau-like tapestry . . . majestic and triumphant."

Wickham, John. "Derek Walcott: Poet and Dramatist." *Bajan* 197 (Jan. 1970): 4-6. Profile of Walcott appreciates his living/working in West Indies while other artists live abroad.

_____. "A Look at Ourselves." Rev. of *The Sea At Dauphin. Bim* 6.22 (June 1955): 128-30. Rev. production of three West Indian plays including *The Sea at Dauphin.*

_____. "Lost in the Enchantment of our Islandness." *Bajan* (Mar. 1979): 38-39.

_____. "Poetry and Politics." Rev. of *The Star-Apple Kingdom. Bajan* 297 (Aug. 1978): 11-12. Title poem based on Jamaica, its political leader, but identifications are symbolic.

_____. "Reflections on the State of Theatre in the Caribbean." *Bim* 17.65 (June 1979): 16-22.

_____. Rev. of *Ti-Jean and His Brothers. Bajan* 204 (Sept. 1970): 22, 24-25.

_____. "Theatre: 'Dream on Monkey Mountain.'" *Bim* 12.48 (Jan.-June 1969): 267-68. Production at Combermere school, Bridgetown, Barbados, Oct. 1968.

Wieland, James. "'Confronting His Madness': History as Amnesia in the Poetry of Derek Walcott." *New Literature Review* 7 (1979): 73-83. Out of contradictory history, "makes something vital and changing."

_____. *The Ensphering Mind: History, Myth, and Fiction in the Poetry of Allen Curnow, Nissim Ezekiel, A. D. Hope, A.N. Klein, Christopher Okigbo and Derek Walcott.* Washington, D. C.: Three Continents Press, 1988. Sees Walcott as pivotal in these writers' efforts to accommodate alien histories, to generate sustaining myth through fictive constructs. Two chapters place extra emphasis on Walcott. Chapter two—"A Blink in the Sad Eye of Time: Attitudes to History in the Poetry of Derek Walcott, Christopher Okigbo, and Nissim Ezekiel." Chapter five—"Adam's Task . . . Myth and Fictions in the Poetry of Derek Walcott."

_____. "Making Radiant the Moment: Towards a Reading of Derek Walcott's *Sea Grapes.*" *ACLALS Bulletin* (Mysore) 5.3 (1981): 112-21.

Williams, Hugo. Rev. of *In a Green Night. London Magazine* 2.4 (July 1962): 77-79.

Willis, Susan. "Caliban as Poet: Reversing the Maps of Domination." *Massachusetts Review* 23.4 (Winter 1982): 615-30. Act of mapping viewed in Third World as record of slavery and expropriation of wealth. Walcott, Césaire, Guillen, Lamming.

Wilson, Judith. Rev. of *The Star-Apple Kingdom. Essence* 11.2 (June 1980): 21.

Wilson, Robert. "West Indian Poet Wins Nobel." *USA Today* 9-11 Oct. 1992: 5D.

"Workshop Takes 'Franklin' to Jamaica." *Trinidad Guardian* 18 June 1973: 7.

"Workshop to Stage Second Season." Trinidad Guardian 18 Mar. 1973: 6.

Wright, Benedict. "Derek Walcott." *Express Independence Magazine* (Trinidad) 31 Aug. 1969: 27. Interview.

Wright, Bruce McM. "No Longer Blinded by Our Eyes. The Poetry of Derek Walcott: The Return of the Exile as Exile." *Shango* 1.1 (1973): 23-27. Walcott remains poet manqué.

Wyke, Clement H. "Divided to the Vein: Patterns of Tormented Ambivalence in Walcott's *The Fortunate Traveller.*" *Ariel* 20.3 (1989): 55-71. Personal uses image clusters, patterns withdrawing and advancing, to form apocalyptic vision. Ambiguous and paradoxical personality emerges.

Zabus, Chantal. "A Calibanic Tempest in Anglophone & Francophone New World Writing." *Canadian Literature* (1985): 35-50. Useful theme, Walcott mentioned in passing. More on Césaire, Fanon, Lamming, C. L. R. James.

(+) indicates that this item is included in the present collection of essays.

(#) indicates that I have been unable to examine this item in its original form of publication. This accounts, in most cases, for missing publication data.

Index